Expert Evidence

Expert Evidence

Andrew W. Jurs

PROFESSOR OF LAW AND ASSOCIATE DEAN
DRAKE LAW SCHOOL

CAROLINA ACADEMIC PRESS
Durham, North Carolina

ISBN   978-1-5310-1045-4
eISBN   978-1-5310-1046-1
LCCN   2018967082

Carolina Academic Press
700 Kent Street
Durham, North Carolina 27701
Telephone (919) 489-7486
Fax (919) 493-5668
www.cap-press.com

Printed in the United States of America

To Katie, Clara, and Milo

Summary of Contents

Contents

Acknowledgments

Creating this text is the consolidation of efforts, thoughts, comments, and support of so many people, and I would like to thank them for their contributions to make this work possible.

I owe my gratitude to a group of research assistants who have, over the years, done any number of projects, both large and small, to assist me in the creation of the law review articles contained herein and the text itself. To those dedicated students, some now lawyers and some still, as of this writing, lawyers-to-be, I say thanks. These students include Aaron Bachmann, Bonnie Yamani, Leonardo Perez, Avery Sander, Krissa LeLacheur Mason, Louis Sloven, Jackson O'Brien, and Spencer Willems.

Over the years, many colleagues have also taken the time to make comments and suggestions on my work and I thank them for their guidance and assistance. At the risk of inadvertently omitting someone, I count among these colleagues: Ronald Wright, Michael D. Green, Sidney Shapiro, Kami Chavis, Scott Shepard, Joseph Sanders, Erica Beecher-Monas, Jagdeep Bhandari, David Caudill, Susan Haack, John Langbein, Benjamin J. Priester, Alan G. Williams, Kevin Saunders, Mark Kende, Miguel Schor, Mack Shelley, Allan Vestal, George Fisher, Anthony Champagne, Jane Campbell Moriarty, Anthony Gaughan, Jerry Anderson, and the faculty of Drake University Law School. Special thanks to my co-author Scott DeVito, for his enthusiasm, dedication, and patience as we engaged in the statistical analysis of legal issues.

I also wish to thank the following authors, publishers, and other copyright holders of works contained herein for permission to reproduce excerpts: Susan Haack, Robert F. Koteles, Jr., Paul Bush. Paul C. Giannelli, Joe S. Cecil, Thomas E. Willging, Frank D. Tinari, Steve Foritano, Robert Epstein, David H. Kaye, William C. Thompson, Ronald M. Sandgrund, Barry M. Wertheimer, Lyn Haber, Ralph Norman Haber, Sophia Gatowski, Jennifer Groscup, George Sensabaugh, David A. Freeman, George Sensabaugh, Simon Ford, Edward J. Imwinkelreid, Joseph Peterson, Andrea Roth, Jane C. Moriarty, John D. North, the Colorado Lawyer, the LexisNexis Group, the National Academies Press, the American Psychological Association,

The staff at Carolina Academic Press has been an invaluable resource for the production of this text, and I thank them for their dedication and efforts.

Finally, I wish to thank Katie, Clara, and Milo, for their support and encouragement during the creation of this work.

Table of Cases

Table of Secondary Authorities

Part I

Foundational
Rules and Principles

Chapter 1

Science and Law as Oil and Water

At the core of nearly every legal dispute is a question of uncertainty: Do we trust the witness who is testifying before the jury? Which manufacturer is to blame for the improper design of a product? Does the prescription medication really cause a disease? For that reason, we will find expert evidence at the core of an enormous number of cases going to trial.

Recent research has shown that expert witnesses appear in as many as 86 percent of cases that go to trial.[1] This number appears nearly identical to the same measurement decades ago.[2] Yet in many law schools, the complexities of expert evidence account for just one of the many subsections in an evidence survey course, and one that is often given less attention than necessary to cover the core issues in detail. This book is an attempt to provide opportunities for detailed focus on this vital area.

Part of the problem with teaching expert evidence is that it is so varied. Think about a series of cases, and how expert testimony would fit within each:

- After an airplane crash, plaintiff claims engine error caused destabilization of the flight while the defense claims pilot error;[3]

- A baby born with limb reduction birth defects claims that an anti-nausea drug caused these injuries, while the defense claims the drug is safe and effective;[4] or

- After a tire fails and causes a serious rollover accident on a highway, the injured family claims the tire was manufactured improperly while the tire company is sure this tire is just as safe as every other one they've produced.[5]

While each of these cases involves drastically different facts, claims, and legal issues—whether it relates to aircraft engine design, pharmaceutical teratogenic effects, or causes of tire decay—at the core of each dispute is the need for an expert to testify on the disputed issue of fact. Underlying the final courtroom testimony is a set of

---

1. Andrew W. Jurs, *Expert Prevalence, Persuasion and Price: What Trial Participants Really Think About Experts*, 91 IND. L.J. 353, 367 (2016).

2. Shari Seidman Diamond, *How Jurors Deal with Expert Testimony and How Judges Can Help*, 16 J.L. & POL'Y 47, 56 (2007) (86% of trials from 1998 sample); Samuel R. Gross, *Expert Evidence*, 1991 WIS. L. REV. 1113, 1119 (1991) (86% of cases reported in *Jury Verdicts Weekly* in 1985–86).

3. Beech Aircraft Corp. v. Rainey, 488 U.S. 153 (1988).

4. Daubert v. Merrell Dow Pharms., Inc., 509 U.S. 579 (1993).

5. Kumho Tire Co. v. Carmichael, 526 U.S. 137 (1999).

uniform rules that regulate who will be able to testify to these issues, what factual and experiential basis they will need to have to testify, and what they will be permitted to tell the jury about their expert opinions. To say this book is about those rules is to say War and Peace is about Russia.[6] Of course it is, but it's a little more complicated than that.

Just as in a survey course about evidence, we will of course be covering the rules of admissibility and procedure surrounding expert testimony. However, you may find this text different in several regards. First, since expert litigation issues are critical to so many types of litigation, they form an enormous part of litigation strategy for litigants. As is often the case for firms, many of the expert issues will be delegated to junior associates by law firm partners. For that reason, we will consistently practice writing throughout the book, by drafting memos, disclosures, motions *in limine*, or bench briefs necessary for expert issues in civil or criminal litigation scenarios.

Second, we will also — particularly in the second half of the book — explore the scientific disciplines that commonly appear in legal cases. Some of these are largely used in criminal cases, like DNA, fingerprints, or other forensic techniques. Because many students do not end up practicing criminal law, we will also cover some common civil litigation expert areas like accident reconstruction or economic valuation. Of course, we cannot cover every expert topic. Instead, these specific topics can serve as a template that can be used to tackle almost any expert issue by analogy.

Meanwhile, as we cover these substantive areas, we will also start to notice some consistent themes that reoccur throughout the book. These are not hidden, nor will I or your professor "hide the ball" and spring them on you later. Instead, these recurring themes get at larger truths about the meaning of science, adjudicative decision-making, and justice. For example, from the very first day of class to the end, we will see a continuous friction between "science" and "the law" — and how courts and litigants manage that friction is an underlying lesson in the cases in the book.

Another theme is the balancing of competing interests in play in any expert case. On one hand, we recognize that a final verdict should reflect the actual reality of what happened in the case and provide an accurate scientific analysis of those facts. On the other hand, the legal system erects impediments to accurate decision-making in the form of substantive and procedural rules, and these rules can sometimes distort the fact-finding process. Ultimately we will need to make value choices about whether "truth" and "justice" have been balanced correctly. This is only the beginning of the trip, however, and so we need not solve those riddles today, if at all.

Instead, we start with a much more fundamental question: What is "science" anyway? One may wonder why such a silly question starts what is otherwise a serious book. The answer is simple: I will assume that upper-division students have some concept of the legal component of the scientific-legal divide, but I cannot assume that they

---

6. Rod Riggs, *My Point of View*, Ames Trib., May 23, 1967, at 7 (including the famous "speed reading War and Peace" joke, although the quotation is often attributed to Woody Allen. *See* https://quoteinvestigator.com/2015/12/08/speed-reading/).

have much exposure to or familiarity with science and the scientific method. Courts will consistently refer to "science" or "the methods and procedures of science," so we must explore what that terminology means, and perhaps more importantly, what it means to whom. In so doing, we will start to see why there is such a serious conflict between the legal and scientific methods, and how that conflict is a result of their underlying principles and values. That friction serves as the spark behind this text.

A. Science and Law—Why Oil and Water?

Taking depositions or testimony from a scientific expert, it is not uncommon for both the lawyer and expert to get frustrated. "Why don't you just let me tell you the whole story?" says the expert, while the lawyer replies, "Please answer my questions." So why is it that science and the law are so often at cross-purposes? In the following excerpt from philosopher Susan Haack, she reaches for an answer to that question.

As you read the passage, make a chart that describes the fundamentals of each process, as follows:

- What is the goal of the inquiry?

- What methods are used to make decisions in this area?

- What values does the inquiry adhere to?

- What is the ultimate result of the inquiry?

Exploring these fundamentals begins to explain the conflict between analytic processes. Afterward, Haack identifies some practical problems that this friction creates.

Susan Haack, *Irreconcilable Differences? The Troubled Marriage of Science and Law*
72-Wtr Law & Contemp. Probs. 1 (2009)[Ed.]

III
The Nature of Science and the Culture of Law

It is sometimes said that science is a search for truth; and this is right, if rightly understood. The core business of the sciences is inquiry; the object of the enterprise is to figure out answers to questions about the world and how it works. Of course, it goes without saying that whenever one wants answers to questions, one wants true answers. This is not to say that scientists seek THE TRUTH, in some quasi-religious sense; nor is it to suggest that scientific truths are the only truths, or that scientific truths are ever known with absolute certainty. But it is to say that when, for example, James Watson and Francis Crick worked to "solve the structure of DNA," what they wanted was to reach the answer that DNA is a double-helical, backbone-out macro-

---

[Ed.] This article is also available in Susan Haack, Evidence Matters: Science, Proof, and Truth in the Law 78–104 (2014).

molecule with like-with-unlike base pairs if DNA is a double-helical, backbone-out macromolecule with like-with-unlike base pairs, to reach the answer that DNA is a triple-helical backbone-in macromolecule with like-with-like base pairs if it is a triple-helical backbone-in, macromolecule with like-with-like base pairs, and so on.

As the example suggests, once scientists have figured out the answer to one question, new questions almost invariably arise—sometimes a whole cascade of them: as, once they had worked out the structure of DNA, molecular biologists next had to tackle the "Coding Problem," which it would take more than a decade to solve. And as this in turn suggests, even though there is no guarantee that every step will be in the right direction, it is in the nature of the scientific enterprise to push forward, to tackle new questions with the help of answers to older ones.

Of course, scientists seek not just true answers, but substantive, explanatory answers ("either DNA is a double-helical, backbone-out macromolecule with like-with-unlike base pairs, or not," though undeniably true, won't do). Although scientific investigation sometimes focuses on particular things or events—a particular planet, earthquake, eclipse, epidemic, or whatever—even when it does, there is always a concern with laws, explanation, prediction; in short, with the general. Medical scientists, for example, might investigate why this individual seems unusually resistant to HIV infection; but the goal would be to figure out what it is about him that makes him less susceptible.

Like historians, investigative journalists, detectives, or anyone seriously trying to figure something out, scientists make informed guesses at the answers to their questions, work out their consequences, seek out evidence to check how well those consequences hold up, and use their judgment as to how to proceed from there. There is no algorithmic "scientific method," no formal, or formalizable, procedure available to all scientists and only to scientists, which, faithfully followed, guarantees success, or even progress. But over centuries of work, scientists have gradually developed a vast array of special tools and techniques: ever more-powerful instruments of observation, ever more-cunning (and sometimes very formally precise) experimental designs, ever more-sophisticated mathematical and statistical techniques, ever fancier computer programs, and so on. These scientific "helps" to inquiry usually develop in an ad hoc way, in response to some problem at hand; and almost always they rely on some earlier scientific innovation, theoretical or practical. The evolution of such "technical" helps to inquiry has been an untidy, pragmatic, fallible, bootstrap process that has gradually made it possible to get more and better-focused evidence and to assess more accurately where evidence leads—in short, to extend and amplify unaided human cognitive powers.

Because the core business of science is inquiry, the core values of science are epistemological: honesty, with oneself and others, about what the evidence is and what it shows, and willingness to make that evidence available to others in the field—essentially the values Robert Merton articulated long ago under the labels "disinterestedness" and "communism."[53] Instilling and sustaining commitment to these values

---

53. Robert K. Merton, Social Theory and Social Structure 307 (1949).

isn't easy; scientists are fallible human beings, with the usual, mixed and sometimes dubious motives, hopes, and fears. Still, besides those technical helps, the sciences have developed informal social mechanisms to enable the pooling of evidence and to provide incentives and disincentives, which, up to a point, harness less-admirable motives, such as vanity or the desire for prestige, to serious scientific work. However, while the technical helps enabling scientists to acquire and assess evidence keep getting better and better, these "social" helps do not; in fact, they are coming under increasing strain both from the ever-growing scale of the scientific enterprise and from the alien values of the governments and large industrial concerns on whose financial support science increasingly depends—especially in the most commercialized areas of science, the medical sciences in particular.

Where all but the very simplest scientific claims and theories are concerned, the evidence will ramify in all directions; it is usually mediated by sophisticated instruments; more often than not it is the shared resource of many people, who may be working together or may be rivals, and who may be working in the same laboratory or thousands of miles or many decades or even centuries apart; it is almost invariably incomplete; and it is quite often ambiguous or misleading. At any time, some scientific claims and theories are so well-established that it would be astounding if they turned out to be wrong, some well- but not quite so well-established, some rather speculative, some very speculative, some highly speculative, and some downright wild and wacky. The proportion of the well-warranted to the highly speculative varies, obviously, from field to field, with some areas of science thus far more speculative than others, and some, arguably, thus far mostly speculative; for some fields of science are more advanced more "mature," as we say, others relatively new and thus-far undeveloped, and some so undeveloped, so entirely speculative, that one might understandably hesitate to call them "sciences" at all. The boundaries of the enormously complex and uneven enterprise referred to by the commodious word "science" are fuzzy, indeterminate, and frequently contested.

When the available evidence on some scientific question is seriously incomplete, those who work in the relevant scientific community—some of them probably more radical in temperament, others more conservative—may reasonably disagree about the likelihood that this or that answer is correct. As new evidence comes in, a consensus may eventually form that this once merely speculative theory is probably right, or that that once seemingly promising approach probably wrong. But there are no rules determining when a scientific claim is well enough warranted by the evidence to be accepted, or badly enough undermined by the evidence to be rejected; and neither, of course, do scientists reach their "verdict" by taking a vote. Instead, consensus arises as a byproduct when enough members of the relevant scientific subcommunity come to see the evidence as strong enough to warrant this claim or that theory.

Ideally, such consensus would form when, and only when, the evidence is sufficient; in practice, acceptance and warrant sometimes come apart. This may be because significant evidence gets lost or neglected; it may be because some widely held but unwarranted assumption skews scientists' judgment; or it may be the result of the influence or the persuasiveness of some individual or group in the field. But what counts in the end is not what person is most powerful or most persuasive, but what approach proves most fruitful, which theory proves to stand up best as evidence comes in. Watson really wanted to beat out Linus Pauling and win a Nobel prize, but it would not have satisfied him to win simply by being more persuasive than Pauling was; the point was to solve the structure of DNA first. Had he aimed only to win the debate, only to persuade others to his point of view, he would have been engaged in sham inquiry, that is, in advocacy disguised as investigation, not the real thing. Indeed, as Michael Polanyi once put it, "Only if scientists remain loyal to scientific ideals rather than try to achieve success with their fellow scientists can they form a community which will uphold those ideals."[61]

Though some science is certainly policy-relevant, scientific investigation is, in an important sense, policy-neutral. Scientists may, for example, explore the risks and benefits of making this or that drug or pesticide available, or the long-run effects of damming that river or of relying on this rather than that energy source; but whether the risks of the drug outweigh the benefits, whether the river should be dammed, whether we should switch to an alternative energy source, are not themselves scientific questions. However, when scientific work bears closely on policy questions, the line between scientific inquiry and policy advocacy can too easily get blurred.

Quite often, a scientist or scientific team will need to come up with some kind of answer on a specific timetable, as when they are working under pressure in an epidemic or in wartime, or simply because they need to report some result at the end of the grant period to the outfit that funded them. But in such circumstances the work is very apt to be skimped; for the unavoidable fact is that scientific inquiry takes the time it takes, and its progress is ragged and unpredictable. It may be possible to say ahead of time how long it will take to run this series of experiments, or how long that epidemiological study will continue; but even the best-informed specialist can make only very tentative and fallible estimates of how long it might be before this problem is solved, that natural phenomenon understood. Moreover, at any time there are many scientific questions to which there is no warranted answer, and to which scientists can only say, "at the moment, we just don't know; we're working on it, but we can't tell you when we will have it figured out."

I have stressed that the core business of science is inquiry; but not all those who describe themselves as scientists are engaged in this core business (and most of those who are will likely be engaged in fairly routine kinds of investigation, not in the profound intellectual work of the heroes of the history of science). Some scientists are mostly occupied with developing new instruments, new techniques of purification, new computer programs, and so forth and so on; another large class of people who might be described as engaged in "scientific work" in an ample sense of that phrase are simply applying well-established scientific techniques in relatively routine kinds of testing; and some have borrowed the honorific description "science" for no better

61. MICHAEL POLANYI, SCIENCE, FAITH AND SOCIETY 40 (1946).

reason than that they rely on scientific equipment of one kind or another—or just because it makes their work seem more respectable.

Nevertheless, the core business of science is inquiry. And scientific inquiry is by nature tentative and thoroughly fallibilist; it focuses on the general law or principle rather than on the particular case; its core values are intellectual honesty and willingness to share evidence; its procedures are problem-oriented and informally pragmatic; it is open-ended and forward-looking; and, though it is quite often relevant to policy, it is policy-neutral. So it is hardly surprising that the legal system has had trouble handling scientific testimony, for the legal culture could hardly be more different: adversarial; focused on the specific case; formally procedurally anchored; valuing promptness and finality; relying on precedent; and not only relevant, but also sensitive, to policy.

Justice Blackmun writes in *Daubert* that there are "important differences between the quest for truth in the courtroom and the quest for truth in the laboratory."[65] That's putting it mildly. The core business of a legal system is to resolve disputes; and a trial aims not to find out whether the defendant is guilty or liable, but to arrive at a determination of the defendant's guilt or liability—"determine," here, probably being closer to "deem" than to "discover." This is not to deny that inquiry plays a role in the legal process—of course it does; nor is it to deny that, although some cases are focused on legal technicalities, others are centrally concerned with factual issues. But it is to deny that inquiry is quite as central to the law as it is to science.

Moreover, as Justice Blackmun intimates, the way our legal system goes about making its "determinations of the truth" is really quite unlike the processes of scientific investigation: the law relies on an adversarial procedure, subject to the relevant standard of proof, under the constraint of rules some of which mandate the exclusion of relevant evidence for reasons that are not even obliquely truth-related. And the advocacy that is at the core of the adversarial process is a very different matter from inquiry. Inquiry starts with a question and seeks out evidence, aiming to arrive at an answer; advocacy, aiming to persuade, starts with a proposition to be defended and marshals the best evidence it can in its favor. The obligation of a scientist, qua inquirer, is to seek out as much evidence as he possibly can and to assess it as fairly as possible. By contrast, the obligation of an attorney, qua advocate, is to make the best possible case for his client's side of the dispute—including playing up the evidence that favors his case, and explaining inconvenient evidence away if he can't get it excluded.

Some, taking for granted that the legal system is in the relevant respects in the same business as the sciences, object that it goes about that business in a peculiar and ineffective way. C.S. Peirce said this quite explicitly: "Some persons fancy that hot and partisan debate is the way to investigate. This is the theory of our atrocious legal procedure. But Logic puts its heel upon this suggestion."[67] Judge Marvin Frankel

---

65. Daubert v. Merrell Dow Pharms., Inc., 509 U.S. 579, 596–97 (1993).

67. CHARLES SANDERS PEIRCE, 2 COLLECTED PAPERS OF CHARLES SANDERS PEIRCE para. 635 (Charles Hartshorne & Paul Weiss eds., 1932).

is only a little more oblique: "We proclaim to each other and to the world that the clash of adversaries is a powerful means for hammering out the truth.... [But] [d]espite our untested statements of self-congratulation, we know that others searching for the truth—in history, geography, medicine, whatever—do not emulate our adversarial system."[68] If the legal system were in the same business as history, geography, or as physics and the other sciences, its way of conducting that business would be peculiar, and inefficient, to say the least. But the law is really not in exactly the same business.

This is not at all to deny that it is desirable that legal determinations of guilt or liability be, so far as possible, factually correct; on the contrary, it is highly desirable. But that "so far as possible" includes "consistent with satisfying such non-truth-related desiderata as reaching a resolution within a reasonable period of time, proceeding in accordance with constitutional constraints, and taking certain policy-related considerations into account." Given that the legal "quest for truth" must be conducted within a relatively short time frame, it could be argued that an adversarial system is a way of ensuring that the search for and scrutiny of evidence is as thorough as possible within those constraints; though only on certain assumptions, among them that the resources available to the parties are roughly equal—assumptions that, sad to say, only too rarely obtain.

Implicit in the previous paragraphs, but needing to be made explicit, are the crucial differences between the legal and the scientific timetables. In the wake of a major discovery, scientific investigation sometimes advances at an impressive pace, rather as filling in a long, central crossword entry sometimes enables you to solve a whole slew of others; often, though, scientific work is halting and fumbling, slowed sometimes by lack of funds or by political resistance to potentially unwelcome results, and often enough by the sheer intellectual difficulty of the task. And there is always, at least in principle, the possibility of having to go back and start over on what had been thought to be settled questions. By contrast, not without reason, we want the legal system to reach its determinations within a reasonable period of time; and, again not without reason, we want those determinations, once the appeals process is exhausted, to stand.

Also implicit in the preceding paragraphs, and also needing to be made explicit, is that the legal process is highly regimented, conducted under formal rules of procedure, and rules of evidence, and so on. Paul Feyerabend, self-styled "court jester" of the philosophy of science, wrote of the "methodological anarchism" of the sciences; and despite his tendency to wild exaggeration, there is a grain of truth in this idea. It is not exactly that absolutely anything goes; but scientific inquiry does have a kind of free-ranging, "just do it," improvising character. By contrast, the regimented procedures of the law look more like a formal dance—a minuet, perhaps.

Also implicit, and also needing to be made explicit, is that some of the questions answers to which are to be determined at trial, will be case-specific: Did his mother's

68. Marvin F. Frankel, *The Search for Truth: An Umpireal View*, 123 U. Pa. L. Rev. 1031, 1036 (1975).

taking Bendectin cause Jeffrey Blum's birth defect? Did his occupational exposure to polychlorinated biphenyls (PCBs) promote Mr. Joiner's cancer? What is the probability that the match between this DNA sample from the crime scene and this defendant is a matter of chance? Moreover, when they are not foreclosed by precedent, legal decisions will often be influenced by policy considerations, for legal concepts are often tinged with policy.

IV

Those "Irreconcilable Differences" at Work

Against this background we can readily see why, as Mr. Humes so bluntly puts it, "courts don't do science very well":[74] why the law has such difficulty in handling scientific testimony, and so often gets less than the best out of science. But it is a very complicated, very tangled tale; for the tensions between science and law interact and reinforce each other. I had hoped to be able to shoehorn the difficulties into simple categories: "finality vs. fallibilism," "advocacy vs. inquiry," "inertia vs. innovation," and so on; but now this seems impossibly neat and tidy. Here, instead, is a not-so-tidy list.

(i) *Because its business is to resolve disputed issues, the law very often calls on those fields of science where the pressure of commercial interests is most severe.* In tort litigation, for example, much of the scientific work bearing on issues of causation may have been conducted by a drug company or a chemical manufacturer, for marketing purposes or, quite often, with an eye to protecting itself against litigation. This is exactly the kind of scientific work in which commercial interests most severely strain the informal scientific mechanisms that encourage honesty and discourage the withholding of evidence. I think in this context of the wave of litigation by plaintiffs alleging that their cardiovascular problems were aggravated by Merck's arthritis drug, Vioxx: for we now know that Merck's first large clinical trial, the VIGOR study, on the basis of which the FDA approved the drug, was designed in such a way as to be more likely to identify favorable than unfavorable trends; and that the APPROVe study, which prompted the withdrawal of the drug, did not use the statistical method the published report of the study said it used, and would have been even less favorable to Vioxx if it had.

(ii) *Because the legal system aspires to resolve disputes promptly, the scientific questions to which it seeks answers will often be those for which all the evidence is not yet in.* The cases that come to trial will normally be those in which the evidence is thus far incomplete and ambiguous. For one thing, plaintiffs must sue before the possibility of redress is legally foreclosed; for another, when the evidence that a drug or chemical is dangerous is overwhelming, plaintiffs' claims are likely to be settled out of court.

(iii) *Because of its case-specificity, the legal system often demands answers of a kind science is not well-equipped to supply; for related reasons, the legal system constitutes virtually the entire market for certain fields of forensic science (or quasi-science), and*

---

74. Edward Humes, Monkey Girl: Evolution, Education, Religion, and the Battle for America's Soul 257 (2007).

for certain psychiatric specialties. The first point is well-illustrated in *Joiner*: by the time of Mr. Joiner's suit, the toxicity of PCBs was well-established; but how much, if at all, Mr. Joiner's occupational PCB exposure contributed to his developing lung cancer? given that he had been a smoker and that he had a family history of lung cancer — was an almost impossibly difficult question.[79] The clearest illustrations of the second point come from such forensic-identification fields as hair or knife-mark analysis, and such psychiatric specialties as the recovery of supposedly repressed memories or, again, prediction of future dangerousness — surely among the weakest of what we sometimes call the "soft," or social sciences.

(iv) *Because of its adversarial character, the legal system tends to draw in as witnesses scientists who are in a sense marginal-more willing than most of their colleagues to give an opinion on the basis of less-than-overwhelming evidence; moreover, the more often he serves as an expert witness, the more unbudgeably confident a scientist may become in his opinion.* An attorney obligated to make the best possible case for his client will have an incentive to call on those scientists who are ready to accept an answer to some scientific question as warranted when others in the field still remain agnostic; and sometimes on scientists whose involvement in litigation has hardened their initially more-cautious attitudes into unwarranted certainty. I think, in this context, of Merrell Dow's Robert Brent, always ready to testify that Bendectin does not cause birth defects,[Ed.] and psychiatrist Dr. James Grigson, testifying over and over in Texas death-penalty hearings that the defendant would, to a psychiatric certainty, be dangerous in future.

The adversarial process may distort even relatively strong science from relatively strong fields, sometimes to such a degree that it creates a kind of artificial scientific doubt, or artificial scientific certainty; and can generate a public perception that this product is well known to be dangerous, or that product well known to be harmless, when really the evidence is weak, ambiguous, or lacking. Public (mis?)perception that silicone breast implants cause systemic connective-tissue disorders, for example, may have been generated in part by the legal system.

Adversarialism can also cause distortions in the forensic sciences, not only by encouraging the startling dogmatism with which knife-mark examiners, for example, routinely assert that they can make a match with one hundred percent certainty, and that they never make mistaken identifications, but also by fostering the kinds of mistakes that can occur in the application even of scientifically very solid forensic-identification techniques, such as DNA analysis, when technicians are too anxious to be "helpful," to get the results law-enforcement needs.

(v) *Legal rules can make it impossible to bring potentially useful scientific information to light; and the legal penchant for rules, "indicia," and the like sometimes transmutes*

---

79. Gen. Elec. Co. v. Joiner, 522 U.S. 136, 139–40 (1997).

[Ed.] *See also* Susan Haack, *What's Wrong with Litigation-Driven Science? An Essay in Legal Epistemology*, 38 Seton Hall L. Rev. 1053, 1063–69 (2008). This article is also available in Susan Haack, Evidence Matters: Science, Proof, and Truth in the Law 180–207 (2014).

scientific subtleties into formulaic legal shibboleths. Courts' obligation to screen out unreliable scientific evidence has amplified the epistemological atomism of the rules of evidence, for judges rule not only on which proffered expert witnesses may testify, but also on whether they may testify to this or that question specifically. This can be a problem: for interlocking pieces of evidence (for example, toxicological information, animal studies, and epidemiological data), none of which is sufficient by itself, may jointly constitute adequate warrant for a claim that this exposure likely caused a plaintiff's injury; but if no individual piece of it is deemed reliable enough to be admissible, a jury might never hear such evidence. The issue of "weight of evidence methodology" was explicit both in the Court of Appeals' reversal of the district court's exclusion of Mr. Joiner's expert testimony and in Justice Stevens's dissent in *Joiner*; but it was already implicit in *Daubert*, having come to the surface when, on remand, reasoning that each and every one of the Dauberts' experts would have to be excluded under *Daubert* as they had been under *Frye*,[Ed.] Judge Kozinski affirmed the district court's grant of summary judgment in favor of Merrell Dow.

Moreover, the legal system has a way of relying on brief verbal formulae to encapsulate key concepts or principles, to provide guidelines, and to give "indicia" of this or that. As a result, the law sometimes "rigidifies" ideas that scientists themselves treat much more flexibly. For example, though peer-reviewed publication is now standard practice at scientific and medical journals, I doubt that many working scientists imagine that the fact that a work has been accepted for publication after peer review is any guarantee that it is good stuff, or that its not having been published necessarily undermines its value. The legal system, however, has come to invest considerable epistemic confidence in peer-reviewed publication—perhaps for no better reason than that the law reviews are not peer-reviewed! Again, though requiring statistical significance is now also routine scientific practice, most scientists are probably aware of the element of arbitrariness in the usual standards; but legal actors sometimes seem to invest statistical significance with—well, with undue significance. And the law sometimes tinges scientific concepts with policy considerations—which partly explains why, for example, legal and scientific conceptions of causation don't quite mesh: the legal conception is informed by considerations about incentives and disincentives, about who should bear the costs of potentially risky enterprises, and sometimes about whose fault it is that evidence is lacking—considerations quite alien to science.

And the brief verbal formulae on which the law often relies can be ambiguous. For example, Justice Blackmun's observations about "peer review and publication"[95] could be taken as requiring that scientific testimony be based on work that has survived the pre-publication peer-review process of scientific journals—which is relatively easy for a court to determine, but a poor indication of reliability. Or they could be taken as requiring that such testimony be based on work that has survived and will

---

[Ed.]. Frye v. United States, 293 F. 1013 (D.C. Cir. 1923).

95. Daubert v. Merrell Dow Pharms., Inc., 509 U.S. 579, 593–94 (1993).

continue to survive the long-run scrutiny of scientists in the field—which is a better (though still imperfect) indication of reliability, but impossible for a court to determine. There is a similar ambiguity in Judge Kozinski's fifth "*Daubert* factor": whether the work on which scientific testimony is based is "litigation-driven."[97] It is reasonably easy for a court to determine whether the work on which testimony is based was undertaken after litigation began, but this is a very weak indicator of unreliability; whether the design or interpretation of the work on which the testimony is based was significantly affected by litigation-related considerations is a better indication of unreliability, but this is much harder for a court to determine.

(vi) *Both because of its concern for precedent, and because of the desideratum of finality, the legal system has a tendency to inertia, and sometimes lags behind science.* The novel scientific testimony excluded by the *Frye* court was proffered by the defense: Mr. Frye had passed a then-new blood-pressure deception test, "monograph" evidence, you might say; but by the time Florida first endorsed the *Frye* test in *Kaminski*, what was at stake was the admissibility of polygraph evidence.[99] The introduction of DNA "fingerprinting" in the late 1980s met with significant resistance in the ensuing "DNA Wars"; and even after the reliability of DNA analysis and its power to enable justice was acknowledged, prosecutors pushed back against requests for post-conviction testing. One might conjecture that *Daubert* and, especially, *Joiner* would have lessened the tendency for courts to follow other courts' rulings about the reliability of this or that kind of scientific evidence; but some commentators argue that *Joiner* has led judges who feel uneasy about the possibility that the very same evidence might be ruled reliable by one court and unreliable by another in the same jurisdiction to treat such evidentiary rulings as precedential.

Notes and Questions

1. How do the answers to our process questions—goal, methods, values, and results—lead to the problems in how law handles science, listed by Haack in Part IV?

2. Are the problems listed in Part IV, in how science is distorted by legal processes, intractable? In a part of the article not excerpted above, Haack suggests that "[since] divorce is out of the question ... [b]oth partners have tried to adapt." *Id.* at 21. For example, if scientific inquiry is ongoing, then legal processes that are inconsistent with that approach (like, say, statutes of limitation) can and have been changed. *Id.* Or if adversarial experts inherently come from the margins of a discipline, judges should appoint independent experts which can be nominated by neutral inquiry. *Id.* (citing efforts by the American Association for the Advancement of Science and the Duke University School of Law to create databases of independent experts and technical advisors). Haack concludes *Irreconcilable Differences* by stating: "Maybe we could learn something from the experiences of other countries

---

97. Daubert v. Merrell Dow Pharms., Inc., 43 F.3d 1311, 1317 (9th Cir. 1995).
99. Kaminski v. State, 63 So. 2d 339, 340 (Fla. 1952).

that are equally technologically advanced, but have different regulatory and legal arrangements; certainly, we would do well to approach these problems in a more empirical, experimental—a more scientific—spirit." *Id.* at 23.

Later in the text, having reviewed specific areas of expertise and their shortcomings, we will return to the question of reform efforts. For now, just keep in mind that the way things have been done is not necessarily the way things need to be.

B. The Practical Implication of Oil and Water in Law

In *Irreconcilable Differences*, Haack provides a list of problems that the "oil & water" effect can have when science is presented in a legal forum. Do those concerns exist, however, outside the realm of philosophical or theoretical analyses? The answer is "yes."

In the following case, we see an example of a court dealing with the "oil & water" effect in a judicial opinion, and see these distortions in action in real litigation. Charged with assessing the scientific evidence in the important Supreme Court case *Daubert v. Merrell Dow Pharmaceuticals, Inc.* after remand, Judge Kozinski, writing for the majority, reflects on the role of a legal arbiter in assessing whether proffered evidence is "good science" or not. This case is not unique, except perhaps for its candor, in expressing confusion and frustration at this difficult (if not impossible) task. Let it serve us as an introduction to those considerations, and as a reminder that this is not a "law school problem" created for 3L writing projects, but a real one that manifests itself in courtrooms across the United States on a regular basis.

Daubert v. Merrell Dow Pharmaceutical, Inc. ("*Daubert II*")

43 F.3d 1311 (9th Cir. 1995)

Kozinski, Circuit Judge.

[The case is a products liability lawsuit for the drug Bendectin, in which the plaintiffs allege that the medication caused birth defects. The case facts appear later in the book, in Chapter 8.B.iii.]

II

A. Brave New World

Federal judges ruling on the admissibility of expert scientific testimony face a far more complex and daunting task in a post-*Daubert* world than before. The judge's task under *Frye* [*v. United States*, 293 F. 1013 (D.C. Cir. 1923),] is relatively simple: to determine whether the method employed by the experts is generally accepted in the scientific community. Under *Daubert*, we must engage in a difficult, two-part analysis. First, we must determine nothing less than whether the experts' testimony reflects "scientific knowledge," whether their findings are "derived by the scientific method," and whether their work product amounts to "good science." [*Daubert v. Merrell Dow Pharms., Inc.*, 509 U.S. 579, 590, 593 (1993)].[Ed.] Second, we must ensure that the proposed expert testimony is "relevant to the task at hand," *id.* at 597, i.e., that it logically advances a material aspect of the proposing party's case. The Supreme Court referred to this second prong of the analysis as the "fit" requirement. *Id.* at 591.

The first prong of *Daubert* puts federal judges in an uncomfortable position. The question of admissibility only arises if it is first established that the individuals whose testimony is being proffered are experts in a particular scientific field; here, for example, the Supreme Court waxed eloquent on the impressive qualifications of plaintiffs' experts. *Id.* at 583 n. 2. Yet something doesn't become "scientific knowledge" just because it's uttered by a scientist; nor can an expert's self-serving assertion that his conclusions were "derived by the scientific method" be deemed conclusive, else the Supreme Court's opinion could have ended with footnote two. As we read the Supreme Court's teaching in *Daubert*, therefore, though we are largely untrained in science and certainly no match for any of the witnesses whose testimony we are reviewing, it is our responsibility to determine whether those experts' proposed testimony amounts to "scientific knowledge," constitutes "good science," and was "derived by the scientific method."

The task before us is more daunting still when the dispute concerns matters at the very cutting edge of scientific research, where fact meets theory and certainty dissolves into probability. As the record in this case illustrates, scientists often have vigorous and sincere disagreements as to what research methodology is proper, what should be accepted as sufficient proof for the existence of a "fact," and whether information derived by a particular method can tell us anything useful about the subject under study.

Our responsibility, then, unless we badly misread the Supreme Court's opinion, is to resolve disputes among respected, well-credentialed scientists about matters squarely within their expertise, in areas where there is no scientific consensus as to what is and what is not "good science," and occasionally to reject such expert testimony because it was not "derived by the scientific method."[Ed.] Mindful of our position in the hierarchy of the federal judiciary, we take a deep breath and proceed with this heady task.

B. Deus ex Machina

The Supreme Court's opinion in *Daubert* focuses closely on the language of Fed. R. Evid. 702, which permits opinion testimony by experts as to matters amounting to "scientific ... knowledge." The Court recognized, however, that knowledge in this context does not mean absolute certainty. 509 U.S. at 590. Rather, the Court said, "in order to qualify as 'scientific knowledge,' an inference or assertion must be derived by the scientific method." *Id.* Elsewhere in its opinion, the Court noted that Rule 702

[Ed.]　The citations to *Daubert* have been updated by the Author to reflect accurate pin citations, which were unavailable at the time of the original case.

[Ed.]　Emphasis added by the Author.

is satisfied where the proffered testimony is "based on scientifically valid principles." *Id.* at 597. Our task, then, is to analyze not what the experts say, but what basis they have for saying it.

Which raises the question: How do we figure out whether scientists have derived their findings through the scientific method or whether their testimony is based on scientifically valid principles? Each expert proffered by the plaintiffs assures us that he has "utiliz[ed] the type of data that is generally and reasonably relied upon by scientists" in the relevant field, and that he has "utilized the methods and methodology that would generally and reasonably be accepted" by people who deal in these matters. The Court held, however, that federal judges perform a "gatekeeping role," *Daubert*, 509 U.S. at 597; to do so they must satisfy themselves that scientific evidence meets a certain standard of reliability before it is admitted. This means that the expert's bald assurance of validity is not enough. Rather, the party presenting the expert must show that the expert's findings are based on sound science, and this will require some objective, independent validation of the expert's methodology.

While declining to set forth a "definitive checklist or test," *id.* at 593, the Court did list several factors federal judges can consider in determining whether to admit expert scientific testimony under Fed. R. Evid. 702: whether the theory or technique employed by the expert is generally accepted in the scientific community; whether it's been subjected to peer review and publication; whether it can be and has been tested; and whether the known or potential rate of error is acceptable. *Id.* at 593–94.[3] We read these factors as illustrative rather than exhaustive; similarly, we do not deem each of them to be equally applicable (or applicable at all) in every case.[4] Rather, we read the Supreme Court as instructing us to determine whether the analysis undergirding the experts' testimony falls within the range of accepted standards governing how scientists conduct their research and reach their conclusions.

One very significant fact to be considered is whether the experts are proposing to testify about matters growing naturally and directly out of research they have conducted independent of the litigation, or whether they have developed their opinions expressly for purposes of testifying. That an expert testifies for money does not necessarily cast doubt on the reliability of his testimony, as few experts appear in court merely as an eleemosynary gesture. But in determining whether proposed expert testimony amounts to good science, we may not ignore the fact that a scientist's normal workplace is the lab or the field, not the courtroom or the lawyer's office.[5]

---

3. These factors raise many questions, such as how do we determine whether the rate of error is acceptable, and by what standard? Or, what should we infer from the fact that the methodology has been tested, but only by the party's own expert or experts? Do we ask whether the methodology they employ to test their methodology is itself methodologically sound? *Such questions only underscore the basic problem, which is that we must devise standards for acceptability where respected scientists disagree on what's acceptable* [emphasis added by the Author].

4. Two of the four factors mentioned by the Supreme Court would be difficult or impossible to apply to the expert testimony in this case....

5. There are, of course, exceptions. Fingerprint analysis, voice recognition, DNA fingerprinting and a variety of other scientific endeavors closely tied to law enforcement may indeed have the court-

That an expert testifies based on research he has conducted independent of the litigation provides important, objective proof that the research comports with the dictates of good science. *See* PETER W. HUBER, GALILEO'S REVENGE: JUNK SCIENCE IN THE COURTROOM 206–09 (1991) (describing how the prevalent practice of expert-shopping leads to bad science). For one thing, experts whose findings flow from existing research are less likely to have been biased toward a particular conclusion by the promise of remuneration; when an expert prepares reports and findings before being hired as a witness, that record will limit the degree to which he can tailor his testimony to serve a party's interests. Then, too, independent research carries its own indicia of reliability, as it is conducted, so to speak, in the usual course of business and must normally satisfy a variety of standards to attract funding and institutional support. Finally, there is usually a limited number of scientists actively conducting research on the very subject that is germane to a particular case, which provides a natural constraint on parties' ability to shop for experts who will come to the desired conclusion. That the testimony proffered by an expert is based directly on legitimate, preexisting research unrelated to the litigation provides the most persuasive basis for concluding that the opinions he expresses were "derived by the scientific method." ... If the proffered expert testimony is not based on independent research, the party proffering it must come forward with other objective, verifiable evidence that the testimony is based on "scientifically valid principles." One means of showing this is by proof that the research and analysis supporting the proffered conclusions have been subjected to normal scientific scrutiny through peer review and publication. HUBER, GALILEO'S REVENGE at 209 (suggesting that "[t]he ultimate test of [a scientific expert's] integrity is her readiness to publish and be damned").

Peer review and publication do not, of course, guarantee that the conclusions reached are correct; much published scientific research is greeted with intense skepticism and is not borne out by further research. But the test under *Daubert* is not the correctness of the expert's conclusions but the soundness of his methodology. That the research is accepted for publication in a reputable scientific journal after being subjected to the usual rigors of peer review is a significant indication that it is taken seriously by other scientists, i.e., that it meets at least the minimal criteria of good science. *Daubert*, 509 U.S. at 593 ("[S]crutiny of the scientific community is a component of 'good science.'"). If nothing else, peer review and publication "increase the likelihood that substantive flaws in methodology will be detected." *Id.* ...

Establishing that an expert's proffered testimony grows out of pre-litigation research or that the expert's research has been subjected to peer review are the two principal ways the proponent of expert testimony can show that the evidence satisfies the first prong of Rule 702. Where such evidence is unavailable, the proponent of expert scientific testimony may attempt to satisfy its burden through the testimony of its own

---

room as a principal theatre of operation. *See, e.g., United States v. Chischilly*, 30 F.3d 1144, 1153 (9th Cir. 1994) (admitting expert testimony concerning a DNA match as proof the defendant committed sexual abuse and murder). As to such disciplines, the fact that the expert has developed an expertise principally for purposes of litigation will obviously not be a substantial consideration.

experts. For such a showing to be sufficient, the experts must explain precisely how they went about reaching their conclusions and point to some objective source—a learned treatise, the policy statement of a professional association, a published article in a reputable scientific journal or the like—to show that they have followed the scientific method, as it is practiced by (at least) a recognized minority of scientists in their field. *See United States v. Rincon,* 28 F.3d 921, 924 (9th Cir.1994) (research must be described "in sufficient detail that the district court [can] determine if the research was scientifically valid").

Notes and Questions

1. In *Daubert II*, we see that, faced with the responsibility of determining what science is "good" and what is not, Judge Kozinski expresses reservations about whether that can be done in a legal forum. To do so, he reiterates the so-called "*Daubert* factors" from the Supreme Court, but adds a new factor of consideration as well: whether the opinions grew out of research previously performed or whether the opinions were created wholly for the purposes of testifying. As a way to evaluate the science, is this new factor helpful in deciding what is "good science" or not? As a legal matter, is it inconsistent with *Daubert* itself to add new variables for consideration? Since *Daubert II*, many courts (but not all) have considered the factor of litigation-driven science in evaluating expert evidence, some calling it the "fifth factor" of consideration after the four from *Daubert* at the Supreme Court. *See, e.g., Johnson v. Manitowoc Boom Trucks, Inc.,* 484 F.3d 426 (6th Cir. 2007). *See also* David S. Caudill, *Expertise, Lab Lit, and the Fantasy of Science Free From Economics,* 33 CARDOZO L. REV. 2471, 2481 (2012).

2. Assume that the "fifth factor" of whether the opinions were created solely for purposes of litigation is legitimate to use in deciding what is "good science." Afterwards, Judge Kozinski then describes, in footnote 5, that:

   > Fingerprint analysis, voice recognition, DNA fingerprinting and a variety of other scientific endeavors closely tied to law enforcement may indeed have the courtroom as a principal theatre of operations.... As to such disciplines, the fact that the expert has developed an expertise principally for purposes of litigation will obviously not be a substantial consideration.

   Daubert II, 43 F.3d at 1317 n. 5. Why would Judge Kozinski make this blanket assertion? As we begin to look at expert evidence in detail later in the course, we will learn that the assumption that forensic evidence is objectively based and without any corrupting influences is naïve at best and tragic at worst.

   In Chapter 2 and again in Chapter 7 on forensic evidence, we will have an opportunity to learn about the sad case of Cameron Willingham. Convicted of murdering his three children in an arson, the State of Texas executed Willingham in April 2004.[7] Evidence at trial included a fire expert testifying that Willingham

---

7. David Grann, *Trial by Fire,* NEW YORKER (Sept. 7, 2009). https://www.newyorker.com/magazine/2009/09/07/trial-by-fire.

must have set the fire intentionally, due to several observations at the scene. Later review of the case debunked these findings, saying they had no scientific basis and that they were more "characteristic of mystics or psychics." The National Academy Report in 2009, speaking of fire investigations in general, found that "Despite the paucity of research, some arson investigators continue to make determinations about whether or not a particular fire was set. However, according to testimony presented to the committee, many of the rules of thumb that are typically assumed to indicate that an accelerant was used have been shown not to be true."[8] What might the Willingham case tell us about whether forensic evidence can be litigation-driven?

3. Fundamentally, the post-*Daubert* world of gatekeeping will require judges to evaluate the merits of complex scientific evidence, even if it requires, as Judge Kozinski states, "resolv[ing] disputes among respected, well-credentialed scientists about matters squarely within their expertise, in areas where there is no scientific consensus as to what is and what is not 'good science' ..." 43 F.3d at 1316. Whether or not that description holds, it is required of judges and will form the core of litigation issues regarding complex expert testimony. We will spend the rest of the semester reviewing the rules of expert analysis and examples of courts grappling with science, and we will see how they do with a "daunting" (but necessary) task.

---

8. NATIONAL RESEARCH COUNCIL, NATIONAL ACADEMY OF SCIENCES, STRENGTHENING FORENSIC SCIENCE IN THE UNITED STATES: A PATH FORWARD 173 (2009).

Chapter 2

Substantive Rules of Admission

Admission of expert testimony depends on compliance with a complex series of both substantive and procedural rules. We will turn to the procedural prerequisites and review them in detail in Chapter 3, but first we need to decide when expert evidence can be admitted under the substantive standards of the Federal Rules of Evidence or similar state rules.

As with all evidentiary issues, the admissibility of expert testimony is largely contextual. This may lead to apparent incongruity, as identical testimony may be admissible in one case but not be in another, or an expert may qualify to testify in one case but be excluded in another. Yet as we evaluate the individual standards for each rule of evidence, we can see that lack of compliance with these principles will provide an opportunity to prevent testimony for a variety of reasons. In that regard, I envision expert admission under the substantive evidentiary standards as a "series of hoops" that the proponent of the testimony must jump through, all of which must be satisfied prior to the admission of the expert testimony.

This chapter will deal with those hoops by defining what each is intended to do, establishing each corresponding legal standard for admission, and then applying those standards to new situations. It may be helpful to recognize that in real litigation, each expert rarely raises concerns in every area. Rather, an advocate will commonly raise one or two issues of import for an individual expert. The back-and-forth discussion of compliance with these evidentiary and procedural rules of admission provide much of the grist for the mill for pretrial litigation.

Any discussion of evidentiary issues regarding expert witnesses must surely begin with the central rule of expert testimony — Federal Rule of Evidence 702. Adopted in the initial set of rules which became effective in 1975, it has been amended several times in the interim. In its current form, the rule provides a template for evaluation of expert testimony:

Federal Rule of Evidence 702:
Testimony by Expert Witnesses

A witness who is qualified as an expert by knowledge, skill, experience, training, or education may testify in the form of an opinion or otherwise if:

(a) the expert's scientific, technical, or other specialized knowledge will help the trier of fact to understand the evidence or to determine a fact in issue;

(b) the testimony is based on sufficient facts or data;

(c) the testimony is the product of reliable principles and methods; and

(d) the expert has reliably applied the principles and methods to the facts of the case.

Unlike many rules of evidence which cover a single substantive standard—hearsay under Rule 802 or habit under Rule 406—the language of Rule 702 contains several different standards, and therefore can be seen as "four rules for the price of one." Each of the four rules in Rule 702 is intended to answer a different question and, alone or in combination with other rules, provides the legal standard for determining admissibility. What are the four questions Rule 702 answers?

– **Question #1**: Will the factfinder need expert testimony to evaluate this issue?

– **Question #2**: Is this person an expert?

– **Question #3**: Does this expert have an adequate factual basis for the opinion?

– **Question #4**: Is the method used by the expert based in reliable principles in general, which have been applied reliably to the specific issue in the case?

Working our way through these questions, each one at a time, comprises the entirety of Chapter 2, and will cover the main tenets of substantive admissibility for expert testimony. The materials in Section A involve evaluation of whether testimony by an expert is necessary to resolve the issues of concern in an individual case. In the cases in Section B, courts will consider whether a particular proposed witness meets the requirements of expertise required by the rules. We will also focus in detail on the borderline between lay and expert witnesses by considering those witnesses who have specialized knowledge due to exposure to subject matter in the course of their work, but who do not meet the classical definition of expertise.

Section C addresses experts who rely on otherwise inadmissible materials in order to form their opinion, and whether those materials can properly form the basis of their opinion. In Section D, the chapter concludes with the most detailed materials of all: evaluating expert reliability. A proponent of an expert must establish reliability of the expert's methodology in general terms—i.e., that accident reconstruction relies on sound principles of engineering—and also that those principles were reliably applied to the situation at hand. We will also consider the methods by which courts resolve contested reliability matters and, in a more general sense, what the effect has been of judicial screening of expert testimony at trial.

A. Will the Factfinder Need Expert Testimony to Evaluate This Issue? The Expert Relevance Question

"… an expert … may testify in the form of an opinion or otherwise if: (a) the expert's … specialized knowledge will help the trier of fact to understand the evidence or to determine a fact in issue." Fed. R. Evid. 702.

In a criminal case, a defendant's trunk contains a spoon and a small sifter-grinder, each with cocaine residue attached. The prosecution calls an experienced narcotic detection officer to the stand to explain to the jury that a sifter-grinder is a tool used by narcotics venders to adulterate cocaine. Can the expert testify to the common use of a sifter in the drug trade?[9]

In a civil case, plaintiff sues a television network for breach of contract and asks for damages in the form of half of the net revenue from the show. Plaintiff calls an expert economist to explain to the jury how he calculated the total loss to the plaintiff by starting with the undisputed revenue total from the show and dividing it by two. Can the expert testify to the damages due to the plaintiff?[10]

At the core of these two scenarios, we must answer the same question: When may expert testimony be presented by a party to help the jury reach a verdict (in their favor, presumably)? In our first of four standards established under Rule 702, the language from the rule envisions two separate scenarios where expert testimony is admissible: a) if the testimony helps the factfinder determine a fact at issue, or b) even if it does not help decide the issue, if it helps the factfinder understand the evidence. Although they are similar, each envisions a different scenario.

Yet even with these limits, two additional factors must also be considered. Even if the testimony helps the factfinder decide the issue—as it would in each of our two examples above—does the jury really need help on the issue? Even when helpful, expert evidence cannot be based on common knowledge. In the second example above, the court excluded the damages testimony after determining that the jury could figure out how to divide net revenue in half. On the other hand, the judge did permit the narcotics detective to explain the use of a sifter in the cocaine trade. We will explore where the line is drawn between different perceptions of common knowledge later in the chapter.

Finally, even if expert testimony is helpful and not common knowledge, it cannot violate a separate limit from Rule 704: it cannot clearly and unequivocally tell the jury what decision to reach. In our cocaine prosecution, if the detective explained that, in addition to sifting cocaine, a sifter is "clearly drug paraphernalia" under the relevant statute, we may exclude that testimony as well. When testimony is more ambiguous than this example, however, the limit of the rule may be unclear.

Together these four principles explain when expert testimony meets standards of relevance under Rule 702.

---

9. United States v. Rivera-Rodriguez, 808 F.2d 886 (1st Cir. 1986).

10. Trademark Props., Inc. v. A&E Television Networks, No. 2:06-CV-2195-CWH, 2008 WL 4811461, at *2 (D.S.C. Oct. 28, 2008).

EEOC v. U-Haul Co. of Texas

No. Civ.A. H-04-3788, 2005 WL 2860987

(S.D. Texas Nov. 1, 2005)

HITTNER, J.

Pending before the Court is EEOC's Motion to Exclude Testimony of Defendant U-Haul Texas's Designated Expert Witness (Document No. 56). Having considered the motion, submissions, and applicable law, the Court determines the motion should be granted.

BACKGROUND

The Equal Employment Opportunity Commission (EEOC) filed the instant suit on September 29, 2004 asserting hostile work environment, sexual harassment, and retaliation claims against U-Haul Co. of Texas.... These claims were brought on behalf of three women who allege a former U-Haul manager acted inappropriately toward them on a number of occasions during the women's course of employment with U-Haul.

On March 31, 2005, U-Haul filed its expert witness designation with this Court. In its designation, U-Haul designated Leticia Flores as its only expert. Flores is an investigator employed by the EEOC, and was involved in the investigation of the allegations that form the basis of the instant lawsuit. In its designation, U-Haul indicates that Flores has expertise in the investigation of discrimination claims and indicates that Flores's "opinions can be found in her deposition ..." [that there was no evidence of sexual or gender discrimination by U-Haul.][Ed.] On September 1, 2005, EEOC filed a motion seeking to exclude Flores's expert witness testimony. EEOC argues that Flores has no specialized knowledge that would assist the trier of fact in understanding the evidence or determining a fact issue. EEOC further argues that even if Flores qualifies as an expert, her testimony is impermissible under Rule 403 of the Federal Rules of Evidence. In response, U-Haul contends that Flores's duties as an EEOC investigator qualify her as an expert. Moreover, U-Haul avers that Flores's testimony is relevant because she investigated the alleged discrimination in this case and ostensibly later changed her opinion about whether U-Haul engaged in culpable conduct.

LAW AND ANALYSIS

EEOC challenges U-Haul's designation of Flores as an expert witness on the grounds that, *inter alia*, Flores's testimony does not comply with the requirements of Rule 702 of the Federal Rules of Evidence. Rule 702 provides "[i]f scientific, technical, or other specialized knowledge will assist the trier of fact to understand the evidence or to determine a fact in issue, a witness qualified as an expert by knowledge,

---

[Ed.] Bracketed material has been moved within the text for clarity, by the Author.

skill, experience, training, or education, may testify thereto in the form of an opinion or otherwise...." Fed. R. Evid. 702. Thus, the testifying individual must both qualify as an expert and her testimony must assist the jury in resolving a fact issue or understanding evidence. *Id.*; *see Daubert v. Merrell Dow Pharms., Inc.*, 509 U.S. 579, 591 (1993). The Court will first analyze whether Flores's testimony will assist the jury in resolving a fact issue or understanding the evidence.

The parties spend little time informing the Court how Flores's testimony will assist the jury as required by Rule 702. U-Haul appears to designate Flores as an expert so that she can opine that insufficient evidence exists indicating wrongdoing by U-Haul. Indeed, U-Haul avers that Flores's deposition testimony makes clear "that the person entrusted by the EEOC to investigate this matter found no evidence of sexual or gender discrimination." Essentially, U-Haul asks the Court to allow Flores to opine on the sufficiency of the evidence.

As other courts have noted, specialized knowledge, without a showing that such knowledge will assist the trier of fact, is insufficient to meet the requirements of Rule 702.... The Court finds the Texas Supreme Court's analysis in the case of *K-Mart Corp. v. Honeycutt*, 24 S.W.3d 357 (Tex. 2000) persuasive on the issue of whether Flores should be permitted to testify. There, the Texas court, in analyzing Texas Rule of Evidence 702, which employs nearly identical language to Federal Rule 702, noted that expert testimony should be excluded if the testimony is within common knowledge of the trier of fact. *Id.* at 360. The Court recognized

> Expert testimony assists the trier-of-fact when the expert's knowledge and experience on a relevant issue are beyond that of the average juror and the testimony helps the trier-of fact understand the evidence or determine a fact issue. When the jury is equally competent to form an opinion about the ultimate fact issues or the expert's testimony is within the common knowledge of the jury, the trial court should exclude the expert's testimony.

Id. (citations omitted). Here, assuming, *arguendo*, Flores qualifies as an expert, the Court determines her testimony would not assist the trier of fact in either resolving the fact issues in this case or understanding the evidence. The issue here is whether U-Haul engaged in discriminatory activities, and the jury is qualified and able to make its own determination as to the sufficiency of the facts underlying this action.

Notes and Questions

1. Was the court correct in deciding that the EEOC investigation evidence would not be relevant under Rule 702? If it is helpful and related to the case, why not admit it? Is there any evidence from an expert like Flores which might be admissible, even if her conclusion was not?

2. Notice in this case that the court makes no attempt to discuss Flores's qualifications as an expert in employment discrimination. Why does it not matter whether she is qualified when deciding admission of the evidence?

Siring v. Oregon State Board of Higher Education
927 F. Supp. 2d 1069 (D. Or. 2013)

SIMON, District Judge.

In this lawsuit alleging employment discrimination based on age and disability, Defendant ... moves to exclude the expert report and testimony of Jean Stockard, Ph.D., Plaintiffs expert relating to the tenure-track review, evaluation, and termination processes and procedures in the Oregon University System and the process and procedure used in Defendant's decision to deny tenure to Plaintiff and terminate her employment....

STANDARDS

Federal Rule of Evidence 702 establishes that expert opinion evidence is admissible if (1) the witness is sufficiently qualified as an expert by knowledge, skill, experience, training, or education; (2) the scientific, technical, or other specialized knowledge will help the trier of fact to understand the evidence or to determine a fact in issue; (3) the testimony is based on sufficient facts or data; (4) the testimony is the product of reliable principles and methods; and (5) the expert has reliably applied these principles and methods. Fed. R. Evid. 702. Under *Daubert* and its progeny, the district court's inquiry into admissibility is a flexible one....

"The trial court must assure that the expert testimony 'both rests on a reliable foundation and is relevant to the task at hand.'" *Primiano v. Cook*, 598 F.3d 558, 565 (9th Cir. 2010) (quoting *Daubert*, 509 U.S. at 597, 113 S. Ct. 2786). "Expert opinion testimony is relevant if the knowledge underlying it has a valid connection to the pertinent inquiry. And it is reliable if the knowledge underlying it has a reliable basis in the knowledge and experience of the relevant discipline." *Id.* at 565.... The judge is "supposed to screen the jury from unreliable nonsense opinions, but not exclude opinions merely because they are impeachable. The district court is not tasked with deciding whether the expert is right or wrong, just whether his [or her] testimony has substance such that it would be helpful to a jury." *Alaska Rent-A-Car*, 709 F.3d at 883.... [W]hen an expert meets the threshold established by Rule 702, the expert may testify and the factfinder decides how much weight to give that testimony.

BACKGROUND

Plaintiff Rosemary Siring was a tenured professor at the University of Montana when she took a position as a tenure-track professor at Eastern Oregon University ("EOU") in 2006. In her third year of instruction at EOU, she was evaluated. At the end of her fourth year of instruction, she was placed on a one-year terminal contract. Siring alleges that she was terminated based on her age and perceived disability.

Plaintiff's proffered expert, Jean Stockard, Ph.D., has worked at the University of Oregon for nearly 40 years. She is a faculty member and served on and chaired the elected personnel committees of the College of Arts and Sciences and the University. Those committees review personnel cases, including tenure and promotion decisions, and make recommendations as to their disposition. During her career, Dr. Stockard has: (1) served as Department Head and Associate Head at the University of Oregon; (2) served as an external reviewer for other universities, where she provided independent reviews of candidates for promotion and tenure; (3) served three terms as President of the University of Oregon chapter of the American Association of University Professors …; (4) served as chair of the AAUP committees charged with addressing issues related to academic freedom and discrimination based on gender; (5) served as a grievance counselor, assisting individuals navigating the University's grievance process; …; (7) developed tenure processes for the University of Oregon in compliance with the Oregon Administrative Rules; (8) reviewed tenure processes for compliance with the OARs; and (9) engaged in scholarly research on the ways in which institutional practices and policies affect the career progression of women in science and engineering sectors of the academy.

Dr. Stockard was provided with more than 5,500 pages of documents from this case.… Dr. Stockard prepared a written opinion and, in response to Defendant's Motion in Limine, a supplemental opinion, in which she opines about the Oregon University System's tenure review process generally and EOU's tenure review process specifically with respect to Siring … [and] concludes, among other things, that there were significant deficiencies in the tenure review process with respect to Siring and that there was "no scholarly reason for Siring's dismissal".…

DISCUSSION

Defendant argues that the Stockard Report is not admissible under FRE 702.… [That is due to the fact that] it will not help a jury understand the evidence or determine a fact at issue in this case … [because it] … [merely substitutes Dr. Stockard's judgment for the jury's because the subject matter of the Stockard Report is within the common knowledge of the average layperson.…][Ed.]

… Expert opinion must have "substance such that it would be helpful to the jury." *Alaska Rent-A-Car* [*v. Avis Budget Group, Inc.*], 709 F.3d at 883 [(9th Cir. 2013)]. In other words, it should "address an issue beyond the common knowledge of the average layman." *Mukhtar v. Cal. State Univ., Hayward*, 299 F.3d 1053, 1065 n. 9 (9th Cir. 2002).…

Defendant argues that the Stockard report (1) will not aid the jury…, and (2) contains legal conclusions and interpretations of Oregon law that usurp the court's role in explaining the law to the jury. Defendant's arguments are unavailing.

The Subject Matter of the Stockard Report Is Not Within the Knowledge of the Average Layperson

The particularized and specialized evaluation and review practices, policies, and procedures relevant to a tenure-track professor are not within the common knowledge of the average layperson. How tenure-track professors are evaluated, reviewed, and promoted in the Oregon University System is not necessarily similar to how a layperson may be evaluated, reviewed, or promoted at his or her job. It is both specialized and specifically governed in the Oregon University System by numerous administrative rules. *See* Or. Admin. R. 580-021-0100 through 580-021-0140. Professorial tenure is

---

[Ed.] The final section of the sentence, beginning with "merely," has been moved within the text, by the Author.

a unique system, and the Court finds that as an expert in the field of tenure-track evaluation, review, and promotion, Dr. Stockard's opinion addresses issues beyond the
common knowledge of the average layperson and will aid a jury in making its determination. Accordingly, Dr. Stockard may testify regarding the Oregon University System
standards and practices for tenure-track review, evaluation, promotion, and termination
and whether EOU complied with those standards in its decisions relating to Siring. *See,
e.g., Hangarter* [*v. Provident Life & Accident Ins. Co.*], 373 F.3d at 1016 [(9th Cir. 2004)].

The Stockard Report does not usurp the Court's role

Defendant also argues that Dr. Stockard's report is not helpful to the jury because
it merely reflects Dr. Stockard's understanding of the law and is improper because an
expert cannot displace the court's role of explaining the law to the jury.... [A]n expert's
opinion that relies in part on the expert's understanding of state law does not improperly
usurp the court's role. *Hangarter*, 373 F.3d at 1017. An expert may "properly be called
upon to aid the jury in understanding the facts in evidence even though reference to
those facts is couched in legal terms" and may "refer to the law in expressing an opinion
without that reference rendering the testimony inadmissible." *Id.* (citation omitted).
The Stockard Report does not improperly invade the province of the Court....

Relevancy and Unfair Prejudice

... Defendant asserts that the Stockard Report merely opines that EOU's procedures
did not comply with "usual" practices in the Oregon University System. Thus, Defendant argues, the Stockard Report is not relevant because it does not opine that
EOU treated Siring differently than any other professor at EOU and, therefore, does
not support an inference of discrimination.

Expert testimony is relevant if it will help the jury understand a fact at issue. *See,
e.g., Cooper v. Brown*, 510 F.3d 870, 942 (9th Cir. 2007); *see also Primiano* [*v. Cook*],
598 F.3d at 565 [(9th Cir. 2010)] (finding that expert testimony "is relevant if the
knowledge underlying it has a valid connection to the pertinent inquiry"). Expert
testimony need not address every element of a claim, but need only help the jury
understand the evidence or "a fact in issue." Fed. R. Evid. 702(a).

Siring proffers Dr. Stockard as an expert in the usual policies and procedures for
tenure review and evaluation in the Oregon University System and to opine on the
ways in which EOU failed to follow those policies and procedures with regard to its
evaluation of Siring. Although Dr. Stockard does not compare how EOU treated
Siring with how EOU treated any other employee, which might more directly support
an implication of discrimination, such a direct link is not required to render Dr.
Stockard's opinion relevant. Siring is allowed to proffer circumstantial evidence to
the jury to assist the jury in determining whether EOU based its employment decision
relating to Siring on legitimate, nondiscriminatory reasons or whether EOU made
its decision with an improper discriminatory or retaliatory motive. *See, e.g., Gay v.
Waiters' & Dairy Lunchmen's Union, Loc. No. 30*, 694 F.2d 531, 550 (9th Cir. 1982)
(finding that when inferring discriminatory intent, all evidence, "direct and circumstantial, statistical and nonstatistical" relevant to such intent should be considered).

Dr. Stockard's testimony that EOU failed to follow the usual and customary procedures and policies of the Oregon University System in EOU's tenure evaluation and review of Siring is information that would be helpful for a jury in determining the propriety of EOU's employment decisions with regards to Siring. *See, e.g., Dukes v. Wal-Mart, Inc.*, 509 F.3d 1168, 1179 (9th Cir. 2007) (rejecting argument that expert report should be excluded because the expert's opinion did not prove discrimination, noting that a jury may agree that the expert's evidence was insufficient to prove discrimination, but that does not warrant excluding the expert testimony); *Suzuki Motor Corp. v. Consumers Union of U.S., Inc.*, 330 F.3d 1110, 1137 n. 14 (9th Cir. 2003) (noting that expert testimony that the defendant departed from professional standards "does shed light on the propriety" of the defendant's actions). Even if Dr. Stockard's report does not, by itself, provide evidence to prove all of the elements of Siring's claim that does not render the opinion irrelevant....

Unfair prejudice and confusion

Defendant also argues that the Stockard Report should be excluded under FRE 403 because it is unfairly prejudicial and confusing to the jury.... The fact that her conclusions are helpful to Siring and not to Defendant does not render her testimony unfairly prejudicial.

CONCLUSION

The Court finds Dr. Jean Stockard to be a qualified expert. Defendant's motion in limine to exclude Dr. Stockard's expert testimony is granted in part and denied in part. Dr. Stockard's testimony as to the intent, motive, or state of mind of Eastern Oregon University and its personnel is excluded, but her remaining testimony is relevant and reliable and will be admitted.

Notes and Questions

1. What will the jury understand after the expert's testimony that the jury did not understand before? How do we know they need assistance on this issue?

2. At trial, the jury hears Dr. Stockard's testimony regarding tenure practices and procedures as permitted in the case. Does it matter that, after hearing Dr. Stockard's testimony, the jury would not yet be able to reach a verdict? Why or why not?

3. If the EEOC evidence was irrelevant and excluded in *U-Haul*, why is evidence of Dr. Stockard's personal investigation into Siring's termination admissible in *Siring*?

4. In some ways, the question of whether an expert's evidence assists the jury depends on whether that expert can provide insight into an unusual or unfamiliar subject such as tenure practices within an academic institution or medical treatment options for a particular disease. As a specialty becomes more complex, the argument that it is "common knowledge" and unhelpful becomes less relevant. However, in some cases, the expert's evidence would assist the jury, but may also be too close to the average layperson's experience to be admissible under Rule 702. We will evaluate this distinction by examining two similar scenarios in the following case and problem.

Godfrey v. Iverson

559 F.3d 569 (D.C. Cir. 2009)

RANDOLPH, Circuit Judge

In the early hours of July 20, 2005, a brawl erupted at the Eyebar, a Washington, D.C. nightclub. Among the injured was Marlin Godfrey, a patron in the Eyebar VIP area that night. He suffered a concussion, a ruptured eardrum, a burst blood vessel in his eye, a torn rotator cuff, various cuts and bruises, and emotional injuries. Godfrey sued Allen Iverson and his bodyguard, Jason Kane, both of whom were in the Eyebar VIP area that night. The amended complaint alleged that Kane and Terrance Williams, who also sometimes acted as Iverson's bodyguard, attacked him and directly caused his physical and emotional injuries, and that Iverson was negligent in failing to stop both men from injuring Godfrey. After a six-day trial, the jury returned a verdict in favor of Godfrey against Kane for assault and battery and intentional infliction of emotional distress, and against Iverson for negligent supervision of Kane.... In response to Iverson's and Kane's appeal, Godfrey filed what may be described as a conditional cross-appeal: if we order a new trial, he would like us to declare that several of the district court's evidentiary rulings were in error. The only issue warranting discussion is Iverson's contention that, absent expert testimony, the evidence was legally insufficient to support the verdict against him for negligent supervision.

Allen Iverson has played professional basketball since the Philadelphia 76ers drafted him in 1996. He now plays for the Detroit Pistons. He often hires bodyguards to accompany him when he attends public events. Iverson's manager Gary Moore was in charge of hiring the bodyguards and telling them when and where to work. Jason Kane has provided security for Iverson in the Washington, D.C. area for some time and was doing so during Iverson's charity weekend events in July 2005.

Iverson and several friends entered the Eyebar nightclub shortly after midnight, with Kane as his bodyguard. They went straight to the small VIP area of the club, where Marlin Godfrey and his party already had a table. Although accounts differed about how the fight started, the evidence indicated that an argument broke out between Godfrey and Williams, Kane's friend who sometimes worked as Iverson's bodyguard and happened to be in the club that night. Witnesses said that Kane and Williams loudly and aggressively ordered patrons, including Godfrey and his party, to leave the VIP area and make room for Iverson and his friends. Soon after Curtis Fitzgerald — an Eyebar security employee and friend of Kane's and Godfrey's — intervened to defuse the situation and move Godfrey's party to a different table, Kane shoved Fitzgerald and a group of others jumped in the attack. When Godfrey, who has significant martial arts training, walked toward the fracas to "help his friend" Fitzgerald, he was attacked and beaten until he became disoriented; he regained his senses in the club's storage room, where he had wandered to get away from the fight. Godfrey received treatment for his injuries that night in the George Washington Hospital emergency room and was released at noon that day.

Williams admitted that he took part in beating up Godfrey. Other witnesses testified that after Kane pushed Fitzgerald, they saw Kane jump into the fight and attack Godfrey, punching him, kicking him, and striking him in the head with a bottle. Iverson stayed out of the fray in the back corner of the VIP area, standing on a couch or bench and observing. He did not say or do anything to try to stop Kane or anyone else from fighting. There was no evidence that any of the club's patrons or employees attacked or threatened Iverson.

[At trial], the case went to the jury with two claims against Kane—assault and battery and intentional infliction of emotional distress—and two claims against Iverson for negligent supervision of Kane and Williams. The jury found Kane liable on both claims against him, and it found Iverson liable for negligently supervising Kane. As to Williams, the jury found that he was not working for Iverson that night. The jury awarded Godfrey $250,000 for pain and suffering and $10,000 for medical expenses....

Liability for negligent supervision arises when an "employer knew or should have known its employee behaved in a dangerous or otherwise incompetent manner, and that the employer, armed with that actual or constructive knowledge, failed to adequately supervise the employee." *Brown v. Argenbright Sec., Inc.*, 782 A.2d 752, 760 (D.C. 2001) (internal quotation marks and citation omitted). Iverson argues that the district court should have granted judgment as a matter of law on the negligent supervision claim because Godfrey did not introduce expert testimony to establish the standard of care Iverson owed in supervising Kane. This argument stems from a peculiar aspect of common law negligence in the District of Columbia. A plaintiff has the burden of proving the applicable standard of care, the defendant's failure to meet that standard, and the causal relationship between that failure and the plaintiff's injury. *Meek v. Shepard*, 484 A.2d 579, 581 (D.C. 1984). In the typical negligence case, the standard of care applicable to a person's conduct is simply that of a "reasonable man under like circumstances." Restatement (Second) of Torts § 283 (1965); *see also id.* § 298. Ordinarily a jury can ascertain this standard without the aid of expert testimony. But "if the subject in question is so distinctly related to some science, profession or occupation as to be beyond the ken of the average layperson," D.C. law requires expert testimony to establish the pertinent standard of care unless it is "within the realm of common knowledge and everyday experience" of the jurors. *District of Columbia v. Arnold & Porter*, 756 A.2d 427, 433 (D.C. 2000) (internal quotation marks and citations omitted).

The expert testimony requirement originated in professional malpractice cases. *See District of Columbia v. Hampton*, 666 A.2d 30, 35 (D.C. 1995) (citing, for example, medical and legal malpractice cases in which expert testimony was required to establish the standard of care). Recently, though, the D.C. Court of Appeals has required expert testimony in a wider variety of cases, *id.*, even in those that might initially seem to fall within jurors' common knowledge. *See Briggs v. Wash. Metro. Area Transit Auth.*, 481 F.3d 839, 845 (D.C. Cir. 2007) (cataloguing various non-malpractice cases in which expert testimony was required to establish the standard of care). And as *Briggs* recognized, "expert testimony is routinely required 'in negligence cases ...

which involve issues of safety, security and crime prevention.'" *Id.* at 845–46 (quoting *Varner v. District of Columbia*, 891 A.2d 260, 267 (D.C. 2006)).

Iverson argues that because this case involves security issues, Godfrey had to establish the standard of care through expert testimony. He relies on a series of district court cases. In *Edwards v. Okie Dokie, Inc.*, plaintiffs sued a nightclub and the District of Columbia for negligently supervising security personnel and police officers who used allegedly unreasonable force to stop an altercation outside a nightclub. 473 F. Supp. 2d 31, 35, 45–46 (D.D.C. 2007). In *Parker v. Grand Hyatt Hotel*, police officers and hotel security personnel forcibly removed the plaintiff from a hotel restaurant under suspicion that he attempted to steal something; he sued the District of Columbia and hotel management for negligently supervising those officers. 124 F. Supp. 2d 79, 83–84 (D.D.C. 2000). In *Farooq v. MDRB Corp.*, the plaintiff brought suit against a hotel for negligently training and supervising security personnel who failed to find a knife that a patron carried into a hotel party and used to kill the plaintiff's son. 498 F. Supp. 2d 284, 285–86 (D.D.C. 2007). The district court granted summary judgment in each of these cases because the plaintiffs failed to present expert testimony establishing the standard of care applicable to a municipality or business entity in training and supervising its police or security officers. *Edwards*, 473 F.Supp.2d at 46; *Parker*, 124 F. Supp. 2d at 90; *Farooq*, 498 F. Supp. 2d at 287.

We do not believe these cases stand for the proposition that expert testimony is always required to establish the standard of care in cases involving supervision of security personnel, much less personal bodyguards. Expert testimony was necessary to establish the standard of care for installation of cushioning under the monkey bars on a playground, *Messina v. District of Columbia*, 663 A.2d 535, 538 (D.C. 1995), but not to establish whether holes in the side rails of a playground slide created an unreasonably dangerous condition, *District of Columbia v. Shannon*, 696 A.2d 1359, 1365–66 (D.C. 1997). As the court put it in *Shannon*, "It takes no expert knowledge of human behavior to know that children stick their fingers in holes." *Id.* at 1365. As to the need for expert testimony, the factual context mattered in those cases and it matters in this one too.

The key distinction between what happened at the Eyebar and the district court cases Iverson cites is that here the individual with the supervisory authority (Iverson) was *present* when his employee (his personal bodyguard Kane) committed the tortious acts. It was this fact, together with the duration of the melee, that led the district court to believe that the jury could find that Iverson had the ability to supervise or control Kane's behavior that night, a mandatory element of the negligent supervision tort. Iverson's presence during the attack also affects the standard of care. A jury may need the aid of expert testimony to evaluate how a hotel should train and otherwise supervise its security guards to ensure that they do not unreasonably use force *on some future date*. But it is a different thing altogether to say such expert assistance is needed to establish the standard of care for an individual who is present while his personal bodyguard, acting on his behalf in clearing a room in a nightclub, beats a customer and causes significant injuries. Iverson has pointed to no case in the District of Columbia—nor have we been able to locate any—dealing with the standard of care a person owes in supervising his personal bodyguard in his presence. The evidence in this case supported the jury's finding that Kane attacked Godfrey in a fight that lasted several minutes, and that Iverson stood and watched without attempting to do anything to stop the beating. *See 2922 Sherman Ave. Tenants' Ass'n v. District of Columbia*, 444 F.3d 673, 679 (D.C. Cir. 2006). We find no error in the district court's ruling that the jury did not need the assistance of expert testimony to determine the standard of care Iverson owed to Godfrey.

People v. Sibrian

207 Cal. Rptr. 3d 428 (Cal. Ct. App. 2016)

BANKE, Judge

INTRODUCTION

Defendant Henry Sibrian appeals from his conviction of resisting an officer.... He contends the trial court erred, first, in allowing expert testimony on excessive force.... We affirm.

FACTUAL AND PROCEDURAL BACKGROUND

Shortly after 1:00 a.m. on October 21, 2013, Sheriff's Sergeant Joseph Buford observed defendant commit various traffic violations. As Buford turned on the flashing lights of his patrol car to initiate a traffic stop, defendant pulled over on his own because he had arrived at his house. Buford ordered defendant to get out of his car, but he refused. Additional deputies arrived, and defendant was wrestled out of the car and detained. During the struggle, defendant and two deputies were injured. The district attorney charged defendant with a single count of resisting an executive officer by the use of force or violence.

Sergeant Buford testified at trial that he first noticed defendant's car when he heard squealing tires. He followed the car about a mile as it ran two red lights and a stop sign and then pulled over and came to a stop on Sheryl Drive in San Pablo. Buford knew the neighborhood, as he had responded to "homicides, domestic violence, stolen vehicles, robberies, fights, [and] drunks" in the area. He drew his firearm at low ready and ordered defendant to show his hands. Defendant stuck both hands out the driver's side window, along with the upper half of his body. Defendant was "slurring and rambling." Buford could not understand him and believed he might be intoxicated.

Buford called for assistance, and Deputy Mitch Moschetti arrived almost immediately. Together, they approached defendant's car, and Buford opened the driver's side door. He ordered defendant "at least five or six times" to get out, but he refused. Defendant smelled of alcohol. He continued to ramble and was "gripping the steering wheel with two hands." Both officers tried to pull defendant out of the car, but he "was flailing his body." Although he suspected defendant was intoxicated, Buford did not conduct a field sobriety test and did not obtain a blood sample.

Deputy Moschetti testified he struggled with defendant for a few seconds, while telling him to stop resisting and get out of the car. Then he "delivered a closed fist strike" to defendant's right eye. He again tried to move defendant, but defendant grabbed Moschetti's arm and moved it "very forcefully." Moschetti punched him in the right eye a second time.

Moschetti retrieved his Taser and told defendant to stop resisting or he would be tased. Defendant grabbed the Taser and tried to pull it from Moschetti's hand. Moschetti tased him in the stomach. By this time, another deputy, Michael Santos, had arrived, and he was able to pull defendant out of the car. Defendant's face and stomach hit the asphalt, and he landed flat on his stomach.

Now on the ground, defendant kept his right arm tucked underneath his stomach and kicked his legs. Moschetti told him to stop resisting and put his hands behind his back. After unsuccessfully trying to pull defendant's right arm out from under his body, Moschetti "delivered a closed fist strike to his right rib cage." Defendant released his right arm, and Moschetti placed him in handcuffs. Defendant became "verbally aggressive" and spat blood on Santos.

Moschetti suffered cuts on his hands and bruises on his shins. Defendant also appeared to be injured. There was blood around his right eye and blood from his nose, and he had injuries on the left side of his head and on his right cheek.

Deputy Santos testified that when he arrived at the scene defendant appeared "aggressive" and was "actively resisting." Defendant scratched Santos with his fingernails, inflicting a four-inch gash on his forearm. After Santos pulled him from the car to the ground, defendant continued to struggle and kick. Another deputy arrived, and Santos, Moschetti, and Trinidad eventually got defendant under control and handcuffed. Defendant continued to be uncooperative—he yelled, failed to follow instructions, and spat a mouthful of blood on Santos's left arm. Santos suffered an open wound on his left hand and wounds on his right hand and arm.

The prosecution also called George Driscoll, a senior inspector with the district attorney's office, whom the trial court permitted to testify as an expert "in the area of law enforcement training, law enforcement tactics, and law enforcement procedures regarding the use of force." Driscoll had 34 years' experience in law enforcement, and has trained law enforcement officers in Fourth Amendment issues and use of force, including specific defensive tactics and methods to overcome resistance. He testified law enforcement officers have a responsibility to enforce the law, and when "they encounter resistance, they're not expected to retreat, they're expected to ensure compliance."

The prosecutor presented a hypothetical scenario of an officer stopping a car for numerous traffic violations at 1:00 a.m. in a medium to high crime area. The prosecutor then questioned Driscoll about hypothetical officer conduct tracking the version of events described by Buford, Moschetti, and Santos. Driscoll opined the officers' conduct in the hypothetical scenario would not be inconsistent "with the industry standard." For example, Driscoll testified when a suspect's unlawful driving threatens the public, an officer is expected to stop that threat by having the suspect stop and step out of the car. If the suspect refuses to leave his car, the officer is at a disadvantage because the suspect has "complete access to everything in the car, and ... maneuverability inside the car." There could be a weapon in the car, or the suspect could start the car and flee. Driscoll opined if the suspect grips his steering wheel and refuses to get out, officers should attempt to grab his arm to break his grip and use a distraction strike only if they are unable to break the suspect's grip on the steering wheel. He explained officers oftentimes have chemical agents and Tasers "as part of their tool system on their belt." The use of a chemical spray "probably wouldn't be a good choice for the officers to select" in the circumstances of the hypothetical because dispersal of the spray in the small area of the suspect's car could impair the officers. But if two distraction strikes are ineffective in removing the suspect's hands from the steering wheel, Driscoll opined use of a Taser would not be inconsistent with industry standard.

On cross-examination, Driscoll stated he had testified 12 times as an expert in the use of force by law enforcement officers. In each case, he concluded the use of force was consistent with industry standards. Revisiting the hypothetical scenario, Driscoll opined that if the first officer were to point his gun at the head of the suspect that would *not* be consistent with industry standards. He was aware of Contra Costa County's policy that Tasers should not routinely be used when subjects are demonstrating passive resistance or are unresponsive.

Israel Herrera, defendant's landlord, testified for the defense. He saw defendant parked outside his house, with police cars behind him. An officer pointed a weapon toward defendant and told Herrera to stay back. Two more officers parked in front of the house. They started to hit defendant inside his car. Herrera never heard the officers telling defendant to get out of the car. "They pulled him out of the car, he was on the floor and then he was handcuffed."

Defendant also testified. Around 10:30 p.m. the night of his arrest, he left work and went to a friend's house in Berkeley. He "might have had a couple of drinks." (Later, he testified he had one 22-ounce beer.) Around 12:30 a.m., he left his friend's house and drove home. He did not run any red lights or stop signs, and did not notice a police officer following him. As soon as he parked, he saw police lights. An officer approached his window, pointed a gun at his face, and ordered him to put out his hands, which he did. Defendant "thought he was going to shoot." Another officer arrived, and the two officers forced him out of his car. The officers never ordered him to exit the car. After he was handcuffed, he felt "a whole bunch of punches just coming in different directions, right, left, temple, jaw, the back of [his] head." He felt a knee hit his eye, and he started yelling "police brutality." Blood filled his mouth, and he spat it out because he could not breathe. He did not intend to get blood on anyone. Then he felt a burning sensation in his chest from a Taser. He was tased three times and taken to jail. From there, he was taken to a hospital, where he stayed from 2:00 a.m. to 5:30 p.m. Photographs showed marks from the Taser on defendant's chest, stomach, and shoulder.

Defendant denied holding on to the steering wheel, denied refusing to exit his car, and denied resisting the officers at any time. "It was like lamb to a slaughter. I gave myself completely to them and ... I did every order they gave me." He plans to file a civil lawsuit against Deputy Moschetti.

The jury found defendant guilty as charged. The trial court placed him on formal felony probation for three years, conditioned on serving 180 days in county jail.

DISCUSSION

A. *Allowing Expert Testimony on the Use of Force*

Defendant maintains the issue of whether the officers used excessive force was not a proper subject for expert testimony under Evidence Code section 801, [the California equivalent of F.R.E. 702]. Alternatively, he contends the trial court should have excluded the testimony ... as unduly prejudicial.

Evidence Code section 801 allows a qualified expert to testify on matters "[r]elated to a subject that is sufficiently beyond common experience that the opinion of an expert would assist the trier of fact." Cal. Evid. Code § 801(a); *People v. Brown*, 94 P.3d 574 (Cal. 2004). "Expert opinion is not admissible," however, "if it consists of inferences and conclusions which can be drawn as easily and intelligently by the trier of facts as by the witness." *People v. Torres*, 39 Cal. Rptr. 2d 103 (Cal. Ct. App. 1995).... We review a decision to admit expert opinion testimony for abuse of discretion. *People v. Prince*, 156 P.3d 1015 (Cal. 2007).

Defendant was charged with "knowingly resist[ing], by the use of force or violence, [an executive] officer, in the performance of his [or her] duty" in violation of section 69. Under this penal code provision, an officer must be acting lawfully when the resistance occurs. *In re Manuel G.*, 941 P.2d 880 (Cal. 1997). An officer using excessive force is not acting lawfully. *People v. Orguin*, 173 Cal. Rptr. 663 (Cal. Ct. App. 1981); *People v. White*, 161 Cal. Rptr. 541 (Cal. Ct. App. 1980). Thus, the prosecution was required to prove beyond a reasonable doubt that the officers acted lawfully, and the jury was instructed "[a] peace officer is not lawfully performing his or her duties if he or she is ... *using unreasonable or excessive force* in his or her duties." (Italics added.)

In response to defendant's motion to exclude Driscoll's testimony, the trial court held ... [a] hearing. Driscoll testified law enforcement officers are required to receive training on the use of force, and the purpose of the training is to enhance the safety of officers, suspects, and the public. An officer's prior "common life experience regarding combative or forceful situations" is not sufficient because a "law enforcement officer has a significant greater responsibility, duty, obligation, regarding the enforcement of the laws" than a lay person. Driscoll explained an officer is expected to overcome a person's noncompliance with lawful commands, and officers receive specialized training to recognize resistance because they "have to try and minimize the escalation of resistance." "[T]heir training will allow them to recognize this, and then use appropriate means to overcome that resistance." He stated officers are taught to escalate their level of force if their tactics are not effective in overcoming resistance. Driscoll gave the example of a suspect who is refusing to follow commands and is on the ground with his hands underneath his body. An officer would recognize the inability to see the suspect's hands is a safety issue, and "would then use greater force to extract the hands."

At this point in Driscoll's testimony, the trial court observed it appeared to be helpful and to cover matters beyond the common experience of an ordinary juror. "[W]hat

I've heard so far, there are many things here that a normal juror does not understand. The principles for escalation of force, for example. That's nothing that's naturally understood by a juror.... Inspector Driscoll gave the example of the suspect who is forced to the ground and was lying on top of his hands. And so because the officer doesn't know what's in his hands, the officer, according to Inspector Driscoll, has more latitude in what he can do. I'm not sure that's something that is naturally known to a jury. I think there are many points like that. So I think subject to further testimony in cross-examination, this information … is something that would be helpful to a jury."

After further testimony by Driscoll, the court heard argument by the parties. It then ruled Driscoll could testify as an expert "because the issues of incremental use of violence and the kind of force that can be used … those are not issues that a jury understands without testimony from an expert." However, Driscoll could not testify that the officers' conduct was either reasonable or constituted excessive force—it would be "up to the jury to decide whether the use of force is reasonable."

Defendant contends Driscoll's testimony "was unnecessary" because "the jury was perfectly capable of evaluating the reasonableness of the force used against [defendant] based on the evidence presented at trial." Necessity, however, is not the measure for the admissibility of expert evidence. "[E]xperts may testify even when jurors are not 'wholly ignorant' about the subject of the testimony.... Rather, the pertinent question is whether, even if jurors have some knowledge of the subject matter, expert opinion testimony would assist the jury." *Prince*, 156 P.3d at 1222.

Here, one of the key issues for the jury was whether the officers acted lawfully in the way in which they detained and arrested defendant. Driscoll's testimony could be of some assistance because, as the trial court observed, jurors would not necessarily know about the need for escalating force in response to a noncompliant suspect or the potential continued danger posed by a suspect after he has been wrestled to the ground. Driscoll also explained the risks of allowing a noncompliant suspect to remain in his car and why the officers may have decided not to use a chemical agent.

Expert testimony "will be excluded *only* when it would add nothing at all to the jury's common fund of information, i.e., when "the subject of inquiry is one of such common knowledge that men of ordinary education could reach a conclusion as intelligently as the witness." *People v. McAlpin*, 812 P.2d 563 (Cal. 1991) (italics added). Because we cannot say Driscoll's testimony "would add nothing at all to the jury's common fund of information," we also cannot say the trial court abused its discretion in deeming it admissible. *Id*; *People v. Farnam*, 47 P.3d 988, 1028 (Cal. 2002).

Defendant's reliance on *Allgoewer v. City of Tracy*, 143 Cal. Rptr. 3d 793 (Cal. Ct. App. 2012), a civil excessive force case, is misplaced. In *Allgoewer*, the trial court granted the defendants' nonsuit motion because the plaintiff had not presented any expert testimony on "what force a reasonable law enforcement officer would have used under the same or similar circumstances." *Id*. at 796. The Court of Appeal reversed, concluding, as have other courts, that there is no per se requirement that a plaintiff must present expert testimony to prove an excessive force claim. *Id*. at 800–01. The appellate court recognized that the "reasonableness" standard applicable to such claims "must be judged from the perspective of a reasonable officer on the scene, rather than with the 20/20 vision of hindsight." *Id.* at 800. And since "the standard is not defined by the generic — a reasonable *person* — but rather by the specific — a reasonable *officer* — it is more likely that [the] line between common and specialized knowledge has been crossed." *Id.* (quoting *Kopf v. Skyrm*, 993 F.2d 374, 378 (4th Cir. 1993). However, "a blanket rule that expert testimony is generally admissible in excessive force cases would be just as wrong as a blanket rule that it is not." *Allgoewer*, 143 Cal. Rptr. 3d at 800. "The facts of every case will determine whether expert testimony would assist the jury." *Id.*

Where the force used consists of only bare hands, the court suggested "expert testimony might not be helpful." *Id.* However, "[a]dd handcuffs, a gun, a slapjack, mace, or some other tool, and the jury may start to ask itself: what is mace? what is an officer's training on using a gun?" *Id.* "Answering these questions may often be assisted by expert testimony." *Id.*

The *Allgoewer* Court went on to conclude that, on the record before it, a nonsuit was not warranted. While the defendant officers argued expert testimony was necessary because the case "involved specialized training and experience regarding police practices and procedures. But beyond that vague assertion, defendants offer no explanation of why or how that was so." *Id.* at 802.

In short, *Allgoewer* holds the admission of expert evidence on police training and practices must be made on a case-by-case basis and, in some civil excessive force cases, as in the case before it, the plaintiff need not present expert testimony to prove his or her case. *Allgoewer* does not hold a plaintiff cannot present such testimony. In fact, it recognizes that, depending on the circumstances, such evidence may be proper....

The instant criminal case presents a different issue than that in *Allgoewer* — did the trial court abuse its discretion in allowing such evidence in this criminal prosecution? Moreover, *Allgoewer* suggests it did not, since more was involved here than force "reduced to its most primitive form — bare hands." *Id.* at 800 (quoting *Kopf*, 993 F.2d at 379). In this case, the officers were dealing with a suspected drunk driver who refused to get out of his car, late at night and in a relatively high crime area. The officers used not only their hands, but also a Taser and handcuffs, and they chose not to use a chemical agent. Driscoll's testimony provided relevant context and a basis for evaluating the officers' handling techniques and choice of assistive tools.

Defendant alternatively maintains that, even if Driscoll's expert testimony had some relevance and was admissible under Evidence Code section 801, it nevertheless should have been excluded ... [as] unduly prejudicial because Driscoll "convey[ed] his belief in the credibility of the officers' testimony." This overstates Driscoll's testimony. When presented with a hypothetical scenario tracking the officers' testimony, Driscoll gave his opinion on the use of force, but he did not suggest either of the arresting officers' version of events was correct or that the officers were credible and defendant was not. Nor, contrary to defendant's claim, did Driscoll refuse "to answer questions based on hypotheticals that contradicted the prosecution's theory." On cross-examination, when asked a different hypothetical, Driscoll opined an officer pointing a firearm at a suspect's head (as defendant testified Sergeant Buford did) would not be consistent with industry standards. Defense counsel then asked if "the officer is able to the see the suspect's hands, and *weapons at that time are not a concern*," would that change Driscoll's opinion? (Italics added.) Driscoll responded "By limiting the factors as you just did, that's inconsistent with all of the factors that the officer is forced to consider." This was not a refusal to answer a question based on a hypothetical scenario different from the prosecution's theory. Rather, Driscoll was pointing out that an officer could not simply put aside concerns about weapons in the hypothetical scenario described.

Defendant also cites to *Thompson v. City of Chicago*, 472 F.3d 444 (7th Cir. 2006), another civil excessive force case, in which the district court excluded proffered testimony by two officers not on the ground it was inadmissible, but on the ground its prejudicial effect outweighed it's probative value. *Id.* at 457. The circuit court of appeals found no abuse of discretion, observing "[i]ntroducing two experts to testify that [the defendant-officer] used excessive force would have induced the jurors to substitute their own independent conclusions for that of the experts." *Id.* at 458.

Generally, "[a] finding of no abuse of discretion in one court's exclusion of evidence has no bearing on whether a different court abused its discretion in admitting evidence in a different trial." *People v. Cordova*, 358 P.3d 518 (Cal. 2015). Here, in contrast to *Thompson*, Driscoll was not called to give his opinion on the legal question of whether the officers used excessive force, but to explain law enforcement tactics and training in the use of force. In fact, the trial court expressly barred Driscoll from rendering any opinion on whether the arresting officers' use of force was reasonable....

The judgment is affirmed.

Notes and Questions

1. In *Sibrian*, Judge Banks allowed the expert testimony to explain why the use of force was reasonable considering the circumstances. Yet in *Godfrey*, the court excluded testimony on use of force standards. Why the distinction? As we consider the distinction between the cases, consider the standard enunciated by Mason Ladd, cited by the advisory committee in their notes for Rule 702:

   > There is no more certain test for determining when experts may be used than the common sense inquiry whether the untrained layman would be qualified to determine intelligently and to the best possible degree the particular issue without enlightenment from those having a specialized understanding of the subject involved in the dispute.

   Mason Ladd, *Expert Testimony*, 5 Vand. L. Rev. 414, 418 (1952). Basically, one must ask whether the jury is capable of figuring out the issue without help or needs specialized assistance. If we apply that standard to *Godfrey* and *Sibrian*, it can help explain why testimony in one is admissible but not the other. In particular, look again at the passage from *Sibrian* about the exclusion of evidence on proper use of force when an officer uses his or her bare hands. Why does that matter?

2. The expert in question in *Sibirian*—George Driscoll—has significant qualifications in the field, but can you think of any other professionals who may also be able to testify on this subject matter? We will evaluate expert qualifications to testify in detail *infra* in Section B, but one should consider that for any given testimony, different experts may suffice.

3. Is there a risk that the expert testimony on law enforcement standards in a case like *Sibrian*—a subject which lay jurors will have little or no experience dealing with—will result in too much deference to the expert? If so, does it infringe upon the jury's role? We will consider the limits of expert testimony relating to a case's ultimate issue next, as we explore the contours of Rule 704.

Federal Rule of Evidence 704:
Opinion on an Ultimate Issue

(a) **In General—Not Automatically Objectionable.** An opinion is not objectionable just because it embraces an ultimate issue.

(b) **Exception.** In a criminal case, an expert witness must not state an opinion about whether the defendant did or did not have a mental state or condition that constitutes an element of the crime charged or of a defense. Those matters are for the trier of fact alone.

Alvarado v. Oakland County
809 F. Supp. 2d 680 (E.D. Mich. 2011)

BORMAN, District Judge

This matter comes before the Court on ... Defendants' Motion to Preclude Plaintiff from Offering the Expert Opinions of Michael D. Lyman, Ph.D at Trial....

I. INTRODUCTION

Plaintiff in this action claims that Defendant Oakland County Deputy Micky Simpkinson used excessive force when he pulled Plaintiff from his vehicle and took him to the ground during a traffic stop on July 23, 2007.... Plaintiff claims that Deputy Simpkinson used excessive force in removing Plaintiff from his vehicle, causing Plaintiff to suffer a separated shoulder, a labral tear and a torn rotator cuff, all of which required repeated surgeries and ultimately forced Plaintiff to take early retirement from his job at General Motors, resulting in economic and non-economic damages. Deputy Simpkinson responds that Plaintiff ignored his repeated and continuous efforts to stop Plaintiff's vehicle through the use of overhead lights, flashing lights and sirens. Deputy Simpkinson contends that Plaintiff attempted to elude the stop for over one-half mile after Deputy Simpkinson first attempted to pull Plaintiff over, before finally bringing his vehicle to a stop. Thus, when Plaintiff finally stopped his vehicle and Deputy Simpkinson approached the vehicle, he did so cautiously, with his weapon drawn, until he could clearly ascertain that neither Plaintiff nor his passenger posed an immediate threat. Deputy Simpkinson further responds that he used a reasonable amount of force, under the circumstances, in removing Plaintiff from his vehicle and placing him in handcuffs....

II. LEGAL STANDARD

"The Federal Rules of Evidence, the Federal Rules of Criminal and Civil Procedure and interpretive rulings of the Supreme Court and this court all encourage, and in some cases require, parties and the court to utilize extensive pretrial procedures — including motions *in limine* — in order to narrow the issues remaining for trial and to minimize disruptions at trial." *United States v. Brawner*, 173 F.3d 966, 970 (6th Cir. 1999). District courts have broad discretion over matters involving the admissibility of evidence at trial. *United States v. Seago*, 930 F.2d 482, 494 (6th Cir. 1991).

III. ANALYSIS

. . .

B. Deputy Simpkinson's Motion to Preclude Plaintiff from Offering the Expert Opinions of Michael D. Lyman, Ph.D at Trial

Federal Rule of Evidence 704 provides in pertinent part: "[T]estimony in the form of an opinion or inference otherwise admissible is not objectionable because it embraces an ultimate issue to be decided by the trier of fact." However, as the advisory committee notes to Rule 704 make clear, the ultimate issue rule does not permit expert opinion testimony that opines on the ultimate legal conclusion which the jury must reach in the case:

> The abolition of the ultimate issue rule does not lower the bars so as to admit all opinions. Under Rules 701 and 702, opinions must be helpful to the trier of fact, and Rule 403 provides for exclusion of evidence which wastes time. These provisions afford ample assurances against the admission of opinions which would merely tell the jury what result to reach, somewhat in the manner of the oath-helpers of an earlier day. They also stand ready to exclude opinions phrased in terms of inadequately explored legal criteria. Thus the question, "Did T have capacity to make a will?" would be excluded, while the question, "Did T have sufficient mental capacity to know the nature and extent of his property and the natural objects of his bounty and to formulate a rational scheme of distribution?" would be allowed.

Fed. R. Evid. 704 Advisory Committee Note.

In sum, the expert's opinion must stop short of embracing the "legal terminology" which frames the ultimate legal conclusion which the jury must reach in the case. *See Torres v. Cty. of Oakland*, 758 F.2d 147, 151 (6th Cir. 1985). In *Torres*, the court concluded that a question posed to an expert, which inquired whether the plaintiff had been discriminated against because of her national origin, ran afoul of the rules of evidence because the question "track[ed] almost verbatim the language of the applicable statute" and the term "discrimination" had a specialized meaning in the law not commonly understood in its lay use. *Id.* "The problem with testimony containing a legal conclusion is in conveying the witness' unexpressed, and perhaps erroneous, legal standards to the jury. This 'invade[s] the province of the court to determine the applicable law and to instruct the jury as to that law.'" *Id.* at 150 (quoting *F.A.A. v. Landy*, 705 F.2d 624, 632 (2d Cir.), *cert. denied,* 464 U.S. 895 (1983)).

In *Berry v. City of Detroit*, 25 F.3d 1342, 1353–54 (6th Cir. 1994), in the context of a § 1983 claim, the Sixth Circuit held that the district court erroneously admitted expert testimony opining that certain conduct by the defendant amounted to "deliberate indifference," which improperly expressed the ultimate legal conclusion at issue in the case. In *Berry,* the court cited the Second Circuit's decision, *Hygh v. Jacobs*, 961 F.2d 359 (2d Cir. 1992), which held that expert testimony on the use of excessive force which embraced the ultimate legal conclusion in the case should have been excluded by the trial court. The expert in *Hygh* was permitted to opine at trial that the defendant's use of a baton to strike a person in the head was unjustified deadly physical force under the circumstances of the case. 961 F.2d at 363. Quoting the following passage from *Hygh,* the Sixth Circuit in *Berry* excluded expert opinion as to "deliberate indifference:"

> Even if a jury were not misled into adopting outright a legal conclusion proffered by an expert witness, the testimony would remain objectionable by communicating a legal standard—explicit or implicit—to the jury. Whereas an expert may be uniquely qualified by experience to assist the trier of fact, he is not qualified to compete with the judge in the function of instructing the jury....
>
> Far more troubling, [the expert] testified that Jacobs' conduct was not "justified under the circumstances," not "warranted under the circumstances," and "totally improper." We have held that an expert's testimony that a defendant was "negligent" should not have been allowed. We see no significant distinction in [the expert's] conclusory condemnations of Jacobs' actions here, which, in the language of the advisory committee, "merely [told] the jury what result to reach."

25 F.3d at 1354 (quoting *Hygh*, 961 F.2d at 364) (internal citations and parenthetical information omitted).

DeMerrell v. City of Cheboygan, 206 Fed. App'x. 418 (6th Cir. 2006), although an unpublished opinion, provides this Court with some helpful guidance on this issue. In *DeMerrell,* the Sixth Circuit, relying on *Berry,* held that expert opinion testimony that expressed a legal conclusion was properly excluded by the district court, explaining:

> In the instant case, Plaintiff-Appellant's expert testified as to a legal conclusion because he stated that "it was objectively unreasonable for Officer White to shoot Mr. DeMerrell." (JA 430). As stated previously, objective reasonableness is the precise legal standard of *Graham* to be used in the qualified immunity inquiry of *Saucier. See Saucier v. Katz*, 533 U.S. 194, 201 (2001); *Graham v. Connor*, 490 U.S. 386, 396 (1989). Additionally, Plaintiff-Appellant's expert's

opinion further states that "a reasonable officer on the scene would not have concluded at the time that there existed probable cause that Mr. DeMerrell posed a significant threat of death or serious physical injury to the officer or others." This testimony also expresses a legal conclusion, going beyond "stating opinions that suggest the answer to the ultimate issue." *Berry*, 25 F.3d at 1353. Still other conclusions by Plaintiff-Appellant's expert were improper legal conclusions, namely that the "use of deadly force by [Officer White] was improper and unnecessary." *See Hygh v. Jacobs*, 961 F.2d 359, 364 (2d Cir. 1992) (precluding expert testimony in a § 1983 excessive force case that an officer's conduct was not "justified under the circumstances," not "warranted under the circumstances," and "totally improper").

206 Fed. App'x. at 426–27....

Cases ... which interpret applicable Sixth Circuit law, indicate that expert testimony regarding recognized police policies and procedures, and specifically continuum of force policies, are appropriate subjects of expert testimony, provided that the experts do not express legal conclusions based on their interpretation of the application of those policies in a particular case.... The Court concludes that Dr. Lyman may testify regarding nationally recognized police standards governing the use of excessive force, as well as the specific OCSD excessive force guidelines to which Deputy Simpkinson was subject.

Lyman will not be permitted, either by his report or his testimony at trial, to opine as to whether Deputy Simpkinson's conduct in arresting Plaintiff was unreasonable under those guidelines or practices. It may be helpful to the jury, for example, to know that Oakland County Deputies are expected to escalate the use of force along a certain a continuum under a certain given set of circumstances. But whether or not Deputy Simpkinson's conduct in this case was unreasonable given those guidelines is a decision that only the jury is competent to make. Accordingly, Dr. Lyman will be prohibited from expressing any legal conclusions, which either explicitly or implicitly embrace the ultimate legal issue in this case of whether Deputy Simpkinson's conduct was reasonable under the totality of the circumstances which he faced. Specifically, Dr. Lyman is prohibited from expressing the following opinions that appear in his report:

- That the applicable "standard of care" to be applied in this case was enunciated by the Court in *Graham v. Connor*, 490 U.S. 396 (1989). Instructing the jury on the law is role of the judge, not the expert.

- That "the level of force used by Deputy Micky Simpkinson against Joseph Alvarado in removing him from his vehicle was excessive, unnecessary and served no objectively reasonable purpose." This is an opinion as to the ultimate legal conclusion called for in this case and is impermissible expert testimony.

- That "there was no reasonable belief on the part of Simpkinson that either occupant of the vehicle was dangerous or otherwise posing a threat." This is simply unhelpful to the jury and also states a legal conclusion regarding the reasonableness of Deputy Simpkinson's belief....

- That "it is [his] opinion, stated within a reasonable degree of professional certainty, considering Alvarado's low if non-existent levels of resistance, that the actions in which [sic] Deputy Simpkinson used to remove him from his vehicle, under the circumstances known to Simpkinson at the time, were excessive, unnecessary and served no legitimate law enforcement purpose. As such, Simpkinson's actions were inconsistent with nationally recognized standards of care, professional policing guidelines and failed to be objectively reasonable."

The Court will permit Dr. Lyman to testify on the use of excessive force but will be vigilant in precluding him for expressing opinions that embrace the actual legal conclusion that the jury is asked to decide in this case, i.e. whether Deputy Simpkinson's conduct in effecting Plaintiff's arrest on the evening in question was unreasonable under the totality of circumstances known to him at the time. Dr. Lyman will be permitted to reference nationally accepted police practices regarding the use of excessive force, as well as the OCSD's policies and procedures regarding the use of excessive force.... Dr. Lyman will be precluded, however, from expressing any opinion as to whether Deputy Simpkinson's conduct was reasonable in light of those policies and guidelines. Deputy Simpkinson will be free to attack on cross-examination both Dr. Lyman's qualifications to render his opinions as well as the allegedly outdated nature of the materials on which he relies. Such matters go to the weight of Dr. Lyman's testimony, not its admissibility.

IV. CONCLUSION

For the foregoing reasons, the Court ... grant in part and denies in part Defendants' Motion to Preclude Dr. Lyman's Opinions at Trial....

Notes and Questions

1. In reaching its decision, the *Alvarado* court relied on *Hygh v. Jacobs*, 961 F.2d 359 (2d Cir. 1992), which drew the line between permissible testimony under 704 and impermissible discussions by citing the advisory committee's notes on the rule:

   > [While Rule 704] has abolished the common law "ultimate issue" rule..., it has not lowered the bar so as to admit all opinions. This circuit is in accord with other circuits in requiring exclusion of expert testimony that expresses a legal conclusion.... We invoke the advisory committee note's illuminating distinction between admissible and excludable versions of an expert's opinion testimony: "Under Rules 701 and 702, opinions must be helpful to the trier of fact, and Rule 403 provides for exclusion of evidence which wastes time. These provisions afford ample assurances *against the admission of opinions which would merely tell the jury what result to reach....*" Fed. R. Evid. 704 advisory committee's note (emphasis added by court).

   Id. at 362. The court in *Alvarado* excludes several pieces of testimony by Dr. Lyman, but did not exclude all his testimony. To clarify what is permitted and not, review the individual pieces of evidence discussed in *Alvarado*, considering the *Hygh* standard. Does *Hygh* contain a more concise standard for what evidence is admissible under 704?

2. Considering the Rule 704 standard, why does the court allow expert testimony on law enforcement use of force in *People v. Sibrian*? What did the court say about the possible limitation of the evidence, based on considerations of ultimate issue under Rule 704?

3. Reread the exception to Rule 704(a) for criminal cases in Rule 704(b). The rule specifically disallows expert testimony on "whether the defendant did or did not have a mental state or condition that constitutes an element of the crime charged or of a defense." While cases where these limitations become important cover many areas of criminal law and procedure, a common problem is expert testimony on "intent to distribute" as an element of an enhanced possession crime. In *United States v. Boyd*, 55 F.3d 667 (D.C. Cir. 1995), the expert on drug packaging and distribution testified—in response to questions about a hypothetical identical to the facts alleged at trial—that the facts demonstrated intent to distribute. In response, the court reversed the conviction, calling it a "flagrant breach of the Rules of Evidence for the Government to elicit the opinion of an expert on the ultimate issue of fact that was for the jury alone to decide." *Id.* at 669. Considering the testimony in question, it is clear that an expert cannot testify in hypothetical form to what an expert cannot testify to directly. However, assume for a moment that Rule 704(b) did not exist. Would the testimony be admitted or remain out? What are the best arguments for admission of the evidence? For exclusion? This issue is not hypothetical; in some states, 704(b) has not been added to the state rules of evidence. *See, e.g.*, Iowa R. Evid. 5.704; Wash. R. Evid. 704. If so, determining admissibility rests on the rules previously discussed. *State v. Montgomery*, 183 P.3d 267 (Wash. 2008); *State v. Dinkins*, 553 N.W.2d 339 (Iowa Ct. App. 1996).

Tying It Together

Your firm has recently been retained by a new client, and you have been assigned to the client's case. In 2015, the Defendant XYZ Television Corp. broadcast a segment on its weekly primetime news broadcast, *60 Primetime XYZ*, which was critical of the ethical behavior of several televangelists, including Rex Tyrone. Rex Tyrone then brought a libel suit against XYZ, claiming that the network broadcast contained several false and negative statements about him.

In a libel case involving a public figure, the plaintiff has the burden of establishing that the statement in question is false and also that the defendant had actual malice when publishing the alleged defamatory statement. Actual malice means that when the defendant published or broadcast the statement, the defendant acted with "knowledge that it was false or with reckless disregard of whether it was false or not." *N.Y. Times v. Sullivan*, 376 U.S. 254, 280 (1964).

To support his claim of libel, Plaintiff Tyrone has endorsed Dr. Louise Little. Little is a Ph.D. linguist who specializes in English syntax and linguistic analysis of communication content, and who regularly serves as an expert witness in cases in involving libel, slander, and copyright infringement. All parties recognize that Dr. Little is well-credentialed in the field of linguistics, and her qualifications are not at issue. Dr. Little has reviewed the *60 Primetime XYZ* segment on Rex Tyrone, and now offers her opinion in support of his claims.

Little's testimony would begin with a general explanation of how certain rhetorical devices or patterns of speech convey implicit meanings. She would then explain that the Defendant's broadcast, with its use of words, patterns of words, position of words, taking of words out of context, and placing of words with visual items all convey meanings to the viewing public. Dr. Little will then explain how those meanings imply defamatory facts, how the average viewer was likely to understand the broadcasts, and that Defendant had knowledge of the falsity of the facts and implied facts presented to the viewing audience. She will conclude that "when XYZ broadcast the segment on Tyrone, it implied facts that were not true. The only way to do this is by an editorial agenda, and to want to show these facts as false."

The Defendant XYZ Television objects to the testimony of Dr. Little in its entirety.

Assignment: Please prepare a 1–2 page brief for the partner, explaining your argument in the context of the cases we have reviewed.

- How will counsel for Plaintiff Tyrone argue that Dr. Little's testimony meets the standards established in the Federal Rules of Evidence for expert testimony, and therefore should be admitted in its entirety?

- As counsel for Defendant XYZ Television, why are you objecting to Dr. Little's testimony, and why should it be excluded from trial?

B. Is This Person an Expert? Qualifications Screening under Rule 702

"A witness who is qualified as an expert by knowledge, skill, experience, training, or education may testify in the form of an opinion or otherwise...." Fed. R. Evid. 702.

Expert testimony conjures images of a bespectacled middle-aged witness in a lab coat, with Excel spreadsheets and a wall of credentials. Clearly that type of expert can qualify to testify under the rules of evidence, but it was plainly written to include a broader range of expertise. An expert may be qualified through educational training alone, ready to opine after receiving a diploma. Experts can also include someone who has never spent a day in the classroom, such as a weekend orienteer or an informally-trained auto-mechanic. Or an expert can be someone with both educational and practical training in the field.

Since the definition of an expert remains so broad, it may become necessary to decide whether a specific witness qualifies at all. So, the rules and case law parse out the distinction, with traditional lab coat experts on one end of the spectrum and non-expert fact witnesses on the other. Drawing the line between these two groups can be difficult, and under certain circumstances, the line may seem arbitrary. Yet the rules ensure that only certain witnesses may be called experts and given leeway to offer specialized opinions in a court of law.

Carter v. State

5 S.W.3d 316 (Tex. App. 1999)

FOWLER, Justice

Over her plea of not guilty, a judge found appellant, Patty Busby Carter, guilty of possession of less than one gram of a controlled substance, namely cocaine…. Appellant appeals on one point of error. We affirm the trial court judgment because we conclude that the bare minimum information was introduced to qualify a chemist as an expert.

THE CONTROVERSY

On July 8, 1997, Houston Police officers were conducting an undercover prostitution investigation. An undercover officer picked up appellant in an unmarked police car. Once in the car, appellant agreed to have sex with the officer for $30. The undercover officer proceeded to a hotel parking lot as directed by appellant. While the undercover officer and appellant were getting out of the car, a uniformed police officer approached the car. When the uniformed police officer informed appellant she was under arrest and that she needed to see her hands, appellant dropped a piece of toilet paper behind her. When the arresting officer picked up the toilet paper, the officer discovered a crack pipe. A field test at the station house revealed that the residue inside the pipe was cocaine. The crack pipe was sent to the crime lab for further examination.

At trial, Edna Black, who is a chemist with the Houston Police Department's Crime Laboratory, testified as an expert as to the tests she ran on the crack pipe. When Black took the witness stand, the prosecutor attempted to prove her expert qualifications. That testimony follows below:

Q: Ma'am, could you state your name for the record, please?

A: My name is Edna Black.

Q: Ms. Black, who are you employed with?

A: I am employed in the City of Houston Police Crime Laboratory.

Q: What are your duties in the Crime Laboratory?

A: I'm a chemist, and as a chemist I receive evidence that is submitted by the police officers, and I do a chemical analysis to determine if that evidence is a controlled substance or not, and I keep a record of my results.

Q: You've testified a few times, have you not?

A: Yes, I have.

Q: How many years you been doing those kind of analyses?

A: Almost seven years

Q: And you have the education that allows you to do that?

A: Yes, I do.

The prosecutor then led Black on a discussion about the crack pipe. When the prosecutor asked for Black's expert opinion as to what the crack pipe contained, appellant objected to Black as an expert witness. However, the trial court overruled the objection and allowed Black to give her expert opinion. It is this ruling which appellant now complains about on appeal.

DISCUSSION AND HOLDING

In her sole point of error, appellant contends the trial court erred in overruling her objection to Black's testimony because the state failed to prove her to be an expert witness. Appellant's objection was reasonable and certainly understandable. The prosecutor did a careless job of qualifying this witness as an expert. But, these things do not necessarily mean that the trial court abused its discretion in allowing the witness to testify as an expert. *See Penry v. State*, 903 S.W.2d 715, 762 (Tex. Crim. App. 1995) (stating that whether a witness offered as an expert possesses the required qualifications is a question which rests largely in the trial court's discretion).

According to Rule 702 of the Texas Rules of Evidence, if scientific, technical, or other specialized knowledge will assist the trier of fact to understand the evidence or to determine a fact issue, a witness qualified as an expert by knowledge, skill, experience, training, or education may testify thereto in the form of an opinion or otherwise. *See* Tex. R. Evid. 702.

> "The opinions of experts are received upon the theory that, by reason of study or experience, they have upon *the subject of inquiry* a special knowledge which *jurors generally do not possess* and are therefore *better equipped* to draw conclusions from the facts *than the jurors themselves.*... [T]he practical test for receiving such opinion is: *On the subject in issue* can the jury receive any *appreciable aid* from the person offered?"

[R. Ray, Law of Evidence, 2 Texas Practice § 1400 (3rd ed. 1980).]

> ... The special knowledge which qualified a witness to give an expert opinion may be derived entirely from a study of technical works, or specialized education, or practical experience or varying combinations thereof; what is determinative is that his answers indicate to the trial court that he possesses knowledge which will assist the jury in making inferences regarding fact issues more effectively than the jury could do so unaided.

Holloway v. State, 613 S.W.2d 497, 501 (Tex. Crim. App. 1981); *see Clark v. State*, 881 S.W.2d 682, 698 (Tex. Crim. App. 1994).

The admission of expert testimony is within the sound discretion of the trial court and will not be disturbed on appeal absent an abuse of discretion. *See Griffith v. State*, 983 S.W.2d 282, 287 (Tex. Crim. App. 1998); *Thomas v. State*, 915 S.W.2d 597, 600 (Tex. App. Houston [14th Dist.] 1996, pet. ref'd). Although the issue here is very close, we do not believe the trial court abused its discretion in overruling appellant's objection to this witness.

As we begin our discussion, we cannot help but note that we have not found a case in which so few qualifications were introduced for a police chemist. Nonetheless, based on the evidence in the record, the trial court heard sufficient testimony to conclude that the witness had seven years of practical experience with the City of Houston crime lab testing substances to determine whether or not they were controlled substances. The court also could make a reasonable inference from the testimony that the witness had testified on other occasions as a chemist.

Rule 702 of the Texas Rules of Evidence authorizes an expert to give an opinion even when it is based solely on practical experience. Rule 702 states the various methods of qualifying a witness—knowledge, skill, experience, training, or education—disjunctively, not conjunctively. Without stating that a witness may be qualified by only one of the methods of qualification, Texas case law has recognized that the bases for qualifying a witness are stated in the disjunctive. *See Penry v. State*, 903 S.W.2d 715, 762 (Tex. Crim. App. 1995); *Clark*, 881 S.W.2d at 698; *Holloway*, 613 S.W.2d at 501; *Thomas*, 915 S.W.2d at 600. Here, the chemist's practical experience was the method of qualification. And clearly, as referred to in *Holloway*, the chemist's practical experience, was in the precise subject at issue—whether or not the substance was a controlled substance.

If Rule 702 and the case law interpreting it mean what they say, experience alone can provide a sufficient basis to qualify a person as an expert. Although we have not found a decision from the Texas Court of Criminal Appeals or one from a Texas Court of Appeals, we have found numerous cases from the federal courts[2] stating that a witness may be qualified on the basis of only one of the five qualifications listed in Rule 702—including practical experience. *See Lauria v. Nat'l R.R. Passenger Corp.*, 145 F.3d 593, 598 (3d Cir. 1998) (stating witnesses can qualify as experts under Rule 702 on the basis of practical experience alone, and a formal degree, title, or educational speciality is not required. *United States v. Abrego*, 141 F.3d 142, 173 (5th Cir. 1998) (stating, although a doctor did not profess to being an "expert" on Valium habituation or dependency, it was not an abuse of discretion for trial court to allow such testimony because the doctor had practical experience sufficient to give his expert opinion); *United States v. Valle*, 72 F.3d 210, 215 n. 4 (1st Cir. 1995) (holding that street savvy and practical experience can qualify a witness as an expert as surely as "'a string of academic degrees or multiple memberships in learned societies'"); *Sullivan v. Rowan Cos.*, 952 F.2d 141, 145 (5th Cir. 1992) (holding that an expert may be qualified on any of the five bases listed in Rule 702 of the Federal Rules of Evidence); *Rogers v. Raymark Indus.*, 922 F.2d 1426, 1429 (9th Cir. 1991) (concluding that a witness can qualify as an expert through practical experience in a particular field, not just through academic training); *Lavespere v. Niagara Mach. & Tool Works, Inc.*, 910 F.2d 167, 176 (5th Cir. 1990) (concluding that since the five qualifications in Rule 702 are stated in the disjunctive, the court must assume the drafters of the rule chose deliberately, and that an expert may be qualified on any one of the five bases listed) ...

Thus, although only one or two more questions about this chemist's educational training and her experience would have been advisable, we cannot say that the trial court abused its discretion in allowing the testimony of this chemist.

In short, because Black had been testing substances for the City of Houston crime lab for the past seven years to determine whether or not they were controlled substances, this practical experience was sufficient for her to testify as an expert witness on the issue of whether a substance was a controlled substance. Thus, the trial court did not abuse its discretion when it overruled appellant's objection to Black as an expert witness. We overrule appellant's sole point of error and affirm the trial court judgment.

WITTIG, Justice, dissenting.

In this instance, the applicable "abuse of discretion" standard requires us to review only the testimony actually elicited from Black on the record before us regarding her expertise. It is from that record we determine whether the trial judge's decision to allow her to testify was "arbitrary and unreasonable and without reference to guiding principles." *Goode v. Shoukfeh*, 943 S.W.2d 441, 446 (Tex. 1997); *Lagrone v. State*, 942 S.W.2d 602, 616 (Tex. Crim. App. 1997), *cert. denied*, 522 U.S. 917, 118 S. Ct. 305, 139 L.Ed.2d 235 (1997)....

As the majority recognizes, the prosecutor brought out no testimony as to Black's training, education, skill, or knowledge in the field of identifying controlled substances. The only testimony as to Black's qualifications as an expert in identifying controlled substances was with regard to her "practical experience." ...

While, in some cases, an expert's qualifications can be established on practical experience alone, Black's nebulous and sketchy testimony about her experience left too much to be inferred about her qualifications as an expert in identifying controlled substances ...

The State simply failed to demonstrate Black had the expertise to identify the particular substance the police officers obtained from appellant was cocaine.... The timely and specific objection to the expertise of Black should have been sustained.

Clena Investments, Inc. v. XL Specialty Insurance Co.
280 F.R.D. 653 (S.D. Fla. 2012)

ROSENBAUM, United States Magistrate Judge.

This matter comes before the Court on Defendant's Amended Motion to Strike Plaintiff's Expert.... The Court has carefully reviewed the pending Motion, all filings in support thereof and in opposition thereto, and the record in this case, and has held an evidentiary hearing ... and being otherwise duly advised in the premises, the

Court now grants in part and denies in part Defendant's Amended Motion to Strike Plaintiff's Expert, as set forth below.

I. *Background*

This case arises out of an insurance dispute between Plaintiff Clena Investments, Inc. and Defendant XL Specialty Insurance Co. In the Complaint, Clena alleges that on October 24, 2005, it sustained damages to a property that was insured by XL. Although the Complaint itself does not specifically identify the source of the alleged damage, Clena's later filings in the case attribute the damages to Hurricane Wilma. According to the Complaint, XL improperly denied Clena's insurance claim for damages.

Therefore, Clena filed this action in the Circuit Court for the Seventeenth Judicial Circuit in and for Broward County, Florida. XL subsequently removed the case, invoking diversity jurisdiction under 28 U.S.C. § 1332.

During the course of discovery, at XL's request, EFI Global conducted an investigation into the origins and causes of damages to the Property. In its report, EFI explained that Richard N. Harb, P.E., had "conducted an origin and cause damage investigation" at the Property. Based on Harb's investigation, EFI opined that only roughly ten square feet of the roof displayed indications consistent with wind damage, constituting "about 0.1 percent of the damage...." The bulk of the damage, which pertained to approximately fifty percent of the roof, was consistent with "normal long term deterioration caused by wear and tear." EFI estimated the roof to be the original roof installed in 1984. EFI also attributed some of the damage to "poor roof installation," "settlement," and "expansion and contraction damage caused by temperature differentials." Ultimately, EFI concluded that the Property's roof was "expired ... [and that it had] exceeded its useful life expectancy."

EFI explained that its report and conclusions were "based on visual inspection of the damages at the ... [Property]. No destructive investigation was performed. No mold investigation was performed. The construction drawings were not reviewed ..." A review of the report also shows that EFI considered certain Florida Building Code requirements, meteorological information obtained from the websites of the National Weather Service Forecast Office and the National Oceanic and Atmospheric Administration, and information from the National Roofing Contractors Association. EFI's report itself appears to set forth all information that EFI obtained from these sources and relied upon in its report.

In response to EFI's report, Clena engaged Vandin Calitu to review and opine on EFI's report and on the probable cause of the damage to the Property. He also looked at and remarked on repair-cost estimates that were submitted to him for review.

Calitu, a professional engineer licensed in Florida, majored in building-construction engineering and graduated from Bucharest Technical University with his Bachelor of Science degree. He later earned his Master of Science degree in civil engineering from the University of Miami. Since 1997, Calitu has worked as an engineer, serving as a project manager on various design and construction projects since 1997. In this capacity, Calitu must account for potential hurricane-force wind impact when building a construction project. He testified during the evidentiary hearing on January 27, 2012, that he ensures building compliance with the Hurricane Code requirements, designed to allow buildings to withstand Category V hurricane winds. In addition to working as a project manager for Malcolm Pirnie (Calitu's current employer), CH2M Hill, CDM, and an engineering firm in Romania at different times, for the past approximately five years, Calitu has also engaged in work as a litigation expert and as a consultant outside of his other employment.

As Calitu describes his work experience, he has dealt with all disciplines of engineering and has developed a particular expertise in the area of heating, ventilation, and plumbing and in geotechnical engineering. According to Calitu, he "work[s] a lot with all sorts of construction companies down here in South Florida, … general contractors, roofers, … pretty much all disciplines, piping" … [and] also conducted roof investigations.

In working on this case, Calitu reviewed EFI's report, including the meteorological and other information contained therein … and photographs with moisture readings taken by Clena's public adjuster … In addition, Calitu visited the Property in July 2011, went up on the roof and visually inspected and photographed it, and spoke with two tenants of the Property who had claimed that Hurricane Wilma left "a bunch of debris … on the roof[,] … and there was a tree that fell on the roof [in connection with Hurricane Wilma]." These tenants also took Calitu inside the Property and showed him water damage.

Based on his investigation, Calitu opined, in relevant part,

> [T]he existing damages of the roof and, in turn, the interior leaks, are likely due to high winds activity in recent years[.] Hurricane Wilma likely caused the existing roof damages and interior leaks at the Property. The effect of such winds on the parapet wall flashing and edge roof membrane and also on the air plenums and air condensing units created the proper conditions for water and air intrusion under the roof membrane. Continuous water and air infiltration has been undermining the membrane, metal deck and overall roof structure.

> At this time, without any documentation, the exact extent of destruction on this roof immediately after a category 2 or up hurricane and the ongoing deterioration thereafter would be quite impossible to estimate. However, the initial cause of damage due to high winds and windborne debris could not be ruled out.

> It is difficult to isolate the roof damages to a particular hurricane event in the last few years, either Katrina, Frances, Irene, Wilma, etc. However, based on several factors and recorded data … that I researched, it is my personal opinion that the probability that hurricane Wilma affected the subject roof is much higher than that of hurricane Franc[e]s.

> … [I]t is highly probable that the wind damages on the subject roof are associated with Hurricane Wilma rather than Frances.

In his deposition testimony and his testimony during the January 27, 2012, evidentiary hearing, Calitu explained that his conclusion that Hurricane Wilma, not Hurricane Frances, inflicted the damage also stemmed from his reasoning that had the current extent of cracking and holes in the roof membrane existed when Hurricane Frances occurred, the roof membrane would have been peeled off by Hurricane Wilma....

Finally, Calitu took issue with certain aspects of EFI's report. Among others, Calitu criticized as "speculative" EFI's assessment that the roof was approximately 26 years old because EFI did not indicate that it had consulted any evidence that would have dated the roof. Calitu further noted the absence in EFI's report of any specific reference to the impact in the analysis of the parapet wall of the roof and of the twelve roof-top-mounted air-condensing units sitting on the otherwise-flat roof. According to Calitu, significant damage to the parapet wall was consistent with "high winds when flying debris would repeatedly hit the parapet wall." Calitu opined that EFI had "conveniently omitt[ed] the deterioration of the parapet wall perimeter flashing and membrane" in concluding that only ten square feet of the Property's roof had been damaged by high winds ...

EFI subsequently prepared a supplemental report ... [and] continued ... to disagree with Calitu's conclusions regarding the cause of damage to the roof, concluding that the parapet wall had actually shielded the roof surface from the direct force of the wind. In addition, EFI insisted that any damage to the roof around the air-condensing units was not caused by wind.

Along with its Motion for Summary Judgment, XL filed its Amended Motion to Strike Plaintiff's Expert ("Amended Motion") ... [which] seeks to strike Calitu and his report and deposition testimony from the record. XL originally took issue with Calitu's qualifications and determinations, complaining that

1) ... Calitu lacks the expertise to provide expert testimony about wind speeds at the insured property, whether the insured building was damaged by wind, and when any damages at the insured property occurred;

2) ... Calitu's opinions are not the product of reliable scientific methodologies;

3) ... Calitu did not base his opinions upon sufficient and reliable facts and data; and

4) ... Calitu's opinions are lay, not expert, opinions and will not assist a lay trier of fact in determining whether the insured property sustained covered damage during the effective period of the policy, and if so, the amount of that damage.

At the evidentiary hearing, however, XL conceded that Calitu possessed the requisite qualifications to opine that wind had inflicted the damage to the Property. XL further clarified that it is not challenging the reliability of the methods Calitu used in opining that wind had damaged the Property, nor is it objecting to the helpfulness of Calitu's opinion in this regard. Instead, during the hearing, XL focused its arguments on Calitu's qualifications to determine that it was more likely that Hurricane Wilma had caused the damage than that any other hurricane had....

In response, Clena argues that, as a professional engineer who personally examined the property, evaluated the materials prepared by Clena's public adjuster, reviewed the applicable weather reports, and applied his observations in light of his professional training and experience, Calitu is qualified to render his expert opinion and to critique the report that XL's retained expert....

II. *Analysis*

Rule 702, Fed. R. Evid., governs the admissibility of expert testimony. It provides,

> If scientific, technical, or other specialized knowledge will assist the trier of fact to understand the evidence or to determine a fact in issue, a witness qualified as an expert by knowledge, skill, experience, training, or education, may testify thereto in the form of an opinion or otherwise, if (1) the testimony is based upon sufficient facts or data, (2) the testimony is the product of reliable principles and methods, and (3) the witness has applied the principles and methods reliably to the facts of the case.

Fed. R. Evid. 702. Under this rule, the party offering the expert testimony bears the burden of laying the proper foundation, and that party must demonstrate admissibility by a preponderance of the evidence. *Rink v. Cheminova, Inc.*, 400 F.3d 1286, 1291–92 (11th Cir. 2005). In determining whether expert testimony and any report prepared by the expert may be admitted, the Court engages in a "rigorous" three-part inquiry into whether (1) the expert is qualified to testify competently regarding the matters he intends to address; (2) the methodology by which the expert reaches his conclusions is sufficiently reliable; and (3) the testimony assists the trier of fact, through the application of scientific, technical, or specialized expertise, to understand the evidence or to determine a fact in issue. *United States v. Frazier*, 387 F.3d 1244, 1260 (11th Cir. 2004).... While some overlap exists among these requirements, the court must individually analyze each concept. *Frazier*, 387 F.3d at 1260.

Under *Daubert*, the court acts as a gatekeeper, but this role "is not intended to supplant the adversary system or the role of the jury." *Quiet Tech.* [*DC-8, Inc. v. Hurel-Dubois, UK Ltd.*], 326 F.3d at 1341 [((11th Cir. 2003)] (quoting *Maiz v. Virani*, 253 F.3d 641, 666 (11th Cir. 2001)).... Thus, the district court cannot exclude an expert because it believes that the expert lacks personal credibility. *Rink*, 400 F.3d at 1293, n. 7. To the contrary, "vigorous cross-examination, presentation of contrary evidence, and careful instruction on the burden of proof are the traditional and appropriate means of attacking shaky but admissible evidence." *Quiet Tech.*, 326 F.3d at 1341.

Here, Defendant challenges on all three prongs ... the expert testimony of Calitu and his Report and deposition testimony as they relate to Calitu's opinion that the wind-inflicted damage to the Property probably occurred as a result of Hurricane Wilma. The Court separately considers each prong.

A. *Calitu's Qualifications*

An expert may be qualified "by knowledge, skill, experience, training, or education." *Furmanite Am., Inc. v. T.D. Williamson, Inc.*, 506 F. Supp. 2d 1126, 1129 (M.D. Fla. 2007) (citing Fed. R. Evid. 702). Moreover, "[a]n expert is not necessarily unqualified simply because [his] experience does not precisely match the matter at hand." *Id.* (citing *Maiz*, 253 F.3d at 665). Where an expert does have congruent experience, "[t]he Committee Note to the 2000 Amendments of Rule 702 ... explains that '[n]oth-ing in this amendment is intended to suggest that experience alone ... may not provide a sufficient foundation for expert testimony.'" *Frazier*, 387 F.3d at 1261 (quoting Fed. R. Evid. 702 advisory committee's note (2000 amends.)).

Determining whether a witness is qualified to testify as an expert "requires the trial court to examine the credentials of the proposed expert in light of the subject matter of the proposed testimony." *Jack v. Glaxo Wellcome, Inc.*, 239 F. Supp. 2d 1308, 1314–16 (N.D. Ga. 2002). In other words, a district court must consider whether an expert is qualified to testify competently regarding the matters he intends to address. *City of Tuscaloosa [v. Harcros Chems., Inc.]*, 158 F.3d at 562–63 [(11th Cir. 1998)]. This inquiry is "'not stringent,' and 'so long as the expert is minimally qualified, objections to the level of the expert's expertise [go] to credibility and weight, not admissibility.'" *Vision I Homeowners Ass'n, Inc. v. Aspen Specialty Ins. Co.*, 674 F. Supp. 2d 1321, 1325 (S.D. Fla. 2009) (citations omitted).... After the district court undertakes a review of all of the relevant issues and an expert's qualifications, the determination regarding qualification to testify rests within the district court's discretion. *See Berdeaux v. Gamble Alden Life Ins. Co.*, 528 F.2d 987, 990 (5th Cir. 1976).

Turning to Defendant's Amended Motion to Strike, the Court has reviewed Calitu's résumé and his deposition testimony further detailing his prior experience as a pro-fessional engineer. The Court has also considered the scope of Calitu's report and EFI's report. In addition, the Court has considered the evidence adduced during the January 27, 2012, *Daubert* hearing, as well as XL's concession that Calitu is qualified to identify wind-inflicted damage. Based on these factors, the Court agrees that Calitu possesses sufficient qualifications to testify that damage to the Property was caused by hurricane-force winds and to opine on the correctness of EFI's conclusions re-garding the same issue. The Court further finds that contrary to XL's suggestion, Calitu also possesses sufficient education, training, and experience to opine that Hur-ricane Wilma more likely caused the damage to the Property than Hurricane Frances or any other preceding hurricane because had the roof suffered from the same of extent of damage that it does now when Hurricane Wilma hit, Hurricane Wilma would have ripped the membrane from the roof.

Calitu appears to possess an appropriate educational and professional background to serve as an expert in these subject areas. In furtherance of obtaining his professional engineer's license, Calitu graduated with both an undergraduate and a graduate degree in engineering. He has also actually worked as a practicing civil and structural engineer for fourteen years. As a professional engineer, Calitu has directed numerous construc-tion projects as the project manager. In this capacity, he has worked with, among others, roofing contractors, and he, as a part of his "side" business, has conducted roof investigations. He has further been responsible for ensuring building-construction compliance with the Hurricane Code. Notably, Calitu possesses precisely the same professional license as Harb, who conducted EFI's investigation in this case for XL.

This is not surprising, as assessing structure-related damages to a building would seem to be a natural fit with the training and experience that a professional civil engineer has. *See, e.g., Broussard v. State Farm Fire & Cas.*, 523 F.3d 618, 631 (5th Cir. 2008) (affirming district court's ruling allowing structural engineer to testify that storm surge and not hurricane-force winds caused damage); *cf. also Traveler Indem. Co. of Conn. v. Centimark Corp.*, 2010 WL 3431159, *2 (S.D. Fla. Aug. 30, 2010) (finding licensed engineer qualified to provide expert opinion that installation of roofing system was faulty). Presumably, XL viewed Harb's professional-engineering license as at least one relevant qualification for assessing the cause of damage to the Property before hiring EFI. No less is true of Calitu's comparable license and experience.

Nor, as XL originally suggested in its Motion, does the fact that Calitu has not previously served as an expert witness in cases involving wind damage render him any less qualified to serve as an expert in this case. Every expert found to be qualified by a court must be so designated a first time. While findings by other courts that Calitu is qualified to serve as an expert witness in the area of wind damage might help to support a finding that Calitu is qualified to opine in this case on the likely cause of the damages to the Property, the absence of such prior court determinations does not preclude the Court from concluding that Calitu is qualified here. Rather, Calitu's education, experience, and professional background can and do, in and of themselves, satisfy the relatively low threshold established by Rule 702 and *Daubert* and its progeny to find Calitu qualified to opine on whether the possible causes of damages to the Property are consistent with hurricane damage....

XL's complaints that Calitu is not an expert in determining when damage occurred or in weather are similarly unavailing. Calitu was not asked to date the damage; instead, Calitu has opined that the type of damages he saw at the Property are consistent with damages inflicted by hurricane-force winds and that had a hurricane preceding Wilma inflicted the damage at issue, Wilma would have caused the roof membrane to be ripped off. Although dating the damage might be helpful to Calitu's analysis, even XL's own expert remarked, "[D]ue to the numerous numbers of storm events during the 2004 and 2005 seasons, it is inconclusive which hurricane caused the observed damage." As for Calitu's lack of weather expertise, Calitu need not be able to predict a hurricane to be able to identify the damages that result from one. Notably, EFI obtained its weather information relating to hurricanes in South Florida from the websites of NWS and NOAA, just as Calitu relied in his report on weather-related information on hurricanes from the National Hurricane Center. In short, Calitu's background, training, education, and professional experience as a practicing, licensed civil engineer sufficiently qualify him to opine on the causes of damages to the Property and the likelihood that a roof in the current condition of that of the Property could not have survived Hurricane Wilma.

B. *Reliability*

... For the same reasons that, as XL concedes, Calitu's experience and inspection of the Property lay a permissible foundation for Calitu's conclusion that wind caused the damage to the Property's roof, they provide an acceptable basis for Calitu's opinion that Hurricane Wilma most probably exacted the damage at issue. More specifically, Calitu testified that, as a result of his training and experience, he knows where to look and what to look for when inspecting a property for damage, and, as a professional engineer, he understands the import of cracks and holes that an untrained person would not. He further appreciates the impact of high winds on property, having to take these effects into account when building to ensure Hurricane Code compliance. For all of these reasons, Calitu may rely upon his training, experience, and inspection of the Property to opine that it is more likely that Hurricane Wilma imposed the Property damage than that any prior hurricane did. And because XL's objection to the second opinion stems only from the fact that that opinion ties the damages to the Property to Hurricane Wilma, the Court similarly overrules XL's challenge to the second opinion set forth above.

C. *Helpfulness*

Expert testimony is helpful to the trier of fact only "if it concerns matters that are beyond the understanding of the average lay person." *Frazier*, 387 F.3d at 1262. In other words, "[p]roffered expert testimony generally will not help the trier of fact when it offers nothing more than what lawyers for the parties can argue in closing arguments." *Id.* at 1262–63 (citing 4 *Weinstein's Fed. Evid.* § 702.03[2][a]). Moreover, where an expert opinion has a tendency to confuse the trier of fact, it may not satisfy the helpfulness prong. *See Frazier*, 387 F.3d at 1258. Finally, "[b]ecause of the powerful and potentially misleading effect of expert evidence," judges must take care not to allow misleading and prejudicial opinions to influence the finder of fact. *See id.* at 1263.

Here, both of the opinions that XL challenges satisfy the helpfulness test. Calitu's knowledge and training that enable him to opine that the roof membrane would have blown off had it been in its current condition prior to Hurricane Wilma are not universally shared and fall outside the realm of the average person's understanding. Similarly, most people do not possess the requisite specialized knowledge and training to determine damages to the Property most probably attributable to Hurricane Wilma....

III. *Conclusion*

... To the extent that Defendant's Amended Motion seeks to strike Calitu's opinion that Hurricane Wilma most likely inflicted the damage to the Property, based on Calitu's experience and training, the Amended Motion is Denied.

Notes and Questions

1. After the chemist's (minimal) testimony in *Carter* about her qualifications, how would each side argue on whether the standard for Rule 702 admission has or has not been met? Under the Federal Rules of Evidence, determinations of admissibility on Rule 702 questions should be determined by a "preponderance of the evidence." *Daubert v. Merrell Dow Pharms., Inc.*, 579 U.S. 509, 592 n. 10 (1993). If that is the standard, would you have admitted the testimony? On appeal, the standard of review is "abuse of discretion." *Gen. Elec. Co. v. Joiner*, 522 U.S. 136 (1997). As an appellate judge, would you affirm?

2. When we evaluate Vandin Calitu's background, what are his formal educational credentials and what is his practical experience in the field? Which of these factors does the court find more persuasive in finding Calitu qualified to testify as an expert here?

3. You will also note that the *Clena Investments* court suggested that Defendant's expert Harb had the same qualifications as Plaintiff's expert Calitu: "XL viewed Harb's professional-engineering license as at least one relevant qualification for assessing the cause of damage to the Property before hiring EFI. No less is true of Calitu's comparable license and experience." *Clena*, 280 F.R.D. at 662. This type of strategic consideration is one factor to consider when an attorney considers filing a pretrial motion.

4. The *Clena* court also makes clear that any proposed expert evidence must meet all of the requirements of Rule 702: qualifications, reliability, and helpfulness to the jury. *Id.* at 660. The court states, with unusual candor, that overlap exists among these requirements, but remember that each section of analysis addresses a separate consideration. As for the third prong of the analysis, we will turn our attention to reliability analysis in Section D, but we have already covered helpfulness in detail in Section A. Independent of the issue of qualifications, how exactly is Calitu's testimony helpful to the jury? What will the jury be able to determine after his testimony that they could not before? Why is that issue not one of common knowledge? Consider the interaction of helpfulness and qualifications in evaluating admissibility of expert testimony in the next case.

Meridia Products Liability Litigation v. Abbott Laboratories
447 F.3d 861 (6th Cir. 2006)

COLE, Circuit Judge.

In this multi-district product liability case, Plaintiffs-Appellants—certain current and past consumers of the diet-drug Meridia, whose actions were transferred to, or originated in, the Northern District of Ohio—appeal the district court's grant of summary judgment in favor of Defendants-Appellees, the pharmaceutical company that marketed and distributed Meridia and its affiliates. Plaintiffs argue on appeal that the district court ... erred in partly excluding the testimony of one of Plaintiffs' experts, and ... erred in granting summary judgment to Defendants as to Plaintiffs' various common law and statutory claims. For the reasons that follow, we affirm the district court's grant of summary judgment.

I.

This litigation was occasioned by the diet-drug Meridia. First developed in 1980 as an anti-depressant by Boots Pharmaceuticals, Meridia works by slowing the body's dissipation of serotonin and norepinephrine, brain chemicals that affect satiety and impulse control. Meridia originally failed to gain Food and Drug Administration approval. In 1990, the rights to Meridia were purchased by Knoll Pharmaceuticals, which began to test the drug's potential to effectuate weight loss. In 1997, the FDA approved the marketing and sale of Meridia as a prescription diet-drug, which Knoll began to market in 1998. In 2001, Abbott Laboratories acquired Knoll. Abbott Labs now markets Meridia to doctors, pharmacies, and directly to consumers.

On March 19, 2002, a consumer watchdog group petitioned the FDA to remove Meridia from the market, alleging the drug to be ineffective and unsafe. In the wake of that petition, plaintiffs across the United States brought suit against Abbott Labs.... The plaintiffs claimed to have incurred various injuries—e.g., heart attack, stroke, tachycardia, palpitations, chest pain, high blood pressure, and death—and claimed that Meridia is ineffective. The plaintiffs also claimed that they were at increased risk of developing a future injury. Some of the claims were filed originally in federal court, and Abbott Labs, which is an Illinois company, removed many of the state court claims on the ground of diversity.

In August of 2002, with the approval of the litigants, the Judicial Panel on Multi-District Litigation transferred the pending federal cases to the United States District Court for the Northern District of Ohio, [where] Plaintiffs filed a Master Class Action and a Motion for Class Certification. The MCA Complaint alleged nine grounds for relief: (1) strict liability, (2) negligence, (3) negligence *per se*, [and] (4) violation of statutory consumer protection.... Plaintiffs requested compensatory damages, punitive damages, attorneys' fees, and "such other or further ... relief as may be appropriate under the circumstances."

Abbott Labs filed various motions in response. First, it filed a motion to exclude all of Plaintiffs' expert witnesses. Second, it filed a motion for summary judgment, pursuant to Federal Rule of Civil Procedure 56(c), with respect to all claims.... The district court denied Abbott Labs's motion to exclude Plaintiffs' experts, except that it granted in part Abbott Labs's motion with respect to Arnold Schwartz, Ph.D.—as a pharmacologist, Dr. Schwartz was not permitted to testify as to the physiological effects of high blood pressure. The court granted Abbott Labs's motion for summary judgment with respect to all issues. *See In re Meridia Prods. Liab. Litig.*, 328 F. Supp. 2d 791 (N.D. Ohio 2004).... This timely appeal followed.

III.

... Plaintiffs also argue that the court erred in its application of the summary judgment standard, and in partially excluding the testimony of one of Plaintiffs' experts. These challenges to the district court's decision fail.

A.

We review a district court's grant of summary judgment *de novo. Miles v. Kohli & Kaliher Assocs., Ltd.*, 917 F.2d 235, 241 (6th Cir. 1990). Summary judgment is appropriate "if the pleadings, depositions, answers to interrogatories, and admissions on file, together with the affidavits, if any, show that there is no genuine issue of material fact and that the moving party is entitled to judgment as a matter of law." Fed. R. Civ. P. 56(c). We "must view all the facts and the inferences drawn therefrom in the light most favorable to the nonmoving party." *Birch v. Cuyahoga Cty. Probate Ct.*, 392 F.3d 151, 157 (6th Cir. 2004). . . .

B.

In the course of granting summary judgment in favor of Abbott Labs, the district court excluded as inexpert part of the testimony of Arnold Schwartz, Ph.D., an indisputably qualified pharmacologist. Specifically, the court would not permit Dr. Schwartz's to testify on the health effects of heightened blood pressure, or to testify that Meridia's health risks outweigh its benefits. We review the exclusion of expert testimony for abuse of discretion, *see Kumho Tire. Co. v. Carmichael*, 526 U.S. 137, 152–53 (1999), even when the exclusion results in the entry of summary judgment for the opposing party, *see Nelson v. Tenn. Gas Pipeline Co.*, 243 F.3d 244, 248 (6th Cir. 2001).

As the Supreme Court explained in *Daubert v. Merrell Dow Pharmaceuticals, Inc.*, 509 U.S. 579, district courts act as gatekeepers to ensure that "any scientific testimony or evidence admitted is not only relevant, but reliable." *Id.* at 589. The *Daubert* Court identified a non-exhaustive list of factors to guide the district court's decision. . . . Ultimately, the district court has "considerable leeway" in making these sorts of determinations. *Kumho Tire Co.*, 526 U.S. at 152.

In this case, the district court found that Dr. Schwartz is a qualified pharmacologist, with an attendant expertise on the effects of drugs on the body. Accordingly, the court admitted his testimony as to what Meridia does: *inter alia*, it temporarily elevates blood pressure in some patients. The court found, however, that Dr. Schwartz is not an expert on the effects of high blood pressure on the human body. Dr. Schwartz testified that Meridia may increase blood pressure, and that this increase poses a risk to heart health that outweighs any corresponding cardiac benefit of weight loss. In excluding that testimony, the court noted that Dr. Schwartz is not a cardiologist, and that he "shows no training or experience allowing him to answer this question." Moreover, the court found that Dr. Schwartz's opinions on this subject lacked foundation and left the court "to rely solely on his subjective judgments." *In re Meridia*, 328 F. Supp. 2d at 806.

In short, the district court did not abuse its discretion; the court faithfully articulated and applied the relevant factors in partially excluding Dr. Schwartz's testimony.

V.

For the preceding reasons, we affirm the district court's grant of summary judgment.

Notes and Questions

1. To understand the interaction of the issue of qualifications and the issue of helpfulness, first ask yourself how exactly the testimony of Dr. Schwartz would be of assistance to the jury in the case. Then examine his qualifications. What are the best arguments to establish that he can testify to everything? Why does the court disagree?

2. Like in *Merida*, the issue of "mismatch" of qualifications often occurs in cases involving very specific medical specialties. Clearly, all physicians have certain spe-

cialized knowledge of physiology or chemistry of the body, but when presenting testimony, the issues become much more specific than those generalities. Consider *Ralston v. Smith & Nephew Richards, Inc.*, 275 F.3d 965 (10th Cir. 2001), in which a patient sued the manufacturer of a surgical nail for defective design. In support of her claim, plaintiff endorsed Dr. Kimberly Templeton, the surgeon who treated the plaintiff. While the court recognized that Dr. Templeton is a board-certified orthopedic surgeon, she was excluded from testifying about the defective design of the surgical nail when she testified she was not an expert on the particular nail in question or in product warnings in general. *Id.* at 969–70. Of course, Dr. Templeton's testimony would have helped the jury decide the case, but again, that is not the question here. Instead, while she had specialized knowledge in the field of orthopedic surgery, her knowledge did not encompass product design and is therefore excluded due to "mismatch." *See also Cleveland ex rel. Cleveland v. United States*, 457 F.3d 397 (5th Cir. 2006) (excluding testimony of an internal medicine physician in evaluating standard of care for an emergency room physician). However, in deciding whether the qualifications match the testimony, courts are careful to require a fact-intensive inquiry and not rely solely on formal certification. *Pages-Ramirez v. Ramirez-Gonzalez*, 605 F.3d 109 (5th Cir. 2009). In *Pages-Ramirez*, the court noted that though the contested expert lacked certification to administer the drug at issue in the case, her expertise regarding the drug's administration rested on a "reliable foundation" that included several related certifications, years of peer-reviewing relevant incidents, and the fact that she published materials on how to administer the drug in question. *Id.* at 116–17.

3. Clearly expertise can mismatch when it fails to meet the specialization required for a particular field, as in *Merida* or *Ralston*. However, instead of hyper-specialization, expertise issues can center around whether expert testimony is required at all. While opinion evidence is commonly considered an expert prerogative, Federal Rule of Evidence 701 does allow lay witnesses to testify to a specialized opinion under limited circumstances. In the following two cases, we will see the type of evidence commonly allowed by Rule 701, and then consider the non-expert "specialized knowledge" issue.

United States v. Tipton
964 F.2d 650 (7th Cir. 1992)

COFFEY, Circuit Judge.

The defendant-appellant, Darryl Tipton, appeals his conviction for embezzling money and evading federal income tax, alleging that the district court abused its discretion in admitting samples of his handwriting in evidence … and that the evidence was insufficient to support a finding of guilt. We affirm.

I. FACTS

On January 4, 1990, a federal grand jury returned a six-count indictment against the defendants Tipton (four counts) and Sam Clark (two counts) for their role in a fraudulent payout scheme involving money from the Department of Housing and Urban Development. Clark pled guilty prior to trial and testified on behalf of the government at Tipton's trial. Tipton was charged with two counts of embezzling money of the United States ... as well as with two counts of evading federal income tax in 1984 and 1985..., and proceeded to trial on August 22, 1990.

The Department of Housing and Urban Development provided the City of Aurora, Illinois with money (as part of an annual entitlement grant) to be used by qualified low income homeowners for repair and/or remodeling work of their homes. Tipton worked for the City of Aurora as a rehabilitation specialist in the division of Neighborhood Services from 1983 to 1985. His responsibilities included assisting qualified homeowners through the housing repair application process as well as training and supervising the work of David Kramer, who also worked on housing rehab projects. Following confirmation of the applicant's income, the rehabilitation specialist (Tipton or Kramer) determined the applicant's eligibility, inspected the applicant's home and prepared a draft-specifications sheet listing the details of the work project. Contractors submitted sealed bids for the projects, and once the bids were opened, the rehabilitation specialist and the homeowner determined whether to proceed. If the homeowner decided to proceed, the rehabilitation specialist assisted in preparing the applicant's written loan proposal, which was in turn forwarded to Tipton's immediate supervisor, Patricia Casler, and ultimately to the City Council of Aurora, Illinois. If the City Council approved the loan, it would adopt a resolution approving a transfer of funds. After the City Council's approval of the transfer of funds from the City's bank account to the homeowner's individual account, the rehab specialist prepared, signed, and submitted a cover letter to the bank enclosing the City's resolution and a "transfer of funds" form requesting that the bank set up an individual account for the homeowner. The "transfer of funds" form directed to the bank was signed by the rehab specialist, the comptroller and the mayor. The approval process did not require independent investigation of the loan proposals submitted by Tipton.

After the project was completed, the contractor was required to forward a signed completion notice to either Tipton or Kramer certifying completion of the contract. The rehabilitation specialist was supposed to inspect the home and verify the completion of the project. Following the verification, the specialist completed a payout authorization form which required three signatures, those of the homeowner, the rehabilitation specialist and Pat Casler (Tipton's immediate supervisor). Casler testified that it was her usual practice not to independently inspect Tipton's work before approving the payout form. Once the payout form was signed by these three, the bank reviewed the form to determine whether it was properly executed. The bank then prepared the check in the name of the homeowner and entered the debit on a ledger card, recording the date of the check, the amount and the name of the contractor paid.

At trial, the government relied extensively on the testimony of Sam Clark, an old friend and distant relative of Tipton. In the early 1980's, Clark was working on a number of rehabilitation projects for the City of Aurora. Clark testified that in the summer of 1983, Tipton suggested a fraudulent payout scheme to him in which several unidentified contractors who lacked the necessary insurance coverage would operate under Clark's name and insurance, and upon receipt of payout authorizations, the City's bank would issue payout checks in Clark's name. Tipton further proposed that Clark cash the checks and give the money to Tipton, who would in turn take care of the uninsured contractors. Clark agreed to the plan, and several months later Tipton called Clark at a job site and asked him to pick up a check at Aurora Federal Savings & Loan. Clark followed Tipton's instructions, picked up and cashed the check, placed the money in an envelope, and delivered it to Tipton. At this time Tipton gave Clark some of the money. Clark testified that this procedure continued from the summer of 1983 to January of 1985. Clark stated he picked up approximately twenty or thirty checks from the Aurora Savings & Loan for work that he never performed, and he received approximately $200 to $300 from Tipton for each check he cashed.

Around May of 1984, assistant rehabilitation specialist David Kramer sent a letter to Georgana Brison, a rehabilitation applicant who had been on his case list since 1983, to determine why she had not completed her rehab application. After a period of time and receiving no answer from Brison, Kramer stated that he reviewed her file and discovered it contained a City Council resolution transferring funds to an account in Brison's name. Kramer testified that he was surprised at this unusual procedure, for he had not done any work to initiate a resolution transferring funds. Kramer stated that he inquired of Tipton concerning the transfer of funds resolution in Brison's file, and Tipton replied that the rehabilitation process had been restructured so that the funds were now approved as soon as the rehabilitation work was identified. Kramer related that he advised Tipton that Brison was not interested in participating in the program and asked him to have the resolution authorizing the transfer of funds to Brison's account rescinded, and Tipton replied that he would take of it. Several months later, Kramer again asked Tipton to have the City cancel Brison's transfer of funds resolution, and Tipton replied once again that he would take care of it. Unbeknownst to Kramer, the bank had transferred the HUD funds from the City's account into Brison's loan account prior to his conversations with Tipton. On April 27, 1984 and May 1, 1984, the bank issued payout checks to Sam Clark for $8,000 and $4,000 respectively, for Brison's alleged home rehabilitation. Clark testified that he gave all the cash from these checks to Tipton.

Patricia Casler testified that her name had been forged on certain payout forms and that she had never authorized anyone to enter her signature on any form indicating approval. In addition, approximately twenty rehabilitation applicants testified and disavowed the authenticity of their respective signatures on payout forms and stated further that the work described as completed in certain invoices or payout forms had never been performed. Kramer testified that certain signatures and handwriting on rehabilitation applicants' bogus "transfer of funds" forms, payout forms and invoices appeared to be Tipton's. Robin Hunton, a forensic document examiner of more than twelve years experience [sic] in the field, who has examined thousands of documents, testified concerning her examination and comparison of various rehabilitation documents with handwriting exemplars supplied by Tipton and likewise stated that Tipton's handwriting appeared on a number of these forged documents.

Joe Mazzura, an agent with the Internal Revenue Service, also testified for the prosecution regarding Tipton's 1984 and 1985 federal tax returns. Mazzura stated that after comparing Tipton's reported income for 1984 and 1985 with the sum of money involved in the embezzled checks Clark cashed and gave to Tipton, he was of the opinion that Tipton failed to report income of $146,715 in 1984 and $14,903.50 in 1985.

Following trial, the jury found the defendant guilty on two counts of embezzling money of the United States and two counts of evading federal income tax in 1984 and 1985. The district court sentenced Tipton to four years imprisonment on the two counts of embezzlement and one count of tax evasion to be served concurrently with each other....

II. ISSUES FOR REVIEW

The defendant raises the following issues on appeal: (1) whether the district court abused its discretion in admitting in evidence the identification of the defendant's handwriting, since Robin Hunton was, in his opinion, unqualified to testify as a handwriting expert, and the probative value of David Kramer's lay opinion of Tipton's handwriting was purportedly outweighed by its prejudicial effect; ... and (3) whether the evidence was sufficient to find him guilty beyond a reasonable doubt.

III. DISCUSSION
A. Handwriting Identification

The defendant contends the district court abused its discretion in admitting the expert testimony of Robin Hunton, a forensic document examiner. In his brief, the defendant asserts that "[o]n a preliminary examination, it may have seemed that Ms. Hunton was a qualified examiner of questioned documents" but "once she was subjected to cross-examination, it became evident that her expertise was only superficial." The district court has broad discretion when deciding to admit expert testimony, and its determination will be affirmed unless it is manifestly erroneous. *Carroll v. Otis Elevator Co.*, 896 F.2d 210, 212 (7th Cir. 1990). Federal Rule of Evidence 702 allows a trial court to admit the testimony of a "witness qualified as an expert by knowledge, skill, experience, training, or education" if his or her expert testimony "will assist the trier of fact to understand the evidence or to determine a fact in issue." *Id.* Courts have found the qualification of a handwriting expert to be sufficient where the expert testifies to related experience, knowledge or training. *United States v. Marler*, 614 F.2d 47, 50 (5th Cir. 1980); *United States v. Green*, 523 F.2d 229, 236–37 (2d Cir. 1975), *cert. denied*, 423 U.S. 1074 (1976); *United States v. Tovar*, 687 F.2d 1210, 1215 (8th Cir. 1982).

At trial, Hunton testified that as a forensic document examiner for the United States Department of the Treasury, she worked in an IRS laboratory examining documentary evidence containing known and questioned handwriting. She has examined documents for more than twelve years and estimated that she has examined thousands of documents. Furthermore, Hunton has testified in judicial proceedings approximately twenty-four times and is a member of many forensic science and document examining societies. She has received additional training, instruction and experience while working as a lab technician in the FBI laboratory (Documents Section) and through her attendance in classes offered by the FBI and related organizations. We agree with the district court that the government's expert witness had more than sufficient training, knowledge, experience and expertise to qualify as an expert regarding forged documents. *See Liquid Air Corp. v. Rogers*, 834 F.2d 1297, 1308 (7th Cir. 1987), *cert. denied*, 492 U.S. 917 (1989) ("Experience and knowledge establish the foundation for an expert's testimony...."). In our opinion, the defendant has failed to demonstrate that the district court's decision to admit the testimony of Robin Hunton as an expert witness in the area of forensic document examination was an abuse of discretion.

The defendant also argues that the trial court improperly admitted the testimony of his co-worker, David Kramer, regarding Tipton's handwriting on several of the forged documents. The defendant alleges in his brief that "Kramer stated that the writing appeared to be that of Tipton..., but he was not certain." The defendant further alleges that the probative value of Kramer's lay opinion as to the handwriting was substantially outweighed by its prejudicial effect and was "therefore violative of Federal Rule of Evidence 403 and [the] defendant's due process rights." The district court's determination on the admissibility of evidence will be upheld unless it appears that the court clearly abused its discretion. *See United States v. Covelli*, 738 F.2d 847, 854 (7th Cir.), *cert. denied*, 469 U.S. 867 (1984). "Generally, an abuse of discretion only occurs where no reasonable person could take the view adopted by the trial court." *United States v. Manos*, 848 F.2d 1427, 1429 (7th Cir. 1988) (citation omitted).

The district court admitted Kramer's testimony regarding his lay opinion as to the identification of Tipton's handwriting on various documents over the defendant's objection. Federal Rule of Evidence 701 provides that:

> If the witness is not testifying as an expert, the witness' testimony in the form of opinions or inferences is limited to those opinions or inferences which are (a) rationally based on the perception of the witness and (b) helpful to a clear understanding of the witness' testimony or the determination of a fact in issue.

... Although we have not previously addressed the issue of lay opinion testimony regarding the identification of handwriting, other circuits have allowed the admission of lay witnesses' handwriting testimony. In *United States v. Barker*, 735 F.2d 1280, 1283 (11th Cir.), *cert. denied*, 469 U.S. 933 (1984), the Eleventh Circuit affirmed the trial court's decision to admit the testimony of two co-workers of the defendant that "they were familiar with the defendant's handwriting and stated that in their opinions it matched or was similar to the handwriting on the checks." The Eleventh Circuit held that this testimony was properly admitted under Federal Rule of Evidence 701 and 901(b)(2). *Id.* Moreover, in *United States v. Whittington*, 783 F.2d 1210, 1214–15 (5th Cir.), *cert. denied*, 479 U.S. 882 (1986), the Fifth Circuit affirmed the trial court's decision to admit a document on the basis of lay opinion testimony identifying the defendant's signature on it. Like the lay witnesses in *Barker*, the witnesses in *Whittington* were also lay co-workers of the defendant who testified that they were familiar with the defendant's signature. The court admitted the document even though the witnesses did not see the defendant sign it because "[a] signature may be identified by testimony of a person familiar with the signature." *Id.* at 1215 (footnote omitted).

Because Kramer was familiar with Tipton's handwriting and signature as a result of observing many of the rehabilitation documents Tipton prepared, we are of the opinion that Kramer was qualified to testify regarding Tipton's signature and handwriting. The trial court did not abuse its discretion in admitting Kramer's testimony identifying Tipton's handwriting or signature on the phony documents.

Tipton's contention that Kramer was not "certain" in his identification of Tipton's handwriting is a mischaracterization of the trial record. On cross-examination Kramer testified to the following questions by counsel:

> DEFENDANT'S COUNSEL: And when you talked [on direct examination] about these signatures here, you always said they appeared to be Mr. Tipton's signature; is that correct?
>
> KRAMER: Yes, I did....
>
> DEFENDANT'S COUNSEL: You don't know for sure that they are; is that correct?
>
> KRAMER: *Unless I absolutely saw him sign it, I can't be absolutely certain.*

(Emphasis added.) On cross-examination Kramer merely related that he could not be "absolutely certain" that a signature was Tipton's unless he observed Tipton actually sign the document. That is the kind of statement we might expect from a truthful witness who wants to be careful to tell the whole truth and nothing but the truth. Without actually observing Tipton sign the documents, certainly it was more accurate and proper for Kramer to state that the signatures "appeared" to be Tipton's than to say that he was "absolutely certain" of the fact....

C. Sufficiency of the Evidence

The defendant contends that the government's evidence was insufficient to prove guilt beyond a reasonable doubt. Specifically, the defendant alleges among other things that with the exception of Sam Clark's testimony, there was no direct evidence of his participation in a scheme to embezzle money provided to the City of Aurora by HUD.... A defendant attacking the sufficiency of the evidence has a heavy burden and "'[o]nly where the record contains no evidence, regardless of how it is weighed, from which the jury could find guilt beyond a reasonable doubt, may an appellate court overturn the verdict.'" *United States v. Redwine*, 715 F.2d 315, 319 (7th Cir.1983), *cert. denied*, 467 U.S. 1216 (1984) (citation omitted). Furthermore, all reasonable inferences must be drawn in favor of the government. *United States v. Douglas*, 874 F.2d 1145, 1151 (7th Cir.), *cert. denied*, 493 U.S. 841 (1989).

The defendant seems to have forgotten that the trial testimony revealed that in 1983, the defendant approached Sam Clark and suggested that Clark cash rehabilitation payout checks and turn the money over to Tipton. Clark testified that he had cashed approximately thirty payout checks at the direction of Tipton for work that had never been performed. In addition, Clark was paid for work never performed, according to the testimony of approximately twenty homeowners. The record establishes that Tipton controlled the transfer and payout and thus had the ability to direct a false transfer and payout scheme. The record further established that the defendant's co-worker, David Kramer, city officials, and committees relied on Tipton to properly prepare the "transfer of funds" forms and the payout forms. A number of applicants testified that documents in their files had been falsified. Kramer identified signatures and handwriting on documents in those files as being Tipton's. The government's handwriting expert, Robin Hunton, a forensic document examiner, identified four signatures on the falsified documents as being Tipton's. This testimony concerning the fraudulent scheme is consistent with other portions of the record dealing with Tipton's ability to direct the unauthorized transfer of funds and payout scheme. Finally, the government presented the testimony of an IRS agent, who stated that Tipton failed to report income of $146,175 in 1984 and $14,903.50 in 1985 on his federal tax returns. We are convinced that the government's overwhelming testimony of Tipton's guilt established that he had fraudulently created, directed and operated a scheme to embezzle thousands of dollars of United States monies and evaded federal income taxes, as set forth in the indictment.

IV. CONCLUSION

The decision of the district court is affirmed.

Lord & Taylor LLC v. White Flint, L.P.
849 F.3d 567 (4th Cir. 2017)

HARRIS, Circuit Judge.

Lord & Taylor, LLC,[Ed.] operates a retail department store along Rockville Pike in Montgomery County, Maryland. From 1977 to 2015, the store was part of the White Flint Shopping Center, an enclosed shopping mall. But in 2015, the Mall's operator, White Flint, L.P., closed the Mall and began demolition in order to make way for a mixed-use redevelopment. L&T sued White Flint, claiming that White Flint had breached the parties' contract by closing the Mall without L&T's consent.

A jury found White Flint in breach of contract and awarded L&T $31 million in damages. Both parties appeal, arguing primarily that the damages award is too high (White Flint) or too low (L&T)....

I.
A.

This is the latest chapter in a long-running dispute between the parties over the planned redevelopment of the Mall site. The Montgomery County Council approved the redevelopment in 2012, as part of a broader plan to revitalize the surrounding area, and litigation commenced soon thereafter.... In 1975, White Flint, then planning

---

[Ed.] The Plaintiff's name has been shortened to L&T in this case for clarity purposes, by the Author.

the development of what would become the Mall, reached an agreement with L&T: L&T would lease land on the Mall site and serve as an "anchor" tenant for the Mall, along with co-anchor Bloomingdale's.... [I]n exchange, White Flint would construct an enclosed "first class" mall and then maintain it until at least 2042. The parties' agreement required White Flint to secure L&T's consent before building any additional structures or making alterations to the Mall's design or appearance.

The Mall opened in 1977 and operated successfully for many years, before more recently experiencing a drop in business. The parties, not surprisingly, disagree about the cause of this decline. According to White Flint, the Mall's struggles reflect the weakening of the mall business generally, as consumer preferences change and e-commerce grows; for L&T, the blame goes to White Flint, for allowing the Mall to fail and even hastening its demise by offering tenant buy-outs, all to facilitate the redevelopment plan. Whatever the cause, in 2012, Bloomingdale's chose not to renew its lease, and by 2013, the vast majority of tenants had left the Mall.

The Mall officially closed in January 2015, leaving L&T the sole business operating on the premises.... Ultimately, the redevelopment plan calls for transforming what once was an enclosed mall into a mixed-use development, complete with residential, retail, recreational and office space.

B.

L&T objected to the redevelopment, arguing that the clear terms of the parties' agreement required White Flint to maintain the Mall, and that the proposed mixed-use alternative would negatively affect its business by making customer access less convenient and denying the store the benefit of foot traffic from Mall customers. Negotiations between the parties proved fruitless, and L&T filed its first complaint against White Flint in July 2013.... L&T amended its complaint to bring the alternative claim ... one for damages resulting from White Flint's alleged breach of contract. And for good measure, L&T added a claim for fraud, as well. According to L&T, White Flint's breach and fraud had cost it somewhere between $70 and $100 million. Specifically, L&T sought damages for lost profits during the construction phase of the redevelopment; for the costs of redesigning and reconstructing its store to conform to the new development; and for the loss of bargained-for property rights, in the form of use restrictions and easements violated by the planned redevelopment.

L&T's case went to trial, where a jury heard evidence and argument for twelve days. On the merits of its breach claim, L&T argued that the proposed redevelopment was a clear violation of its contract with White Flint, and that White Flint had hastened the Mall's decline in order to reap the rewards of redevelopment. In response, White Flint argued that any breach of contract should be excused by reason of impossibility. According to White Flint, economic trends combined with the departure of co-anchor Bloomingdale's made continued operation of the Mall impossible, and its substitute mixed-use redevelopment would be an overall economic boon to the area.

Much of the trial, however, focused on the question of damages, with L&T presenting two distinct theories under which it sought recovery. First, L&T claimed damages for lost profits during the demolition and construction phase of the project, when customer access would be disrupted and the store would lose the benefit of foot traffic in the area. L&T's expert calculated lost profits of up to $31 million, on the assumption that the construction phase would last for between ten and thirteen years, starting with the alleged breach in 2012.

White Flint took issue with L&T's calculations, and presented expert testimony of its own projecting a construction period of only three and a half years and estimating damages using a significantly lower profit margin than that employed by L&T's expert. White Flint also insisted that any damages award should reflect not only lower profits during construction, but also the greater profits that would accrue to L&T in subsequent years, once construction was complete and the store became part of a successful mixed-use development. The district court disagreed, holding that any such future benefits were too speculative to be the basis of a damages award, and instructing the jury to that effect.

L&T's second damages theory centered around the costs of reconfiguring its store to take account of the fact that it no longer would be part of an enclosed mall. L&T presented testimony from Kerry Mader, a long-time store executive responsible for renovations, who explained the extensive redesign that would be required to accommodate the shift from a multi-entrance mall store to a stand-alone store, and calculated construction costs of between $30 and $36 million. White Flint did not present evidence of its own regarding construction costs or argue for a different cost estimate. But it did object to the admission of Mader's testimony, arguing that Mader was offering expert opinion without having been qualified as an expert under Rule 702 of the Federal Rules of Evidence. The district court rejected that argument, concluding that Mader was offering lay rather than expert testimony, based on Mader's own previous experience and "day-to-day work with the company," and that any shortcomings in his cost estimate should be addressed by "spirited cross-examination" of the witness.

After several days of jury deliberation and an agreement by the parties to accept a non-unanimous verdict, the jury found White Flint in breach of contract, rejected White Flint's defenses, and awarded L&T $31 million in damages. The $31 million figure is consistent with both L&T's estimate of lost profits (up to $31 million) and its estimate of construction costs (between $30 and $36 million), and the jury's general verdict form did not specify the theory on which damages were awarded....

II.
A.

District courts have broad discretion to manage jury trials. Accordingly, we review a district court's jury instructions, evidentiary rulings, and discovery rulings for abuse of discretion only. *See Gen. Elec. Co. v. Joiner*, 522 U.S. 136, 141 (1997) (evidentiary rulings)....

B.

We begin with White Flint's appeal. White Flint does not challenge the jury's finding that it breached its contract with L&T. Instead, it challenges the $31 million damages award, raising two arguments, each aimed at one of L&T's theories of recovery. With respect to lost profits, White Flint argues that the district court erred by instructing the jury not to consider, in calculating damages, the redevelopment's potential positive impact on L&T's profits. And with respect to renovation costs, White Flint argues that Mader's construction cost estimate was improperly admitted as lay opinion testimony. For the reasons given below, we find neither argument persuasive.

1.

In response to L&T's expert testimony on lost profits, White Flint presented its own expert, Scott DeCain, to testify to the future benefits of the redevelopment project for L&T's bottom line. DeCain acknowledged that L&T's sales would decline during the construction period, which he estimated at three and a half years. But according to DeCain, once construction on the redevelopment was complete, L&T's net profits would *increase*—in the amount of $10 million over five years.... White Flint argued, any damages award based on lost profits should include an offset or deduction to account for these future economic benefits.

The district court disagreed. Under Maryland law, the district court explained in an oral ruling, damages must be proved with "reasonable certainty." White Flint's evidence of future benefit to L&T, the court concluded, was "entirely too speculative" to meet that standard....

We find no abuse of discretion in the district court's determination. As the parties agree, this case is governed by Maryland law. And under Maryland law, it is clear that damages related to lost profits "may not be recovered unless they can be proved with 'reasonable certainty.'" Complete certainty is not required, and reasonable inferences may be drawn from the evidence. *See M & R Contractors & Builders v. Michael*, 215 Md. 340, 138 A.2d 350, 355 (1958)....

The district court properly applied that standard and concluded that on the record before it, White Flint could not establish to a "reasonable certainty" whether and to what extent L&T would benefit from the redevelopment. We have no basis for disturbing that judgment.... None of this, to be clear, is to fault DeCain or his work. A real estate development of the scale contemplated here is an inherently risky endeavor, extending years into the future and marked by significant uncertainty. Any prediction of the degree of success, no matter how sophisticated, necessarily will rest on assumptions about a long list of contingencies. At bottom, deciding when anticipated future profits from such an enterprise have been established as "reasonably certain" is a fact-intensive judgment call, within the sound discretion of a trial court. The district court did not abuse that discretion here.

2.

L&T separately claimed damages for the cost of reconfiguring and renovating its store to accommodate the new site plan and, in particular, the loss of several entrances that had connected it to the original Mall. To support this second theory of damages, L&T offered the testimony of Kerry Mader, an executive of L&T's parent company responsible for store design, store construction, and facilities, who opined that construction costs would fall between $30 and $36 million. White Flint objected, arguing that Mader's proposed testimony was expert in nature and that Mader had not been qualified as an expert under [702].

The district court rejected that claim and allowed Mader to testify as a lay opinion witness under Federal Rule of Evidence 701. The court recognized that Rule 702's reliability requirements may not be circumvented by allowing unqualified expert testimony in the guise of lay testimony. And the court understood that there may be a "fine line" between Rule 701 lay opinion and Rule 702 expert testimony. In this case, however, the district court concluded that because Mader's testimony was based on Mader's own experience — his "day-to-day work" as an officer of L&T — it was admissible as lay testimony, without the necessity of qualifying Mader as an expert.

Again, we have no basis for disturbing the district court's judgment. It is true, as White Flint argues, that Mader was not qualified as an expert under Federal Rule of Evidence 702, which governs testimony by "expert" witnesses that is based on "scientific, technical, or other specialized knowledge." But Federal Rule of Evidence 701 permits a lay witness — with no need for expert qualification — to give opinion testimony that is "rationally based on the witness's perception" and helpful to determining a fact in issue, so long as it is not based on the same "scientific, technical, or other specialized knowledge" covered by Rule 702. And while the line between the two, as the district court recognized, can be "a fine one," *see United States v. Perkins*, 470 F.3d 150, 155 (4th Cir. 2006) (internal quotation marks and citation omitted), the key to Rule 701 lay opinion testimony is that it must arise from the personal knowledge or firsthand perception of the witness. *See id.* at 155–56; *MCI Telecommunications Corp. v. Wanzer*, 897 F.2d 703, 706 (4th Cir. 1990) (allowing lay opinion testimony under Rule 701 where it is "well founded on personal knowledge as distinguished from hypothetical facts" and based on "relevant historical or narrative facts that the witness has perceived") (internal quotation marks omitted).

We have applied that general rule to permit business employees — like Mader — to opine on accounting projections under Rule 701, so long as their opinions are based on their first-hand experience on the job. *See MCI Telecommunications*, 897 F.2d at 706 (holding that business bookkeeper may give lay opinion testimony on projected profits on the "basis of facts and data perceived by him" in his role as bookkeeper). Indeed, in an unpublished opinion that is directly relevant here, we have allowed lay testimony as to projected *construction* costs when it is based on the witness's personal experience with similar projects. *See Lake Ridge Apartments, LLC v. Bir Lakeridge, LLC*, 335 Fed. Appx. 278 (4th Cir. 2009) (unpublished).

The district court did not abuse its discretion when it concluded that under this line of authority, Mader's testimony was admissible under Rule 701 as lay opinion testimony. With 38 years of industry experience, Mader supervises store design and construction at L&T on a "day-to-day" basis. Drawing on personal knowledge gleaned from that on-the-job experience—including "relevant historical ... facts" regarding the more than 50 redesign projects he has overseen, *see MCI Telecommunications*, 897 F.2d at 706—Mader described past L&T renovation projects, outlined the kinds of changes necessitated by the loss of mall entrances, and explained the increased construction costs customarily associated with renovations to a store that remains open for business. The district court reasonably could conclude that like the witness in *Lake Ridge Apartments*, Mader's ultimate projection of construction costs was predicated on his "previous experience," and "personal knowledge and perception," rather than the kind of specialized reasoning process subject to Rule 702 as expert testimony.

We note, as did the district court, that this determination is consistent not only with our precedent but also with the advisory committee's Note to Rule 701. That Note recognizes that "most courts have permitted the owner or officer of a business to testify to the value or projected profits of the business, without the necessity of qualifying the witness as an accountant, appraiser, or similar expert." Fed. R. Evid. advisory committee's note to 2000 amendment. Such testimony, the Committee explains, is admissible under Rule 701 because it is based not on "experience, training or specialized knowledge within the realm of an expert," but on "the particularized knowledge that the witness has by virtue of his or her position in the business." *Id.* It requires nothing more than acknowledgement of an accounting identity—that the "profits" referenced in the Note equal revenue minus cost—to see that the cost estimate offered by Mader, an officer at L&T, falls squarely under this contemplated category of permissible lay testimony.

White Flint argues strenuously that Mader's hands-on experience is insufficient to substantiate his testimony because, for instance, Mader visited the store only once, and had never before estimated costs for a Maryland project. But those arguments go to the weight to be given Mader's testimony, not to its lay character or admissibility....

III.

For the foregoing reasons, we affirm in full the judgment of the district court.

Notes and Questions

1. In *Tipton*, the prosecution offered two different witnesses—Robin Hunton and David Kramer—who both testified that the signature on the documents belonged to the Defendant. What was the objection to each witness? Ultimately, the court permitted both to testify, but for different reasons. Considering the exact content of the testimony of each witness, why were they admitted?

2. In *Lord & Taylor*, each litigant offered the testimony of a witness on the issue of damages. What was the objection to each witness here? Ultimately, the court rejected the testimony of Scott DeCain as violating of Rule 702, but Kerry Mader—who admittedly does not meet the standards of Rule 702—is permitted to testify. What is going on here?

3. In their notes on the amendments to Rule 701 in 2000, the advisory committee explained the distinction between Rule 701 and Rule 702 opinion testimony as follows:

> Rule 701 has been amended to eliminate the risk that the reliability requirements set forth in Rule 702 will be evaded through the simple expedient of proffering an expert in lay witness clothing. Under the amendment, a witness' testimony must be scrutinized under the rules regulating expert opinion to the extent that the witness is providing testimony based on scientific, technical, or other specialized knowledge within the scope of Rule 702. *See generally Asplundh Mfg. Div. v. Benton Harbor Eng'g*, 57 F.3d 1190 (3d Cir. 1995). By channeling testimony that is actually expert testimony to Rule 702, the amendment also ensures that a party will not evade the expert witness disclosure requirements set forth in Fed. R. Civ. P. 26 and Fed. R. Crim. P. 16 by simply calling an expert witness in the guise of a layperson. *See* Gregory P. Joseph, *Emerging Expert Issues Under the 1993 Disclosure Amendments to the Federal Rules of Civil Procedure*, 164 F.R.D. 97, 108 (1996).

> The amendment is not intended to affect the "prototypical example[s] of the type of evidence contemplated by the adoption of Rule 701 relat[ing] to the appearance of persons or things, identity, the manner of conduct, competency of a person, degrees of light or darkness, sound, size, weight, distance, and an endless number of items that cannot be described factually in words apart from inferences." *Asplundh Mfg.*, 57 F.3d at 1196.

> For example, most courts have permitted the owner or officer of a business to testify to the value or projected profits of the business, without the necessity of qualifying the witness as an accountant, appraiser, or similar expert. *See, e.g., Lightning Lube, Inc. v. Witco Corp.*, 4 F.3d 1153 (3d Cir. 1993) (no abuse of discretion in permitting the plaintiff's owner to give lay opinion testimony as to damages, as it was based on his knowledge and participation in the day-to-day affairs of the business). Such opinion testimony is admitted not because of experience, training or specialized knowledge within the realm of an expert, but because of the particularized knowledge that the witness has by virtue of his or her position in the business. The amendment does not purport to change this analysis....

The "particularized knowledge" rule is therefore not an exception to Rule 702, but rather a recognition that — as a result of repeated exposure to a particular issue — one gains knowledge that others could have gained had they been in the same position. Jack Weinstein has suggested the dividing line between the two depends on the type of reasoning necessary to reach the conclusion: if any person exposed to the same information could reach the same level of knowledge, then it remains a lay 701 opinion, but if the opinion reflects reasoning that can only be mastered by specialists in the field, it becomes an expert 702 opinion. 4 WEINSTEIN'S FED. EVID. § 701.03[1].

4. Examples of "particularized knowledge" cases, where testimony was admitted even if not obvious to the general public, are as varied as specialty professions. Yet a selection of these cases firmly supports the distinction suggested by WEIN-STEIN's, *supra*, that the key issue is the type of reasoning required to complete the opinion:

   a) *United States v. Graham*, 796 F.3d 332, 365 (4th Cir. 2015): Cell phone company employee permitted to testify to mechanism of cell phone connection to cell tower, based on particularized knowledge as an employee but "not conclusions [he] drew based on any specialized reasoning or assessment…."

   b) *Montgomery v. Gooding, Huffman, Kelly & Becker*, 163 F. Supp. 2d 831, 838 (N.D. Ohio 2001): Land developers could testify as to marketability of land parcels allegedly devalued by defendant's breach; this testimony is not specialized knowledge requiring disclosure under 702.

   c) *Astro-Tel v. Verizon Florida, LLC*, 979 F. Supp. 2d 1284, 1293 (M.D. Fla. 2013): Court rejects attempt to proceed on antitrust claim without expert testimony; no witness testifying based on "particularized knowledge" will be sufficient to prove the claim ("Due to the complex web of telecommunications providers at hand and the varied products and services offered to consumers, expert testimony is a necessity for defining the relevant antitrust geographic and product markets.").

   d) *Chen v. Mayflower Transit*, 224 F.R.D. 415, 419–20 (N.D. Ill. 2004): President of related trade association may not testify to pricing practices in the moving industry under Rule 701; witness has no "personal knowledge and day-to-day experience with the business" in question, so cannot testify as a lay witness.

   e) *Tampa Bay Shipbuilding & Repair v. Cedar Shipping, Co.*, 320 F.3d 1213, 1223 (11th Cir. 2003): Company president and others with extensive ship building and repair experience may testify under Rule 701 that services were charged at a fair rate.

5. Remember, however, that evidentiary rulings will be reviewed under an "abuse of discretion" appellate standard, so the trial judge will have significant authority to decide on what side of the specialized/particularized knowledge line any particular testimony falls. *Gen. Elec. Co. v. Joiner*, 522 U.S. 136, 141 (1997).

Tying It Together

Eddie Eagle was finally facing the charges he had feared for most of his career: conspiracy to distribute heroin, possession of heroin with intent to distribute, and RICO counts, all with a possibility of life in prison. But as a precautionary measure, Eddie was always careful on the phone. When he discussed a deal, Eddie would always use lingo instead of real words for drugs. For example, when he said "Would you like to come over for breakfast?," he was asking if they needed a delivery the next morning, at a pre-determined drop location.

Special Prosecutor Jane Jones has seen drug gangs that think they're smarter than they actually are. In response, she endorses Joe L. Inguist as her expert. Inguist is a 30-year veteran of the FBI, who has worked major cocaine cases in South Florida since 1990 or so. Inguist personally has worked undercover within drug rings, and also listened to wiretaps on over 500 phones of dealers. He also trains new drug agents at the annual FBI summer camp in Quantico.

Inguist will testify to two things, based on his experience:

- 1) He will interpret the lingo contained within Eddie's wiretap calls, telling the jury that "breakfast" means a morning delivery, etc.; and
- 2) That the dangerousness of the operation was considerably higher since there were multiple members of the conspiracy.

When Jones endorses Inguist, the defense files a motion asking for his testimony to be excluded.

Assignment: Please prepare a 1–2 page brief explaining your argument in the context of the cases we have reviewed.

- As an assistant prosecutor in Jones's office, why does Inguist's testimony meet the standards established in the Federal Rules of Evidence for admission? Why should the court admit all of his testimony?
- As defense counsel for Eagle, why are you objecting to Inguist's testimony and why should it be entirely excluded from trial?

C. Does This Expert Have an Adequate Factual Basis for the Opinion? Rule 702 and 703 Standards for Foundational Bases

"… an expert … may testify in the form of an opinion or otherwise if: … (b) the testimony is based on sufficient facts or data…." Fed. R. Evid. 702.

Federal Rule of Evidence 703:
Bases of an Expert's Opinion Testimony

An expert may base an opinion on facts or data in the case that the expert has been made aware of or personally observed. If experts in the particular field would reasonably rely on those kinds of facts or data in forming an opinion on the subject, they need not be admissible for the opinion to be admitted. But if the facts or data would otherwise be inadmissible, the proponent of the opinion may disclose them to the jury only if their probative value in helping the jury evaluate the opinion substantially outweighs their prejudicial effect.

Unlike determining whether an expert would be helpful to a factfinder or whether an expert is sufficiently qualified, the Rule that evaluates whether an expert has a factual or empirical basis to testify is not contained within Rule 702. Rather, this question appears separately in Rule 703, which envisions three different options for the source of information that an expert can rely upon in forming her opinion:

1) Inadmissible Evidence, Not a Type Reasonably Relied Upon in Field,

2) Inadmissible Evidence, But Reasonably Relied Upon in Field, or

3) Admissible Evidence Only.

The rule informs us how to handle each of these scenarios, although only explicitly listing the first two. Let us review each, to decide how a court would handle them.

The first scenario envisions an expert who is relying on materials that were not admissible in evidence at trial, and these materials are not something that an expert would reasonably rely upon in the field of expertise. Imagine a family physician relying on astrology charts in determining the proper course of treatment for a child with a cough. In this scenario, Rule 703 will disallow the expert opinion in its entirety, and the underlying information—since it is already inadmissible—cannot be admitted either. *See, e.g., In re Agent Orange Prod. Liab. Litig.*, 611 F. Supp. 1223, 1245 (E.D.N.Y. 1985). This situation involves complete exclusion.

Conversely, the third scenario will permit the admission of both the expert opinion but also the (previously admissible) underlying evidence. Imagine here an expert who is asked to opine on a medical issue at trial, based on a series of hypotheticals that match the evidence already given to the jury in court. In this scenario, the expert opinion rests on a proper basis: if it is good enough for the jury, it is good enough for the expert. Therefore, the opinion and underlying facts are all admitted for jury consideration. *See, e.g., United States v. Clay*, 832 F.3d 1259, 1317 (11th Cir. 2016) (finding forensic accounting expert's testimony admissible when based on defendant's financial restatement, since restatement was admissible as a business record under Rule 803(6)); *Bouygues Telesom, S.A. v. Tekelec*, 472 F. Supp. 2d 722, 728 (E.D.N.C. 2007) ("Generally, Rule 703 permits expert opinion to be based upon personal knowledge, *admissible evidence*, or inadmissible evidence if it is 'of a type reasonably relied upon by experts in the particular field in forming opinions of inferences upon the subject.' Fed. R. Evid. 703") (emphasis added).

Finally, the second scenario is the most complicated but also the one discussed in most detail in the rule. Imagine an ER physician who relies upon oral statements of other medical providers—EMTs, radiologists, or nursing staff—and those other providers will not be called to testify at trial. Even though their statements are (largely) inadmissible hearsay, any doctor deciding a course of action for a patient must reasonably rely on them. In fact, they make life-or-death decisions based on these types of data. *See* Fed. R. Evid. 703 advisory committee's note (citing Paul D. Rheingold, *The Basis of Medical Testimony*, 15 Vand. L. Rev. 473, 489 (1962); McCormick on Evidence § 15). With this commonsense basis, Rule 703 explicitly allows the *expert opinion* in these circumstances to be admitted. However, there is a complication. The expert is relying on previously inadmissible material, and before 2000, courts varied on whether the admission of the opinion now "bootstrapped" the underlying facts into admissibility as well. Fed. R. Evid. 703 advisory committee's note to 2000 amends. Recognizing the prior ambiguity in the rule, the advisory committee amended the rule to clearly state that admission of the opinion is *not* enough to admit the underlying facts. Instead, the underlying evidence is presumptively *in*admissible unless it meets a very high standard of balancing: the probative value of the evidence in evaluating the opinion of the expert *substantially outweighs* the prejudicial effect of the evidence. Fed. R. Evid. 703. Prejudice can take any form common in the rules of evidence (like propensity, for example), but the advisory committee clearly envisioned the most common prejudice to be misuse for substantive purposes instead of the proper purpose of evaluation of the expert opinion. Fed. R. Evid. 703 advisory committee's note to 2000 amends. As we will see, the reality is that this balancing test ensures that in these types of situations, underlying evidence will rarely be admitted over objection, unless a high probative value exists in its value to explain the expert opinion. Without that, the opinion is admitted without basis. With our ER physician then, while the opinion evidence will be admissible, the underlying data will likely not be unless it has particular probative value for assessing the opinion.

But does that mean the underlying evidence is *verboten* and will be unlikely to be discussed under most circumstances? No, as it turns out. Remember that Rule 703 is only concerned with the admission by the *proponent* of the evidence, as the rulebook makes clear shortly thereafter, in Rule 705:

Federal Rule of Evidence 705:
Disclosing the Facts or Data Underlying an Expert's Opinion

Unless the court orders otherwise, an expert may state an opinion — and give the reasons for it — without first testifying to the underlying facts or data. But the expert may be required to disclose those facts or data on cross-examination.

Let us consider these rules, and how the courts handle expert opinion based on varying factual bases, with the following cases.

Bernhardt v. Richardson-Merrell, Inc.
723 F. Supp. 1188 (N.D. Miss. 1988)

BIGGERS, District Judge.

… The court has before it the defendant's motion to reconsider the court's denial of its motion for summary judgment and the defendant's motion to strike the plaintiffs' submission of the affidavit of Dr. Stuart Newman. Having considered the parties' memoranda and supporting exhibits, the court is in a position to rule on the merits.

I.

Dana Michelle Bernhardt and her parents brought this suit against the manufacturer of the drug Bendectin asserting that Bendectin caused a deformity of Michelle's hand and arm. Mrs. Bernhardt took Bendectin during her pregnancy with Michelle after her doctor, Dr. Hal P. James, prescribed it for morning sickness. The parties rely on the testimony of medical experts who reached opposite conclusions in determining whether Bendectin caused the plaintiff's birth defects. The defendant relies on the affidavit of Dr. John Jackson, a professor of medical genetics at the University of Mississippi. In his affidavit, Dr. Jackson indicated that certain parts of the body are completely formed during gestational stages and the formation cannot be reversed except by a traumatic event. According to Dr. Jackson, the arm buds begin to form on the fetus within thirty days from conception, the hand plate is formed by the thirty-eighth day and the elbow has formed and finger rays have split into fingers by the forty-fourth day after conception. Utilizing this information, Dr. Jackson concluded that Bendectin could not have caused Michelle's deformity because her mother took the drug fifty-four or fifty-five days after the conception of Michelle. Dr. Jackson also opined that Bendectin was not a teratogen, a drug which affects limb development.

In opposition to the defendant's motion for summary judgment, the plaintiffs submitted answers to the defendant's interrogatories which contained summaries of the plaintiffs' expert testimony. According to the plaintiffs, Dr. Melnick, Dr. Lord, Dr. Thiersch, Dr. Glauser, Dr. Brownlee, and Dr. Newman would testify that, based upon in vitro and in vivo animal studies, Bendectin was a teratogen which could affect limb formation within the first ten weeks of pregnancy. The plaintiffs also indicated that several doctors would testify that taking Bendectin during pregnancy as "prescribed by Dr. Clark (the prescribing obstetrician)" created a risk of the birth defects. (In fact, Dr. Hal Pearson James treated and prescribed Bendectin to Mrs. Bernhardt during her pregnancy). Dr. McBride, Dr. Done, Dr. Brownlee, Dr. Thomas, Dr. Melnick, Dr. Newman, Dr. Glauser and Dr. Lord would testify "with reasonable medical certainty, the cause of the limb defect that the infant plaintiff was born with was Bendectin."

II.

Since the plaintiffs must establish that Bendectin caused the birth defect by reasonable medical certainty, they must present sufficient evidence to establish the existence of causation in order to survive the defendant's motion for summary judgment. *Celotex Corp. v. Catrett*, 477 U.S. 317, 322 (1986). *Washington v. Armstrong World Indus., Inc.*, 839 F.2d 1121, 1123 (5th Cir. 1988).

Initially, the court denied the defendant's motion for summary judgment because Dr. Jackson based his opinion upon an assumption of when the conception of Michelle occurred. The defendant asked for reconsideration of its motion for summary judgment because Dr. Jackson based his assumption of when conception occurred on the plaintiff's answers to interrogatories. After considering the defendant's motion, the court gave the plaintiffs the opportunity "to rebut the defendant's contention that the fingers of a fetus were developed by the forty-fourth day after conception [by pointing out] in writing what expert testimony [the plaintiffs had] to rebut this conclusion." Instead of pointing out what evidence the plaintiff had … the plaintiffs submitted an affidavit of Dr. Newman which indicated that Bendectin was a teratogen and it can affect the limb development within fifty days after conception. Dr. Newman also opined that "scientific studies and observations have shown" limb development can vary plus or minus ten days. The defendant moved to strike Dr. Newman's affidavit....

III.

The parties support their positions in this case by conflicting expert testimony. In addressing the motion for summary judgment, the court must consider the reliability and foundation of the experts' opinions. Fed. R. Evid. 703; *Washington v. Armstrong World Indus., Inc.*, 839 F.2d at 1123. An expert opinion must be based upon data reasonably relied upon by experts in the particular field of expertise testified to. Thus, the scientific theory on which an expert bases his opinion must be sufficiently recognized in his field. Fed. R. Evid. 703; *Soden v. Freightliner Corp.*, 714 F.2d 498, 505 (5th Cir. 1983). Since conjecture, speculation, and conclusory opinions have insufficient probative value, the court must determine whether the expert opinions have a scientific basis and factual basis.

The plaintiffs' experts have not indicated whether or not the animal studies upon which they rely are reasonably relied upon by experts in the field of embryology, epidemiology, or pharmacology. Fed. R. Evid. 703. Additionally, the plaintiffs' experts have not indicated what scientific material supports their conclusion linking Bendectin's effect on rats and rabbits to their conclusion that the drug similarly affects human fetuses. A conclusion that Bendectin could cause deformities in animals does not support a conclusion that *it does* cause birth defects in humans. *Lynch v. Merrell-Nat'l Labs.*, 830 F.2d 1190 (1st Cir. 1987). The courts in *Richardson v. Richardson-Merrell, Inc.*, 857 F.2d 823 (D.C. Cir. 1988), and *Hull v. Merrell-Dow Pharmaceuticals*, 700 F. Supp. 28 (S.D.Fla.1988), noted that the overwhelming scientific data demonstrated that Bendectin was not a teratogen. In this case, there is nothing to indicate that the plaintiffs' expert opinions are based on studies generally accepted in the field of epidemiology, embryology, or pharmacology. In the absence of such proof, the court cannot conclude that the opinions of the plaintiffs' experts meet minimum standards of reliability.

Even if the court assumed Bendectin was a teratogen, the plaintiff failed to present a factual basis upon which an expert could conclude that it probably caused the plaintiff's deformities. According to Doctors Swan and Done, ingesting Bendectin during Mrs. Bernhardt's pregnancy created a risk of birth defects. Dr. Swan indicated the risk was statistically significant enough to establish a probable link between Bendectin and the plaintiff's birth defects. However, none of these doctors indicated whether the studies they relied upon were generally accepted in their fields of expertise. Moreover, the court cannot be sure the experts based their conclusions upon a diagnosis of Michelle Bernhardt because the experts assumed a Dr. Clark prescribed Bendectin to Mrs. Bernhardt, when, in fact, Dr. James prescribed Bendectin to Mrs. Bernhardt. There is no indication in the evidence before the court of who Dr. Clark is. The plaintiffs' experts simply concluded this drug caused the plaintiffs' injuries without applying an accepted scientific theory to an objective medical diagnosis of the plaintiff.

Trial courts cannot "accept uncritically any sort of opinion espoused by an expert merely because his credentials render him qualified to testify...." Whether an expert's opinion has an adequate basis and whether without it an evidentiary burden has been met are matters of law for the court to decide. *Richardson by Richardson v. Richardson-Merrell, Inc.*, 857 F.2d 823, 829 (D.C. Cir. 1988). In this case the plaintiffs failed to show an adequate factual and scientific basis to support their expert's conclusions. Consequently, the plaintiffs failed to present proof that would establish the issue of causation which is essential to their case. Accordingly, the defendant is entitled to summary judgment and its motion to reconsider will be granted....

State v. Heine

844 N.W.2d 409 (Wis. Ct. App. 2014)

FINE, J.

Peter T. Heine appeals the judgment convicting him of first-degree reckless homicide, as party to a crime, in connection with his sale of heroin to a person who died as a result of ingesting the heroin. is only claim on this appeal is that the trial court deprived him of his constitutional right of confrontation by receiving into evidence a toxicology report, which analyzed blood and urine the physician performing the autopsy recovered from the victim's body, without requiring the testimony of those involved in analyzing the specimens. Significantly, the report, although it was received into evidence, *was neither introduced nor received into evidence to trace or identify the specific heroin* the State said that Heine sold to the victim. As we show below, we need not analyze who among the many persons who participated in the toxicology analyses had to testify in order to satisfy Heine's right to confrontation because the physician who performed the autopsy testified at the trial and could, consistent with Heine's right of confrontation, rely on the report in giving his medical opinion that the victim died from a heroin overdose.

I.

Heine's main brief on this appeal does not challenge that there was sufficient evidence that he sold heroin to the victim shortly before the victim died.... Thus, Heine focuses on the State's burden to prove that the victim died from a heroin overdose, not that the heroin ingested by the victim was sold to him by Heine.

Three persons from the toxicology laboratory testified, none of whom had any hands-on testing duties. The first person testified that he was a "toxicologist" with the testing laboratory who "reviews and releases forensic cases that come to our laboratory," which he said was "certified" by various certifying organizations. He testified on cross-examination that fourteen persons, as phrased by Heine's trial lawyer, "touched these samples in this case." The witness conceded that he did not review the raw data, but only "sign[ed] off on the final report."

The second person from the toxicology laboratory to testify certified the analysis of the victim's urine. She explained, however, that she did "not work in the lab" and was not, as phrased by the prosecutor, "familiar with the lab processes as it relates to the calibration of" the machine used for, again as phrased by the prosecutor, "the urine opiates confirmation." The third person from the laboratory to testify was the person who certified the "opioid testing" of the victim's blood. She explained her duties to the jury: "I have to review all of the data and I look at the chain of custody, make sure that it's complete as it went through the lab from each person. I verify the sequence table to make sure that there is nothing wrong with it and I review the entire batch, so I basically reanalyze it, if you want to think of it that way." She testified, though, that her review of the data was limited to checking "the chain of custody," and that their "analysts [had] run a calibration." The trial court received the toxicology report into evidence over the objection of Heine's trial lawyer, opining that the jury could give the report whatever "weight" it deemed fit.

Vincent Tranchida, M.D., the Chief Medical Examiner of Dane County, autopsied the victim. He told the jury that he had been Dane County's Chief Medical Examiner since January 1, 2011, and had been "a Senior medical examiner in the Office of Chief Medical Examiner of New York City from 2003 until 2010." Before that, he "worked as a resident in anatomic and clinical pathology at the University of Michigan at Ann Arbor." He told the jury that he had done "[a]proximately 2,000" autopsies before he assumed his Dane County duties, and that he had done "over 500" autopsies since then. Heine did not and does not on this appeal challenge Dr. Tranchida's qualifications to testify as an expert....

In the course of the autopsy, Dr. Tranchida noted that there were "four fresh punctures" in the front of the victim's elbow, as well as scarring from old punctures. He also found "white frothy foam" in the tube that had been used in an attempt to resuscitate the victim, that "the white frothy foam [went] all the way down deep into his airways, his trachea and his bronchi," and that the victim's lungs were "full of fluid." Dr. Tranchida also told the jury that the victim had an inordinate amount of urine in his bladder: in "my examination of [the victim]'s bladder I found that it was distended with urine. Most people tend to go to the bathroom when their urine — when the bladder starts to fill with about 200 milliliters of urine. He had 400 milliliters of urine, almost twice that amount."

Dr. Tranchida testified that he read the toxicology laboratory report, and that he regularly relied on toxicology results for, as phrased by the prosecutor's question, "purposes of completing [his] final diagnosis." Dr. Tranchida testified that the report indicated that a sample of the victim's blood revealed the presence of "morphine" and a "specific metabolite for heroin," as well as "codeine, which is also a contaminant often used in heroin." He also noted that the laboratory report said that the metabolite, which, he testified, "has a very short half-life," was in the victim's urine, as was "quite a lot of morphine." Dr. Tranchida opined that the substances found by the laboratory were "very consistent with a heroin intoxication." Dr. Tranchida explained that heroin kills by affecting the lungs' ability to breathe: "What it's causing is it's causing the capillaries in the lungs to dilate but causing contraction of the veins in the lungs. So as a result the fluid is pumping into the lungs but it's not coming out and being drawn back into the circulation, so the lungs get wetter and wetter with fluid." He recounted what he saw during the autopsy:

> In addition to this, the person is struggling to breathe. And the proteins that line the insides of the air sacs start to get churned up, so you start to get this froth as the person is having trouble breathing and the lungs are getting wetter and more full of fluid.... Now, in addition to this, we see the urine continue to accumulate.... So that's why we see foam in the airways, we see wet lungs and we see them accumulating urine in the bladder, because over this period of time they're still alive, they're still processing the heroin, it's still being cleared from their system, but they sustain the dangerous anoxic brain injury and as a result they're going into progressive respiratory failure.

The prosecutor asked Dr. Tranchida for his opinion as to why the victim died:

> **Q.** In terms of the physical examination you conducted of [the victim] combined with the toxicology results were you able to form any conclusion to a reasonable degree of medical certainty regarding [the victim]'s cause of death?
>
> **A.** Yes, I was.
>
> **Q.** What was your conclusion?
>
> **A.** My conclusion to a reasonable degree of medical certainty for [the victim]'s death is that his cause of death is an acute heroin intoxication.

Heine's trial lawyer did not object to Dr. Tranchida's opinion and does not challenge it on this appeal.

II.

As we have seen, Heine contends that the toxicology report's receipt into evidence violated his right to confront his accusers. The Sixth Amendment to the United States Constitution provides:

> In all criminal prosecutions, the accused shall enjoy the right to a speedy and public trial, by an impartial jury of the State and district wherein the crime shall have been committed, which district shall have been previously ascertained by law, and to be informed of the nature and cause of the accusation; *to be confronted with the witnesses against him;* to have compulsory process for obtaining witnesses in his favor, and to have the Assistance of Counsel for his defense.

State v. Deadwiller, 820 N.W.2d 149, 151 (Wis. App. 2012) (emphasis by *Deadwiller*), *aff'd,* 834 N.W.2d 362 (Wis. 2013). We review *de novo* the trial court's decision to receive the report into evidence over the confrontation objection of Heine's trial lawyer. *See State v. Williams,* 644 N.W.2d 919, 924 (Wis. 2002).

"The confrontation right applies to statements that are 'testimonial.' *Davis v. Washington,* 547 U.S. 813, 821 (2006); *Crawford v. Washington,* 541 U.S. 36, 68–69 (2004) ('Where testimonial statements are at issue, the only indicium of reliability sufficient to satisfy constitutional demands is the one the Constitution actually prescribes: confrontation.')." *Deadwiller*, 820 N.W.2d at 151 (internal parallel citations omitted). Thus, certifications by a laboratory of tests received as substantive evidence, or the testimony by someone who did not perform the tests received as substantive evidence may violate a defendant's right to confrontation. *See Melendez-Diaz v. Massachusetts*, 557 U.S. 305, 308, 311 (2009) (sworn certifications) ("In short, under our decision in *Crawford* the analysts' affidavits were testimonial statements, and the analysts were 'witnesses' for purposes of the Sixth Amendment. Absent a showing that the analysts were unavailable to testify at trial *and* that petitioner had a prior opportunity to cross-examine them, petitioner was entitled to 'be confronted with' the analysts at trial.") (one set of internal quotation marks omitted; emphasis by *Melendez-Diaz*); *Bullcoming v. New Mexico*, 564 U.S. 647 (2011) (certificate of laboratory analysis testified-to by a person who did not do the analysis but was familiar with the laboratory's testing procedures) ("We hold that surrogate testimony of that order does not meet the constitutional requirement. The accused's right is to be confronted with the analyst who made the certification, unless that analyst is unavailable at trial, and the accused had an opportunity, pretrial, to cross-examine that particular scientist.").

The confrontation issue was revisited in *Williams v. Illinois*, 567 U.S. 50 (2012), where the lead opinion on behalf of three other justices in support of the judgment determined that an expert could, under Rule 703 of the Federal Rules of Evidence, give an opinion based on a laboratory report even though neither the analysts nor the report's author testified, and the report could be "disclosed" to the factfinder "to show that the expert's reasoning was not illogical, and that the weight of the expert's opinion does not depend on factual premises unsupported by other evidence in the record—not to prove the truth of the underlying facts." *See also Deadwiller*, 834 N.W.2d at 369–73; *Deadwiller*, 820 N.W.2d at 151–53. A post-*Williams v. Illinois* analysis by the United States Court of Appeals for the Tenth Circuit is helpful:

> A prime example of where an out-of-court statement might be admitted for a purpose other than to establish its substantive truth, and one pertinent to this case, is when an expert witness testifies regarding the out-of-court development of facts or data on which the expert's opinions were based. Federal Rule of Evidence 703 authorizes an expert to testify to an opinion even if that opinion is based on otherwise inadmissible facts or data, which at times may include out-of-court testimonial statements. *See Williams*, 567 U.S. at 50. Although an expert often will not disclose this otherwise inadmissible information to a jury, Rule 703 permits disclosure to the jury if "the court determines that [its] probative value in assisting the jury to evaluate the expert's opinion substantially outweighs [its] prejudicial effect." However, the disclosure of this otherwise inadmissible information is to assist the jury in evaluating the expert's opinion, not to prove the substantive truth of the otherwise inadmissible information. *See Williams*, 567 U.S. at 50.

United States v. Pablo, 696 F.3d 1280, 1287–88 (10th Cir. 2012) (bracketing and parentheticals by *Pablo*).

Rule 703 of the Federal Rules of Evidence provides:

> An expert may base an opinion on facts or data in the case that the expert has been made aware of or personally observed. If experts in the particular field would reasonably rely on those kinds of facts or data in forming an opinion on the subject, they need not be admissible for the opinion to be admitted. But if the facts or data would otherwise be inadmissible, the proponent of the opinion may disclose them to the jury only if their probative value in helping the jury evaluate the opinion substantially outweighs their prejudicial effect.

WIS. STAT. § 907.03 ... is substantially similar:

> The facts or data in the particular case upon which an expert bases an opinion or inference may be those perceived by or made known to the expert at or before the hearing. If of a type reasonably relied upon by experts in the particular field in forming opinions or inferences upon the subject, the facts or data need not be admissible in evidence in order for the opinion or inference to be admitted. Facts or data that are otherwise inadmissible may not be disclosed to the jury by the proponent of the opinion or inference unless the court determines that their probative value in assisting the jury to evaluate the expert's opinion or inference substantially outweighs their prejudicial effect.

As we see, WIS. STAT. § 907.03 has two parts: (1) a properly qualified expert witness may rely on inadmissible material if that material is "of a type reasonably relied upon by experts in the particular field in forming opinions or inferences upon the subject"; and (2) the material may be revealed to the factfinder by the opinion's proponent *only* if "the court determines that their probative value in assisting the jury to evaluate the expert's opinion or inference substantially outweighs their prejudicial effect." The first part of the Rule rests on the commonsense reality that a testifying expert could not be required to replicate all of the experiments and personally make all of the observations either underlying the development of the expert's field or otherwise relevant to the expert's opinion. Thus, Isaac Newton observed: "If I have seen a little further it is by standing on the shoulders of Giants." Certainly, a courtroom would be overflowing if *every* giant who developed the field had to testify, and, also, few expert witnesses would be able to testify at all if they had to personally reproduce the experiments and analyses that underlay developments in their field. *See, e.g., Williams*, 644 N.W.2d at 928 ("Section 907.03 implicitly recognizes that an expert's opinion may be based in part on the results of scientific tests or studies that are not her own. It is rare indeed that an expert can give an opinion without relying to some extent upon information furnished by others."); *Walworth Cty. v. Therese B.*, 671 N.W.2d 377, 382 (Wis. App. 2003) ("It is well settled that it is 'proper for a physician to make a diagnosis based in part upon medical evidence of which he has no personal knowledge but which he gleaned from the reports of others.'") (quoted source omitted). Thus, permitting the expert to rely on inadmissible material in accordance with 907.03 does not violate a defendant's right to confrontation. *Williams*,

644 N.W.2d at 931. *See also Williams v. Illinois*, 567 U.S. at ___ (in connection with Rule 703 of the Federal Rules of Evidence) (the lead opinion on behalf of three other justices in support of the judgment).

The second part of the rule is designed to prevent the expert from being a mere conduit for inadmissible material. *See Williams*, 644 N.W.2d at 926 ("[O]ne expert cannot act as a mere conduit for the opinion of another."); *Walworth Cty.*, 671 N.W.2d at 382 ("[A]lthough Wis. Stat. §907.03 allows an expert to base an opinion on hearsay, it does not transform the hearsay into admissible evidence.").

Rule 703 of the Federal Rules of Evidence has, as we see, the same cautionary instruction, and we have also seen that the lead opinion on behalf of three other justices in support of the judgment in *Williams v. Illinois* approved disclosing the data on which the expert relied in order to "to show that the expert's reasoning was not illogical, and that the weight of the expert's opinion does not depend on factual premises unsupported by other evidence in the record." *Williams*, 567 U.S. at ___. At least under §907.03, the trial court must first determine that the "probative value in assisting the jury to evaluate the expert's opinion or inference substantially outweighs their prejudicial effect" before the opinion's proponent may disclose the inadmissible material to the jury. As we have seen, the trial court received the toxicology reports into evidence. Assuming without deciding that receipt of the toxicology report into evidence was error under both *Bullcoming* and *Melendez-Diaz*, and that the trial court received the report into evidence in order to explain a foundation for Dr. Tranchida's testimony, it did not make the required finding under §907.03, we agree with the State that the errors, if they were errors, were harmless beyond a reasonable doubt because under §907.03, Dr. Tranchida's testimony that he regularly relied on toxicology results in forming his final opinion as to cause of death laid the proper foundation for him to have relied on the toxicology report irrespective of whether that report was admissible into evidence or disclosed to the jury. *See Deadwiller*, 834 N.W.2d at 377 ("For an error to be harmless, the party who benefitted from error must show that 'it is clear beyond a reasonable doubt that a rational jury would have found the defendant guilty absent the error.'") (one set of internal question marks and quoted source omitted)....

As seen from our extensive review of Dr. Tranchida's testimony, he was no mere conduit for the toxicology report; rather, he fully explained why *he,* based on his education and experience, honed in on heroin as the cause of the victim's death: the fresh elbow punctures, the "white frothy foam" that extended "down deep into [the victim's] airways, his trachea and his bronchi," that the victim's lungs were "full of fluid," and the victim's inordinate retention of urine. It was perfectly reasonable and consistent with both Wis. Stat. Rule 907.03 and Heine's right to confront his accusers, for Dr. Tranchida to take into account the toxicology report in firming up his opinion as to why the victim died. Heine was fully able to confront Dr. Tranchida and challenge his opinion and his supporting reasons. Heine was not deprived of his right to confrontation, and the trial court's receipt of the toxicology report into evidence was harmless beyond a reasonable doubt because, as we have already noted, Dr. Tranchida could have given his opinion exactly as he gave it without referring to the report. Thus, we affirm.

Notes and Questions

1. The discussion of the admissibility of the expert opinions in *Bernhardt* brings up a central underlying consideration in expert witness issues: the burden of proof. The expert opinions claiming that Bendectin causes birth defects were based on animal studies, but the proponent of the evidence never attempted to prove that researchers in the field would reasonably rely on those studies in determining birth defect causation in humans. If they had attempted to do so, what sources might they rely on to establish reasonable reliance?

2. Compare the factual basis in *Heine* to *Bernhardt*. Independent of the Confrontation Clause issue, why is the factual basis relied upon by the expert to testify in *Heine* proper? Does it matter if the toxicology report itself was admitted into evidence at trial?

3. Assume for a moment that the toxicology report was not admitted into evidence in *Heine*, but that Dr. Tranchida relied on it for his opinions. What standard applies to admission of the report at this point in trial? If admitted, what is it admitted to demonstrate?

Tying It Together

"Touchdown Tom" had been a star at Central Valley University, leading the Cougars to several Tulip Bowl championships in the 1980s. By the early 2000s, however, his right knee was arthritic and painful. Even though he had a lot of hesitation, he agreed to the knee replacement surgery recommended by his orthopedic surgeon, Dr. Dominguez. It didn't go as planned. Even when he woke up from the surgery, Tom could sense something wrong, and as the days stretched to weeks, his knee mobility never improved, while the pain was unmanageable. Tom decided to consult with a lawyer, and eventually, Tom sued Dr. Dominguez for malpractice.

To prove his case, Tom hired two different board-certified orthopedic surgeons—Drs. Adams and Baker—as his experts. To formulate their opinion on the case, each expert relied on Dr. Dominguez's surgical report, Dr. Dominguez's deposition testimony from the lawsuit, and post-operative photographs of Tom's knee. In addition to those reports, Dr. Baker also reviewed some reports written by Dr. Chen, who Tom saw after the surgery for follow-up treatment. Dr. Chen dies from a serious car accident, and so the case must proceed without his testimony.

Assignment: Please prepare a one to two-page brief explaining your argument in the context of the cases we have reviewed.

 — As defense counsel for Dr. Dominguez, why are you objecting to Tom's expert testimony, and why should it be excluded from trial?

 — As Tom's attorney, why does each expert meet the standards established in the Federal Rules of Evidence for admission, so that each may testify?

D. Is the Method Used by the Expert Based on Reliable Principles in General, Which Have Been Applied Reliably to the Specific Issue in the Case? *Frye*, *Daubert*, and Judicial Gatekeeping of Scientific Merit

"… an expert … may testify in the form of an opinion or otherwise if: … (c) the testimony is the product of reliable principles and methods; and (d) the expert has reliably applied the principles and methods to the facts of the case." Fed. R. Evid. 702.

In a criminal case, an expert for the defense has decades of experience in astrology, trained under a well-regarded master of the field, and is certified by the International Society for Astrological Research.[11] If permitted to testify, he will state that defendant did not commit the violent crime charged since his astrological sign would indicate he is a peaceful man.

In a products liability action, plaintiff intends to call the Fire Chief—who has twenty-five years of experience in investigating fires—to testify to the origin of the fire at plaintiff's house.[12] The Chief will testify that the fire started from a malfunctioning electric blanket, based on visual inspection of the blanket and the house. Conditions in the house also might suggest a separate possible electric source for the fire, and plaintiff testified to an unsuccessful attempt to light a candle at the house on the night in question.

Our final Rule 702 consideration for expert testimony involves a two-step judicial assessment of the methodology used by the expert in forming his or her opinions. The rule explicitly requires, per section (c), an evaluation of whether the scientific or specialized doctrine, *in general*, is proper in this case. In addition, section (d) requires an evaluation of whether that field has been ***properly applied*** to the specifics of the case. In our examples, we may decide to exclude our astrologer from testifying about criminal guilt because, while the expert is both qualified and would assist the jury in deciding a fact in question (guilt), there is not a proven connection between astrological signs and individual behavior on a particular day. This is a failure of the reliability of the field, **in general**, to address criminal guilt. In comparison, our Fire Chief may be well qualified, helpful to the jury, and fire origin investigation may be a reliable field, yet we can still exclude the testimony, since the generally reliable field has not been properly applied to the issues **in the case**. His failure to address alternative causes would violate the "application of the field" concerns of subsection (d).

---

11. INT'L SOC'Y FOR ASTROLOGICAL RESEARCH, www.isarastrology.com.

12. This is based on Pekarek v. Sunbeam Prods., Inc., 672 F. Supp. 2d 1161 (D. Kan. 2008).

While these examples may seem (and be) simplistic, they recognize a fundamental truth about the jury system: that it mistrusts juries to be able to handle experts on their own. In a world where all jurors could see "junk science" for what it is, we would not need the Rule 702(c) & (d) limitations since they would discredit the expert opinion *sua sponte*. Yet our rules assume jurors facing an unreliable expert may be — for whatever reason — unable to disregard the expert's opinion. Thus, we require judicial screening or "gatekeeping," so jurors consider only reliable-enough science.

Based on that fundamental truth, we entrust our judges to screen expert testimony for reliability — both "in general" and "as applied" — prior to admission of expert opinions into evidence. This may seem simple enough, but the reality is that judicial gatekeeping requires a great deal of detailed evaluation of complex science by judges, so that they can ascertain the merit of the science being proffered. Whether they are trained in science or not, judges will break down the reasoning, basis, and methodology of the scientific expert presented by a party, and must decide ultimately: Is this "good science" or not? Recognizing this as a difficult challenge, the Supreme Court in *Daubert* nonetheless stated "We are confident that federal judges possess the capacity to undertake this review." *Daubert v. Merrell Dow Pharms., Inc.*, 509 U.S. 579, 593 (1993). Yet while noting his confidence in judges, Chief Justice Rehnquist questioned whether the majority opinion would require them to become "amateur scientists" to perform the gatekeeping role.[13]

Twenty-five years after *Daubert*, the gatekeeping role continues to place judges in a difficult position, one which many of them are not scientifically prepared to perform. It also creates long and often complex case law, which we will examine to learn how judges approach gatekeeping issues. After we cover those legal standards in detail, we will then consider some of the practical implications of reliability screening. As we evaluate the following cases, remember that judicial reliability screening, at its core, is about one fundamental consideration: Is this "good science" that the jury should consider?

i. The Original *Frye* Standard

Reliability screening in its modern form began to take shape in the later years of the 20th Century, although prior to the 1980s and 1990s debate over "junk science,"[14] some methodologies and some experts did receive judicial examination in depth. We will therefore look back almost a century, to examine *Frye v. United States* and its lessons for judges. After, we will then consider the application of the *Frye* standard in more modern contexts, and finish with its relevance today. As we do so, remember to consider the fundamental question about reliability screening: Will this result in only "good science" being presented to the jury?

---

13. Daubert v. Merrell Dow Pharms., Inc., 509 U.S. 579, 600–01 (1993) (Rehnquist, C.J., concurring in part and dissenting in part).

14. Peter Huber, Galileo's Revenge: Junk Science in the Courtroom (1991).

Frye v. United States

293 F. 1013 (D.C. Cir. 1923)

Van Orsdel, Associate Justice.

Appellant, defendant below, was convicted of the crime of murder in the second degree, and from the judgment prosecutes this appeal.

A single assignment of error is presented for our consideration. In the course of the trial counsel for defendant offered an expert witness to testify to the result of a deception test made upon defendant. The test is described as the systolic blood pressure deception test. It is asserted that blood pressure is influenced by change in the emotions of the witness, and that the systolic blood pressure rises are brought about by nervous impulses sent to the sympathetic branch of the autonomic nervous system. Scientific experiments, it is claimed, have demonstrated that fear, rage, and pain always produce a rise of systolic blood pressure, and that conscious deception or falsehood, concealment of facts, or guilt of crime, accompanied by fear of detection when the person is under examination, raises the systolic blood pressure in a curve, which corresponds exactly to the struggle going on in the subject's mind, between fear and attempted control of that fear, as the examination touches the vital points in respect of which he is attempting to deceive the examiner.

In other words, the theory seems to be that truth is spontaneous, and comes without conscious effort, while the utterance of a falsehood requires a conscious effort, which is reflected in the blood pressure. The rise thus produced is easily detected and distinguished from the rise produced by mere fear of the examination itself. . . .

Prior to the trial defendant was subjected to this deception test, and counsel offered the scientist who conducted the test as an expert to testify to the results obtained. The offer was objected to by counsel for the government, and the court sustained the objection. Counsel for defendant then offered to have the proffered witness conduct a test in the presence of the jury. This also was denied.

Counsel for defendant, in their able presentation of the novel question involved, correctly state in their brief that no cases directly in point have been found. The broad ground, however, upon which they plant their case, is succinctly stated in their brief as follows:

> The rule is that the opinions of experts or skilled witnesses are admissible in evidence in those cases in which the matter of inquiry is such that inexperienced persons are unlikely to prove capable of forming a correct judgment upon it, for the reason that the subject-matter so far partakes of a science, art, or trade as to require a previous habit or experience or study in it, in order to acquire a knowledge of it. When the question involved does not lie within the range of common experience or common knowledge, but requires special experience or special knowledge, then the opinions of witnesses skilled in that particular science, art, or trade to which the question relates are admissible in evidence.

Numerous cases are cited in support of this rule. Just when a scientific principle or discovery crosses the line between the experimental and demonstrable stages is difficult to define. Somewhere in this twilight zone the evidential force of the principle must be recognized, and while courts will go a long way in admitting expert testimony deduced from a well-recognized scientific principle or discovery, the thing from which the deduction is made must be sufficiently established to have gained general acceptance in the particular field in which it belongs.

We think the systolic blood pressure deception test has not yet gained such standing and scientific recognition among physiological and psychological authorities as would justify the courts in admitting expert testimony deduced from the discovery, development, and experiments thus far made.

The judgment is affirmed.

United States v. Lewellyn
723 F.2d 615 (8th Cir. 1983)

FAGG, Circuit Judge.

Gary Lewellyn, a Des Moines stockbroker, was indicted on nine counts of embezzlement, three counts of making a false statement, and three counts of mail fraud, for converting over $17 million in money and securities from two Iowa banks. In response to the government's pretrial motion the district court ruled that Lewellyn could not rely on a defense of insanity by reason of pathological gambling and excluded evidence related to that defense. Lewellyn then waived a jury trial and was convicted on all counts following a trial to the court based primarily on stipulated evidence. On appeal Lewellyn contends that the district court committed error in precluding his insanity defense. We affirm.

As a preliminary matter, we decline the government's invitation to modify or abandon the American Law Institute (ALI) insanity test as adopted by this court in *United States v. Frazier*, 458 F.2d 911 (8th Cir. 1972):

> (1) A defendant is insane ... if, at the time of the alleged criminal conduct, as a result of mental disease or defect he lacks substantial capacity either to appreciate the wrongfulness of his conduct or to conform his conduct to the requirements of law.
>
> (2) As used in this Article, the terms "mental disease or defect" do not include any abnormality manifested only by repeated criminal or otherwise antisocial conduct. Model Penal Code § 4.01 (Final Draft 1962).

Id. at 918 (footnote omitted). As a panel we are without authority to modify the insanity standard established in this circuit. Only the court *en banc* is empowered to change an existing rule of law. *See United States v. Howard*, 706 F.2d 267, 269 (8th Cir. 1983). Consequently, the *Frazier* test provides the framework for our decision in the present case.

Lewellyn does not contend that he suffered a mental condition which entailed a lack of substantial capacity to appreciate the wrongfulness of his conduct. Rather, he claims that he should have been allowed to present evidence that as a pathological, or compulsive, gambler he lacked substantial capacity to conform his conduct to the requirements of law. Of necessity, his position is that not only did his mental condition render him unable to abstain from gambling, but that he also lacked substantial capacity to avoid breaking the law to obtain the funds required for gambling.

The district court held a pretrial hearing that emphasized three questions: (1) whether pathological gambling is a mental disease or defect within the meaning of the ALI rule, (2) whether a pathological gambler is unable to resist impulses to gamble, and (3) whether a pathological gambler lacks substantial capacity to refrain from engaging in criminal activity such as embezzlement and similar offenses. At the hearing Lewellyn introduced as an exhibit the Diagnostic and Statistical Manual of Mental Disorders (3d ed. 1980) (DSM-III) published by the American Psychiatric Association, in which pathological gambling is classified and described as a disorder of impulse control. In addition Lewellyn adduced expert testimony which indicated that pathological gambling, although classified as a mental disorder, is the equivalent of a mental disease within the meaning of the ALI insanity rule. Lewellyn's expert witnesses further testified that some pathological gamblers are unable to refrain from gambling and that some pathological gamblers are unable to resist engaging in criminal activities to support their gambling compulsion....

The district court observed that factual issues had been raised on the three questions that had been the subjects of the pretrial hearing and noted that perhaps these factual issues should be presented to a jury by allowing Lewellyn to rely on an insanity defense at trial. The district court was concerned, however, with the relationship between the mental condition asserted, pathological gambling, and the crimes charged. Accordingly, the district court noted that to allow the insanity defense in this case would amount to "a revolutionary expansion of the defense of insanity ..." and held "that a defense of insanity, based upon a disorder of impulse control in the form of pathological gambling, is not available to a Defendant charged with embezzlement even if there is evidence which would support a finding that he lacked substantial capacity to conform his conduct to the requirement[s] of the law." The district court then granted the government's motion to exclude evidence pertaining to a defense of insanity by reason of pathological gambling.

As the district court recognized, the central question in this case is the link between pathological gambling and criminal activity such as embezzlement. We will therefore make some assumptions for the sake of discussion and put aside some issues that need not be addressed in this case. We will assume that Lewellyn is himself a pathological gambler. We will also assume for purposes of this case that some pathological gamblers are unable to resist impulses to gamble. We are able to glean from the record that the largest share of the embezzled funds was used to finance stock and commodities speculation through various brokerage house accounts under Lewellyn's control, and we will assume that his speculative endeavors constituted gambling behavior.

The district court held as a matter of law that in a prosecution for embezzlement a defendant may not rely on a theory of insanity by reason of pathological gambling, and accordingly precluded evidence to support this theory, even after the court concluded that Lewellyn had made a sufficient showing that a pathological gambler charged with embezzlement fits within the language of the ALI rule. In our view, however, this case may be resolved without reaching the question whether as a matter of law such a limitation should be placed on the availability of the insanity defense. Hence, while we agree with the result reached by the district court, we note the well-established rule that we may affirm on any ground supported by the record, even though that ground was not relied on by the district court. *See Blum v. Bacon*, 457 U.S. 132, 137 n. 5 (1982); *Brown v. St. Louis Police Dep't*, 691 F.2d 393, 396 (8th Cir. 1982), *cert. denied*, 461 U.S. 908 (1983).

We have recognized that in order to raise the issue of insanity a defendant must make a minimum showing. A defendant is presumed sane, but the introduction of evidence of insanity dispels the presumption and subjects the prosecution to the burden of proving sanity beyond a reasonable doubt. *United States v. Dresser*, 542 F.2d 737, 742 (8th Cir. 1976) (citing *Davis v. United States*, 160 U.S. 469, 486–88 (1895)). In *Dresser* we referred to this threshold showing as a "prima facie case of insanity." 542 F.2d at 742 n. 7....

In the present case we need not decide whether pathological gambling may never be grounds for an insanity defense. In the particular circumstances of this case we are concerned with the connection between pathological gambling and collateral criminal activity. To make the required minimum showing of insanity Lewellyn had to show that at least some pathological gamblers lack substantial capacity to conform their conduct to the requirements of laws prohibiting criminal activities like embezzlement. We now turn to the record to determine whether Lewellyn made a showing which would have allowed him to rely on an insanity defense at trial.

DSM-III contains the following description of pathological gambling:

> The essential features are a chronic and progressive failure to resist impulses to gamble and gambling behavior that compromises, disrupts, or damages personal, family, or vocational pursuits. The gambling preoccupation, urge, and activity increase during periods of stress. Problems that arise as a result of the gambling lead to an intensification of the gambling behavior. Characteristic problems include loss of work due to absences in order to gamble, defaulting on debts and other financial responsibilities, disrupted family relationships, borrowing money from illegal sources, forgery, fraud, embezzlement, and income tax evasion.

> Commonly these individuals have the attitude that money causes and is also the solution to all their problems. As the gambling increases, the individual is usually forced to lie in order to obtain money and to continue gambling, but hides the extent of the gambling. There is no serious attempt to budget or save money. When borrowing resources are strained, antisocial

behavior in order to obtain money for more gambling is likely. Any criminal behavior—e.g., forgery, embezzlement, or fraud—is typically nonviolent. There is a conscious intent to return or repay the money.

Id. at 291....

The language of DSM-III does not establish that pathological gamblers may lack substantial capacity to refrain from engaging in embezzlement and similar criminal activities. Portions of DSM-III no doubt indicate that criminal activity is often associated with pathological gambling. DSM-III does not state, however, that pathological gamblers who engage in criminal conduct do so because they lack substantial capacity to conform their conduct to the requirements of law, nor does it state anything of equivalent meaning. It is not remarkable, though, that the language of DSM-III does not conform to the legal principles embodied in the ALI insanity rule.

> The purpose of DSM-III is to provide clear descriptions of diagnostic categories in order to enable clinicians and investigators to diagnose, communicate about, study, and treat various mental disorders. The use of this manual for nonclinical purposes, such as determination of legal responsibility, competency or insanity ... must be critically examined in each instance within the appropriate institutional context.

Id. at 12. When we examine DSM-III carefully within the context of the criminal law we conclude that its language does not establish a relationship between pathological gambling and criminal activity sufficient to constitute insanity under the ALI standard. As a consequence, DSM-III does not alone supply the minimum showing Lewellyn was required to make before he could rely on an insanity defense.

Expert testimony adduced by Lewellyn, couched in terms more like those of the ALI insanity rule, does suggest the requisite connection between pathological gambling and criminal activity because it supports the proposition that some pathological gamblers lack substantial capacity to resist engaging in embezzlement and similar offenses. Dr. Julian Taber, a psychologist, testified that in some instances pathological gamblers are incapable of conforming their conduct to the requirements of law, and are unable to avoid behavior such as forgery, fraud, and embezzlement. Dr. Robert Custer, a psychiatrist, testified that in the late stage of pathological gambling individuals are unable to resist activities like embezzlement or fraud because they have to gamble and they have to obtain money in order to gamble.

Lewellyn is dependent on this scientific expert testimony to sustain his burden of making the required minimum showing that would permit him to rely on an insanity defense at trial. The expert testimony is essential because it supports a proposition not established in DSM-III: that some pathological gamblers lack substantial capacity to refrain from committing embezzlement and similar offenses. We note, however, that established principles control admissibility of scientific evidence. "[W]hile courts will go a long way in admitting expert testimony deduced from a well-recognized scientific principle or discovery, the thing from which the deduction is made must be sufficiently established to have gained general acceptance in the particular field in which it belongs." *Frye v. United States,* 293 F. 1013, 1014 (D.C. Cir. 1923). In deciding whether a scientific principle meets the *Frye* standard we have recognized reliability as "one of the most important factors" that should be considered. *United States v. Alexander,* 526 F.2d 161, 163 (8th Cir. 1975). Because our analysis of the *Frye* rule would govern the admission at trial of expert testimony similar to that given at the pretrial hearing, this analysis is equally applicable in determining whether expert testimony adduced by Lewellyn is sufficient to constitute the required minimum showing of insanity.

Pathological gambling has received relatively little scientific attention. Dr. Custer testified that pathological gambling has only recently been recognized as a disease. Both Dr. Taber and Dr. Custer cited the inclusion of pathological gambling in DSM-III, published in 1980, as evidence that the condition is generally accepted as a mental disease by mental health professionals. Pathological gambling was not listed, however, in DSM-II, published in 1968.

From the testimony at the pretrial hearing it is apparent that few psychologists or psychiatrists have had much experience dealing with pathological gamblers. Dr. Taber estimated that there may be perhaps 20 psychologists with some in-depth experience working with pathological gamblers, but he said that to his knowledge he was the only psychologist devoted full-time to their treatment. Dr. Taber knew of no psychiatrist who would work full-time with pathological gamblers. Dr. Custer stated that probably not more than 20 or 25 doctors have had experience with pathological gambling.

There is accordingly little knowledge about pathological gambling within the community of mental health professionals. Dr. Taber testified that in talking with physicians, social workers, and psychologists, he had "found very prevalent ignorance or just lack of concern with the problem." Dr. Custer indicated that it is necessary to spend a significant amount of time working with pathological gamblers in order to understand the problem "because it is so new and there is so very little that has been known about it." Dr. Custer said he does not think many doctors know about pathological gambling, and that as a result they do not recognize it as a disease.

In order to make the necessary minimum showing of insanity Lewellyn was required to demonstrate that there is general acceptance in the fields of psychiatry and psychology of the principle that some pathological gamblers lack substantial capacity to conform their conduct to the requirements of laws prohibiting embezzlement and similar offenses. There is no evidence in the record, however, either in DSM-III or the expert testimony, that this principle is generally accepted in the mental health professions. Indeed, the record shows that the pathological gambling disorder itself has only recently been recognized in DSM-III, and that there is scant experience and limited knowledge concerning this problem. In our view, Lewellyn has failed to show that the opinions espoused by his expert witnesses possess the requisite indicia of scientific reliability.

Because we find that Lewellyn did not make the required minimum showing of insanity, we affirm the district court's exclusion of evidence pertaining to a defense of insanity by reason of pathological gambling.

Notes and Questions

1. Prior to the *Frye* case in 1923, reliability screening—if done at all—was performed using a combination of relevance determinations (does it help the jury?) and the "commercial marketplace test" (if the expert succeeds in the profession, they must be qualified to do so as an expert). DAVID H. KAYE ET AL., THE NEW WIGMORE: A TREATISE ON EVIDENCE § 1.2.1, at 6–7 (2004); David L. Faigman, Elise Porter & Michael J. Saks, *Check Your Crystal Ball at the Courthouse Door, Please: Exploring the Past, Understanding the Present, and Worrying About the Future of Scientific Evidence*, 15 CARDOZO L. REV. 1799, 1804 (1994). Are these tests going to be effective in deciding what is "good science" and what is not?

2. While it may be tempting to consider the timeline of reliability analysis to proceed from commercial marketplace ideas to general acceptance to *Daubert* screening, researchers have consistently demonstrated that judges applied the *Frye* general acceptance test only to criminal cases until the 1980s. *See, e.g.*, Michael J. Saks, *Judging Admissibility*, 35 J. CORP. L. 135, 139 (2009); Michael D. Green, *The Road Less Well Traveled (and Seen): Contemporary Lawmaking in Products Liability*, 49 DEPAUL L. REV. 377, 399 n. 114 (1999) (reviewing in detail the limited application of *Frye* to civil cases before 1990); Paul C. Giannelli, Daubert: *Interpreting the Federal Rules of Evidence*, 15 CARDOZO L. REV. 1999, 2008 (1994). In the absence of true gatekeeping, judges instead would focus on the qualifications of the expert instead of the reliability of the technique. Michael D. Green & Joseph Sanders, *Admissibility Versus Sufficiency: Controlling the Quality of Expert Witness Testimony*, 50 WAKE FOREST L. REV. 1057, 1058 (2015). Only in the late 1980s did courts begin to apply gatekeeping standards in complex civil litigation, namely toxic torts. David E. Bernstein, Frye, Frye, *Again: The Past, Present, and Future of the General Acceptance Test*, 41 JURIMETRICS J. 385, 390–92 (2001). As we will see, this shift marks the beginning of the "junk science" debate of the pre-*Daubert* era.

3. Under the general acceptance test, who has the ultimate authority to decide when a methodology is "good science"? Considering the structure of the standard, what would happen in the case of a scientist who rejects convention with a new theory (i.e., Galileo, Copernicus, Einstein, etc.)? We must contemplate this balance of power within the general acceptance test as we consider the following cases questioning that approach:

United States v. Downing
753 F.2d 1224 (3d Cir. 1985)

BECKER, Circuit Judge.

… The most important justification for the *Frye* test is that it provides a *method* by which courts can assess the reliability of novel scientific expert testimony. *See United States v. Addison*, 498 F.2d 741, 743–44 (D.C. Cir. 1974). The general acceptance standard in effect permits the experts who know most about a procedure to form a "technical jury," whose positive assessment of the scientific status of a procedure becomes a necessary prerequisite to the admissibility of expert testimony based on the procedure. *See People v. Barbara*, 255 N.W.2d 171, 194 (Mich. 1977). Adherents of the general acceptance standard also argue that it guarantees the existence of a coterie of experts qualified to testify about the status of a particular scientific technique and, in theory at least, promotes uniformity of decision. *United States v. Addison*, 498 F.2d at 744; *Reed v. State*, 391 A.2d 364, 371–72 (Md. 1978).

The general acceptance standard also safeguards against the possible prejudicial effects of testimony based upon "an unproved hypothesis in an isolated experiment." *United States v. Brown*, 557 F.2d 541, 556 (6th Cir. 1977). The concern over potentially specious expert testimony assumes particular importance in the criminal context, where the general acceptance standard has had its most substantial impact. When the government seeks to introduce novel scientific evidence, for example, a possible tension between the defendant's right to a fair trial, on the one hand, and the trend toward admissibility of expert testimony embodied in the Federal Rules of Evidence, is apparent in many of the cases discussing *also* [sic] Paul C. Giannelli, *The Admissibility of Novel Scientific Evidence:* Frye v. United States, *A Half Century Later*, 80 COLUM. L. REV. 1197, 1246 (1980) (introduction of unreliable evidence increases the likelihood of an erroneous verdict). *Cf. id.* at 1248 (suggesting that, in the criminal context, the defendant be allowed to introduce novel scientific evidence on the basis of a less stringent foundational showing than that required of the prosecution). This concern is also reflected by those courts that highlight the potentially prejudicial effect on the jury arising from the "aura of special reliability and trustworthiness" of scientific expert testimony. *United States v. Amaral*, 488 F.2d 1148, 1152 (9th Cir. 1973). *See also Addison*, 498 F.2d at 744 (scientific evidence may "assume a posture of mythic infallibility in the eyes of a jury of laymen.").

Notwithstanding the valid evidentiary concerns subsumed in the general acceptance standard, critics of the standard have cited two general problems with it: its vagueness and its conservatism. *See, e.g.,* 1 [D. LOUISELL & C. MUELLER, FEDERAL EVIDENCE,] § 105, at 821 [(1977)]. Professor Giannelli's excellent and comprehensive article catalogues the numerous difficulties that have arisen in applying the test. Giannelli, *supra*, at 1208–28. First, the vague terms included in the standard have allowed courts to manipulate the parameters of the relevant "scientific community" and the level of agreement needed for "general acceptance." Thus, some courts, when they wish to admit evidence, are able to limit the impact of *Frye* by narrowing the relevant scientific community to those experts who customarily employ the technique at issue. *See, e.g., People v. Williams*, 331 P.2d 251 (Cal. Ct. App. 1958) (in admitting results of the Nalline test for narcotics use, the court held that the *Frye* test was satisfied upon showing of general acceptance by those who are expected to be familiar with the use of the technique, although the prosecution's own expert had conceded the lack of acceptance within the medical profession generally). Judicial interpretation of the "general acceptance" component of the test has yielded even more disparate results. One court has described "general acceptance" as "widespread; prevalent; extensive though not universal," *United States v. Zeiger*, 350 F. Supp. 685, 688 (D.D.C.), *rev'd*,

475 F.2d 1280 (D.C. Cir. 1972), while another has suggested that the test requires agreement by a "substantial section of the scientific community." *United States v. Williams*, 443 F. Supp. 269, 273 (S.D.N.Y. 1977), *aff'd*, 583 F.2d 1194 (2d Cir. 1978), *cert. denied*, 493 U.S. 1117 (1979).

Professor Giannelli and others have discussed other problems that arise in applying the *Frye* test: the selectivity among courts in determining whether evidence derives from "novel" principles; the inadequacy of expert testimony on many scientific issues; an uncritical acceptance of prior *judicial*, rather than scientific, opinion as a basis for finding "general acceptance"; and the narrow scope of review by which some appellate courts review trial court rulings. *See* Giannelli, *supra*, at 1208–21. All of these problems contribute to the "essential vagueness" of the *Frye* test. 1 LOUISELL & MUELLER, *supra*, at 821.

Apart from these various difficulties in implementation, moreover, *Frye*'s general acceptance standard has been found to be unsatisfactory in other respects. Under *Frye*, some have argued, courts may be required to exclude much probative and reliable information from the jury's consideration, thereby unnecessarily impeding the truth-seeking function of litigation. *See, e.g.*, *United States v. Sample*, 378 F. Supp. 44, 53 (E.D. Pa. 1974) (*Frye* "precludes too much relevant evidence"); *see also* 1 LOUISELL & MUELLER, *supra*, at 822; Frederick D. Lacey, *Scientific Evidence*, 24 JURIMETRICS J. 254, 265 (1984) (*Frye* jurisdictions will always lag behind advances in science). *But see United States v. Addison*, 498 F.2d 741, 743 (D.C. Cir. 1974) (consequence that *Frye* standard retards the admissibility of scientific evidence is not an "unwarranted cost").

United States v. Smith

869 F.2d 348 (7th Cir. 1989)

KANNE, Circuit Judge.

Defendant Tamara Jo Smith was charged in the Northern District of Illinois with conspiracy to commit bank and wire fraud, and substantive counts of bank, credit card and wire fraud. She was convicted of 31 of the 37 counts with which she was charged. Smith challenges the use of a spectrographic voice identification expert at trial.... We affirm.

I. Facts

Tanya and Tamara Smith are identical twins who are commonly mistaken for one another. Some of their friends, however, could distinguish them by a small scar on Tanya's forehead.

In their scheme, the two women posed as bank employees and telephoned banks authorizing them to make fictitious wire transfers of nonexistent funds. They then arranged for various individuals to pick up the money at transferee banks or at Western Union. These persons would keep a small portion for themselves and turn the bulk over to the twins.

The two women were indicted and tried together. Because identity[1] was a core dispute at trial, the government called a spectrographic voice identification expert to testify. The original voice identification expert, who prepared the spectrograms at issue here, was unable to testify at the last minute. The expert who testified was a substitute who was called in for the trial. Tamara challenges this expert testimony. She protests the use of spectrographic voice identification testimony in general, alleging that it is not generally accepted by the scientific community.…

II. Voice Identification Expert Testimony

Dr. Hirotaka Nakasone testified as an expert witness and voice examiner. He compared the recorded voices of Tanya and Tamara Smith to the recorded voice of the person who called the Harris Bank on November 23, 1984 and falsely identified herself as a bank employee attempting to arrange a wire transfer. He concluded that it was highly probable that this was Tanya Smith and highly probable that it was not Tamara Smith. He found that it was probable that Tanya, not Tamara, telephoned Northern Trust Bank on May 21 and 22, 1985. Dr. Nakasone found that it was probably Tamara, and probably not Tanya, who called the American National Bank regarding a separate wire, and probably Tanya, and probably not Tamara, who made another call to a New Jersey bank.

Smith challenges the district court's admission of this evidence against her on two grounds [including] the lack of general acceptance of spectrograms by the scientific community.… The government disputes these contentions.

In discussing the admissibility of this evidence in general, both parties cite *Frye v. United States*, 293 F. 1013 (D.C. Cir. 1923) in which the court stated that:

> Just when a scientific principle or discovery crosses a line between experimental and demonstrable stages is difficult to define. Somewhere in this twilight zone the evidential forces of a principle must be recognized, and while courts will go a long way in admitting expert testimony deduced from a well-recognized scientific principle or discovery, the thing from which the deduction must be made must be sufficiently established to have gained general acceptance in a particular field in which it belongs.

Id. at 1014.

Although the validity of the judge-made rule in *Frye* has been criticized by some courts and commentators for numerous reasons, this circuit has continued to affirm (and to apply) the *Frye* standard. *United States v. Carmel*, 801 F.2d 997, 999 (7th Cir. 1986); *United States v. Tranowski*, 659 F.2d 750, 755–56 (7th Cir. 1981). Under the *Frye* test, several other circuits have held expert testimony concerning spectrographic voice identification admissible. *See, e.g., United States v. Williams*, 583 F.2d 1194, 1198–1201 (2d Cir. 1978), *cert. denied*, 439 U.S. 1117 (1979); *United States v. Baller*, 519 F.2d 463, 465–67 (4th Cir.), *cert. denied*, 423 U.S. 1019 (1975); *United States v. Franks*, 511 F.2d 25, 32–34 (6th Cir.), *cert. denied*, 422 U.S. 1042 (1975). We join these circuits today,

---

1. Several witnesses made mistaken identifications as between the twins.

and hold that expert testimony concerning spectrographic voice analysis is admissible in cases where the proponent of this testimony has established a proper foundation.

A. *General Considerations*

With respect to admission of expert testimony in general, Federal Rule of Evidence 702 provides:

> If scientific, technical, or other specialized knowledge will assist the trier of fact to understand the evidence or to determine a fact in issue, a witness qualified as an expert by knowledge, skill, experience, training, or education, may testify thereto in the form of an opinion or otherwise.

Under this rule, trial courts have broad discretion to admit or exclude evidence, and their rulings will not be reversed absent an abuse of that discretion. *See, e.g., Simplex, Inc. v. Diversified Energy Sys., Inc.*, 847 F.2d 1290, 1292 (7th Cir. 1988) (decision of trial court is to be affirmed unless "manifestly erroneous"); *United States v. Lundy*, 809 F.2d 392, 394–95 (7th Cir. 1987) (same).... In *Lundy*, this court summed up many of the predicates for admission of expert testimony when it said:

> Because experts are given special latitude to testify based on hearsay and third-hand observations and to give opinions, *see* Fed. R. Evid. 702, courts have cautioned that an expert must be qualified as an expert, provide testimony that will assist the jury and rely only on evidence on which a reasonable expert in the field would rely.... Courts agree that it is improper to permit an expert to testify regarding facts that people of common understanding can easily comprehend.

809 F.2d at 395 (citations omitted).

In discussing whether expert testimony concerning spectrographic voice identification in particular is admissible under *Frye*, other circuits seem to have focused upon whether the technique is (a) reliable and (b) likely to mislead the jury. *Williams*, 583 F.2d at 1198–1200.

Regarding the reliability of such evidence, we make the observation made by other circuits that:

> [N]either newness nor lack of absolute certainty in a test suffices to render it inadmissible in court. Every useful new development must have its first day in court. And court records are full of the conflicting opinions of doctors, engineers and accountants....

United States v. Stifel, 433 F.2d 431, 437 (6th Cir. 1970), *cert. denied*, 401 U.S. 994 (1971); *Franks*, 511 F.2d at 33. Unanimity of opinion is not necessary among the scientific community to deem evidence reliable. *Baller*, 519 F.2d at 466; *Williams*, 583 F.2d at 1198 ("A determination of reliability cannot rest solely on a process of 'counting (scientific) noses.'"). The technique, moreover, need not be infallible to be reliable. *Williams*, 583 F.2d at 1198.

In *Williams*, the court noted several indicia of reliability of a given scientific technique. They include the potential rate of error, the existence and maintenance of standards, the care and concern with which a scientific technique has been employed (and whether it appears to lend itself to abuse), and its analogous relationship with other types of scientific techniques. A final factor is the presence of "fail-safe" characteristics: characteristics the variability of which will lead to different, rather than similar, results. 583 F.2d at 1198–99. The court in *Williams* opined that these indicia were present with regard to spectrograms.

The tendency of testimony on scientific techniques to mislead the jury relates to the fact that, because of the apparent objectivity of opinions with a scientific basis, the jury may cloak such evidence in an "aura of mystic infallibility." *Williams*, 583 F.2d at 1199; *Baller*, 519 F.2d at 466.... The tendency of such evidence to mislead the jury is reduced, however, by factors such as the comprehensibility of the technique, the ability of the jury to make the same comparisons as the expert, and the instruction of the jury by the trial judge as to their responsibility to discredit such evidence if they find it unconvincing. The weight of such testimony can be attacked, moreover, by cross-examination and refutation. *Williams*, 583 F.2d at 1199–1200; *Baller*, 519 F.2d at 466–67; *Franks*, 511 F.2d at 32–34.

B. *Admissibility in This Case*

Smith's principal argument is that spectrographic voice identification has not received sufficient general in the scientific community to be admissible under *Frye*. She contends that in cases where courts have admitted voice identification testimony, these courts have too narrowly defined the relevant scientific community to include only those scientists who use the technique, and not those who oppose its use. The relevant scientific community includes not only those who utilize spectrographic voice identification techniques, but linguists, psychologists and engineers as well.

Smith also cites a 1979 report of the National Research Council, *On the Theory and Practice of Voice Identification*, saying that there is a wide disparity in this field between the development of the theories behind voice identification and its practice, the latter being more developed than the former. She also criticizes the fact that Nakasone, who never before had been qualified as a voice identification expert in a court of law, was allowed to testify. Smith also seizes on the fact that Nakasone admitted in his testimony that the field itself was controversial and that some studies had found high error rates. She acknowledges *Williams* and *Stifel*, discussed above, which advocate a flexible approach to applying the *Frye* test, but urges that "it is equally true that a scientific procedure must be accepted and proved reliable before it is brought into a courtroom lest the integrity of the judicial process succumb to charlatans and quacks."

As the government points out in its brief, Smith misconceives the manner in which the *Frye* test is to be applied. Under her view, it would seem, if there is any disagreement at all as to the reliability or validity of a scientific technique, the disputed evidence should not come in. This court has not applied the *Frye* test in such a manner. Polygraph (lie detector) test results long have been admissible in this circuit under the sound discretion of the trial judge, provided that this discretion is not abused. *See, e.g., United States v. Williams,* 737 F.2d 594, 610–11 (7th Cir. 1984), *cert. denied,* 470 U.S. 1003 (1985).... Polygraph tests are still of disputed reliability.

Turning finally to the instant case, we hold that the district judge did not abuse his discretion in admitting the testimony. Sufficient evidence of the reliability of this technique was adduced at trial. Moreover, this technique is not, under the proper circumstances, likely to mislead the jury. We hold that such circumstances existed here.

The government presented ample evidence of the reliability of spectrographic voice identification at trial. In addition to describing the principles behind and the technique used to make spectrograms,[9] Dr. Nakasone testified as to their reliability. He himself had performed spectrographic analysis and produced his own opinion thereon in 150 instances, even though he never before had testified as a voice identification expert in a court of law. In none of these cases had he been informed that he had made a misidentification.

Nakasone also testified as to studies performed in the field. He first discussed a study performed by Professor Oscar Tosi of Michigan State University in conjunction with the Michigan State Police from 1968 to 1970. Of the 35,000 comparisons made in this study, the error rate for false identifications was 2.4% and the error rate for false eliminations was about 6%. This study previously has been cited as authoritative by other federal courts of appeal. *See, e.g., Williams,* 583 F.2d at 1198; *Baller,* 519 F.2d at 465. A follow-up to that study conducted by Dr. Tosi involving only actual cases examined by trained voice examiners found no errors whatsoever.

Nakasone also discussed a more recent report published by the FBI in June, 1987 in the Journal of the Acoustical Society of America. The cases in that report which were submitted to actual determinations yielded a .31% rate of false identifications and a .53% rate of false eliminations. Finally, Nakasone testified that variations, such as use of tapes not recorded under laboratory conditions and attempts by the speaker to disguise her voice, will increase the error rate of false eliminations. That is, instead of resulting in more false identifications, these variations will result in more false eliminations.

On cross-examination as to his qualifications, Dr. Nakasone readily admitted that no one's voice is one-hundred percent unique, and that the field of voice identification is not one-hundred percent reliable. He also indicated his awareness of other studies, the Campbell study and the Hazzen study. These studies had higher error rates than those cited by him, purportedly of 62.7 percent and 83.33 percent respectively. Nakasone also mentioned that no studies involving black females, which both of the defendants are, had been performed.

During subsequent cross-examination, Nakasone answered questions regarding the study performed by the National Research Council cited to by Smith in her brief.

---

9. A spectrogram is, according to Dr. Nakasone, a graphic display of sound in three dimensions: frequency in hertz, time in seconds and different levels of energy. Spectrograms display the fundamental frequency (pitch) of a voice and its resonating characteristics, as well as rate of speech. Different formations of words result in different patterns on the spectrogram. Spectrograms are made by transferring a recorded voice to a machine, called a sound spectrograph, that transforms the sounds on tape into electrical coordinates....

He also testified extensively as to intraspeaker and interspeaker variation. Nakasone agreed that no one says the same word exactly the same way twice and that it is currently only an assumption that interspeaker variation is sufficiently greater than intraspeaker variation for spectrographic analysis to be able to distinguish one person's voice from that of another.

We conclude that the district judge did not abuse his discretion in admitting Nakasone's testimony into evidence. This testimony contained many of the indicia of reliability discussed by the Second Circuit in *Williams, supra.* A thorough examination of the record reveals both that this technique is not one-hundred percent infallible and that the entire scientific community does not support it. As we discuss above, however, neither infallibility nor unanimity is a precondition for general acceptance of scientific evidence under *Frye.* We also note, as the government points out in its brief, that spectrographic identification is similar to lay identification of voices, which is admissible in this circuit. *See, e.g., United States v. Gironda,* 758 F.2d 1201, 1218 (7th Cir.), *cert. denied,* 474 U.S. 1004 (1985).

Since sufficient indicia of reliability were present in this case, it was proper for the district judge to let this evidence go to the jury, in order for it to make the ultimate determination as to the credibility of Nakasone's testimony. *Williams,* 583 F.2d at 1200.

This testimony, moreover, was not likely to mislead the jury. The jury had the opportunity in this case to hear both the voice exemplars and the recorded conversations, and to see the spectrograms. Although the district judge did not give a specific instruction on Nakasone's testimony, he properly instructed the jury as to their sole prerogative to judge credibility of the witnesses and the weight of their testimony, and as to their right to reject expert testimony. Dr. Nakasone, moreover, was very candid at trial about the limitations of spectrography. He also was subject to rigorous cross-examination.... We thus conclude that this testimony was admissible....

IV. Conclusion

The admission in this case by the judge of the testimony of a spectrographic voice identification expert was not an abuse of his discretion....

Notes and Questions

1. We can see that even prior to *Daubert,* cases like *Downing* recognized significant criticism of the *Frye* standard and confusion on how to apply it. In a recent article on forensic voice comparison techniques like those used in *Smith,* Geoffrey Morrison and William Thompson raise these concerns about *Frye*:

    > The outcome of a judicial inquiry into "general acceptance" often depends on the judge's determinations of what must be accepted and by whom.

    > What exactly is "the thing from which the deduction is made" in the context of forensic voice comparison? Is it the approach, the framework, the system as applied in a particular case, or, as we would argue, all of these? The assessment of "general acceptance" may well depend on the answer to this question.

In the context of forensic voice comparison, who must generally accept this thing? That is, what class of experts constitutes the "relevant scientific community" whose views are to be examined to determine "general acceptance"? Is it practitioners of a particular approach, researchers who publish specifically on forensic voice comparison, researchers in the broader scientific community? The assessment of "general acceptance" will also depend on the answer to this question.

If the goal of the inquiry is to ensure the trustworthiness of forensic voice comparison evidence, then we suggest courts look to a relatively broad scientific community. Spectrographic analysis is undoubtedly accepted among the community of spectrographic analysts (just as astrology is generally accepted among astrologers and phrenology among phrenologists), but history suggests that acceptance of a particular approach among enthusiastic promoters or users of the approach, who often have a financial stake it its success, provides little assurance that it is trustworthy....

Ultimately, however, we think that general acceptance is a very poor indicator of scientific validity, especially during a period in which a paradigm shift is underway, as is now the case in forensic science in general and forensic voice comparison in particular. One should not prefer an earth centered model of the universe, or prefer an approach to forensic voice comparison based on subjective judgment, because it is the preference of the majority of scientists and/or practitioners, one should prefer the model or approach which shows the greatest promise or which is ultimately demonstrated to make the most valid and reliable predictions....

Geoffrey S. Morrison & William C. Thompson, *Assessing the Admissibility of a New Generation of Forensic Voice Comparison Testimony*, 18 COLUM. SCI. & TECH. L. REV. 326, 388–90 (2017). Of course, these exact questions can apply to any discipline, and raise many of the weaknesses in the *Frye* approach to reliability screening. *See generally* Paul C. Giannelli, *The Admissibility of Novel Scientific Evidence:* Frye v. United States, *A Half-Century Later*, 80 COLUM. L. REV. 1197, 1208–23 (1980).

2. Removing the issue of general acceptance away from science altogether, let us instead consider this hypothetical: What is "generally accepted" in a house? Look at the list of items below, and decide which are and are not generally accepted in a home.

Hot Water Heater	Gold Trim	High-speed internet
Land-line Telephone	Wine Fridge	Movie Theatre
Sauna	Refrigerator	Granite countertops
Dishwasher	Three-car garage	Personal Computer

What does this tell us about the general acceptance standard that we did not know before?

3. In our next section, D(ii), we will consider *Daubert*, subsequent case law after 1993, and, afterward, how judges perform their gatekeeping role. But before we leave

Frye, we must recognize that even if *Daubert* screening applies in federal court (and many states), some states have affirmatively decided to remain *Frye* adherents. That means that when they interpret their own rules of evidence—often modeled after the Federal Rules of Evidence—they see *Frye* and general acceptance as the appropriate standard for reliability screening. Before we move to 1993's *Daubert* case, let us consider for a moment why a state would retain *Frye*, with the following case:

People v. Leahy

882 P.2d 321 (Cal. 1994)

Lucas, C.J.

INTRODUCTION

The issues addressed by the Court of Appeal in this case were (1) whether the results of a horizontal gaze nystagmus (HGN) field sobriety test are admissible in the absence of a *Kelly/Frye* foundational showing, that is, foundational evidence disclosing general acceptance of the test within the relevant scientific community (see *People v. Kelly*, 549 P.2d 1240 (Cal. 1976) [hereafter *Kelly*]; *Frye v. United States*, 293 F. 1013, 1014 (D.C. Cir. 1923) [hereafter *Frye*]), and (2) whether a police officer without scientific expertise is qualified to give an opinion concerning the results of the HGN test. The Court of Appeal answered both questions in the negative and reversed defendant Leahy's convictions for driving under the influence of alcohol.

We granted review and asked for supplemental briefing on the question whether the *Kelly/Frye* standard for admitting the results of new scientific techniques should be modified following the United States Supreme Court's decision in *Daubert v. Merrell Dow Pharms., Inc.*, 509 U.S. 579 (1993) (hereafter *Daubert*), holding that *Frye* was abrogated by Rule 702 of the Federal Rules of Evidence. As will appear, after reviewing such additional briefing and argument, we conclude that the *Kelly/Frye* formulation (or now more accurately, the *Kelly* formulation) should remain a prerequisite to the admission of expert testimony regarding new scientific methodology in this state. We further conclude, consistent with the Court of Appeal's conclusions herein, that the HGN test is a "new scientific technique" within the scope of *Kelly*, and that the trial court improperly admitted police testimony regarding that technique without first requiring compliance with *Kelly*.

Accordingly, we affirm the judgment of the Court of Appeal reversing defendant Leahy's conviction on the ground of failure to comply with *Kelly*, and direct a remand to the trial court for a *Kelly* hearing in accordance with our opinion.

FACTS

The following facts were taken largely from the Court of Appeal opinion.... Leahy was stopped after a police officer observed him driving a car traveling 55 miles per hour in a 25-mile-per-hour zone. Leahy's face was flushed, his eyes were red and watery, his speech was slurred, his balance was unsteady, and he exuded the odor of alcohol. Despite these relatively conventional indicia of intoxication, the officer was not convinced defendant was under the influence of alcohol. The officer decided to give defendant some field sobriety tests.

Defendant passed two such tests, the "internal clock" test and the "alphabet" test. He was also required, however, to take the HGN test. As a recent appellate decision explains, "Nystagmus is an involuntary rapid movement of the eyeball, which may be horizontal, vertical, or rotary. [Citation.] An inability of the eyes to maintain visual fixation as they are turned from side to side (in other words, jerking or bouncing) is known as horizontal gaze nystagmus, or HGN. [Citation.] Some investigators believe alcohol intoxication increases the frequency and amplitude of HGN and causes HGN to occur at a smaller angle of deviation from the forward direction. [Citation.]" *People v. Ojeda*, 275 Cal. Rptr. 472 (Cal. Ct. App. 1990).

In the present case, the officer believed that defendant failed the HGN test, and accordingly he arrested defendant. A subsequent intoxilyzer breath test revealed a .10 percent blood-alcohol level. Accordingly, defendant was charged with driving under the influence of alcohol and driving with a blood-alcohol level in excess of .08 percent. Defendant made a motion *in limine* to bar evidence of the HGN test result based on *Kelly* & *Frye*. The trial court denied the motion....

COURT OF APPEALS DECISION

... The Court of Appeal agreed with [prior state rulings regarding officer testimony] and concluded "[i]t was error to admit HGN evidence as either lay or expert testimony without a proper scientific foundation. The usual field sobriety tests are grounded in common knowledge, i.e., that intoxicated persons will often demonstrate lack of concentration, judgment, balance, and coordination. HGN is not."

Consequently, at least as the law of California currently stands, it will be error in the event of any retrial to permit such evidence as the basis of an opinion concerning intoxication without a *Kelly-Frye* foundation, i.e., proof of general acceptance of HGN in the scientific community....

DISCUSSION

We will first discuss the background leading to adoption of the *Kelly/Frye* formulation and then outline some of the considerations which militate for or against its retention. We next will address the *Daubert* decision and its effect on that formulation. As will appear, we conclude, consistent with the views of *both* parties herein, that *Daubert* affords no compelling reason for abandoning *Kelly* in favor of the more "flexible" approach outlined in *Daubert*. Then we will turn to the question whether the trial court erred in permitting the officer to testify regarding the results of the HGN test given to defendant, and whether that error requires reversal of the judgment against defendant.

1. *People* v. *Kelly* — Our unanimous 1976 *Kelly* decision involved the admissibility of *voiceprint* evidence produced by a technique used to identify voices by spectrographic analysis. That case first set forth certain "general principles of admissibility" of expert testimony based on new scientific techniques, including the following "traditional" two-step process: "(1) The *reliability of the method* must be established, usually by expert testimony, and (2) the witness furnishing such testimony must be properly *qualified as an expert to give an opinion* on the subject. Additionally, the proponent of the evidence must demonstrate that correct scientific procedures were used in the particular case. [Citations.]"

Kelly next considered the appropriate test for determining the reliability of a new scientific technique. We recognized that one possible approach would be to leave questions of admissibility to the discretion of the trial court in the first instance, "in which event objections, if any, to the reliability of the evidence (or of the underlying scientific technique on which it is based) might lessen the weight of the evidence but would not necessarily prevent its admissibility."

We rejected the foregoing approach, however, and confirmed allegiance to the "germinal" *Frye*, and its formulation, as follows: "Just when a scientific principle or discovery crosses the line between the experimental and demonstrable stages is difficult to define. Somewhere in this twilight zone the evidential force of the principle must be recognized, and while courts will go a long way in admitting expert testimony deduced from a well-recognized scientific principle or discovery, the thing from which the deduction is made must be *sufficiently established to have gained general acceptance in the particular field in which it belongs.*" *Frye*, 293 F. at 1014, *italics added and quoted in Kelly*, 549 P.2d at 1244.

In *Kelly*, we explained that prior California cases, and "most" sister state cases, have followed *Frye* and "assigned the task of determining reliability of the evolving technique to members of the scientific community from which the new method emerges." We observed that the *Frye* standard holds several advantages, including (1) assuring that those persons most qualified to assess the validity of a scientific technique would have the determinative voice, (2) providing a "minimal reserve of experts" to critically examine each technique in a particular case, (3) promoting uniformity of decision based on finding a consensus in the scientific community, and (4) protecting the parties by its "essentially conservative nature."

Expounding on the last factor, we noted that "[s]everal reasons ... support a posture of judicial caution in this area. Lay jurors tend to give considerable weight to 'scientific' evidence when presented by 'experts' with impressive credentials. We have acknowledged the existence of a '... misleading aura of certainty which often envelops a new scientific process, obscuring its currently experimental nature.' [Citation.]" We further noted that once a trial court has admitted evidence derived from a new technique and the decision is affirmed on appeal in a published opinion, it will become precedent controlling subsequent trials. Thus, it is essential that the decision to admit such evidence is carefully considered.

For all the foregoing reasons, in *Kelly* we deemed the more cautious *Frye* formulation preferable to simply submitting the matter to the trial court's discretion for decision in each case. We now review that conclusion in light of a recent decision by the United States Supreme Court.

2. *Daubert* v. *Merrell Dow Pharms., Inc.* — In *Daubert*, plaintiffs sued the manufacturer (Merrell Dow) of the anti-nausea drug Bendectin, alleging its ingestion caused birth defects. Merrell Dow moved for summary judgment, submitting an affidavit from an expert epidemiologist, Dr. Lamm, who stated that none of the 30 pertinent published studies had ever found Bendectin capable of causing malformations in fetuses. Rather than directly contest Dr. Lamm's factual statements, plaintiffs responded with their own experts' declarations to the effect that their unpublished studies, and reanalyses of published studies, indicated a link between Bendectin and fetal malformation.

The federal district court granted Merrell Dow's motion for summary judgment on the basis that the scientific theories of plaintiffs' experts failed to meet *Frye*'s "general acceptance" standard. *See Daubert v. Merrell Dow Pharms., Inc.*, 727 F. Supp. 570, 572–76 (S.D. Cal. 1989). The Ninth Circuit Court of Appeals affirmed. *See Daubert v. Merrell Dow Pharms., Inc.*, 951 F.2d 1128 (9th Cir. 1991).…

The Supreme Court observed that although the *Frye* standard has been the "dominant" one in the 70 years since its formulation, it has come under "increasing attack of late." *Daubert v. Merrell Dow Pharms., Inc.*, 509 U.S. 579, 585 (1993). Indeed, according to the high court, "The merits of the *Frye* test have been much debated, and scholarship on its proper scope and application is legion." *Id.* The court, however, found it unnecessary to resolve the debate. Instead, the court concluded that the *Frye* test had been *superseded* by adoption of the Federal Rules of Evidence in 1975.…

[T]he Supreme Court in *Daubert* relied on Rule 702 of the Federal Rules of Evidence, governing expert testimony: "If scientific, technical, or other specialized knowledge will assist the trier of fact to understand the evidence or to determine a fact in issue, a witness qualified as an expert by knowledge, skill, experience, training, or education, may testify thereto in the form of an opinion or otherwise." As the court explained, "[n]othing in the text of this Rule [Rule 702] establishes 'general acceptance' as an absolute prerequisite to admissibility.… Given the Rules' permissive backdrop and their inclusion of a specific rule on expert testimony that does not mention 'general acceptance,' the assertion that the Rules somehow assimilated *Frye* is unconvincing."

The high court in *Daubert* concluded that *Frye*'s "austere standard" was "absent from and incompatible with the Federal Rules of Evidence, [and] should not be applied in federal trials." In the following portion of its opinion, the court expounded on the screening functions federal courts should perform under rule 702 to assure that "any and all scientific testimony or evidence admitted is not only relevant, but reliable." … We now turn to an analysis of the California statutory provisions governing the admissibility of expert evidence and address the question whether *Daubert*'s holding provides an appropriate analogy supporting the abrogation of the *Kelly* formulation in this state.

3. California Provisions on Admissibility — *Daubert*, dealing with federal law, offers at most only persuasive authority to assist us in determining whether to reconsider our *Kelly* decision. We first review the California statutory provisions to determine whether the *Kelly* standard is "absent from and incompatible with" the California Evidence Code provisions regarding the admissibility of expert testimony.…

Sections 720 and 801 are the California provisions regarding admissibility of expert testimony. Section 720, subdivision (a), provides that "A person is qualified to testify as an expert if he has special knowledge, skill, experience, training, or education sufficient to qualify him as an expert on the subject to which his testimony relates...." Subdivision (b) of that section provides that "[a] witness' special knowledge ... may be shown by any otherwise admissible evidence, including his own testimony."

Section 801 permits an expert to state an opinion that is "(a) Related to a subject that is sufficiently beyond common experience that the opinion of an expert would assist the trier of fact; and (b) Based on matter (including his special knowledge ...) perceived by or personally known to the witness..., whether or not admissible, *that is of a type that reasonably may be relied upon by an expert* in forming an opinion upon the subject to which his testimony relates, unless an expert is precluded by law from using such matter as a basis for his opinion." (Italics added.) ... "The applicable rule in this state ... is that the admissibility of evidence based on a new scientific technique is determined under the principles of *Frye v. United States*, 293 F. 1013, 1014...." *People v. Harris*, 767 P.2d 619, 649 (Cal. 1989).

4. *Survival of* Kelly — Sections 720 and 801, in combination, seem the functional equivalent of Federal Rules of Evidence, rule 702, as discussed in *Daubert*. Although some language in section 801 is broad enough to include a *Frye* standard of general acceptance (matter "of a type that reasonably may be relied upon by an expert"), nothing in these sections expressly establishes general acceptance as an absolute prerequisite to admissibility, and nothing in the legislative history leading to adoption of the Evidence Code indicates that a general acceptance standard was intended. To paraphrase *Daubert*, the drafting history makes no mention of *Frye*, and a rigid general acceptance requirement might seem at odds with the liberal thrust of the Evidence Code and its general approach of relaxing the traditional barriers to "opinion" testimony.

Thus, were we approaching the question afresh, without the benefit of our analysis and holding in *Kelly*, we might reasonably conclude, by analogy to *Daubert*, that the framers of the Evidence Code did not intend to adopt a general acceptance standard. But *Kelly* was decided in 1976, 11 years *after* the adoption of the Evidence Code and its provisions governing the admissibility of expert testimony. *See Fishback v. People*, 851 P.2d 884, 890 (Colo. 1993) (retaining *Frye* on similar analysis). We were presumably well aware in *Kelly* that the *Frye* "general acceptance" standard arguably was "absent from and incompatible with" the preexisting California statutory provisions. Nonetheless, we concluded otherwise and found *Frye* compatible with those provisions, which we cited in our opinion. No significant relevant developments have occurred in this state since *Kelly* was decided to justify abandoning its conclusions. Thus, the principle of stare decisis appears applicable here, unless the criticism of the *Frye* doctrine cited in *Daubert* and in other sources persuades us otherwise.

Both defendant and the People herein urge us to retain our *Kelly* holding. Defendant encourages us to preserve the "cautious" and "conservative" approach we deliberately chose in *Kelly*. The People ... agree, stating, "there must be some standard test for the trial courts to follow to minimize the influx of what has come to be known as 'junk science' into the courtrooms of this state. The *Kelly/Frye* test, while not perfect, has acted to keep such unreliable evidence from the jury." Amici curiae Los Angeles District Attorney (LADA), Criminal Justice Legal Foundation (CJLF), California

Public Defenders' Association, and Product Liability Advisory Counsel have also submitted briefs supporting the retention of *Kelly*.

LADA takes the position that for us to adopt *Daubert* would "ignore over forty years of precedent based upon policy considerations which have not changed, and without any compulsion to do so from the California Legislature or from the voters." In the view of CJLF, "California should retain the *Kelly* rule as an important safeguard against untested and unproven scientific theories." The other two above mentioned amici curiae are in general agreement.

The foregoing position, however, is not unanimous. Other amici curiae (namely, the State Attorney General and the Appellate Committee of the California District Attorneys Association (ACCDA)) urge us to employ the *Daubert* analogy and either discard, or substantially alter, our *Kelly* holding. It seems apparent from their briefs, however, that the primary concern of these amici curiae involves the interpretation and application of *Kelly* in the context of the deoxyribonucleic acid (DNA) cases. These amici seem more concerned with the narrow issue of the exclusion of DNA test evidence ... than with the general question of the retention of *Kelly*.

Amicus curiae ACCDA asserts that *Kelly* is unclear as to the proper standard for proving general acceptance by the scientific community. *Compare People v. Shirley*, 723 P.2d 1354 (Cal. 1982) (opposition by scientists "significant either in number or expertise"), *with People v. Guerra*, 690 P.2d 635 (Cal. 1984) (unanimity of opinion unnecessary if use of technique supported by "clear majority" of the scientific community)....

Additionally, ACCDA suggests it is unclear how to apply that correct scientific procedures be employed in the case.... Amicus curiae Attorney General echoes the concerns of ACCDA, and asserts that *Kelly/Frye* (1) emphasizes "nose counting" of the scientific community rather than focusing directly on the reliability of the challenged technique, thereby excluding "demonstrably reliable, highly probative evidence, as it has in the case of DNA evidence," (2) is premised on an unrealistic model of a "relatively monolithic scientific community," (3) improperly defers to scientists the legal question of the admissibility of evidence; and (4) unduly penalizes crime victims, their families and friends by excluding relevant evidence of guilt.

The Attorney General also observes that the *Kelly/Frye* test is uncertain in various respects, such as (1) whether, and to what extent, it applies to expert testimony, (2) whether there must be general acceptance of the scientific technique itself or merely the scientific principle underlying it, (3) whether "probability estimates" (e.g., in DNA cases) are subject to *Kelly/Frye,* (4) what is the "relevant" scientific community, and (5) what constitutes "general acceptance" (e.g., a simple majority, a consensus, or a significant minority).

The Attorney General further suggests that the supposed benefits of *Kelly/Frye* (e.g., minimizing undue influence on juries, leaving scientific questions to qualified scientists, avoiding multiple suits, and promoting uniformity of decision) can be alternatively achieved by giving the trial courts broad discretion to decide admissibility questions, subject to vigorous cross-examination of experts, full presentation of contrary evidence, and careful jury instructions on the burden of proof. According to the Attorney General, the DNA cases demonstrate that *Kelly/Frye* does not guarantee against multiple litigation or conflicting decisions.

As with amicus curiae ACCDA, the Attorney General urges us to clarify or "fix" our *Kelly* rule in the following respects, should we elect not to abandon it entirely:

First, we should make clear that "general acceptance" does not require unanimity, a consensus of opinion, or even majority support by the scientific community. The Attorney General argues that general acceptance should mean that the technique "is accepted by other well credentialed scientists *outside the testing laboratory....*" (Italics in original.)

Second, according to the Attorney General, we should clarify that *Kelly* does not apply to "probability estimates" such as those given in DNA cases, and we should hold that *Kelly* is inapplicable to the "particular standardized protocol" used to perform the test in the case at hand, rather than to the "fundamental validity" of the technique itself.

Finally, the Attorney General suggests we should adopt an abuse of discretion standard of appellate review, rather than permit a de novo review at the appellate level....

In sum, rather than raise fundamental defects in our approach in *Kelly*, these amici curiae appear more concerned with clarifying or modifying our *Kelly* standard for use in future cases.... We turn, then, to the commentators critical of the *Frye* formulation itself.

The critics of *Frye* focus primarily on its conservative nature: As previously noted, the doctrine contemplates an undefined period of testing and study by a community of experts before a new scientific technique may be deemed "generally accepted," thus delaying the admissibility of evidence derived from the technique. (*See, e.g.,* Bert Black, *A Unified Theory of Scientific Evidence,* 56 FORDHAM L. REV. 595, 636–637 (1988) [Black]; Paul C. Giannelli, *The Admissibility of Novel Scientific Evidence:* Frye v. United States, *a Half-Century Later,* 80 COLUM. L. REV. 1197, 1223–24, 1248 (1980) [Giannelli]; Roger S. Hanson, *James Alphonzo* Frye *is Sixty-Five Years Old; Should He Retire,* 16 WESTERN ST. U. L. REV. 357, 367–68 (1989) [Hanson]; Note, *Leading Cases,* 101 HARV. L. REV. 119, 125–27 (1987) [Harvard Note]; *Daubert, supra,* 509 U.S. at 586–87 nn.4–5.) These commentators observe that conceivably, a reliable, readily provable, technique could nonetheless remain unknown and untested by the relevant scientific community, thereby indefinitely delaying its use in the courtroom. (Hanson, at 367–68.) ...

But we acknowledged the foregoing basis for criticism in *Kelly,* noting that "[s]ome criticism has been directed at the *Frye* standard, primarily on the ground that the test is too conservative, often resulting in the prevention of the admission of relevant evidence. [citations]" We nonetheless concluded that "there is ample justification for the exercise of considerable judicial caution in the acceptance of evidence developed by new scientific techniques." As we have previously indicated, *Kelly* set forth at length its reasons for adopting a more cautious approach to the admission of new scientific evidence. Nothing occurring in the years since *Kelly* was decided requires us to reconsider that conclusion....

As previously noted, amicus curiae Attorney General criticizes *Kelly* on the additional ground that it requires the trial judge to defer admissibility questions to a "nose count" of scientists rather than allowing the judge or jury to directly confront the issue of the reliability of the evidence. But, as we observed in *Kelly*, it may be preferable to let admissibility questions regarding new scientific techniques be settled by those persons most qualified to assess their validity. Some commentators have questioned the ability of trial judges, often wholly unschooled in scientific areas, to evaluate highly technical scientific material. As the Harvard Note, *supra*, observes, "The *Frye* rule ensures that judges and juries with little or no scientific background will not attempt to resolve technical questions on which not even experts can reach a consensus...." (Harvard Note, at 127.) ... Moreover, most critics of *Frye* acknowledge the test has several positive aspects and operates well in many situations. (*See* Hanson, at 361–63, 458–60; Harvard Note, at 127; Black, at 637–38.)

For example, the Hanson article lists the following positive features of the *Frye* doctrine: "(a) The time and cost of proving and establishing new scientific principles are transformed from a courtroom ... to a laboratory.... (b) Each court thus need not confront the principle *de novo*, and may draw from other court decisions, the applicable literature, ... and if offered, additional expert testimony.... (c) Presumably a battery of well-qualified scientific and medical personnel are available to support the principle...." (Hanson, at 458–59.)

The Harvard Note is likewise predominantly favorable toward *Frye*. The author states that, "[d]espite the[] criticisms, however, the *Frye* rule plays a vital role in the trial process.... Although the *Frye* test may be difficult to apply and at times may exclude relevant evidence, it has proven its value for over sixty years. It has prevented justice from becoming a matter of amateur guesswork based on unreliable techniques and has helped to assure that determinations of guilt or innocence are not influenced by the vagaries of pseudoscience. [*Frye* is] ... a wise rule that contributes greatly to the integrity of the criminal process." (Harvard Note, at 127.)

Even Professor Giannelli, *Frye*'s severest critic, acknowledges that *Frye*'s requirement of a "special burden" as a prerequisite to admissibility of a new scientific technique has merit, and that if a "relevancy" test is chosen as an alternative (as in *Daubert*), special steps should be taken to assure the reliability of the evidence, including requiring the prosecutor to prove the validity of the technique beyond a reasonable doubt. (Giannelli, at 1248–50.)

Despite the criticism of *Kelly/Frye*, this court has had numerous occasions to review and apply the doctrine, and has done so without apparent difficulty or critical comment.... Additionally, we observe that the Legislature has had ample opportunity to amend the Evidence Code provisions to abrogate or modify the general acceptance standard that *Kelly* found implicit within them.... In sum, *Kelly* sets forth the various reasons why the more "conservative" *Frye* approach to determining the reliability of expert testimony regarding scientific techniques represents an appropriate one. *Daubert*, which avoided the issue of *Frye*'s "merits," presents no justification for reconsidering that aspect of our holding in *Kelly*. Thus, we conclude that the *Kelly* formulation survived *Daubert* in this state, and that none of the above described authorities critical of that formulation persuades us to reconsider or modify it at this time. Accordingly, we turn next to the question of the application of that standard to the facts of the present case.

5. *HGN test is a new scientific test under* **Kelly**—After reviewing the briefs and applicable cases, we conclude the Court of Appeal correctly decided that the HGN test was a "new scientific technique" within the scope of the *Kelly* formulation, and for that reason proof was required of its general acceptance by the scientific community....

6. *Police Officer Testimony is Insufficient to Establish General Acceptance*—The People concede that "most states have determined the [HGN] test is a scientific test" under *Frye*. They nonetheless insist that testimony by the officers administering the HGN test is sufficient to establish *Kelly* compliance. They rely on our statement in *People v. Stoll*, 783 P.2d 698, 710 (Cal. 1989), that "absent some special feature which effectively blindsides the jury, expert opinion testimony is not subject to *Kelly/Frye*." The People observe that the officers who administered the tests are subject to cross-examination, and that the jury is not likely to accord their opinions regarding HGN test results the same weight as a scientist's opinion on the same subject. According to the People, field sobriety tests such as the HGN test merely "rely on the experience of a police officer in observing the performance of persons who may or may not be intoxicated.... There is nothing more scientific about the HGN test than the other field sobriety tests."

The People also rely on language in *Ojeda*, 275 Cal. Rptr. at 474, that "police officers who deal daily with intoxicated persons become expert at recognizing the physical effects of intoxication.... This does not make them scientists." The People cite cases from other states holding either that the HGN test is not a "scientific" test or that the testimony of police officers regarding administration of the HGN test is sufficient compliance with the *Frye* standard.... [These] decisions, however, do not explain how police officers are competent to establish general acceptance of HGN testing *in the scientific community*, or how they are qualified to relate the scientific bases underlying the nystagmus test....

7. *Limited Remand Appropriate*—In accord with our foregoing discussion, we conclude that the Court of Appeal was correct in reversing both counts of defendant's conviction, for no evidence was elicited to show that HGN testing had been generally accepted in the scientific community, and the error was clearly prejudicial. As the Court of Appeal concluded, "it is reasonably probable a different result would have been achieved on both counts but for the HGN evidence [citation]. Leahy passed the other field sobriety tests. His blood-alcohol level was said to be .10, only .02. over the statutory maximum; and criminalists generally concede a margin of error of at least plus or minus .01. Also, the passage of time between arrest and test can account for even more than that, up or down. About 90 minutes went by between arrest and Leahy's encounter with the intoxilyzer. Depending on when he had his last drink and a host of other factors, his blood-alcohol level could have risen or fallen several points in that time."

We accept, however, the People's suggestion that an entire retrial of the case may be unnecessary. Instead, we will direct the Court of Appeal to reverse defendant's conviction and remand the case to the trial court for a *Kelly* hearing in accordance with our opinion....

Notes and Questions

1. The court notes that California adopted its Evidence Code in 1965, eleven years before the decision in *Kelly* that adopted the *Frye* reasoning. Because of the timing, the court must evaluate the weight of *Kelly* under the doctrine of stare decisis. Is that the only reason that the court continues with *Frye*? With an alternate timeline of the Evidence Code and *Kelly*, would the court have decided to follow *Daubert*?

2. Are the requirements for admission under the *Frye/Kelly* test clear enough after *Leahy* to apply to new and different situations? What guidance has the court given to trial judges in making determinations of general acceptance?

3. California is not the sole state to retain *Frye* after challenges to scientific standards arose after *Daubert* in 1993. In those years, state courts in New York, Pennsylvania, Illinois, Florida, Washington, Maryland and others all decided to retain *Frye* analysis. *See Grady v. Frito-Lay*, 839 A.2d 1038 (Pa. 2003); *Donaldson v. Cent. Ill. Pub. Serv. Co.*, 767 N.E.2d 314 (Ill. 2002); *Burral v. State*, 724 A.2d 65, 80 (Md. 1999); *State v. Copeland*, 922 P.2d 1304 (Wash. 1996); *People v. Wesley*, 633 N.E. 2d 451 (N.Y. 1994); *Flanagan v. State*, 625 So. 2d 827 (Fla. 1993). Some state legislatures attempt to adopt *Daubert* by statute, in lieu of judicial intervention. *See, e.g.*, Ga. Code Ann. §24-7-702(f) (2018). For a detailed review of the breakdown of the states and their admissibility standards, see David H. Kaye Et Al., The New Wigmore: A Treatise on Evidence §6.4.2, at 225–26 (2004).

4. As we consider *Daubert* in more detail in Section D(ii), below, consider how admissibility issues will be resolved in those circumstances, and then how a court in a state that retains *Frye* would handle the same issue. They may not be entirely similar, but are they entirely different either?

ii. The *Daubert* Decision and Aftermath

Even in the pre-*Daubert* years, many commentators strongly criticized the *Frye* general acceptance standard. We saw many of those criticisms in Section D(i) above, in cases like *Downing* or *Leahy*, in legal scholarship like the Morrison & Thompson article excerpted after *Smith*, or in Giannelli's work cited in many of these cases. As *Frye* began to be applied more frequently to civil cases, as it had not been prior to the mid-1980s, the debate over admission of so-called "junk science" intensified. Peter Huber, Galileo's Revenge: Junk Science in the Courtroom (1991); David E. Bernstein, Frye, Frye, *Again: The Past, Present, and Future of the General Acceptance Test*, 41 Jurimetrics J. 385, 390–92 (2001) (timing *Frye* use in civil cases); Kenneth

J. Chesebro, *Galileo's Retort: Peter Huber's Junk Scholarship*, 42 Am. U. L. Rev. 1637 (1993); Barry M. Epstein & Marc S. Klein, *The Use and Abuse of Expert Testimony in Product Liability Actions*, 17 Seton Hall L. Rev. 656 (1987).

The Supreme Court took notice, wading into the debate on scientific reliability soon thereafter. With their "*Daubert* trilogy" of case opinions, the Court altered the landscape of expert admissibility. But in so doing, significant new questions would arise as well.

As we look at these cases, remember the fundamental question about reliability screening: Will this result in only "good science" being presented to the jury?

Daubert v. Merrell Dow Pharmaceuticals., Inc.
509 U.S. 579 (1993)

Blackmun, J.

In this case we are called upon to determine the standard for admitting expert scientific testimony in a federal trial.

I

Petitioners Jason Daubert and Eric Schuller are minor children born with serious birth defects. They and their parents sued respondent in California state court, alleging that the birth defects had been caused by the mothers' ingestion of Bendectin, a prescription antinausea drug marketed by respondent. Respondent removed the suits to federal court on diversity grounds.

After extensive discovery, respondent moved for summary judgment, contending that Bendectin does not cause birth defects in humans and that petitioners would be unable to come forward with any admissible evidence that it does. In support of its motion, respondent submitted an affidavit of Steven H. Lamm, physician and epidemiologist, who is a well-credentialed expert on the risks from exposure to various chemical substances. Doctor Lamm stated that he had reviewed all the literature on Bendectin and human birth defects—more than 30 published studies involving over 130,000 patients. No study had found Bendectin to be a human teratogen (*i.e.,* a substance capable of causing malformations in fetuses). On the basis of this review, Doctor Lamm concluded that maternal use of Bendectin during the first trimester of pregnancy has not been shown to be a risk factor for human birth defects.

Petitioners did not (and do not) contest this characterization of the published record regarding Bendectin. Instead, they responded to respondent's motion with the testimony of eight experts of their own, each of whom also possessed impressive credentials. These experts had concluded that Bendectin can cause birth defects. Their conclusions were based upon "in vitro" (test tube) and "in vivo" (live) animal studies that found a link between Bendectin and malformations; pharmacological studies of the chemical structure of Bendectin that purported to show similarities between the structure of the drug and that of other substances known to cause birth defects; and the "reanalysis" of previously published epidemiological (human statistical) studies.

The District Court granted respondent's motion for summary judgment. The court stated that scientific evidence is admissible only if the principle upon which it is based is "'sufficiently established to have general acceptance in the field to which it belongs.'" 727 F. Supp. 570, 572 (S.D. Cal. 1989), quoting *United States v. Kilgus*, 571 F.2d 508, 510 (9th Cir. 1978). The court concluded that petitioners' evidence did not meet this standard.... The United States Court of Appeals for the Ninth Circuit affirmed. 951 F.2d 1128 (1991). Citing *Frye v. United States*, 293 F. 1013, 1014 (1923), the court stated that expert opinion based on a scientific technique is inadmissible unless the technique is "generally accepted" as reliable in the relevant scientific community. 951 F.2d at 1129–30. The court declared that expert opinion based on a methodology that diverges "significantly from the procedures accepted by recognized authorities in the field ... cannot be shown to be 'generally accepted as a reliable technique.'" *Id.*, at 1130, quoting *United States v. Solomon*, 753 F.2d 1522, 1526 (9th Cir. 1985).... The court concluded that petitioners' evidence provided an insufficient foundation to allow admission of expert testimony that Bendectin caused their injuries and, accordingly, that petitioners could not satisfy their burden of proving causation at trial.

We granted certiorari in light of sharp divisions among the courts regarding the proper standard for the admission of expert testimony.

II

A

In the 70 years since its formulation in the *Frye* case, the "general acceptance" test has been the dominant standard for determining the admissibility of novel scientific evidence at trial. *See* E. Green & C. Nesson, Problems, Cases, and Materials on Evidence 649 (1983). Although under increasing attack of late, the rule continues to be followed by a majority of courts, including the Ninth Circuit.

The *Frye* test has its origin in a short and citation-free 1923 decision concerning the admissibility of evidence derived from a systolic blood pressure deception test, a crude precursor to the polygraph machine. In what has become a famous (perhaps infamous) passage, the then Court of Appeals for the District of Columbia described the device and its operation and declared:

> Just when a scientific principle or discovery crosses the line between the experimental and demonstrable stages is difficult to define. Somewhere in this twilight zone the evidential force of the principle must be recognized, and while courts will go a long way in admitting expert testimony deduced from a well-recognized scientific principle or discovery, *the thing from which the deduction is made must be sufficiently established to have gained general acceptance in the particular field in which it belongs.* (emphasis added).

Because the deception test had "not yet gained such standing and scientific recognition among physiological and psychological authorities as would justify the courts in admitting expert testimony deduced from the discovery, development, and experiments thus far made," evidence of its results was ruled inadmissible. *Id.*

The merits of the *Frye* test have been much debated, and scholarship on its proper scope and application is legion.[4] Petitioners' primary attack, however, is not on the content but on the continuing authority of the rule. They contend that the *Frye* test was superseded by the adoption of the Federal Rules of Evidence. We agree.

We interpret the legislatively enacted Federal Rules of Evidence as we would any statute. *Beech Aircraft Corp. v. Rainey*, 488 U.S. 153, 163 (1988). Rule 402 provides the baseline:

> All relevant evidence is admissible, except as otherwise provided by the Constitution of the United States, by Act of Congress, by these rules, or by other rules prescribed by the Supreme Court pursuant to statutory authority. Evidence which is not relevant is not admissible.

"Relevant evidence" is defined as that which has "any tendency to make the existence of any fact that is of consequence to the determination of the action more probable or less probable than it would be without the evidence." The Rule's basic standard of relevance thus is a liberal one.

Frye, of course, predated the Rules by half a century. In *United States v. Abel*, 469 U.S. 45 (1984), we considered the pertinence of background common law in interpreting the Rules of Evidence. We noted that the Rules occupy the field but, quoting Professor Cleary, the Reporter, explained that the common law nevertheless could serve as an aid to their application....

Here there is a specific Rule that speaks to the contested issue. Rule 702, governing expert testimony, provides:

> If scientific, technical, or other specialized knowledge will assist the trier of fact to understand the evidence or to determine a fact in issue, a witness qualified as an expert by knowledge, skill, experience, training, or education, may testify thereto in the form of an opinion or otherwise.

Nothing in the text of this Rule establishes "general acceptance" as an absolute prerequisite to admissibility. Nor does respondent present any clear indication that Rule 702 or the Rules as a whole were intended to incorporate a "general acceptance" standard. The drafting history makes no mention of *Frye*, and a rigid "general acceptance" requirement would be at odds with the "liberal thrust" of the Federal Rules and their "general approach of relaxing the traditional barriers to 'opinion' testimony." *Beech Aircraft Corp. v. Rainey*, 488 U.S. at 169 (citing Rules 701 to 705). See also Jack B. Weinstein, *Rule 702 of the Federal Rules of Evidence is Sound; It Should Not Be Amended*, 138 F.R.D. 631 (1991) ("The Rules were designed to depend primarily upon lawyer-adversaries and sensible triers of fact to evaluate conflicts"). Given the Rules' permissive backdrop and their inclusion of a specific rule on expert testimony that does not mention " 'general acceptance,' " the assertion that the Rules somehow assimilated *Frye* is unconvincing. *Frye* made "general acceptance" the exclusive test for admitting

---

4. Michael D. Green, *Expert Witnesses and Sufficiency of Evidence in Toxic Substances Litigation: The Legacy of Agent Orange and Bendectin Litigation*, 86 Nw. L. Rev. 643 (1992).

expert scientific testimony. That austere standard, absent from, and incompatible with, the Federal Rules of Evidence, should not be applied in federal trials.

B

That the *Frye* test was displaced by the Rules of Evidence does not mean, however, that the Rules themselves place no limits on the admissibility of purportedly scientific evidence. Nor is the trial judge disabled from screening such evidence. To the contrary, under the Rules the trial judge must ensure that any and all scientific testimony or evidence admitted is not only relevant, but reliable.

The primary locus of this obligation is Rule 702, which clearly contemplates some degree of regulation of the subjects and theories about which an expert may testify. "*If scientific*, technical, or other specialized *knowledge will assist the trier of fact* to understand the evidence or to determine a fact in issue" an expert "may testify *thereto*." (Emphasis added.) The subject of an expert's testimony must be "scientific ... knowledge." The adjective "scientific" implies a grounding in the methods and procedures of science. Similarly, the word "knowledge" connotes more than subjective belief or unsupported speculation. The term "applies to any body of known facts or to any body of ideas inferred from such facts or accepted as truths on good grounds." Webster's Third New International Dictionary 1252 (1986). Of course, it would be unreasonable to conclude that the subject of scientific testimony must be "known" to a certainty.... But, in order to qualify as "scientific knowledge," an inference or assertion must be derived by the scientific method. Proposed testimony must be supported by appropriate validation—*i.e.*, "good grounds," based on what is known. In short, the requirement that an expert's testimony pertain to "scientific knowledge" establishes a standard of evidentiary reliability.

Rule 702 further requires that the evidence or testimony "assist the trier of fact to understand the evidence or to determine a fact in issue." This condition goes primarily to relevance. "Expert testimony which does not relate to any issue in the case is not relevant and, ergo, non-helpful." 3 Weinstein & Berger 702[02], p. 702–18. *See also United States v. Downing*, 753 F.2d 1224, 1242 (3d Cir. 1985) ("An additional consideration under Rule 702—and another aspect of relevancy—is whether expert testimony proffered in the case is sufficiently tied to the facts of the case that it will aid the jury in resolving a factual dispute"). The consideration has been aptly described by Judge Becker as one of "fit." *Id.* "Fit" is not always obvious, and scientific validity for one purpose is not necessarily scientific validity for other, unrelated purposes. See Starrs, Frye v. United States *Restructured and Revitalized: A Proposal to Amend Federal Evidence Rule 702*, 26 Jurimetrics J. 249, 258 (1986). The study of the phases of the moon, for example, may provide valid scientific "knowledge" about whether a certain night was dark, and if darkness is a fact in issue, the knowledge will assist the trier of fact. However (absent creditable grounds supporting such a link), evidence that the moon was full on a certain night will not assist the trier of fact in determining whether an individual was unusually likely to have behaved irrationally on that night. Rule 702's "helpfulness" standard requires a valid scientific connection to the pertinent inquiry as a precondition to admissibility.

That these requirements are embodied in Rule 702 is not surprising. Unlike an ordinary witness, see Rule 701, an expert is permitted wide latitude to offer opinions, including those that are not based on firsthand knowledge or observation. Presumably, this relaxation of the usual requirement of firsthand knowledge ... is premised on an assumption that the expert's opinion will have a reliable basis in the knowledge and experience of his discipline.

Faced with a proffer of expert scientific testimony, then, the trial judge must determine ... whether the expert is proposing to testify to (1) scientific knowledge that (2) will assist the trier of fact to understand or determine a fact in issue. This entails a preliminary assessment of whether the reasoning or methodology underlying the testimony is scientifically valid and of whether that reasoning or methodology properly can be applied to the facts in issue. We are confident that federal judges possess the capacity to undertake this review. Many factors will bear on the inquiry, and we do not presume to set out a definitive checklist or test. But some general observations are appropriate.

Ordinarily, a key question to be answered in determining whether a theory or technique is scientific knowledge that will assist the trier of fact will be whether it can be (and has been) tested. "Scientific methodology today is based on generating hypotheses and testing them to see if they can be falsified; indeed, this methodology is what distinguishes science from other fields of human inquiry." Green, 83 Nw. L. Rev. at 645. *See also* C. Hempel, Philosophy of Natural Science 49 (1966) ("[T]he statements constituting a scientific explanation must be capable of empirical test"); Karl Popper, Conjectures and Refutations: The Growth of Scientific Knowledge 37 (5th ed. 1989) ("[T]he criterion of the scientific status of a theory is its falsifiability, or refutability, or testability") (emphasis deleted).

Another pertinent consideration is whether the theory or technique has been subjected to peer review and publication. Publication (which is but one element of peer review) is not a *sine qua non* of admissibility; it does not necessarily correlate with reliability, see S. Jasanoff, The Fifth Branch: Science Advisors as Policymakers 61–76 (1990), and in some instances well-grounded but innovative theories will not have been published, see Horrobin, *The Philosophical Basis of Peer Review and the Suppression of Innovation*, 263 JAMA 1438 (1990). Some propositions, moreover, are too particular, too new, or of too limited interest to be published. But submission to the scrutiny of the scientific community is a component of "good science," in part because it increases the likelihood that substantive flaws in methodology will be detected....

Additionally, in the case of a particular scientific technique, the court ordinarily should consider the known or potential rate of error, *see, e.g., United States v. Smith*, 869 F.2d 348, 353–54 (7th Cir. 1989) (surveying studies of the error rate of spectrographic voice identification technique), and the existence and maintenance of standards controlling the technique's operation, see *United States v. Williams*, 583 F.2d 1194, 1198 (2d Cir. 1978) (noting professional organization's standard governing spectrographic analysis), *cert. denied*, 439 U.S. 1117 (1979).

Finally, "general acceptance" can yet have a bearing on the inquiry. A "reliability assessment does not require, although it does permit, explicit identification of a relevant scientific community and an express determination of a particular degree of acceptance within that community." *United States v. Downing*, 753 F.2d at 1238. *See also* 3 WEINSTEIN & BERGER 702[03], pp. 702–41 to 702–42. Widespread acceptance can be an important factor in ruling particular evidence admissible, and "a known technique which has been able to attract only minimal support within the community," *Downing*, 753 F.2d at 1238, may properly be viewed with skepticism.

The inquiry envisioned by Rule 702 is, we emphasize, a flexible one. Its overarching subject is the scientific validity and thus the evidentiary relevance and reliability — of the principles that underlie a proposed submission. The focus, of course, must be solely on principles and methodology, not on the conclusions that they generate.

Throughout, a judge assessing a proffer of expert scientific testimony under Rule 702 should also be mindful of other applicable rules. Rule 703 provides that expert opinions based on otherwise inadmissible hearsay are to be admitted only if the facts or data are "of a type reasonably relied upon by experts in the particular field in forming opinions or inferences upon the subject." Rule 706 allows the court at its discretion to procure the assistance of an expert of its own choosing. Finally, Rule 403 permits the exclusion of relevant evidence "if its probative value is substantially outweighed by the danger of unfair prejudice, confusion of the issues, or misleading the jury...." Judge Weinstein has explained: "Expert evidence can be both powerful and quite misleading because of the difficulty in evaluating it. Because of this risk, the judge in weighing possible prejudice against probative force under Rule 403 of the present rules exercises more control over experts than over lay witnesses." Weinstein, 138 F.R.D. at 632.

III

We conclude by briefly addressing what appear to be two underlying concerns of the parties and *amici* in this case. Respondent expresses apprehension that abandonment of "general acceptance" as the exclusive requirement for admission will result in a "free-for-all" in which befuddled juries are confounded by absurd and irrational pseudoscientific assertions. In this regard respondent seems to us to be overly pessimistic about the capabilities of the jury and of the adversary system generally. Vigorous cross-examination, presentation of contrary evidence, and careful instruction on the burden of proof are the traditional and appropriate means of attacking shaky but admissible evidence. See *Rock v. Arkansas*, 483 U.S. 44, 61 (1987). Additionally, in the event the trial court concludes that the scintilla of evidence presented supporting a position is insufficient to allow a reasonable juror to conclude that the position more likely than not is true, the court remains free to direct a judgment, Fed. R. Civ. P. 50(a), and likewise to grant summary judgment, Fed. Rule Civ. P. 56; ... Green, 83 Nw. L. REV. at 680–81. These conventional devices, rather than wholesale exclusion under an uncompromising "general acceptance" test, are the appropriate safeguards where the basis of scientific testimony meets the standards of Rule 702.

Petitioners and, to a greater extent, their *amici* exhibit a different concern. They suggest that recognition of a screening role for the judge that allows for the exclusion of "invalid" evidence will sanction a stifling and repressive scientific orthodoxy and will be inimical to the search for truth. It is true that open debate is an essential part of both legal and scientific analyses. Yet there are important differences between the quest for truth in the courtroom and the quest for truth in the laboratory. Scientific conclusions are subject to perpetual revision. Law, on the other hand, must resolve disputes finally and quickly. The scientific project is advanced by broad and wide-ranging consideration of a multitude of hypotheses, for those that are incorrect will eventually be shown to be so, and that in itself is an advance. Conjectures that are probably wrong are of little use, however, in the project of reaching a quick, final, and binding legal judgment — often of great consequence — about a particular set of events in the past. We recognize that, in practice, a gatekeeping role for the judge, no matter how flexible, inevitably on occasion will prevent the jury from learning of authentic insights and innovations. That, nevertheless, is the balance that is struck by Rules of Evidence designed not for the exhaustive search for cosmic understanding but for the particularized resolution of legal disputes.[13]

IV

To summarize: "General acceptance" is not a necessary precondition to the admissibility of scientific evidence under the Federal Rules of Evidence, but the Rules of Evidence — especially Rule 702 — do assign to the trial judge the task of ensuring that an expert's testimony both rests on a reliable foundation and is relevant to the task at hand.... The inquiries of the District Court and the Court of Appeals focused almost exclusively on "general acceptance," as gauged by publication and the decisions of other courts. Accordingly, the judgment of the Court of Appeals is vacated, and the case is remanded for further proceedings consistent with this opinion.

It is so ordered.

REHNQUIST, C.J., concurring in part and dissenting in part.

... The Court concludes, correctly in my view, that the *Frye* rule did not survive the enactment of the Federal Rules of Evidence, and I therefore join Parts I and II-A of its opinion....

Questions arise simply from reading this part of the Court's opinion, and countless more questions will surely arise when hundreds of district judges try to apply its teaching to particular offers of expert testimony. Does all of this *dicta* apply to an expert seeking to testify on the basis of "technical or other specialized knowledge" —

---

13. This is not to say that judicial interpretation, as opposed to adjudicative factfinding, does not share basic characteristics of the scientific endeavor: "The work of a judge is in one sense enduring and in another ephemeral.... In the endless process of testing and retesting, there is a constant rejection of the dross and a constant retention of whatever is pure and sound and fine." B. CARDOZO, THE NATURE OF THE JUDICIAL PROCESS 178, 179 (1921).

the other types of expert knowledge to which Rule 702 applies — or are the "general observations" limited only to "scientific knowledge"? What is the difference between scientific knowledge and technical knowledge; does Rule 702 actually contemplate that the phrase "scientific, technical, or other specialized knowledge" be broken down into numerous subspecies of expertise, or did its authors simply pick general descriptive language covering the sort of expert testimony which courts have customarily received? The Court speaks of its confidence that federal judges can make a "preliminary assessment of whether the reasoning or methodology underlying the testimony is scientifically valid and of whether that reasoning or methodology properly can be applied to the facts in issue." The Court then states that a "key question" to be answered in deciding whether something is "scientific knowledge" "will be whether it can be (and has been) tested." Following this sentence are three quotations from treatises, which not only speak of empirical testing, but one of which states that the "'criterion of the scientific status of a theory is its falsifiability, or refutability, or testability.'"

I defer to no one in my confidence in federal judges; but I am at a loss to know what is meant when it is said that the scientific status of a theory depends on its "falsifiability," and I suspect some of them will be, too.

I do not doubt that Rule 702 confides to the judge some gatekeeping responsibility in deciding questions of the admissibility of proffered expert testimony. But I do not think it imposes on them either the obligation or the authority to become amateur scientists in order to perform that role. I think the Court would be far better advised in this case to decide only the questions presented, and to leave the further development of this important area of the law to future cases.

General Electric Co. v. Joiner
522 U.S. 136 (1997)

REHNQUIST, C.J.

We granted certiorari in this case to determine what standard an appellate court should apply in reviewing a trial court's decision to admit or exclude expert testimony under *Daubert v. Merrell Dow Pharms., Inc.*, 509 U.S. 579 (1993). We hold that abuse of discretion is the appropriate standard. We apply this standard and conclude that the District Court in this case did not abuse its discretion when it excluded certain proffered expert testimony.

I

Respondent Robert Joiner began work as an electrician in the Water & Light Department of Thomasville, Georgia (City), in 1973. This job required him to work with and around the City's electrical transformers, which used a mineral-oil-based dielectric fluid as a coolant. Joiner often had to stick his hands and arms into the fluid to make repairs. The fluid would sometimes splash onto him, occasionally getting into his eyes and mouth. In 1983 the City discovered that the fluid in some of the transformers was contaminated with polychlorinated biphenyls (PCB's). PCB's are widely considered to be hazardous to human health. Congress, with limited exceptions, banned the production and sale of PCB's in 1978.

Joiner was diagnosed with small-cell lung cancer in 1991. He sued petitioners in Georgia state court the following year. Petitioner Monsanto manufactured PCB's from 1935 to 1977; petitioners General Electric and Westinghouse Electric manufactured transformers and dielectric fluid. In his complaint Joiner linked his development of cancer to his exposure to PCB's and their derivatives.... Joiner had been a smoker for approximately eight years, his parents had both been smokers, and there was a history of lung cancer in his family. He was thus perhaps already at a heightened risk of developing lung cancer eventually. The suit alleged that his exposure to PCB's "promoted" his cancer; had it not been for his exposure to these substances, his cancer would not have developed for many years, if at all.

Petitioners removed the case to federal court. Once there, they moved for summary judgment. They contended that (1) there was no evidence that Joiner suffered significant exposure to PCB's, furans, or dioxins, and (2) there was no admissible scientific evidence that PCB's promoted Joiner's cancer. Joiner responded that there were numerous disputed factual issues that required resolution by a jury. He relied largely on the testimony of expert witnesses. In depositions, his experts had testified that PCB's alone can promote cancer and that furans and dioxins can also promote cancer. They opined that since Joiner had been exposed to PCB's, furans, and dioxins, such exposure was likely responsible for Joiner's cancer.

The District Court ruled that there was a genuine issue of material fact as to whether Joiner had been exposed to PCB's. But it nevertheless granted summary judgment for petitioners because ... the testimony of Joiner experts had failed to show that there was a link between exposure to PCB's and small-cell lung cancer. The court believed that the testimony of respondent's experts to the contrary did not rise above "subjective belief or unsupported speculation." 864 F. Supp. 1310, 1326 (N.D. Ga. 1994). Their testimony was therefore inadmissible.

The Court of Appeals for the Eleventh Circuit reversed. It held that "[b]ecause the Federal Rules of Evidence governing expert testimony display a preference for admissibility, we apply a particularly stringent standard of review to the trial judge's exclusion of expert testimony." *Id.*, at 529. Applying that standard, the Court of Appeals held that the District Court had erred in excluding the testimony of Joiner's expert witnesses.... We granted petitioners' petition for a writ of certiorari and we now reverse.

II

Petitioners challenge the standard applied by the Court of Appeals in reviewing the District Court's decision to exclude respondent's experts' proffered testimony. They argue that that court should have applied traditional "abuse-of-discretion" review. Respondent agrees that abuse of discretion is the correct standard of review. He contends, however, that the Court of Appeals applied an abuse-of-discretion standard in this case. As he reads it, the phrase "particularly stringent" announced no new standard of review. It was simply an acknowledgment that an appellate court can and will devote more resources to analyzing district court decisions that are dispositive of the entire litigation. All evidentiary decisions are reviewed under an abuse-of-discretion standard. He argues, however, that it is perfectly reasonable for appellate courts to give particular attention to those decisions that are outcome determinative.

We have held that abuse of discretion is the proper standard of review of a district court's evidentiary rulings. *Old Chief v. United States*, 519 U.S. 172, 174 n. 1 (1997); *United States v. Abel*, 469 U.S. 45, 54 (1984).... The Court of Appeals suggested that *Daubert* somehow altered this general rule in the context of a district court's decision to exclude scientific evidence. But *Daubert* did not address the standard of appellate review for evidentiary rulings at all. It did hold that the "austere" *Frye* standard of "general acceptance" had not been carried over into the Federal Rules of Evidence. But the opinion also said:

> "That the *Frye* test was displaced by the Rules of Evidence does not mean, however, that the Rules themselves place no limits on the admissibility of purportedly scientific evidence. Nor is the trial judge disabled from screening such evidence. To the contrary, under the Rules the trial judge must ensure that any and all scientific testimony or evidence admitted is not only relevant, but reliable." 509 U.S. at 589 (footnote omitted).

Thus, while the Federal Rules of Evidence allow district courts to admit a somewhat broader range of scientific testimony than would have been admissible under *Frye*, they leave in place the "gatekeeper" role of the trial judge in screening such evidence. A court of appeals applying "abuse-of-discretion" review to such rulings may not categorically distinguish between rulings allowing expert testimony and rulings disallowing it. *Compare Beech Aircraft Corp. v. Rainey*, 488 U.S. 153, 172 (1988) (applying abuse-of-discretion review to a lower court's decision to exclude evidence), *with United States v. Abel, supra*, at 54 (applying abuse-of-discretion review to a lower court's decision to admit evidence). We likewise reject respondent's argument that because the granting of summary judgment in this case was "outcome determinative," it should have been subjected to a more searching standard of review. On a motion for summary judgment, disputed issues of fact are resolved against the moving party — here, petitioners. But the question of admissibility of expert testimony is not such an issue of fact, and is reviewable under the abuse-of-discretion standard.

We hold that the Court of Appeals erred in its review of the exclusion of Joiner's experts' testimony. In applying an overly "stringent" review to that ruling, it failed to give the trial court the deference that is the hallmark of abuse-of-discretion review.

III

We believe that a proper application of the correct standard of review here indicates that the District Court did not abuse its discretion. Joiner's theory of liability was that his exposure to PCB's and their derivatives "promoted" his development of small-cell lung cancer. In support of that theory he proffered the deposition testimony of expert witnesses. Dr. Arnold Schecter testified that he believed it "more likely than not that Mr. Joiner's lung cancer was causally linked to cigarette smoking and PCB exposure." Dr. Daniel Teitelbaum testified that Joiner's "lung cancer was caused by or contributed to in a significant degree by the materials with which he worked."

Petitioners contended that the statements of Joiner's experts regarding causation were nothing more than speculation. Petitioners criticized the testimony of the experts in that it was "not supported by epidemiological studies ... [and was] based exclusively on isolated studies of laboratory animals." Joiner responded by claiming that his experts had identified "relevant animal studies which support their opinions." He also directed the court's attention to four epidemiological studies on which his experts had relied.

The District Court agreed with petitioners that the animal studies on which respondent's experts relied did not support his contention that exposure to PCB's had contributed to his cancer. The studies involved infant mice that had developed cancer after being exposed to PCB's. The infant mice in the studies had had massive doses of PCB's injected directly into their peritoneums or stomachs. Joiner was an adult human being whose alleged exposure to PCB's was far less than the exposure in the animal studies. The PCB's were injected into the mice in a highly concentrated form. The fluid with which Joiner had come into contact generally had a much smaller PCB concentration.... The cancer that these mice developed was alveologenic adenomas; Joiner had developed small-cell carcinomas. No study demonstrated that adult mice developed cancer after being exposed to PCB's....

Respondent failed to reply to this criticism. Rather than explaining how and why the experts could have extrapolated their opinions from these seemingly far-removed animal studies, respondent chose "to proceed as if the only issue [was] whether animal studies can ever be a proper foundation for an expert's opinion." Of course, whether animal studies can ever be a proper foundation for an expert's opinion was not the issue. The issue was whether *these* experts' opinions were sufficiently supported by the animal studies on which they purported to rely. The studies were so dissimilar to the facts presented in this litigation that it was not an abuse of discretion for the District Court to have rejected the experts' reliance on them....

Respondent points to *Daubert*'s language that the "focus, of course, must be solely on principles and methodology, not on the conclusions that they generate." 509 U.S. at 595. He claims that because the District Court's disagreement was with the conclusion that the experts drew from the studies, the District Court committed legal error and was properly reversed by the Court of Appeals. But conclusions and methodology are not entirely distinct from one another. Trained experts commonly extrapolate from existing data. But nothing in either *Daubert* or the Federal Rules of Evidence requires a district court to admit opinion evidence that is connected to existing data only by the *ipse dixit* of the expert. A court may conclude that there is simply too great an analytical gap between the data and the opinion proffered....

We hold, therefore, that abuse of discretion is the proper standard by which to review a district court's decision to admit or exclude scientific evidence. We further hold that, because it was within the District Court's discretion to conclude that the studies upon which the experts relied were not sufficient, whether individually or in combination, to support their conclusions that Joiner's exposure to PCB's contributed to his cancer, the District Court did not abuse its discretion in excluding their testimony....

BREYER, J, concurring.

The Court's opinion, which I join, emphasizes *Daubert*'s statement that a trial judge, acting as "gatekeeper," must "'ensure that any and all scientific testimony or evidence admitted is not only relevant, but reliable.'" This requirement will sometimes ask judges to make subtle and sophisticated determinations about scientific methodology and its relation to the conclusions an expert witness seeks to offer—particularly when a case arises in an area where the science itself is tentative or uncertain, or where testimony about general risk levels in human beings or animals is offered to prove individual causation. Yet, as amici have pointed out, judges are not scientists and do not have the scientific training that can facilitate the making of such decisions.... Of course, neither the difficulty of the task nor any comparative lack of expertise can excuse the judge from exercising the "gatekeeper" duties that the Federal Rules impose—determining, for example, whether particular expert testimony is reliable and "will assist the trier of fact"....

... It is, thus, essential in this science-related area that the courts administer the Federal Rules of Evidence in order to achieve the "end[s]" that the Rules themselves set forth, not only so that proceedings may be "justly determined," but also so "that the truth may be ascertained." Fed. R. Evid. 102.

I therefore want specially to note that, as cases presenting significant science-related issues have increased in number, judges have increasingly found in the Rules of Evidence and Civil Procedure ways to help them overcome the inherent difficulty of making determinations about complicated scientific or otherwise technical evidence. Among these techniques are an increased use of Rule 16's pretrial conference authority to narrow the scientific issues in dispute, pretrial hearings where potential experts are subject to examination by the court, and the appointment of special masters and specially trained law clerks....

Notes and Questions

1. In *Daubert*, did the Court lower or heighten the bar of admission for expert evidence and/or testimony? Will the new gatekeeping standard let in more or less evidence than the general acceptance standard that preceded it? Regardless of the Court's intent, we will examine the "true effect" of *Daubert* in Part 2.D(iii).

2. Chief Justice Rehnquist asked an important question about the applicability of the so-called *Daubert* factors in his concurrence and dissent: "Does all of this *dicta* apply to an expert seeking to testify on the basis of 'technical or other specialized knowledge'—the other types of expert knowledge to which Rule 702 applies—or are the 'general observations' limited only to 'scientific knowledge'?" After 1993, federal appellate courts split on this issue, with some finding that gatekeeping applied to all experts and others finding it applied only to "scientific" experts. *Compare, e.g., Watkins v. Telsmith, Inc.*, 121 F.3d 984 (5th Cir. 1997)

(finding gatekeeping applies to all experts), *with Compton v. Subaru of Am., Inc.*, 82 F.3d 1513 (10th Cir. 1996) (gatekeeping only for scientific experts).

In 1999, the Supreme Court resolved the dispute in *Kumho Tire Co. v. Carmichael*, 526 U.S. 137 (1999), the final "*Daubert* trilogy" case. In the opinion, Justice Breyer explains why gatekeeping analysis must apply to all expert testimony under Rule 702:

> In *Daubert*, this Court held that Federal Rule of Evidence 702 imposes a special obligation upon a trial judge to "ensure that any and all scientific testimony ... is not only relevant, but reliable." 509 U.S. at 589. The initial question before us is whether this basic gatekeeping obligation applies only to "scientific" testimony or to all expert testimony. We, like the parties, believe that it applies to all expert testimony.
>
> For one thing, Rule 702 itself says:
>
> If scientific, technical, or other specialized knowledge will assist the trier of fact to understand the evidence or to determine a fact in issue, a witness qualified as an expert by knowledge, skill, experience, training, or education, may testify thereto in the form of an opinion or otherwise.
>
> This language makes no relevant distinction between "scientific" knowledge and "technical" or "other specialized" knowledge. It makes clear that any such knowledge might become the subject of expert testimony. In *Daubert*, the Court specified that it is the Rule's word "knowledge," not the words (like "scientific") that modify that word, that "establishes a standard of evidentiary reliability." 509 U.S. at 589–90. Hence, as a matter of language, the Rule applies its reliability standard to all "scientific," "technical," or "other specialized" matters within its scope. We concede that the Court in *Daubert* referred only to "scientific" knowledge. But as the Court there said, it referred to "scientific" testimony "because that [wa]s the nature of the expertise" at issue. *Id.* at 590, n. 8.
>
> Neither is the evidentiary rationale that underlay the Court's basic *Daubert* "gatekeeping" determination limited to "scientific" knowledge." ... The Rules grant that latitude to all experts, not just to "scientific" ones.
>
> Finally, it would prove difficult, if not impossible, for judges to administer evidentiary rules under which a gatekeeping obligation depended upon a distinction between "scientific" knowledge and "technical" or "other specialized" knowledge. There is no clear line that divides the one from the others....

Kumho Tire Co., 526 U.S. at 147–48. Per *Kumho*, all expertise should be subjected to reliability analysis prior to admission. Yet when looking at the *Daubert* factors, they were clearly authored with the labcoat-and-beaker-type science in mind. So how do these factors apply practically? First, it is necessary to recognize that the *Daubert* factors are factually relevant to the proffered evidence in a specific dispute. So, in a similar case involving facts or evidence that heavily rely on science and lab-work (our "labcoat-and-beaker" body of evidence), those factors would likely provide significant guidance. However, in a case where an expert relies on specialized knowledge which is not lab-tested, those factors may or may not help at all. In *Kumho*, Breyer recognized this concern by highlighting that: "the test of reliability is flexible, and *Daubert*'s list of specific factors neither necessarily nor exclusively applies to all experts or in every case. Rather, the law grants a district court the same broad latitude when it decides *how* to determine reliability as it enjoys in respect to its ultimate reliability determination." *Kumho*, 526 U.S. at 141–42. Really, what courts need to avoid is allowing experts to testify based on the *ipse dixit* of the expert ("Because I said so"). *Id.* at 158 (citing *Joiner*, 522 U.S. at 146). As we will examine later, this *ipse dixit* basis for testimony will give courts difficulty, particularly in experience-based fields like some forensic fields.

3. In *Joiner*, the Court adopts the "abuse of discretion" standard for appellate review of a trial court's decision on reliability under Rule 702 and *Daubert*. What were the other options? What was the effect of the Court choosing this appellate standard, as compared to the alternative? Ultimately, one must consider *why* the Court adopted a high bar for an appeals court to overturn a lower court's review of evidence. What message is the Court sending to the District Court judges with this opinion?

4. Any time a litigant challenges expert testimony as unreliable, the judge will admit or exclude the evidence with findings on the record. Judges have significant leeway in performing this gatekeeping function, under *Daubert* and *Joiner*. Faced with a new and complex science, what do judges do? What factors are most important to them? Before reading Part 2.D(iii) below, think about how you, as a judge, might approach this task.

Tying It Together

Donna Dean had a tough day at work, and after agreeing to take several co-workers home at the end of the day, she was regretting the decision. On Long Branch Road—a country road with one lane of traffic in each direction—she spotted Wendy driving ahead of her. As a prank, she decided to pass Wendy's car on the left as coworkers shouted at Wendy. Donna's passing speed is disputed in the case, but by all accounts, she clearly exceeded the 40-mph limit. After the prank, she re-entered the right lane ahead of Wendy and then started to slow down. It was too late.

Violet Vargas had also had a tough day at work, and she was eager to get home. When she approached the intersection of Long Branch Road and Third Avenue, Violet stopped and turned left onto Long Branch Road at or near the time Donna had passed Wendy. Only three seconds after she turned left, Donna's car clipped Violet's, spinning it 180 degrees and causing a rollover. Violet died instantly in the crash, and Donna's car careened off the road into a field.

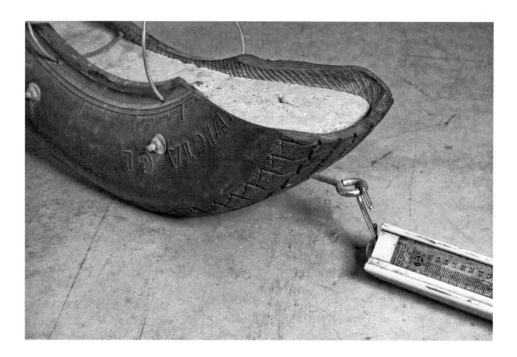

Captain Charles of the Polk County Police, an accident reconstructionist certified by the Institute of Police Technology and Management,[15] visited the scene, reviewed evidence already gathered by the responding law enforcement officials, and performed on-site testing. As part of his process, he pulled a drag sled—a weighted sled with attached scales (see photo above)[16]—over the road and grass surfaces where the vehicles had traveled. He used a mathematical formula to determine the "drag factor," or the amount of friction existing between a moving vehicle and the ground, generated by these surfaces. He incorporated the drag factors, estimated vehicle weights, post-crash travel distances, and braking estimates into other formulas to calculate the momentum required to move the vehicles from the point of impact over those surfaces to their final resting positions. Working backward from these calculations, and accounting for the energy absorbed by the crash, the officer concluded that Donna was driving 61 mph at the time of the collision. The District Attorney charged Donna with negligent homicide in the death.

Before trial, Donna filed a motion *in limine* asking for exclusion of Capt. Charles's speed calculation for failing to meet the requirements of *Daubert*. At a subsequent *Daubert* hearing, Charles testified that the mathematical formulas used to calculate defendant's speed are standardized, tested, published, and nationally accepted within his field, with a potential margin of error that he mitigated by using conservative estimates when making assumptions about certain variables. He also testified that he applied these calculations to the facts of the collision in accordance with his crash reconstruction training. He agreed that using a drag sled on grass instead of pavement

---

15. INST. OF POLICE TECH. & MGMT., http://iptm.unf.edu/default.aspx.
16. Photo used with permission of the photographer, Steve Foritano.

was not ideal, but explained that it was the best technique available to him to estimate the drag factor—an essential factor in his speed calculations—of that surface. In response, Donna called Jane Jackson, a leading expert in the field of accident reconstruction, to testify that drag sleds can precisely determine drag factor over dry, paved surfaces, but that they lack accuracy on other surfaces. In fact, she testified that even the American Prosecutor's Research Manual unequivocally states "The drag sled should not be used to measure the drag factor on wet roads … [or] on grass, as it cannot accurately produce the same friction as a full-sized vehicle, whose weight furrows the tires into the ground when it travels."[17]

After the hearing, Judge Roy Bean found that Charles's analysis could be presented at trial. The jury convicted Donna of the charge of negligent homicide, and she appealed.

Assignment: Please prepare a memo evaluating the testimony of Capt. Charles in the case of *State of Polk v. Donna Dean*, from the perspective of either the prosecution or defense.

iii. Empirical Data on Gatekeeping Factors and Methodology

Andrew W. Jurs, *Gatekeeper with a Gavel:*
A Survey Evaluating Judicial Management of Challenges to Expert Reliability and Their Relationship to Summary Judgment
83 Miss. L.J. 325 (2014)

Daubert's gatekeeping standard has, since 1993, granted judges extraordinary authority to screen expert evidence in federal court. To screen the evidence, judges have been given a series of substantive factors to consider, and the Supreme Court has suggested several procedural methods to evaluate complex evidence. Beyond that guidance, judges have a wide range of discretion to do their work.

In the decade after *Daubert*, a series of studies inquired into judicial handling of the new gatekeeping authority. The studies evaluated the frequency of motions challenging expert evidence, the procedural methods used to evaluate evidence, and the substantive factors judges used to decide contested expert issues.… But many studies explicitly recognize that additional research is needed, and the age of the studies suggest updating their findings.…

Using a survey methodology, this Study will analyze reliability motions in trial courts by examining the frequency, procedural methodology, and substantive factors used to handle those motions. That portion of the Study will update the prior research in the area, shed light on the judicial handling of reliability motions now that *Daubert* is twenty years old, and provide a comparison to previous data to see if judicial gatekeeping has changed.…

---

17. *Crash Reconstruction Basics for Prosecutors: Targeting Hardcore Impaired Drivers*, Am. Prosecutors Research Inst. (Mar. 2003), https://ndaa.org/wp-content/uploads/crash_reconstruction_basics.pdf.

I. PRIOR STUDIES ON JUDICIAL HANDLING OF RELIABILITY MOTIONS

The Supreme Court decision in *Daubert v. Merrell Dow Pharms., Inc.* was a watershed moment for expert evidence in federal court.... The gatekeeping function would permit judges to assess the merits of the science offered in court to ensure it met minimum standards.

To these ends, the Court has suggested both substantive factors to consider in gatekeeping and procedural methods to assist in that decision. To evaluate the reliability of evidence, the Court offered the following substantive factors: technique can and has been tested, peer review and publication, known or potential rate of error, standards for controlling the technique, and general acceptance within the scientific community. In a later case, *General Electric Co. v. Joiner*, Justice Breyer offered thoughts on the procedures that may assist a judge in those findings. Justice Breyer suggested that judges could use special masters, pretrial conferences, questioning from the bench, or independent experts to make findings on reliability;[15] each of these methods is contained within the Rules of Civil Procedure or Evidence.

Between 1993 and 2002, scholars and researchers repeatedly evaluated the effect of the change in judicial screening mandated by *Daubert*.... These studies were critically important in measuring the initial effects of *Daubert* and understanding how it changed ... gatekeeping....

A. *Reliability Motions — Empirical Studies*

To evaluate these studies, I will break them into several different subjects, discussing first the frequency of reliability issues ... then reviewing the procedures judges use [for] gatekeeping. Finally, I ... recap the prior work discussing the substantive factors used by judges to decide reliability.

1. Frequency of *Daubert* Gatekeeping Questions in Court

One question researchers wanted to measure was how often a reliability issue would arise in court. To measure the frequency, different studies used distinct methodologies.

Lloyd Dixon and Brian Gill measured the frequency of reliability determinations using statistical analysis of cases appearing on a computerized database in their 2001 study.[17] By using this method, the researchers could measure the absolute frequency of the motions, as well as the change in the frequency over time. In their analysis, they found that, not only had the rate of reliability assessment risen after *Daubert*, but that the rate of excluding evidence as unreliable also was increasing. For example, the likelihood of a reliability issue being raised was between 68% and 71% in the four years prior to *Daubert*, and 76% to 89% in the four years afterward. Similarly, the likelihood of evidence being found unreliable went from 36%–39% to 51%–70% in the same time period. Dixon and Gill conclude "the results ... suggest that the standards for reliability tightened in

---

15. Gen. Elec. Co. v. Joiner, 522 U.S. 136, 147–50 (1997) (Breyer, J., concurring).

17. Lloyd Dixon & Brian Gill, RAND Institute for Civil Justice, Changes in the Standards for Admitting Expert Evidence in Federal Civil Cases Since the *Daubert* Decision 15–24 (2001).

the years after the *Daubert* decision. The success rate for challenges rose, encouraging an increase in the proportion of challenges that targeted reliability." ...

In a study from 2002, Carol Krafka and her colleagues used a survey methodology to measure how often judges reported facing a reliability motion.[23] While Krafka is careful to note that the survey cannot measure the absolute frequency of reliability issues arising, the survey could measure the frequency judges report reliability issues arising in their most recent expert case, and compare the results to a pre-*Daubert* survey result. The 1998 survey finds that expert admissibility questions, when raised, were handled more often by a motion *in limine* (72% of cases) than at trial (64%). This contrasts greatly with survey data from 1991, when Krafka reports judges handled expert admissibility at trial in 79% of cases, while addressing it in a motion *in limine* in 32% of cases....

One final study, also from 2002, again addresses the frequency of reliability challenges. Using a database analysis technique evaluating reported cases, Jennifer Groscup and her colleagues evaluated how often *Daubert* issues arose in criminal cases.[28] In reviewing state and federal cases, Groscup found that over 74% of experts had been admitted at the trial court level. At the appellate level, the rate of admittance remained very high, at 69.1%. Groscup found that these rates did not change based on the *Daubert* shift, but that the party offering the testimony did demonstrate an effect; prosecution experts were significantly more likely to be admitted (95.8%) than defense experts (7.8%) at the trial level.

So while Dixon and Gill, Krafka, and Groscup provide some data on the frequency of *Daubert* reliability challenges, the data is far from complete. In addition, the studies rely on surveys from 1991 and 1998 or a database of cases decided between 1980–1999 (Dixon and Gill) or 1988–1998 (Groscup)....

2. Procedural Methodology of Handling Gatekeeping

Prior studies did not just analyze the frequency of reliability motions, but they also measured the procedures used by judges to decide them. In this area, survey research was particularly important in measuring how judges report their handling of the motions.

Krafka's 2002 study evaluated data from a 1998 survey of federal judges, which asked them about the methods used in court addressing expert issues. Krafka asked judges about many methods, including: clarifying questions from the bench, expert reports under Fed. R. Civ. P. 26, *Daubert* hearings, pretrial conferences under Fed. R. Civ. P. 16, independent experts, special masters under Fed. R. Civ. P. 53, and others. Judges used some of the techniques, such as questions from the bench, *Daubert* hearings, or pretrial conferences, in any case involving an expert. The judges reserved other methods for complex ... [cases, including]: independent experts, special masters, or requesting instruction from the parties on their expertise....

---

23. Carol Krafka et al., *Judge and Attorney Experiences, Practices, and Concerns Regarding Expert Testimony in Federal Civil Trials*, 8 PSYCHOL. PUB. POL'Y & L. 309, 321 (2002).

28. Jennifer Groscup et al., *The Effects of* Daubert *on the Admissibility of Expert Testimony in State and Federal Criminal Cases*, 8 PSYCHOL. PUB. POL'Y & L. 339, 342–44 (2002).

State court judges handle reliability inquires as well. Shirley Dobbin and her colleagues reported on state court judges' responses to a survey in a 2007 study. Dobbin found that state court judges are less likely to use clarifying questions from the bench (69% would use).[38] State court judges were also less likely to ask for special instruction from the parties (29% would use, vs. 39% of federal judges). However, state judges are more likely to use an independent expert, since 36% would do so (compared to 26% of federal judges).... Krafka and Dobbin provide a snapshot of the methodology of handling expert reliability motions ... [but as] with the research on frequency of reliability issues arising, the surveys rely on data from the 1990s....

B. *Substantive Factors Used to Evaluate Reliability*

Beyond how often and by what methods judges evaluate reliability, empirical research has also evaluated the substantive factors judges use in deciding expert motions. *Daubert* itself suggested five factors for judges to consider, but research would be needed to decide if these factors are being used and which are most helpful.

Using statistical tools to analyze their database of published cases, Dixon and Gill could measure how often the *Daubert* factors appeared in reported case decisions. Not surprisingly, after 1993's *Daubert* decision, the incidence of the five factors increased dramatically. Dixon and Gill found a statistically significant rise in the mention of the factors in the years after 1993, particularly in the period two-to-four years after *Daubert*. After 1997, the incidence of the factors appearing lessens, perhaps due to a more experienced judicial gatekeeper narrowly focusing on the contested issue. Finally, Dixon and Gill found the two factors of general acceptance and peer review remain most relevant to judicial inquiries in the last measured period, in that order.

Groscup's work mirrors this result about relative importance of the factors, again using analysis of published opinions from a major commercial database. When analyzing the importance of the *Daubert* factors, Groscup found that the importance of all factors was low in comparison with other non-factor considerations such as relevance, reliability, or expert qualifications. But when comparing solely the *Daubert* factors, the two factors that seem to be most important in assessing expert admissibility are general acceptance and peer review.... [B]oth Dixon and Gill and Groscup have found, using statistical assessment of different opinions in a computerized database, that error rate and falsifiability are the less-helpful factors.

Survey data support these findings as well. In her 2001 study, Sophia Gatowski and her research group surveyed 400 state court judges about scientific evidence and gatekeeping.[51] Of the four factors, Gatowski also found general acceptance to be the most likely *Daubert* factor to be used by a judge in assessing reliability. Of all judges

38. Shirley A. Dobbin et al., *Federal and State Trial Judges on the Proffer and Presentation of Expert Evidence*, 28 Just. Sys. J. 1 (2007).

51. Sophia Gatowski et al., *Asking the Gatekeepers: A National Survey of Judges on Judging Expert Evidence in a Post-Daubert World*, 25 Law & Hum. Behav. 433, 441 (2001).

surveyed, 93% found general acceptance useful in assessing the merits of scientific evidence, with 64% finding the factor very useful. Slightly fewer judges, at 92%, felt that peer review was useful at all, with 52% finding it was very useful. Error rate at 91% (and 54% very useful) and falsifiability at 88% (38% very useful) were less often cited as critical to assessing expert evidence.

Just as with the studies on the frequency of reliability assessment and procedural methods of handling reliability issues, the data on substantive factors is very helpful but ... dated....

III. A NEW SURVEY ON JUDICIAL HANDLING OF GATEKEEPING

Considering the coverage and age of prior research on expert reliability motions, I decided to empirically study the frequency of, procedural methodology for, and substantive factors relevant to deciding challenges to expert reliability....

A. *Study Methodology*

To these ends, I created a survey for state court trial judges.... I ... wanted to pick states that had different standards for determining the reliability of scientific evidence, so that some judges would have *Daubert* as their home standard and others would not. This would allow for analysis of variations in handling motions based on the home-state standard. States were then grouped by region, and for each region I needed a state that had a *Daubert* admissibility standard and one that retained the *Frye* standard so that I could cross-compare different factors. Finally, each state would need to have similar evidentiary and procedural rules in the relevant areas including: independent experts, pretrial conferences, questions from the bench, and special masters. With all these considerations, choosing states involved substantial background research.

Based on an initial analysis of potential states, I chose the following states for the survey: Alabama, Mississippi, New Mexico, Arizona, Minnesota, and Michigan. The sample included three states that have adopted the *Daubert* standard—Mississippi, New Mexico, and Michigan—and three states that have continued using the *Frye* standard—Alabama, Arizona,[Ed.] and Minnesota. The states also break into three distinct regions—South (AL & MS), West (AZ & NM), and Midwest (MN & MI)—each with one *Daubert* and one *Frye* state. Finally, each state has similar rules of evidence and procedure in the important areas of summary judgment, independent experts, questions from the bench, pretrial conferences, and special masters. The states selected offered the best available combination of the important factors.... The initial survey group included a total of 996 participants.

Every judge meeting the sample qualifications received an initial letter explaining the survey and its general goals, along with an explanation of how to participate.... Following the second round of participation, the Study includes a final survey group of 158 judges....

[Ed.] Arizona used the *Frye* standard until January 1, 2012.

Figure 1: Frequency of Motions Challenging Expert Reliability,
in All Cases with Experts

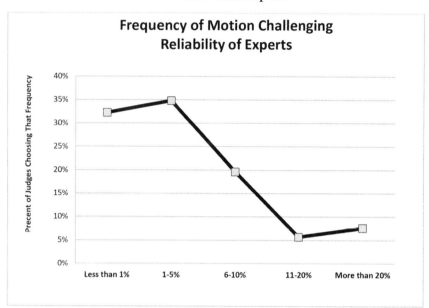

C. *Judicial Handling of Reliability Motions*

Judges taking the survey answered a variety of questions discussing reliability motions challenging expert testimony, starting with questions about their frequency. The first question on frequency of motions asked judges: "In what percentage of cases with expert witnesses do you see a motion challenging the reliability of expert testimony?" A substantial majority of judges believed such motions occurred in less than 5% of cases with experts, with 32% answering that the motion occurred in less than 1% of cases ($n = 51$), and an additional 35% answering that the motion occurred between 1% and 5% of the time ($n = 55$). This compares to a total of 33% who believed the motions were in 6% or more of cases with experts ($n = 52$).

After asking about the frequency with which judges see reliability motions, the survey asked all judges what substantive factors they believe are helpful in deciding the motion. The possible responses included the "*Daubert* factors" of: technique can and has been tested, subjected to peer review and publication, known or potential rate of error, existence of standards controlling the technique, and general acceptance. Judges were instructed to choose any factors they believed were helpful [or could choose "other" and explain].... Judicial responses are recorded below in Figure 2, with the most helpful factors being general acceptance and testing while the least helpful factor was rate of error.

... For those judges who have ruled on a motion challenging expert reliability, the survey then asked what procedural techniques were helpful in ruling on the motion. The possible responses to this question included the suggested methods of Justice Breyer from *Joiner*: questioning a witness from the bench, independent expert, special

Figure 2: Substantive Factors Judges Believe Are Helpful to Decide a Motion Challenging Expert Reliability

	Number Who Believe the Factor is Helpful	Percentage
Technique Can And Has Been Tested	143	90.5
Subjected To Peer Review And Publication	139	87.8
Known Or Potential Rate Of Error	111	70.2
Existence Of Standards Controlling The Technique	128	81.0
General Acceptance	152	96.2
Other	8	5.1
	Total = 158	

master, or hearings (with or without testimony presented).[112] Judges were again instructed to choose any factors they believed were helpful....

Judicial responses to this question are recorded below in Figure 3. Judges who have ruled on reliability motions are most likely to use a hearing with testimony to decide the motion, and least likely to use a special master under Rule 53 or an Independent Expert under Rule 706.

Besides asking specifically about the procedural methods and substantive considerations in deciding expert reliability motions, the survey also asked judges to rate their overall comfort with that type of motion. For this question, and for all questions asked about judicial comfort with evaluating or granting motions, the survey asked judges to rate their comfort level on a scale from one to seven, with one being "Entirely Comfortable" and seven being "Not Comfortable." This question was asked of all judges taking the survey.

When asked to rate their comfort level with reliability challenges on this scale, a majority (55%; $n = 87$) answered the question with one or two, with 20.3% at "1" and 34.8% at "2" (1: $n = 32$; 2: $n = 55$). Other answers were less frequent, with 18.4% answering "3" ($n = 29$), 12% answering "4" ($n = 19$), and 7% answering both "5" and "6" (5: $n = 11$; 6: $n = 11$). One judge answered "7" on this question.

...

F. Comparing Judges Based on Home-State Admissibility Standard

In addition to reviewing the responses of all judges, I also decided to break the judges into groups based on their home-state expert admissibility standard, to determine if there are any statistically significant differences between the judges applying a different standard. Differences between judges applying different standards could signal the importance of the change in the substantive law of admissibility after *Daubert*....

---

112. *Joiner*, 522 U.S. at 147–50 (Breyer, J., concurring).

Figure 3: Procedural Methods Used by Judges to
Decide Reliability Motions

	Number Who Have Used the Technique	Percentage
Hearing With Testimony Presented	101	85.6
Hearing Without Testimony Presented	63	53.4
Questioning a Witness From the Bench	64	54.2
Independent Expert	9	7.6
Special Master	4	3.4
Other	10	8.4
	Total = 118	

In analyzing the response data, many areas did not show statistically significant differences.... However, there are some interesting and significant differences between the judges based on their home-state reliability standard.... On the critical issue of which gatekeeping standard is more likely to exclude evidence, judges from *Daubert* jurisdictions and judges from *Frye* jurisdictions ... differed significantly. When asked directly which standard is the stricter one for analyzing reliability, *Frye* judges were nearly evenly split: 50.4% believed that *Daubert* is the stricter standard, while 49.6% chose the *Frye* standard ($n = 57, 56$). On the other hand, judges who serve in a

Figure 4: Comfort Level with a Motion Challenging Reliability of
Expert Evidence, All Judges

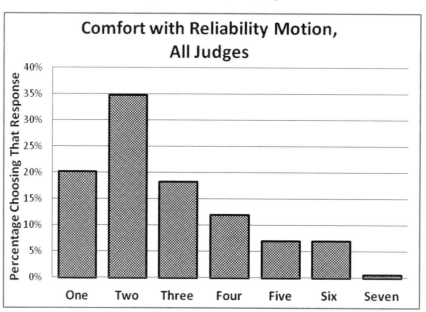

Daubert jurisdiction, and who therefore would have more familiarity with how that standard worked, were not evenly divided. A supermajority of 87% of those *Daubert* judges chose the *Daubert* standard as stricter, while only 13% chose *Frye* ($n = 39, 6$). This difference is statistically significant....

Notes and Questions

1. The data in the study above provides some indication of which substantive factors and which procedural methodologies judges use in evaluating reliability motions. Are these data consistent with the findings of the earlier studies? In what ways do they differ?

2. When we consider the comfort level of judges in deciding reliability motions, what conclusions can we draw? Are these data helpful to litigants when they consider filing a motion challenging or defending expert reliability? For a deeper discussion of judicial comfort with reliability, and background to perform these tasks, see *infra*, Part 2.D(iv).

3. In *Gatekeeper with a Gavel*, the survey asked judges which standard—*Frye* or *Daubert*—is more likely to exclude evidence. Overall, the results did not show a large difference, until they were broken down by "home state" standard. Judges from *Frye* states evenly split between *Frye* and *Daubert*, but judges from *Daubert* states overwhelmingly chose their home-state *Daubert* standard. Why might this be so? If asked which standard is "stricter," what then does this data suggest? Think about this issue as we examine that puzzle in a different way with the studies in Part 2.D(iv) below.

iv. Problems with Judicial Gatekeeping

Figure 4 in *Gatekeeper with a Gavel* examines the judicial comfort level with deciding reliability motions. It turns out that judges are less comfortable with reliability motions than they are with motions for summary judgment: 86% of judges were at levels 1 & 2 for summary judgment, but only 55% were at 1 or 2 for reliability analysis. Why might this be so?

Two studies bear upon this question, each discussing the judicial background and fitness for the task of gatekeeping. As we examine those studies below, think about the *Daubert* Court's statement: "We are confident that federal judges possess the capacity to undertake this review."[17] Should we be confident, or recognize the concerns of the Chief Justice when he said "... I do not think [Rule 702] imposes on [judges] either the obligation or the authority to become amateur scientists."[18] Can judges perform gatekeeping without becoming amateur scientists? Or do we expect too much of them? If we do not expect deep scientific knowledge, then what tools do judges have to assist them, and will they use them?

---

17. *Daubert*, 509 U.S. at 593.
18. *Daubert*, 509 U.S. at 600–01 (Rehnquist, C.J., concurring in part and dissenting in part).

Sophia Gatowski, et al., *Asking the Gatekeepers: A National Survey of Judges on Judging Expert Evidence in a Post-*Daubert *World*

25 Law & Hum. Behav. 433 (2001)[Ed.]

In the wake of *Daubert* and subsequent cases upholding and extending its scope and applicability, a large body of scholarship continues to debate the merits of the *Daubert* criteria as judicial decision-making guidelines. Included in this debate are discussions of the relative importance of each of the criteria to the admissibility decision and procedures for their application, [and] the extent to which judges understand and can properly apply the criteria when assessing the validity and reliability of proffered scientific evidence.... Although almost all of this past discourse about *Daubert* and its progeny recognizes that judges are central and active figures in admissibility decision-making, and becoming increasingly more so as a result of recent legal decisions, rarely have judges themselves been asked for their opinions and experiences with respect to *Daubert*, their gatekeeping role, and the admissibility decision-making process.

Typically, empirical research about the impact of *Daubert* has focused on analysis of published appellate opinions, often imposing artificial criteria to infer conclusions about the utility and relevance of *Daubert* to admissibility decisions, the scientific literacy of judges, and the extent to which there is a differential application of *Daubert* to different domains of expert testimony. While providing important insight regarding the influence of *Daubert*, an empirical analysis of published case law is, by its very nature, restricted to an analysis of post hoc justifications of those writing a decision in a particular.... Thus, information about judges' decision-making processes obtained from judicial opinions may differ in important ways from information obtained when judges are simply asked to talk about the process of making admissibility decisions in a survey.... Although judges who are being surveyed or interviewed are still speaking from their position as a judge, they may be less constrained because their anonymity is protected and the potential for appellate review is removed....

To add to what is being learned from analyses of case law and in order to shed light on the judicial perspective with respect to current debates about *Daubert*, we turned to the gatekeepers themselves with the following overarching questions in mind.

- What do judges think about the intent and value of *Daubert*?

- Do judges see the role of "gatekeeper" as an appropriate one?

- Can judges operationalize *Daubert*'s scientific concepts and appropriately use them as decision-making guides? ...

Drawing on the responses provided by a national survey of state trial court judges (N = 400), this paper presents empirical evidence regarding judicial opinions about the *Daubert* criteria, their utility as decision-making guidelines, and their applicability to different domains of expert knowledge. By asking judges directly, the results of this national survey provide important information about whether judges are able to operationalize the *Daubert* criteria....

METHOD

The primary purpose of the national survey was to assess the level to which the judiciary understand the scientific meaning of the *Daubert* guidelines and how they might apply them when evaluating the admissibility of scientific evidence. In addition to assessing the scientific literacy of judges, the survey also asked respondents for their opinions about the relevance and utility of the *Daubert* criteria to the judicial gatekeeping role ...

Survey Sample

Construction of the sampling frame began with the generation of a list of eligible sample elements using the 1997–1998 edition of THE AMERICAN BENCH.... To be included in the sampling frame, a judge either had to be sitting on the bench of the state trial court of general jurisdiction or on the bench of a court of special jurisdiction hearing a docket likely to contain the types of evidence of interest to this research.... Given the complexity and length of the telephone survey, and the status and professional distance of the sample population, an estimated sample size of 1,264 was drawn in order to achieve the goal of 400 completed interviews ...

Can Judges Operationalize *Daubert*'s Scientific Concepts and Appropriately Use Them as Decision-Making Guides?

Falsifiability

The majority of the judges surveyed (88%, n = 352), regardless of the admissibility standard followed in their state, believed falsifiability to be a useful guideline for determining the merits of proffered scientific evidence. In fact, only 8% (n = 32) of the judges surveyed reported that falsifiability was "not at all useful" as a decision-making tool.

As a follow-up to the question about the utility of the guideline, judges were asked to discuss how they would apply the guideline of "falsifiability" in determining the admissibility of proffered scientific evidence....

From the answers that were provided, the researchers could only infer a true understanding of the scientific meaning of falsifiability in 6% (n = 23 of 400) of the judges' responses. In fact, for the 352 judges who indicated that falsifiability was a useful criterion, the coders could only infer a true understanding of the concept in 4% of the responses elicited.... Just over one third of the judges (35%, n = 140 of 400) provided a response that clearly indicated that the judge did not understand the scientific meaning of falsifiability.... Interestingly, despite the general sense of hesitancy in providing a response regarding how they would use the criterion of falsifiability when making an admissibility decision, only 16% of the judges surveyed asked for a definition or further explication of the guideline....

Error Rate

The vast majority of judges (91%, n = 364) indicated that a consideration of error rate was useful when determining the merits of proffered scientific evidence, with just over half (54%, n = 214) stating that it was "very useful."

Despite the general agreement that examining error rates when making an admissibility decision was useful, once again the responses revealed a general lack of understanding of the scientific meaning of error rate.... When asked a question about how they would apply the concept of error rate to a determination of admissibility, a clear understanding was revealed in only 4 % (n = 16) of the responses. For the 364 judges who indicated that error rate was a useful criterion, the coders could only infer a true understanding of the concept in 4% (15 of 364) of the responses provided. In 86% of the responses (n = 344 of 400) the judges' understanding of the concept was questionable at best ... and in 10% of responses (n = 40 of 400) judges clearly had little understanding of the scientific meaning of error rate.... [D]espite the general sense of hesitancy in providing a response regarding how they would use the criterion of error rate when making an admissibility decision, only one judge asked for a definition ... of the guideline....

Peer Review and Publication

The majority of the judges surveyed (92%, n = 368), regardless of admissibility standard followed in their state, felt that the concept of peer review was useful for determining the admissibility of expert evidence, with just over half (52%, n = 208) reporting that it was a "very useful" guideline. Only 6% (n = 24) of judge-respondents overall indicated that peer review was "not at all useful" in determining the admissibility of scientific evidence.

The majority of judges noted that they would be highly likely to reject anything not subjected to rigorous peer review analysis, and comments such as "substantial weight should be given to peer review as it gives the evidence credibility" were frequent. When asked how they might apply the concept of peer review to a determination of the admissibility of proffered evidence, most judges (71%, n = 284 of 400) provided responses that demonstrated a clear understanding of the scientific peer review process.... Only 10% of the respondents (n = 39) gave a response that clearly reflected a lack of understanding with respect to the application of peer review and publication in the decision-making process. Five percent of the respondents asked for a definition of "peer review and publication" before providing a response.

General Acceptance

Not surprisingly, the vast majority of judges (93%, n = 371), regardless of operating admissibility standard, indicated that general acceptance was a useful criterion for determining the merits of the proffered scientific evidence, with 64% (n = 254) indicating that it was a "very useful" guideline. Again, not surprisingly given its relation to the *Frye* standard, the majority of judges (82%, n = 328) also demonstrated a clear understanding of the concept of general acceptance when asked to discuss how they would apply the guideline to the admissibility of expert evidence. In fact, no judge asked for a definition of general acceptance before providing a response....

Andrew W. Jurs, *Questions from the Bench and Independent Experts: A Study of the Practices of State Court Judges*

74 U. Pitt. L. Rev. 47 (2012)

Research conducted since 1993 demonstrates that judges see themselves as generally more active in gatekeeping since *Daubert*.[1] Yet, nearly twenty years later, very few studies have tested the specific methods used by judges in their gatekeeping role. In *General Electric Co. v. Joiner*, Justice Breyer's concurrence noted that while judges may lack a background in complex science, the Rules of Evidence and Rules of Civil Procedure already contain methods helpful for *Daubert* gatekeeping. Breyer suggests that any judge facing an issue involving expert testimony may wish to resort to advanced fact-finding techniques including: examination of the potential expert by the court, appointment of an independent expert to assist the court, use of additional pretrial conferences, or delegation to special masters. Do judges follow this advice?

This Study helps to answer that question by investigating the actual judicial use of, frequency of use of, and reasons for use of advanced fact-finding methodologies. Specifically, the Study focuses on the two evidentiary methods suggested by Justice Breyer—judicial questioning under Rule 614 and appointment of independent experts under Rule 706— ... to [help] determine whether the judiciary has the tools necessary to perform gatekeeping....

III. A NEW SURVEY REGARDING EVIDENCE RULES 614 AND 706

To further evaluate the use of advanced fact-finding techniques in the Rules of Evidence, this Study asked state court judges in the Midwestern United States about their use of these techniques....

A. Methodology

This IRB-approved Study assesses the use, frequency of use, and reasons for use of advanced fact-finding methodologies in the Rules of Evidence by state trial court judges. To achieve that goal, the Study surveyed state trial court judges in several states to determine their usage of judicial questioning from the bench and appointment of independent experts.

i. *Selection of Methods to Study*

Prior to the design of a survey or the selection of a sample, the Study initially had to determine which advanced fact-finding methods to evaluate. The final selection included the judicial use of questioning from the bench and the appointment of in-

---

1. *See, e.g., The Changing Role of Judges in the Admissibility of Expert Evidence*, Civil Action (Nat'l Ctr. for St. Cts., Williamsburg, Va.) Spring 2006, at 1, 1–4 (hereinafter *Changing Role*) (showing through a survey of judges that judges believe they have a more active role since *Daubert*); Carol Krafka et al., *Judge and Attorney Experiences, Practices, and Concerns Regarding Expert Testimony in Federal Civil Trials*, 8 Psychol. Pub. Pol'y & L. 309 (2002) (same); Sophia Gatowski et al., *Asking the Gatekeepers: A National Survey of Judges on Judging Expert Evidence in a Post-*Daubert *World*, 25 Law & Hum. Behav. 433 (2001) (same).

dependent experts. A brief word of explanation details why these specific methods were to be used.

Several factors led to the Study including solely these methods. First, both methods have long-standing precedent in common law prior to their inclusion in the Federal Rules of Evidence and similar state rules.... Second, the two methods included were the only methods from the Rules of Evidence to be specifically endorsed by Justice Breyer in *Joiner*.... A third reason to study these methods, particularly at this point in time, involves the age and timing of the previous studies.... Fourth, as *Daubert* ages, data suggest judges may be experiencing difficulty with managing complex evidence in the courtroom.[47] If judges are having difficulty with science and statistics, then judges themselves, along with policymakers and court administrators, should have accurate information on how other judges manage expert testimony in the courtroom. With appropriate data, parties can analyze if change is either mandated or desirable....

ii. *Selection of Sample*

To collect data on the use of advanced fact-finding, I began with lists of currently-appointed state court judges in three Midwestern states: Iowa, Nebraska, and North Dakota ... The initial survey group contained a total of 209 participants.

The three states selected for the Study—Iowa, Nebraska, and North Dakota—were selected due to several factors. First, each of the three selected states has Rules of Evidence for judicial questioning and independent experts that are nearly identical to each other and the Federal Rules of Evidence. Second, the states occupy a similar geographic area which may limit any effect of regional or cultural differences on the use of these techniques....

iii. *Survey Instrument and Response Rate*

Every judge meeting the sample qualifications received an initial survey, accompanied by a cover letter explaining the Study and its goals, and a stamped return envelope. The survey asked judges about their use of, and opinions regarding, advanced fact-finding methods.... Following the second wave of responses, the Study resulted in a final response group of 118 judges, for a total response rate of 56%.

B. Analysis of Survey Responses

Following collection of the survey responses, I analyzed the patterns of use for these fact-finding techniques among all respondents....

---

47. *See, e.g.*, Richard Lempert, *Befuddled Judges: Statistical Evidence in Title VII Cases*, *in* Legacies of the 1964 Civil Rights Act 263, 278 (Bernard Grofman ed., 2000); National Research Council, National Academy of Sciences, Evolving Role of Statistical Assessments as Evidence in the Courts 72 (S.E. Fienberg ed., 1989) ("[S]tatistical evidence poses problems for courts."); Stephen E. Fienberg, *The Increasing Sophistication of Statistical Assessments as Evidence in Discrimination Litigation*, 77 J. Am. Stat. Ass'n 784, 784 (1982) ("[C]ourts are increasingly presented with complex issues of measurement, sampling methodology, and statistical inference.")....

Figure 1: Percentage of Judges Who Use Each Fact-Finding Technique

	Number Who Have Used the Method	Percentage
614: Fact Witness	99	83.8
614: Expert Witness	69	58.4
706: Independent Expert	26	22.0
	Total Responses = 118	

i) *Do Judges Question Witnesses and Appoint Independent Experts?*
If So, How Often and Why?

Judges' use of the three methods of fact-finding varied widely between methods. Judges were much more likely to question a fact witness from the bench using Rule 614 than appoint an independent expert witness.

A substantial majority of the judges in the survey have used the authority of Rule 614 to question a fact witness from the bench. Of the judges surveyed, 84% have used this fact-finding tool (*n* = 99). This compares to 57% of judges who have questioned an expert witness pursuant to Rule 614, and 22% who have ever appointed an independent expert pursuant to Rule 706.

… In addition, since prior studies demonstrated that a majority of judges have not appointed an independent expert using Rule 706, the survey also asked judges to choose explanations why independent experts are not often used. The judges could choose from four specific options that might explain the rarity of independent expert appointment: lack of knowledge about the procedure, concern about interference with adversarial norms, rarity of cases where a Rule 706 expert is necessary, and the use of party experts make independent experts unnecessary. Judges could select any they deemed appropriate, or select an open-ended "other" category.

In comparing the reasons, the sole explanation that a substantial majority of judges believed explained the lack of use of Rule 706 was "concern about interference with the adversarial system," which 77% of judges chose (*n* = 91). A small majority of judges — 58% — also selected "rarity of cases which make a Rule 706 expert necessary" as an explanation (*n* = 69). Judges were almost evenly divided on whether "party experts make Rule 706 experts unnecessary," with 52.5% selecting this response (*n* = 62) while 47.5% did not (*n* = 56). A majority of judges rejected "lack of knowledge about the procedure" as the explanation for lack of use of the rule, with only 31% agreeing with this reason (*n* = 37). Finally, many of the judges who selected "other" as an explanation mentioned one issue — cost or payment of expenses — as the reason for lack of use of Rule 706….

Notes and Questions

1. Under *Daubert*, judges clearly have been given significant authority to decide whether proffered expert testimony meets the reliability standard, and is therefore

"good science." Whether judges have the skills and knowledge to effectively screen out unreliable scientific methodology is a question that has been debated since 1993. The Supreme Court in *Daubert* expressed high confidence in judges' abilities, although the Chief Justice suggested that perhaps this reliability screening would require judges to become "amateur scientists." Do judges have what it takes to perform gatekeeping skillfully? Empirical evidence on this question is mixed, although the Gatowski article provides some reason to be skeptical. While judges overwhelmingly endorsed the "*Daubert* factors" as helpful in deciding contested reliability questions, almost all judges could not demonstrate understanding of two of those factors: error rate and falsifiability. When asked if their background adequately prepared them to deal with scientific evidence in the courtroom, the Gatowski study found judges were evenly split—52% to 48%—on the question. Other studies provide similar evidence.

A comparable study in 2007 found judges possessed a similar level of math and science training as the general jury pool, but less than the college-educated component of the jury pool. Valerie P. Hans, *Judges, Juries, and Scientific Evidence*, 16 J. L. & Pol'y 19, 28–31 (2007). When asked questions about a hypothetical case involving DNA evidence, judges performed worse than college-educated jurors in analyzing scientific evidence. *Id.* at 37–38; *see also* Richard Lempert, *Befuddled Judges: Statistical Evidence in Title VII Cases*, in Legacies of the 1964 Civil Rights Act app. 2, at 263, 278 (Bernard Grofman ed., 2000); National Research Council, National Academy of Sciences, The Evolving Role of Statistical Assessments as Evidence in the Courts 72 (Stephen E. Fienberg ed., 1989). Justice Breyer has concluded, based on his assessment of the situation, that "[M]ost judges lack the scientific training that might facilitate the evaluation of scientific claims or the evaluation of expert witnesses who make such claims." Stephen Breyer, *Introduction*, in Fed. Jud. Ctr., Reference Manual on Scientific Evidence 1, 4 (2d ed. 2000).

2. If judges are asked to address difficult questions about admissibility, and may have inadequate preparation to do so, then how are they to perform their gatekeeping responsibilities? Justice Breyer's concurrence in *Joiner* offered some suggestions: ask questions from the bench (Fed. R. Evid. 614), hold pretrial conferences (Fed. R. Civ. P. 16), appoint special masters to oversee scientific questions (Fed. R. Civ. P. 53), or appoint an independent expert (Fed. R. Evid. 706). The last of these techniques—appointing an independent expert—is similar to how civil law nations handle complex science: by the appointment of an expert to assist the judge in handling the issues in the case. *See* Andrew W. Jurs, *Balancing Legal Process with Scientific Expertise: A Comparative Assessment of Expert Witness Methodology in Five Nations, and Suggestions for Reform of Post-Daubert U.S. Reliability Determinations*, 95 Marq. L. Rev. 1329, 1407 (2012). Could the civil law approach work here?

The judicial survey data from *Questions from the Bench and Independent Experts* seem to indicate the answer is no. In that survey, only 22% of judges had ever appointed an independent expert, and a majority stated that "concern about interference with the adversarial system" explains why judges do not appoint experts under Rule 706. *Jurs,* 74 U. PITT. L. REV. at 64. If this result is consistent with the experiences of most judges, then Justice Breyer's suggestion that judges use management tools in gatekeeping seems to fall on deaf ears.

3. Judges potentially lacking preparation to deal with complex science combined with infrequent use of techniques designed to assist them in the gatekeeping function has led many commentators to push for reform. We will discuss these reform suggestions in great detail in Chapter 11, once we have reviewed specific disciplines of expertise. Even at this early stage, however, we can wonder what effect *Daubert* has had, or is having, on real cases, and if judges are finding reliability screening difficult. Do they simply allow more evidence and let the jury sort it out? Or do they provide a significant road block to evidence admissibility, excluding it until proven reliable to a higher standard? Let us turn to that issue, as we finish our reliability section with a fundamental question:

v. Does it Matter? The Practical Effect of *Daubert* in the Judicial System

Andrew W. Jurs & Scott DeVito, *The Stricter Standard: An Empirical Assessment of* Daubert's *Effect on Civil Defendants*

62 CATH. U. L. REV. 675 (2013)

The question of whether *Daubert v. Merrell Dow Pharmaceuticals, Inc.* adopted a more lenient or more stringent standard for testing the reliability of expert evidence has dogged academics, practitioners, and researchers for twenty years. Research since 1993, using a variety of methodologies, has been largely inconsistent. Some quantitative studies show that the *Daubert* standard has had no effect on the admission of expert evidence. Other quantitative studies find the opposite, that *Daubert* is a more stringent standard of admissibility. *Daubert* cannot be both meaningless and more restrictive, and determining which of these two conclusions is correct will have enormous implications.

If the shift to *Daubert* had no effect on the judicial management of evidence or trial outcomes, the choice between the *Daubert* standard and the traditional *Frye* test for admissibility is without consequence. Perhaps, if this is true, reformers should abandon efforts to change the tort system through doctrinal modifications and seek redress elsewhere. Moreover, an impotent *Daubert* would also indicate that the controversy in evidence law about expert admissibility has been much ado about nothing.

However, if *Daubert* is a more stringent standard, the implications are enormous. It would indicate that—at the time of its decision—the Supreme Court badly misjudged what effect *Daubert* would have on the admissibility of scientific evidence. At the time, the Court believed that the decision would be consistent with "the liberal thrust of the Federal Rules [of Evidence] and their general approach of relaxing the traditional barriers to opinion testimony." If this were not true, the Court would need to revisit expert reliability standards, to clarify the standard by either affirming the new reality or insisting upon the lenient standard initially envisioned. A stricter *Daubert* standard would also have an enormous effect on substantive tort law … Therefore, the interpretation of the *Daubert* standard is important, especially in an era when expert witness testimony is as prevalent as it is today.

In this Article, we answer the question: Did *Daubert* have a measurable effect on expert admissibility, and if so, did it adopt a stricter or more lenient standard for admissibility? To make this determination, this Article builds on a methodology used in a 2005 study by Edward Cheng and Albert Yoon.[12] … Cheng and Yoon first suggested that the effect of *Daubert* could be measured across the judicial system by reviewing removal rates from state to federal court in multiple jurisdictions. We also believe that removal rates offer a very accurate method of measuring the systematic effect of *Daubert*….

To this end, we created a database of approximately 4 million cases and calculated removal rates during the period from 1990 to 2000. Based on our two-step analysis of that data, we conclude that *Daubert* is a stricter standard than *Frye* for the admissibility of expert testimony….

II. REMOVAL RATE APPROACH TO ANALYZING *DAUBERT*

B. *The Promise of Removal Rate Analysis*

We believe that the removal rate metric is the most important innovation of the Cheng and Yoon study and that it offers significant benefits over alternative methods, such as survey work or case studies. The power of the removal rate approach lies in the scope of cases included in the analysis. Under the removal rate approach, we can capture *Daubert*'s effect on a larger body of cases, not just those that went to trial or resulted in appellate decisions. In our analysis…, we could include an aggregate total of 3,997,970 cases…. Additionally, the removal rate approach avoids the potential shortcomings of quantitative survey research. Namely, the removal rate analysis measures the true test of litigants' opinions—their actions when their self-interest is in play…. Finally, as Cheng and Yoon noted in their work, the removal rate metric also removes one potential distorting factor from consideration.[108] Because removal occurs early in the litigation process, the strength of the evidence in a specific case is likely unknown at the time of removal. As such, a litigant's removal decision usually cannot be based on case-specific evidentiary concerns, but rather represents a general opinion of the relative merits of state or federal court…. With these benefits, we are convinced that the removal rate metric offers the best opportunity to measure the true effect of the *Daubert* decision.

---

12. Edward K. Cheng & Albert H. Yoon, *Does* Frye *or* Daubert *Matter? A Study of Scientific Admissibility Standards*, 91 Va. L. Rev. 471, 482–84 (2005).

108. *Id.* at 484.

C. *Our Analysis of Removal Rates Shows That a State's Adoption of* Daubert *Does Effect the Rate of Removal*

... Our ... statistical analysis demonstrates that defendants respond to a state's adoption of *Daubert* or *Frye* in precisely the way one would intuitively expect if defendants think that the *Daubert* standard is stricter than the *Frye* standard.

1. *Two Thought Experiments and the Expected Consequences of* Daubert's *Adoption: Flight-from-Frye and Flight-to-State-Court*

To understand the true effect of *Daubert* on removal rates, we must focus on what removal rates were intended to measure—defense attorneys' views as to the relative strictness of the *Daubert* and *Frye* standards—and ask what the world would be like if defense attorneys believe that *Daubert* is a stricter standard. In engaging in this process we used two thought experiments. The first thought experiment, "Flight-from-*Frye*," is based on two assumptions. First, if defense attorneys believe that *Daubert* is a stricter standard than *Frye*, then, in cases where the admissibility standard matters, they should remove the case from a *Frye* jurisdiction to a *Daubert* jurisdiction. Second, although there is a cost to remove a case ... it is not excessive.

If these assumptions are true, then we should expect to see the following: if state A is a *Frye* jurisdiction at time t_1 through t_{10} and if the federal courts adopt *Daubert* at time t_5, then the rate of removals from state court to federal court should increase after time t_5, with a steep increase initially followed by gradual tapering. Graphically, this should look something like:

Figure 1: The "Flight-from-*Frye*" Theoretical Effect in Years 1 to 10

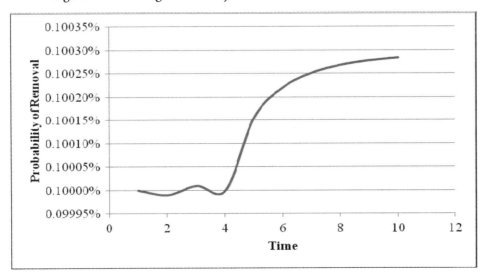

This trend follows naturally from our first assumption: that defense attorneys believe that the *Daubert* standard will keep out more evidence than the *Frye* standard. Thus, when it matters, defense attorneys will remove a case to federal court more frequently after the federal courts adopt *Daubert* to take advantage of the stricter standard even if it costs something to do so. Moreover, the change will be an increase in the rate of removals.

Let us now reverse this in the "Flight-to-State-Court" thought experiment. Under the Flight-to-State-Court experiment, the two basic assumptions of Flight-from-*Frye* remain the same. Now, assume that state A is a *Frye* jurisdiction at time t_1 through t_{10}, the federal courts adopted *Daubert* at time t_5, but then state A adopts *Daubert* at time t_{11}. As noted in the Flight-from-Frye experiment, there should be an increase in the rate of removals occurring after time t_5. But, because state A adopts *Daubert* at time t_{11}, there is no longer any evidentiary advantage to removing from state court to federal court because the state and federal courts now will apply the same expert admissibility standard.... [W]e should see a decrease in the rate of removals after time t_{11} because of the lost evidentiary benefit of removal plus the cost of removal. Graphically, this should look something like:

Figure 2: The "Flight-to-State-Court" Theoretical Effect in Years 1 to 15

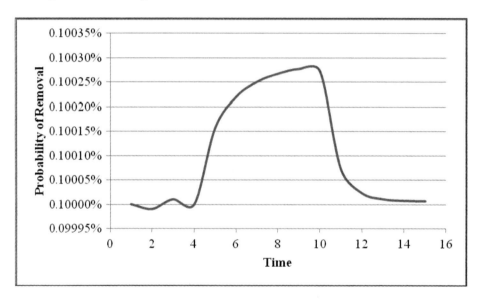

2. *Analysis of Removal Rate Data Demonstrates Litigants Act in the Same Way as the Flight-from-Frye Thought Experiment*

In the Flight-from-Frye experiment, we expect to see the rate of removals increase in states that do not change from *Frye* to *Daubert* during a period before and after the federal courts adopt *Daubert*. Our analysis clearly demonstrates this effect.

Our first step is to attempt to confirm (or deny) the Flight-from-Frye thought experiment. In doing so we are attempting to measure *only* the effect the *federal courts'* adoption of *Daubert* has on removal rates. To measure this impact, we identified 13 states that were *Frye* states both before and for some period after ... *Daubert*. Using these states, we engaged in two identical analyses: one of pure federal data, and the

Figure 3: Fixed-Effects Analysis on Removal Rate
Using Federal Data Only

Daubert Adopted in U.S. Court	Probability of Removal
No	0.259268
Yes	0.327401

Figure 4: Fixed-Effects Analysis on Removal Rate Using
State and Federal Data

Daubert Adopted in U.S. Court	Probability of Removal
No	0.004517
Yes	0.005297

other of mixed federal and state data.... The pure federal dataset contained entries using the Federal Database to calculate the number of cases removed, the number of tort cases filed, and the removal rate. The mixed dataset contained entries using the State Database to calculate the number of tort cases filed, the Federal Database to calculate the number of cases removed, and both ... to calculate the removal rate....

... Using [the federal] data, we performed a fixed-effects analysis using logistic regression. This provided statistically significant results showing that the probability that a case in federal court was removed from state court increased after *Daubert* was adopted.

Next, we reproduced this analysis using the mixed Federal and State Database. This analysis also produced statistically significant results demonstrating that the adoption of *Daubert* increases the probability of removal to federal court.... These results unequivocally demonstrate that in states using the *Frye* standard, the adoption of *Daubert* by the federal courts results in an increased rate of removals to the federal courts.

3. Analysis of Removal Rate Data Also Demonstrates Litigants Act in the Same Way as the Flight-to-State-Court Thought Experiment

The Flight-to-State-Court thought experiment proposed that, if the state court was initially a *Frye* state, remained a *Frye* state for a period of time after the federal courts adopted *Daubert*, but eventually adopted *Daubert*, the rate of removals should decrease. Looking at actual case data, litigants' actual behavior mirrored this result.

We used 5 states that adopted *Daubert* from 1994 to 2000—a period after the federal courts adopted *Daubert*—and 8 states that did not adopt *Daubert* through 2000 as controls. Once again, we engaged in two sequences of analysis: one using pure federal data and the other using mixed federal and state data.

Using the pure federal data, we performed a fixed-effects analysis using a logistic regression and produced a statistically significant result, at the $p \leq .05$ level, demon-

Figure 5: Fixed-Effects Analysis on Removal Rate Using Federal Data Only

Daubert Adopted by State	Probability of Removal
No	0.303158
Yes	0.25104

strating that adoption of a *Daubert* standard by state courts *after* the federal courts results in a decreased probability of removal.

Remarkably, the results in Figure 5 show that the rate of removal *reverts* to the levels of pre-federal adoption once the state also adopts *Daubert*. This is precisely what we expected to find under the Flight-to-State-Court thought experiment. Such a result strongly supports the underlying thesis that defense attorneys believe *Daubert* is the stricter standard. Next, we reproduced this analysis using the combined federal and state dataset but found *no* statistically significant relationships.

4. The Empirical Evidence of Actual Removal Rates Demonstrates Litigants Behavior After the Adoption of Daubert *Mirrored Our Thought Experiments*

By analyzing the removals from 1990 to 2000, we can demonstrate that those litigants in the dataset acted in the manner predicted by the Flight-from-*Frye* and Flight-to-State-Court thought experiments. This result strongly supports the conclusion that litigants themselves believe that the *Daubert* standard is stricter than the *Frye* standard.

Andrew W. Jurs & Scott DeVito, *Et Tu, Plaintiffs? An Empirical Analysis of* Daubert's *Effect on Plaintiffs, and Why Gatekeeping Standards Matter (a Lot)*
66 ARK. L. REV. 975 (2013)

... Just this year, the authors of this article offered a new empirical analysis of *Daubert*'s effect. Our study postulated that the effect of the adoption of the *Daubert* scientific admissibility standard could be measured through aggregation and analysis of civil defendants' decisions to remove their cases to federal court ... [and] we found that civil defendants demonstrated by their actions that *Daubert* is the stricter gatekeeping standard.... Yet, even after that study, significant questions remained, and we wondered if we could replicate the results using a different metric.

In this article, we answer that question by applying the fixed-effects statistical model to a new and different dataset. Instead of measuring the removal decisions of civil defendants, we will measure the filing decisions of civil plaintiffs and compare their choices before and after *Daubert*'s adoption. By doing so, we can quantify whether civil plaintiffs demonstrate — through their actions in millions of cases — agreement with defendants that *Daubert* represents a stricter admissibility standard. After evaluating the data, we find that after federal courts adopted *Daubert* in 1993, civil plaintiffs increased the rate at which they filed cases in a state court adhering to the older *Frye* standard. This data alone is enough to demonstrate that civil plaintiffs collectively act in ways demonstrating *Daubert* is a stricter standard.

In addition to civil plaintiffs' initial reactions to *Daubert*, we can confirm our theory by demonstrating a counter-effect that occurs in the event a state changes to the same admissibility standard used in federal courts. When a state court adopts a *Daubert*-like standard that mirrors the federal standard, a plaintiff no longer receives a strategic advantage through choice of venue. When we evaluated the data after 1993, we found exactly this counter-effect: plaintiffs' filing choices shift in those states that adopt *Daubert* after 1993, eliminating the post-*Daubert* change and returning to the pre-*Daubert* filing pattern. This counter-effect confirms that civil plaintiffs— through their collective behavior in millions of actual cases—act in ways showing *Daubert* is the stricter standard....

III. EMPIRICAL ANALYSIS OF PLAINTIFF FILING PATTERNS

... Our analysis tests whether attorneys representing plaintiffs in civil cases act in ways consistent with *Daubert* being a stricter standard than the alternatives. The key to this analysis is quantifying attorneys' opinions by aggregating and assessing their collective judgment on how *Daubert* works. Such an analysis produces a clear result: Just as with civil defendants, civil plaintiffs believe *Daubert* is a stricter standard for expert gatekeeping.

A. Thought Experiment: How Would Plaintiffs Act If *Daubert* Is a Stricter Standard?

In order to measure whether *Daubert* is a stricter standard, we must first understand how the data might look with *Daubert* as a stricter standard. Doing so requires re- membering that attorneys file where they think they can win. When attorneys rely on expert testimony in their cases, they may have the option to file in federal or state court. Because federal and state courts have different gatekeeping standards, all else being equal, attorneys will likely file in the jurisdiction with the weakest gatekeeping standard—i.e., the one with the lowest probability of excluding the evidence. In short, when a gatekeeping gradient exists—i.e., an advantage in gatekeeping that is accessible through venue choice—plaintiffs' attorneys should file in the venue with the weaker gatekeeping standard in order to increase their chances of success.

By observing where attorneys file their cases, we can use the creation and destruc- tion of the gatekeeping gradient to determine whether attorneys act as if *Daubert* is the stricter standard. For example, assume that before 1993 both the federal and state courts in State A applied the pre-*Daubert*, federal standard of "general acceptance" under *Frye*. Assume further that in 1993—when *Daubert* changed the federal gate- keeping standard—State A's state courts continued to use the *Frye* standard. Thus, beginning in 1993, State A's federal and state courts applied different gatekeeping standards for expert evidence, creating a gatekeeping gradient.

Prior to 1993, filing in federal court, rather than state court, did not yield a *Daubert-Frye* evidentiary standard type of gatekeeping advantage. Therefore, before 1993 the probability of filing in federal court should appear fairly constant. But when

Figure 1. The "Flight to *Frye*" Theory: Effect on Filings in
State A from 1990 to 1997

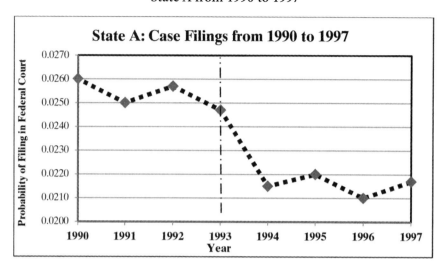

the gatekeeping systems are different—as they would be in our post-*Daubert* hypothetical—plaintiffs' attorneys could choose to file in either a state court applying
Frye or a federal court applying *Daubert*. If attorneys believe that *Daubert* applies a
stricter gatekeeping standard, the data should demonstrate a shift in where attorneys
file their cases as plaintiffs' attorneys choose to remain in state court because of its
more lenient standard. This effect should, relative to the pre-1993 period, produce
a decrease in the probability of filing in federal court. Graphically, the result would
look similar to Figure 1—the "Flight to *Frye*" Theory.

On the other hand, if plaintiffs' attorneys believe that application of *Daubert* and
Frye have nearly identical effects on the exclusion of evidence, the probability of filing
in federal court should remain stable—a generally flat pattern ... one would not expect to see a downward-shifting pattern like Figure 1.

The destruction of the gatekeeping gradient provides another opportunity to determine whether attorneys believe *Daubert* is a stricter standard. Assume that after
the federal courts adopted *Daubert* in 1993, State B retained the *Frye* gatekeeping
standard until finally adopting the *Daubert* gatekeeping standard in 1997. In this scenario—although State B would have experienced a decrease in filings in federal court
after the federal courts adopted *Daubert* in 1993—plaintiffs' attorneys, by 1997,
could no longer take advantage of the gatekeeping gradient through venue choice
because it would not exist. Having lost this advantage, the probability of plaintiffs
filing in federal court should increase to a level similar to the previous period ... [we]
refer to this effect as the "Return to Federal Court" Theory, and graphically, it would
look similar to Figure 2.

Once again, if plaintiffs' attorneys believe that application of *Daubert* and *Frye*
have nearly identical effects on the exclusion of evidence, the probability of filing in

Figure 2. The "Return to Federal Court" Theory: Effect on Filings in
State B from 1994 to 2001

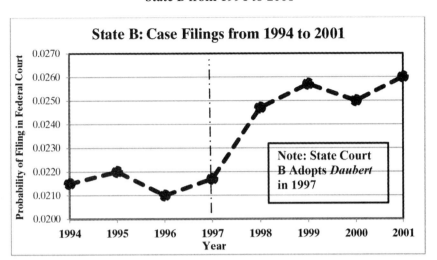

federal court should remain stable — a generally flat pattern ... [and the] pattern in
Figure 2 should not occur.

As the following section will demonstrate, the changes depicted in Figure 1 and
Figure 2 actually occurred as litigants in real cases reacted to the shifting gatekeeping
standards in federal and state court. This effect confirms that plaintiffs' attorneys believe — as evinced by their actions — the *Daubert* standard is stricter than the *Frye*
standard.

B. Analysis of Case Data Shows That Adoption of *Daubert* Affects Plaintiffs' Venue
Choices

To test the validity of the "Flight to *Frye*" and "Return to Federal Court" theories,
we first created a database of cases filed in the relevant period. Next, we statistically
analyzed that database to measure plaintiffs' reactions as different venues adopted
Daubert....

The fixed-effects analysis of the "Flight to *Frye*" and "Return to Federal Court"
groups produced statistically significant effects that support this study's hypothesis —
that *Daubert* is the stricter standard. In the case of the "Flight to *Frye*" group, the
probability of filing in federal court decreased by nearly 21% when the federal courts
began to use *Daubert*:

Table 1. Effect of *Daubert* on the Probability of Filing in Federal Court

Daubert Adopted by Federal Courts	Probability of Filing in Federal Court
No	0.014113
Yes	0.011683

To ensure that a shift in population over the ten-year period did not cause these effects, we normalized the data to eliminate population growth as a factor. Using this normalized data, the fixed-effects analysis produced a similar 20% decrease in the probability of filing in federal courts when the federal courts began to use *Daubert*:

Table 2. Effect of *Daubert* on the Probability of Filing in Federal Court — Data Normalized for Population Growth

Daubert Adopted by Federal Courts	Probability of Filing in Federal Court
No	0.014128
Yes	0.011750

These results match precisely what one would expect if attorneys believe that *Daubert* is a stricter standard than *Frye* and depict a situation just like Figure 1.

In the case of the "Return to Federal Court" group, the probability of filing in federal court increased by nearly 22% when the state courts adopted *Daubert* a few years after the federal courts began to use *Daubert*:

Table 3. Effect of State-Court Adoption of *Daubert* on the Probability of Filing in Federal Court

Daubert Adopted by State Court	Probability of Filing in Federal Court
No	0.011551
Yes	0.014065

After normalizing the data to account for population growth, we found a nearly 17% increase in the probability of filing in federal court given that the state court also applied *Daubert*:

Table 4. Effect of State-Court Adoption of *Daubert* on the Probability of Filing in Federal Court — Data Normalized for Population Growth

Daubert Adopted by State Court	Probability of Filing in Federal Court
No	0.011867
Yes	0.013835

The rise in probability matches the results one would expect if attorneys believe that *Daubert* is a stricter standard, and the results depict a situation just like Figure 2. Moreover, the rise in probability corresponds closely to the decrease in probability caused during the "Flight to *Frye*" period, further supporting the view that state adoption of *Daubert* in the "Return to Federal Court" period eliminated the advantage that drove attorneys to file in federal court during the "Flight to *Frye*" period. These results strongly support the view that attorneys believe *Daubert* is a stricter standard than *Frye* and that their filing choices changed pursuant to that belief.…

Jennifer Groscup et al., *The Effects of* Daubert *on the Admissibility of Expert Testimony in State and Federal Criminal Cases*

8 Psychol. Pub. Pol'y & L. 339 (2012)[Ed.]

Scientific and technical advances are being made daily; therefore, keeping up to date on all, or even most, of these advancements is nearly impossible. In courts, these advancements affect the evidence that is presented, including expert testimony. Determining which expert evidence is admissible and which is "junk" is a daunting task, particularly for the trial judges who are responsible for making these decisions. Not only must judges decipher complex issues in fields of study that are possibly unfamiliar to them in order to determine admissibility, but their decisions to admit or exclude expert testimony may affect the outcome of the case. In civil cases, this could result in an injured plaintiff who is denied compensation for some grievous harm; in criminal cases, expert testimony could convince a jury to convict a defendant, depriving him or her of freedom or even of life. Recent changes in admissibility standards have made expert testimony admissibility an important field of study.…

… The main focus of the *Daubert* opinion was to encourage courts to evaluate scientific evidence based on the methodology used and not the conclusions derived by the researcher. However, most judges are not trained in scientific methodology. To assist judges who lack scientific training in their "gatekeeping" task of evaluating the reliability of scientific evidence, the Court created a nonexclusive list of factors to be considered.… The Court reasoned that this type of evaluation, in conjunction with Rule 702, would provide a more flexible standard than that derived from *Frye*.

The *Daubert* decision and its potential effects on the general admissibility of expert testimony created an explosion of discussion in both legal and scientific communities. There was little agreement concerning the likely future effects of the *Daubert* decision, and several questions were raised.…

Although *Daubert* concerned a civil matter, its ruling extends to criminal as well as civil cases. The influence of *Daubert* on the admissibility of expert testimony in criminal cases is especially important because of the significance of a potentially unfavorable outcome for the defendant. In a criminal case, the outcome of the decision to admit or exclude expert testimony could affect the defendant's freedom, liberty, and life. The expert evidence proffered can range from testimony about complex procedures such as DNA testing to common events such as the observations of a police officer.…

Our investigation of *Daubert* (and continuing investigation of *Kumho*) attempts to shed some light on these issues. In the present study, we address the questions raised by *Daubert* as they pertain to criminal cases. Are judges in appellate courts discussing *Daubert* or paying attention to the decision's suggestions? ... Finally, how has the admissibility of expert testimony been affected by the *Daubert* decision?

Method

In our efforts to determine the actual effects of the *Daubert* decision, we studied appellate court opinions concerning expert testimony. Appellate court decisions were selected because of their potential to demonstrate trends in judicial decision making about expert testimony. Decisions involving expert testimony were located with the Westlaw database using the search term "admiss! 5 expert & witness," which garnered the most relevant cases. Searches were limited to those cases decided within the 5½ years prior to *Daubert* (decision issued on June 28, 1993) and those decided within the 5½ years following *Daubert*, totaling 11 years of appellate court opinions. Cases that were included in the study contained substantive discussion of expert testimony admissibility.... Once a case was selected for evaluation, it was coded for content by one of three independent raters. If a case contained substantive admissibility discussion of more than one expert, then each expert was coded separately.... The total number of experts coded was 1,184, drawn from both civil and criminal appellate cases. There were 693 criminal appellate cases. The 491 experts discussed in civil ... cases are not included in the analysis....

The coding scheme consisted of over 100 variables relating to the admissibility of expert testimony, only some of which are reported here.... Because *Daubert* focused on expert testimony issues, the characteristics of the experts in appellate cases are of interest, such as the qualifications of the experts proffered. Coded information about the expert included the domain of the expert's testimony, the number of experts testifying for each of the parties, the party for whom the key expert testified, and the basis for the expert's knowledge (i.e., theory, body of research, case specific research, experience, education, and case specific experience). Some of the more intense post-*Daubert* controversy centered around rates of admission. Coded information about the admission decision included the trial court admission decision and the appellate court admission decision....

Results

Description of the Cases

Of the 693 criminal cases examined, 372 were from federal appellate courts, and 321 were from state appellate courts....

Rates of Admission and the Appellate Standard of Review

One of the main concerns raised about the *Daubert* decision was its potential effect on the admissibility of expert testimony. Trial court and appellate court admission decisions were recorded. It is noteworthy to recall that these rates of admission are only for cases that were appealed, not for all cases in which an expert was presented in a trial court. Of the cases that were appealed, 74.3% (*n* W 513) of the experts were admitted at the trial court level. At the criminal appellate court level for those cases, 69.1% (*n* W 465) of the experts were admitted. We computed chi squares to determine the patterns of relationship between (a) admissibility and timing and (b) admissibility and type of testimony at the trial and appellate court levels. Contrary to the predictions of most commentators, the basic rates of admission at the trial and the appellate court levels did not change significantly after *Daubert* in criminal cases on appeal. There were also no significant changes in admission rates across the three post *Daubert* time periods at either adjudicative level. However, different rates of admission at the trial court, $p < .001$, and the appellate court, $p < .001$, levels occurred depending on the type of testimony presented. At both the trial court and appellate court levels, technical testimony was admitted at a higher-than-average rate. Medical — mental health, scientific, and business testimony were all admitted at a lower-than-average rate. Within each type of testimony, there were no significant changes in admission over time at either the trial or the appellate court levels....

One explanation for the lack of any changes in the observed rates of admission before versus after *Daubert* is that admissibility depends on the party offering the testimony. The party for whom the key expert testified was significantly related to admission at both the trial court, $p < .001$, and the appellate court levels, $p < .001$. At both adjudicative levels, experts proffered by the prosecution were more likely to be admitted than experts proffered by defendants. At the trial court level, prosecution experts were admitted 95.8% of the time, and defendant — appellant experts were admitted only 7.8% of the total number of times they were offered. This pattern was slightly less pronounced at the appellate level, with prosecution experts admitted 85.1% of the time and defense experts admitted 18.8% of the total number of times they were offered. This indicates the reversal of some trial court decisions by the appellate court. Appellate courts do not simply affirm trial court judgments regarding expert testimony....

Discussion and Conclusions

The *Daubert* decision and subsequent Supreme Court decisions on expert testimony created a flurry of scholarship predicting the effects of those landmark decisions. The purpose of this study was to assess the effects of these decisions on criminal appellate courts' treatment of expert evidence and on the admissibility of expert testimony. Given the importance of the *Daubert* decision, we expected to find ... some changes in admissibility as a result of *Daubert* following the *Daubert* decision. Unexpectedly, no change in the overall rate of admission for all types of expert evidence was observed....

Notes and Questions

1. How have researchers tried to quantify the effects of *Daubert* in the foregoing studies and the research they describe? For each methodology, can you think of a benefit and a drawback in using that study design? Later in the text, when we review specific areas of expertise, we will revisit the issue of methodological choices, but it is important to think about the underlying structure of a study to consider its value in support of a proposition.

2. Jurs & DeVito found that *Daubert* increased reliability standards in evaluating experts, but the Groscup study found no effect. How can both of those findings be true?

3. Initially, commentators had some expectation that *Daubert* would be applied to forensic sciences, and therefore lead to an evaluation of their reliability and sci-

entific merit. We will discuss scientific bases for forensics later, in Chapters 5 (DNA), 6 (fingerprints) and 7 (hair and tool mark). In 2002, Judge Louis Pollak turned the gatekeeping power of *Daubert* on fingerprint analysis. *United States v. Llera Plaza*, 179 F. Supp. 2d 492 (E.D. Pa. 2002). Applying the *Daubert* factors to ACE-V print analysis, Judge Pollak held:

> ACE-V does not adequately satisfy the "scientific" criterion of testing (the first *Daubert* factor) or the "scientific" criterion of "peer review" (the second *Daubert* factor). Further, the court finds that the information of record is unpersuasive, one way or another, as to ACE-V's "scientific" rate of error (the first aspect of *Daubert*'s third factor), and that, at the critical evaluation stage, ACE-V does not operate under uniformly accepted "scientific" standards (the second aspect of *Daubert*'s third factor).

Id. at 516. Based on those considerations, the court would not allow testimony of a print "match." *Id.* Once the decision was issued, the government appealed. Several months later, the judge issued a new ruling permitting the evidence. *United States v. Llera Plaza*, 188 F. Supp. 2d 549, 576 (E.D. Pa. 2002). Courts since then have given *Daubert* little effect in evaluating forensic experts, a fact that has not gone unnoticed by scholars and researchers in the field. In 2009, the National Academy of Sciences Committee on Forensics bemoaned the lack of attention to forensics, in their scathing report *Strengthening Forensic Science in the United States: A Path Forward*, NATIONAL RESEARCH COUNCIL, NATIONAL ACADEMY OF SCIENCES, STRENGTHENING FORENSIC SCIENCE IN THE UNITED STATES: A PATH FORWARD (2009). They found that "[f]ederal appellate courts have not with any consistency or clarity imposed standards ensuring the application of scientifically valid reasoning and reliable methodology in criminal cases involving *Daubert* questions." *Id.* at 96. The Report suggested that, "using *Daubert* as a guide, the least that the courts should insist upon from any forensic discipline is certainty that practitioners in the field adhere to enforceable standards, ensuring that any and all scientific testimony or evidence admitted is not only relevant, but reliable." *Id.* at 101. We will revisit the NAS report in detail many times in this text when discussing specific forensic disciplines. However, the judicial failure to require reliability of forensics prior to admission has enormous real-world effects, as the case of Cameron Willingham demonstrates.

4. The State of Texas executed Cameron Willingham in April 2004 following his murder convictions in the deaths of his three children in a house fire in 1991. *See* David Grann, *Trial by Fire*, NEW YORKER (Sept. 7, 2009). At trial, the fire investigator testified that, based on his training and experience, the fire was intentional due to two factors: the presence of accelerant at the scene and lack of injury to Willingham. Later review of the case debunked these findings, saying they had no scientific basis and that they were more "characteristic of mystics or psychics." *Id.* The National Academy Report in 2009, speaking of fire investigations in general, found that "[d]espite the paucity of research, some arson investigators continue to make determinations about whether or not a particular fire was set. However,

according to testimony presented to the committee, many of the rules of thumb that are typically assumed to indicate that an accelerant was used have been shown not to be true." NATIONAL RESEARCH COUNCIL, NATIONAL ACADEMY OF SCIENCES, STRENGTHENING FORENSIC SCIENCE IN THE UNITED STATES: A PATH FORWARD 173 (2009). For a detailed review of the Willingham case, read the Grann article or Paul Giannelli's law review article detailing the evidence, excerpted in Chapter 7: Paul C. Giannelli, *Junk Science and the Execution of an Innocent Man*, 7 N.Y.U. J. L. & LIBERTY 221 (2013). PBS Frontline also covered the case in 2010, and the program is available on their website: http://www.pbs.org/wgbh/pages/frontline/death-by-fire/. Consider this case and its meaning as we return to forensics in Chapters 5 through 7.

Tying It Together

About ten years ago, John Porter started going to the doctor a lot, complaining of pain, limb weakness, and fatigue. It was odd for Porter, who had led a very active life and continued to do so as a teacher at Polk City High. In the last ten years, Porter's condition worsened. By the time of his 60th birthday in 2015, the joint pain was becoming excruciating, and his regular doctor had referred him to a specialist: Dr. Inga Douglas. As a board-certified orthopedic surgeon with 20 years of experience at Polk University Hospital, Douglas works with all types of joint abnormalities. Her initial examination of Porter led to the conclusion that he suffered from rheumatoid arthritis, a degenerative autoimmune disease that leads to chronic inflammation of joints, usually resulting in significant joint damage. Douglas also concluded that Porter's right hip already had significant damage due to the disease, but also due to injuries Porter sustained as a football player at Polk University in the 1970s. Her recommendation for Porter was to monitor his arthritis in general, but also to receive a hip replacement. Porter agreed to the surgery, which was set for December 31, 2015, at Polk University Hospital.

On that day, the surgery began uneventfully. Douglas prepared the hip for placement of the FlexaHip 2300 Artificial Joint—a procedure she had performed dozens of times before—and then inserted the device in the place of Porter's original joint. Thinking all was well, Douglas finished the surgery, wrote her surgical report as required by hospital rules, and went home.

Porter was most definitely not fine. As soon as he awoke, his wife could tell something was amiss. Douglas had told Porter to expect pain, but when he awoke the pain was excruciating. Sally Porter and her husband assumed it would go away, but it didn't, even despite extensive rehabilitation and multiple post-operative appointments with other doctors. Months later, John was still unable to get out of bed, walk, or drive a car. In April 2016, when Polk High told him he was out of sick leave, he told them that he couldn't work and resigned. Financially desperate, Porter called Getta, Lotta & Dough—a respected plaintiff's firm—and spoke with Pat Dough.

Only two months later, in June 2016, Dr. Douglas answered a knock on the door and was served with a lawsuit. In the suit, Porter alleged negligence in the performance of the hip surgery, resulting in over $1 million in damages. Knowing that she needed a lawyer fast, Dr. Douglas retained the experienced defense firm of Gotta, Outta & Trouble.

Since the initial filing of *Porter v. Douglas*, the parties have engaged in significant discovery, and have recently endorsed several witnesses for trial. Porter's disclosures include his wife, Sally Porter, but also an expert physician, Dr. Patrick Payola. Their endorsements indicate that they will testify to the following:

— **Sally Porter**: When asked about how the surgery on her husband went, Porter will say: "Right in the recovery room he didn't look right. I knew there was no way that went according to plan. Dr. Douglas messed it up!"

— **Patrick Payola**: Payola has been retained as an expert in orthopedic surgery, having earned his M.D. in 1976, after which he has worked at Smalltown General Hospital. To review the *Porter* case, Payola reviewed the report that Dr. Douglas wrote immediately after the surgery, reports from other physicians and rehabilitation staff about Porter's condition after the surgery, and medical journal articles regarding the FlexaHip 2300 from 1998. Dr. Payola will state: "The procedure was done incorrectly, but shouldn't have been done at all. Based on my experience and the articles about the FlexaHip 2300 from when it came on the market in 1998, it shouldn't be used with rheumatoid arthritis patients. Beyond that, later reports indicate that the device was incorrectly placed at the joint."

For the defense, Dr. Douglas has endorsed an expert witness of her own, Dr. Dana David:

— **Dana David**: David has been retained as an expert in orthopedic surgery. She is a board-certified orthopedic surgeon, having graduated from Stanford Medical School in 2005 and with post-graduate residencies at Harvard and Yale for five more years. In assessing this case, Dr. David looked at reports on Porter from Dr. Douglas and all other treaters, plus a 2014 article about the FlexaHip 2300 from the *New England Journal of Medicine*. She will testify that: "The surgery was done correctly. Originally, the FlexaHip has been considered unsafe for patients like Porter, but more recent research has shown that it is safer than all alternatives. In addition, I have reviewed lab testing of Porter from his post-op rehab doctors, and a new DNA test they did indicates that he has a particularly virulent form of arthritis. In my opinion, his hip was unusable without surgery anyway."

Assignment: As the newest attorney in your firm, you have been assigned to evaluate what the opponent might attack about your case, if those attacks have merit, and also if your firm can attack the opponent's evidence.

— As John Porter's attorney at Getta, Lotta & Dough, what parts of your case might the defense attack, and do those attacks have merit? Also consider whether your firm can file a motion to limit Dr. Douglas's case.

— As Dr. Douglas's attorney at Gotta, Outta & Trouble, what parts of your case might the plaintiff attack, and do those attacks have merit? Also consider whether your firm can file a motion to limit Porter's case.

Chapter 3

Procedural Rules Regarding Expert Testimony

Expert witness testimony must, as we have seen, comply with a series of substantive standards to be admitted at trial. Adherence to the substantive Rules of Evidence, however, is not the only requirement—the evidence must also meet procedural requirements as well.

The discovery process in any legal dispute will place strict timelines on both sides to provide mandatory disclosures of evidence to one another. Civil disclosures, as we will see, are commonly expansive, while criminal disclosure rules require less mandatory discovery and are more varied by jurisdiction. By either standard, though, a litigant who fails to provide required information has invited judicial sanction, up to and including exclusion of the evidence at trial. Judges are often uncompromising on these requirements.

In a civil case, initial disclosures are often followed with depositions of important fact witnesses; afterward the parties exchange expert disclosures, followed by additional depositions of these witnesses. Depositions are often taught to law students as a "skills-only" issue, but as we shall see, the substantive and procedural rules for depositions are critical for any case involving expert witnesses.

In this chapter, we will proceed through the discovery process, from the initial witness disclosures through depositions, defining the rules for each step and then applying them to new situations. When we discussed the substantive rules of evidence discussed in Chapter 2, I suggested that any particular expert would likely raise one or two issues, but not every issue. With procedural considerations, however, the rules are more likely to apply to every expert in every case.

Working our way through these questions, each one at a time, provides the entirety of Chapter 3, and will cover the main procedural requirements for admission of expert testimony. We will begin in Section A with discussion of civil discovery rules, a more-familiar starting point for any student who has completed civil procedure as a 1L. The cases and materials of Section B will contrast the criminal disclosure rules, and we will find that the default "everybody gets everything" standards of civil disclosure no longer apply. Yet expert disclosures remain critically important components of criminal discovery and often raises constitutional due process considerations as well. The chapter will conclude with a discussion of rules for depositions, and it will offer practice exercises in the area to apply those rules contextually.

A. Rules of Disclosure in Civil Cases

Any discussion of civil discovery rules will begin with the central rule of expert disclosure, Federal Rule of Civil Procedure 26. As you examine the rule—and it is quite detailed about its requirements—be sure to spot how it treats different witnesses with different standards. There are three distinct types of witnesses covered by the rule, and each has separate requirements of disclosure.

Federal Rule of Civil Procedure 26:
Duty to Disclose; General Provisions Governing Discovery

(a) REQUIRED DISCLOSURES.

(1) *Initial Disclosure.*

(A) *In General.* Except as exempted by Rule 26(a)(1)(B) or as otherwise stipulated or ordered by the court, a party must, without awaiting a discovery request, provide to the other parties:

(i) the name and, if known, the address and telephone number of each individual likely to have discoverable information—along with the subjects of that information—that the disclosing party may use to support its claims or defenses ...;

(ii) a copy—or a description by category and location—of all documents, electronically stored information, and tangible things that the disclosing party has in its possession, custody, or control and may use to support its claims or defenses ...;

(iii) a computation of each category of damages claimed by the disclosing party—who must also make available for inspection and copying as under Rule 34 the documents or other evidentiary material, unless privileged or protected from disclosure, on which each computation is based ...; and

(iv) for inspection and copying as under Rule 34, any insurance agreement under which an insurance business may be liable to satisfy all or part of a possible judgment in the action or to indemnify or reimburse....

(B) *Proceedings Exempt from Initial Disclosure.* The following proceedings are exempt from initial disclosure:

(i) an action for review on an administrative record;

(ii) a forfeiture action in rem arising from a federal statute;

(iii) a petition for habeas corpus ...;

(vii) an action by the United States to collect on a student loan guaranteed by the United States; ...

(C) *Time for Initial Disclosures—In General.* A party must make the initial disclosures at or within 14 days after the parties' Rule 26(f) conference unless a different time is set by stipulation or court order, or unless a party objects during the conference that initial disclosures are not appropriate in this action and states the objection in the proposed discovery plan. In ruling on the objection, the court must determine what disclosures, if any, are to be made and must set the time for disclosure.

(D) *Time for Initial Disclosures—For Parties Served or Joined Later.* A party that is first served or otherwise joined after the Rule 26(f) conference must make the initial disclosures within 30 days after being served or joined. . . .

(E) *Basis for Initial Disclosure; Unacceptable Excuses.* A party must make its initial disclosures based on the information then reasonably available to it. A party is not excused from making its disclosures because it has not fully investigated the case or because it challenges the sufficiency of another party's disclosures or because another party has not made its disclosures.

(2) *Disclosure of Expert Testimony.*

(A) *In General.* In addition to the disclosures required by Rule 26(a)(1), a party must disclose to the other parties the identity of any witness it may use at trial to present evidence under Federal Rule of Evidence 702, 703, or 705.

(B) *Witnesses Who Must Provide a Written Report.* Unless otherwise stipulated or ordered by the court, this disclosure must be accompanied by a written report—prepared and signed by the witness—if the witness is one retained or specially employed to provide expert testimony in the case or one whose duties as the party's employee regularly involve giving expert testimony. The report must contain:

(i) a complete statement of all opinions the witness will express and the basis and reasons for them;

(ii) the facts or data considered by the witness in forming them;

(iii) any exhibits that will be used to summarize or support them;

(iv) the witness's qualifications, including a list of all publications authored in the previous 10 years;

(v) a list of all other cases in which, during the previous 4 years, the witness testified as an expert at trial or by deposition; and

(vi) a statement of the compensation to be paid for the study and testimony . . .

(C) *Witnesses Who Do Not Provide a Written Report.* Unless otherwise stipulated or ordered by the court, if the witness is not required to provide a written report, this disclosure must state:

> (i) the subject matter on which the witness is expected to present evidence under Federal Rule of Evidence 702, 703, or 705; and

> (ii) a summary of the facts and opinions to which the witness is expected to testify.

(D) *Time to Disclose Expert Testimony.* A party must make these disclosures at the times and in the sequence that the court orders. Absent a stipulation or a court order, the disclosures must be made:

> (i) at least 90 days before the date set for trial or for the case to be ready for trial; or

> (ii) if the evidence is intended solely to contradict or rebut [expert evidence] … within 30 days after the other party's disclosure.

(E) *Supplementing the Disclosure.* The parties must supplement these disclosures when required under Rule 26(e).…

(e) SUPPLEMENTING DISCLOSURES AND RESPONSES.

(1) *In General.* A party who has made a disclosure under Rule 26(a) — or who has responded to an interrogatory, request for production, or request for admission — must supplement or correct its disclosure or response:

> (A) in a timely manner if the party learns that in some material respect the disclosure or response is incomplete or incorrect.…

Under this rule the authors envision three different types of witnesses, each with distinct requirements for disclosure under the rule. Under Rule 26, litigants measure timelines from two base points: the filing of the case (or 26(f) scheduling conference) and the date of trial. As we will see, disclosure for each set of witnesses will occur at a specific time envisioned by the rules. The three types of witnesses, and the default time setting for their disclosures, are:

a) **Standard Fact Witnesses in 26(a)(1)(A):** "within 14 days after the parties' Rule 26(f) conference," which by Rule 26(f)(1) is to occur "as soon as is practicable";

b) **Non-Retained Expert Witnesses under 26(a)(2)(C):** disclosures must occur "at least 90 days before the date set for trial or for the case to be ready for trial"; and

c) **Retained Expert Witnesses under 26(a)(2)(B):** disclosures must occur "at least 90 days before the date set for trial or for the case to be ready for trial."

We will proceed through these groups in order, evaluating the substantive requirements of disclosure for each type of witness in Parts 3.A.i & ii. We will finish our examination of the civil disclosure rules with a detailed discussion of judicial responses for untimeliness or lack of substance in disclosures, when we review sanctions under Rule 37 in Part 3.A.iii.

Together these rules provide the procedural timeline and disclosure requirements covering all civil litigation, including cases involving expert witnesses.

i. Fact Witness Disclosure and Fed. R. Civ. P. 26(a)(1)

Federal Rule of Civil Procedure 26(a) REQUIRED DISCLOSURES.

(1) *Initial Disclosure.*

(A) *In General.* Except as exempted by Rule 26(a)(1)(B) or as otherwise stipulated or ordered by the court, a party must, without awaiting a discovery request, provide to the other parties:

(i) the name and, if known, the address and telephone number of each individual likely to have discoverable information — along with the subjects of that information — that the disclosing party may use to support its claims or defenses . . . ;

Poitra v. Denver County School District No. 1

311 F.R.D. 659 (D. Colo. 2015)

SHAFFER, United States Magistrate Judge

Rarely, if ever, do "two wrongs make a right." The court's challenge, in the discovery or case management context, comes in untying the Gordian knot that the two wrongs create. This case presents just such a problem.

Pending before the court is Defendant School District No. 1's (hereinafter "DPS") Motion for Sanctions Pursuant to Federal Rule of Civil Procedure 37. . . . This motion seeks an order striking Rebecca Ortega, James Woods, Kao Vang and Ben Gallegos from Mr. Poitra's list of trial witnesses . . . based on Plaintiff's failure to properly and timely disclose those individuals pursuant to Federal Rule of Civil Procedure 26(a)(1) and (e). . . . Plaintiff Michael G. Poitra filed his Response to Motion for Sanctions . . . and argues that "listing . . . the four employees as witnesses on the pretrial order complies with the disclosure requirements pursuant to Rule 26(e)(1) as the individuals were discussed during depositions of both the Plaintiff and DPS management, were listed in interrogatory responses, and were the subject of documents provided by DPS, thus making them otherwise known to the Defendant." In the alternative, Plaintiff argued that any prejudice arising from the inclusion of these individuals on Mr. Poitra's witness list "nine months prior to trial could be cured by interviewing those employees. . . .

This court set the matter for a hearing . . . [and a]t that time, counsel for Defendant advised that her client's motion for sanctions now was only directed to Ms. Rebecca Ortega, since Mr. Poitra had agreed to remove the other three individuals from his "final" witness list. In response to questioning from this court, Plaintiff's counsel conceded that she had never formally disclosed Ms. Ortega pursuant to Rule 26(a)(1). However, counsel argued that Ms. Ortega had been referenced in Mr. Poitra's December 16, 2015 deposition and in Ms. Anita Marchant's deposition on January 5,

2015.... Plaintiff's counsel also suggested that Ms. Ortega's inclusion in the Final Pretrial Order sufficed to give Defendant proper notice....

PROCEDURAL BACKGROUND

... Mr. Poitra commenced this litigation on March 27, 2014 with the filing of a Complaint that generally alleged that he was the victim of employment discrimination and tortious conduct while employed by the Denver Public Schools. Throughout the relevant time period, Anita Marchant was Mr. Poitra's supervisor. The Complaint asserts that in February 2013, one of Mr. Poitra's co-workers, Etoi Montgomery, advised Ms. Marchant of certain allegations regarding Plaintiff's interactions with a female co-worker. Ms. Marchant allegedly placed Mr. Poitra on administrative leave without first interviewing the Plaintiff. An investigation of those allegations subsequently was conducted.... Ms. Marchant ultimately made the decision to terminate Mr. Poitra and he received a letter to that effect on April 2, 2013, in which Ms. Marchant stated that Plaintiff had "engaged in inappropriate workplace conduct and then failed to fully cooperate with the District's investigation of the allegations against you."

The Complaint named as defendants Denver County School District No. 1 and Anita Marchant.... The First Claim alleged tortious interference with contract by Defendant Marchant. The Second Claim was brought under 42 U.S.C. § 1983 and asserted a violation of Plaintiff's liberty and property interests under the Fourteenth Amendment. The Third and Fifth Claims asserted race discrimination and gender discrimination, respectively, under Title VII....

On June 13, 2014, this court held a [Rule 16] scheduling conference and entered a case management order establishing certain pretrial deadlines. At the scheduling conference, counsel indicated that [Rule 26(a)(1)] disclosures had been made on or before June 6, 2014.... The court adopted, without change, the December 6, 2014 discovery cutoff proposed by the parties, as well as their proposed dispositive motion deadline of January 15, 2015. Consistent with [Rule 30], each party was permitted to take ten depositions without leave of court.... On April 30, 2015, the parties submitted their proposed Rule 16(d) Final Pretrial Order. This court held a final pretrial conference on May 5, 2015. The District Court's Instructions for Preparation of Final Pretrial Order require each party to separately list their witnesses "who will be present at trial" and those witnesses "who may be present at trial if the need arises." For both "will call" and "may call" witnesses, the designating party also must provide "a short statement as to the nature and purpose of the witness' testimony." In the Final Pretrial Order submitted by the parties, Mr. Poitra's counsel listed 22 "will call" witnesses, 18 "may call" witnesses, and one "will call" expert witness who will "offer testimony and expert opinions regarding the economic losses suffered by Plaintiff." Defendants listed 4 "will call witnesses" and 7 "may call" witnesses.

In the Final Pretrial Order submitted to the court, Defendants noted their objection to the following individuals included on Plaintiff's "will call" witness list, "because such witnesses have never been disclosed by either party:" Rebecca Ortega, James

Woods, Ben Gallegos, Kao Vang.... Plaintiff's counsel conceded that these individuals, including Ms. Ortega, had not been formally disclosed previously. Counsel also suggested that she would be revisiting her witness list and would likely pare that list down. While the court heard from each side on the matter of the previously undisclosed witnesses, I emphasized that I was not privy to all discovery in this case and was not making any ruling because no motion challenging the inclusion of these individuals on Plaintiff's witness list had been filed.

On May 8, 2015, Judge Daniel [set] ... this matter for a ... jury trial to commence on January 11, 2016, and setting a final trial preparation conference for December 17, 2015. Defendant DPS filed the instant motion ... on November 16, 2015....

ANALYSIS

This court, in *Sender v. Mann*, 225 F.R.D. 645 (D.Colo.2004), discussed at length the standards governing Rule 26(a)(1)(A) of the Federal Rules of Civil Procedure. That discussion bears repeating. Rule 26(a)(1) provides, in pertinent part, that a party must disclose, without awaiting a formal discovery request, "the name ... of each individual likely to have discoverable information—*along with the subjects of that information—that the disclosing party may use to support its claims or defense....*" Rule 26(a)(1)(A)(i) does not require the identification of every individual that may know something about the matter in dispute. Rather, the disclosure obligation is limited to those individuals who are likely to have discoverable information "that the disclosing party may use" to support its claims or defenses....

... Rule 26(a)(1) disclosures are designed to accelerate the exchange of basic information and "help focus the discovery that is needed, and facilitate preparation for trial or settlement." *See* Advisory Committee Notes to 1993 Amendments to Fed.R.Civ.P. 26(a). To that end, initial disclosures should provide an opposing party "with information essential to the proper litigation of all relevant facts, to eliminat[e] surprise, and to promot[e] settlement." *Windom v. FM Industries, Inc.*, No. 8:00CV580, 2003 WL 21939033, at *2 (D.Neb. Aug. 12, 2003) (quoting *Rolscreen Co. v. Pella Prods. of St. Louis, Inc.*, 145 F.R.D. 92, 94 (S.D.Iowa 1992)).... More to the point, initial disclosures should be "complete and detailed," and should "give the opposing party information as to the identification and location of persons with knowledge so that they can be contacted in connection with the litigation." *Crouse Cartage Co. v. National Warehouse Investment Co.*, No. IP02-071CTK, 2003 WL 23142182, at *1 (S.D.Ind. Jan. 13, 2003) (quoting *Biltrite Corp. v. World Road Markings, Inc.*, 202 F.R.D. 359, 362 (D.Mass.2001)). "Indicating briefly the general topics on which such persons have information should not be burdensome, and will assist other parties in deciding which depositions will actually be needed." *See* Fed. R. Civ. P. 26(a) advisory committee's note to 1993 amendment....

In short, the Rule 26(a)(1) disclosure requirements should "be applied with common sense ... keeping in mind the salutary purposes that the rule is intended to accomplish. The litigants should not indulge in gamesmanship with respect to the disclosure obligations." *See* Fed. R. Civ. P. 26(a) advisory committee's note to 1993 amendment.... Counsel who make the mistake of treating Rule 26(a)(1) disclosures as a technical formality, rather than as an efficient start to relevant discovery, do their clients no service and necessarily risk the imposition of sanctions.

Fed. R. Civ. P. 26(e) imposes a self-executing obligation to supplement initial disclosures to the extent their disclosures are "incomplete or incorrect." *See A PDX Pro Co., Inc. v. Dish Network Service, LLC,* 311 F.R.D. 642, 647 n. 5 (D.Colo. Nov. 30, 2015).... There is, however, no affirmative duty to supplement initial disclosures "if the additional or corrective information" has "otherwise been made known to the other parties during the discovery process or in writing." *See* Fed. R. Civ. P. 26(e)(1)(A).

It is undisputed that Plaintiff Poitra did not include Ms. Ortega in his initial Rule 26(a)(1) disclosures or in any written supplemental disclosure provided to Defendants prior to the final pretrial conference on May 5, 2015. In opposing Defendant's motion to strike Ms. Ortega, Plaintiff's counsel points to specific deposition testimony from Mr. Poitra and Ms. Marchant as satisfying her client's supplementation obligation. Resolution of the pending motion for sanctions thus turns on the application of Rule 26(e)(1)(A).

Defense counsel deposed Mr. Poitra on December 16, 2014. That deposition lasted for approximately four hours, during which Plaintiff's counsel asked a total of 12 questions; none of which referenced Ms. Ortega or prompted a response that mentioned Ms. Ortega. The passages referring to Ms. Ortega are found on all or portions of 18 pages of a 161-page deposition transcript.... Mr. Poitra testified that he had discussed his case with Ms. Ortega and others, but also conceded that it "has probably been a year" since he spoke last to Ms. Ortega. According to Plaintiff, Ms. Ortega was interested in knowing whether he "was going to pursue a case" and expressed her opinion that he should.... In response to defense counsel's questions, Mr. Poitra testified that Ms. Ortega had been one of "his supports in vending," but that he had not made the decision to hire her and initially believed she "was [not] going to be a good fit for my team, but yet I was forced to make her part of my team." ... Mr. Poitra described Ms. Ortega's attitude toward Anita Marchant. According to Plaintiff, Ms. Ortega "didn't like Anita at all" and "would complain about Anita." Mr. Poitra recalled that Ms. Ortega would tell him to "watch" his back and describe Ms. Marchant as "really controlling." ...

Ms. Marchant made only one reference to Ms. Ortega during her January 5, 2015 deposition.... Approximately four months after Ms. Marchant's deposition and the discovery cutoff, Plaintiff's counsel listed Ms. Ortega in the Final Pretrial Order as a "will call" witness....

... In suggesting that her client complied with his supplementation obligations under Rule 26(e), Plaintiff argues that "[b]oth parties and their counsel were present when Ortega ... [was] discussed in the context of this case, not simply as [an individual] who might now something but within the specific factual parameters relevant to this case." ... Reduced to its essence, Plaintiff's argument maintains that a party's duty to supplement Rule 26(a)(1)(A)(i) disclosures is satisfied if an individual that may have relevant information is mentioned, even in passing, during a deposition. That argument is predicated on an incomplete reading of Rule 26(a)(1)(A)(i) and would effectively undermine the very purpose for initial disclosures. Rule 26(a)(1)(A)(i) requires more than simply a laundry list of potentially knowledgeable individuals. Rather, a party is duty-bound to disclose those individuals "likely to have discoverable information" that the disclosing party "may use to support its claims or defenses." To complete the disclosure obligation, the party must also identify "the subjects of [the discoverable] information" that the putative witness may provide.

Rule 26(e) must be construed and applied against the backdrop of the very specific requirements set forth in Rule 26(a)(1)(A)(i). Indeed, the elements of Rule 26(e) are quite clear. First, to trigger the duty to supplement, a party's initial disclosures must, in some respect, be incomplete or incorrect. Here, that element is not in dispute, for Plaintiff concedes that Ms. Ortega was not identified in Mr. Poitra's ... disclosures.... Second, Rule 26(e)(1)(A) requires that supplemental disclosures occur "in a timely manner." ... As the court noted in *Auraria Student Housing at the Regency, LLC v. Campus Village Apartments, LLC*, 2014 WL 2933189, at *2 (D.Colo. June 30, 2014), "knowledge of the existence of a person is distinctly different from knowledge that the person will be relied upon as a fact witness." ...

The facts in this case are distinguishable from those in *Llewellyn v. Allstate Home Loans, Inc.*, 795 F.Supp.2d 1210 (D.Colo.2011), *aff'd in part, rev'd in part on other grounds*, 711 F.3d 1173 (10th Cir.2013). In the latter case, the defendants moved to strike a declaration offered by the plaintiff in response to the defendants' motion for summary judgment. That declaration had been signed by the plaintiff's accountant, an individual who had not been formally disclosed under Rule 26(a)(1) as a fact witness or disclosed in the plaintiff's discovery responses. In denying the motion to strike, the court noted that the accountant had been a topic of questioning during the plaintiff's deposition and that defense counsel specifically had asked the plaintiff about "a produced document that had been previously created [by the accountant] for purposes of the litigation." The court emphasized that defense counsel "knew during [p]laintiff's deposition that [the accountant] had discoverable information related to [p]laintiff's purported damages." In contrast, Mr. Poitra's deposition testimony could be reasonably interpreted to suggest that Ms. Ortega was disinclined to play any role at trial.

... For the foregoing reasons, I find that Mr. Poitra failed to comply with his disclosure obligations under Rule 26(a)(1)(A)(i), as well as his duty to supplement those disclosures in a timely manner pursuant to Rule 26(e)(1)(A).

... Sanctions should not be imposed under Rule 37(c)(1) where the failure to disclose was substantially justified.... After carefully considering the facts in this case, the applicable Rules, ... and the pertinent case law, I hereby grant Defendant's motion for sanctions and strike Ms. Ortega as a substantive or merits witness in this action....

Morgan v. U.S. Xpress, Inc.

No. 4:03-CV-88-1 (CAR), 2006 WL 278398, at *1
(M.D. Ga. Feb. 3, 2006)

ROYAL, J.

I. Defendant's Motion to Strike

A. Background

This case involves a motor vehicle accident between Plaintiff Wes Morgan's semi-oil tanker and a semi-truck of disputed identity. The accident at issue occurred on February 11, 2003 in Talbot County, Georgia. Shortly after the accident, Plaintiffs came to believe that the unidentified semi-truck belonged to Defendant, U.S. Xpress. Plaintiffs notified Defendant of the accident on May 10, 2003, and Defendant denied that any of its trucks were involved. Plaintiffs subsequently filed the present lawsuit against Defendant in June 2003.

Through the course of discovery, Plaintiffs sought information that would enable them to identify the U.S. Xpress truck allegedly involved in the accident. Plaintiffs discovered that U.S. Xpress, like many trucking companies, monitors the geographic location of its trucks using a satellite positioning system. Plaintiffs requested that Defendant produce truck positioning data from the date of the accident. Defendant declined to produce this data, claiming that any information recorded on its system on the date of the accident would have been routinely purged fourteen days later, on February 25, 2003, and therefore was unavailable in May and June 2003 when Defendant was notified of the accident and when it was served with the present lawsuit.

Plaintiffs theorize that this information was available to Defendant at least in May and June 2003, if not during the time Plaintiffs were seeking it through discovery. Plaintiffs contend that Defendant intentionally hid or destroyed the information, refused to produce it, and misled the Court about its availability. One of the central issues in this case, then, is whether Defendant had the ability to access and retrieve truck positioning data from its satellite tracking system.

To support their contentions, Plaintiffs offer the testimony of four witnesses: Jim Coppinger, Kevin R. DeBinder, Jim Clerc, and Kenneth Michael Schulz. Each is a former information technology employee of Defendant.... Plaintiffs designated these witnesses as expert witnesses in accordance with Rule 26 of the Federal Rules of Civil Procedure.

Defendant deposed each of the witnesses and paid the requested expert fees. Defendant now seeks to strike Plaintiffs' Rule 26 designations on the grounds that these four witnesses are purely "fact witnesses" rather than "expert witnesses" within the meaning of Rule 26.[1] ... Defendant [also] seeks to recover the fees paid to each wit-

---

1. Defendant does not raise the issue of whether the witnesses are qualified to provide expert testimony pursuant to Rules 702, 703, and 705 of the Federal Rules of Evidence.

ness on the grounds that the amount paid is greatly above the amount due to a "fact witness."

As primary evidence that the witnesses are purely fact witnesses, Defendant offers the witnesses' admissions that their testimony is based on personal knowledge. Defendant also cites Jim Coppinger's statement that his testimony relates to "facts … not opinions … [but] facts," and points to a remark by Plaintiffs' counsel suggesting that Coppinger's testimony is not opinion testimony. After considering the applicable law, the experts' affidavits and resumes, excerpts of their deposition testimony…, and the live testimony of Jim Coppinger and Kevin DeBinder given during a hearing…, the Court now turns to the merits of Defendant's Motion to Strike.

B. Expert and Fact Witnesses Under the Federal Rules

Rule 26 of the Federal Rules of Civil Procedure and Rules 701, 702 and 703 of the Federal Rules of Evidence distinguish between "lay" or "fact" witnesses and expert witnesses. Among other differences, the two are subject to different disclosure requirements, and expert witnesses are entitled to receive a "reasonable fee" rather than the $40.00 per diem statutory fee … [for] lay witnesses.

Rule 26 references the Federal Rules of Evidence to identify which witnesses are expert witnesses. *See* Fed.R.Civ.P. 26(a)(2)(A) & 1993 advisory committee's note (explaining that the term "expert" refers to "those persons who will testify under Rule 702 of the Federal Rules of Evidence with respect to scientific, technical, and other specialized matters"). The Federal Rules of Evidence define a fact witness as one whose testimony is rationally based on his perception. *See* Fed. R. Evid. 701. In contrast, the rules define experts by reference to their knowledge, skill, or training. *See* Fed. R. Evid. 702. Further, they define expert testimony by looking at whether the opinions offered draw on that expertise. *See* Fed. R. Evid. 703.

While the Eleventh Circuit has not specifically addressed the criteria necessary to determine whether a particular witness is a "fact" witness or an "expert witness" under Rule 26, courts in other jurisdictions consistently have held that a witness is not an expert witness merely by virtue of his specialized training and knowledge in a particular field. *Fisher v. Ford Motor Co.,* 178 F.R.D. 195, 197 (N.D. Ohio 1998); *accord Sipes v. United States,* 111 F.R.D. 59, 61 (S.D. Cal. 1986). Instead, a witness with specialized knowledge and training may be a pure "fact witness" when a witness is a direct participant in the events about which he is testifying. *Gomez v. Rivera Rodriguez,* 344 F.3d 103, 113 (1st Cir. 2003). However, if the testimony consists of "opinions based on scientific, technical, or other specialized knowledge," the opinions may be considered expert testimony, regardless of whether those opinions were formed during the scope of interaction with a party prior to litigation. *Musser v. Gentiva Health Servs.,* 356 F.3d 751, 757 n. 2 (7th Cir.2004) (distinguishing cases holding that a treating physician is not an expert witness if his or her testimony is based on observations made during treatment). Thus, to determine whether a particular witness is a "fact" witness or an "expert witness" under Rule 26, a court should look to the nature of the testimony being given. *Gomez,* 344 F.3d at 113 ("[T]he triggering mechanism for application of Rule 26's expert witness requirements is not the status of the witness but rather the essence of the proffered testimony.").

C. Classification of Witnesses

1. *Jim Coppinger*

Having reviewed Coppinger's affidavit and the portions of his deposition testimony provided to the Court, it is clear that Coppinger's testimony is sufficiently based on his technical knowledge of fleet tracking systems in general, and Defendant's system in particular, to classify him as an expert witness. Coppinger opined that, contrary to Defendant's contentions, the truck positioning data was not purged from Defendant's computer system fourteen days after the data was recorded. He also opined that Defendant would have retained a back-up of the data from the date in question and could have accessed that data from the back-up tapes it maintains. Finally, Coppinger gave his opinion about other information Defendant could have used to determine the locations of U.S. Xpress trucks on the date of the accident.

Coppinger's opinion is based on his years of experience working with computer systems in the fleet tracking industry. He is the co-inventor and patent-holder of a truck communications system. He also was the "architect of the [U.S. Xpress] computer system" and was responsible for converting the system to the type.... Defendant uses today. In his affidavit, Coppinger offers an extensive explanation of "how the system really works." Furthermore, in his deposition, he responded to several hypothetical questions posed by defense counsel about how data and codes would be interpreted. Accordingly, Coppinger's testimony is based on his "scientific, technical, [and] specialized knowledge" about how fleet tracking systems generally operate, and about how Defendant's system, in particular, operates.

Though he has personal knowledge of Defendant's computer system as the "architect" of that system, Coppinger's testimony is based on his understanding of "how the system really works" rather than on his personal experience in accessing the particular data at issue in this case. Furthermore, his testimony likely will assist the jury in understanding the complex computer issues and terminology in this case....

2. *Jim Clerc*

Like Jim Coppinger, Jim Clerc is properly classified as an expert witness. Clerc opined that Defendant could have accessed and produced the electronic tracking data and satellite positioning data for every truck in its fleet on the dates in question. He also gave his opinion as to the type of data that would have been saved to the back-up tapes.

Clerc's opinions are based primarily on his years of experience with Defendant's computer system and his knowledge of computer systems in general. Clerc designed and developed numerous satellite tracking applications while employed by Defendant. He also was responsible for creating the satellite tracking ... file in Defendant's computer system.

Though Clerc's affidavit contains factual assertions about the instructions he was given by U.S. Xpress executives in setting up Defendant's computer system, this testimony does not defeat his classification as an expert witness. Clerc's opinions are based on his specialized knowledge and understanding of the inner-workings of Defendant's computer system rather than on his particular experience in accessing and retrieving the specific data at issue in this case. ...

3. *Kevin DeBinder*

Kevin DeBinder is more properly designated as a fact witness rather than an expert witness. In May and June 2003, when Defendant first learned of the accident and the lawsuit, DeBinder was working on a project for U.S. Xpress that required him to access, retrieve, and analyze satellite positioning data from the U.S. Xpress system. He opined that the truck positioning data was not routinely purged from Defendant's system fourteen days after the accident. His opinion is based on his experience accessing and using the satellite positioning data contained in U.S. Xpress's databases. More specifically, it is based on the fact that he had accessed satellite tracking data older than fourteen days from Defendant's system on previous occasions.

While DeBinder has excellent professional credentials, including a computer science degree and over twenty years of experience as a computer programmer and systems analyst, his knowledge and experience does not form the basis of his testimony in this case. Furthermore, though DeBinder, like Coppinger, explained some of the technical aspects of the U.S. Xpress computer system, his opinions are not based on any technical or specialized knowledge of its inner-workings. Instead, they are based on the fact that he previously had accessed similar data that was older than fourteen days during the relevant time period.

Because DeBinder's opinion is based primarily on the fact that he previously accessed similar data from Defendant's computer system, he is a fact witness, not an expert witness. ...

4. *Kenneth Michael Schulz*

Kenneth Michael Schulz also is more properly designated as a fact witness rather than an expert witness. Like DeBinder, Schulz worked on a project for U.S. Xpress that required him to access, retrieve, and analyze satellite positioning data stored in the U.S. Xpress computer system. Schulz opined that satellite positioning data older than fourteen days was available for viewing on Defendant's computer system in May and June 2003. His opinion is based on the fact that he had accessed data older than fourteen days on previous occasions. ...

D. Amount of Witness Fees

Having determined that DeBinder and Schulz are fact witnesses rather than expert witnesses for the purpose of Rule 26, the Court must now consider whether Defendant is entitled to a refund of the money paid to those witnesses in excess of the witness and mileage fees they were entitled to receive as fact witnesses. ...

Under 28 U.S.C. § 1821, fact witnesses are entitled to receive only reasonable compensation for their time and expenses. This includes a per diem allowance of $40.00 and actual reasonable travel expenses. While 28 U.S.C. § 1821 sets forth the minimum amount a fact witness is entitled to receive, there is nothing in the statute prohibiting the parties from agreeing to pay a higher amount. *See Baker v. Taco Bell Corp.,* 163 F.3d 348, 352 (D. Colo.1995).

Under the statute, Defendant was required to pay only the $40.00 per diem allowance and actual reasonable travel expenses to DeBinder and Coppinger. Prior to their depositions, however, Defendant agreed to pay them more. Defendant agreed to pay DeBinder and Schulz $300.00 per hour before the depositions were taken, and provided them with a check before the deposition began.

Though Defendant now claims that its counsel asked Plaintiffs' counsel to strike DeBinder and Schulz as experts during a telephone meeting with Plaintiff's counsel one day before the depositions were scheduled, Defendant did not raise the issue with the Court at that time. In the majority of cases involving a challenge to the amount of fees payable to a witness, the challenge was mounted before the deposition occurred or before payment was made. *See, e.g., Fisher v. Ford Motor Company,* 178 F.R.D. 195, 196–97 (N.D. Ohio 1998); *Baker,* 163 F.R.D. at 349. Defendant has cited no case in which a court adjusted the amount of fees retroactively after the court determined a witness was a lay witness rather than an expert. In its own research, this Court found only one case in which a court did so, and in that case counsel objected to the amount of the fees requested by the witness before the witness was deposed. *DeMar v. United States,* 199 F.R.D. 617, 617–18 (N.D. Ill.2001). Defendant's discontent with the amount of the witness fees should have been brought to the attention of the Court before the witnesses were deposed.... By moving forward with the depositions and paying the fees they agreed to pay, Defendant waived its objection to the amount of the fees.... Defendant cannot now complain of something that easily could have been resolved before the depositions took place.

Notes and Questions

1. As we saw in *Poitra,* failure to disclose a fact witness under Rule 26(a)(1) can result in a court striking the witness at trial. However, as the *Poitra* court alluded to, there is the potential for a litigant to waive the sanction. In *Llewellyn v. Allstate Home Loans, Inc.,* 795 F.Supp.2d 1210 (D. Colo. 2011), the defense inquired about an undisclosed accountant's report during the deposition of the plaintiff. In denying relief, the court noted that the defense "knew during [p]laintiff's deposition that [the accountant] had discoverable information related to [p]laintiff's purported damages." *Id.* at 1220. As we will see in the discussion of depositions in Part 3.C, *infra,* these split-second decisions during questioning can have significant impacts later in the case. It seems clear that the defense in the case should have either refrained from questioning about the accountant's report or asked for supplemental discovery after the deposition under Rule 26(e). What they could not do was ask about the report and later also ask for the court to strike the accountant.

2. In some situations, it may be unclear whether a witness is solely a fact witness or will testify as an expert. The *Morgan* court clearly finds that a witness "is not an expert witness merely by virtue of his specialized training and knowledge in a particular field." For example, a physician walking his dog observes a serious car

accident. When called to relay the movement of the cars, the physician is acting as a fact witnesses, not an expert. But will the physician be a fact or expert witness when she is called to the stand to discuss the injuries she observed to a driver? To decide when the line has been crossed, the *Morgan* court wants us to examine the substance of the proposed testimony. Clearly some serious line-drawing must occur, and the *Morgan* court attempts to do so with the various computer systems analysts. Is the line dividing those witnesses into separate categories clear?

3. The examination of the substance of the witness testimony—which is required in order to separate Rule 26(a)(1) fact witnesses from 26(a)(2) expert witnesses—will also become an issue as we need to distinguish between retained experts under Rule 26(a)(2)(B) and non-retained experts under Rule 26(a)(2)(C). We discuss this issue next, in Part 3.A.ii.

ii. Expert Disclosures: Retained and Non-Retained Experts with Rule 26(a)(2)

Federal Rule of Civil Procedure 26(a) REQUIRED DISCLOSURES.

(2) *Disclosure of Expert Testimony.*

(A) *In General.* In addition to the disclosures required by Rule 26(a)(1), a party must disclose to the other parties the identity of any witness it may use at trial to present evidence under Federal Rule of Evidence 702, 703, or 705.

(B) *Witnesses Who Must Provide a Written Report.* Unless otherwise stipulated or ordered by the court, this disclosure must be accompanied by a written report—prepared and signed by the witness—if the witness is one retained or specially employed to provide expert testimony in the case or one whose duties as the party's employee regularly involve giving expert testimony ...

(C) *Witnesses Who Do Not Provide a Written Report.* Unless otherwise stipulated or ordered by the court, if the witness is not required to provide a written report, this disclosure must state:

(i) the subject matter on which the witness is expected to present evidence under Federal Rule of Evidence 702, 703, or 705; and

(ii) a summary of the facts and opinions to which the witness is expected to testify.

McFerrin v. Allstate Property & Casualty Co.
29 F.Supp.3d 924 (E.D. Ky. 2014)

Van Tatenhove, District Judge.

This case began with an automobile accident in Leslie County, Kentucky. After the accident, insurance claims were asserted both against the tortfeasor's insurance company and against Plaintiff Brandon McFerrin's insurance company. This litigation arises out of the latter claim. Presently before the Court is Defendant Allstate Property & Casualty Insurance Company's Motion for Partial Summary Judgment....

I

On June 6, 2010, Plaintiff McFerrin and another driver were in a motor vehicle accident. The investigating officer who arrived at the scene detected no injuries to either driver. McFerrin denied any need for treatment and drove his car to his mother's place of employment ... At the urging of his family members, McFerrin eventually reported to the emergency room at the Mary Breckinridge Hospital later that day, reporting pain in his upper back, left shoulder, and left elbow. At the hospital, McFerrin had X-rays of his shoulder and elbow, and a CT scan of his spine. According to the reviewing radiologists at the Mary Breckinridge hospital, both the X-rays and the CT scan were interpreted as normal studies with no injuries. Curiously, however, despite the negative results, McFerrin was transferred to the University of Tennessee Medical Center where he was examined by an orthopedist, Dr. Richard Smith.

The record reflects that Dr. Smith examined McFerrin on the next day, June 7, 2010, and that his report directly contradicts the findings of the radiologists at Mary Breckinridge. Neither party explains why McFerrin was transferred to another hospital after the negative results on his initial X-rays, nor why Dr. Smith examined McFerrin, nor have they indicated whether Dr. Smith analyzed different X-rays or CT scans than the ones that were done at Mary Breckinridge. The record presented to the Court also does not explain these facts. Doctor Smith states in his June 7, 2010 assessment that McFerrin had a "[l]eft scapula fracture and [p]ossible T12 fracture." The report further states that "X-rays show a moderate deformity at T12 which may be due to acute fracture *or could possibly be an old injury*." Doctor Smith ordered a brace for McFerrin, and then saw him in a follow-up visit later that month. The report from the follow-up visit states that McFerrin could walk "without any difficulty" and that his fractures were healing. Doctor Smith reported that an X-ray showed the "T12 fracture in good alignment" and notes that he could not even see the fracture present on the CT scan. McFerrin received pain medication and was told to start "weaning himself off" of the brace. On July 21, 2010, after another follow-up visit, Dr. Smith reported that McFerrin's back "is not really bothering him at all," and that he had some tightness in his left shoulder and about 80% of his normal range of motion.... McFerrin returned to his normal work duties on July 21, 2010 with no listed work restrictions.

Allstate emphasizes, and McFerrin does not dispute, that prior to the accident in June, 2010, McFerrin had suffered significant back injuries. In March, 2001, McFerrin was treated at Mary Breckinridge Hospital for a neck injury and other minor lacerations suffered in a car accident.... In July, 2007, the Mary Breckinridge emergency records report that McFerrin came in twice—once with further complaints of severe back pain and once because of musculoskeletal back pain and recurrent seizure activity, probably due to his fall from a ladder. After his fall from the ladder, McFerrin was transferred to Wellmont Holston Valley Medical Center where he stayed for five days. At the time of his discharge, his pain was described as "rather severe" and he had to walk with a walker. The medical records, dated July 21, 2007, state that his medical history includes chronic back pain and seizures. In September, 2007, McFerrin began seeing chiropractor Dale Williams for "severe" pain in his lower back.... That same month, McFerrin saw another doctor, Dr. George Chaney, who gave him further injections of pain medication and referred him to a neurosurgeon.... In November, 2007, neurosurgeon Dr. James Bean attributes McFerrin's pain to his fall from the ladder in July of that year and notes that although he was being treated with high dose narcotics he was still not getting relief and still walking with a walker. Doctor Bean diagnosed McFerrin as a "[l]eft scapular region thoracic pain syndrome, *etiology unknown.*" McFerrin states in his answers to interrogatories that at least one doctor had suggested exploratory surgery, but he had refused....

Within a few months after the accident at issue in this case, the other driver's insurance company settled McFerrin's claims for personal injuries up to the $25,000 policy limits. Thereafter, McFerrin alleged that the amount was insufficient and notified Allstate that he desired to claim against the underinsured motorist policy covering the truck McFerrin was driving when the accident occurred. A dispute about the dollar value of McFerrin's claim ensued, and McFerrin filed the instant suit.... Now, Allstate moves the Court to grant summary judgment in its favor on McFerrin's damages claim[s]....

II
A

Summary judgment is appropriate when there are no genuine issues of material fact, and the moving party is entitled to judgment as a matter of law. Fed.R.Civ.P. 56(c); *Celotex Corp. v. Catrett,* 477 U.S. 317, 323–25 (1986). Summary judgment is improper, however, if genuine factual issues exist that "may reasonably be resolved in favor of either party".... *Anderson v. Liberty Lobby, Inc.,* 477 U.S. 242, 250 (1986). In applying the summary judgment standard, the Court must review the facts and draw all reasonable inferences in favor of the non-moving party. *Logan v. Denny's, Inc.,* 259 F.3d 558, 566 (6th Cir.2001) (citing *Liberty Lobby,* 477 U.S. at 255).

The moving party has the initial burden of demonstrating the basis for its motion and identifying those parts of the record that establish the absence of a genuine issue of material fact. *Chao v. Hall Holding Co., Inc.,* 285 F.3d 415, 424 (6th Cir.2002).... Once the movant has satisfied this burden, the nonmoving party must go beyond the pleadings and come forward with specific facts to demonstrate that a genuine issue exists. *Chao v. Hall Holding Co., Inc.,* 285 F.3d 415, 424 (6th Cir.2002) (citing *Celotex Corp.,* 477 U.S. at 324, 106 S.Ct. 2548). Yet even when construing the evidence in the light most favorable to the non-moving party, the non-moving party still "must do more than simply show that there is some metaphysical doubt as to the material facts." *Matsushita Elec. Indus. Co., Ltd. v. Zenith Radio Corp.,* 475 U.S. 574, 587 (1986). Rather, the Federal Rules of Civil Procedure require the non-moving party to present "specific facts showing that there is a genuine issue for trial." *Id.* (citing Fed.R.Civ.P. 56(e)).

While Kentucky's substantive law governs the issues involved in McFerrin's UIM and personal injury claim, federal procedural law governs the rules of practice concerning disclosure of witnesses and evidence. *See Hayes v. Equitable Energy Resources, Co.,* 266 F.3d 560, 566 (6th Cir.2001). In Kentucky, "the interpretation of insurance contracts is a matter of law for the Court" to decide, and is appropriately determined through summary judgment when there are no other factual issues in dispute. *West Am. Ins. Co. v. Prewitt,* 401 F.Supp.2d 781, 783 (E.D.Ky.2005), *aff'd,* 208 Fed.Appx. 393 (6th Cir.2006).

B

Allstate primarily contends that McFerrin cannot establish his claims for personal injury damages in this case because such claims require the presentation of expert testimony, and McFerrin has not provided the required information to Allstate concerning any experts that he anticipates calling at trial. To analyze this claim, it is necessary to explain some of the discovery process that has occurred thus far. Allstate served McFerrin with its first set of interrogatories in April, 2013, which included a request for McFerrin to state whether he expected to call any expert witnesses at trial, medical or otherwise, and if so to state the expert's identity, and the subject matter and grounds for their testimony. McFerrin responded to this question simply by stating "Will Supplement." Allstate has since submitted written inquiries requesting more completed responses, but counsel for McFerrin never supplemented his answer to the Interrogatory No. 5 concerning expert witnesses, nor has he in any other way identified any medical experts or otherwise addressed his failure to do so other than to say that he would "probably just use a treating Doc as witness." The deadlines in the Court's Scheduling Order specified that McFerrin had to disclose information concerning witnesses who may offer expert testimony by November 25, 2013. Allstate filed the instant motion in February, 2014, claiming that in reliance on McFerrin's failure to disclose any expert witnesses, Allstate also has not named any opinion witnesses when making its own timely expert disclosures.

On February 28, 2014, McFerrin filed his response to Allstate's motion for summary judgment, along with a motion to supplement his answers to the interrogatories. In the proposed supplemental answers, however, McFerrin lists the names and addresses of people who are witnesses to the incident out of which the instant litigation arose, but in response to the question about expert witnesses, McFerrin's answer states, "No experts have been retained, nor will be retained." McFerrin reiterates in his responsive brief that he does not plan to retain any expert witness for purposes of trial, and contends that Dr. Smith "is well able to testify" as to McFerrin's injuries, treatment, and the reasonability of treatment costs. Allstate maintains, however, that McFerrin must present medical expert testimony in order to establish a prima facie claim for personal injury, and that as McFerrin's treating physician, Dr. Smith is prohibited from offering opinion testimony addressing the issue of causation of McFerrin's injuries because such evidence must be introduced through an expert witness disclosed according to [Rule 26(a)(2)]....

1

The first point of analysis is the requirements for disclosure of witnesses under the Federal Rules of Civil Procedure. Under Federal Rule 26, potential witnesses are divided into three categories for purposes of disclosure. *Musser v. Gentiva Health Servs.*, 356 F.3d 751, 756 (7th Cir.2004). First, for fact witnesses, the parties must disclose the name and contact information "of each individual likely to have discoverable information—along with the subjects of that information—that the disclosing party may use to support its claims or defenses...." Fed. R. Civ. P. 26(a)(1)(A). The parties must disclose this first group of potential witnesses "at or within 14 days" after the parties Rule 26(f) conference unless otherwise specified by the court. Fed. R. Civ. P. 26(a)(1)(C). Rule 26(a)(2)(A) governs disclosures of the second group of potential witnesses, pursuant to which the parties "must disclose *the identity of any witness it may use* at trial to present evidence under Federal Rule of Evidence 702, 703, or 705." Fed. R. Civ. P. 26(a)(2) (emphasis added). These witnesses are in addition to the fact witnesses who must be disclosed under Rule 26(a)(1). The final group includes those expert witnesses who have been "retained or specially employed to provide expert testimony in the case," and the disclosure of such witnesses "must be accompanied by a written report" that has been "prepared and signed" by the expert witness. Fed. R. Civ. P. 26(a)(2)(B).

It is particularly important to note that the Federal Rules specify two categories of expert witnesses, and that only those who have been specifically retained for trial need to provide the accompanying report. However, witnesses who will provide expert testimony still must be disclosed as expert witnesses even if they were not retained for purposes of trial, at least under the provision in Rule 26(a)(2)(A). The Federal Rules of Evidence referenced by Federal Rule of Civil Procedure 26(a)(2)(A) determine what must be disclosed as expert testimony. "Expert testimony is designated as such by its reliance on 'scientific, technical, or other specialized knowledge.'" *Musser*, 356 F.3d at 757 n. 2 (quoting Fed. R. Evid. 702). For those witnesses who will provide such expert testimony but who need not provide a written report, the disclosure still must state "the subject matter on which the witness is expected to present evidence" and "a summary of the facts and opinions to which the witness is expected to testify." Fed. R. Civ. P. 26(a)(2)(C). Thus, a party must disclose the identity, subject matter, and a summary of the expected testimony for any witness who will give opinion testimony relying on "scientific, technical, or other specialized knowledge," even if that witness has not been specifically retained for trial. Fed. R. Evid. 702; *see also Musser*, 356 F.3d at 757. Parties are required to make these disclosures "at the times and in the sequence that the court orders," but "at least 90 days before" trial, or within 30 days after the other party's disclosure if the witness is intended solely to rebut the other party's evidence. Fed. R. Civ. P. 26(a)(2)(D).

Federal Rule 26 also contemplates the need for supplementation of these disclosures by requiring parties to "supplement or correct" their disclosures, as well as their responses to interrogatories and requests for production, "in a timely manner" whenever the party realizes that its disclosure or response "is incomplete or incorrect".... Whenever a party fails to disclose a witness in any of the three categories ... or when the party fails to supplement as required by Rule 26(e), the Federal Rules prohibit that party from using such information or witness to give evidence at trial "unless the failure was substantially justified or is harmless." Fed. R. Civ. P. 37(c)(1).

Here, the record reflects that Allstate timely filed their initial disclosures pursuant to Federal Rule 26(a)(1) on June 10, 2013, but that McFerrin apparently never filed such initial disclosures. Allstate had previously served interrogatories on McFerrin in April, 2013, specifically requesting the names and addresses of any fact witnesses, to which McFerrin simply responded by stating "Will Supplement, if any," and then named only "Brandy Pence who came to the scene of accident," and whose address would be provided "when I can find it." McFerrin apparently never supplemented any of these answers to the interrogatories. McFerrin also never filed any expert disclosures under Rule 26(a)(2)(A) or (a)(2)(B). Allstate has timely notified the Court that "[i]n reliance upon [McFerrin's] apparent position that he will not present any evidence pursuant to Federal Rules of Evidence 702, 703, or 705," Allstate has also not disclosed or retained any expert witnesses. The deadlines for all disclosures, discovery, and supplementation have long since passed, and to the Court's knowledge, McFerrin has not submitted any Rule 26 disclosures in any of the required forms. On February 28, 2014, McFerrin filed a motion for an order permitting him to file supplemental answers ... McFerrin's proposed supplementation only provides the names and contact information of Brandon McFerrin, Stephanie Clemons, Rebecca Creech, Brandy Pence, and Dr. Richard Smith, and then later states that "No experts have been retained, nor will be retained."

Given the standard explained above, in order to avoid the sanction mandated by Federal Rule of Civil Procedure 37(c)(1), McFerrin has the burden of establishing that his failure to supplement the interrogatories was either "substantially justified or is harmless." Fed. R. Civ. P. 37(c)(1); *Roberts v. Galen of Va., Inc.,* 325 F.3d 776, 782 (6th Cir.2003). The only justification provided for this failure is McFerrin's statement that the deadlines for filings were changed once, and that a staff member of his counsel's law office had the responsibility to answer or supplement the interrogatories but had left the office without doing so. McFerrin's counsel acknowledges that this oversight "should have been caught and reviewed but was not." McFerrin's counsel argues, however, that this oversight is "harmless" because Allstate has possessed information concerning McFerrin's medical bills and records for three years, and thus there "have been no secrets about Plaintiff's treatment or the costs incurred." Moreover, McFerrin's counsel seems to assert that because no expert has been retained specifically for purposes of trial, there is no need to file any disclosure concerning witnesses beyond the simple list of names and contact information listed in his proposed answers to the interrogatories....

First, it is important to note that the standard for whether supplementation should be permitted is whether the failure is "harmless," not whether Allstate has been prejudiced by it. *Sommer v. Davis,* 317 F.3d 686, 692 (6th Cir.2003). The purpose of Rule 26 disclosures of witnesses, both fact witnesses and expert witnesses, is to enable the parties to adequately prepare for trial. The commentary to Rule 26 states that the duty to disclose "extends to witnesses that the other party already knows of and to documents that the other party already knows of or even possesses." Even if Allstate could have guessed that McFerrin would call Dr. Smith as a witness, the commentary further explains as follows:

> The fact that the other party already knows of a potential witness or has a document, does not, by itself, achieve a critical purpose of the Rule 26(a)(1)(A) disclosures, which is to inform the other parties which witnesses and documents the disclosing party may use to support its claim or defenses.

Fed. R. Civ. P. 26, Practice Commentary. The Rule itself also provides that "all disclosures under Rule 26(a) must be in writing, signed, and served." Rule 26(a)(4). Thus, neither the fact that Allstate may have known the identities of several doctors who had examined McFerrin, nor the fact that Allstate was in possession of a large number of medical records is enough to discharge McFerrin's duty to properly and formally disclose witnesses, records, and other evidence.... McFerrin has not met his burden [to establish] ... his failure to disclose Dr. Smith under Rule 26(a)(1) nor his failure to supplement ... was substantially justified or harmless.

For the sake of argument, however, even if McFerrin is allowed to supplement his responses, the information he wishes to include still fails to meet the requirements of Rule 26(a), and is also insufficient to overcome Allstate's motion for summary judgment. Crucial to this determination is who qualifies as an "expert" for purposes of Rule 26(a)(2) disclosures. McFerrin's responsive brief seems to assume that the definition of "expert" depends only on whether a witness has been specifically retained for purposes of trial, thus requiring an accompanying expert report as described in Rule 26(a)(2)(B). However, as explained above, the relevant inquiry as to whether a witness is considered an expert, and is required to be disclosed under Rule 26(a)(2), "is the *nature of the testimony* rather than the *status of the witness*."[Ed.] The Commentary to Rule 26 explains that just because a witness has a certain expertise does not make him an expert witness "so long as his testimony is going to be limited to that of a fact witness." If, on the other hand, the witness is going to testify as to his opinion concerning "scientific, technical, or other specialized knowledge," then such witnesses "must be identified as such under Rule 26(a)(2)(A) even if they were previously disclosed as individuals with discoverable information under Rule 26(a)(1)," because listing someone "as a supporting witness does not alert the opponent to the possible need to take the types of countermeasures specially associated with experts." Fed. R. Civ. P. 26, Commentary; *see also Musser*, 356 F.3d at 757–758. Although McFerrin is correct that the requirement of an expert report as described in Rule 26(a)(2)(B) depends on whether the witness has been specifically retained for purposes of trial, he must still disclose anyone giving expert testimony under 26(a)(2)(A) even if the report is not required....

[Ed.] Emphasis added by Author.

Interestingly, McFerrin does not request leave to supplement his expert disclosures. Instead, McFerrin requests to supplement his answers to interrogatories, presumably in lieu of supplementing his Rule 26(a)(1) disclosures. Additionally, McFerrin does not differentiate among any of the three categories of witnesses discussed above. Instead McFerrin insists that Dr. Smith is not going to testify as an expert witness,[7] and further contends that as McFerrin's treating physician, Dr. Smith "is well able to testify to the broken bones, the injuries, the course of Plaintiff's treatment, and the reasonableness of the costs set out in the records."

There are two main problems with this position. First, although treating physicians do not automatically have to be disclosed as experts under Rule 26(a)(2), treating physicians and treating nurses "must be designated as experts if they are to provide expert testimony" as defined in Federal Rule of Evidence 702 discussed above. *Musser*, 356 F.3d at 758. McFerrin is correct that an expert report is generally not required for a treating physician who will testify regarding the course of treatment. If, however, the treating physician testifies "beyond the scope" of the treatment rendered and gives opinion testimony based on his "scientific, technical, or otherwise specialized knowledge," then the treating physician is still testifying as an expert witness, and at the very least must be disclosed according to the requirements in Rule 26(a)(2)(A) and (C), and Rule 26(a)(4), which McFerrin has not done with regard to Dr. Smith. *Fielden v. CSX Transp. Inc.*, 482 F.3d 866, 869 (6th Cir. 2007); *Musser*, 356 F.3d at 757. Accordingly, if the Court allows supplementation ... and if Dr. Smith is not going to give expert testimony as McFerrin claims he will not, then Dr. Smith will be limited to providing testimony only as a fact witness.... Courts are often concerned that permitting treating physicians to testify without providing expert reports can allow parties to circumvent the purposes of Rule 26....

To summarize, McFerrin has not properly disclosed Dr. Smith as a witness according to the requirements of Rule 26(a) for any of the three categories of witnesses. If the Court allows the supplementation McFerrin has requested, the proposed answers to interrogatories still do not satisfy the requirements for either fact witnesses or expert witnesses. If the Court were to construe the proposed answers as sufficient to at least allow Dr. Smith to testify as a fact witness under Rule 26(a)(1), and as McFerrin seems to request, then Dr. Smith still will be prohibited from presenting opinion testimony as contemplated by the Federal Rules of Evidence because McFerrin has not, nor does he intend to, introduce Dr. Smith as an expert witnesses in either of the two categories described in Fed. R. Civ. P. 26(a)(2).[8] Thus, Dr. Smith will only be

---

7. The Court presumes that such a statement must mean that McFerrin intends Dr. Smith to testify only as a fact witness under the first category in Rule 26(a)(1).

8. The Court need not reach the issue of whether McFerrin can supplement his disclosures in order to introduce Dr. Smith as an *expert* witness under Rule 26(a)(2) because McFerrin has affirmatively stated that he does not intend to do so. Were he to request such permission, however, the motion would be denied because McFerrin could not meet the standard of showing substantial justification or harmlessness, especially....

allowed to testify as a fact witness under Rule 26(a)(1), and, as such, will be limited to testifying as to the course of treatment and to what he directly observed while Mc-Ferrin was under his care.

2

Such limitations on Dr. Smith's testimony bring us to the second problem with McFerrin's position. McFerrin has presented claims for medical expenses, pain and suffering, and lost wages, all based on his personal injury claims. Kentucky law generally requires expert testimony to prove claims of personal injury such as are advanced in this case. *See Blair* [*v. GEICO Gen. Ins. Co.*], 917 F.Supp.2d at 655 [(E.D. Ky. 2013)]. In personal injury cases, Kentucky allows recovery of "necessary and reasonable expenses for medical services." *Langnehs v. Parmelee*, 427 S.W.2d 223, 224 (Ky.1967). However, to establish such a claim, McFerrin must demonstrate that the injury for which he incurred the medical expenses at issue was caused by the car accident. In a UIM claim such as this, "Kentucky law usually requires expert or medical testimony to establish that an incident legally caused a medical injury." *Blair,* 917 F.Supp.2d at 657 (quoting *Lacefield v. LG Electronics, Inc.,* 2008 WL 544472, at *3 (E.D. Ky. Feb. 26, 2008)). Kentucky courts recognize an exception to this rule for "situations in which causation is so apparent that laymen with general knowledge would have no difficulty in recognizing it." *Id.* Except for such situations, however, the general rule is that "the causal connection between an accident and an injury must be shown by medical testimony and the testimony must be that the causation is probable and not merely possible." *Jarrett v. Saltz,* 2007 WL 4355449, at *3 (Ky. App. Dec. 14, 2007)....

Here, to the Court's knowledge, Allstate has made no express admissions as to causation of McFerrin's injuries, and McFerrin has stated that Dr. Smith will not be providing expert testimony in this case. Thus, McFerrin can only establish causation if his situation fits into the exception to the general rule explained above—i.e., if the cause of his injuries is so apparent that lay members of the jury could easily determine whether and to what extent the June 6, 2010 accident caused those injuries. However, McFerrin's situation is clearly not one in which causation is so apparent that expert testimony is unnecessary because of his extensive history of back problems, and because the reports of the doctors analyzing his initial X-rays contradict Dr. Smith's later diagnosis....

Moreover, McFerrin does not dispute that he must demonstrate causation in order to establish his UIM claim, nor does he contend that the issue of causation is "so apparent" that a lay jury would "have no difficulty in recognizing it" such that he can present the issue to a jury apart from medical expert testimony. *Jarboe* [*v. Harting*], 397 S.W.2d at 778 [(Ky. App. 1965)].... Accordingly, McFerrin has not met his burden of presenting at least some specific facts showing that a genuine dispute exists, and summary judgment must be entered in favor of Allstate. *See Celotex Corp.,* 477 U.S. at 324, 106 S.Ct. 2548 ...

Andrew W. Jurs, *The Expert Heightened Disclosure Requirement and the Physician-Defendant in Medical Negligence Cases*

28 J. LEGAL MED. 521 (2007)

... Treating physicians use their medical expertise to testify about the facts in a case. Retained experts evaluate medical records, prepare opinions on standard of care and causation, and present complex medical issues to a jury at trial. Medical experts in a medical negligence lawsuit provide crucial testimony that is often case determinative.

Therefore, parties must adhere to the procedural requirements for expert testimony. The stakes are high; failure to appropriately disclose expert testimony or provide expert reports under applicable heightened disclosure standards can result in witness preclusion, crippling a litigant's case or even resulting in summary judgment or a dismissal.

In federal court, expert disclosure is handled through Rule 26 of the Federal Rules of Civil Procedure. Rule 26(a) divides disclosures into two distinct categories: initial disclosures under Rule 26(a)(1) and expert disclosures under Rule 26(a)(2). Experts are divided into two categories: standard disclosure and heightened disclosure experts requiring a report.

Federal court decisions evaluating Rule 26(a)(2) have established a substance-based interpretation for determination of which experts must provide heightened disclosures. This interpretation provides that, based on the anticipated testimony of the expert..., the expert may be required to provide heightened disclosures.... Recent case law from the substance-based perspective has expanded which experts need to provide heightened disclosures....

I. THE FEDERAL RULES

Federal Rule of Civil Procedure 26 provides the framework for disclosures and discovery in civil litigation. In determining the logistics of expert disclosures, the rule provides a framework for determining which experts require the standard disclosures and which require heightened disclosures....

Litigants must decide the critical issue of which experts qualify for heightened disclosure well before trial. When determining whether heightened requirements apply, litigants know failure to abide by the requirements of the rule regarding expert disclosures exposes them to sanctions, including witness preclusion, under Rule 37.

To guide the distinction between heightened and standard expert disclosures, the Advisory Committee for the 1993 amendments briefly addressed the difference between the two groups. The Committee stated:

> The requirement of a written report in paragraph (2)(B), however, applies only to those experts who are retained or specially employed to provide such testimony in the case or whose duties as an employee of the party regularly

involve the giving of such testimony. *A treating physician, for example, can be deposed or called to testify at trial without any requirement for a written report.*

The Committee advised that the purpose of the amendment, to characterize heightened versus standard disclosures based on the status of the expert ... is in contrast to the former Rule 26 prior to the 1993 amendments.... The current rule language therefore avoids an analysis of the substance of the testimony, focusing on the expert's status as retained, specially employed, or regularly giving testimony....

The Advisory Committee notes to the 1993 amendments underscore the standard disclosures for the physician-defendant, plainly stating that, for the treating expert, no report is required. However, the status-based solution established by Rule 26(a)(2) after the 1993 amendments, and the workable dichotomy between heightened and standard disclosure requirements, would not last for long.

II. JUDICIAL INTERPRETATION OF RULE 26(a)(2)

Federal courts interpreting Rule 26(a)(2) faced a clear status-based distinction between retained experts with heightened disclosure requirements and all other experts for whom there is only a requirement for standard disclosures. It would not take long for courts to expand the number of experts requiring heightened disclosure.

A. Federal Courts First Adopt the Substance-Based Approach

Federal courts first interpreted the heightened disclosure requirement of Rule 26 from a substance-based perspective in May of 1995. In the case of *Wreath v. United States*, Magistrate Newman addressed a defense motion to compel disclosures pertaining to expert witnesses.[14] The plaintiff had disclosed her treating physician as an expert who would testify regarding the nature, extent, and cause of her damages. The defense claimed the treating expert's testimony required an expert report under Rule 26(a)(2)(B).

To resolve the motion, the court cited extensively from Rule 26(a)(2)(B) and the Advisory Committee notes, and determined "treating physician[s] testifying only to the care and treatment afforded to a party were intended to be excluded from the requirements of Fed. R. Civ. P. 26(a)(2)(B)."[17] However, the court ... continued:

> [W]hen the physician's proposed opinion testimony extends beyond the facts made known to him during the course of the care and treatment of the patient and the witness is specially retained to develop specific opinion testimony, he becomes subject to the provisions of Fed. R. Civ. P. 26(a)(2)(B). *The determinative issue is the scope of the proposed testimony.*[18]

By these words, the court acknowledged that a treating physician, who by his or her status clearly is not under the requirements of Rule 26(a)(2)(B), may nonetheless fall under the heightened disclosure requirement if two conditions are met: (a) facts

---

14. Wreath v. United States, 161 F.R.D. 448 (D. Kan. 1995).

17. *Id.* at 449.

18. *Id.* at 450 (emphasis added).

are made known to the witness beyond the facts needed for treatment; and (b) he or she is retained to develop specific opinion testimony. The divide between heightened and regular disclosure, then, depends on a factual determination about the scope of the testimony. As the court continued: "[A] treating physician requested to review records of another health care provider in order to render opinion testimony concerning the appropriateness of the care and treatment of that provider would be specially retained notwithstanding that he also happens to be the treating physician."

... A similar result is seen in *Baker v. Taco Bell Corp.*[20] In the *Baker* case, the court faced a motion to compel reimbursement for expert expenses and the reimbursement depended on the witness' status as standard or heightened disclosure experts. As the court in *Wreath* had done, the *Baker* court chose to look at the substance of the experts' testimony to determine whether they were standard or heightened disclosure experts. Specifically, the court found the experts

> are witnesses testifying to the facts of their examination, diagnosis and treatment of a patient. It does not mean that the treating physicians do not have an opinion as to the cause of an injury based upon their examination of the patient or to the degree of injury in the future. These opinions are a necessary part of the treatment of the patient.[23]

The court focused on the substance of the testimony in analyzing whether Rule 26(a)(2)(B) applies. In doing so, the court determined that standard treating experts, testifying as to information based on their patient examination regarding the cause and prognosis of an injury, do not fall under heightened disclosure requirements. If the substance of the testimony comes from outside sources beyond ... examination, or the ... opinions expand beyond the extent, cause, and prognosis of the injury, then the expert would be subject to the Rule 26(a)(2)(B) heightened disclosure requirement.

B. *Wreath* and *Baker* Provide Early Precedent

In the spring of 1995, the *Wreath* and *Baker* decisions established the substance-based approach as the federal test for requiring either standard or heightened disclosure. Other courts quickly followed the lead of these decisions on Rule 26(a)(2)(B) expert issues.

For example, the court in *Salas v. United States*, faced with a motion to compel expert reports under Rule 26(a)(2)(B) from treating physicians, cited the language of the rule but then the decisions in *Wreath* and *Baker*.[25] The *Salas* court found the treating physicians would testify as to their treatment of the patient and also about the cause

---

20. Baker v. Taco Bell Corp, 163 F.R.D. 348 (D. Colo. 1995).
23. *Id.* at 349.
25. Salas v. United States, 165 F.R.D. 31 (W.D.N.Y. 1995).

of the injuries. *Salas* stated the general rule, established by a majority of courts including *Wreath* and *Baker*, is to look at the substance of the expert testimony, because "a treating physician considers not just the plaintiff's diagnosis and prognosis, but also the cause of the plaintiff's injuries." The court concluded that "questioning these [treating] physicians as to whether the injuries for which they treated the plaintiff can be causally related to the accident would appear to be within the scope of the patient's care and treatment," and therefore the witnesses need not be disclosed with a Rule 26(a)(2)(B) report.[28]

The court reached a similar conclusion in *Mangla v. University of Rochester*, where it flatly stated: "Treating physicians, however, testifying to their personal consultation with a patient are not considered expert witnesses pursuant to [Rule 26]."[29] The court first looked at the source of the witnesses' opinions, noting that a treating physician's testimony is based on the physician's personal knowledge of the patient derived from the examination and not from outside sources. In addition, the court addressed the scope of a treating witness' testimony, finding the cause of an injury and degree of injury in the future both are part of the treatment of the patient and knowledge of those factors does not make a witness a Rule 26(a)(2)(B) expert requiring heightened disclosure.[31]

As a result of the decisions in *Wreath, Baker, Salas,* and *Mangla*, a court faced with a request for heightened disclosure would examine the substance and source of the testimony of the witness. The court would order Rule 26(a)(2)(B) heightened disclosure if the witness' anticipated testimony is beyond the limits of treatment, causation, and prognosis or is based on information beyond that derived from the examination performed by the physician.

C. The Substance-Based Approach Becomes Standard

The maturation of the early decisions on standard versus heightened disclosure requirements into clear precedent on the issue can be seen almost immediately after the first set of decisions was published. *Brown v. Best Foods, Inc.* contains the most detailed review of the early case law in this area, providing a comprehensive substance-based framework....[32]

Many other courts have made similar findings when addressing Rule 26(a)(2) issues involving the distinction between standard and heightened disclosure experts.... According to *Sircher v. City of Chicago*, "... a witness such as Dr. Ferraro, whose proposed opinion testimony will come from his knowledge acquired as a treating physician, is not someone from whom a Rule 26(a)(2)(B) formal report is required."[42] In *Washington*

---

28. *Id.* at 33.

29. Mangla v. Univ. of Rochester, 168 F.R.D. 137 (W.D.N.Y. 1996) (citing *Salas*, 165 F.R.D. at 32; *Baker*, 163 F.R.D. at 352).

31. *Id.* at 139.

32. Brown v. Best Foods, Inc., 169 F.R.D. 385 (N.D. Ala. 1996).

42. Sircher v. City of Chicago, No. 97-C-6694, WL 560568, at *2 (N.D. Ill. July 27, 1999).

v. Arapahoe County Department of Social Services, the court held: "If a treating physician offers expert testimony concerning matters which are not based on his or her observations during the course of treating the party designating them, however, an expert report which complies with the requirements of Rule 26(a)(2)(B) is required."[43]

Judge Ponsor in *Garcia v. City of Springfield Police Dep't* summed up the precedent established by post-1993 Rule 26 case law regarding heightened versus standard disclosures . . . :

> The common rule distilled from the above decisions is that so long as the expert care-provider's testimony about causation and prognosis is based on personal knowledge and on observations obtained during the course of care and treatment, and he or she was not specially retained in connection with the litigation or for trial, a Rule 26 expert report is not necessary.[46]

. . . In 1998, the court in *Sprague v. Liberty Mutual Insurance Co.* provided a brief analysis of the reasons behind the substance-based approach.[51] In that case, the court reasoned that the substance-based approach was needed to provide effective cross-examination tools for attorneys. Normally a treating expert has created medical records based on his or her examination "from which any competent attorney can effectively cross-examine." Because a retained expert has not created such records from a contemporaneous patient examination, the expert "is required to provide the report to enable effective cross-examination." Under the . . . substance-based approach, the courts . . . require a Rule 26(a)(2)(B) report to figuratively "level the playing field" for cross-examination. . . .

Notes and Questions

1. In *McFerrin*, the court neatly lays out the three different types of witnesses under Rule 26(a), and the disclosure requirements of each. Look at the analysis for Dr. Smith's testimony in detail: is the court telling us that a doctor can never be a 26(a)(1) fact witness? It seems that the answer is no. A physician, even a treating physician, could be a standard fact witness, so long as her testimony is solely limited to facts. The *McFerrin* court indicates that the testimony would probably be limited only to the "course of treatment and to what he directly observed." Can you argue that the court is being overly inclusive in allowing the doctor to testify to those two issues?

2. Independent of the line between fact witnesses under Rule 26(a)(1) and expert witnesses under Rule 26(a)(2), the court also divides the category of experts into retained and non-retained groups. The plaintiff in *McFerrin* appears to miss the

---

43. Washington v. Arapahoe Cty. Dep't of Soc. Serv., 197 F.R.D. 439, 442 (D. Colo. 2000) (citing Bucher v. Gainey Transp. Serv. of Indiana, Inc., 167 F.R.D. 387, 390 (M.D. Penn. 1990)).
46. Garcia v. City of Springfield Police Dep't, 230 F.R.D. 247, 249 (D. Mass. 2005)
51. Sprague v. Liberty Mut. Ins. Co., 177 F.R.D. 78, 80 (D.N.H. 1998).

category of non-retained experts, as the court notes: "Moreover, McFerrin's counsel seems to assert that because no expert has been retained specifically for purposes of trial, there is no need to file any disclosure concerning witnesses beyond … [Rule 26(a)(1) requirements]." *McFerrin,* 29 F.Supp.3d at 931. He is half-right. The court clearly agrees that an expert report under Rule 26(a)(2)(B) is not required for anyone who is not a retained expert, the court also makes clear: "… he must still disclose anyone giving expert testimony under 26(a)(2)(A) even if the report is not required.…" That disclosure must include basic identifying information but also a summary of facts and opinions, as stated in Rule 26(a)(2)(C). This requirement is less onerous than the requirements of a retained expert, but it still requires minimal disclosure by a party to avoid witness preclusion under Rule 37.

3. Since the plaintiff in *McFerrin* asserted Dr. Smith remained solely a fact witness rather than an expert, the court did not need to dive into details on whether his testimony would require an expert report under Rule 26(a)(2)(B). But **when** is an expert "retained" and when is she not? The standard rule—as reiterated by *McFerrin*—requires court to look at the **substance of the testimony** rather than the **status of the witness.** Considering the language of Rule 26(a)(2)(B), how can this be so?

   The article *The Expert Heightened Disclosure Requirement* describes how multiple courts have handled the same issue: by relying on substance of the testimony instead of status. Considering that standard, think about how judges will evaluate future expert witnesses in deciding whether they cross the line and become retained experts.

4. While the rules require limited disclosures for non-retained experts, the requirements for the subset of expert witnesses who are retained or specially employed under Rule 26(a)(2)(B) are quite detailed and specific.

Federal Rule of Civil Procedure 26(a) Required Disclosures.

(2) *Disclosure of Expert Testimony.*

   (B) *Witnesses Who Must Provide a Written Report.* Unless otherwise stipulated or ordered by the court, this disclosure must be accompanied by a written report—prepared and signed by the witness—if the witness is one retained or specially employed to provide expert testimony in the case or one whose duties as the party's employee regularly involve giving expert testimony. The report must contain:

      (i) a complete statement of all opinions the witness will express and the basis and reasons for them;

      (ii) the facts or data considered by the witness in forming them;

      (iii) any exhibits that will be used to summarize or support them;

      (iv) the witness's qualifications, including a list of all publications authored in the previous 10 years;

(v) a list of all other cases in which, during the previous 4 years, the witness testified as an expert at trial or by deposition; and

(vi) a statement of the compensation to be paid for the study and testimony....

Robinson v. District of Columbia

75 F.Supp.3d 190 (D.D.C. 2014)

BOASBERG, U.S. District Judge.

On March 6, 2009, Arnell Robinson was riding his motorcycle down O Street in Northwest Washington, when he was involved in a fatal collision with an unmarked police car. Later that year, his mother, Plaintiff Caroline Robinson, brought this suit against the Metropolitan Police Department officer who was driving the car and the District of Columbia. A pivotal question in the case is how the accident transpired. Now that the parties have completed extensive discovery, Robinson moves to strike Defendants' accident-reconstruction expert, Wendell Cover. She argues that Defendants and Cover failed to comply with certain disclosure requirements for expert witnesses.... While the Court agrees that Defendants should have exercised more care in complying with the rules of expert discovery, it believes that striking Cover's participation is unnecessarily draconian. The Court will thus deny Plaintiff's Motion, although it will permit her to re-open Cover's deposition to inquire further about certain limited topics.

I. Procedural Background

While some cases may proceed on an express route, this one has not. Like the slowest local, this train has stopped at every possible station along the way. Expert discovery was initially scheduled to close on August 30, 2011, over three years ago. Upon requests from both parties, however, the Court has extended the deadlines for expert reports and expert discovery on more than fifteen occasions....

One of the experts whom Defendants identified is Wendell Cover. He was retained "to evaluate and reconstruct, to the degree possible, [the] motor vehicle collision that occurred on Friday, March 06, 2009." Defendants provided a copy of his report to Robinson on February 21, 2013. But by May 1, 2014 — the final deadline for expert discovery — Defendants had yet to make him available for a deposition.

As a result, on May 6, 2014, Plaintiff filed a motion to strike Cover's report and testimony. The motion sought to exclude him on several grounds, including that Defendants had failed to produce him for a deposition before the relevant cutoff date; he had not provided certain materials before the expert-report deadline; his analysis was deficient in certain respects; and he lacked the necessary qualifications to serve as an expert. The Court dismissed that motion without prejudice and ordered that Cover's deposition take place in early June 2014. Shortly after the deposition was completed, Plaintiff filed the present Motion, again seeking to bar Cover's report and testimony.

II. Analysis

While this Court has previously cautioned Plaintiff about submitting digressive and prolix filings, that admonition appears to have struck stony ground. Instead, Robinson has submitted a lengthy Motion to Strike, which frequently veers off into discussions of the merits of the case and often skips back and forth among various arguments. The filing, as a result, is difficult to decipher. The Court was, nevertheless, able to discern ... grounds on which Robinson challenges Cover's report and proposed testimony. First, she asserts that Defendants and Cover failed to comply with [Rule 26(a)]....

A. *Compliance with Rule 26(a)*

Rule 26(a)(2) provides that "a party must disclose to the other parties the identity of any witness it may use at trial to present evidence under Federal Rule of Evidence 702, 703, or 705," which are the rules that govern expert testimony. For proposed experts who regularly provide expert testimony or who have been specifically retained to do so, this disclosure must ordinarily be supplemented by a written report, prepared and signed by the witness, which includes the substance of the expert's opinions and the "basis and reasons for them." The report must additionally contain "the facts or data considered by the witness," "any exhibits that will be used to summarize or support" his opinions, and certain information about the witness's qualifications, his past history as an expert, and his compensation. "The purpose of Rule 26(a)(2) is to prevent unfair surprise at trial and to permit the opposing party to prepare rebuttal reports, to depose the expert in advance of trial, and to prepare for depositions and cross-examination at trial." *Minebea Co., Ltd. v. Papst*, 231 F.R.D. 3, 5–6 (D.D.C.2005)....

Under Rule 37(c)(1), if a party fails to comply with these disclosure requirements, "the party is not allowed to use that ... witness to supply evidence on a motion, at a hearing, or at a trial, unless the failure was substantially justified or is harmless." "In addition to or instead of this sanction," courts may provide alternative sanctions, including informing the jury of the party's failure, awarding costs and attorney fees to the prejudiced party, or any of the other sanctions listed in Rule 37(b)(2)(A)(i)–(vi).

Here, Robinson contends that Cover's disclosures fell short of Rule 26(a)'s demands in several respects. She claims, for instance, that his report does not adequately delineate the bases for his opinions. She also argues that he did not produce his CV, a list of cases in which he had previously served as an expert, and certain models, photographs, and other data prior to the June 28, 2013, deadline for Defendants' expert reports. Instead, he produced his CV on April 14, 2014, his list of prior cases on May 16, 2014, and the photographs, models, and exhibits on June 5, 2014, the day of his deposition. She further notes that he never produced court records related to a "friendly" lawsuit he filed in D.C. Superior Court to recover his fees from the District. For all of these reasons, Robinson believes Cover's report and proposed testimony must be struck....

While the Court agrees that some of the materials were produced after they should have been, it does not believe that any of these transgressions, singly or in concert, provide a basis for excluding Cover. First, Plaintiff's allegation that the report contains insufficient detail holds no water. She complains, for example, that he used photographs to locate the police cruiser's final "rest position" and to evaluate the damage to the cruiser and Robinson's motorcycle, but his report does not identify the specific photographs that he relied upon. As another example, she argues that his report did not include the variables he used to calculate the motorcycle's speed at the time of the crash. From these complaints, it is clear that Robinson believes an expert's report must be so detailed as to completely eliminate the need for a deposition. But that is not what Rule 26 requires. *See Evans v. Washington Metro. Area Transit Auth.,* 674 F.Supp.2d 175, 180–81 (D.D.C.2009); *Romero v. ITW Food Equip. Grp. LLC,* 289 F.R.D. 387, 389 (D.D.C.2013). Courts in this District have "reject[ed] the idea that 'an expert report must be sufficiently complete that no deposition of the expert should be needed to prepare to cross examine him.'" *Heller v. Dist. of Columbia,* 952 F.Supp.2d 133, 138 (D.D.C.2013) (quoting *Evans,* 674 F.Supp.2d at 180). Indeed, "[t]he expert report ... is not the end of the road, but a means of providing adequate notice to the other side to enable it to challenge the expert's opinions and prepare to put on expert testimony of its own." *Id.* at 139. Cover's report does just that. It provides a complete description of the opinions he plans to offer at trial and it explains how he arrived at them. While it may not provide the most comprehensive explanation of his planned testimony, it is sufficient.

Turning next to Cover's failure to produce his CV and list of prior cases before the relevant deadline, the Court finds that such deficiencies were harmless. As Defendants point out, Plaintiff received Cover's CV and case list several weeks in advance of his deposition. As a result, she had ample time to prepare for it. This is reflected in the fact that she was able to question Cover about his involvement in previous cases and about his qualifications. Plaintiff's Memorandum and her Reply, moreover, focus solely on whether the violations were substantially justified; she does not provide any indication that she was *prejudiced* by receiving these documents when she did. The late productions of the CV and case list, therefore, do not provide a basis to strike Cover. *See* Fed. R. Civ. P. 37(c)(1) (allowing party to use witness so long as violations of Rule 26(a) or (e) are "substantially justified or ... harmless")....

The non-production of the friendly-lawsuit documents is similarly harmless. Putting aside the parties' disagreement about whether Defendants even had an obligation to produce these documents, Plaintiff was able to obtain them. She was aware of the lawsuit prior to Cover's deposition and she had the opportunity to question him about it. The Court, therefore, finds that Plaintiff was not prejudiced by Defendants' decision not to produce these documents.

The Court moves, finally, to Cover's failure to produce certain photographs, diagrams, and 3-D models in advance of his deposition. According to Robinson, Cover arrived at his deposition with 256 photographs, six photogrammetric diagrams, and at least two 3-D models, which required proprietary software to view. She argues that "[g]etting this voluminous wealth of information was impossible to digest on the spot in the deposition." She complains, additionally, that because she did not receive these materials in advance, her experts were unable to review them and help her prepare for the deposition.

With respect to the late-produced photographs, Plaintiff was not prejudiced. She concedes that she had previously received the "police on-scene photos." It thus appears that the only photographs to which she did not have access prior to the deposition were photographs that Cover took while inspecting the damage to Arnell Robinson's motorcycle. Since the motorcycle itself was in Plaintiff's possession, it is difficult to see how she was harmed by Cover's failure to produce these. Robinson and her experts had the ability to examine the motorcycle and prepare to depose him about his description of its damage.

The exhibits and models, however, present a slightly different story. Cover generated 3-D models of the accident site to demonstrate that two witnesses could not have seen the collision. He also used photogrammetry to diagram the accident scene. By not receiving these data in advance of Cover's deposition, Robinson was unable to consult her experts about them. And although there are perhaps better and more efficient ways Plaintiff could have handled Defendants' failure to produce these data, it was Defendants' obligation under Rule 26(a) to provide them with Cover's report. Their failure to do so was not entirely harmless.

Striking Cover, however, is far too harsh a penalty. The harm was not great, and the "preclusion of evidence is an extreme sanction." *Richardson v. Korson,* 905 F.Supp.2d 193, 200 (D.D.C.2012). Because a trial date has not yet been set, the Court believes that any possible prejudice to Plaintiff can be eliminated by giving her the opportunity to further depose Cover about these late-produced materials. It will, accordingly, allow Plaintiff an additional two hours to depose Cover about the diagrams and models. In the interests of fairness and preventing any prejudice to Plaintiff, the Court will also require that Defendants pay the costs associated with this deposition. *See id.* at 201.... In declining to strike Cover, the Court cautions Defendants that it does not condone their shortcomings here. It expects litigants, especially repeat players like the District, to comply with the Rules.

III. Conclusion

For the foregoing reasons, the Court will deny Plaintiff's Motion to Strike.

Notes and Questions

1. When the deposition is reopened in *Robinson,* what topics can plaintiff ask the expert about? Why is the court limiting the reopened deposition to only that topic? And why is that specific material different than, say, the CV or photographs, which the court finds harmless and which will not be discussed in the new deposition?

2. The requirements of a retained expert report under Rule 26(a)(2)(B) are extensive, yet the court is careful to mention they are not required to be "so detailed as to completely eliminate the need for a deposition." And so, like in *Robinson,* courts must review the disclosures provided, what was not provided, the context of the case, and the timeline of events to decide whether the disclosures are inadequate

and whether there is prejudice. We will review sanctions in our next section, Part 3.A.iii, but note that the *Robinson* court reminds us evidence preclusion is a severe penalty, one the court avoids by reopening the deposition and awarding costs for that deposition to the party in error.

Tying It Together

At the end of Chapter 2, we learned about the *John Porter v. Inga Douglas, M.D.* case involving surgical implantation of a replacement hip and subsequent complications. As the case proceeds toward trial, we now need to consider the discovery obligations of the parties under Rule 26.

Assignment: Assume you are an associate at Gotta, Outta & Trouble. Dr. Douglas will need to disclose witnesses pursuant to Rule 26, and so you have been assigned the task of writing draft disclosures for three witnesses, who will discuss the following:

- **Sally Porter**: will testify about her husband's condition leading up to the surgery;

- **Inga Douglas, M.D.**: will testify about the surgery she performed on Porter; and

- **Dana David, M.D.**: will testify about Porter's hip condition and that the surgery was performed correctly, as discussed in detail in Chapter 2.

Please note that should you need any additional information required to complete the disclosures, please add that information to the case (so long as it is not inconsistent with the given facts).

Please prepare the draft disclosures.

iii. Sanctions under Fed. R. Civ. P. 37

Federal Rule of Civil Procedure 37:
Failure to Make Disclosures or to Cooperate in Discovery; Sanctions

(a) MOTION FOR AN ORDER COMPELLING DISCLOSURE OR DISCOVERY.

(1) *In General.* On notice to other parties..., a party may move for an order compelling disclosure or discovery. The motion must include a certification that the movant has in good faith conferred or attempted to confer with the person or party failing to make disclosure or discovery in an effort to obtain it without court action.

(2) *Appropriate Court.* A motion for an order to a party must be made in the court where the action is pending. A motion for an order to a nonparty must be made in the court where the discovery is or will be taken.

(3) *Specific Motions.*

(A) *To Compel Disclosure.* If a party fails to make a disclosure required by Rule 26(a), any other party may move to compel disclosure and for appropriate sanctions.

(B) *To Compel a Discovery Response.* A party seeking discovery may move for an order compelling an answer, designation, production, or inspection....

(5) *Payment of Expenses; Protective Orders.*

(A) *If the Motion Is Granted (or Disclosure or Discovery Is Provided After Filing).* If the motion is granted — or if the disclosure or requested discovery is provided after the motion was filed — the court must, after giving an opportunity to be heard, require the party or deponent whose conduct necessitated the motion ... to pay the movant's reasonable expenses incurred in making the motion, including attorney's fees. But the court must not order this payment if:

(i) the movant filed the motion before attempting in good faith to obtain the disclosure or discovery without court action;

(ii) the opposing party's nondisclosure, response, or objection was substantially justified; or

(iii) other circumstances make an award of expenses unjust.

(B) *If the Motion Is Denied.* If the motion is denied, the court may issue any protective order authorized under Rule 26(c) and must, after giving an opportunity to be heard, require the movant, the attorney filing the motion, or both to pay the party or deponent who opposed the motion its reasonable expenses incurred in opposing the motion, including attorney's fees. But the court must not order this payment if the motion was substantially justified or other circumstances make an award of expenses unjust....

(b) FAILURE TO COMPLY WITH A COURT ORDER.

...

(2) *Sanctions Sought in the District Where the Action Is Pending.*

(A) *For Not Obeying a Discovery Order.* If a party or a party's officer, director, or managing agent ... fails to obey an order to provide or permit discovery, including an order under Rule 26(f), 35, or 37(a), the court where the action is pending may issue further just orders. They may include the following:

(i) directing that the matters embraced in the order or other designated facts be taken as established for purposes of the action, as the prevailing party claims;

(ii) prohibiting the disobedient party from supporting or opposing designated claims or defenses, or from introducing designated matters in evidence;

(iii) striking pleadings in whole or in part;

(iv) staying further proceedings until the order is obeyed;

(v) dismissing the action or proceeding in whole or in part;

(vi) rendering a default judgment against the disobedient party; or

(vii) treating as contempt of court the failure to obey any order except an order to submit to a physical or mental examination.

(B) *For Not Producing a Person for Examination.* If a party fails to comply with an order under Rule 35(a) requiring it to produce another person for examination, the court may issue any of the orders listed in Rule 37(b)(2)(A)(i)–(vi), unless the disobedient party shows that it cannot produce the other person.

(C) *Payment of Expenses.* Instead of or in addition to the orders above, the court must order the disobedient party ... to pay the reasonable expenses, including attorney's fees, caused by the failure, unless the failure was substantially justified or other circumstances make an award of expenses unjust.

(c) FAILURE TO DISCLOSE, TO SUPPLEMENT AN EARLIER RESPONSE, OR TO ADMIT.

(1) *Failure to Disclose or Supplement.* If a party fails to provide information or identify a witness as required by Rule 26(a) or (e), the party is not allowed to use that information or witness to supply evidence on a motion, at a hearing, or at a trial, unless the failure was substantially justified or is harmless. In addition to or instead of this sanction, the court, on motion and after giving an opportunity to be heard:

(A) may order payment of the reasonable expenses, including attorney's fees, caused by the failure;

(B) may inform the jury of the party's failure; and

(C) may impose other appropriate sanctions, including any of the orders listed in Rule 37(b)(2)(A)(i)–(vi)....

Pacific Indemnity Co. v. Nidec Motor Corp.
203 F. Supp. 3d 1092 (D. Nev. 2016)

GORDON, Judge.

This case arises out of a fire that took place in July 2012 at a theater at Caesar's Palace in Las Vegas. Plaintiff Pacific Indemnity Company's insured owns the show that was performing in the theater and the insured suffered losses when the fire damaged the theater and disrupted the performance of future shows. Pacific contends the fire was caused by a defect in a Re-Fan II Turbo fan or its component parts.... Defendant Nidec manufactured the fan motor. Pacific sued ... Nidec for strict products liability, alleging that the fan motor was defective. Pacific also asserts claims for negligence and breach of implied warranty....

Under the scheduling order, the parties had until April 20, 2015 to disclose experts. On April 17, 2015, the parties stipulated to extend the discovery deadlines for sixty days while the parties pursued settlement discussions. They proposed to extend the expert disclosure deadline to June 19, 2015. The Magistrate Judge denied without prejudice the parties' stipulation to extend the initial expert disclosure deadline because the parties failed to address whether there was excusable neglect for failing to move to extend the deadline earlier. The parties did not file another stipulation or motion to extend the deadline. Thus, April 20 remained the date for initial expert disclosures.

On June 19, 2015, Pacific designated Erik Christiansen as a retained expert and Amy Saenz and "Clark County Fire Department Investigators with designation CC906 and CC902" as non-retained experts. Pacific provided an expert report prepared by Christiansen. In his report, Christiansen stated that the fan motor was severely damaged by heat and fire, that the bearings no longer would spin freely, and that heat patterns observed on the motor's interior were "consistent with internal failure, as opposed to external fire attack." Christiansen also noted a thermal cut-off switch was in the closed position. Christiansen opined that:

> [b]ased on the damage to the fan, the most likely cause of the fire was a failure of the fan motor. The motor shows internal damage consistent with an over-heating event. Additionally, the thermal switch that protects the motor from overheating was found to be failed closed, and therefore would not disconnect power to the fan motor as intended during an over-temperature situation.[1]

Pacific also provided a report from the Clark County Fire Department. The investigators who prepared the report are identified only as CC906 and CC902. According to that report, the fire occurred while the theater was empty. The investigators found burned chairs and "what looked like fan parts lying on the chairs." The investigators reviewed video footage but the video did not have a direct view of the fire. Instead, they could see from reflections where the fire had occurred. The investigators examined where the fan had been suspended from the ceiling.... The fan motor showed "signs of heavy fire damage to the motor and metal parts." "The fan motor would not spin" when the investigator tried to turn it. The investigators also examined the light board and noticed that dimmer #48 had been tripped, while all other dimmers remained in the on position. A stage hand informed the investigators that an electrician had wired the fan into dimmer switch #48. The investigators concluded that the "area of origin is on or in the fan motor on the east side of the theater." They further concluded that the "cause of the fire is most probably [an] overheating/failure of the electrical motor."

The day before Pacific designated its initial experts, Nidec disclosed its rebuttal expert, Kenneth Theis, even though there was no expert to rebut at that time. According to Theis, the motor's rotor would not rotate, but he concluded it was "the result of external heat damage to the bearings and loss of an end shield, not internal

---

1. In a separate affidavit, Christiansen stated:
   [t]o a reasonable degree of engineering and scientific certainty, the most likely cause of the fire was a failure of the fan motor. The motor shows internal damage consistent with an overheating event....

heat generated by the motor itself." Theis noted that the damage was more pronounced on one side of the motor and the opposite side "showed no internal heating." He also concluded that the electrical resistance measurements of the motor's windings were consistent with original factory specifications and there was no other evidence of internal heat consistent with being a fire source. Theis thus concluded:

> [t]he resistance measurements and lack of internal shorting of the coils of the subject motor rules out heat generation internal to the [Nidec] motor. There is no other objective evidence or condition of the motor that would suggest it was the cause of the fire.

Theis also concluded the motor had no defects in its design or manufacture, and the "[d]amage to the subject [Nidec] motor was not the cause of the fire, but the result of fire and heat after the fire began external to the motor." He bases his conclusion on the fact that there was "no heat ... generated internal to the [Nidec] motor sufficient to compromise insulation or the other internal components." Instead, he suggests other components of the fan could have been the source ... Nidec noticed Christiansen's deposition for August 17, 2015 ... [which] would have fallen within the time remaining in the discovery period. This deposition never took place.

Nidec moves for summary judgment, arguing that Pacific did not timely disclose any experts and thus Pacific will not be able to show the fan motor was defective or that it caused the fire. Nidec argues that even if the court allows Pacific's untimely expert disclosures, Pacific's designated expert does not opine the motor was defective or caused the fire and the other identified experts did not provide reports.

Pacific responds by arguing the late designation was harmless because the parties had agreed to extend the deadlines while they pursued settlement efforts, Nidec designated its own expert only one day prior, and Nidec was already aware of most of the information disclosed in Pacific's expert designation. Pacific also contends Nidec had the opportunity to depose Christiansen within the discovery period and had scheduled a deposition, but then decided not to proceed with it. Pacific acknowledges the parties should have sought relief from the court regarding the deadlines, but instead the parties resumed settlement talks.

As to whether there is evidence the motor was defective, Pacific argues that it does not necessarily need an expert because the mere fact of the fire shows a defect. Pacific also asserts both the fire investigators and Christiansen opine that the fire started in the motor. Finally, Pacific contends that causation is a question of fact for the jury.

II. ANALYSIS

A. Failure to Timely Disclose Expert

A party must disclose the identity of any expert witness it intends to use at trial and must provide the expert's written report. Fed. R. Civ. P. 26(a)(2)(A)–(B).... When a party fails to do so, that party is "not allowed to use the information or witness to supply evidence ... at trial, unless the failure was substantially justified or is harmless." Fed. R. Civ. P. 37(c)(1). The party facing the sanction bears the burden of showing substantial justification or harmlessness. *See Yeti by Molly, Ltd. v. Deckers Outdoor Corp.,*

259 F.3d 1101, 1107 (9th Cir.2001). "Harmlessness may be established if a disclosure is made sufficiently before the discovery cutoff to enable the movant to depose the expert and challenge his expert report." *Boliba v. Camping World, Inc.*, No. 2:14-CV-01840-JAD-NJK, 2015 WL 3916775, at *2 (D.Nev. June 25, 2015) (citations omitted).

However, even if a party cannot show harmlessness or substantial justification, I am not required to exclude evidence as a sanction. *Jackson v. United Artists Theatre Circuit, Inc.*, 278 F.R.D. 586, 594 (D.Nev.2011). Other potential sanctions under Rule 37(c)(1) include payment of reasonable expenses incurred and any other "appropriate" sanction, including those listed in Rule 37(b)(2)(A)(i)–(vi). I have wide discretion in determining the appropriate sanction. *See Yeti*, 259 F.3d at 1106. In making that determination, I consider: (1) "the public's interest in expeditious resolution of litigation;" (2) "the court's need to manage its docket;" (3) the risk of prejudice to the party seeking sanctions; (4) "the public policy favoring disposition of cases on their merits;" and (5) "the availability of less drastic sanctions." *See Wendt v. Host Int'l, Inc.*, 125 F.3d 806, 814 (9th Cir.1997). When excluding evidence would "amount[] to dismissal of a claim, the district court [is] required to consider whether the noncompliance involved willfulness, fault, or bad faith." *R&R Sails, Inc. v. Ins. Co. of Penn.*, 673 F.3d 1240, 1247 (9th Cir.2012).

Pacific concedes it failed to timely disclose its expert. That failure was not completely harmless because Nidec expended resources filing a summary judgment motion based on the fact that Pacific had not timely designated any experts. However, the untimely disclosure was not sufficiently prejudicial to Nidec to justify excluding Christiansen; that remedy is too harsh under the circumstances. Doing so would, by Nidec's own argument, amount to dismissal of Pacific's claims. There is no evidence of willfulness or bad faith to support case-ending sanctions. Moreover, Nidec was already aware of Christiansen's identity because he was present when the parties and their respective experts examined and tested the fan in September 2013. The parties were attempting to settle this matter without the need to expend resources on costly expert reports but were unable to do so by the disclosure deadline. Although the parties should have obtained court approval of an extended deadline, Nidec still had time during the discovery period to depose Christiansen. Indeed, Nidec had noticed his deposition but, for reasons unknown, cancelled it. Additionally, Nidec did not disclose Theis by the initial expert disclosure deadline even though his report reads more like an initial expert report than a rebuttal report and there was nothing for Theis to rebut at the time his report was disclosed....

Although I decline to exclude Christiansen, the late disclosure is sanctionable. In an effort to mitigate any prejudice to Nidec, I will extend the discovery deadline only to allow Nidec to depose Christiansen if it chooses to do so and for Theis to update his rebuttal report in response. Because Nidec could have deposed Christiansen during the discovery period, I will not award Nidec fees and costs associated with Christiansen's deposition if Nidec opts to depose him. However, I will award Nidec its reasonable attorney's fees and costs for preparing the summary judgment motion because Nidec would not have had a basis to make that motion if Pacific had timely disclosed its initial expert designations.

Notes and Questions

1. In deciding on a sanction under Rule 37, the court has a variety of options as well as a variety of factors to consider. Clearly, a court has the power to exclude a witness (or other evidence) when it has not been timely disclosed unless the proponent of the evidence can establish it is either 1) substantially justified, or 2) harmless to the opponent. Even without these, Judge Gordon affirms that judges have wide discretion to decide an appropriate sanction, and will consider the *Wendt* factors to guide their decision. How do each of these factors relate to appropriateness of a sanction? Note also how—in a situation where preclusion would end the case—that a court should consider "willfulness, fault, or bad faith." *Pacific Indemn. Co.*, 203 F. Supp. 3d at 1097 (citing *R & R Sails, Inc. v. Ins. Co. of Pa.*, 673 F.3d 1240, 1247 (9th Cir. 2012)). Is a different standard here fair, since the preclusion of the witness will be measured by the same *Wendt* factors?

2. Consider the range of sanctions available to a court, in addition to witness preclusion. A court, under Rule 37(c)(1):

    (A) may order payment of the reasonable expenses, including attorney's fees, caused by the failure;

    (B) may inform the jury of the party's failure; and

    (C) may impose other appropriate sanctions, including any of the orders listed in Rule 37(b)(2)(A)(i)–(vi) ...

    [which include:

    (i) directing that the matters embraced in the order or other designated facts be taken as established for purposes of the action, as the prevailing party claims;

    (ii) prohibiting the disobedient party from supporting or opposing designated claims or defenses, or from introducing designated matters in evidence;

    (iii) striking pleadings in whole or in part;

    (iv) staying further proceedings until the order is obeyed;

    (v) dismissing the action or proceeding in whole or in part;

    (vi) rendering a default judgment against the disobedient party; or

    (vii) treating as contempt of court the failure to obey any order except an order to submit to a physical or mental examination.]

    Whether any of these sanctions is appropriate will be largely contextual, which explains why the court examined the claims, timelines, and evidence in *Pacific Indemnity* in such detail. This is typical for cases with contested discovery issues under Rule 37.

3. Unlike *Pacific Indemnity*, where Judge Gordon writes that courts retain the discretion to not preclude evidence even when substantial justification or harmless-

ness have not been shown, other judges see preclusion of evidence as a default sanction unless those exceptions are proven by the opponent of the sanction. *Klonoski v. Mahlab*, 156 F.3d 255, 269 (1st Cir. 1998) (finding Rule 37(c)(1) "clearly contemplates stricter adherence to discovery requirements, and harsher sanctions for breaches of [the] rule, and the required sanction in the ordinary case is mandatory preclusion."). *See also Santiago-Diaz v. Laboratorio Clinico y de Referencia del Este*, 456 F.3d 272, 276 (1st Cir. 2006) (same); *Lohnes v. Level 3 Communications, Inc.*, 272 F.3d 49, 60 (1st Cir. 2001) (same). Any sanctions are reviewed under an abuse of discretion standard deferential to the trial court judge. *Esposito v. Home Depot U.S.A.*, 590 F.3d 72, 78 (1st Cir. 2009). As such, the individual preferences and default position on preclusion for a particular judge may be the most important factor of all.

B. Rules of Disclosure in Criminal Cases

Criminal discovery rules, under the Federal Rules and most state rules or codes on disclosure, limit mandatory disclosure drastically compared to the civil rules we have covered. Some types of inculpatory information will be disclosed by the prosecution to the defense, and importantly for our purposes, the requirements of disclosure include materials pertaining to expert tests, examinations, and witnesses. After reading the rule, we will consider the scope of those disclosure requirements and court sanctions for failure to comply. We will finish with a review of disclosure requirements for exculpatory information under *Brady*[19] and other cases.

Federal Rule of Criminal Procedure 16:
Discovery and Inspection

(a) GOVERNMENT'S DISCLOSURE.

(1) *Information Subject to Disclosure.*

    (A) *Defendant's Oral Statement.* Upon a defendant's request, the government must disclose to the defendant the substance of any relevant oral statement made by the defendant, before or after arrest, in response to interrogation by a person the defendant knew was a government agent if the government intends to use the statement at trial.

    (B) *Defendant's Written or Recorded Statement.* Upon a defendant's request, the government must disclose to the defendant, and make available for inspection, copying, or photographing, all of the following:

        (i) any relevant written or recorded statement by the defendant if:

           • the statement is within the government's possession, custody, or control; and

---

19. Brady v. Maryland, 373 U.S. 83 (1963).

• the attorney for the government knows—or through due diligence could know that the statement exists;

(ii) the portion of any written record containing the substance of any relevant oral statement made before or after arrest if the defendant made the statement in response to interrogation by a person the defendant knew was a government agent; and

(iii) the defendant's recorded testimony before a grand jury relating to the charged offense....

(D) *Defendant's Prior Record.* Upon a defendant's request, the government must furnish the defendant with a copy of the defendant's prior criminal record that is within the government's possession, custody, or control if the attorney for the government knows—or through due diligence could know—that the record exists.

(E) *Documents and Objects.* Upon a defendant's request, the government must permit the defendant to inspect and to copy or photograph books, papers, documents, data, photographs, tangible objects, buildings or places, or copies or portions of any of these items, if the item is within the government's possession, custody, or control and:

(i) the item is material to preparing the defense;

(ii) the government intends to use the item in its case-in-chief at trial; or

(iii) the item was obtained from or belongs to the defendant.

(F) *Reports of Examinations and Tests.* Upon a defendant's request, the government must permit a defendant to inspect and to copy or photograph the results or reports of **any physical or mental examination and of any scientific test or experiment**[Ed.] if:

(i) the item is within the government's possession, custody, or control;

(ii) the attorney for the government knows—or through due diligence could know—that the item exists; and

(iii) the item is material to preparing the defense or the government intends to use the item in its case-in-chief at trial.

(G) *Expert Witnesses.* At the defendant's request, the government must give to the defendant a written summary of any testimony that the government intends to use under Rules 702, 703 or 705 of the Federal Rules of Evidence during its case-in-chief at trial.... The summary provided under this subparagraph must describe the witness's opinions, the bases and reasons for those opinions, and the witness's qualifications.

[Ed.] Emphasis added by Author.

(2) *Information Not Subject to Disclosure.* Except as permitted by Rule 16(a)(1)(A)–(D), (F), and (G), this rule does not authorize the discovery or inspection of reports, memoranda, or other internal government documents made by an attorney for the government or other government agent in connection with investigating or prosecuting the case.

United States v. Pembrook

119 F. Supp. 3d 577 (E.D. Mich. 2015)

MICHELSON, District Judge.

On April 22, 2014, four men attempted to rob a jewelry store in Grand Rapids, Michigan, but, after one was shot by a store owner, they fled without merchandise. Later that same day, three men stole $1,500,000 in Rolex watches from a jewelry store in West Bloomfield, Michigan. Defendants Nathaniel Pembrook, David Briley, Shaeed Calhoun, and Orlando Johnson are charged with multiple criminal offenses arising out of these robberies (the first might have only been an attempt, but, for convenience, the Court will, as the parties do, refer to the Grand Rapids and West Bloomfield incidents as robberies). The Government believes Defendants are responsible for the robberies in part because of what it learned from data it obtained—without a warrant—from cellular-phone service providers. In particular, logs from the cell towers close by the two jewelry stores allegedly indicate that a phone used by Johnson was in the area of both stores at the time of the two robberies. Other cell-site data purportedly shows that Calhoun, Briley, and Pembrook traveled together (at least roughly) from Philadelphia, Pennsylvania, to Wisconsin, to the location of the two robberies, and then back to Philadelphia.

Calhoun says that by obtaining the cell-site data without a warrant, the Government conducted a search prohibited by the Fourth Amendment. So he moves to suppress the cell-site data. Calhoun also seeks to exclude from trial the testimony of the Government's cell-site data expert [under Rule 16]....

I.

A.

Some background on how cellular towers communicate with cellular phones helps to understand how the Government used cell-site data to investigate the two jewelry-store robberies and the associated expert testimony the Government plans to elicit at trial.

For a cellular phone to receive a call, send a text message, or download a webpage, it must communicate with a cellular tower. A cellular phone automatically searches for a signal from nearby towers and "[o]nce the phone locates a tower, it submits a unique identifier—its 'registration' information—to the tower so that any outgoing and incoming calls can be routed through the correct tower." *United States v. Powell,* 943 F.Supp.2d 759, 767 (E.D.Mich.2013) (citing Timothy Stapleton, Note, *The Electronic Communications Privacy Act and Cell Location Data,* 73 Brook. L.Rev. 383, 387 (2007)). "Nearby" is a relative term: it can range from a block (maybe less) to a couple miles (maybe more) depending on the tower density in the area. *See United States v. Davis,* 785 F.3d 498, 503 & n. 7 (11th Cir.2015) (en banc); *In re Application of U.S.,* 405 F.Supp.2d 435, 437 (S.D.N.Y.2005). Further, although a cell phone often registers with its closest tower, "a variety of factors including physical obstructions and to-pography can determine which tower services a particular phone." *United States v. Evans,* 892 F.Supp.2d 949, 952 (N.D.Ill.2012).

Cellular service providers (e.g., Verizon Wireless) keep track of cell-phone com-munications with their towers; courts refer to these logs as "cell-site data" or "cell-site location information" ("CSLI" for short), *see e.g., In re Application of the U.S. for Historical Cell Site Data,* 724 F.3d 600 (5th Cir.2013); *In the Matter of the Application of the U.S.A. for an Order Authorizing Disclosure of Historical Cell Site Information,* 40 F.Supp.3d 89 (D.D.C.2014). Although, a cell phone "regularly communicates with cell towers in its network" even in "idle" mode, *Evans,* 892 F.Supp.2d at 952, the Gov-ernment avers that the cell-site data at issue in this case only corresponds to active cell-phone use, for example, receiving a call or sending a text. Cell-site data might also include the "sector" of a tower to which the phone connected. For example, a tower's 360 degree coverage area might be partitioned into three 120 degree sectors.... This cell-site data permits investigators to determine the location of a cell phone at a particular time. Assume cell-cite data show that, on June 1, 2015, a cell phone using the phone number (734) xxx-1234 initiated a call via a tower located at Liberty Street and 1st Street, in Ann Arbor, Michigan at 12:00 p.m. and terminated that call while connected with a tower located at Liberty and 5th Avenue at 12:04 p.m. With a map showing that Liberty runs east-west (with 1st Street intersecting Liberty west of 5th Avenue) and with information from the cellular-service provider that the (734) xxx-1234 account is John Smith's, this cell-site data indicates (but does not conclusively prove) that Smith's phone traveled east on Liberty (or a parallel street) in Ann Arbor just after noon on June 1, 2015. An examination of the sector information might allow further refinement of the phone's geographic location....

In this case, the Government obtained cell-site data without obtaining a warrant upon a showing of probable cause.... Six days after the robberies, the Government sought an order directing a number of cellular-service providers to produce the phone numbers of the cellular devices that, around the time of the two robberies, had con-nected to cell towers servicing the two jewelry stores.

In support of its request, the Government provided some details of the crime. It informed the reviewing magistrate judge that on April 22, 2014, around 12:30 p.m., "a jewelry store located at 4518 Plainfield Ave NW, Grand Rapids, Michigan, was robbed by four males." "An employee of the business shot at, and possibly hit, one of the suspects," the Government averred. "After the gunfire[,] all four suspects fled without any merchandise." Further, said the application, "at approximately, 5:00pm, a jewelry store located at 6637 Orchard Lake Road, West Bloomfield Township, Michi-gan, was robbed by three men.... A review of video confirms that the three suspects were also involved in the robbery earlier that day in Grand Rapids, Michigan." The Government further informed that it "believe[d] that cell tower information in the two locations may reveal a common number that was active at each location around the time of the crime." ...

On April 28, 2014, a federal magistrate judge granted the Government's application.... She thus ordered Metro PCS, AT & T, Verizon, Sprint, and T-Mobile to disclose "all records and other information (not including the contents of communications) about all communications made using" the cell towers providing service to the Grand Rapids store between 10:00 a.m. and 1:00 p.m. on April 22, 2014 and the towers providing service to the West Bloomfield store between 4:00 and 5:15 p.m. on April 22, 2014. Although the magistrate judge's order included the phone numbers of each wireless device that "registered" with the towers during the two time periods, the Government advises that "[t]he data at issue in this case only includes location information for the cellular device when that device is in active use, that is, when someone is sending or receiving a call or text." ...

Almost four weeks later, on May 22, 2014, the Government filed a second ... application. In addition to the details of the robberies set out in its first application, the Government added that on April 28, 2014, "a Court Order was obtained ... authorizing the FBI to obtain data from cell phone towers near the two robberies at the times the robberies occurred. From that data it was determined that one telephone number was active at both locations during [the] time frame of each robbery, (424) 302-1434." ...

To summarize the Government's use of cell-site data in this case, it first obtained data associated with the towers around the site of the two robberies and determined that the cell phone with the number (424) 302-1434 connected to towers in the vicinity of the Medawar's jewelry store in Grand Rapids, Michigan around 12:30 p.m. and the Tapper's jewelry store in West Bloomfield, Michigan around 5:00 p.m. The Government then sought records associated with the 1434 number, which the Government now says was Defendant Johnson's and determined that the 1434 number had frequently called (872) 999-0033 around the time of the two robberies and that both those numbers had called two Philadelphia numbers. So the Government sought cell-site data from April 21 to May 21, 2014 for the 0033 number, which the Government now believes was used by Calhoun. Then, based on surveillance video, the Government concluded that Calhoun and Briley were involved in the robberies.... [From the cell data,] it appears that the Government could determine Calhoun's approximate location between April 15 and May 30, 2014, a six-week period, and Johnson's approximate location for an eight-week period.

D.

At trial, the Government intends to call Christopher Hess, a special agent with the FBI, to testify about his analysis of the cell-site data obtained during the Government's investigation.

Pursuant to Federal Rule of Criminal Procedure 16, on April 6, 2015, the Government sent Defendants' counsel a letter summarizing Hess' testimony. The letter explained, "SA Hess will specifically testify to cell site location data for four cell phones for the period of April 18–23, 2014. Using call detail records provided by the telecommunication companies that include information related to the cellular towers that a particular cellular telephone is communicating with, SA Hess will plot out the locations of the four cellular phones from April 18–23, 2014." The letter identified four phone numbers and their alleged users: [including Briley, Johnson & Calhoun].... The Government's April 6, 2015 letter also attached a document titled "Basic Principals [*sic*] Utilized in Record Analysis" prepared by Hess. In it, Hess provides how cell phones communicate with cell towers. Much of the information is similar to that presented above, but Hess included some additional detail about cellular communications.... [He] also included four maps prepared by Hess— one for each of the four phone numbers referenced in the Government's letter. Each map shows data points at Philadelphia, Pennsylvania, South Bend, Indiana, Grand Rapids, Michigan, and West Bloomfield, Michigan. Underneath the maps, Hess wrote three statements: "Preliminary analysis identified similar travel patterns of the referenced numbers"; "Travel originated and terminated in Philadelphia, PA"; and "The phones traveled to WI then to MI and utilized towers consistent with the geographic area encompassing robbery locations in Grand Rapids and Southfield, Michigan."

Finally, the Government's Rule 16 letter included Hess' curriculum vitae. It states, among other things, that Hess is educated in criminal justice and has received over 400 hours of training in various cellular protocols and radio frequency theory. The Government informs that "Hess has testified as an expert in historical cell site analysis in over 25 criminal trials," including before five different judges of this judicial district.

II.

The Court starts with Calhoun's motion to suppress.... Calhoun's primary argument is that the Court must suppress the cell-site data that the Government obtained pursuant to the April 28, August 5, and September 17, 2014 orders because that data was obtained via a search prohibited by the Fourth Amendment.

The Fourth Amendment to the United States Constitution provides, "[t]he right of the people to be secure in their persons, houses, papers, and effects, against unreasonable searches and seizures, shall not be violated." A "search []" within the meaning of the Amendment occurs when "Government physically occupie[s] private property for the purpose of obtaining information." *See United States v. Jones*, 565 U.S. 400 (2012).[Ed.] And, under *Katz v. United States*, 389 U.S. 347 (1967), a "search" also occurs "when the government infringes upon an expectation of privacy that society is prepared to consider reasonable."

Calhoun relies on the latter formulation. Combining the two concurring opinions in *United States v. Jones*, 565 U.S. 400 (2012), Calhoun asserts that five justices believe that people have a legitimate expectation of privacy in their hour-by-hour whereabouts over an extended period, such as the six- and eight-week periods at issue in this case.... Calhoun argues that because potentially hundreds of wireless devices were

[Ed.] The citations here and five lines lower than this have been updated by the Author, to reflect the Reporter cite.

connected to the towers proximate to the two jewelry stores around the time of the robberies, the "cell tower [data] dump" obtained pursuant to the April 28, 2014 order was a "dragnet" search that violated the Fourth Amendment.

It is not necessary to directly address these arguments. The question presented is whether the cell-site evidence the Government has already obtained should be suppressed, not whether an application for that data should be granted. And suppression is not an automatic remedy for a Fourth Amendment violation. *Herring v. United States*, 555 U.S. 135, 140 (2009). The Supreme Court has directed lower courts to ensure that suppression will have "[r]eal deterrent value" and to be mindful that the "bottom-line effect [of exclusion], in many cases, is to suppress the truth and set the criminal loose in the community without punishment." *Davis v. United States*, 564 U.S. 229 (2011) (citation and internal quotation marks omitted). The balance has been articulated this way: When law enforcement "exhibit[s] deliberate, reckless, or grossly negligent disregard for Fourth Amendment rights, the deterrent value of exclusion is strong and tends to outweigh the resulting costs," but when law enforcement "act[s] with an objectively reasonable good-faith belief that their conduct is lawful ... the deterrence rationale loses much of its force, and exclusion cannot pay its way." *Id.* Suppression is a remedy of "last resort."

... [At] the time the Government obtained the cell-site data at issue in this case, there was no binding authority holding that obtaining cell-site data, even cell-site data revealing an individual's whereabouts over an extended period or his presence in a private place, required a warrant supported by probable cause. Further, as will also be explained, the persuasive authority available at the time was mixed. As such, the Court finds that the Government could not have been "deliberate, reckless, or grossly negligent," *Davis*, 131 S.Ct. at 2427, in violating Calhoun's Fourth Amendment rights (assuming, without deciding, that it did violate them).

III.

Remaining for resolution is Calhoun's motion to exclude the Government's cell-site data expert, Christopher Hess, from testifying at trial or, in the alternative, to limit his testimony, or, in further alternative, for additional discovery relating to Hess' testimony.

Calhoun raises four arguments. First, he says that the Government's Federal Rule of Criminal Procedure 16 letter and the accompanying report by Hess "fail[] to provide any details describing the bases and reasons" for Hess' conclusions, thereby depriving the Court of the ability to determine whether his methods are reliable. Second, Calhoun says that Hess' opinion is based on the "theory of granulization"—a theory untested by the scientific community. Third, Calhoun argues that Hess' testimony is not admissible under Federal Rule of Evidence 701 as lay-witness testimony. Finally, Calhoun asserts that if the Court allows Hess to testify, he would like additional discovery so that he can effectively cross-examine Hess at trial.

The Court begins with Calhoun's third point because the Government agrees with it: the Government acknowledges that Hess' testimony is not lay-witness testimony and so Hess must pass this Court's screening of expert witnesses. So the question is whether Hess' testimony satisfies the standards set out in Federal Rule of Evidence 702 and *Daubert v. Merrell Dow Pharms., Inc.*, 509 U.S. 579 (1993).... Or more concisely stated, the question is whether Hess' expert opinion "rests on a reliable foundation and is relevant to the task at hand." *Daubert*, 509 U.S. at 597. It is the Government's burden to persuade the Court that the answer is likely "yes." But exclusion remains the exception, as "[v]igorous cross-examination, presentation of contrary evidence, and careful instruction on the burden of proof are the traditional and appropriate means of attacking shaky but admissible evidence," *Daubert*, 509 U.S. at 596.

The basis for Calhoun's second argument, that Hess' testimony relies on an untested theory, is a single case: *United States v. Evans*, 892 F.Supp.2d 949 (N.D.Ill.2012). There, the Government sought to rely upon the testimony of a cell-site expert to show that the criminal defendant, Antonio Evans, was in the area where a kidnapping took place. *Id.* at 951. The court explained that the theory of granulization involved (1) identifying the cell tower, sector, and sector-coverage direction used by the phone during the relevant time period; (2) estimating "the range of each [sector's] coverage based on the proximity of the tower to other towers in the area"; and (3) predicting "where the coverage area of one tower will overlap with the coverage area of another." *Id.* at 952. Applying this theory to the facts at hand, the Government's expert intended to testify that Evans' cell-phone used two towers at the time of the kidnapping and that "[t]he building where the victim was held [fell] squarely within the coverage overlap of [those] two towers." *Id.* The court found one significant problem was that the expert's coverage-overlap theory assumed that Evans' phone "used the towers closest to it at the time of the calls" without accounting for the possibility that Evans' might have connected to other towers because of signal obstruction or network traffic. *Id.* at 956. "Second," the court reasoned, "the granulization theory remains wholly untested by the scientific community, while other methods of historical cell site analysis can be and have been tested by scientists." *Id.* "Given that multiple factors [could] affect the signal strength of a tower and that [the expert's] chosen methodology ha[d] received no scrutiny outside the law enforcement community," the court concluded that the Government had not carried its burden in establishing that the granulization method was reliable. *Id.* at 957.

Hess' proposed testimony is not similar enough to that excluded in *Evans* to justify that result here. The Government explains that it "is not attempting to put a particular cell phone in [a] very specific location via Agent Hess' testimony"; instead, it "is attempting to show how the four phones in question originated in the Philadelphia, Pennsylvania [*sic*] on April 21, 2014, traveled in a similar pattern over the next few days, were in the Grand Rapids and West Bloomfield areas around the time of the robberies, and traveled back to Philadelphia on April 2223, 2014." The Government "concedes" that cell-site data cannot place Defendants "in a precise location." Thus, to the extent that Hess' testimony essentially consists of placing the four cell phones at issue in this case within a general geographic region, i.e., within a couple miles of a particular tower, the Court is not persuaded that Hess' testimony is based on the granulization theory or that *Evans* is on point.

As for testimony more akin to Hess'—that, because a log shows that a particular phone connected to a particular tower at a particular time, it can be inferred that a phone was within that tower's coverage area at that time—a number of courts have found such testimony to be based on reliable methods. *See, e.g., United States v. Schaffer*, 439 Fed.Appx. 344, 347 (5th Cir.2011) (finding that agent's testimony demonstrated that determining a phone's location based on cell-site data is "neither untested nor unestablished")....

As for Calhoun's argument that the Court cannot even tell if Hess' testimony is based on reliable methods because the Government's Rule 16 letter lacks sufficient disclosure, the Court mostly disagrees. As explained at the outset, at a basic level, Hess' method is straightforward: a cell phone has to connect to a cell tower to make a cellular communication; the cell tower is fixed somewhere (e.g., the roof of a building); the cell tower has a limited coverage area; and the service provider logs the connection (which phone, which tower, and when). This basic method is adequately disclosed in Hess' "Basic Princip[le]s Utilized in Record Analysis." In particular, Hess explains that "[t]he tower with the best signal is the one the handset will use for service, this is the serving cell and will be used to make and receive calls," that each cell tower "has its own unique identifier, this identifier is used to track which towers the handsets use," that towers can be "located anywhere (church steeples, water towers, [etc.])," and that some service providers' logs show both the tower a phone used to initiate a call and the one used when the call ended. This information, at least when coupled with publicly available information in any number of cases involving using cell-site data, sufficiently discloses Hess' method so that the Court can determine its reliability and fulfill its gatekeeper duties under Rule 702 and *Daubert*.

It appears that Calhoun's real complaint with the Government's Rule 16 disclosure is that Hess did not disclose the "source" of certain assertions. The following are among Hess' assertions that Calhoun complains of: even if the phone has a better signal to a tower different than the one providing service, "the phone will not randomly reselect to an adjacent tower unless the tower is on its 'neighbor list' which is controlled by the network service provider"; "[a]s the phone moves, it will choose a new serving cell based on signal strength and neighbor list"; a cell tower can be located anywhere; there are more towers in urban areas than in rural ones; and "[a] typical cell tower has THREE, 120° sectors." Calhoun says that Hess has not disclosed "any source for these so-called 'principals.'"

On this limited point the Court agrees with Calhoun. Although Federal Rule of Criminal Procedure 16 does not require detailed disclosure, *United States v. Campbell*, No. 1:04-CV-0424-RWS, 2006 WL 346446, at *1 (N.D.Ga. Feb. 13, 2006), it does demand that the Government "describe ... the bases and reasons for [its expert's] opinions," Fed.R.Crim.P. 16, and, according to the accompanying advisory committee note, that description "should cover not only written and oral reports, tests, reports, and investigations, but any information that might be recognized as a legitimate basis for an opinion under Federal Rule of Evidence 703," Fed.R.Crim.P. 16 advisory committee note (1993). Indeed, at oral argument, counsel for the Government indicated that they would explore whether more detailed information could be provided. Thus, the Court will order that the Government supplement its Rule 16 disclosure to explain the source of Hess' "Basic Princip[le]s Utilized in Record Analysis."

United States v. Douglas

862 F. Supp. 521 (D.D.C. 1994), *aff'd*,
70 F.3d 638 (D.C. Cir. 1995)

LAMBERTH, District Judge.

... Mr. Gregory Moss is a police officer in the Metropolitan Police Department. In August, 1992, Officer Moss was detailed out of the patrol section in order to work ... undercover officer with the Vice Office.... His assignment was to investigate the defendant, Mr. Neil Douglas. Mr. Douglas became a targeted suspect following a series of complaints from citizens of the area around 14th and Sheperd Streets. Officer Moss viewed two police photographs of Mr. Douglas in order to help him identify the suspect.

Officer Moss first encountered Mr. Douglas on November 2, 1992. Moss asked to buy half an ounce of cocaine from Mr. Douglas, who responded that Moss should meet him at the 1300 block of Randolph Street. When Moss arrived there, however, he met Robert Johnson instead. The two men had a brief exchange and Mr. Johnson asserted that he would go and "speed up" Mr. Douglas. A few minutes later, Mr. Johnson returned, entered the car in which Officer Moss sat, and gave Moss a white rock-like substance in exchange for five hundred dollars. Officer Moss then returned to the Fourth District Police Station and gave the package to the narcotics division. The substance tested positive for crack cocaine.

On November 10, 1992, Officer Moss was in the area of 3933 Fourteenth Street, N.W., Washington, D.C. Officer Goodwin, another member of the Metropolitan Police Department, had arrived earlier in order to videotape the events. Moss met Mr. Douglas and asked to buy a half-ounce of cocaine from him. Mr. Douglas explained that he would first need to buy a scale to measure the cocaine. The two men got into Moss' unmarked police car and drove around the block to a corner store on Fourteenth and Spring Road. (The videotape recording cuts off when the car went around the block, and resumes when the car is parked at 3933 Fourteenth Street.) Mr. Douglas acquired a scale and the two men drove back.... Moss and Douglas got out of the car and entered the building. Mr. Douglas then went up to the second level, where he remained for approximately three to five minutes. When he returned, he handed Moss a white rock-like substance in exchange for five hundred dollars. Moss then returned to his car and drove to the Fourth District Police Station. The substance tested positive for crack cocaine.

On November 16, 1992, Officer Moss returned to the 3900 block of Fourteenth Street, this time wearing a small tape recorder. He met with Mr. Douglas and had a brief conversation. Moss asked Mr. Douglas if he had seen Mr. Johnson. Douglas responded that Mr. Johnson had just left. The two men then conversed briefly … Officer Moss next saw Mr. Douglas on November 25, 1992, from an observation post. He identified all target suspects, including Mr. Douglas, and they were arrested.… [Defendant was] indicted for unlawfully, knowingly and intentionally distributing a mixture and substance containing a detectable amount of cocaine base, also known as crack. On May 12, 1993, Mr. Sussman, defense counsel for Mr. Douglas, wrote a letter to Mr. Glenn Ivey, the prosecutor handling the case at that time. In the letter, Mr. Sussman asked Mr. Ivey to confirm his understanding that the Government had no tapes. Mr. Ivey never responded to Mr. Sussman's letter.

Mr. Stephen McCool subsequently assumed responsibility for this case from Mr. Ivey. Mr. McCool learned of the tapes on July 9, 1993, immediately informed Mr. Sussman of their existence and invited him to inspect the tapes. Mr. Douglas comes now before this court seeking a new trial on the basis of prejudicial prosecutorial misconduct. The court analyzes Mr. Douglas' claims and their merits.

Mr. Douglas argues that the prosecutor's deliberate and prejudicial misconduct denied him a fair trial. Mr. Douglas argues … prosecutorial misconduct [due to] the discovery delay.…

A. DISCOVERY DELAYS

Mr. Douglas asserts that the government's initial failure, and ensuing delay, in disclosing its videotape and audiotape to defense counsel was a flagrant violation of its discovery obligations under Fed.R.Crim.P. 16(a)(1)(A) and 16(a)(1)(C). The government readily concedes this point. Fed.R.Crim.P. 16(d)(2) provides several possible sanctions to enforce the discovery rules. These include granting a continuance, permitting the other party to discover or inspect the evidence, and suppressing the evidence. Fed.R.Crim.P. 16(d)(2). Mr. Douglas moved to suppress the videotape, audiotape and DEA-7 (drug chemical analysis). The court denied his motion. Mr. Douglas argues that the court's refusal to suppress the evidence overlooked the government's disregard for his discovery rights, prejudiced his substantial rights, and denied him a fair trial. The court cannot agree.

"Relief for violations of discovery rules lies within the discretion of the trial court." *United States v. Rodriguez,* 799 F.2d 649, 652 (11th Cir.1986). *Accord Northrop v. McDonnell Douglas,* 751 F.2d 395, 399 (D.C.Cir.1984) (deferring to trial court's discretion in discovery sanctions). The trial court's discretion, however, is influenced by a principle of restraint. The court should impose the "least severe sanction necessary to ensure prompt and complete compliance with its discovery orders." *United States v. Turner,* 871 F.2d 1574, 1580 (11th Cir.1989), *cert. denied,* 493 U.S. 997 (1989). *See generally United States v. Euceda-Hernandez,* 768 F.2d 1307, 1312 (11th Cir.1985).

Mindful of this principle, the court evaluates four factors: (1) the reason for the violation (delay), (2) any bad faith by the violating party, (3) whether the defendant suffered any prejudice, and (4) the feasibility of curing the prejudice with a continuance. *United States v. McCrory,* 930 F.2d 63, 69–70 (D.C.Cir.1991), *cert. denied,* 502

U.S. 1037 (1992); *United States v. Mavrokordatos,* 933 F.2d 843, 847 (10th Cir.1991); *United States v. Christopher,* 923 F.2d 1545, 1554–55 (11th Cir.1991). The court considers each factor in light of the record.

1. Reason for Delay

The Government characterized its failure to respond to Mr. Sussman's letter of May 12, 1993, as an "honest mistake." Motions Hearing — II at 17. The court accepts the Government's representation that the mistake was an "honest" one. Nevertheless, the Government's failure to respond to defense counsel's letter, especially in regards to such an important matter, betrays flawed procedures and a reckless disregard for the defendant's discovery rights. The Government's negligence, therefore, is the only reason — albeit a bad one — for the delay.

2. Bad Faith

This court held a hearing pursuant to Mr. Douglas' Motion for Discovery Sanctions. Mr. Ivey appeared and responded to the court's questions at the hearing. Mr. Ivey knew that the tapes existed and failed to provide them to the defense. He also failed to respond to Mr. Sussman's letter in writing, although he recalls talking with Mr. Sussman on the telephone (but not about the tapes). Finally, Mr. Ivey stated that his failure was not motivated by any bad faith or a desire to "sandbag" the defendant. It was, he claims, an "honest mistake" and an "oversight."

The court finds no reason to disbelieve Mr. Ivey's statements that there was no wilful misconduct. He was credible and accepted responsibility for his mistake. There is, of course, no question that Mr. Ivey was negligent. Negligence, however, is not necessarily polluted by the stain of bad faith. *See Unigard Security Insurance Company, Inc. v. North River Insurance Company,* 4 F.3d 1049, 1069 (2d Cir.1993). Indeed, the court's finding is supported by Mr. McCool's ensuing conduct: upon assuming the case, he *immediately* informed Mr. Sussman of the tapes.

A court should pause before imposing a sanction in the absence of bad faith. *See United States v. Augello,* 451 F.2d 1167, 1170 (2d Cir.1971) (refusing to suppress officers' testimony in absence of bad faith or negligence in their destruction of tapes); *Turner,* 871 F.2d at 1580 (admitting testimony of officer concerning taped conversations despite government's failure to provide tapes to defense, due to the absence of bad faith).

3. Prejudice and Potential Cure

Mr. Sussman argues that if the government had disclosed the tapes in time, "no doubt the quality of the defense would have been altered." Mr. Sussman contends that his defense strategies were severely limited and his efforts largely misfocused. For these reasons, Mr. Sussman argues, the admission of the tapes severely prejudiced Mr. Douglas. The court has already determined that the delay did not prejudice the defendant. Nevertheless, an analysis of the potential cure (a continuance) for any such prejudice will serve as an instructive examination of the court's finding.

A continuance is the preferred sanction for a discovery delay. *Euceda-Hernandez,* 768 F.2d at 1312. In *Euceda-Hernandez,* the trial court had suppressed certain post-arrest statements made by the defendants to federal agents because the prosecutor failed to provide defense counsel with the substance of the statements until three days prior to trial. The appeals court reversed: "By suppressing the Government's evidence rather than granting a continuance or recess, a trial judge may achieve a speedier resolution to a criminal case and reduce his docket, but he does so at the expense of sacrificing the fair administration of justice and the accurate determination of guilt and innocence."

In *United States v. White*, 846 F.2d 678 (11th Cir.1988), *cert. denied*, 488 U.S. 984 (1988), the court declared that any prejudice caused by the Government's late (discovery) production can be allayed by granting a continuance. A continuance, the court explained, provides defense counsel with additional time in which to alleviate the prejudice. The suppression of evidence, therefore, works against the goals of Rule 16, which is the fair administration of justice.

Mr. Sussman did not go so far as to *request* a continuance. Instead, he declared, "I don't think a continuance is going to help me along." This declaration is antithetical to Mr. Sussman's concerns of "substantial prejudice" to Mr. Douglas. Several courts have held that when defense counsel fails to request a continuance after a discovery delay, such failure erases any potential prejudice created by the delay. *See De Laval Turbine, Inc. v. West India Industries, Inc.*, 502 F.2d 259, 263 n. 6 (3d Cir.1974) ("Any claim of prejudice (surprise) is belied by the fact that Henry Lift's counsel did not request a continuance ..."). Mr. Sussman not only failed to request a continuance, but characterized it as "useless." On the one hand, Mr. Sussman asserts that a continuance would not be helpful. On the other hand, he maintains that the delay has substantially prejudiced his client. In conjunction, these representations carelessly abandon the boundaries of reason and consistency.

The court has analyzed the four factors to consider when imposing discovery sanctions and finds that although the Government had no good reason for the discovery delay, there was no bad faith. The court also finds that Mr. Sussman's failure to request a continuance belies any claim of prejudice to Mr. Douglas. The court therefore rejects Mr. Douglas' claim of prejudice from the Government's discovery delay.

. . .

CONCLUSION

Mr. Douglas claims that the prosecutor's misconduct denied him a fair trial. Mr. Douglas bases this claim on ... [several points, including the] ... discovery delay.... The charge of prejudicial prosecutorial misconduct is a very serious one, as a fair trial is essential to due process. The Supreme Court has made the point: "Society wins not only when the guilty are convicted but when criminal trials are fair." *Brady v. Maryland*, 373 U.S. 83, 87 (1963).

The court has carefully examined each claim in light of the record and has, indeed, found occasions of prosecutorial misconduct. Nevertheless, within the context of the entire trial, the prosecutorial impropriety does not amount to prejudicial error....

Notes and Questions

1. Cell phone location information has become a critically important tool in law enforcement in the past decade or so, although the legal lines for its use have only recently been clarified. In *Pembrook*, the court handles two considerations raised by the defense: the Fourth Amendment implications of cell phone data as well as the disclosure issues. At the time of the case, the Fourth Amendment issue remained unresolved, but in June 2018, the Supreme Court decision in *Carpenter v. United States* made clear that cell phone location data is protected by the Fourth Amendment and therefore subject to the warrant requirement.[20] The *Pembrook* court decided that, due to the unclear state of the law at the time, the officers' conduct was not clearly wrongful and moved on to the expert issue. The court then found that not only must a report contain the expert's ultimate conclusion, but must also include "written and oral reports, tests, reports, and investigations, [and] any information that might be recognized as a legitimate basis for an opinion under Federal Rule of Evidence 703." *Pembrook*, 119 F. Supp. 3d at 598. In fact, some courts will expand this discovery to include not only the bases of actual testimony, but all preparatory materials (lab notes, etc.) as well. *See United States v. Zanfordino*, 833 F.Supp. 429 (S.D.N.Y. 1993) (relying on Fed. R. Civ. Pro. 26, court ordered pretrial disclosure of all preparatory materials for expert). Under the abuse of discretion review standard, the individual preferences of the judge become critical.

2. The *Douglas* court evaluated whether the [former] prosecutor's failure to disclose tapes under Rule 16(a)(1)(C) merited sanctions. Of course, this is not a case directly dealing with expert disclosures under Rule 16(a)(1)(G), but does provide several important baseline considerations for all discovery review. Just as with the evaluation of sanctions in civil case law, the issue here is within the trial court's discretion. However, the court also argues for a "principle of restraint," whereby the least severe sanction necessary should be used. *See also United States v. Golyanski*, 291 F.3d 1245, 1249 (10th Cir. 2002) ("In the absence of a finding of bad faith, the court should impose the least severe sanction that will accomplish prompt and full compliance with the discovery order.").

    To decide the sanction, a court will use four factors to weigh the severity of conduct and the impact of the wrongdoing on the opponent. Considering the restraint principle, however, evidence or witness exclusion will remain unlikely in the absence of bad faith or direct prejudice. *Golyanski*, 291 F.3d at 1249 ("It would be a rare case where, absent bad faith, a district court should exclude evidence rather than continue the proceedings."). This is why Sussman's lack of a request for a continuance, and characterization as it being "useless," undercuts Douglas's appeal.

3. Remember, the Rule 16 standard applies to the disclosure of *inculpatory* materials from the prosecution to the defense. For disclosures from the defense to the pros-

---

20. Carpenter v. United States, 585 U.S. ___, 138 S. Ct. 2206 (2018).

ecution, they can be more limited but often rely on a principle of reciprocity: if the defense asks for prosecution disclosures, then the defense must also be willing to disclose information as well. Such reciprocity does *not* violate a defendant's due process or self-incrimination rights. *Wardius v. Oregon*, 412 U.S. 470, 472, 475 (1973) (finding mandatory defense disclosures do not violate due process, although discovery should normally be a "two-way street").

Independent of these rules for inculpatory materials, the Supreme Court has also created a series of constitutionally mandated rules regarding prosecution disclosure of *exculpatory* materials to the defense. These rules provide mandatory disclosure with severe sanctions to the non-disclosing prosecutor, starting with dismissal of the case and then leading up to and including disbarment.[21] *See* Robert Mosteller, *Exculpatory Evidence, Ethics, and the Road to Disbarment of Mike Nifong: The Critical Importance of Full Open-File Discovery*, 15 Geo. Mason L. Rev. 257 (2008).

An overview of the rules — starting with *Brady* — will highlight the basic principles of exculpatory discovery, but any student hoping to practice in the criminal law area should review more specific or localized standards in detail.

Brady v. Maryland
373 U.S. 83 (1963)

Douglas, J.

Petitioner and a companion, Boblit, were found guilty of murder in the first degree and were sentenced to death, their convictions being affirmed by the Court of Appeals of Maryland. Their trials were separate, petitioner being tried first. At his trial Brady took the stand and admitted his participation in the crime, but he claimed that Boblit did the actual killing. And, in his summation to the jury, Brady's counsel conceded that Brady was guilty of murder in the first degree, asking only that the jury return that verdict 'without capital punishment.' Prior to the trial petitioner's counsel had requested the prosecution to allow him to examine Boblit's extrajudicial statements. Several of those statements were shown to him; but one dated July 9, 1958, in which Boblit admitted the actual homicide, was withheld by the prosecution and did not come to petitioner's notice until after he had been tried, convicted, and sentenced, and after his conviction had been affirmed.

Petitioner moved the trial court for a new trial based on the newly discovered evidence that had been suppressed by the prosecution. Petitioner's appeal from a denial of that motion was dismissed by the Court of Appeals without prejudice to relief under the Maryland Post Conviction Procedure Act. The petition for post-conviction relief was dismissed by the trial court; and on appeal the Court of Appeals held that suppression of the evidence by the prosecution denied petitioner due process of law. . . .

---

21. North Carolina State Bar Disciplinary Commission Amended Findings of Fact, Conclusions of Law, and Order of Discipline, N.C. State Bar v. Nifong (July 24, 2007).

The crime in question was murder committed in the perpetration of a robbery. Punishment for that crime in Maryland is life imprisonment or death, the jury being empowered to restrict the punishment to life by addition of the words 'without capital punishment.' In Maryland, by reason of the state constitution, the jury in a criminal case are 'the Judges of Law, as well as of fact.' The question presented is whether petitioner was denied a federal right....

We agree with the Court of Appeals that suppression of this confession was a violation of the Due Process Clause of the Fourteenth Amendment. The Court of Appeals relied in the main on two decisions from the Third Circuit Court of Appeals — *United States ex rel. Almeida v. Baldi*, 195 F.2d 815, and *United States ex rel. Thompson v. Dye*, 221 F.2d 763 — which, we agree, state the correct constitutional rule.

This ruling is an extension of *Mooney v. Holohan*, 294 U.S. 103, 112, where the Court ruled on what nondisclosure by a prosecutor violates due process:

> It is a requirement that cannot be deemed to be satisfied by mere notice and hearing if a state has contrived a conviction through the pretense of a trial which in truth is but used as a means of depriving a defendant of liberty through a deliberate deception of court and jury by the presentation of testimony known to be perjured. Such a contrivance by a state to procure the conviction and imprisonment of a defendant is as inconsistent with the rudimentary demands of justice as is the obtaining of a like result by intimidation.

In *Pyle v. Kansas*, 317 U.S. 213, 215–216, we phrased the rule in broader terms:

> Petitioner's papers are inexpertly drawn, but they do set forth allegations that his imprisonment resulted from perjured testimony, knowingly used by the State authorities to obtain his conviction, and from the deliberate suppression by those same authorities of evidence favorable to him. These allegations sufficiently charge a deprivation of rights guaranteed by the Federal Constitution, and, if proven, would entitle petitioner to release from his present custody. *Mooney v. Holohan*, 294 U.S. 103.

The Third Circuit in the *Baldi* case construed that statement in *Pyle v. Kansas* to mean that the 'suppression of evidence favorable' to the accused was itself sufficient to amount to a denial of due process. 195 F.2d, at 820. In *Napue v. Illinois*, 360 U.S. 264, 269, we extended the test formulated in *Mooney v. Holohan* when we said: 'The same result obtains when the State, although not soliciting false evidence, allows it to go uncorrected when it appears.' And see *Alcorta v. Texas*, 355 U.S. 28; *Wilde v. Wyoming*, 362 U.S. 607. Cf. *Durley v. Mayo*, 351 U.S. 277, 285 (dissenting opinion).

We now hold that the suppression by the prosecution of evidence favorable to an accused upon request violates due process where the evidence is material either to guilt or to punishment, irrespective of the good faith or bad faith of the prosecution.

The principle of *Mooney v. Holohan* is not punishment of society for misdeeds of a prosecutor but avoidance of an unfair trial to the accused. Society wins not only when the guilty are convicted but when criminal trials are fair; our system of the administration of justice suffers when any accused is treated unfairly. An inscription on the walls of the Department of Justice states the proposition candidly for the federal domain: 'The United States wins its point whenever justice is done its citizens in the courts.'[2] A prosecution that withholds evidence on demand of an accused which, if made available, would tend to exculpate him or reduce the penalty helps shape a trial that bears heavily on the defendant. That casts the prosecutor in the role of an architect of a proceeding that does not comport with standards of justice, even though, ... his action is not 'the result of guile,' to use the words of the Court of Appeals....

McDowell v. Dixon
858 F.2d 945 (4th Cir. 1988)

WINTER, Chief Judge.

Robert Henry McDowell was convicted of first degree murder and felonious assault in the Superior Court of Johnston County, North Carolina on December 10, 1979. He was sentenced to death for the murder conviction and to a term of twenty years for the assault conviction. McDowell pursued state postconviction remedies, and, after an evidentiary hearing, the trial court granted him a new trial. The Supreme Court of North Carolina vacated the trial court's order, and on remand the trial court denied any further relief. The Supreme Court of North Carolina declined to review the denial of relief, and a petition for a writ of certiorari was denied by the Supreme Court of the United States. *McDowell v. North Carolina*, 476 U.S. 1165 (1986). McDowell then filed a petition for writ of habeas corpus in the district court, which was denied. The court also denied a motion to alter or amend its judgment of denial.

McDowell appeals, and we reverse. We conclude that the nondisclosure of exculpatory evidence by the prosecutor denied McDowell due process of law. We direct that the writ issue unless McDowell is tried anew in a reasonable period to be allowed by the district court.

I.

During the night of July 14, 1979, someone entered the bedroom of fourteen-year-old Patsy Mason and four-year-old Carol Ann Hinson at their residence in Sanford, North Carolina and assaulted them with a large knife. Patsy suffered serious injuries, but survived. Carol Ann was killed. The only direct evidence linking McDowell to the crime was Patsy's testimony identifying him as the assailant. Circumstantial evidence against McDowell consisted of the testimony of his girlfriend, Frances Jenkins, that

---

2. Judge Simon E. Sobeloff when Solicitor General put the idea as follows in an address before the Judicial Conference of the Fourth Circuit on June 29, 1954:

> The Solicitor General is not a neutral, he is an advocate; but an advocate for a client whose business is not merely to prevail in the instant case. My client's chief business is not to achieve victory but to establish justice. We are constantly reminded of the now classic words penned by one of my illustrious predecessors, Frederick Lehmann, that the Government wins its point when justice is done in its courts.

McDowell had arrived at their home at 1:45 a.m., later than usual, and had behaved suspiciously. Police conducted a search of McDowell's dwelling and seized a machete knife, an instrument capable of having inflicted the type of wounds suffered by Patsy and Carol Ann, as well as nunchukhs and a flashlight, items which according to Patsy her assailant had possessed. The prosecution could adduce no evidence of fingerprints, blood, hair, body secretions or other physical evidence linking McDowell to the crime. There was also no evidence of any inculpatory statements made by McDowell.

In addition to the identification testimony of Patsy, the prosecution presented the testimony of Marvin Stone, who, shortly after midnight, had "caught glimpses of a silhouette of a person on a bicycle" leaving the Mason home and pedaling down the street. About five minutes later he heard some screaming, and he investigated. Stone peered into a glass storm door into one of the Masons' bedrooms, and saw a small girl and a child lying on the floor. He returned home because there did not appear to be anything amiss. Several minutes later he heard more screaming. He awakened his parents and was returning to the Masons' when the police arrived.

Also present in the Mason house on the evening of July 14, 1979 were Patsy's parents, John and Sarah Mason, and her baby brother, Jerome. John Mason testified that he fell asleep watching television at 11:00 p.m. and awoke at 1:00 a.m. He made no claim that he awakened because of the screams. After waking, Mr. Mason checked on the children as he usually did before he went to bed for the evening, and upon discovering that they had been injured, he called for an ambulance. He then awakened his wife, who was still sleeping.

II.

McDowell contends that he was denied a fair trial, and hence due process of law, because the prosecution had in its file exculpatory evidence not disclosed to the defendant's counsel, despite a general request therefor, and that this evidence was not otherwise brought out at trial. He thus claims that the prosecution has violated the principles of *Brady v. Maryland,* 373 U.S. 83 (1963) and its progeny, by failing to disclose evidence material to guilt or punishment. He also argues that the prosecution violated the principle first enunciated in *Mooney v. Holohan,* 294 U.S. 103 (1935) that knowing use of false testimony is inconsistent with due process, because, in his trial, it permitted its witnesses to give a false impression of what transpired when it possessed evidence to indicate that falsity. . . .

There were three separate items of undisclosed evidence. First, there existed direct evidence potentially damaging to the reliability of Patsy's identification of McDowell as her attacker and Patsy's credibility or memory. Patsy was initially questioned about the identity of her attacker in the early morning hours of July 15, 1979, less than three hours after the attack, by Sanford police officer W.A. Baker in the Lee County Hospital. The following exchange occurred:

Q. Do you know who did this to you?

A. Patsy motioned with her head in a negative manner.

Q. Does he live in your neighborhood?

A. Motioned with her shoulder, I don't know.

Q. Was he black or white?

A. *White.* (emphasis added)

An interview conducted by SBI agent Stewart with Terry Hinson, (Carol Ann's mother and Patsy's stepsister), disclosed that she "knew that Patsy had already told that the people who did it were white." Patsy's description to SBI officer Scheppf on July 17, 1979, was that she was uncertain as to whether the man was black or white. Subsequently, on July 18, 1979, Patsy stated that her attacker had been black, with a medium afro and a medium build, and that she did not know the man. Patsy later identified McDowell from a photo spread. Defense counsel were apprised only of Patsy's July 18 description that her assailant was black, and of the results of the photo spread. At trial Patsy testified that she had always described her attacker as a black man with *flat* hair, big eyes and a flat nose, and that she had seen McDowell before briefly on only one occasion.

The second item of undisclosed evidence came from an interview between Agent John Walker and an eleven-year-old neighbor of the Masons, Jerry Stone. Stone reported seeing a black male approach the Mason home riding a bicycle "white in color," at about 11:30 p.m. on July 14. According to Stone, the bicyclist was "approximately 6'0", 20 years old, very skinny, very dark skinned, no hat, no shirt, light green medium cutoff shorts and believed to be wearing shoes, possibly black boots up to one foot high." The bicyclist shone a flashlight at the Mason residence, approached the front door, and was admitted into the house. Stone then examined the ten-speed bicycle, which he described as "a Huffy brand ... white in color, ... no fenders, no horn and no front headlight." Stone then knocked on Patsy's side door, and when she opened the door, asked her "who the colored boy was on the white ten speed bicycle." Patsy replied that she did not know, and that he might be talking with her parents. Jerry Stone then left and went home. Several minutes later, he heard "a ten speed bicycle travelling real fast down Third Street."

The final item of undisclosed evidence consisted of police reports prior to July 14 of white intruders in the Mason home. Hope Spivey and Sheila Jackson, young cousins of Patsy, told of two separate incidents, one several weeks prior to the crime, and one just a few hours before the crime. A police report revealed that on June 25, according to Hope, Hope, Patsy and Sheila had been in an upstairs bedroom when they were distracted by a noise outside their room. They turned toward the bedroom door and suddenly saw a man, whose face was covered by a mask or was "red", peering in their bedroom door. The girls screamed and the intruder left. John Mason summoned the police, who came and made a written report of the incident.

The second incident occurred on July 14, when Patsy's cousins observed a "white/male" intruder near the Masons' basement stairway, wielding a knife. Again, the police were summoned and, despite the girls' vivid recollection ... the police dismissed the girls' accounts after an investigation of the basement turned up no evidence to support the story.

III.

The law to be applied when the prosecution fails to disclose exculpatory evidence to a defendant is relatively uncomplicated. *Brady v. Maryland,* 373 U.S. 83 (1963), held, as an extension of *Mooney v. Holohan,* 294 U.S. 103 (1935), that

> The suppression by the prosecution of evidence favorable to an accused upon request violates due process where the evidence is material either to guilt or to punishment, irrespective of the good faith or bad faith of the prosecution.

Id. 373 U.S. at 87. The Court explained the rationale of the rule as "not punishment of society for misdeeds of a prosecutor but avoidance of an unfair trial to the accused.... A prosecution that withholds evidence on demand of an accused which, if made available, would tend to exculpate him or reduce the penalty ... casts the prosecutor in the role of an architect of a proceeding that does not comport with standards of justice...," even though the prosecutor's failure to divulge was not intentionally deceptive. *Id.* at 87–88.

The *Brady* doctrine was restated and amplified in *United States v. Agurs,* 427 U.S. 97 (1976). It acknowledges that *Brady* applies in four different situations: first, where the undisclosed evidence demonstrates that the prosecution's case includes perjured testimony. In those instances the conviction is "fundamentally unfair, and must be set aside if there is any reasonable likelihood that the false testimony could have affected the judgment of the jury." *Id.* at 103 (footnotes omitted). The *Brady* doctrine also applies when there has been suppression of *specific* evidence described in a pretrial request. In that event, the Court held, the conviction or the punishment, as the case may be, cannot stand if the suppressed evidence is material. *Brady* also applies in two other instances where the defense makes no pretrial request for exculpatory evidence or where, lacking specific knowledge of what to request, the defense makes only a general request for exculpatory material.

In none of the three latter cases does the defendant need to demonstrate that the suppressed evidence would have resulted in acquittal. This very strict standard would not sufficiently encourage the "prosecutor's obligation to serve the cause of justice." *Id.* at 111. The Court has framed the issue instead by holding that:

> The proper standard of materiality must reflect our overriding concern with the justice of the finding of guilt. Such a finding is permissible only if supported by evidence establishing guilt beyond a reasonable doubt. It necessarily follows that if the omitted evidence creates a reasonable doubt that did not otherwise exist, constitutional error has been committed

Id. at 112 (footnote eliminated).

United States v. Bagley, 473 U.S. 667 (1985), considered the standard of materiality to be applied in determining whether a conviction should be reversed because the prosecution failed to disclose requested evidence that could have been used to impeach prosecution witnesses. The Court rejected any distinction between impeachment evidence and exculpatory evidence, and upheld its prior ruling in *Giglio v. United States,* 405 U.S. 150, 154 (1972), that "'nondisclosure of evidence affecting credibility falls within th[e] general rule [of *Brady*].'" 473 U.S. at 677. Elaborating on *Agurs*, the Court concluded that "evidence is material only if there is a reasonable probability that, had the evidence been disclosed to the defense, the result of the proceeding would have been different. A 'reasonable probability' is a probability sufficient to undermine confidence in the outcome." The Court stated that this standard is identical to that adopted in *Strickland v. Washington*, 466 U.S. 668 (1984), to determine the propriety of granting a new trial due to incompetence of counsel. A court's inquiry in determining the materiality of the undisclosed evidence, as in *Strickland*, should "consider directly any adverse effect that the prosecutor's failure to respond might have had on the preparation or presentation of the defendant's case." *Bagley*, 473 U.S. at 683. The Court also held that this standard is applicable to "no request", "general request", and "specific request" cases of prosecutorial nondisclosure. *Id.* at 682.

As we have already mentioned, the standard of materiality on appeal is not altered because of the lack of misconduct on the part of the prosecution. *Agurs* directly addressed this issue, and determined that "[i]f the suppression of evidence results in constitutional error, it is because of the character of the evidence, not the character of the prosecutor." 427 U.S. at 110. It follows that insignificant evidence deliberately withheld by a vindictive prosecutor who believes it to be important will not give rise to constitutional error, but if "evidence highly probative of innocence is in his file, he should be presumed to recognize its significance *even if he has actually overlooked it.*" *Id.* (Emphasis added). It is therefore no argument that, in this or any other criminal case, the prosecution did not recognize the importance of the undisclosed evidence, or would not have withheld the evidence had it been requested. "The *Brady* rule is based on the requirement of due process. Its purpose is not to displace the adversary system as the primary means by which truth is uncovered, but to ensure that a miscarriage of justice does not occur." 473 U.S. at 675. It is the fairness of the trial, not of the prosecutor's conduct which is at issue.

Agurs has clearly indicated that not all evidence favorable to the defendant will create a reasonable doubt. *Agurs* itself rejected the claim of the defendant that evidence of the homicide victim's prior record of weapons violations created a reasonable doubt where none before had existed. The Court noted that the prior record "did not contradict any evidence offered by the prosecutor, and was largely cumulative...." 427 U.S. at 113–4.

By contrast, in *Norris v. Slayton*, 540 F.2d 1241 (4 Cir.1976), we considered a set of circumstances very similar to those at issue here. In *Norris*, the investigating officer had stated in a report that the rape victim had been unsure whether the defendant was her assailant when the police first asked her to identify him. The prosecution knew of this report but failed to furnish a copy of it to the defense. The victim subsequently testified at trial that when she first confronted Norris, she was certain that he was her assailant. We concluded that the report "was evidence which had a direct bearing upon the critical issue in the case and might 'reasonably have weakened or overcome testimony adverse to the defendant.'" *Id.* at 1244. The report would have weakened the victim's credibility, as well as the accuracy of her identification of the defendant as her assailant. In an addendum to our opinion in *Norris,* we further stated that since the omitted evidence "was of such a nature as to raise a substantial likelihood that it would have affected the result in Norris' trial"....

In the case at bar the critical issue was the identity of the assailant. Robert Mc-Dowell is unmistakably black, and Patsy Mason first claimed that her assailant was white. Originally she claimed that he had shoulder length hair, later that he had an afro, and ultimately that his hair was flat. The state attempts to distinguish *Norris* from this case by stressing that Patsy has always *identified* McDowell as her attacker when shown pictures of him. This contention unjustifiably diminishes the value of the prior inconsistent description in impeaching Patsy's credibility, or memory or both, and ignores the fact that, "[i]mpeachment evidence, however, as well as exculpatory evidence, falls within the *Brady* rule." *Bagley,* 473 U.S. at 676. Whether Patsy testified truthfully and accurately determined the guilt or innocence of Robert McDowell. Hers was the sole identification testimony and where it was not, as here, incontestably corroborated by circumstantial evidence, the conclusion is inescapable that had the jury known of her prior inconsistent identifications, there was a reasonable probability that the outcome of McDowell's trial might have been different. Certainly it was enough to create a reasonable doubt of McDowell's guilt that did not otherwise exist.

The prosecution also argues that Patsy's first account is not material because Officer Baker described her as "semi-conscious" when she uttered the fact that her assailant had been white, although several physicians testified that she had been alert and conscious at the time. We recognize that had Patsy's prior inconsistent identifications been proved, there was evidence to minimize or explain away their damaging effect on the prosecution's case. But that evidence is not so overwhelming that we can say that the jury inevitably would have been persuaded that her in-court identification was entirely truthful and conclusive, and that her memory and credibility were beyond reproach. Thus we are not persuaded that the inconsistent prior identifications were not material as defined in *Bagley* and *Agurs.*

Another significant aspect of Patsy's account of her assailant's features concerns her prior acquaintance with McDowell. We do not doubt that the strategy counsel used to defend McDowell was influenced by their lack of knowledge of Patsy's first identifications of her attacker, and that the trial might have taken a different course "had the defense not been misled by the prosecutor's incomplete response." *Bagley* at 683. At trial, Patsy testified that she had seen McDowell once before the night of the attack, but only briefly. In fact, defense counsel had evidence that Patsy had frequented "Black" nightspots around Sanford, and the owner of such a nightspot told police that the two knew each other, as did a friend of Terry Hinson's. Although the defense counsel thus knew of this discrepancy in her testimony, we surmise that they chose not to prove it, because prior acquaintance between victim and defendant would have tended to support Patsy's ability to identify her assailant accurately. In light of Patsy's first description of her assailant as a white man, however, of which defense counsel was ignorant, Patsy's prior association with McDowell makes her subsequent identification of him as the attacker even less credible, and the likelihood of a different result in a new trial even greater.

While we think that suppression of the evidence of inconsistent identification alone is sufficient to vitiate McDowell's conviction, that conclusion is reinforced by consideration of other exculpatory evidence that was suppressed.

Jerry Stone's account of the events which occurred at the Mason home on July 14 is evidence which the jury was entitled to hear. His account calls Patsy's version of the night into question in two different respects. First, Patsy gave no account of Jerry Stone's visit in her own testimony which tracked her recollection of that evening from 6:00 p.m. until she lost consciousness from her wounds. Moreover, Jerry Stone's description of the man who visited the Mason home differs from Patsy's initial identification in several significant respects.... If a jury found Jerry Stone credible, the fact that John Mason ... admitted a black male into his house when he claims to have been asleep might seriously undermine his credibility as a witness as well.

Finally, evidence of a white intruder in the Mason home hours before the attack demonstrates that there might have been another person who had motive or opportunity to commit the crime.... It is the province of the jury to determine whether it believed the story, and if so, whether the incident had any bearing on the subsequent crime.

We summarize by stating there is not insubstantial evidence that Robert McDowell murdered Carol Hinson and assaulted Patsy Mason. However, the only direct evidence presented by the prosecution is the eyewitness identification made by Patsy Mason. There is no evidence of matching fingerprints, bloodstains, body secretions, hair or fibers. The omitted evidence was not cumulative, and it was unquestionably contradictory of the prosecution's case against McDowell. In our view, the omitted evidence could have created a reasonable doubt in the minds of the jurors. We cannot say that even if the jury had been aware of the undisclosed evidence, it still would have had no reasonable doubt of McDowell's guilt of the crimes committed against Patsy and Carol Ann. It follows that McDowell was denied due process of law in his trial by the nondisclosure of the evidence that we have described....

Notes and Questions

1. The *Brady* case makes clear that evidence that is both material and exculpatory must be disclosed to the defense, otherwise the conviction has been obtained in violation of due process. Yet more recent caselaw since *Brady* has expanded that basic principle, as *McDowell* makes clear and as we will explore briefly in these notes. In *United States v. Agurs*, the court made clear that the *Brady* requirement applies regardless of any request from the defense (as the defense had made in *Brady* itself). 427 U.S. 97, 106–107 (1976). *Agurs* also mentioned that the standard for materiality was not "the result would have been different," which sets too high a standard, but instead is "any reasonable likelihood that the false testimony could have affected the judgment of the jury," a much lower standard and one the *Bagley* court later connected to the standard for ineffective assistance of counsel under *Strickland v. Washington*, 466 U.S. 668 (1984). *Id.* at 120; *see also United States v.*

Bagley, 473 U.S. 667, 682 (1985). These standards make clear the expansive nature of disclosure and its self-executing nature.

2. *Brady* itself rested on a prior precedent, *Mooney v. Holohan*, 294 U.S. 103 (1935), in which the court held a prosecutor's use of perjured testimony violated due process rights of the defendant. *Mooney* has since been expanded, as the *McDowell* court makes clear, to include situations where the prosecutor later learns of the false testimony and does not notify the court and counsel of that fact. *Napue v. Illinois*, 360 U.S. 264, 269 (1959). This result underscores the fact that the consideration in these cases is not the *mens rea* of the prosecutor, since the cases do not require bad faith or knowing concealment of the testimony (they couldn't, since due process can be violated even if the DA learns of the perjury after trial). Instead, *Agurs* states flatly that suppression is based on "the character of the evidence, not the character of the prosecutor." 427 U.S. at 110.

3. As we consider all materials and issues broadly labeled as *Brady* claims, we must also examine impeachment materials. In *Giglio v. United States*, 405 U.S. 150 (1972), the Supreme Court decided that impeachment materials, i.e., used to attack the credibility, bias, or motivation of the testifying witness, must be disclosed under *Brady*, so long as they meet the materiality test for *Brady* material ("reasonable likelihood that they would affect the judgment of the jury"). In *Giglio* itself, the prosecutor (who was unaware of the promise made by another prosecutor) failed to disclose a promise of leniency for a critical prosecution witness. The Court reversed the conviction as a due process/*Brady* violation.

4. Finally, unrelated to witness testimony, the Court has also discussed due process in the context of preservation of evidence. *Arizona v. Youngblood*, 488 U.S. 51 (1988). The *Youngblood* court is very clear that its ruling does not affect *Brady* materials, instead it deals with evidence that has not yet been shown to be exculpatory but could be had it been preserved. In these circumstances, the court *will* look at the motives of the police and prosecutor, and a due process violation occurs only if they acted in bad faith. *Youngblood*, 488 U.S. at 58. In essence, negligent or even reckless destruction of evidence will not suffice. Of course, in our era of DNA exonerations, one might reasonably wonder if that standard should remain for all types of evidence.

Tying It Together

On routine patrol in Polk City one night, Officer Alvarez and Officer Bhandari observe a man walking along Polk Boulevard wearing jeans, a white t-shirt and a vest. Upon closer examination, Alvarez could see a black semi-automatic handgun in the rear waistband area, and stopped the car in order to speak with the man. At this point, the pedestrian—Dave Davis—ran east through an alley with Bhandari in hot pursuit, while Alvarez called for backup. During the chase, Bhandari saw the handgun fall from Davis' waistband as he continued pursuit. Four blocks later, Davis was apprehended by several officers and a K-9 unit, and later Bhandari recovered the discarded pistol. It turns out that Dave Davis has a prior felony conviction for auto theft, which makes it a crime for him to possess a firearm. He is booked on felon in possession of a firearm, 18 U.S.C. §922(g).[22]

In anticipation of trial, the Assistant U.S. Attorney files a Rule 16 endorsement for Specialist Roger Karp as an expert in fingerprint analysis. The AUSA endorsement states that Karp will testify to the following at trial:

- his educational and work background;

- his training and experience as a fingerprint examiner;

- the difference between latent fingerprints and ink fingerprints;

- "the likelihood of obtaining a fingerprint of comparable value on a handgun is usually less than 5%";

- "the likelihood of obtaining a fingerprint of comparable value on a firearm component is less than 5%";

- he examined the firearm, magazine, and cartridges in this case for fingerprints; and

- since the firearm had been touched prior to testing, there is not enough of a latent print to make a comparison to Davis' fingerprints.

In addition, the AUSA also attaches a "Statement of Qualifications" to the endorsements. This document is contained in the text in Appendix A.

Assignment: Please prepare a 1–2 page brief explaining your argument in the context of the cases we have reviewed.

- As defense counsel for Davis, why are you objecting to Karp's testimony and why should it be entirely excluded from trial?

- As an assistant prosecutor on the case, why is Karp's testimony admissible?

C. Rules and Strategy for Depositions — Fed. R. Civ. P. 30

In a civil case, after each set of disclosures (fact witnesses and expert witnesses), litigants will evaluate the disclosures and seek further discovery by taking testimony at a deposition.[23] Deposition strategy, coverage, and specificity will almost always depend on the context of the case, and the witness's role in it. Taking depositions is also a discrete skill, different from paper discovery, because it depends on interpersonal

---

22. 18 U.S.C. §922(g): It shall be unlawful for any person—
   (1) who has been convicted in any court of, a crime punishable by imprisonment for a term exceeding one year ... to ... possess ... any firearm or ammunition; or to receive any firearm or ammunition which has been shipped or transported in interstate or foreign commerce.

23. With few exceptions, depositions are largely limited to civil cases. *But see* FED. R. CRIM P. 15 (allowing depositions of witnesses when necessary based on "exceptional circumstances and in the interests of justice."); IOWA R. CRIM. P. 2.13 (granting defense choice to take depositions of prosecution witnesses, although if done, then prosecution gets ability to depose defense witnesses).

skills, but also different from trial testimony, because here one need not be (directly) cognizant of the factfinder. Many law schools teach depositions as a skills-based course, or skip it altogether based on a metaphorical theory that you can't teach dancing by reading a book. Maybe so.

Yet we will cover the rules and basic standards covering depositions, then consider deposition objectives and strategies. We will finish with some video excerpts of depositions for discussion purposes. As we explore these cases and exercises, remember to keep in mind the context of the case and the purpose of the evidence at issue.

Federal Rule of Civil Procedure 30: *Depositions by Oral Examination*

(a) WHEN A DEPOSITION MAY BE TAKEN

(1) *Without Leave.* A party may, by oral questions, depose any person, including a party, without leave of court except as provided in Rule 30(a)(2). The deponent's attendance may be compelled by subpoena under Rule 45.

(2) *With Leave.* A party must obtain leave of court, and the court must grant leave to the extent consistent with Rule 26(b)(1) and (2):

   (A) if the parties have not stipulated to the deposition and:

      (i) the deposition would result in more than 10 depositions being taken under this rule ... by the plaintiffs, or by the defendants, or by the third-party defendants;

      (ii) the deponent has already been deposed in the case; or

      (iii) the party seeks to take the deposition before the time specified in Rule 26(d), unless ... [out of the country]; or

   (B) if the deponent is confined in prison.

(b) NOTICE OF THE DEPOSITION; OTHER FORMAL REQUIREMENTS.

(1) *Notice in General.* A party who wants to depose a person by oral questions must give reasonable written notice to every other party. The notice must state the time and place of the deposition and, if known, the deponent's name and address....

(2) *Producing Documents.* If a subpoena duces tecum is to be served on the deponent, the materials designated for production, as set out in the subpoena, must be listed in the notice or in an attachment....

(3) *Method of Recording.*

   (A) *Method Stated in the Notice.* The party who notices the deposition must state in the notice the method for recording the testimony....

(4) *By Remote Means.* The parties may stipulate—or the court may on motion order—that a deposition be taken by telephone or other remote means. For the purpose of this rule ... the deposition takes place where the deponent answers the questions....

(c) EXAMINATION AND CROSS-EXAMINATION; RECORD OF THE EXAMINATION; OBJECTIONS; WRITTEN QUESTIONS.

(1) *Examination and Cross-Examination.* The examination and cross ... of a deponent proceed as they would at trial.... After putting the deponent under oath or affirmation, the officer must record the testimony by the method designated under Rule 30(b)(3)(A)....

(2) *Objections.* An objection at the time of the examination—whether to evidence, to a party's conduct, to the officer's qualifications, to the manner of taking the deposition, or to any other aspect of the deposition—must be noted on the record, but the examination still proceeds; the testimony is taken subject to any objection. An objection must be stated concisely in a nonargumentative and nonsuggestive manner. A person may instruct a deponent not to answer only when necessary to preserve a privilege, to enforce a limitation ordered by the court, or to present a motion ... [regarding termination].

(d) DURATION; SANCTION; MOTION TO TERMINATE OR LIMIT.

(1) *Duration.* Unless otherwise stipulated or ordered by the court, a deposition is limited to 1 day of 7 hours....

(2) *Sanction.* The court may impose an appropriate sanction—including the reasonable expenses and attorney's fees ... —on a person who impedes ... [an exam of] the deponent.

(3) *Motion to Terminate or Limit.*

(A) *Grounds.* At any time during a deposition, the deponent or a party may move to terminate or limit it on the ground that it is being conducted in bad faith or in a manner that unreasonably annoys, embarrasses, or oppresses the deponent or party....

(B) *Order.* The court may order that the deposition be terminated or may limit its scope and manner....

International Union of Electric, Radio and Machine Workers v. Westinghouse Electric Corp.

91 F.R.D. 277 (D.D.C. 1981)

FLANNERY, District Judge.

This matter comes before the court on defendant Westinghouse Electric Corporation's motion to compel discovery and for sanctions against plaintiffs, International Union of Electrical, Radio and Machine Workers (hereinafter "IUE") and its Local 186. In particular, defendant seeks to compel plaintiffs' representative to answer certain questions propounded to him on deposition.

FACTS

This dispute arises out of the failure of plaintiffs' representative, Mr. Willis Robinson, to answer certain questions asked by defendant on deposition.... Mr. Robinson refused to answer defendant's questions based upon instructions from plaintiffs' counsel not to do so. Plaintiffs' counsel instructed Mr. Robinson not to answer sixteen of defense counsel's questions on the basis of objections to the relevancy of these questions. Plaintiffs maintain that defense counsel's questions are directed to an issue, whether the original certification of IUE as the collective bargaining representative for the Charlotte Apparatus Repair Plant was proper, which has already been litigated between the parties[2] and which therefore, according to principles of res judicata and/or collateral estoppel, cannot be relitigated by defendant in this court. As such, plaintiffs maintain that inquiry into this area is irrelevant to the case at bar and that discovery on this issue is therefore improper under Federal Rule of Civil Procedure 26(b)(1).

Defendant maintains, however, that the disputed issue can be relitigated before this court and that the information requested is therefore relevant. This response to plaintiffs' objection notwithstanding, defendant further maintains that it was improper for plaintiffs' counsel to instruct Mr. Robinson not to answer the proposed questions since under Federal Rule of Civil Procedure 30(c) the proper course of conduct is for counsel to note an objection to the question, but then to allow the answer to be given, subject of course to later exclusion by the court at a ruling on the merits of the objection.

DISCUSSION

I. Motion to Compel

The issue in this case presents a direct clash between two provisions of the Federal Rules of Civil Procedure: 1) Rule 26(b)(1) which provides that "(p)arties may obtain discovery regarding any matter, not privileged, which is relevant to the subject matter involved in the pending action," and 2) Rule 30(c) which provides that upon examination at a deposition "(e)vidence objected to shall be taken subject to the objections." Confronting an objection based on relevancy, the two rules appear to be mutually exclusive. Following Rule 30(c) to the letter makes discovery of irrelevant material possible in contravention of Rule 26(b)(1); conversely, permitting a refusal to answer questions directed at arguably irrelevant material expressly violates the strictures of Rule 30(c). The determination of which rule should control the instant situation involves an analysis of the policies underlying the Federal Rules.

Rule 30(c)

The provisions of Rule 30(c) are obviously intended to expedite and ... simplify ... discovery....

> At the taking of a deposition, the witness will be examined and cross-examined by counsel for the parties in the same fashion as at a trial, with one important exception. If there is objection to a question, the reporter will simply note the objection in the transcript and the witness will answer the question despite

---

2. This issue has been litigated three times according to plaintiffs.

the objection. The court can consider the objection if the deposition is offered at the trial, and at that time will refuse to allow reading of the answer to any question which was properly objectionable. If the witness refuses to answer a question put at a deposition, the examination may be adjourned, or completed on other matters, and application then made to the court to compel an answer. This is undesirable, since it delays the deposition and brings the court into a process which is intended to work largely without judicial supervision.

Wright, Law of Federal Courts 420, Oral Depositions s 84 (3d ed. 1976); accord *W.R. Grace & Co. v. Pullman, Inc.*, 74 F.R.D. 80, 84 (D. Okla. 1977). The sole case in this jurisdiction discussing this issue agrees that answering the question, despite the objection, is the better policy.

> Finally, the Court would observe that in most cases … the better practice is for attorneys to note their objections, but permit their clients to answer questions leaving resolution of the objection to pre-trial or trial. This approach conserves the parties' or witnesses' time and money, as well as judicial resources, and expedites the trial of the lawsuit. Furthermore, the objections may become moot by disposition of the case before trial or abandonment by the party at the time of trial.

Drew v. Sulphite & Paper Mill Workers, 37 F.R.D. 446, 449–50 (D.D.C. 1965). The *Drew* court also referred specifically to a refusal to answer on grounds of irrelevancy: "(p)laintiff also objected on the ground of irrelevancy, which is clearly proper within Rule 26. However, such an objection does not warrant a refusal to answer questions...." *Id.*

The cases from other jurisdictions which have construed Rule 30(c) in the context of an attorney instructing a witness not to answer particular questions take even a stronger stance on upholding the provisions of the rule. See, e. g., *Ralston Purina Co. v. McFarland*, 550 F.2d 967, 973 (4th Cir. 1977) (counsel's action indefensible and utterly at variance with Rules' discovery provisions); *Lloyd v. Cessna Aircraft Co.*, 74 F.R.D. 518, 519 (E.D.Tenn.1977) (government counsel's conduct wholly improper); *Shapiro v. Freeman*, 38 F.R.D. 308, 311–12 (S.D.N.Y. 1965) (counsel had no right whatever to instruct witnesses not to answer). Further, in a recent opinion relying on the above-noted principles to overrule a challenge to his own court order requiring all attorneys to refrain from instructing witnesses not to answer questions, Judge Edelstein cited these principles as being well-established. *United States v. International Business Machines Corp.*, 79 F.R.D. 378, 381 (S.D.N.Y. 1978); accord Wright & Miller, Federal Practice and Procedure § 2113 at 419 n.22 (1970).

Although the above-noted principles establish that Rule 30(c) should be followed whenever possible, it is nonetheless clear that a firm application of the rule should not be followed in every case. For example, Rule 30(c) should not mandate disclosure of trade secrets or privileged information merely because such information is sought through a question asked on deposition, see *Perrignon v. Bergen Brunswig Corp.*, 77 F.R.D. 455, 460–61 n.4 (N.D. Cal. 1978); strict application of the rule in these contexts would undermine the values traditionally thereby protected. In some cases then, the mere fact of revelation of some types of information, regardless of its later use or non-use at trial, is sufficiently onerous to justify an exception to the policies of Rule 30(c). Recognizing this, however, the bounds of these exceptional situations must be structured so as not to emasculate the rule. Therefore, the touchstone for determining the existence of such an exception to Rule 30(c) should be the potential harm from disclosure, cf. *Preyer v. United States Lines, Inc.*, 64 F.R.D. 430, 431 (E.D. Pa. 1973) (indicating rule might not be applicable where refusal to answer is based upon claim of privilege); in the absence of a showing of some serious harm likely to result from responding to any given question, the policies behind Rule 30(c) require the answer to be given.[2]

Ordinarily, therefore, objections based merely on an assertion of irrelevance, such as that in the instant case, will not be exempted from the provisions of the rule. See *id.* (when objection merely based on irrelevance, rule should be strictly applied). Although use of this approach may lead to the disclosure of some material arguably protected from discovery under another provision of the Federal Rules (i.e. disclosure of irrelevant, nonharmful material), it must be recognized that only through such a compromise is it possible to avoid totally eviscerating either Rule 30(c) or the corresponding protections of another discovery rule, such as Rule 26(b)(1).

II. Motion for Sanctions

Defendant has also requested this court to impose sanctions, in the form of costs and attorney's fees, upon plaintiffs because, in defendant's opinion, there was no authority whatsoever justifying plaintiffs' counsel's conduct. The award of such sanctions is governed by Federal Rule of Civil Procedure 37(a)(4), which provides, in pertinent part:

> If the motion is granted, the court shall, after opportunity for hearing, require the party or deponent whose conduct necessitated the motion or the party or attorney advising such conduct or both of them to pay to the moving party the reasonable expenses incurred in obtaining the order, including attorney's fees, unless the court finds that the opposition to the motion was substantially justified or that other circumstances make an award of expenses unjust.[Ed.]

Upon consideration of the precedents discussed in part one of this Opinion and the explicit language of Rule 30(c), this court finds no substantial justification for the action of plaintiff's counsel in this case. Further, there is no indication of any other mitigating circumstances such as might make an award of expenses unjust.

---

2. When such harm can be shown, however, the objecting attorney should normally also seek a protective order under Rule 30(d).

[Ed.] Author note: this language now also appears in the deposition rule, Fed. R. Civ. P. 30(d)(2).

Ronald M. Sandgrund,
Your First Expert Witness — Part II
40 COLO. LAW. 93 (2011)[Ed.]

Effective expert testimony boils down to one thing: a credible, prepared expert witness. This two-part article describes the essential principles a new lawyer should consider when retaining, preparing, deposing, and examining expert witnesses. Part I discussed why expert testimony is useful, when expert testimony is advisable, who might qualify as an effective expert witness, [and] how to locate and retain qualified experts.... This second part examines [multiple issues, including] preparing your own and the opposition's expert witnesses for deposition and trial examination....

Deposition and Trial Testimony: Preparing the Expert and Examining the Opposing Expert

There are many similarities between preparing your own expert to give testimony and preparing for the opposing expert's testimony. The steps necessary to organize and execute such preparation are discussed below.

Reviewing Your Expert's Work File

When preparing to defend your own expert's deposition, you should review the expert's file to gauge and anticipate how opposing counsel might use its contents to challenge the expert, and then prepare the expert accordingly. In some rare cases, due to monetary constraints or your expert's lack of full cooperation, such as some treating health care providers in personal injury cases, preparing the expert to testify may not be feasible. For the most part, though, preparing to ask your own expert appropriate follow-up questions to minimize harm and to bolster the expert's credibility usually is prudent.

If your expert's file will be produced for inspection to opposing counsel, you must ensure that the integrity of the file's contents and order is preserved, that the expert is not deprived of access to the file during his or her own deposition or trial preparation, and that any materials added to the file since the date of its original production to opposing counsel are easily identified. If anything is missing or has been removed, it is up to you to find out why and consider whether to add the materials to the file.

Reviewing Your Expert's Résumé

Confirm with your expert that his or her résumé is accurate, complete, and up-to-date. Are there weaknesses in your expert's credentials that can be addressed simply by expanding on or rewording the expert's résumé without tampering with the truth? Trial court judges can be persnickety when asked to qualify expert witnesses to testify to the precise subject matter on which they were endorsed to testify. Following are

---

examples of rulings that might reflect how a judge's broad discretion in qualifying an expert might affect the scope of the expert's actual trial testimony.

- A court accepts an elevator mechanic with twenty-five years' experience as an expert in how elevators and their safety mechanisms function, but not in what actually may have caused a particular elevator to operate as it did on the day of the plaintiff's alleged "free-fall" accident.

- A court accepts an architect and structural engineer as an expert on a home builder's standard of care, but not regarding the builder's subcontractors' standards of care.

- A court accepts a lawyer who did work for liability insurers and wrote insurance coverage books as an expert on an insurer's "bad faith" claims handling, but not regarding an individual claims adjuster's standard of care or what a particularly confusing policy provision meant.

- A court accepts a construction cost estimator as an expert regarding repair costs, but not regarding the need for the repair plan to comply with the building code.

There is no guarantee that an ample résumé will be sufficient for a trial court to qualify an expert in a particular field. A judge may be more likely to qualify an expert in a subject matter to which another judge previously has qualified the expert to testify

Reviewing Your Expert's Report and Preparing the Expert for Deposition

When preparing your expert for deposition, view him or her through opposing counsel's critical eye and prepare accordingly. In addition, treat the expert as you would any witness being prepared for deposition and as your experience and training dictate. One commentator suggests "address[ing] any authorities within the same field who disagree with the expert's ultimate opinion," so that attacks based on these authorities—along with possible responses—can be explored.

It is prudent to advise your expert to bring to the deposition only his or her file pertaining to the case and not extraneous materials that could lead to unanticipated inquiries by opposing counsel. Consider preparing your expert for opposing counsel's examination style to reduce your expert's anxiety. Caution your expert against submitting to deposition in his or her office, because the examining lawyer will scan the workplace for useful information and question the expert about it.

Preparing Your Expert for Trial Examination

Encourage your expert to educate the jury by presenting his or her findings in an absorbing manner. However, do not allow an expert's cogent and far-ranging dissertation to cause you to forget to elicit the entire substance of the expert's opinions. Checking off a list of those opinions as they are expressed is one way to ensure all desired opinions have been presented. Remind your expert not to become combative or sarcastic; this could damage the expert's credibility. Leave the bad manners to opposing counsel. You should almost never accept opposing counsel's offer to stipulate to the qualifications of your expert to render opinion testimony, because this will eliminate the opportunity to start building your expert's credibility with the jury by presenting his or her substantial credentials.

It may be a good idea to have another lawyer from your office conduct an abbreviated mock examination of your expert, allowing you to focus on observing and listening to the expert testify, thereby allowing a better, more objective critique. It often is unwise to overly stage or rehearse your expert's trial testimony, and it is almost always a bad idea to supply the expert with a list of questions in advance. Generally, counsel should resist the urge to videotape the expert, even if the witness might benefit from seeing himself or herself testifying, because the expert may be asked about this choreographed "rehearsal" on the stand, and the videotaped record may become discoverable....

Preparing for the Opposing Expert's Deposition and Trial Testimony

The 2007 article "Your First Deposition"[23] provides a starting point for new lawyers who want to learn the basics of preparing for depositions, and includes guidelines for deposing expert witnesses and creating deposition question outlines. This section complements material presented in that article, although it is not a comprehensive discussion of expert witness cross-examination.

If opinions helpful to your case are obtained from the opposing expert during deposition and these opinions extend beyond the scope of the expert's ... [initial] disclosure, the other side must be supplied with a supplemental disclosure of the testimony to be offered at trial.

Reviewing the Opposing Expert's Work File

Arrangements should be made to examine and, if desired, to obtain a copy of the opposing expert's entire file long before he or she is deposed. This can be accomplished by mutual agreement, a provision in the Case Management Order, or subpoena. Access to all digitized information, photos, real evidence samples, and even computer modeling software also should be arranged. Sometimes, it may be necessary to have your own or a consulting expert examine, interpret, and comment on the file contents....

Reviewing the Opposing Expert's Résumé

The opposing expert's *curriculum vitae* will reflect both the areas of the expert's expertise and areas in which necessary specialized knowledge may be lacking. If there are aspects of the case that require specialized knowledge the expert does not have but that are necessary to render the opinions, these areas should be identified and explored. Any opinions that exceed the scope of his or her expertise should be examined during deposition and the introduction of such opinions during trial vigorously resisted.

Reviewing the Opposing Expert's Prior Testimony and Reports

Because an expert's opinions often are fact-specific, reviewing prior testimony and reports in dissimilar cases rarely uncovers significant inconsistencies. Such

---

23. Ronald M. Sandgrund, *Your First Deposition*, 36 COLO. LAW. 119 (Nov. 2007), www.cobar. org/tcl/tcl_articles.cfm?articleid=5327.

review will, however, help identify potential biases due to concentrated work for a particular law firm, insurer, or industry, or due to philosophical orientation, such as traditionalist versus "new school" approaches in a particular field. Perhaps the greatest benefit of reviewing earlier deposition and trial testimony is to see how the expert skirts the difficult questions so you can anticipate and neutralize these strategies....

Reviewing the Opposing Expert's Report and Reading Between the Lines

When reviewing an opposing expert's report, there are several actions you will want to take. Among them are the following:

- Identify all of the expert's discrete opinions—that is, every conclusion the expert describes.

- Determine whether there are specific matters on which the expert should have opined but failed to do so. Later, you must decide whether to steer clear of these unstated opinions during deposition, in hopes that the trial court will preclude trial testimony on these matters. This may turn into a game of brinkmanship. In pursuing this strategy, there is a risk that opposing counsel will raise these omitted opinions during his or her deposition examination and that you will have to rely on the trial court to strike them as untimely and prejudicial. Otherwise, you might end up having to examine the witness on these newly disclosed opinions without an adequate opportunity to prepare for that examination. If you elect to examine the expert, however, be sure to note on the record that you are not waiving your right to move for sanctions due to ... untimely disclosure....

- Identify the factual and scientific assumptions on which the expert is relying, with an eye toward having the expert acknowledge that the jury may view the facts differently and why this would erode or invalidate the expert's opinions in whole or in part.

- Determine whether any drafts of the expert's report were generated in any form and what happened to them. As noted above, most experts have developed their own report-drafting process.... If early drafts can be found, they may contain interesting edits or omissions when compared to the final draft.

- Identify the common-sense limits of the expert's opinions. A hired gun who fails to recognize that his or her unconditional testimony, when taken to its logical limit, may seem unreasonable to a jury, undermining his or her own credibility.

Preparing the Opposing Expert's Deposition Question Outline

... In many cases, you may want to meet with your own testifying expert or to hire a consulting expert to help interpret and attack the opposing expert's report. Even though it is impossible for a lawyer to develop the depth of knowledge equal to that of the expert sitting across the table, if you are armed with advance knowledge of the subject matter and you ask pointed, technically accurate questions, such cross-examination often induces the witness to be less evasive and easier to control.

If resources allow, it might be helpful to have your expert attend the deposition of the opposing party's expert, particularly if your expert ... [will also serve as] a rebuttal expert. In the right case, your expert could prove helpful by suggesting questions....

Inevitable Surprises and Necessary Follow Up

Expert depositions rarely go completely as planned. Often, stray pages, studies, and photos may first turn up during deposition, and other materials may be identified for the first time but have never been produced. As noted above, testimony regarding new or previously undisclosed opinions may occur. Difficult decisions may have to be made on the spot regarding (1) how to react, including whether to lodge a detailed objection on the record; (2) whether to question the witness about the newly disclosed opinions or information (and thereby, perhaps, implicitly waive any objections to their untimely disclosure); (3) whether to refrain from questioning the witness about the newly disclosed opinions or information and instead seek a remedial preclusion order, knowing that the order could be denied; and (4) whether to suspend rather than terminate the deposition until after the court rules on a remedial preclusion motion.

Notes and Questions

1. For most objections during deposition, an attorney must state the basis of the objection on the record, and then the witness must answer the question, as *Westinghouse* makes clear. However, as Rule 30(c)(2) makes clear, a party need not answer when the objection is to assert a claim of privilege (or to enforce a court order limiting examination, or to terminate the deposition). The *Westinghouse* court appears to broaden the rule slightly, although the "bounds of these exceptional situations must be structured so as not to emasculate the rule." As such, Judge Flannery directs that the consideration will be a more expansive analysis of the potential harm from disclosure, along with the policy considerations of the rule.

   Should an issue of privilege arise, however, an attorney can instruct a witness not to answer, and then file a motion for a protective order at an appropriate time, should the opponent persist with the questioning. Rule 30(d)(3)(A) seems to suggest an additional response to end questioning, when the deposition is "being conducted in bad faith or in a manner that unreasonably annoys, embarrasses, or oppresses the deponent." Attorney misconduct during depositions is not unheard of, and often brings with it judicial attention and even the potential for sanctions. *See Redwood v. Dobson*, 476 F.3d 462 (7th Cir. 2007) (applying a sanction of censure for harassing questions); *Paramount Commc'n Inc. v. QVC Network*, 637 A.2d 34 (Del. 1994) (expounding on possible sanctions for misconduct in response to "outrageous and unacceptable" conduct of out-of-state counsel; the notorious "Joe Jamail" case).

2. As for strategy of deposition preparation, Sandgrund makes some helpful suggestions that may seem obvious but are often overlooked. First, he appropriately mentions that any new opinions that the opposing expert helpfully offers the questioning attorney must be disclosed anew in a supplemental disclosure. Failure to do so may result in their exclusion from trial. Second, Sandgrund highlights

an excellent method of getting "inside" information on how to attack the opposing expert: use your own expert. He suggests this will limit evasive answers and lead to better control of the situation, but it can also lead to unexpected admissions, helpful limitations on the other expert's testimony, or disclose new bases of testimony previously unknown. It is never possible to "outexpert the expert," but a prepared attorney—with help of their expert—is the next best thing.

3. In *Successful First Depositions*, the authors suggest a three-step procedure for approaching depositions. I call it "Collect, Prepare, and Purpose" for the three critical components. Bradley Clary, Sharon Reich Paulsen & Michael J. Vanselow, Successful First Depositions 163–81 (3d. ed. 2011). First, to prep any deposition, one must collect *every possible source* of information about that expert. Clearly that includes their disclosure report and C.V., but also any prior publications, prior testimony, or other materials can lead to unexpected gems. Next, after collecting everything, it is time to prepare; your job is to review those materials with an eye toward your case. Are there facts from an article that mirror your case? Did the expert get snippy in a prior deposition? Has a prior study by the expert been debunked? You never know until you examine the materials in detail. Finally, it is time for "purpose," that is, to decide what your objective will be for the deposition. Do you need to know what facts the expert's opinion was based on? Do you need to know more about his or her background? Do you just want to see their demeanor, how they would present before a jury? Or has your preparation allowed you to try to "score points," meaning, to get them locked into overclaiming something, underclaiming the scope of the opinion, leaving out important bases of opinion, or getting defensive? You won't know which will work until you finish a thorough preparation, but in an individual case, that preparation and execution can be dispositive.

Tying It Together

We are going to watch several excerpts from expert depositions, and in each of them we need to focus on the conduct of the attorney asking questions. In each case, we will discuss what the attorney does well, what the attorney does poorly, and whether these depositions comply with the Federal Rules as we have learned them.

Lawsuit #1: This is a medical malpractice case that plaintiff filed against an emergency room physician for injuries sustained in the ER. We will watch the deposition of the plaintiff's medical expert, being asked questions by the defense attorney.

Lawsuit #2: This is an auto-accident case, in which plaintiff claims damages from the defendant's car striking her in an intersection. We will watch the deposition of the defense's accident reconstruction expert taking questions from the plaintiff's attorney.

Chapter 4

Statistics — The Universal Language of (Many) Experts

"It was my understanding that there would be no math."[24]

We have so far covered the substantive rules of evidence governing expert testimony, and the procedural rules managing discovery. Before we continue in Part 2 to evaluate specific areas of expertise, we must cover a final underlying principle of expert testimony: statistics.

Rule 702 makes clear that expertise can be based on "knowledge, skill, experience, training, or education," and so statistics do not form the foundation of all expert testimony. An auto mechanic discussing an improper brake repair job does not normally rely on statistical inference, nor does a treating physician responding to a car accident victim's injuries (at least not overtly). But while there are exceptions, wide areas of expert testimony — and many we will discuss and dissect in Part 2 — lay upon a foundation of statistical analysis.

It may seem odd to cover statistical inference in law school, and for students with undergraduate majors in the physical sciences or mathematics, it may seem basic; but it is absolutely necessary to cover. Innumeracy and an approach of "I don't understand/want to think about math" simply cannot do, and can lead to disaster in deposition or trial.

We will therefore cover several areas of statistical analysis commonly used by experts, and therefore commonly discussed in legal cases. The approach here is not to be able to do the statistical analysis oneself (although of course that would also be helpful) but instead to understand the underlying principles and assumptions of the methodology used in each analysis, and how courts have approached such mathematical concepts. We will cover three separate concepts: Statistical Correlation, Statistical Significance, and Regression Analysis. We cannot review every type of mathematical or statistical analysis available to experts, but using these three as a template will provide a framework for handling other types of analysis not discussed.

In each area, we will start with some descriptive reading explaining the technique and what it is trying to measure, before looking at caselaw where judges evaluate the

---

24. *Saturday Night Live! Lily Tomlin & James Taylor* (NBC television broadcast Sept. 18, 1976) (Chevy Chase famously channeling Gerald Ford in a Presidential Debate sketch).

issue in real cases. We will finish each section with a practical exercise as well. Again, the focus here is not on performing the mathematical calculation itself, but instead how these concepts are used—and sometimes misused—in litigation.

A. Correlation

In many areas of statistical analysis, we measure the differences between two (or more) groups and try to decide if the difference is meaningful. We will get to that analysis next, but will start first with the measurement of the association of two variables: their "correlation."

Correlation is defined as "a measurement of the linear association of two variables," and is usually denoted by the correlation coefficient: "a number between -1 and 1 that indicates the extent of the linear association between [those] two variables."[25] To understand correlation in the real world, think of a few examples of factors that might be associated:

- Are law school grades related to bar passage scores?

- Are LSAT scores related to bar passage scores?

- Does more education result in higher incomes?

- Does the height of a person help predict their weight?

For each of these examples, we may have a common-sense understanding of how the association works. One might expect that people with more education have higher incomes, or that tall people are often heavier. Then again, what about the incomes of Ph.D. students teaching as adjuncts (with terrible wages)? What about extremely slight but tall athletes (like high jumpers at the Olympics), or short but heavy people? Even if the overall connection of education to income may be positive, it is not absolute. This is why correlation (and its coefficient) is a helpful tool.

Let us consider the example of bar passage. One might expect that people with higher grades in law school would have higher bar pass rates, and that people with higher incoming LSAT scores might also have higher bar pass rates. In fact, this is true. But what if we want to compare them? Which factor has a *stronger* connection to bar passage? Statistics can help us compare those factors and lead to an objective answer, based on the available data.

As we consider the passage from Kaye and Freeman, think about correlations other than these examples, and start to think about how strongly they might be connected. Afterward, we'll look at courts evaluating and interpreting correlation data in a civil rights case.

---

25. David Kaye & David A. Freeman, *Reference Guide on Statistics, in* REFERENCE MANUAL ON SCIENTIFIC EVIDENCE 211, 286 (3d ed. 2011).

David H. Kaye & David A. Freeman, *Reference Guide on Statistics*

REFERENCE MANUAL ON SCIENTIFIC EVIDENCE
261–64 (3d ed. 2011)[Ed.]

B. CORRELATION COEFFICIENTS

Two variables are positively correlated when their values tend to go up or down together.... The correlation coefficient (usually denoted by the letter r) is a single number that reflects the sign of an association and its strength. Figure 7 shows r for three scatter diagrams: In the first, there is no association; in the second, the association is positive and moderate; in the third, the association is positive and strong.

A correlation coefficient of 0 indicates no linear association between the variables. The maximum value for the coefficient is +1, indicating a perfect linear relationship: The dots in the scatter diagram fall on a straight line that slopes up. Sometimes, there is a negative association between two variables: Large values of one tend to go with small values of the other. The age of a car and its fuel economy in miles per gallon illustrate the idea. Negative association is indicated by negative values for r. The extreme case is an r of -1, indicating that all the points in the scatter diagram lie on a straight line that slopes down.

Figure 7. The correlation coefficient measures the sign of a linear association and its strength.[Ed.]

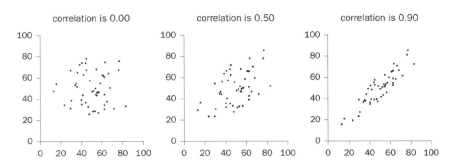

Weak associations are the rule in the social sciences.... [T]he correlation between income and education is about 0.4. The correlation between college grades and first-year law school grades is under 0.3 at most law schools, while the correlation between LSAT scores and first-year grades is generally about 0.4.[126] The correlation between heights of fraternal twins is about 0.5. By contrast, the correlation between heights of identical twins is about 0.95.

[Ed.] Reprinted with permission from the National Academy of Sciences, Courtesy of the National Academies Press, Washington, D.C.

[Ed.] Figure 7 has been moved within the text for clarity, by the Author.

126. LISA ANTHONY STILWELL ET AL., LAW SCH. ADMISSION COUNCIL, PREDICTIVE VALIDITY OF THE LSAT: A NATIONAL SUMMARY OF THE 2001–2002 CORRELATION STUDIES 5, 8 (2003). [Author note: these studies are released every year, and are available here: https://www.lsac.org/lsacresources/research/all/tr.]

1. *Is the association linear?*

The correlation coefficient has a number of limitations, to be considered in turn. The correlation coefficient is designed to measure linear association. Figure 8 shows a strong nonlinear pattern with a correlation close to zero. The correlation coefficient is of limited use with nonlinear data.

Figure 8. The scatter diagram shows a strong nonlinear association with a correlation coefficient close to zero. The correlation coefficient only measures the degree of linear association.[Ed.]

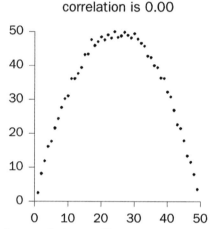

2. *Do outliers influence the correlation coefficient?*

The correlation coefficient can be distorted by outliers—a few points that are far removed from the bulk of the data. The left-hand panel in Figure 9 shows that one outlier (lower right-hand corner) can reduce a perfect correlation to nearly nothing. Conversely, the right-hand panel shows that one outlier (upper righthand corner) can raise a correlation of zero to nearly one. If there are extreme outliers in the data, the correlation coefficient is unlikely to be meaningful.

Figure 9. The correlation coefficient can be distorted by outliers.[Ed.]

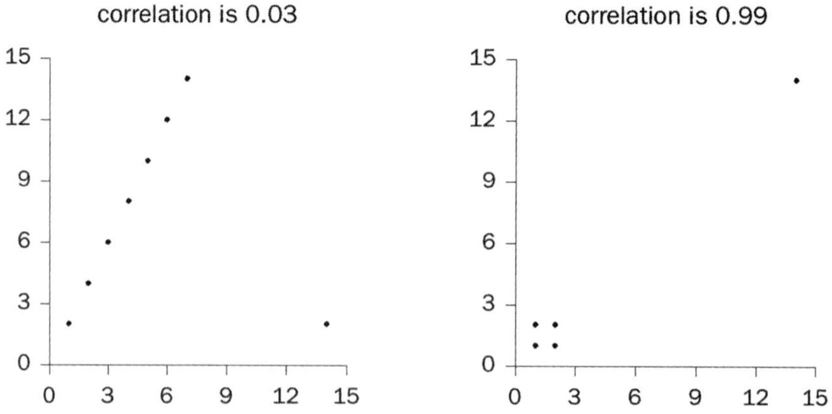

[Ed.] Figure 8 has been moved within the text for clarity by the Author.
[Ed.] Figure 9 has been moved within the text for clarity by the Author.

3. *Does a confounding variable influence the coefficient?*

The correlation coefficient measures the association between two variables. Researchers—and the courts—are usually more interested in causation. Causation is not the same as association. The association between two variables may be driven by a lurking variable that has been omitted from the analysis.... For an easy example, there is an association between shoe size and vocabulary among schoolchildren. However, learning more words does not cause the feet to get bigger, and swollen feet do not make children more articulate. In this case, the lurking variable is easy to spot—age. In more realistic examples, the lurking variable is harder to identify.

In statistics, lurking variables are called confounders or confounding variables. Association often does reflect causation, but a large correlation coefficient is not enough to warrant causal inference. A large value of r only means that the dependent variable marches in step with the independent one: Possible reasons include causation, confounding, and coincidence. Multiple regression is one method that attempts to deal with confounders....

Williams v. Ford Motor Co.
187 F.3d 533 (6th Cir. 1999)

BATCHELDER, Circuit Judge.

   ...

A. Procedural Background

This case is one of many employment discrimination cases in multidistrict litigation against Ford Motor Co. The complaint in the case before us here (hereinafter "*Williams*"), is a state-law employment discrimination class action ... which was originally filed by Michael Williams ... [and others] in Common Pleas Court in Lorain County, Ohio, and removed on diversity grounds to the U.S. District Court.... After Ford moved to consolidate the case with three others, *Jones v. Ford Motor Co., Rose v. Ford Motor Co., and Glinton v. Ford Motor Credit Co.*, the multidistrict panel transferred all four of the cases to the Eastern District of Michigan. The multidistrict panel did not, however, consolidate the cases.

Shortly after the *Williams* plaintiffs filed a motion for class certification, Alan Dale and Bryan Thomas filed a tag-along action ("*Dale*"), claiming that "Ford Motor Company discriminates on the basis of race against Afro-American applicants for unskilled hourly employment through the use of its [pre-employment] test...." The district court entered an order in *Williams*, certifying a class consisting of "all African American applicants for unskilled hourly employment with Ford from 1989 to the present who scored low on the unskilled pre-employment test and who were thereby excluded from unskilled employment with Ford within the state of Ohio." In its order certifying the class, the court noted that [several of the original plaintiffs did not qualify for this class designation, but that] the plaintiffs in *Dale* are adequate class representatives. In that same order, the court denied plaintiffs' motion to consolidate the case with [the other three cases] because "the nature of *Williams* is clearly different...."

Ford filed a motion for summary judgment "on each and every claim asserted in plaintiff's Complaint," which the district court granted in its entirety....

B. Factual Background

Ford operates seven plants in Ohio where motor vehicles and/or their component parts are manufactured and/or assembled. Each plant employs unskilled hourly workers. Ford began using a pre-employment test referred to as the Hourly Selection System Test Battery ("HSSTB") around 1989 to screen applicants for the unskilled hourly positions. Candidates receiving a "low" score are not allowed to proceed in the application process though these applicants may retest, except at Ford's Sandusky plant. The HSSTB measures five areas: reading comprehension, arithmetic, parts assembly, visual speed and accuracy, and precision/manual dexterity. The manual dexterity test may be measured by an apparatus-based test or a paper and pencil test requiring precise finger/hand movement. A score above the 50th percentile on the HSSTB is classified as "high;" a score between the 25th and 50th percentile is classified as "medium." The "low" scoring candidates ... are those who score below the 25th percentile.

Prior to implementation of the HSSTB, Ford utilized referrals from the Ohio Bureau of Employment Services ... [who] administered a General Aptitude Test Battery ("GATB") to prospective candidates. When OBES began to restrict the use of GATB in late 1988, Ford decided to develop its own test. In early 1989, Ford hired Personnel Designs, Inc., which became HRStrategies, Inc.... to develop an interim and long-term selection test for hourly production employees. Because Ford's hourly production employees rotate among assignments and applicants do not apply for positions within specific job classifications, Ford instructed HR to develop a single test battery for all hourly production employees at its facilities. After visiting over a dozen representative Ford facilities to collect information on the content of the Ford hourly jobs, HR developed an interim test battery that was administered in June 1989 at the Lorain and Ohio Assembly Plants. The final test battery, which differed in a number of respects from the interim test, was implemented in late 1989 as a component of Ford's ... hiring process.

In developing the final HSSTB, HR conducted an extensive job analysis to identify the knowledge, skill and ability requirements of Ford hourly production jobs. From December 1989 through May 1990, Ford supervisors participated in job analysis inventories; the supervisors then rated each job requirement and job ability identified in the inventories on its importance to the job category. HR assessed the reliability of the ratings and analyzed the data to identify key job requirements and abilities, and on the basis of the analysis, developed specific tests to measure the skills necessary to perform the job requirements that had been rated as "important" by the experts across all the job categories.

In 1993, Ford directed HR to conduct a criterion-related study, that is a statistical analysis of the relationship between performance on the test and performance on the job. A sample of 105 hourly employees were evaluated on their job performance by 46 selected supervisors; HR analyzed the relationship between the employees' HSSTB scores (pre-employment) and their job performance ratings. HR reported "criterion-related validity analyses with data collected to date show a strong pattern of significant correlations between the tests and performance ratings made by supervisors." Both the initial study and a supplemental study demonstrated a correlation of .30 between the test battery score and overall job performance rating; the supplemental study concluded that "[t]he obtained validity (correlation) coefficient of .30 is both statistically and practically significant and is evidence of the validity and appropriateness of the Ford Hourly Selection Battery for selecting candidates for further consideration for hourly production jobs...."

HR also conducted a validity generalization study called "meta-analysis" in which HR examined literature on sixty-one studies to determine whether similar tests used by other employers predicted employee performance in similar jobs....

Ford's expert, Dr. Wayne Cascio, reviewed and analyzed the test development process and HR's studies and found the test "was developed in a manner consistent with sound professional practice" and "the totality of the evidence for the validity of the HSS supports its continued use." By contrast, Dr. Charles Cranny, expert for the plaintiffs, found numerous problems with the test development and validation studies conducted by HR, concluding that the results of the job analysis fail to demonstrate a clear linkage of specific requirements to job duties and the criterion-related evidence from the preliminary study is inadequate to demonstrate the job-relatedness of the HSSTB.

II.

A. Standard of Review

We review de novo the district court's grant of summary judgment. The proper inquiry on appeal from a grant of summary judgment is "whether the evidence presents a sufficient disagreement to require submission to a jury or whether it is so one-sided that one party must prevail as a matter of law." *Anderson v. Liberty Lobby, Inc.*, 477 U.S. 242, 251–52 (1986). Summary judgment is proper only if there is no genuine issue as to any material fact, and the moving party is entitled to judgment as a matter of law. Fed.R.Civ.P. 56(c). In reviewing a grant of summary judgment, the moving party's evidence "must be viewed in the light most favorable to the [nonmoving] party." *Matsushita Elec. Indus. Co. v. Zenith Radio Corp.*, 475 U.S. 574, 587 (1986); *Adickes v. S.H. Kress & Co.*, 398 U.S. 144, 157 (1970). However, if the nonmoving party failed to make a sufficient showing on an essential element of the case with respect to which the non-movant has the burden, the moving party is entitled to summary judgment as a matter of law. *Celotex Corp. v. Catrett*, 477 U.S. 317, 322–23 (1986).

B. Analysis

The *Williams* action was initiated generally pursuant to Ohio Rev.Code Ann. § 4112.02(A) which provides:

It shall be an unlawful discriminatory practice:

(A) For any employer, because of the race, color, religion, sex, national origin, handicap, age, or ancestry of any person, to discharge without just cause, to refuse to hire, or otherwise to discriminate against that person with respect to hire, tenure, terms, conditions, or privileges of employment, or any matter directly or indirectly related to employment.

The *Williams* plaintiffs alleged no specific practice which would violate the statute—indeed, they alleged no specific practice of any kind—claiming only that each of them has unsuccessfully sought employment with Ford at its Lorain County facility, and that

> Ford Motor Company, due to race/color, has refused to hire them. Plaintiffs further state that other less qualified applicants, and/or others who applied after them but were white, were hired.... Plaintiffs also state that this defendant has engaged in a pattern, practice and course of conduct of not hiring individuals who are black or Afro-American, and in giving preferential treatment to white applicants.

The *Dale* complaint, however, claims that the employment test utilized by Ford discriminates against African American applicants for unskilled hourly positions.

The Ohio courts have held that the evidentiary standards and burdens of proof applicable to a claimed violation of Title VII of the Civil Rights Act of 1964 are likewise applicable in determining whether a violation of Ohio Rev.Code § 4112 has occurred. Thus, the federal case law governing Title VII actions is generally applicable to cases involving alleged violations of Chapter 4112.... In *Albemarle Paper Co. v. Moody*, 422 U.S. 405, 425 (1975), the Supreme Court outlined the applicable burdens of the parties in test-related disparate impact cases:

> Title VII forbids the use of employment tests that are discriminatory in effect unless the employer meets "the burden of showing that any given requirement [has] ... a manifest relationship to the employment in question." This burden arises, of course, only after the complaining party or class has made out a prima facie case of discrimination, i.e., has shown that the tests in question select applicants for hire or promotion in a racial pattern significantly different from that of the pool of applicants. If an employer does then meet the burden of proving that its tests are "job related," it remains open to the complaining party to show that other tests or selection devices, without a similarly undesirable racial effect, would also serve the employer's legitimate interest....

Id. at 425 (internal citations omitted). The Supreme Court made it clear in *Wards Cove* that once a plaintiff has made out a prima facie case, it is not the burden of persuasion which shifts to the employer; instead, at that point, the employer bears the burden of production of evidence demonstrating a business justification for the challenged employment practice. "[T]he ultimate burden of proving that discrimination against a protected group has been caused by a specific employment practice remains with the plaintiff *at all times*." *Wards Cove Packing Co. v. Atonio*, 490 U.S. 642, 659–60 (1989) (emphasis in original).

Therefore, to prove a selection procedure is job-related, the employer must show "by professionally acceptable methods, [that the test is] predictive of or significantly correlated with important elements of work behavior which comprise or are relevant to the job or jobs for which candidates are being evaluated." *Black Law Enforcement*

Officers Ass'n v. City of Akron, 824 F.2d 475, 480 (6th Cir.1987) (brackets in original). In order "to assist employers … to comply with requirements of Federal law prohibiting employment practices which discriminate on grounds of race, color, religion, sex, and national origin … [and] to provide a framework for determining the proper use of tests and other selection procedures," the Equal Employment Opportunity Commission ("EEOC") developed the Uniform Guidelines, a set of standards for establishing the validity of these tests and procedures. A test which is shown to have an adverse impact on hiring of members of any race or ethnic group is deemed "discriminatory" unless it is "validated" in accordance with the guidelines. 29 C.F.R. § 1607.3(A); *Gonzales v. Galvin*, 151 F.3d 526, 529 n. 4 (6th Cir.1998).…

Employers may use three types of studies to validate an employee selection procedure under the Guidelines: content, construct, or criterion-related validity studies. 29 C.F.R. § 1607.5(A).… The Guidelines also set forth specific documentary requirements for each type of study. § 1607.15.… A test will have content validity if there is a direct relationship between the test contents and the job contents. *Police Officers for Equal Rights v. City of Columbus*, 644 F.Supp. at 414. Content validity may be demonstrated through data showing that the skills tested are representative of skills important to the job for which the applicants are to be evaluated.… It is not appropriate, however, for an employer to test for those skills that can readily be learned on the job. 29 C.F.R. §§ 1607.5(B), (F).

A construct validity study evaluates procedures that test for abstract qualities which may be important characteristics for proper job performance but are challenging to test. Such studies are appropriate where the necessary qualities, such as creativity, cannot be measured directly; construct validity studies are usually not appropriate for validating physical exams because these physical qualities and abilities may be readily observed and quantified.…

A criterion-related study evaluates whether performance on the test adequately correlates with performance of the job. *Gillespie v. Wisconsin*, 771 F.2d 1035, 1040 n. 3 (7th Cir.1985). The guidelines provide that a criterion-related study "should consist of empirical data demonstrating that the selection procedure is predictive of or significantly correlated with important elements of job performance." 29 C.F.R. § 1607.5(B). An employment test has criterion-related validity when the data demonstrates a significant positive correlation between degree of success on the test and the degree of success in some measure of job performance. This relationship is expressed as a "correlation coefficient." A correlation coefficient of -1.0 indicates a completely negative relationship: the better one does on the test, the worse one performs on the job. A correlation coefficient of +1.0 indicates a complete identity between relative test scores and relative job performance. *Clady v. Cty. of L.A.*, 770 F.2d 1421, 1426 n. 5 (9th Cir.1985), citing B. SCHLEI & P. GROSSMAN, EMPLOYMENT DISCRIMINATION LAW 114 (2d ed. 1983).…

In its motion for summary judgment, Ford focused on two issues: (1) whether plaintiffs [could show a *prima facie* case] … and (2) whether Ford is entitled to summary judgment on plaintiffs' test-based disparate impact claim where the undisputed facts demonstrate that the test is valid and job-related and that there is no equally valid test available that would produce less disparate impact. Plaintiffs opposed the motion, relying principally on the affidavit of Dr. Charles Cranny who asserted that Ford's pre-employment test was not properly validated.

Treating Ford's first claim as a claim that the plaintiffs had failed to make out a prima facie case of test-based discrimination, the district court held that Ford was not entitled to summary judgment on that basis.... The district court then turned to Ford's claim that it is entitled to summary judgment on plaintiffs' test-based disparate impact claim because it is undisputed that the test has been properly validated and there has been no showing of an alternative test that is both equally valid and less adverse in its impact on African Americans than the HSSTB. Noting that although the burden of persuasion continued with the plaintiffs to demonstrate that the test fails to serve in a significant way the legitimate goals of the employer, the court examined the record evidence, including the "Project Technical Report" detailing the technical research and validation data supporting the HSSTB and the reports of Ford's independent experts evaluating that data, to determine whether Ford had produced evidence of a legitimate business justification for its use of the test. The court concluded that the HSSTB had been developed by professionals and appropriately validated through content-related studies and criterion-related studies. Further, the court concluded that Ford had demonstrated that the job analysis was not race-biased, and had met its burden of showing that the HSSTB is both job-related and a valid predictor of the likelihood of success on the job.... Finding that Ford had shown to a reasonable degree of statistical certainty that its test is a legitimate and valid indicator of future performance on the job, the district court held that Ford was entitled to summary judgment because, although the test does disparately impact African American test-takers, it does not violate Ohio Rev.Code § 4112.02.

On appeal, plaintiffs argue that the district court erred in granting summary judgment to Ford because in so doing, the district court ignored the fact that plaintiffs presented expert testimony that conflicted with Ford's expert testimony ...; the district court erroneously found that the test has both content validity and criterion-related validity which is not supported by the evidence and in any event is a determination to be made by the trier of fact; and the district court applied an incorrect legal standard.... For the reasons that follow, we hold that the district court correctly concluded that Ford was entitled to summary judgment.

1. Content Validity of the HSSTB

The district court correctly concluded that the HSSTB is content valid. The Uniform Guidelines state that "[a] selection procedure can be supported by a content validity strategy to the extent that it is a representative sample of the content of the job." 29 C.F.R. § 1607.14(C)(1). We conclude that content-validity is an appropriate method of validation of the test at issue here, and that Ford has demonstrated that the test has such validity.

The record demonstrates that Ford utilized HRStrategies, a professional test developer, to conduct a job analysis that complied with the technical standards contained in the Guidelines. HR began with Ford's requirement that applicants for employment in hourly positions are not hired for a specific position but, depending upon such variables as production requirements and other employees' exercise of seniority rights under the collective bargaining agreement, must be able to rotate among numerous job classifications. Using the Dictionary of Occupational Titles as a guide, HR assigned each of Ford's roughly 1000 hourly positions into one of 13 categories; HR then utilized 238 Ford supervisors at 18 separate Ford locations, 211 of whom had at least 10 years tenure at Ford and 125 of whom had at least 10 years in their current jobs at Ford, to rate each of the job activities contained in the respective categories, first, as to the extent to which each activity was part of the jobs within the category, and second, as to the importance of each activity to the jobs within the category. These raters were further presented with a list of 59 different job requirements, identical across all jobs, and asked to rate each requirement as to its contemporaneous importance to the job and its anticipated importance five years hence. HR then performed overlap analyses of those ratings to determine the extent to which there was agreement across raters, examining the overlap among raters in the same Ford plant rating the same job, the overlap among raters in different plants of the same type with regard to each job group, and the overlap across different plant types for each job category and across the 13 categories. Finally, HR computed a job requirement profile for each job category by averaging the job requirement ratings for all of the experts in the respective category and, after performing a series of cluster analyses to determine which categories of jobs should be combined, resolved the 13 categories into three rationally based clusters: jobs related to machining/finishing/testing operations and processes; jobs related to off-line support for manufacturing processes; and jobs directly related to the assembly line and the assembly process. HR then determined which job requirements had a mean importance rating of 2 or higher, indicating that the requirement was important—both now and 5 years hence—to the jobs in the respective cluster, and which skill requirements were important across the clusters. From those findings, HR determined which skills would be assessed by the test to be administered by Ford.

Against this evidence, the plaintiffs presented the report and affidavits of their expert, Dr. Cranny. The district court found, and we agree, that Dr. Cranny's opinions are wholly insufficient to create a genuine issue with regard to the content validity of the HSSTB. Dr. Cranny's criticisms of the content-validity study are entirely conclusory, are unsupported by any specific data, and are premised on the unsupportable factual assertion that the data was collected after the test had been administered....

... In challenging Ford's motion for summary judgment the plaintiffs are not required to prove their claims, but they are required to present enough specific facts as to raise a genuine issue material to the relationship between the HSSTB and the job activities and requirements of Ford's hourly production jobs. Plaintiffs cannot challenge the motion for summary judgment by relying on allegations contained in their complaint or on affidavits that merely state conclusory allegations. Ford correctly asserts and the district court correctly found that Dr. Cranny's affidavit did not raise a genuine issue of fact material to the content validity of the HSSTB....

2. Criterion-related validity of the HSSTB

Having concluded that Ford had demonstrated that the HSSTB is content valid, the district court went on to determine whether the test had criterion-related validity. Neither the case law nor the Uniform Guidelines purports to require that an employer must demonstrate validity using more than one method.... Ford appears to concede that, under 29 C.F.R. § 1607.14(C), to the extent that the HSSTB purports to assess or to draw inferences about "mental processes," the test must be shown to have validity beyond mere content validity. That section says that "a content strategy is not appropriate for demonstrating the validity of selection procedures which purport to measure traits or constructs, such as intelligence, aptitude, personality, commonsense, judgment, leadership, and spatial ability." 29 C.F.R. § 1607.14(C)(1). Further, § 1607.14(C)(4) says that "[i]n the case of a selection procedure measuring a knowledge, skill, or ability, the knowledge, skill, or ability being measured should be operationally defined.... As the content of the selection procedure less resembles a work behavior, or the setting and manner of the administration of the selection procedure less resemble the work situation, or the result less resembles a work product, the less likely the selection procedure is to be content valid, and the greater the need for other evidence of validity." ... The district court found that Ford had adequately demonstrated that the HSSTB has criterion-related validity ... [and] ... we conclude that the district court did not err in that conclusion.

Ford's criterion-related study was conducted by the same professional test developer, HRStrategies. HR selected 105 employees, representing four different Ford plants, to participate in the study. These employees had been on the job for three months, were white (53%), African American (38%) and Hispanic (9%), male and female, under and over 40 years old, and had varying degrees of education. HR then utilized 46 Ford supervisors, identified by local Ford personnel as being knowledgeable about the job performances of the employees participating in the study. The supervisors were carefully educated about the study, its purpose and its content; they were required to supply extensive demographic information about themselves; they were instructed in detail on how they were to evaluate the performance of the employees with whom they were familiar and given the procedure to use in the event they were uncomfortable rating any particular employee. The supervisors then rated the job performance of their respective assigned employees on a defined scale for each item within each of eight job requirement dimensions being evaluated, and provided as well a rating of overall performance within each dimension and an overall rating of job performance across dimensions. The job performances of these 105 employees and their HSSTB scores (which were neither revealed nor available to the supervisors evaluating the job performances) were analyzed to examine the relationship between test score and job performance.

The statistical analysis performed by HR showed that the supervisors rating job performance did not rate white employees and African American employees differently; the ratings did not differ based on the race of the rater; raters did not rate study participants of the same race systematically higher than they rated study participants of a different race. Further, the statistical analysis showed a correlation coefficient—the correlation between test performance and job performance—of .30. It is undisputed that a correlation coefficient of .30 is statistically significant and sufficient to establish job-relatedness.[13]

Plaintiffs again presented little more than conclusory and factually unsupported or legally incorrect criticisms of the criterion-related study, including that the study was flawed because it did not include persons who scored "low" on the HSSTB; that several individuals who had scored "low" on the test had succeeded in unskilled positions with employers other than Ford; ... and that the study was flawed because it was conducted after the HSSTB had been implemented as a selection procedure at Ford.

We conclude that the district court was correct in its determination that plaintiffs simply failed to provide the kind of specifics necessary to raise a genuine issue with regard to whether the HSSTB has criterion-related validity. The law does not require that an employer, simply in order that low scorers may be included in validation studies, hire individuals who do not pass a pre-employment test. *See Clady v. Cty. of L.A.*, 770 F.2d 1421, 1431 (9th Cir.1985) (rejecting the contention that a validity study must include individuals who failed the challenged test); *see also* 29 C.F.R. § 1607.14B(1) ("These guidelines do not require a user to hire or promote persons for the purpose of making it possible to conduct a criterion-related study."). Neither does the law require that a criterion-related study be performed before the test is utilized. *See Albemarle Paper Co.*, 422 U.S. at 433, n. 32, 95 S.Ct. 2362 (noting only that the study in that case had been prepared immediately before trial, and studies "closely controlled by an interested party in litigation must be examined with great care.").... Plaintiffs did present the affidavits of several individuals who scored "low" on the HSSTB but who were ultimately successful in working unskilled jobs in the employ of companies other than Ford. Plaintiffs point us to no authority, however, and we have found none, to support their position that such affidavits are sufficient to create a genuine issue with regard to the test's content validity, i.e., the statistically significant correlation between the specific skills assessed by the test and the specific skills important to job performance....

We hold that the district court did not err in concluding that Ford had sustained its burden of demonstrating that the HSSTB has criterion-related validity, that is, Ford has demonstrated through empirical data "that the selection procedure is predictive of or significantly correlated with important elements of job performance." 29 C.F.R. § 1607.5(B). Plaintiffs have failed to raise any genuine issue for trial with regard to the criterion-related validity of the test.... Accordingly, we affirm the district

---

13. Specifically, the HR study found that the .30 correlation coefficient was statistically significant at the 0.01 level, which means that there is less than one chance in one hundred that the .30 correlation coefficient was the product of chance. The Uniform Guidelines provide that "a selection procedure is considered related to the criterion ... when the relationship between performance on the procedure and performance on the criterion measure is statistically significant at the 0.05 level of significance, which means that it is sufficiently high as to have a probability of no more than one (1) in twenty (20) to have occurred by chance." 29 C.F.R. § 1607.14(B)(5).

court's judgment that the HSSTB, although it may have a disparate impact on African American test-takers, does not violate Ohio Rev.Code §4112.02.

Notes and Questions

1. In *Williams*, the court makes clear that once a plaintiff or plaintiffs show a *prima facie* case for employment discrimination under Title VII, the burden of production shifts to the employer to demonstrate that the test given—even if it discriminates—accurately measures employment requirements for the job. They can satisfy this burden in a variety of ways, and you can see that Ford presents affirmative evidence of two methodologies. Why did they decide to offer both? Furthermore, the criterion-related study of the HSSTB test showed a correlation coefficient of 0.3. What is the proper interpretation of that number? And how does that relate to the validation of the HSSTB test for employment purposes?

2. In the Kaye & Freeman excerpt, they mention that correlation coefficients in the social sciences are often low: "Weak associations are the rule in the social sciences." For example, they mention that the association of college grades and first-year grades in law school is under 0.3 at most law schools. Why might the connection be weak (or at least weaker then we might have predicted, especially when compared to the LSAT correlation coefficient of 0.4)? Note also that the Ford HSSTB test has a correlation coefficient of 0.3—does that indicate it does a good or poor job of predicting success at the next employment position? How do you think that Ford managed to create a test with a coefficient this high?

3. Inevitably, when discussing associations between variables and correlation coefficients, someone will (helpfully?) remind us that "correlation is not causation." In some cases, that statement seems so simple as to be tautological. Of course, the HSSTB test in *Williams* does not *cause* high scores on employment ratings afterward. As Kaye & Freeman note, however, there are many cases where a positive association can appear causative but instead is the result of an interfering variable: "For an easy example, there is an association between shoe size and vocabulary among schoolchildren. However, learning more words does not cause the feet to get bigger, and swollen feet do not make children more articulate. In this case, the lurking variable is easy to spot—age." Kaye & Freeman, *supra*. Another example could be ice cream sales at the state park and drowning deaths. Eating ice cream does not make one more likely to drown, but instead the intervening variable is temperature—when the temperature is hot, more people come to the park to swim, and when more people come to swim, they buy more ice cream and there are more swimming accidents. On the other hand, Kaye and Freeman mention the truth in most social science research, which is: "In more realistic examples, the lurking variable is harder to identify." *Id.*

    A helpful (and fun way) to visualize this distinction is to take a moment to review the website *Spurious Correlations*, at http://www.tylervigen.com/spurious-correlations, and look at connections between variables that are supported by a strong statistical relationship but almost certainly not meaningful one. Several examples from the site demonstrate very high correlation coefficients:

- ◦ U.S. spending on science, space and technology & suicides by hanging, strangulation, or suffocation. $r = 0.997$ (!)
- ◦ Number of people who drowned by falling into a pool & films Nicolas Cage appeared in. $r = 0.666$; and
- ◦ Divorce rate in Maine & per capita consumption of margarine. $r = -0.993$ (!)

Even with these very high r-values, no one is ready to stop spending on NASA to prevent suicides nor does Nicholas Cage need to stop appearing in films, at least not in order to prevent drownings. Even with high correlation, these associations are (unless I am seriously misinformed) pure coincidence.

B. Statistical Significance

Correlation is the assessment of the linear association between two variables, and we saw that in employment discrimination cases, it provides a useful measurement of employment test "validation" (whether the test is associated with positive employment performance). While correlation provides a useful entry point to the issue of statistics in the law, a much more common topic—and the one we turn to now—is statistical significance.

When we consider the differences between two variables, does it represent a "true result" or is it a product of random chance? Think about these examples:

- – At A's workplace, male employers are paid more than female employees;
- – When B's case went to trial, women comprised 77% of the venire group;
- – Measurements of students in C's class at lunch indicate that female students are on average 3 inches taller than male students.

Is each of these observations of difference between the groups real, or is it merely a product of chance? For example, in A's workplace, did they record the salaries of all employees, or just some? How do we know which employees made the "sample" and which did not? If we learned that only men on the board of directors were polled, and women in the mail room, that might make a huge difference in deciding if men are paid more than women throughout the company. In example B, if we learned that the jury trial took place in a small rural town that has a large and well-regarded women's college in it, that might change our perception of the jury venire. If I told you that C's class was in fifth grade, we might have a different overall impression of the data difference we observed than if the class was in graduate school.

So when we examine data and find a difference between two variables, we are left to wonder: is it a "true" result showing an actual difference or is it merely a result of sample selection and chance? The concept of statistical significance assists us in answering that question. To learn what statistical significance means, and how it compares the results versus random chance, we will review another passage from Kaye

& Freeman from *The Reference Guide on Statistics*. Afterward, we will look at courts evaluating and interpreting statistical significance in an employment discrimination case occurring at a university.

David H. Kaye & David A. Freeman,
Reference Guide on Statistics
REFERENCE MANUAL ON SCIENTIFIC EVIDENCE
249–53 (3d ed. 2011)[Ed.]

B. SIGNIFICANCE LEVELS AND HYPOTHESIS TESTS

1. *What is the* p-*value?*

In 1969, Dr. Benjamin Spock came to trial in the U.S. District Court for Massachusetts. The charge was conspiracy to violate the Military Service Act. The jury was drawn from a panel of 350 persons selected by the clerk of the court. The panel included only 102 women—substantially less than 50%—although a majority of the eligible jurors in the community were female. The shortfall in women was especially poignant in this case: "Of all defendants, Dr. Spock, who had given wise and welcome advice on child-rearing to millions of mothers, would have liked women on his jury."

Can the shortfall in women be explained by the mere play of random chance? To approach the problem, a statistician would formulate and test a null hypothesis. Here, the null hypothesis says that the panel is like 350 persons drawn at random from a large population that is 50% female. The expected number of women drawn would then be 50% of 350, which is 175. The observed number of women is 102. The shortfall is $175 - 102 = 73$. How likely is it to find a disparity this large or larger, between observed and expected values? The probability is called p, or the p-value.

The p-value is the probability of getting data as extreme as, or more extreme than, the actual data—given that the null hypothesis is true. In the example, p turns out to be essentially zero. The discrepancy between the observed and the expected is far too large to explain by random chance. Indeed, even if the panel had included 155 women, the p-value would only be around 0.02, or 2%.[98] (If the population is more than 50% female, p will be even smaller.) In short, the jury panel was nothing like a random sample from the community.

Large p-value indicate that a disparity can easily be explained by the play of chance: The data fall within the range likely to be produced by chance variation. On the other hand, if p is very small, something other than chance must be involved: The data are far away from the values expected under the null hypothesis. Significance testing often seems to involve multiple negatives. This is because a statistical test is an argument by contradiction.

[Ed.] Reprinted with permission from the National Academy of Sciences, Courtesy of the National Academies Press, Washington, D.C.

98. With 102 women out of 350, the p-value is about 2/10[15] where 10[15] is 1 followed by 15 zeros, that is, a quadrillion....

With the Dr. Spock example, the null hypothesis asserts that the jury panel is like a random sample from a population that is 50% female. The data contradict this null hypothesis because the disparity between what is observed and what is expected (according to the null) is too large to be explained as the product of random chance. In a typical jury discrimination case, small p-value help a defendant appealing a conviction by showing that the jury panel is not like a random sample from the relevant population; large p-value hurt. In the usual employment context, small p-value help plaintiffs who complain of discrimination—for example, by showing that a disparity in promotion rates is too large to be explained by chance; conversely, large p-value would be consistent with the defense argument that the disparity is just due to chance.

Because p is calculated by assuming that the null hypothesis is correct, p does not give the chance that the null is true. The p-value merely gives the chance of getting evidence against the null hypothesis as strong as or stronger than the evidence at hand. Chance affects the data, not the hypothesis. According to the frequency theory of statistics, there is no meaningful way to assign a numerical probability to the null hypothesis. The correct interpretation of the p-value can therefore be summarized in two lines:

p is the probability of extreme data given the null hypothesis.

p is not the probability of the null hypothesis given extreme data.

To recapitulate the logic of significance testing: If p is small, the observed data are far from what is expected under the null hypothesis—too far to be readily explained by the operations of chance. That discredits the null hypothesis.

Computing p-values requires statistical expertise. Many methods are available, but only some will fit the occasion. Sometimes standard errors will be part of the analysis; other times they will not be. Sometimes a difference of two standard errors will imply a p-value of about 5%; other times it will not. In general, the p-value depends on the model, the size of the sample, and the sample statistics.

2. Is a difference statistically significant?

If an observed difference is in the middle of the distribution that would be expected under the null hypothesis, there is no surprise. The sample data are of the type that often would be seen when the null hypothesis is true. The difference is not significant, as statisticians say, and the null hypothesis cannot be rejected. On the other hand, if the sample difference is far from the expected value—according to the null hypothesis—then the sample is unusual. The difference is significant, and the null hypothesis is rejected. Statistical significance is determined by comparing p to a preset value, called the significance level. The null hypothesis is rejected when p falls below this level.

In practice, statistical analysts typically use levels of 5% and 1%.[101] The 5% level is the most common in social science, and an analyst who speaks of significant results

---

101. The Supreme Court implicitly referred to this practice in Castaneda v. Partida, 430 U.S. 482, 496 n.17 (1977), and Hazelwood School District v. United States, 433 U.S. 299, 311 n.17 (1977). In these footnotes, the Court described the null hypothesis as "suspect to a social scientist" when a statistic from "large samples" falls more than "two or three standard deviations" from its expected value under the null hypothesis. Although the Court did not say so, these differences produce p-

without specifying the threshold probably is using this figure. An unexplained reference to highly significant results probably means that p is less than 1%. These levels of 5% and 1% have become icons of science and the legal process. In truth, however, such levels are at best useful conventions.

Because the term "significant" is merely a label for a certain kind of p-value, significance is subject to the same limitations as the underlying p-value. Thus, significant differences may be evidence that something besides random error is at work. They are not evidence that this something is legally or practically important. Statisticians distinguish between statistical and practical significance to make the point. When practical significance is lacking—when the size of a disparity is negligible—there is no reason to worry about statistical significance.[102]

It is easy to mistake the p-value for the probability of the null hypothesis given the data.... Likewise, if results are significant at the 5% level, it is tempting to conclude that the null hypothesis has only a 5% chance of being correct.[103] This temptation should be resisted. From the frequentist perspective, statistical hypotheses are either true or false. Probabilities govern the samples, not the models and hypotheses. The significance level tells us what is likely to happen when the null hypothesis is correct; it does not tell us the probability that the hypothesis is true. Significance comes no closer to expressing the probability that the null hypothesis is true than does the underlying p-value.

3. *Tests or interval estimates?*

How can a highly significant difference be practically insignificant? The reason is simple: p depends not only on the magnitude of the effect, but also on the sample size (among other things). With a huge sample, even a tiny effect will be highly significant. For example, suppose that a company hires 52% of male job applicants and 49% of female applicants. With a large enough sample, a statistician could compute an impressively small p-value. This p-value would confirm that the difference does not result from chance, but it would not convert a trivial difference (52% versus 49%) into a substantial one. In short, the p-value does not measure the strength or importance of an association.

A "significant" effect can be small. Conversely, an effect that is "not significant" can be large. By inquiring into the magnitude of an effect, courts can avoid being misled by p-values. To focus attention on more substantive concerns—the size of the effect and the precision of the statistical analysis—interval estimates (e.g., confidence intervals) may be more valuable than tests. Seeing a plausible range of values for the quantity of interest helps describe the statistical uncertainty in the estimate.

---

values of about 5% and 0.3% when the statistic is normally distributed. The Court's standard deviation is our standard error.

102. E.g., Waisome v. Port Auth., 948 F.2d 1370, 1376 (2d Cir. 1991) ("though the disparity was found to be statistically significant, it was of limited magnitude.")....

103. E.g., Waisome, 948 F.2d at 1376 ("Social scientists consider a finding of two standard deviations significant, meaning there is about one chance in 20 that the explanation for a deviation could be random....").

4. *Is the sample statistically significant?*

Many a sample has been praised for its statistical significance or blamed for its lack thereof. Technically, this makes little sense. Statistical significance is about the difference between observations and expectations. Significance therefore applies to statistics computed from the sample, but not to the sample itself, and certainly not to the size of the sample. Findings can be statistically significant. Differences can be statistically significant.... Estimates can be statistically significant.... By contrast, samples can be representative or unrepresentative. They can be chosen well or badly.... They can be large enough to give reliable results or too small to bother with.... But samples cannot be "statistically significant," if this technical phrase is to be used as statisticians use it.

Tagatz v. Marquette University

861 F.2d 1040 (7th Cir. 1988)

POSNER, Circuit Judge.

Dr. Glenn Tagatz, a professor in the Marquette University education school, brought suit against Marquette under Title VII of the Civil Rights Act of 1964 and the Age Discrimination in Employment Act of 1967. He charged that he had received smaller pay raises than colleagues who were either Catholic or under 40 years of age. Judge Warren, after a bench trial, entered judgment for Marquette, and Tagatz appeals.

The case is remarkable because, for the first time ever so far as we know, the plaintiff testified as his own expert witness.... Dr. Tagatz, a specialist in statistical evidence in employment discrimination cases, prepared the statistical evidence on which his case rides, and was permitted to introduce the evidence as an expert witness. Rule 702 of the Federal Rules of Evidence, which governs the qualification of expert witnesses, is latitudinarian, and nothing in its language suggests that a party cannot qualify as an expert; nor did Marquette object to Dr. Tagatz's testifying as an expert witness. As Dr. Tagatz's counsel pointed out at argument, the fact that a party testifying as his own expert is not disinterested does not distinguish him from any other party who testifies in his own behalf; and hired experts, who generally are highly compensated—and by the party on whose behalf they are testifying—are not notably disinterested. There is a rule against employing expert witnesses on a contingent-fee basis (that is, against paying them more for their testimony if the party that hired them wins), and this rule might be thought to imply that a party—whose "reward" for testifying depends, of course, on the outcome of the suit—is not eligible to be an expert witness. But it is a rule of professional conduct rather than of admissibility of evidence. It is unethical for a lawyer to employ an expert witness on a contingent-fee basis, 3 WEINSTEIN'S EVIDENCE 706[03] at pp. 706-23 to 706-24 (1987), but it does not follow that evidence obtained in violation of the rule is inadmissible. See *United States v. Cervantes-Pacheco*, 826 F.2d 310, 316 (5th Cir.1987) (en banc) (concurring opinion). The trier of fact should be able to discount for so obvious a conflict of interest. In any event, there was no objection to Dr. Tagatz's testifying as an expert witness, so we need not delve deeper into this intriguing subject.

Because the case was tried, the intricate issues concerning prima facie case that Dr. Tagatz presses on us are irrelevant.... The only question is whether Judge Warren's determination that Dr. Tagatz had not proved that he received smaller raises than he would have if he had been either Catholic or young was clearly erroneous. Although Dr. Tagatz attempts to present a disparate-impact claim, he has not identified any specific employment practice that he contends has a discriminatory effect. See *Watson v. Fort Worth Bank & Trust*, 487 U.S. 977 (1988). The only issue, therefore, is whether he proved deliberate discrimination either against non-Catholic, or against middle-aged, faculty.

Marquette is a Jesuit institution. See *Maguire v. Marquette University*, 814 F.2d 1213, 1214 (7th Cir.1987). It gives preference to Catholic applicants for teaching jobs in fields where Catholic doctrine is important, such as theology and philosophy, as it is permitted to do by the exemption in Title VII for religious institutions. See 42 U.S.C. § 2000e-2(e)(2).... But its stated policy is not to discriminate against non-Catholics once they are hired; and whether because of this policy or otherwise, Marquette declined to plead the religious exemption as a defense to Dr. Tagatz's claim of religious discrimination.

Dr. Tagatz, who is 54 and an Episcopalian, received his doctorate in educational psychology from the University of Wisconsin and was hired by Marquette as an associate professor in 1968. In 1971 he was made chairman of the department of psychology in the education school but he was removed from that job in 1974. In 1976 he published a book that received a single, brutally unfavorable review, though the dean of the school of education said he rather liked it; since then Dr. Tagatz has published only one article in a professional journal. According to the Social Science Citation Index, Dr. Tagatz's book has never been cited in a scholarly publication; and none of his articles has been cited since 1982.

Beginning in 1976 the dean placed annual raises on an explicitly meritocratic basis. Scholarly output (quality as well as quantity), teaching quality, and administrative and related service to the school or university are the criteria that the dean uses to determine how large a raise to give each member of the department. Between 1976 and 1981, Dr. Tagatz received average annual raises greater than some members of the department, but below the average. He brought this suit in 1982.

The evidence of discrimination is almost entirely statistical. It consists of a series of tables, prepared by Dr. Tagatz, that compare salary raises for Catholic and non-Catholic, over-40 and under-40 faculty members in the school of education. The samples are small, because the school of education has only a small faculty. In the table that Dr. Tagatz's counsel told us at argument contained the strongest evidence for his client, the salary raises between 1975 and 1985 of each of the 28 faculty members were compared with the faculty member's religion. The comparison showed that, on average, the Catholic members of the faculty received significantly larger annual raises than the non-Catholic ones. A similar table showed larger annual raises on a percentage basis for faculty members under 40 compared to those over 40. Marquette did not offer expert testimony, although Dr. Tagatz is incorrect to say that it offered no statistical evidence. It presented a table showing that the most productive scholars in the school of education, as measured by number of publications, happened to be Catholics. (Dr. Tagatz's own conspicuous lack of scholarly productivity—attributed by the school's dean to Dr. Tagatz's having "gone on strike" after he was fired as department chairman—helped depress the average for the non-Catholic members of the department.) Another table presented by Marquette compared Dr. Tagatz's numerical teaching evaluations with the average for the school's faculty, and showed that in the six periods for which comparable data were available the average score was 57.02, but his score was only 53.07. There was testimony that in addition to being a below-average teacher and at the bottom of the faculty in productivity, Dr. Tagatz was a poor citizen of the school—refusing an important committee assignment, failing to go through proper channels, enlisting students in his vendettas against other faculty members..., and generally behaving in trying ways. Against this there was testimony that Dr. Tagatz is a prominent member of the department and leads it in the number and size of research grants received.

Dr. Tagatz's main argument is that if the plaintiff in a Title VII case presents evidence that passes standard tests of statistical significance, the defendant must present a statistically significant rebuttal or lose. This argument misunderstands the significance of statistical significance, both generally and in this case. One of Dr. Tagatz's tables comparing salary raises for Catholic and for non-Catholic faculty in the school of education reveals a difference (favoring the Catholics) that is significant at the .0048 level. This means (speaking very crudely—see Kruskal, *Tests of Significance,* in 2 Int'l Encyclopedia of Statistics 944, 957 (1978)) that there is a probability of less than 5 in 1,000 that the difference is due to chance. But to infer as Dr. Tagatz would that there is a less than 5 in 1,000 chance (in the absence of contrary evidence) that the group that received the higher raises was favored because it was composed of *Catholics* is erroneous. All that the data show is that there is in all likelihood a *real,* not a spurious, difference between the means of the samples compared. The data do not show that the difference is due to a particular attribute (namely, being Catholic) which the members of the better-off group have and the members of the worse-off group lack. Correlation is not causation. *Ste. Marie v. Eastern R.R. Ass'n,* 650 F.2d 395, 400 (2d Cir.1981) (Friendly, J.). Members of each group may have other things in common, and one or more of those other things, rather than religion, may have caused the difference in mean salary increases. Marquette's evidence suggests that the better-off group is not only Catholic but also more productive, and the group's higher average annual salary raises may be due to its members' greater productivity rather than to their religion. Dr. Tagatz does not question the proposition that "scholarly achievement is clearly recognized as a nondiscriminatory reason for personnel action in academic settings." *Anderson v. University of Northern Iowa,* 779 F.2d 441, 443 (8th Cir.1985); see also *Lieberman v. Gant,* 630 F.2d 60, 66 (2d Cir.1980) (Friendly, J.).

All this is not to say that Dr. Tagatz's tables are *no* evidence. Cf. *MacDissi v. Valmont Industries, Inc.,* 856 F.2d 1054, 1058 (8th Cir.1988). Correlations can be suggestive of causality; scientific induction *means* inferring causality from correlation. Having shown a correlation between religion and salary raises, Dr. Tagatz has shown that it is possible that notwithstanding Marquette's stated policy of treating its Catholic and non-Catholic faculty members alike, Marquette is discriminating against non-Catholics. But it is only a possibility. There are many other possibilities. One is that a Catholic university such as Marquette is more attractive to Catholic academics than to non-Catholic ones; this might explain why the Catholics in the school of education are more productive on average than the non-Catholics. Maybe it is a pure coincidence that the most productive members of the school of education are Catholic; for the sample on which both parties' tables are based is very small. Certainly in a case such as this where the plaintiff's statistical evidence is weak and equivocal, the defendant can rebut it by casual statistical evidence of its own, by nonstatistical evidence, or by a combination of the two types. Then it is up to the district judge to decide whether the plaintiff has carried his burden....

Dr. Tagatz objects very strongly to Judge Warren's attempt to do a little statistical analysis of his own. One of Dr. Tagatz's tables compares the salary raises for the five Catholic and five non-Catholic faculty members who had been continuously employed since 1969, and shows that over this period the average salary raise for the Catholics was higher than for the non-Catholics (including Dr. Tagatz). All five Catholics were full professors at the end of the period, while only two of the non-Catholics were; and Judge Warren noted that if one compared the five Catholic full professors with the two non-Catholic full professors the latter group had done better. Dr. Tagatz points out correctly that a larger sample is more reliable than a smaller one, and complains that Judge Warren made an already very small sample significantly smaller by casting out three of its ten observations. "It is an unacceptable statistical procedure to turn a large sample into a small one by arbitrarily excluding observations." *Washington v. Electrical Joint Apprenticeship & Training Comm., supra,* 845 F.2d at 713. And perhaps the exclusion of the three non-Catholic professors of lower rank was arbitrary. But Dr. Tagatz's failure to control for differences in rank, like his failure to control for differences in scholarly productivity and teaching evaluations, made his table essentially worthless—and such variables *can* be controlled for. See, e.g., Tuckman, Gapinski & Hagemann, *Faculty Skills and the Salary Structure in Academe: A Market Perspective,* 67 AM. ECON. REV. 692 (1977). Judge Warren's reworking of the table was a means of demonstrating just how worthless the table was rather than an impermissible exercise in generating factual data on which the parties were given no opportunity to comment.

Judges, by the way, are not wallflowers or potted plants; and a district judge's effort to test the strength of a party's statistical evidence by determining how sensitive it is to the design of the sample—a standard method of evaluating statistical evidence—is rather to be commended than condemned.

We have focused on the evidence of religious discrimination. The evidence of age discrimination was if anything less impressive. The discovery that young faculty members receive larger annual raises *on a percentage basis* is no evidence at all of age discrimination. As is well known, the professoriat, like the Roman Catholic hierarchy, has only a few ranks. And unlike the Catholic hierarchy, the top rank—full professor—is normally reached relatively early in the academic's career (Dr. Tagatz became a full professor in 1970, when he was 36). This rank structure implies, and one observes, that academics' salaries tend to rise rapidly in the early stages of their career and to reach a plateau when the academic becomes a full professor; and this regardless of age. The phenomenon of diminishing returns to years of experience is well documented in studies of academic salaries. Of course there are exceptions, but Dr. Tagatz's evidence was only of averages. It is unlikely—and there is no evidence—that the characteristic age profile of academic salaries reflects age discrimination. Among alternative explanations, tenure—and the job security that results from it—tends to take some of the edge off academic ambition. So we would expect tenured faculty to be somewhat less productive on average than nontenured faculty, and of course most nontenured faculty are under 40, and most faculty over 40 have tenure. A countervailing factor is that tenured faculty have passed a more careful screening process than untenured. A comparison not between a faculty member before and after he got tenure but between tenured and (different) nontenured faculty members might therefore reveal that tenured faculty were more productive. Cutting back the other way is the possibility that new faculty are more mobile than old—another reason why one might expect the new (who generally are younger) to receive higher raises. A further consideration is that tenure itself is a form of compensation, a substitute for money; this may be another reason why salary increases are higher on a percentage basis for nontenured than for tenured faculty. Given plausible (we do not suggest compelling) explanations unrelated to age discrimination for the results of Dr. Tagatz's statistical comparisons, we can hardly say that Judge Warren committed a clear error in refusing to infer, from evidence unusually meager, that Marquette was discriminating against Dr. Tagatz because of his age.

Dr. Tagatz attempted to bolster his weak statistical evidence of religious and age discrimination with shards of testimonial evidence. There was testimony that the dean had suggested to one of the non-Catholic faculty members that she not wear her Masonic ring (the Catholic Church once regarded the Masons as dangerous heretics, and the Masons returned the compliment); that he told the faculty that Catholic doctrine should be taught wherever possible; and that the younger members of the faculty were more productive than the older ones. Judge Warren was not required to give controlling weight to such evidence, especially since Dr. Tagatz teaches statistics and there is no suggestion that the dean wanted statistics taught with a Catholic slant (e.g., regression of angels on the heads of pins).

Finally, Dr. Tagatz complains that Marquette discriminates in favor of Jesuit members of the faculty by giving them free housing and other (free) benefits. It is a nice question, not necessary to answer, whether discrimination in favor not of a religion but of a religious order is within the scope of Title VII. The discrimination in favor of Jesuits, if that is what it is, is as costly to the Catholic members of the faculty, except those who are Jesuits, as it is to non-Catholics such as Dr. Tagatz. In any event, he failed to prove discrimination. It is true that the Jesuits receive various benefits that the other faculty members do not receive. But this is not the whole picture. Jesuits do not receive their salaries. Instead the university pays those salaries to an association which maintains the residence where the Jesuits live. The association deducts the cost of feeding and housing the Jesuits and various other expenses and returns the balance to the university. The amount returned is about $4,000 per year per Jesuit. So while the Jesuits do get free housing, it is not at the expense of the university; and while they get health insurance and other fringe benefits without contributing (as other faculty members do) to the cost of those benefits, there is no evidence that these benefits cost the university more than the amount that it receives from the association. So far as appears, far from discriminating in favor of its Jesuit faculty members Marquette is obtaining their services at lower cost than the services of its other faculty members.

Despite his use of the expert of his choice, Dr. Tagatz presented a weak case which was properly dismissed....

Notes and Questions

1. In *Tagatz*, the court noted that the plaintiff's statistical analysis showed a difference between Catholic members of the Marquette education faculty and non-Catholic members of the Marquette education faculty at the 0.0048 significance level. Since this clearly meets the conventional level for statistical significance per Kaye & Freeman, why did the court reject plaintiff's evidence and grant summary judgment? To answer the question, start by asking: What does the data on salaries show? Then ask whether, given those results, the plaintiff has made a *prima facie* case.

2. A *p*-value of 0.05, or a 5% likelihood of the result being a product of chance, is the most common level of significance, as Kaye & Freeman make clear. Meeting the level of significance set by convention will result in a researcher reporting results as "statistically significant" or not. However, in some types of situations, we are not as interested in whether the research met that standard for significance, but instead want to characterize the observed results as extremely unusual. For example, Dr. Spock's jury venire of 107 women out of 350 total potential jurors—how unlikely is that result, if we assume everything was done fairly? In footnote 8, Kaye & Freeman inform us that the result is 2/10,15 or a 2 in a quadrillion (one in a 500 trillion) chance this result would occur assuming everything was fair. This venire was very unlikely to be a product only of chance.

   One way to measure the unlikelihood of events is to measure their "standard deviation." To find standard deviation, one must start by calculating the sum of squared deviations between all observations and the mean of the observations, and then divide that sum by the sample size of the observations minus one. The final step is to take the square root of that dividend, which is the standard deviation. ALAN AGRESTI & CHRISTINE FRANKLIN, STATISTICS 57–8 (2007). After mathematically defining the term, Agresti & Franklin then colloquially describe standard deviation as "a typical distance of an observation from the mean," and that "[t]he larger the standard deviation, the greater the spread of the data." *Id.* at 58.

   Another principle of standard deviations helpful to analysis, and often discussed in legal situations, is the so-called "empirical rule." *Id.* at 60. The empirical rule tells us that when we know the standard deviation for a given set of data, a fixed percentage of the data points will fall within 1, 2, or 3 standard deviations, so long

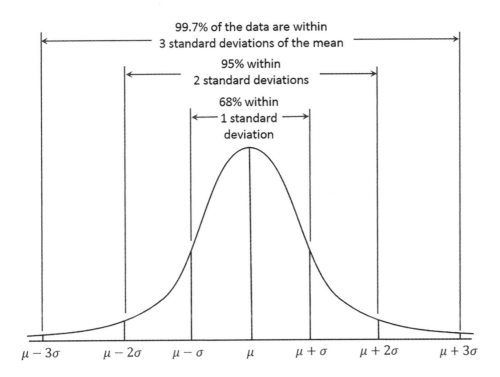

as one assumes the distribution of the data set is "normal" (i.e., bell-shaped). *Id.* The figure above nicely summarizes those percentages for each unit of deviation.[Ed.]

3. In *Casteneda v. Partida*, 430 U.S. 482 (1977), the Supreme Court connected the standard deviation calculation to the legal standard for proving a case. They decided that, "As a general rule for such large samples, if the difference between the expected value and the observed number is greater than two or three standard deviations, then the hypothesis … [that this is random chance] would be suspect to a social scientist." *Id.* at 496 n. 17. At this level, the court reasoned, the plaintiff in a discrimination case has rejected the null hypothesis, and allowed other options (including discrimination) to be considered. Therefore, the plaintiff has made a *prima facie* showing of discrimination in grand jury selection. *Guardians Assoc. of N.Y.C. Police Dep't v. Civil Service Comm'n*, 630 F.2d 79, 86 (2d Cir. 1980) (quoting *Castaneda v. Partida*, 430 U.S. 482, 496, n. 17 (1977)) ("[I]n cases involving large samples, 'if the difference between the expected value (from a random selection) and the observed number is greater than two or three standard deviations,' a prima facie case is established."). This *Casteneda* principle is not a mathematical principle, but a statement of law. JOHN CONLEY & JANE C. MORIARTY, SCIENTIFIC AND EXPERT EVIDENCE 145 (2d ed. 2011). *See also* Robert Nelson, *To Infer or Not to Infer a Discriminatory Purpose: Rethinking Equal Protection Doctrine*, 61 N.Y.U. L. REV. 334 (1986). For an example of a court examining statistical evidence of discrimination in detail, see *United States v. City of New York*, 637 F. Supp. 2d 77 (E.D.N.Y. 2009).

[Ed.} Copyright Daniel Kernler and made available under a Creative Commons Share Alike license.

4. Since *Tagatz* had some statistical data, but not enough, what type of data *could* he have used to establish his case against his employer? While the court does not directly address the issue, it seems clear that despite a statistically-significant difference between Catholic and non-Catholic faculty at the education department, we needed to know *why* the salaries are different. Could it be, as the court suggests, more productivity? Or seniority? Or is it discrimination? When we consider multiple factors that may affect another's income, we need to start considering regression analysis, the statistical tool used to assess these factors in combination.

C. Regression Analysis

To decide whether improper discrimination is the source of the salary imbalances in *Tagatz* or a similar case, a statistical analysis must take into account a variety of relevant variables: seniority, experience, productivity, evaluations, and the like. Doing so requires an analysis called multiple regression.[26] In multiple regression, one can evaluate a series of different independent variables (like our examples for *Tagatz*), and measure each variable's effect on the dependent variable (salary). Because it can take into account so many possible explanatory factors, multiple regression can be a very powerful tool for evaluating which factors do and do not affect the dependent variable. For this reason, scientific research in general, and expert testimony in particular, often contains statistical information from regression analysis.

We will start regression analysis by reading an excerpt from Judge Higginbotham's opinion in *Vuyanich v. Republic National Bank of Dallas*, in which the judge explains regression analysis in detail. Afterward, we will review a case of employment discrimination occurring at a university, *Smith v. Virginia Commonwealth University*, which discusses a defendant's analysis involving multiple regression. Note how the *Smith* case explores the salary imbalances in a way that *Tagatz* does not, and how that makes all the difference to the result.

Vuyanich v. Republic National Bank of Dallas
505 F. Supp. 224 (N.D. Tex. 1980), *vacated*,
723 F.2d 1195 (5th Cir. 1984)

HIGGINBOTHAM, District Judge.

[This is a class action lawsuit for employment discrimination.]

D. The Mathematics of Regression Analysis.

In today's society, among those who claim special insight denied the common run of men, the "esoteric language is mathematics; the special means of inspiration, the

---

26. ALAN AGRESTI & CHRISTINE FRANKLIN, STATISTICS 578–617 (2007) (where they define multiple regression as an analysis that relates the mean of a quantitative response variable to a set of explanatory variables).

computer, the forbidden path of truth, science." B. ACKERMAN, ET AL., THE UNCERTAIN SEARCH FOR ENVIRONMENTAL QUALITY 1 (1974). Econometricians—who with multiple regression analysis can provide an important addition to the judicial toolkit necessary for reconstructing from bits and pieces of data the framework of past events— are no exception.

The practical use of multiple regression has grown markedly over the past 25 years due to the development of statistical methodology itself, increasing availability of statistical data, and most importantly, the development of the computer. Fisher, *Multiple Regression in Legal Proceedings*, 80 COLUM. L. REV. 702, 702 (1980). Regression analysis is increasingly being used in legal proceedings and commentary. *Id.*; *Statistical Evidence on the Deterrent Effect of Capital Punishment: Editors' Introduction*, 85 YALE L.J. 164, 167 n.15 (1975) (Editor's Introduction). To record this court's understanding, correct or not, of the regression analyses presented by the experts in this case, and the limitations of those analyses—an understanding made necessary by technically complex trial challenges to their validity—we here describe how they are used, how they work, and when they do not. Cf. *id.* at 167 n.15 & 169; Fisher, *supra*, at 702.[45]

1. Uses of Multiple Regression.

The two primary uses of multiple regression analysis can be illustrated through the following examples where such analyses have actually been used:

> (i) For years after the disappearance of coal-burning locomotives, there was dispute on the preservation of the jobs of railroad firemen. One issue was whether the presence of a fireman on trains contributed to railroad safety.

> (ii) Cable television systems (CATVs) have been involved in administrative proceedings where one issue is the magnitude of the effect of the entry and activity of CATVs upon the profits and growth of broadcast television stations. This issue presents such questions as the influence of CATVs on the viewing audience of particular stations and the effect of changes in a station's audience on its revenues. Of course some claim that such effects are small while others insist they are large.

Fisher, *supra*, at 703.

In the first case, multiple regression is being used to "test hypotheses"—does a particular variable (presence or absence of firemen) have any effect on some other variable (railroad safety). In the second case, multiple regression is being used for "parameter estimation"—there being little doubt that audience size affects television revenue, and the real question being how much. Fisher, supra, at 704.

Both the firemen and CATV cases above involve "conditional forecasting"—a prediction of what will happen to the "dependent variable" (such as railroad safety) if an "independent variable" (such as the number of firemen) is changed or, looking retrospectively, what would have happened to the dependent variable had the value of an independent variable been different. Fisher, supra.

---

45. The following discussion of the mathematics of regressions draws heavily … on Fisher, *supra*.

Determining whether firemen do affect railroad safety faces two difficulties in the absence of multiple regression analyses. First, the factor whose influence one wishes to test or measure is usually not the only major factor affecting the dependent variable. Thus, for instance, the amount of traffic on the railroads affects accidents as well. If we could make controlled experiments, it would be easy to quantify the relationship. A controlled experiment here would involve varying number of firemen, traffic on railroads, and the other variables expected to affect the number of accidents one at a time, holding everything else constant and observing the resulting number of accidents. This would be difficult and costly. We are left then with analyzing nature's experiments. See *id.* at 705; cf. R. WONNACOTT & T. WONNACOTT, ECONOMETRICS 7 (2d ed. 1979). Second, even if the effects of other systematic factors can be accounted for, there typically remain elements of chance. *Id.* Falling objects follow a physical law, but the behavior of individuals does not. Cf. R. WONNACOTT & T. WONNACOTT, *supra* at 6.

2. *Econometrics and the Ordinary Least Squares Form of Multiple Regression Analysis*

Put in more formal terms, econometrics may be viewed as the science of model building, using quantitative tools used to construct and test mathematical representations of parts of the real world. R. PINDYCK & D. RUBINFELD, ECONOMETRIC MODELS AND ECONOMIC FORECASTS xi (1976). The fundamental underpinning of econometrics is the basic idea of relationships among economic variables. Relationships are grouped to form a model, the number of relationships included in an economic model depending on the objectives for which the model is constructed and the degree of explanation that is being sought.

The models presented in this case involve, for the most part, one type of econometric modeling. They are "single-equation regression models." R. PINDYCK & D. RUBINFELD, *supra*, at 1. Most of the single equation regression models are of a common variety: the behavior of the "endogenous" variable (a variable determined within the economic system under study) is assumed to be a linear function of a set of "exogenous" variables (those determined outside the system), and the variables are assumed to possess certain other properties such that the convenient "ordinary least squares" method of estimating the relationships among those variables can be used. R. PINDYCK & D. RUBINFELD, *supra*, at 1, 225 …

Multiple regression begins by specifying the major variables believed to affect the dependent variable. Fisher, *supra*, at 705. For instance, in our railroad example, we may wish to include as explanatory variables the number of firemen and the amount of railroad traffic, using as the dependent variable the number of railroad accidents. This involves using independent variables which reflect the important or systematic influences that may affect railroad safety. The "minor influences" are placed in a "random disturbance term," treating their effects as due to chance. *Id.* at 705–06. The relationship between the dependent variable and the independent variable of interest—for example, the relationship between the number of accidents and the number of firemen—is then estimated by culling the effects of the other major variables. Multiple regression is thus a substitute for controlled experimentation. *Id.* at 706. The results of multiple regressions—such as what we will call "coefficients" in the ordinary least square methodology—can be read as showing the effect of each independent variable on the dependent variable, holding the other independent variables constant. Moreover, relying on statistical inference, one can make statements about the probability that the effect described is due only to a chance fluctuation.

Central to the validity of any multiple regression model and resulting statistical inferences is the use of a proper procedure for determining what explanatory variables should be included and what mathematical form the equation should follow. The model devised must be based on theory, prior to looking at the data and running the model on the data. If one does the reverse, the usual tests of statistical inference do not apply. And proceeding in the direction of data to model is perceived as illegitimate. Indeed it is important in reviewing the final numerical product of the regression studies that we recall the model's dependence upon this relatively intuitive step.

a. Estimating Multiple Regressions.

If the relationship of interest is to include only one independent variable ("x_1") to explain the behavior of a dependent variable ("Y"), and it is believed that the relationship of Y to x_1 is a straight line, then the relationship is expressed mathematically as:

(1) $Y = a + b_1 x_1$

where a and b_1 are constants, Y is the dependent variable, and x_1 is the independent variable. Diagrammatically, the relationship is illustrated by the straight line in Figure 1. The econometrician thus seeks to determine the value of "a" (called the "intercept" or "constant") and the value of "b_1" (the "coefficient" or "slope" of x_1). Once he obtains these two numbers, for any value of x_1, he would know the exact value of Y.... Because there are random influences in life, it is unlikely that the relationship between Y and x_1 will be so exact. Instead, plotting values of Y against values of x_1 will likely produce a scatter of points as in Figure 2. Thus the correct relationship is not described by equation (1) but instead by:

(2) $Y = a + b_1 x_1 + u$

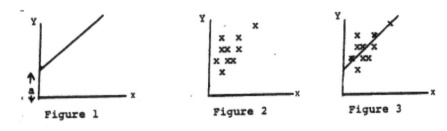

Figure 1   Figure 2   Figure 3

where u represents random influences and is called the "residual" or "error." ... The econometrician attempts to cut through the noise generated by these random disturbances and extract the "signal"—that is, the line around which the points are scattered. He passes the line through the points so that it is as close as possible to the scatter of points, in the sense that the sum of the squared deviations between the predicted and actual Y values is minimized. Not inappropriately, this is called "least squares regression." ... See Figure 3.

In general, numerical estimates of a and b_1 are obtained by entering the scatter of points in a computer programmed to perform "least squares" calculations. These empirical estimates, based on the relatively crude "least squares" method of processing empirical observations, will be "good"—in that they are likely to be quite close to the true values—if and only if certain assumptions hold as to the nature of and relationship among the dependent variable, the independent variable(s), and the error term. See, e.g., R. PINDYCK & D. RUBINFELD, *supra*, at 20–24, 55; R. WONNACOTT & T. WONNACOTT, *supra*, at 55–69 ...

Regressions involving more than one explanatory variable (e.g. number of firemen as well as railroad traffic) are more frequently used and are known as "multiple regressions." *Id.*; R. WONNACOTT & T. WONNACOTT, *supra*, at 71. To illustrate, we may assume that there is a suspected relationship between Y, the dependent variable, and the explanatory variables, x_1, x_2, x_3, ... x_k, such that:

(3) $Y = a + b_1x_1 + b_2x_2 + b_3x_3 + ... + b_kx_k + u$

where a, b_1, b_2, b_3, ... b_k are constants. As with a model with only one explanatory variable, a is called the intercept or constant; b_1, the coefficient of x_1; b_1, the coefficient of x_1; and so forth; and u, the "error term" or "residual." When empirical observations are placed in the computer programmed to do least squares manipulations (just as we input the "points" in the model with one explanatory variable), it will generate numerical estimates of a, b_1, b_2, ... b_k based on how the dependent variable changes when the independent variables move in a variety of ways.... These numerical estimates of b_1, b_2, b_3 ... b_k, are analogous to the b_1 in Figure 3. When only one explanatory variable is used, b_1 is the slope of the line: that is, it tells us how much Y will change for a unit change in the value of x_1. With a multiple regression, b_1 tells how much Y will change for a unit change in the value of x_1, holding the other explanatory variables constant; b_2 is the change in Y corresponding to a unit change in the value of x_2, holding the other explanatory variables constant; and so forth. Thus if the proper model for railroad safety were described by:

(4) $Y = a + b_1x_1 + b_2x_2 + u$

where Y is the number of railroad accidents, x_1 is the number of firemen, and x_2 the miles of railroad traffic, we can "run" this model on the appropriate data, and obtain, for example, $Y = 50 - \frac{1}{2}x_1 + \frac{3}{4}x_2$. This equation tells us, among other things, that with each additional fireman, the number of railroad accidents is reduced by 1/2 of an accident, while with each additional mile of railroad traffic, the number of railroad accidents is increased by 3/4 of an accident.

b. Statistical Inference.

With certain assumptions about the particular probability distribution of the error term, one can go beyond estimating effects of independent variables on the dependent variable to gauging the certainty or accuracy of those effects.... For instance, one can perform calculations that support statements about the range of values likely to contain the true coefficient of any of the explanatory variables.

In particular, one can determine the size of the interval on either side of the estimated coefficient which has a given probability (e.g., .95) of containing the true parameter. This range of variables is referred to as a "confidence interval." R. PINDYCK & D. RUBINFELD, *supra*, at 31. For example, after performing the appropriate calculations, we might find that there is a 95% chance that the true coefficient of firemen in our railroad example is larger than 1/4 and smaller than 3/4. In other words, the 95% confidence interval for the firemen coefficient is 1/2 1/4.

One can also perform calculations to test the hypothesis, at a given level of statistical significance, that the true coefficient is actually zero; that is, that the independent variable to which it corresponds has no effect on the dependent variable. Fisher, *supra*, at 717. If what is known as the "t-statistic" for the particular coefficient is large enough, then we can reject the hypothesis that the true coefficient of the variable in question is equal to zero.... For example, if a 5% level of significance is used, a sufficiently large t-statistic for the coefficient indicates that the chances are less than one in 20 that the true coefficient is actually zero.... The magnitude of the t-statistic necessary to reject such hypothesis varies with the desired level of significance. Thus the t-statistic would need to be larger with a 5% level of significance than with a 10% level of significance.

The magnitude of the t-statistic is also dependent on the particular type of hypothesis to be tested. When an analyst uses a "two-tailed hypothesis"—that is, where he wishes to determine whether there is any relationship, positive or negative, between the independent and the dependent variable—a t-statistic of approximately two means (in the case of large samples) that the chances are less than one in 20 that the true coefficient is actually zero. An explanatory variable is, however, usually included in the equation because of a prior theoretical reason for expecting it to affect the dependent variable in a specific direction.... For instance, we expect additional firemen to decrease, not to increase, the number of accidents. In such situations, we test a more specific hypothesis—a "one-tailed hypothesis"—not whether or not a particular coefficient is positive or negative as with the two-tailed test, but whether or not, in our railroad example, it is negative or zero. In this circumstance, the "one-tailed test" is one in which 5% would be the probability of observing some negative coefficient if the true value were zero.... The t-statistic required for significance at the 5% level on a one-tailed test is only approximately 1.6. Fisher, *supra*, at 717 n.26.

Speaking purely from a statistical point of view, this does not mean that only results significant at the 5% level should be considered; less significant results may be suggestive. *Id.* at 718–19. Thus even if the t-statistic is small for a particular dependent variable, this does not mean there is no relationship between that dependent variable and the independent variable.... This is so because the size of the t-statistic corresponding to statistical significance is ultimately dependent on the level at which statistical significance is arbitrarily set. "The most commonly used significance level is five percent, but this is purely arbitrary." ... It follows that in many instances, reporting only whether a particular coefficient is significant or not should be avoided; it is more informative to report confidence intervals, test statistics, or other quantitative measures of significance. *Id.* at 45–46.

Moreover, significance tests and confidence intervals are controversial when the test data includes an entire universe of decisions. For example, in a promotion case, data on every promotion decision may be available, rather than a mere random sample of such decisions. When all such data are available, some statisticians argue that statistical tests are either meaningless or misleading, while others say that they can be useful.... [C]onsidering the arbitrary nature of the adoption of the 5% level of significance, it is not surprising that courts show flexibility in determining what level of significance to be required in a legal context. Cf., e.g., *United States v. Georgia Power Co.,* 474 F.2d 906, 915 n.11 (5th Cir. 1973).... Indeed, the Fifth Circuit has specifically stated that a 10% level of significance rather than the statisticians' more conventional and more stringent 5% level "*might* be acceptable" in the context of the validity of job tests under Title VII. *Watkins v. Scott Paper Co.,* 530 F.2d 1159, 1187 n.40 (5th Cir.), *cert. denied,* 429 U.S. 861 (1976) (emphasis in original).

Statistical tests more elaborate than t-statistics and confidence intervals for individual coefficients are also available. For instance, "R^2" is often calculated; this is a statistic which provides an overall index of how well Y can be explained by all the independent variables, that is, now well a multiple regression fits the data.... The higher the R^2, the greater the association between movements in the dependent and independent variables. Fisher, *supra,* at 720. There are problems, however, associated with the use of R^2. A high R^2 does not necessarily indicate model quality.... For instance, the addition of more explanatory variables to the regression equation can never lower R^2 and is likely to raise it. Thus one could increase R^2 by simply adding more variables, even though, because of "over-inclusion" and "multicollinearity" (terms we will later describe) it may be improper econometrically to do so....

3. *What Can Go Wrong?*

A "perfect" model would explain completely the process under study. While such models are found in the physical sciences, they are rare in the social sciences.... Indeed, it has been argued that no model in the social sciences ever meets the requirements for a perfect regression analysis.... But this does not mean that because a model is subject to challenge, its results are valueless.... Small departures from assumptions necessary for a perfect regression may have small deleterious effects....

The value of a regression would obviously be affected by problems in the underlying data or by mismeasurements of the explanatory variables.... And, as discussed earlier, the model must be one justified by theory. We turn here to a few of the less intuitively obvious ways in which ordinary least squares can provide unreliable results important to this case.

In a perfect regression model using the ordinary least squares technique, three major assumptions would hold:

(a) that the effects of the random disturbance term are independent of the effects of the independent variable; (b) that the values of the random term for different observations are not systematically related and that the average squared size of the random effect has no systematic tendency to change over observations; and (c) that the sum of random effects embodied in the disturbance term is distributed normally, in the "bell curve" generally characteristic of the distribution of the sum of independent random effects.

Fisher, *supra*, at 708.

One way the first assumption may be violated is if some relevant explanatory variable has been left out of the analysis. This is one type of "misspecification" or "specification error." For instance, if yield of a crop is dependent on both amount of fertilizer and rainfall, and if in our regression we include only fertilizer, there will be improper omission of an explanatory variable. The problem caused by omission of variables is that the regression coefficient(s) of the included explanatory variable(s) (e.g., of fertilizer) would be "biased" (that is, not likely to be correct "on the average"), and the usual tests of significance concerning the included regression coefficient(s) (such as calculation of a confidence interval) will be invalid. . . . Certain statistical tests are available to suggest whether this sin of omission has occurred. . . .

However, in at least one circumstance, this problem may not be a serious one in cases where the issue is whether discrimination exists or does not exist. Where it is possible to use as proxy for the presence (or absence) of discrimination against a particular group a "dummy" or "group status" explanatory variable, such an omission will not threaten the validity of the group status coefficient (and hence, the validity of the model's suggestion of the existence or nonexistence of discrimination) unless the omitted variable is related to the group status variable. . . . Thus, here, where the plaintiffs' model had compensation as its dependent variable, and various explanatory variables (including dummy variables for race and sex), Dr. Madden stated:

> **Q.** Do you agree that your report would have been more valid if you measured all potential productivity?
>
> **A.** Well, since my purpose was to analyze sex and race my report would have been more valid had there—to the extent that there are any omitted productivity variables that are correlated with race or sex. To the extent they're not correlated with race or sex (it) makes no difference whatsoever.

Another type of specification error occurs when one or more irrelevant variables are included in the model. This overinclusion by itself causes fewer problems than underinclusion. . . . Overinclusion of variables, however, increases the risk of "multicollinearity."

Multicollinearity refers to a situation where due to the high (but not perfect) correlation of two or more variables (or combination of variables), it becomes difficult to disentangle their separate effects on the dependent variable. . . . Multicollinearity creates broad confidence intervals, and estimates of coefficients become sensitive to particular sets of sample data: a multicollinear model makes it difficult to establish that an individual explanatory variable influences the dependent variable.... Thus, even if two explanatory variables should be included in the regression, if multicollinearity is serious it may be necessary to drop one of them. This, in turn, may cause problems associated with omission of variables, but those problems might in certain circumstances be acceptable in the face of more serious problems of multicollinearity.... There are some rough rules of thumb to judge whether multicollinearity is serious or not.... Thus, in a discrimination model, when too many qualification variables are included, the patterns of correlation among the explanatory variables will be such that the confidence interval of the group status coefficient is inflated.... Hence, if multicollinearity exists, the probability will be increased that the net impact of group status will be judged statistically nonsignificant, even in cases where there are actual differences in the treatment.

Another form of specification error, occurs in the case where the analyst chooses to use a regression equation that is linear in the explanatory variables when the true regression model is nonlinear in the explanatory variables. For instance, the analyst may think the relationship is best described by, and thus runs the regression on:

(5) $Y = a + b_1x_1 + u$

while the true relationship is:

(6) $Y = a + b_1x_1 + b_2(x_1)^2 + b_3(x_1)^2 + u$

Specification of a linear model when the model is nonlinear—an error in the "form" of the specification—can lead to biased estimates....

We have discussed the first major assumption underlying ordinary least squares with reference to specification errors. When the second assumption is violated, i.e., when the scatter or variance of the error terms about zero (the point of perfect prediction) is not approximately the same for all values of each independent variable, "heteroscedasticity" is said to exist.... Heteroscedasticity can produce errors such as errors in confidence intervals....

The third major assumption underlying ordinary least squares is that the error term follows the "normal distribution." With respect to this assumption, basic least squares regression models are "quite 'robust' in that they will tolerate substantial deviations without affecting the validity of the results."... Nonnormality of errors can be detected, through the use of [specific mathematical techniques]....

Smith v. Virginia Commonwealth University
84 F.3d 672 (4th Cir. 1996)

WILLIAMS, Senior District Judge.

Plaintiffs-appellants are five male professors at Virginia Commonwealth University ("VCU") who brought this action under Title VII of the Civil Rights Act of 1964 in the Eastern District of Virginia. The appellants objected to pay raises that VCU gave to its female faculty in response to a salary equity study conducted at the university. Both parties moved for summary judgment. The district court, finding a statistically demonstrated disparity between female and male faculty salaries, denied the appellants' motion and granted VCU's motion.... [W]e reverse the district court's grant of summary judgment.

I.

VCU is a state institution of higher learning located in Richmond, Virginia. In the spring of 1988, several groups called on VCU to evaluate its pay structure to determine whether female professors were victims of sex based discrimination in pay. VCU appointed a Salary Equity Study Committee to investigate, and a Salary Equity Advisory Committee to review the findings of the Study Committee.

The Study Committee chose to employ a multiple regression analysis, which compares many characteristics within a particular set of data and enables the determination of how one set of factors is related to another, single factor. The VCU study controlled for such differences as doctoral degree, academic rank, tenure status, number of years of VCU experience, and number of years of prior academic experience. Any difference in salary after controlling for these factors was attributed to sex. The study included only tenured or tenure-eligible instructional faculty at the rank of assistant professor or higher. The first regression study in the summer of 1989 showed a $1,354 difference in salaries not attributable to permissible factors. A second analysis run in the summer of 1991 showed a difference of $1,982.

Until the study, the compensation system at VCU had been based on merit alone. A professor was awarded a pay increase after a detailed annual review, if funds were available. Merit factors considered in the annual review were teaching load, teaching quality, quantity and quality of publications, quantity and quality of research, and service to the community (the "performance factors"). The department chair recommended pay raises to the dean, and the dean awarded raises, subject to approval from VCU's Board of Visitors. Salaries vary widely from department to department.

The multiple regression analysis did not include the performance factors because VCU contended that these would be too difficult to quantify. VCU maintained that indirect performance variables were already included in the study in the form of academic rank, status, and experience. The study also did not take into account a faculty member's prior service as an administrator. Administrators are paid higher wages, and faculty members retain this increase in salary when they return to teaching, thus inflating faculty salaries. Most of the faculty that had previously served as administrators were men. Furthermore, the study did not include career interruptions when measuring academic experience. Finally, the Study Committee worked under the assumption that there was no reason to suspect that female faculty members were less productive on the average than male faculty members.

After the study was completed, VCU approved more than $440,000 to increase female faculty salaries. These funds were outside of the normal salary process. The pay increases were implemented by the Salary Equity Implementation Committee made up of three women. Female faculty members had to apply for a pay increase by submitting a curriculum vitae or a narrative statement and a vitae. Of the 201 women eligible for salary review, 172 requested it. All women who requested a review received an increase in salary.

After the district court's denial of the plaintiffs' motion for summary judgment and the grant of VCU's motion, the plaintiffs filed a motion to alter or amend the judgment. In this motion, the plaintiffs offered the affidavit of expert witness Dr. Fred McChesney. McChesney contended that the performance factors VCU claimed it could not quantify had in fact been included in several studies of various faculty systems, and that the inclusion of the performance factors and other variables was necessary to ensure accurate statistical data. McChesney also contended that there was data to dispute VCU's assumption that women were as equally productive as men. In response, VCU's expert witness, Dr. Rebecca Klemm, stated that she ran several various statistical studies with VCU's raw data and found a salary gap to be consistent with that found in the study. McChesney never conducted a pay study himself. The district court denied the motion to alter or amend the judgment.

II.

This case comes to us on the district court's grant of a motion for summary judgment. A motion for summary judgment should be granted only where there is no dispute as to material fact and the moving party is entitled to judgment as a matter of law. *Shaw v. Stroud,* 13 F.3d 791, 798 (4th Cir.), *cert. denied,* 513 U.S. 813 (1994). We review the district court's grant of summary judgment *de novo. Tuck v. Henkel Corp.,* 973 F.2d 371, 374 (4th Cir.1992), *cert. denied,* 507 U.S. 918 (1993). The evidence must be viewed in the light most favorable to the non-moving party. *Ross v. Communications Satellite Corp.,* 759 F.2d 355, 364 (4th Cir.1985).

Under Title VII of the Civil Rights Act, employers are prohibited from discriminating on the basis of sex with respect to compensation. 42 U.S.C. § 2000e-2(a)(1) (1992). On its face, an affirmative action plan that provides for pay raises to only female faculty members violates this provision. However, courts may remedy a violation of § 2000e-2(a)(1) by instituting an appropriate affirmative action plan. 42 U.S.C § 2000e-5(g)(1). Also, the Supreme Court has determined that in certain circumstances, an employer may voluntarily establish an affirmative action plan without violating Title VII. *United Steelworkers v. Weber,* 443 U.S. 193, 197 (1979).

According to *Weber,* an employer's voluntary affirmative action plan is not a violation of Title VII if (1) its purpose is similar to that of Title VII, namely to "break down old patterns" of discrimination; (2) the plan does not "unnecessarily trammel" the rights of those outside the group that it is designed to protect; and (3) it is designed to eliminate a manifest racial or sexual imbalance. *Id.* at 208, 99 S.Ct. at 2729–30; *Johnson v. Transportation Agency,* 480 U.S. 616, 628–31 (1987). The burden of establishing that an employer's voluntary affirmative action plan violates Title VII is on the plaintiff:

> "Once a plaintiff establishes a prima facie case that race or sex has been taken into account in an employer's employment decision, the burden shifts to the employer to articulate a nondiscriminatory rationale for its decision. The existence of an affirmative action plan provides such a rationale. If such a

plan is articulated as the basis for the employer's decision, the burden shifts to the plaintiff to prove that the employer's justification is pretextual and the plan is invalid." *Johnson,* 480 U.S. at 626.

The appellants assert that there is a material question of fact as to whether all the *Weber* requirements are met. Specifically, whether there was a manifest imbalance in pay between male and female faculty members, and whether the plan instituted by VCU unnecessarily trammelled the rights of male faculty. We agree that there is a material question of fact as to whether there was a manifest imbalance in compensation between the male and female faculty and therefore do not reach the question of whether the plan … [violated] the rights of the male faculty.

VCU relied solely on its multiple regression analysis to determine manifest imbalance and to grant the pay increases to the female faculty. The district court also relied on the multiple regression analysis to conclude that VCU had statistically shown an imbalance between male and female faculty salaries. Therefore, the validity of VCU's affirmative action plan depends upon the accuracy of the multiple regression analysis.

The Supreme Court dealt with the use of multiple regression analyses in *Bazemore v. Friday,* 478 U.S. 385 (1986). In *Bazemore,* the Fourth Circuit disallowed the use of a multiple regression analysis at trial because the analysis failed to include all measurable factors that could have an effect on the result of the analysis. The Supreme Court reversed, holding that the multiple regression analysis should have been admitted:

> "While the omission of variables from a regression analysis may render the analysis less probative than it otherwise might be, it can hardly be said, absent some other infirmity, that an analysis which accounts for the major factors 'must be considered unacceptable as evidence of discrimination.' Normally, failure to include variables will affect the analysis' probativeness, not its admissibility. Importantly, it is clear that a regression analysis that includes less than 'all measurable variables' may serve to prove a plaintiff's case." *Id.* at 400 (citation omitted).

Bazemore was not decided at the summary judgment stage, however. The Supreme Court held that the regression analysis was to be considered in light of all the other evidence in the record. *Id.* at 401. VCU cannot rely on *Bazemore* at summary judgment to establish as a matter of law that the multiple regression analysis was sufficient to determine manifest imbalance.

The appellants question several aspects of the multiple regression analysis. Most importantly is the study's failure to account for the performance factors. *Bazemore* and common sense require that any multiple regression analysis used to determine pay disparity must include all the *major* factors on which pay is determined. The very factors (performance, productivity, and merit) that VCU admittedly considered in determining prior pay increases were left out of the study. VCU maintains that it included what it called "crude proxies" for these factors, because, due to their subjective nature, the performance factors are not suitable for statistical analysis. The appellants' expert stated that the study was not valid without adding the performance factors, and that studies performed by disinterested outside researchers "have regularly included productivity measures such as teaching loads and publications," and these studies have shown that productivity has a positive effect on the level of faculty compensation. We find that the questions of whether these proxies for performance were sufficient to account for merit and whether the actual performance factors could and should have been included in the study are questions of material fact.

Also at issue is the fact that the study included male faculty members who had returned from higher paying positions in the VCU administration but kept the higher salary. The study did not account for this salary differential.[2] This, according to the appellants, leads to an illogical comparison involving an inflated pool of faculty members; eighty-five percent of the faculty whose salaries were increased because of prior service as administrators were male. An inflated pool can undermine the validity of a statistical study to determine imbalances. *Johnson*, 480 U.S. at 636; *see E.E.O.C. v. Sears, Roebuck & Co.*, 839 F.2d 302, 322–24 (7th Cir.1988). Appellants' expert, Dr. McChesney, stated that failure to include a faculty member's status as a former administrator could easily have caused a salary differential that was not attributable to sex. Dr. Henry, the man who designed VCU's regression study, stated that inclusion of this factor in the study would have had an effect on the study, and that if he had had the information, he would have included it. The appellants clearly produced evidence to support a finding that the pool was inflated, and this would skew the result.

The study also failed to measure the amount of time *actually* spent in teaching as opposed to the lapse of time since the professor began teaching. Once again, the effect of these issues on the validity of the study is a question of material fact.

Given the number of important variables omitted from the multiple regression analysis, and the evidence presented by the appellants that these variables are crucial, a dispute of material fact remains as to the validity of the study to establish manifest imbalance. Therefore, the decision of the district court granting VCU's motion for summary judgment is reversed.

MICHAEL, Circuit Judge, dissenting.

With all respect to my colleagues on the other side of this case, I am compelled to register a firm dissent. Women faculty members at VCU were paid less just because they were women. This fact was established by VCU's multiple regression study. The plaintiffs' expert argued that the study results would have been different if more factors had been included. But the expert totally failed to back up his opinion with facts or data showing that any allegedly omitted factor was a major one, that is, one that would be "statistically significant" in showing that gender had no effect on salaries. *See Bazemore v. Friday*, 478 U.S. 385 (1986). The district court was therefore exactly right in awarding summary judgment to VCU.

---

2. The study included 770 full-time, tenure-track faculty members. Of this group, 187 were female. There were 82 members of the study pool who were paid more because they had held administrative posts. Of this group, 71 were male.

Apart from their failure to apply *Bazemore* and established summary judgment principles, I believe that the collective opinions of my colleagues are quite disturbing for another reason: in one form or another they all criticize VCU's Study for not taking into account performance factors and, therefore, accept (at least tacitly) the male plaintiffs' argument that a salary equity study cannot assume that men and women on the average are equally productive. Somehow we should be far beyond that point today.

... In *Bazemore v. Friday,* a unanimous Supreme Court determined that this circuit erred in holding that a multiple regression analysis was unacceptable evidence of discrimination. 478 U.S. at 387. The Court flatly rejected our conclusion that "'[a]n appropriate regression analysis of salary should ... include *all* measurable variables thought to have an effect on salary level.'" *Id.* at 399 (quoting *Bazemore v. Friday,* 751 F.2d 662, 672 (4th Cir.1984)) (emphasis supplied by the Supreme Court). To the contrary, a regression analysis provides admissible evidence of discrimination—or, in this case, evidence of a manifest imbalance—if it "accounts for the major factors" relevant in determining whether a disparity exists in salary, and the results ... show that the disparity exists based on an impermissible factor such as gender or race. *Id.* at 400.

This case therefore turns on whether VCU's regression analysis accounted for the "major" factors when determining that a disparity exists in the pay between male and female faculty members. Based on Dr. McChesney's opinion, the plurality says that is a question for the trier of fact because the analysis should have included additional independent variables such as performance, any prior administrative service, and the amount of time a faculty member actually spent teaching (as opposed to ... time since the faculty member began teaching). I disagree.

Bazemore made clear that statistical significance is the wedge that divides "major" factors from other "measurable" factors. Indeed, the Court in *Bazemore* criticized the governmental respondents for a trial strategy that "made no attempt—statistical or otherwise—to demonstrate that when these [omitted, but allegedly important] factors were properly organized and accounted for there was no significant disparity between the salaries of blacks and whites." 478 U.S. at 403 n. 14. In addition, the Court noted three times that the regression analyses in *Bazemore* showed that the salary disparities were "statistically significant." *Id.* at 399 n. 9, 401, 404 n. 15. *Bazemore* ... clearly signals that "major" factors are statistically significant factors.

In this case Dr. McChesney points to additional independent variables that he believes VCU should have included in its regression analysis. He opines that if these variables were included the results of the analysis would have been different. Yet, Dr. McChesney offers *no* evidence showing that the allegedly omitted variables are statistically significant, that is, evidence showing that the allegedly omitted factors are "major." Accordingly, when the trier of fact hears Dr. McChesney's testimony, it will have no evidentiary basis whatsoever for concluding that any or all of the allegedly omitted variables are "major." In fact, because Dr. McChesney offers only his opinion, unsupported by any evidence of statistical significance, it is pure speculation for him to say that the outcome of VCU's regression analysis would have been different had the variables been included. It is therefore error to conclude that under the Supreme Court's teachings in *Bazemore* a genuine issue of material fact is presented here.

At the heart of this case is the plaintiffs' argument that VCU's regression analysis was flawed because it assumed that male and female faculty members are on the average equally productive. Because the plurality and concurring opinions all criticize VCU's Study for not taking into account performance factors, the only conclusion I can draw is that they accept (at least tacitly) the male plaintiffs' argument that a salary equity study cannot assume that men and women on the average are equally productive. I, however, cannot accept the plaintiffs' argument, and I believe that it was completely proper for VCU to assume, when conducting its Study, that men and women are on the average equally productive....

This case should be decided on the record. It establishes that women faculty members at VCU were paid less because they were women. As a matter of law, the plaintiffs have offered no evidence that disputes that fact. The district court's award of summary judgment to VCU should therefore be affirmed.

HALL, MURNAGHAN, ERVIN, and MOTZ, Circuit Judges, joined in this dissent.

Notes and Questions

1. In regression analysis, the selection of the independent variables is critical to a meaningful result at the end of the calculation. In *Smith*, the VCU Salary Equity Study Committee regression included a series of variables that would be helpful in deciding the source of salary differences at that university. The regression variables contained within the committee's study included: doctoral degree, academic rank, tenure status, number of years of VCU experience, and number of years of prior academic experience. However, they did not include so-called "performance factors": teaching load, teaching quality, quantity and quality of publications, quantity and quality of research, and service to the community. To the majority, the regression analysis missed major factors, and so a dispute of material fact remained as to the validity of the study to establish the imbalance of salaries that required remedial salary increases to female faculty members. Why was the court so sure that these "performance factors" were *major* factors, requiring them to be included? Is their assessment correct, or was the dissent right in suggesting that the regression as performed by the committee did establish a pay imbalance meriting adjustments? Remember that *Smith* cites *Bazemore* as holding "major" factors are "statistically significant factors."

2. Another issue to consider in the selection of independent variables in regression is the issue of "multicollinearity," mentioned in the excerpt from *Vuyanich*: "Multicollinearity refers to a situation where due to the high (but not perfect) correlation of two or more variables (or combination of variables), it becomes difficult to disentangle their separate effects on the dependent variable." *Vuyanich*, 505 F. Supp. at 274. *See also* Daniel L. Rubinfeld, *Reference Guide on Multiple Regression*, *in* REFERENCE MANUAL ON SCIENTIFIC EVIDENCE 303, 324–5 (3d ed. 2011).

For example, in a salary study of faculty at a university, the independent variables might include "years since faculty member started teaching" (as the VCU study did) but also "years faculty member actually taught full time." These variables (obviously) overlap, so a finding of salary difference for years of teaching cannot be attributed to one variable or the other, instead the result is tangled within both variables.

In these situations, the court informs us how a researcher might handle the issue of collinearity: "even if two explanatory variables should be included in the regression, if multicollinearity is serious it may be necessary to drop one of them. This, in turn, may cause problems associated with omission of variables, but those problems might … be acceptable in the face of more serious problems of multicollinearity." *Vuyanich*, 505 F. Supp. at 275. When designing a study, researchers must use their judgment and experience to decide when a variable must be dropped, and if so, which variable to eliminate.

3. What if we thought that a university salary regression should include many variables, as the *Smith* court suggests, but that there are major considerations that cannot be quantified into a discrete independent variable? For example, what if we thought that, in addition to every other factor, we should include "collegiality" or physical appearance?[27] How do you think the *Smith* court might approach that issue?

4. Unlike in *Smith* (and *Tagatz* before it), courts often accept statistical evidence as *prima facie* evidence of a litigant's claim or defense. *Hazelwood Sch. Dist. v. United States*, 433 U.S. 299, 307–08 (1977) ("Where gross statistical disparities can be shown, they alone may in a proper case constitute prima facie proof of a pattern or practice of discrimination.") (citing *International Bhd. of Teamsters v. United States*, 431 U.S. 324 (1977)); *Carmichael v. Chappius*, 848 F.3d 536, 545 (2d Cir. 2015) ("We have held, however, that statistical evidence alone may, in some circumstances, suffice to establish a prima facie case of discrimination during jury selection."); *Diaz v. A.T.&T.*, 752 F.2d 1356, 1363 (9th Cir. 1985) ("In some cases, statistical evidence alone may be sufficient to establish a prima facie case.") (*citing O'Brien v. Sky Chefs, Inc.*, 670 F.2d 864, 866 (9th Cir. 1982)). Of course, whether a court can do so depends on the strength of the inference from the regression analysis, which is largely dependent on the study's design.

5. For a (much) more detailed description of multiple regression in general, regression models, interpreting regression results, and other important considerations, see Daniel L. Rubinfeld, *Reference Guide on Multiple Regression*, in REFERENCE MANUAL ON SCIENTIFIC EVIDENCE 303 (3d ed. 2011).

---

27. A body of research has shown that physical appearance has a large effect on teaching evaluations. *See, e.g.* Daniel Hamermesh & Amy M. Parker, *Beauty in the Classroom: Professors' Pulchritude and Putative Pedagogical Productivity*, 24 ECON. EDUC. REV. 369 (2005). The effect is also discriminatory against women and teachers of color. *See, e.g.* Meera E. Deo, *A Better Tenure Battle: Fighting Bias in Teaching Evaluations*, 31 COLUM. J. GENDER & L. 7, 27 (2015). Presumably, the use of this factor in the study would be to "correct" for these considerations.

Tying It Together

As long as he could remember, Carlos Chavez had always wanted to be a lawyer and to improve the conditions in Polk City. After college at Leafy State University, the Polk State University College of Law offered him a scholarship to attend, and he immediately accepted. Carlos worked very hard in his core 1L classes, and finished the year with a GPA in the top 10% of his class. Encouraged by this success, Carlos decided to apply to law review. Like many law reviews, Polk State's Law Review has a competitive process for application, and the board would vote on applications after candidates submitted a detailed application with an essay attached.

The law review denied Carlos's application, but afterward a member of the board told him, "Your application is the closest one we've ever had, for a person of color." Carlos couldn't believe it, until he looked at the membership of law review for the last few years. No people of color had served on law review in recent memory! Knowing that he came to school to right wrongs in this world and appalled by the law review's decision, Carlos filed a discrimination suit against the law review. His lawyer even successfully defended against a 12(b)(6) motion, claiming the law review wasn't covered by discrimination law. It was time for discovery.

Carlos and his attorney have collected data on all law review applicants going back to 1980, and found that there is a statistically significant difference in acceptance rates between white applicants and applicants of color ($p = 0.0002$). Only a few people of color had ever been on law review, and none in recent years.

> **Issue #1:** Let's assume that discovery stops at this point and the defense files a motion for summary judgment. As the judge's clerk, draft a 2-page brief explaining why summary judgment would be appropriate in *Carlos Chavez v. Polk State University Law Review*.

For this question only, assume that Polk State never filed for summary judgment because discovery has only begun. Carlos' attorneys are concerned that the statistical analysis they have performed might not be enough, and so want to design a regression analysis to show that selection on law review is driven by discrimination.

> **Issue #2:** If we were to design a regression model for the plaintiff, what are the independent variables we will include in our analysis?

Part II

Specific Areas of Expertise

Chapter 5

DNA Analysis

In Part I, we evaluated the underlying substantive and procedural rules that govern admission of all expert evidence. We also reviewed some fundamental principles of statistical analysis common to many types of expert analysis. Having reviewed these generally-applicable rules and principles, we will now turn our focus to evaluating specific types of evidence.

Part II consists of chapters that are narrowly focused on one or a few closely-related types of expert evidence. For our future criminal lawyers (and devotees of *Law & Order*), our focus will first turn to criminal forensic evidence. We will evaluate DNA evidence first, as the quintessential example of a rigorous, statistically-driven discipline of individualization—even though we will soon learn that even this area has multiple pitfalls. Our forensic focus will then shift to other, less statistically-driven areas, first with fingerprints—a commonly-accepted type of forensic analysis—and then finishing with forensic analyses that have been harshly criticized in recent years, such as hair and handwriting comparison as well as tool mark identification. After reviewing forensic science and its emphasis on criminal law applications, we then shift focus to evaluate expert evidence common in civil litigation. In contrast to criminal law, we will start with the more complex and less definitive analyses of medical negligence standards and accident reconstruction, and then finish the civil litigation materials with the more mathematical field of economic valuation and damage calculations.

In each of these fields, our assessment of the issue will begin with an introduction to the underlying scientific principles of the discipline, followed by materials related to controversies of the field. While any particular attorney would be unlikely to use all of these disciplines in their practice, the structure of the text seeks to touch on subjects commonly encountered by associates or junior attorneys, and provides a template of evaluation for any other field not specifically covered in this text. In that regard, these chapters contain both controversies of the field but also methodologies of evaluation (or attack) that are replicable to other fields. As always, we will also focus on practical exercises as well, learning to write about expert evidence as we simultaneously learn the substantive law.

Our starting point will be DNA evidence. Anyone familiar with *Law & Order, CSI,* or modern television in general will no doubt have some idea what DNA evidence can do; it is perceived as the quintessential methodology of individual identification, excluding all others (except in the inevitable "identical twin episode"). The National Academy of Sciences 2009 report, *Strengthening Forensic Science in the United States: A Path Forward,* highlights the strong basis of DNA analysis in comparison to other forensic fields: "With the exception of nuclear DNA analysis, however, no forensic method has been rigorously shown to have the capacity to consistently, and with a high degree of certainty, demonstrate a connection between evidence and a specific individual or source."[28] As we will see, however, there are no absolutes in expert evidence. Clearly, DNA has the potential for remarkable specificity, and when done correctly, provides highly probative evidence for the proponent of the testimony. Yet even here, we will find significant potential for errors.

To explore the field, we will first assess the underlying science of DNA analysis, starting with methods commonly used in the early days of forensic DNA analysis, and the legal issues raised by those methods. We will then consider the types of DNA analysis available today, and explore the legal issues that remain salient even in modern litigation. As with the chapter on statistical analysis, the focus here is not on being able to personally perform the comparison of samples, but instead on how the science is used—and sometimes misused—in litigation.

David H. Kaye & George Sensabaugh, *Reference Guide on DNA Identification Evidence*
REFERENCE MANUAL ON SCIENTIFIC EVIDENCE
136–39 (3d ed. 2011)[Ed.]

... The DNA molecule is made of subunits that include four chemical structures known as nucleotide bases. The names of these bases (adenine, thymine, guanine, and cytosine) usually are abbreviated as A, T, G, and C. The physical structure of DNA is often described as a double helix because the molecule has two spiraling strands connected to each other by weak bonds between the nucleotide bases. As shown in Figure 1, A pairs only with T and G only with C. Thus, the order of the single bases on either strand reveals the order of the pairs from one end of the molecule to the other, and the DNA molecule could be said to be like a long sequence of As, Ts, Gs, and Cs.

Most human DNA is tightly packed into structures known as chromosomes, which come in different sizes and are located in the nuclei of cells. The chromosomes are numbered (in descending order of size) 1 through 22, with the remaining chromosome being an X or a much smaller Y. If the bases are like letters, then each chromosome is like a book written in this four-letter alphabet, and the nucleus is like a bookshelf in the interior of the cell. All the cells in one individual contain identical copies of the same collection of books. The sequence of the As, Ts, Gs, and Cs that constitutes the "text" of these books is referred to as the individual's nuclear genome.

All told, the genome comprises more than three billion "letters" (As, Ts, Gs, and Cs). If these letters were printed in books, the resulting pile would be as high as the

---

28. NATIONAL RESEARCH COUNCIL, NATIONAL ACADEMY OF SCIENCES, STRENGTHENING FORENSIC SCIENCE IN THE UNITED STATES: A PATH FORWARD 7 (2009).

[Ed.] Reprinted with permission from the National Academy of Sciences, Courtesy of the National Academies Press, Washington, D.C.

Figure 1. Sketch of a small part of a double-stranded DNA molecule. Nucleotide bases are held together by weak bonds. A pairs with T; C pairs with G.[Ed.]

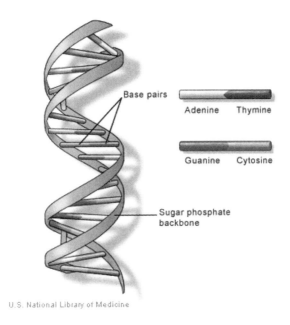

U.S. National Library of Medicine

Washington Monument. About 99.9% of the genome is identical between any two individuals. This similarity is not really surprising—it accounts for the common features that make humans an identifiable species (and for features that we share with many other species as well). The remaining 0.1% is particular to an individual. This variation makes each person (other than identical twins) genetically unique. This small percentage may not sound like a lot, but it adds up to some three million sites for variation among individuals.

The process that gives rise to this variation among people starts with the production of special sex cells—sperm cells in males and egg cells in females. All the nucleated cells in the body other than sperm and egg cells contain two versions of each of the 23 chromosomes—two copies of chromosome 1, two copies of chromosome 2, and so on, for a total of 46 chromosomes. The X and Y chromosomes are the sex-determining chromosomes. Cells in females contain two X chromosomes, and cells in males contain one X and one Y chromosome. An egg cell, however, contains only 23 chromosomes—one chromosome 1, one chromosome 2, ... and one X chromosome—each selected at random from the woman's full complement of 23 chromosome pairs. Thus, each egg carries half the genetic information present in the mother's 23 chromosome pairs, and because the assortment of the chromosomes is random, each egg carries a different complement of genetic information. The same situation exists with sperm cells. Each sperm cell contains a single copy of each of the 23 chromosomes

---

[Ed.] Picture from U.S. Library of Medicine substituted for original Figure 1, for clarity purposes.

selected at random from a man's 23 pairs, and each sperm differs in the assortment of the 23 chromosomes it carries. Fertilization of an egg by a sperm therefore restores the full number of 46 chromosomes, with the 46 chromosomes in the fertilized egg being a new combination of those in the mother and father. The process resembles taking two decks of cards (a male and a female deck) and shuffling a random half from the male deck into a random half from the female deck, to produce a new deck.

During pregnancy, the fertilized cell divides to form two cells, each of which has an identical copy of the 46 chromosomes. The two then divide to form four, the four form eight, and so on. As gestation proceeds, various cells specialize ("differentiate") to form different tissues and organs. Although cell differentiation yields many different kinds of cells, the process of cell division results in each progeny cell having the same genomic complement as the cell that divided. Thus, each of the approximately 100 trillion cells in the adult human body has the same DNA text as was present in the original 23 pairs of chromosomes from the fertilized egg, one member of each pair having come from the mother and one from the father.

A second mechanism operating during the chromosome reduction process in sperm and egg cells further shuffles the genetic information inherited from mother and father. In the first stage of the reduction process, each chromosome of a chromosome pair aligns with its partner. The maternally inherited chromosome 1 aligns with the paternally inherited chromosome 1, and so on through the 22 pairs; X chromosomes align with each other as well, but X and Y chromosomes do not. While the chromosome pairs are aligned, they exchange pieces to create new combinations. The recombined chromosomes are passed on in the sperm and eggs. As a consequence, the chromosomes we inherit from our parents are not exact copies of their chromosomes, but rather are mosaics of these parental chromosomes.

The swapping of material between chromosome pairs (as they align in the emerging sex cells) and the random selection (of half of each parent's 46 chromosomes) in making sex cells is called recombination. Recombination is the principal source of diversity in individual human genomes.

The diverse variations occur both within the genes and in the regions of DNA sequences between the genes. A gene can be defined as a segment of DNA, usually from 1,000 to 10,000 base pairs long, that "codes" for a protein. The cell produces specific proteins that correspond to the order of the base pairs (the "letters") in the coding part of the gene. Human genes also contain noncoding sequences that regulate the cell type in which a protein will be synthesized and how much protein will be produced. Many genes contain interspersed noncoding, nonregulatory sequences that no longer participate in protein synthesis. These sequences, which have no apparent function, constitute about 23% of the base pairs within human genes. In terms of the metaphor of DNA as text, the gene is like an important paragraph in the book, often with some gibberish in it.

Proteins perform all sorts of functions in the body and thus produce observable characteristics. For example, a tiny part of the sequence that directs the production of the human group-specific complement protein (a protein that binds to vitamin D and transports it to certain tissues) is

G C A A A A T T G C C T G A T G C C A C A C C C A A G G A A C T G G C A.

This gene always is located at the same position, or locus, on chromosome 4. As we have seen, most individuals have two copies of each gene at a given locus—one from the father and one from the mother.

A locus where almost all humans have the same DNA sequence is called monomorphic ("of one form"). A locus where the DNA sequence varies among significant numbers of individuals (more than 1% or so of the population possesses the variant) is called polymorphic ("of many forms"), and the alternative forms are called alleles. For example, the GC protein gene sequence has three common alleles that result from substitutions in a base at a given point. Where an A appears in one allele, there is a C in another. The third allele has the A, but at another point a G is swapped for a T. These changes are called single nucleotide polymorphisms (SNPs, pronounced "snips").

If a gene is like a paragraph in a book, a SNP is a change in a letter somewhere within that paragraph (a substitution, a deletion, or an insertion), and the two versions of the gene that result from this slight change are the alleles. An individual who inherits the same allele from both parents is called a homozygote. An individual with distinct alleles is a heterozygote.

DNA sequences used for forensic analysis usually are not genes. They lie in the vast regions between genes (about 75% of the genome is extragenic) or in the apparently nonfunctional regions within genes. These extra- and intragenic regions of DNA have been found to contain considerable sequence variation, which makes them particularly useful in distinguishing individuals. Although the terms "locus," "allele," "homozygous," and "heterozygous" were developed to describe genes, the nomenclature has been carried over to describe all DNA variation—coding and noncoding alike. Both types are inherited from mother and father in the same fashion.

A. Restriction Fragment Length Polymorphism (RFLP) Analysis in the 1980s and 1990s

William C. Thompson & Simon Ford, *DNA Typing: Acceptance and Weight of the New Genetic Identification Tests*

75 Va. L. Rev. 45 (1989)

RFLP Analysis

The standard method for RFLP analysis can be broken into seven distinct scientific procedures, which are performed sequentially. Unreliability in any one of these procedures can compromise the overall validity of the test. Like a chain, the RFLP approach is only as strong as its weakest link. This section will therefore describe separately each procedure used in RFLP analysis and its acceptance in the scientific community.

Step 1: Extraction of DNA

Forensic evidence often consists of a biological material, such as blood or semen, dried onto a solid surface, such as clothing. The first stage in RFLP analysis involves washing the biological material from the surface and bursting the cells by treatment with chemicals and enzymes to release the DNA. The DNA is then 'cleaned up' using enzymes and organic solvents. At this stage, the amount of DNA obtained is estimated to insure that enough intact DNA is present to proceed with the analysis.

Two types of problems may arise in DNA extraction. First, the DNA may be of insufficient quality. In biological specimens that are old or poorly preserved, the long DNA molecules tend to break into shorter fragments. If the fragments are too short, the specimen cannot be accurately typed with RFLP analysis. The short DNA fragments are said to be degraded or to have 'low molecular weight.' An analyst can easily determine whether the DNA in a sample is of sufficient quality for analysis, through the use of standard control procedures. If the DNA is not of sufficient quality, the analyst should simply report that the test is inconclusive. Degraded DNA is likely to cause problems only if the analyst fails to recognize it as such.

A second problem is that the DNA may be contaminated with other chemical or biological agent which could interfere with the reliability of subsequent procedures in the RFLP analysis. For example, detergent and inorganic solvents have been shown to produce aberrant results during restriction digestion, the second step of RFLP analysis. These chemicals could easily appear in forensic samples due to their ubiquitous presence in carpet and floor cleaning fluids, washing detergents and dry cleaning fluids. The DNA extraction procedures used by Cellmark and Lifecodes include a stage in which DNA is purified. The effectiveness of this purification step in removing the sorts of contaminants which might affect the reliability of the tests on forensic samples will undoubtedly be an important issue in the admissibility of DNA typing evidence.

DNA extraction procedures have been described in a number of textbooks and are well accepted among molecular and cell biologists. But these scientists typically use the procedures on clean, fresh samples of blood, while the samples analyzed in crime labs may be quite different.

> The evidence that is picked up at crime scenes is a far cry from anything I ever saw in a research lab.... It is not your typical nice clean laboratory sample and the types of environmental conditions that these evidentiary strains have been exposed to can vary widely.... There is no telling what happened to these things before we get them.

Because the samples analyzed in crime laboratories may be different from those analyzed in research laboratories, the acceptance of DNA extraction techniques in research laboratories may not prove their reliability for forensic use.

Ideally, the reliability of DNA typing on contaminated samples should be established by validation research. A few validation studies have already been published.... Ideally, validation studies of this type should be conducted by independent research laboratories which do not have a financial stake in the acceptance of the procedure....

Step 2: Restriction Digestion

After the DNA is extracted from the specimen and cleaned, it is next cut into fragments by fixing its with 'restriction enzymes' in a test tube. Restriction enzymes are like biological scissors which cut the DNA chains at specific sites, producing a large number of DNA pieces which vary in length, called restriction fragments. Although some of the fragments contain polymorphic DNA segments, most do not. Because the polymorphic segments differ markedly from one individual to the next, the length of the restriction fragments containing these key DNA segments is likely to differ among individuals as well.

The use of restriction enzymes to cut DNA molecules is well accepted in contemporary biology. Restriction enzymes have been used in research laboratories for over fifteen years. In fact, a leading textbook on genetic engineering declares that 'present-day DNA technology is totally dependent upon our ability to cut DNA molecules at specific sites with restriction endonucleases.'

Although restriction digestion is well accepted and widely used, it is nevertheless regarded as a rather tricky procedure which can yield spurious results if performed in a manner which departs even slightly from an exacting protocol. The presence of contaminants in a biological sample also may lead to spurious results. The 'specificity' of restriction enzymes may be impaired by a variety of contaminants, including organic solvents, detergents, and salt. These contaminants may cause the restriction enzymes to cut the DNA at the wrong places, producing restriction fragments of the wrong size and, as a result, incorrect bands on the DNA print.

Consequently, some special concerns may arise about the use of restriction digestion for criminal identification, notwithstanding its general acceptance in the scientific community. Research validating the reliability of RFLP analysis on contaminated samples, however, would respond to concerns about contamination. General concerns about the difficult nature of the procedure and its susceptibility to error can most likely be addressed only through blind proficiency testing of the analysts who actually perform the tests in forensic laboratories. Courts may feel, however, that concerns at this level go more to the weight than to the admissibility of the tests.

Step 3: Gel Electrophoresis

After the DNA is digested, the resulting restriction fragments are separated according to size, using a technique known as 'agarose gel electrophoresis.' This procedure involves placing the DNA in a slab of agarose gel and then applying an electrical current across the gel, causing the DNA fragments to move toward the positive electrode. The speed with which the DNA fragments move depends upon their length, with shorter fragments moving more quickly than longer fragments. At the end of electrophoresis, therefore, the DNA fragments are arrayed across the gel in positions which correspond to their lengths.

The use of electrophoresis as a technique for sorting DNA fragments is broadly accepted in the field of molecular biology. Indeed, there are few important experiments in the field of molecular biology that have not relied, at least in part, on DNA electrophoresis.

Although electrophoresis is accepted for laboratory experiments, questions may arise concerning whether the procedure is sufficiently precise for the demands of forensic DNA typing. There is always a possibility that minor variations in electrophoresis conditions may cause a 'shift' in the position of the bands. During electrophoresis, standard DNA markers of known size are generally run next to laboratory samples. These markets are used for calibration when determining the size of the fragments in an unknown sample. The major danger is that something will cause the bands in an unknown sample to shift relative to the markers. Such a shift could, in effect, change one DNA type into another.

Among experts on DNA typing, there appears to be a difference of opinions as to whether a 'shift' is possible. Dr. Bruce Budowle, who is conducting research on DNA typing at the FBI laboratories at Quantico, Virginia, has stated that the bands of DNA prints are 'steady as a rock … nothing makes them move [relative to the standard markers].' On the other hand, Dr. Michael Baird, chief scientist at Lifecodes, recently admitted that Lifecodes has had a problem with shifting bands, though he claimed that the problem is usually detectable, particularly where the samples being compared are run on the same gel. This issue should clearly receive further scrutiny at *Frye* hearings in the future.

Step 4: Southern Transfer

After completion of the electrophoresis, a permanent 'copy' is made of the array of DNA fragments in the gel. To accomplish this, a sheet of nylon membrane is placed in contact with the gel, and a method known as 'Southern transfer' is used to move the DNA fragments from the gel to the membrane. The DNA fragments attach themselves to the membrane in the same positions they had previously occupied on the gel. The resulting copy is known as a 'blot.' Also during this step, the double-stranded DNA molecules are treated with a chemical which causes them to unzip, or separate into single strands, which are ready for hybridization with a genetic probe.

Southern transfer has been used to investigate the length of restriction fragments containing specific DNA sequences in numerous studies. Because its reliability has never been questioned, Southern transfer must be regarded as a well-accepted procedure. Furthermore, because the use of Southern transfer in RFLP analysis of forensic samples apparently does not differ significantly from its use in other areas of biology, the reliability of this procedure is unlikely to be at issue in hearings on the admissibility of DNA typing.

Step 5: Hybridization

At this point, finding the key polymorphic segments among all the other DNA segments on the blot is like finding a needle in a haystack. One way to find the needle would be to spread out the hay and pass a magnet over it. Similarly, in RFLP analysis, the DNA is spread out by electrophoresis and a genetic probe acts as a 'biological magnet.' The probe will lock onto the key polymorphic segments, but will not lock onto all the other 'hay' DNA in the sample. The probes have been 'tagged' with a radioactive marker so that, after they lock onto the polymorphic segments, their positions on the blot can be determined. Hybridization is the process by which the probe locks onto the polymorphic DNA segments on the blot....

Probes have been used by molecular biologists over the past fifteen years for a variety of purposes. The use of genetic probes to identify specific DNA segments is clearly a well-accepted scientific practice. The probes used in DNA typing, however, differ significantly from the types of probes used in most other applications. DNA typing relies on special probes which lock onto polymorphic DNA segments, those segments which differ from individual to individual. An important issue which may arise with regard to the admissibility of RFLP analysis is whether the DNA fragments identified by these probes are truly polymorphic—that is, whether differences among individuals in the segments identified by the probes are as marked as proponents of the technique claim.

The existence of polymorphic DNA regions has been established by a number of research studies, and the concept of polymorphisms within DNA is well accepted. To date, however, there have been relatively few studies of the performance of the particular probes used in DNA typing. The few studies in existence have been conducted by employees of companies marketing DNA typing tests or by individuals with a financial stake in the technique, who may not be viewed as 'disinterested and impartial' by the courts.

There is an urgent need for independent validation studies. Since the ability of each probe to discriminate between individuals is likely to be an intrinsic property of that probe, each probe presented should be assessed independently. First, it should be demonstrated that the restriction fragments identified by the probes show marked polymorphism in terms of length. Second, the DNA polymorphism should be characterized such that meaningful statistics can be given on the incidence of the DNA polymorphism in the population, as well as in important population subgroups, such as racial minorities.

Step 6: Autoradiography

After they are located by the probes, the position of the polymorphic DNA segments can be visualized through a photographic process, known as 'autoradiography.' During this process, the blot is placed on a piece of X-ray film. Energy from the radioactively-tagged probe exposes the film, producing a pattern of bands known as a 'DNA print.' The position of each band on the DNA print indicates the location of a polymorphic segment on the blot. The location of each segment on the blot is, in turn, an indication of the length of the DNA fragment which contains the segment. Because individuals vary in the length of the DNA fragments containing the polymorphic DNA segments, individuals tend to differ in the position of their bands on a DNA print.

Autoradiography is a simple procedure which has been used for over fifteen years in order to visualize the location of radioactive labels. It clearly must be regarded as a well-accepted scientific practice. The use of autoradiography in forensic science does not differ from the way it is used in medical and biological research. It should not, therefore, be in issue in hearings on the admissibility of DNA typing evidence.

Figure 1: Example of an autoradiogram using RFLP technology.[Ed.]

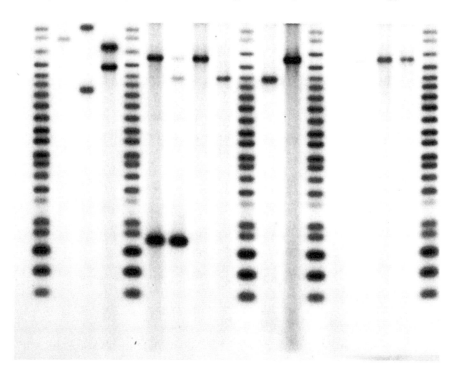

Step 7: Interpretation of the DNA print

The final step in RFLP analysis is to compare two DNA prints to see if they match, and therefore could have originated in the same individual. In most cases, DNA prints are simply eyeballed to see whether they match. The comparison can also be done by machines, which read DNA prints and convert each print into a numerical code. Numerical codes can be compared with one another by computer to determine the degree to which two prints match. Moreover, the use of numerical codes makes possible the creation of large computerized data bases of DNA prints which can be searched to find a match for a given specimen.

The use of simple visual comparisons to determine whether two prints match is widespread in biology and appears to be well-accepted, even though it relies, to some extent, on the analyst's subjective judgment. In scientific publications, the conclusion that two DNA patterns match (or differ) is often supported by photographs of the blots which allow other scientists to draw their own conclusions. A forensic scientist, when testifying in court, could also use photographic evidence to support his or her

---

[Ed.] Example added by the Author. Available at: http://www.rcmp-grc.gc.ca/pubs/nddb-bndg/ ann-13-14/index-eng.htm.

conclusions. Members of a jury, however, are unlikely to have as much experience interpreting prints as the readers of scientific journals. Hence, it seems unlikely that jurors will second guess an expert's conclusions....

Machines capable of reading and comparing DNA prints are new and not widely used. The technology used by the machines is, however, similar to that used in scintillation counting, a procedure accepted and used in medical diagnostics and is biological research involving radioactive isotopes. The only feature of these machines that might raise concerns is the computer software used to compare numerical representations of the DNA prints. This software is designed to compensate for minor inconsistencies between two prints which may arise due, for example, to differing gel conditions. Whether this compensation can be made without altering the probability of a coincidental match between unrelated individuals is an issue that warrants consideration.

People v. Wesley
633 N.E.2d 451 (N.Y. 1994)

KAYE, C.J.

The primary issues on this appeal are whether DNA profiling evidence is admissible in this State and, if so, whether it should have been admitted against defendant in this case. Because such evidence has been accepted and found reliable by the relevant scientific community and because no error was committed in the circumstances of this case, we affirm.

Facts

Defendant appeals, by permission of a Judge of this Court, from an order affirming his conviction for murder in the second degree, rape in the first degree, attempted sodomy in the first degree and burglary in the second degree. On September 15, 1987, 79-year-old Helen Kendrick was found dead in her apartment in the City of Albany. The investigation of her death focused on defendant when caseworkers from the Albany City Hostel, an organization which served developmentally disabled persons, during a routine check of defendant's apartment, found a bloodstained T-shirt with gray and white hairs on it, bloodstained underwear and bloodstained sweatpants. Both defendant and the deceased were clients of the organization.

Even without the DNA profiling evidence, proof of defendant's guilt is compelling. The day after the victim's body was found, defendant told a social worker that he did not know the decedent, even though he had visited her in her apartment only three days before. During questioning by one of the detectives, defendant gave at least three conflicting accounts of how his shirt became bloodied. Defendant also gave an implausible account of how the decedent sustained her injuries. According to a detective, defendant stated that he "tripped" the decedent and she fell to the floor. Defendant noticed blood on the floor so he attempted to check her pulse by feeling in her vaginal area. Because he could not detect a pulse in the victim, he moved toward her chest area and attempted CPR. Unsuccessful in that attempt, he picked her up, thereby staining his clothes with her blood, dropped her to the floor, placed her face down and left the apartment. Defendant volunteered that he "didn't choke her" although the detective never mentioned that she was choked. Defendant also offered that he did not have sexual intercourse with the victim although the detective made no mention of a sexual crime. Defendant told the detective, "I didn't do it. I turned my head when somebody else did it."

In addition, a microscopist testified that nylon from the carpet in the decedent's apartment was on the decedent's dress and on defendant's T-shirt, underpants and sweatpants. She testified that fibers from a blanket in defendant's bedroom were located on the decedent's dress and underpants and on defendant's T-shirt and underpants as well.

The DNA Issue

As stated, the primary issue on this appeal is the introduction of DNA profiling evidence. Such evidence, consisting of unique genetic characteristics belonging to an individual, can provide strong evidence of a person's presence at and participation in a criminal act. In this case, DNA comparison was made of a bloodstain taken from defendant's T-shirt, hair follicles taken from the deceased and blood drawn from the defendant. The conclusion was that the DNA print pattern on the defendant's T-shirt matched the DNA print pattern from the deceased and that the DNA print pattern from the blood of the defendant was different from that of the decedent.

Prior to the trial, a hearing was held to determine whether or not the DNA evidence proffered should be admissible. Following that hearing the trial court ruled the evidence admissible and the defendant was convicted at a subsequent. The Appellate Division affirmed.

Because the issue here is novel, we will discuss (1) the standard to be used in determining admissibility, (2) the use of DNA evidence in this case and (3) whether the standard was met here.

The Standard of Admissibility

It should be emphasized that the inquiry here is into the reliability of the DNA evidence at the time of the proceedings in this case in 1988 and 1989. The DNA evidence was presented as novel scientific evidence requiring a determination as to its reliability ... While foundation concerns itself with the adequacy of the specific procedures used to generate the particular evidence to be admitted, the test pursuant to *Frye v. United States*, 293 F. 1013 poses the more elemental question of whether the accepted techniques, when properly performed, generate results accepted as reliable within the scientific community generally. Only that *Frye* question is before us. The issues of a proper foundation and of the adequacy of laboratory procedures here are not before us, though some of the arguments made by the parties appear not to make this distinction.

In determining whether the DNA profiling evidence was properly admissible, attention must focus on the acceptance of such evidence as reliable by the relevant scientific community. The long-recognized rule of *Frye v. United States (supra)* is that expert testimony based on scientific principles or procedures is admissible but only after a principle or procedure has "gained general acceptance" in its specified field. In *Frye*, the court stated:

> Just when a scientific principle or discovery crosses the line between the experimental and demonstrable stages is difficult to define. Somewhere in this twilight zone the evidential force of the principle must be recognized, and while courts will go a long way in admitting expert testimony deduced from a well-recognized scientific principle or discovery, the thing from which the deduction is made must be *sufficiently established to have gained general acceptance in the particular field in which it belongs*" (emphasis supplied).

The *Frye* court rejected evidence that a person's truthfulness could be determined by a study of systolic blood pressure.

This Court has noted that the particular procedure need not be "unanimously indorsed" [sic] by the scientific community but must be "generally acceptable as reliable."[2] Thus, the issue here concerns the acceptance by the relevant scientific community of the reliability of DNA evidence.

The Use of DNA Evidence in this Case

Prior to the trial in this case, a *Frye* hearing was held to determine whether the relevant scientific community had accepted DNA evidence as reliable. The trial court found that DNA evidence was accepted as reliable. Lifecodes Corporation (Lifecodes) was then asked to perform DNA fingerprint identification on items of biological evidence in this case. Specifically, Lifecodes was asked to analyze a bloodstain on a T-shirt belonging to defendant, hair follicles which were taken from the victim, and whole blood that was drawn from the defendant. At trial, after the *Frye* hearing had been held and the trial court had found DNA evidence to be reliable and in order to lay a foundation for its admission at trial, Dr. Michael Baird, Director of Forensic and Paternity Testing at Lifecodes, explained how each piece of evidence was analyzed. He stated that, in each instance, DNA was extracted from the nucleus of a cell and purified to get a fairly pure DNA sample, free of contaminants. Using a restrictive enzyme that recognizes a particular sequence of DNA, the DNA was then cut into shorter pieces. Agarose gel was then used to separate the DNA pieces by length. The DNA pieces were then stained with ethidium bromide to permit increased visibility using ultraviolet light and to determine whether the separation by size was correctly done. Thereafter, the DNA was split into single strands and transferred from the gel to a nylon membrane. Next, a DNA probe, which had been labelled with radioactive phosphate, was applied to the nylon membrane, causing the probe to bind with the complementary, single-stranded pieces of DNA. Any DNA probe that did not bind, as well as any excess DNA, were washed away. The nylon membrane was then placed on a piece of X-ray film and the pieces of the DNA probe that had been bonded to the membrane were revealed. The X-ray film, now referred to as an autorad, was then analyzed and compared with a known sample. This process is referred

---

2. Daubert v. Merrell Dow Pharms., Inc., 509 U.S. 579 (1993) is not applicable here....

to as autoradiography. Dr. Baird concluded that the DNA print pattern that was generated from the bloodstain on the T-shirt matched the DNA print pattern from the victim's hair follicles, and that pattern was different from the DNA pattern from defendant's blood.

Application of the Standard to the Facts Here

Contrary to the contentions of the defendant, DNA profiling evidence is generally accepted as reliable by the relevant scientific community and was so accepted at the time of the *Frye* hearing in 1988. There was sufficient evidence in the record to support the hearing court's determination on general reliability as a matter of law and, second, the determination comported with generally accepted scientific authority.

The testimony in this case met the applicable standard of reliability. Several experts, including Dr. Sandra Nierzwicki-Bauer, Dr. Richard John Roberts, Dr. Michael Baird, and Dr. Kenneth Kidd, testified to the acceptance of DNA profiling evidence by the relevant scientific community and to its reliability, as well as to the reliability of the procedures used by Lifecodes.

We hold that since DNA evidence was found to be generally accepted as reliable by the relevant scientific community and since a proper foundation was made at trial, DNA profiling evidence was properly admitted at trial. It was admitted under customary foundation principles. The foundation included testimony that the appropriate steps were taken in analyzing the DNA evidence and an analysis and explanation of the assumptions underlying the probability calculations. The foundation did not and should not include a determination of the court that such evidence is true. That function should be left to the jury.

With respect to the assertion in the concurring opinion that the prosecution did not show that the relevant scientific community had accepted Lifecodes' protocols for determining a match, it is clear that the testimony supported the conclusion that the procedures used by Lifecodes were generally accepted by the scientific community. The defendant did not raise the specific problem of matching at the *Frye* hearing, through its expert testimony or examination of the prosecution's experts.

Moreover, the record supports the view that visual matching was accepted by the scientific community in 1988. "The use of simple visual comparisons to determine whether two prints match is widespread in biology and appears to be well-accepted, even though it relies, to some extent, on the analyst's subjective judgment" (Thompson and Ford, *DNA Typing: Acceptance and Weight of the New Genetic Identification Tests*, 75 Va.L.Rev. 45, 75 [1989]). According to the Thompson and Ford article, which was written around the same time the trial court decided this case, the Lifecodes test had been admitted in 22 criminal trials by October of 1988. The same article made the observation that matching could be done either visually or by machine:

> The final step in RFLP analysis is to compare two DNA prints to see if they match, and therefore could have originated in the same individual. In most cases, DNA prints are simply eyeballed to see whether they match. The com-

parison can also be done by machines, which read DNA prints and convert each print into a numerical code. Numerical codes can be compared with one another by computer to determine the degree to which two prints match. Moreover, the use of numerical codes makes possible the creation of large computerized data bases of DNA prints which can be searched to find a match for a given specimen. *Id.*, at 74–75.

It should be noted that novel scientific evidence may be admitted without any hearing at all by the trial court (*see, e.g., Matter of Lahey v. Kelly*, 518 N.E.2d 924; *People v. Middleton*, 429 N.E.2d 100). Moreover, the modern trend in the law of evidence has been away from imposing a special test on scientific evidence and toward using the "traditional standards of relevancy and the need for expertise" (1 McCormick, Evidence § 203, at 873–874 [4th ed. 1992]).

Thus, the general reliability of DNA matching was established at the hearing. The *Frye* test—the sole issue before us—requires no more, despite the new and more stringent requirements that would be added under the test proposed by the concurring opinion. It is important to note that some of defendant's other objections, which were made at the *Frye* hearing but not at trial, are actually matters going to trial foundation or the weight of the evidence, both matters not properly addressed in the pretrial *Frye* proceeding.

As to the procedures used by Lifecodes, the only expert witness for the defense on this issue, Dr. Neville Colman, opined that the procedures, methodology, and quality control used by Lifecodes were inadequate to assure the accuracy and reliability of its testing results. However, three of the prosecution's expert witnesses, Dr. Richard J. Roberts, Dr. Kenneth K. Kidd, and Dr. Sandra Nierzwicki-Bauer, reviewed Lifecodes' written laboratory protocols and concluded that the practices and procedures used by Lifecodes in its DNA fingerprinting were generally accepted by the scientific community as accurate, reliable and appropriate.

Dr. Michael Baird, who is responsible for Lifecodes' standards of quality control, testified that Lifecodes' quality control program (1) analyzes the quality of the DNA that has been isolated from a piece of evidence to make sure that DNA is of appropriate quality for fingerprinting tests, (2) examines the enzyme digestion to make sure that the correct digestion and fragmentation has taken place, (3) evaluates the DNA fragment separation, the DNA probe and data analysis, and (4) monitors the maintenance of equipment being used throughout the test, as well as the preparation of any reagents.

As for peer review of Lifecodes' procedures in performing DNA fingerprint testing, even the defense expert agreed that no peer review articles have discredited the RFLP procedures used by Lifecodes.

Defendant's challenges to the population studies relied on by Lifecodes to estimate the probability of a coincidental match go not to admissibility, but to the weight of the evidence, which should be left to the trier of fact. These challenges were never made by the defendant at trial. Such challenges were, however, made at the *Frye* hearing and were answered by the prosecution. To the extent the defendant at the *Frye* hearing focused on the inadequacy of the DNA population studies done by Lifecodes as indicative of the unreliability of DNA evidence in general, defendant did not prevail. Once there was testimony as to the reliability of the statistical population studies, the trial court was justified in admitting that testimony. Assuming that the defendant had presented evidence of the inadequacy of those studies, defendant would have been entitled to have the jury consider them, not exclude their admissibility entirely. In any event, the record before us indicates that defendant's challenge ... lacks merit.

Dr. Richard Borowsky, who was called as a witness for the defense, testified that the population genetics studies performed by Lifecodes were inadequate, and in many ways incorrect. Specifically, Dr. Borowsky stated that the data base used was too small to obtain a Hardy-Weinberg equilibrium or linkage disequilibrium. On the other hand, Dr. Kidd stated that in his opinion, and in the opinion of the scientific community in general, the data base used by Lifecodes was sufficiently large for such experiments, and a review of the data submitted by Lifecodes regarding its population genetics study revealed no linkage disequilibrium. Furthermore, Dr. Kidd testified that since there are individual genotypes that have been observed to occur more frequently than expected and others that have been observed to occur less frequently than expected, an adjustment in the claimed mean power of certainty of identification should be made. He opined that the adjustment warranted was much less than a factor of 10, but gave that amount as "the largest estimate" of a possible deviation. A factor of 10 reduced the mean power of certainty of identification for American Blacks from 1 in 1.4 billion to 1 in 140 million and for Caucasoids from 1 in 840 million to 1 in 84 million. Here, statistical evidence was admitted based upon expert testimony as to its reliability.

Finally, no support exists in the record for defendant's claim that Lifecodes may have tried to correct "bandshifting" in this case.

After the *Frye* inquiry, the issue then shifts to a second phase, admissibility of the specific evidence—i.e., the trial foundation—and elements such as how the sample was acquired, whether the chain of custody was preserved and how the tests were made. This distinct voir dire foundation is presented at the trial and is the same as that applied to all evidence, not just to scientific evidence. This was not part of the *Frye* hearing or ruling and was not addressed by the trial court here. Indeed, Lifecodes had not completed all the testing here at the time of the *Frye* hearing. Once *Frye* has been satisfied, the question is "whether the accepted techniques were employed by the experts in this case." The focus moves from the general reliability concerns of *Frye* to the specific reliability of the procedures followed to generate the evidence proffered and whether they establish a foundation for the reception of the evidence at trial. The trial court determines, as a preliminary matter of law, whether an adequate foundation for the admissibility of this particular evidence has been established.

At trial, the prosecution laid a foundation for the introduction of DNA evidence, but the defendant made no objection at trial that a proper foundation was lacking.

Once the *Frye* reliability and the trial foundation have been established, the evidence is admissible. At this third stage, the jury is left to hear the testimony and consider the weight of the evidence—i.e., "possible infirmities in the collection and analysis of data" (1 McCormick, Evidence §203, at 877 [4th ed. 1992] …)

CPL Article 440 Motion

Defendant contends that the trial court erred in denying his CPL 440.10(1)(g) motion to vacate the judgment of conviction based on newly discovered evidence that would have dictated a more favorable result for him at trial. According to defendant, Lifecodes' practice of visually matching bands on autorads, rather than using a computer digitized apparatus to declare matches that fell within three-standard deviations of error, rendered the results of DNA forensic testing performed by that company unreliable under New York State law. Defendant asserted further that he would have received a more favorable verdict if the autorads used by Lifecodes had been produced, and if defense experts, who were unavailable at the time of the trial, had been permitted to properly examine the actual sizing reports. Defendant's assertions were based on another case, *People v. Castro*, 545 N.Y.S.2d 985, which was decided after County Court decided this case.

Defendant's reliance on *Castro* is misplaced. In that case, the court concluded that there is general scientific acceptance of the theory underlying DNA identification, and that DNA forensic identification techniques and experiments are generally accepted in the scientific community and can produce reliable results. As for the techniques utilized in that case, however, the court concluded that Lifecodes failed in several major respects to use the generally accepted scientific techniques and experiments for obtaining reliable results, within a reasonable degree of scientific certainty. In this case, the evidence at both the *Frye* hearing and at trial was that the procedures used by Lifecodes met standards of scientific acceptance and reliability.

Accordingly, the order of the Appellate Division should be affirmed.

Notes and Questions

1. Thompson and Ford provide an overview of the first commonly-accepted DNA identification methodology admitted in court, RFLP, and the procedural steps necessary to make an analysis between a known and unknown sample. The article states that at the time (1989), "Machines capable of reading and comparing DNA prints are new and not widely used." Thompson & Ford, 75 Va. L. Rev. at 75. This indicates that the RFLP analysis at the time relied on visual comparison of the radiograph images: "The use of simple visual comparisons to determine whether two prints match is widespread in biology and appears to be well-accepted, even though it relies, to some extent, on the analyst's subjective judgment." *Id.* This type of analysis, without computer-aided analysis of statistical likelihood of "match," is a historical artifact, one that no longer remains relevant to DNA assessments by courts today. In fact, courts will now reject DNA evidence that does not contain a statistical assessment of the likelihood of a match. *See,*

e.g. State v. Williams, 574 N.W.2d 293, 298 (Iowa 1998) (holding "that the admission of evidence of a DNA match without accompanying statistical probability of a random match is error").

2. The trial court admitted Dr. Baird's opinion that the DNA matched, based on the visual inspection method. To make that finding, what scientific admissibility standard is the court applying, and under that standard, how did the court decide that the RFLP evidence should have been admitted?

3. In the *Wesley* case, the court cites Thompson and Ford in noting that the comparison of the known and unknown samples involves subjective visualization. *Supra* note 1. The case is also a notable example of the "Wild West" days of DNA evidence; even between the time of the admission of the evidence at trial (in 1989) and the time of the decision (1994), courts in New York had already addressed the issue of scientific reliability in the *Castro* case, and therefore rejected the argument proposed by the appellant in *Wesley*.

4. If RFLP is an outdated technology not used in modern identification, then why did we evaluate these early cases? One reason is to recognize that in forensic analysis, a methodology will not appear in its final, incontestable form at first instance. It takes time, and the steps along the way can show how courts deal with the initial uncertainties of the technology. Additionally, even in the early days and even with the flaws identified in the readings, it was clear from the very beginning that DNA identification science had enormous implications in the criminal field. As we transition to modern STR/PCR analysis, consider that DNA is not only helpful when presented by the prosecutor in the assessment of likelihood of guilt, the classic use, but can also be a powerful tool for the defense for exoneration purposes years later.

B. Modern STR/PCR Analysis

David H. Kaye & George Sensabaugh, *Modern Scientific Evidence*

4 MODERN SCIENTIFIC EVIDENCE
§§ 30:42, 30:50, and 30:54 (2016–2017 ed.)[Ed.]

§ 30:42. Scientific principles — What are DNA polymorphisms and how are they detected?

By determining which alleles are present at strategically chosen loci, the forensic scientist ascertains the genetic profile, or genotype, of an individual (at those loci). Although the differences among the alleles arise from alterations in the order of the ATGC letters, genotyping does not necessarily require "reading" the full DNA sequence.

[Ed.] Used with the permission of Thomson Reuters.

Here we outline the major types of polymorphisms that are … used in identity testing and the methods for detecting them.

Sequencing. Researchers are investigating radically new and efficient technologies to sequence entire genomes, one base pair at a time, but the direct sequencing methods now in existence are technically demanding, expensive, and time-consuming for whole-genome sequencing. Therefore, most genetic typing focuses on identifying only those variations that define the alleles and does not attempt to "read out" each and every base pair as it appears. The exception is mitochondrial DNA.... As next-generation sequencing technologies are perfected, however…, this situation could change....

VNTRs and RFLP testing. Another category of DNA variations comes from the insertion of a variable number of tandem repeats (VNTR) at a locus. These were the first polymorphisms to find widespread use in identity testing and hence were the subject of most of the court opinions on the admissibility of DNA in the late 1980s and early 1990s. The core unit of a VNTR is a particular short DNA sequence that is repeated many times end-to-end. The first VNTRs to be used in genetic and forensic testing had core repeat sequences of 15–35 base pairs. In this testing, bacterial enzymes (known as "restriction enzymes") were used to cut the DNA molecule both before and after the VNTR sequence. A small number of repeats in the VNTR region gives rise to a small "restriction fragment," and a large number of repeats yields a large fragment. A substantial quantity of DNA from a crime scene sample is required to give a detectable number of VNTR fragments with this procedure.

The detection is accomplished by applying a probe that binds when it encounters the repeated core sequence. A radioactive or fluorescent molecule attached to the probe provides a way to mark the VNTR fragment. The probe ignores DNA fragments that do not include the VNTR core sequence. (There are many of these unwanted fragments, because the restriction enzymes chop up the DNA throughout the genome—not just at the VNTR loci.) The restriction fragments are sorted by a process known as electrophoresis, which separates DNA fragments based on size. Many early court opinions refer to this process as RFLP testing.

STRs. Although RFLP-VNTR profiling is highly discriminating, it has several drawbacks. Not only does it require a substantial sample size, but it also is time-consuming and does not measure the fragment lengths to the nearest number of repeats. The measurement error inherent in the form of electrophoresis used (known as "gel electrophoresis") is not a fundamental obstacle, but it complicates the determination of which profiles match and how often other profiles in the population would be declared to match. Consequently, forensic scientists have moved from VNTRs to another form of repetitive DNA known as short tandem repeats (STRs) or microsatellites. STRs have very short core repeats, two to seven base pairs in length, and they typically extend for only some 50 to 350 base pairs. Like the larger VNTRs, which extend for thousands of base pairs, STR sequences do not code for proteins, and the ones used in identity testing convey little or no information about an individual's propensity for disease. Because STR alleles are much smaller than VNTR alleles, however, they can be amplified with PCR designed to copy only the locus of interest. This obviates the need for restriction enzymes, and it allows laboratories to analyze STR loci much more quickly. Because the amplified fragments are shorter, electrophoretic detection permits the exact number of base pairs in an STR to be determined, allowing alleles to be defined as discrete entities. Figure 2 illustrates the nature of allelic variation at an STR locus found on chromosome 16.

Figure 2: Three Alleles of the D16S539 STR.[6]

> Nine-repeat allele:
>
> GATAGATAGATAGATAGATAGATAGATAGATAGATA
>
> Ten-repeat allele:
>
> GATAGATAGATAGATAGATAGATAGATAGATAGATAGATA
>
> Eleven-repeat allele:
>
> GATAGATAGATAGATAGATAGATAGATAGATAGATAGATAGATA

Although there are fewer alleles per locus for STRs than for VNTRs, there are many STRs, and they can be analyzed simultaneously. Such "multiplex" systems now permit the simultaneous analysis of 16 loci. A subset of 13 is standard in the United States and the Federal Bureau of Investigation is considering adding seven new core loci to CODIS. These are capable of distinguishing among almost everyone in the population....

§ 30:50. Statistical analysis—What constitutes a match or an exclusion?

When the DNA from the trace evidence clearly does not match the DNA sample from the suspect, the DNA analysis demonstrates that the suspect's DNA is not in the forensic sample. Indeed, if the samples have been collected, handled, and analyzed properly, then the suspect is excluded as a possible source of the DNA in the forensic sample. As a practical matter, such exclusionary results normally would keep charges from being filed against the excluded suspect.

At the other extreme, the genotypes at a large number of loci can be clearly identical. In these cases, the DNA evidence is quite incriminating, and the challenge for the legal system lies in explaining just how probative it is. Naturally, as with exclusions, inclusions are most powerful when the samples have been collected, handled, and analyzed properly. But there is one logical difference between exclusions and inclusions. If it is accepted that the samples have different genotypes, then the conclusion that the DNA in them came from different individuals is essentially inescapable. In contrast, even if two samples have the same genotype, there is a chance that the forensic sample came not from the defendant, but from another individual who has the same genotype. This complication has produced extensive ar-

---

6. The core sequence is GATA. The first allele listed has 9 tandem repeats, the second has 10, and the third has 11. The locus has other alleles (different numbers of repeats), shown in Figure [2].

guments over the statistical procedures for assessing this chance or related quantities. This problem of describing the significance of an unequivocal match is the subject of the remaining parts of this section.

Some cases lie between the poles of a clear inclusion or a definite exclusion. For example, when the trace evidence sample is small and extremely degraded, STR profiling can be afflicted with allelic "drop-in" and "drop-out," requiring judgments as to whether true peaks are missing and whether spurious peaks are present. Experts then might disagree about whether a suspect is included or excluded—or whether any conclusion can be drawn.

§ 30:54. Statistical analysis—The product rule for estimating genotype frequencies from samples

… If we take a DNA molecule's view of the population, human beings are containers for DNA and machines for copying and propagating them to the next generation of human beings. The different DNA molecules are swimming, so to speak, in a huge pool of humanity. All the possible alleles (the fives, sixes, sevens, and so on) form a large population, or pool of alleles. Each allele constitutes a certain proportion of allele pool. Suppose, then, that a five-repeat allele represents 12% of all of the allele pool, a six-repeat allele contributes 20%, and so on, for all the alleles at a locus.

The first step in computing a random-match probability is to estimate these allele frequencies. Ideally, a probability sample from the human population of interest would be taken. We would start with a list of everyone who might have left the trace evidence, take a random sample of these people, and count the numbers of alleles of each length that are present in the sample. Unfortunately, a list of the people who comprise the entire population of possible suspects is almost never available; consequently, probability sampling from the directly relevant population is impossible. Probability sampling from a comparable population (with regard to the individuals' DNA) is possible, but it is not the norm in studies of the distributions of genes in populations. Typically, convenience samples (from blood banks or paternity cases) are used. Relatively small samples can produce fairly accurate estimates of individual allele frequencies. Once the allele frequencies have been estimated, the next step in arriving at a random-match probability is to combine them. This requires some knowledge of how DNA is copied and recombined in the course of sexual reproduction and how human beings choose their mates.

The product rule for a randomly mating population. All scientists use simplified models of a complex reality. Physicists solve equations of motion in the absence of friction. Economists model exchanges among rational agents who bargain freely with no transaction costs. Population geneticists compute genotype frequencies in an infinite population of individuals who choose their mates independently of their alleles at the loci in question. Although geneticists describe this situation as random mating, geneticists know that people do not choose their mates by a lottery. "Random mating" simply indicates that the choices are uncorrelated with the specific alleles that make up the genotypes in question.

In a randomly mating population, the expected frequency of a pair of alleles at any single locus depends on whether the two alleles are distinct. If the offspring happens to inherit the same allele from each parent, the expected single-locus genotype frequency is the square of the allele frequency ($p2$). If a different allele is inherited from each parent, the expected single-locus genotype frequency is twice the product of the two individual allele frequencies (often written as $2p1p2$).[1] These proportions are known as Hardy-Weinberg proportions. Even if two populations with distinct allele frequencies are thrown together, within the limits of chance variation, random mating produces Hardy-Weinberg equilibrium in a single generation.

Once the proportion of the population that has each of the single-locus genotypes for the forensic profile has been estimated, the proportion of the population that is expected to share the combination of them—the multilocus profile frequency—is given by multiplying all the single-locus proportions. This multiplication is exactly correct when the single-locus genotypes are statistically independent. In that case, the population is said to be in linkage equilibrium. Early estimates of DNA genotype frequencies assumed that alleles were inherited independently within and across loci (Hardy-Weinberg and linkage equilibrium, respectively). Because the frequencies of the VNTR loci then in use were shown to vary across census groups (whites, blacks, Hispanics, Asians, and Native Americans), it became common to present the estimated genotype frequencies within each of these groups (in cases in which the "race" of the source of the trace evidence was unknown) or only in a particular census group (if the "race" of the source was known)....

State v. Roman Nose
649 N.W.2d 815 (Minn. 2002)

ANDERSON, J.

Tony Allen Roman Nose, appellant, appeals from his conviction of first-degree murder during the commission of criminal sexual conduct ... for the July 11, 2000, killing of Jolene Stuedemann. Appellant claims that the trial court erred by failing to conduct a pretrial *Frye-Mack* hearing on the general acceptance within the relevant scientific community of the PCR-STR method of testing deoxyribonucleic acid (DNA) used by the Minnesota Bureau of Criminal Apprehension (BCA) in this case. Appellant also claims that the trial court erred by admitting the DNA evidence in this case, arguing that the state failed to show reliability under the second prong of the *Frye-Mack* standard, and by admitting certain other evidence.... We conclude

---

1. Suppose that 10% of the sperm in the gene pool of the population carry allele 1 (A1), and 50% carry allele 2 (A2). Similarly, 10% of the eggs carry A1, and 50% carry A2. (Other sperm and eggs carry other types.) With random mating, we expect 10% × 10% = 1% of all the fertilized eggs to be A1A1, and another 50% × 50% = 25% to be A2A2. These constitute two distinct homozygote profiles. Likewise, we expect 10% × 50% = 5% of the fertilized eggs to be A1A2 and another 50% × 10% = 5% to be A2A1. These two configurations produce indistinguishable profiles—a peak, band, or dot for A1 and another mark for A2. So the expected proportion of heterozygotes A1A2 is 5% + 5% = 10%.

that the trial court erred when it failed to conduct a *Frye-Mack* hearing on the general acceptance within the relevant scientific community of the method of testing DNA used here and remand for hearing to determine if the PCR-STR method of testing DNA has obtained general acceptance within the relevant scientific community....

On July 11, 2000, the body of 17-year-old Jolene Stuedemann, an apparent homicide victim, was found by her sister in their home in Woodbury, Minnesota. A medical examiner determined, based on an examination of the body at the scene and an autopsy, that Stuedemann had been beaten and stabbed multiple times with a screwdriver, had been sexually assaulted, and that she bled to death as a result of multiple stab wounds inflicted during the sexual assault. An investigation led authorities to appellant.

Appellant, who was 17 years old when Stuedemann was killed, was a resident of a group home in Woodbury during the school year. Appellant normally returned to Montana during the summer months. Appellant testified that on the night before Stuedemann's body was discovered he decided to break group home rules so that he would be returned to Montana. On the evening prior to Stuedemann's homicide, appellant went to the home of his friend, Andy Reiman, who was dating Stuedemann and who lived about a mile from the group home. Reiman and Stuedemann returned to Reiman's home, where they encountered appellant in the driveway, listening to his walkman. All three went into Reiman's home where they drank beer and watched television. Appellant claimed that Stuedemann also gave him some marijuana and that Stuedemann and he did some "coke."

Appellant testified that he was sitting on the couch listening to music with his eyes shut, and that when he opened his eyes, Reiman and Stuedemann were engaged in sexual intercourse. According to appellant, he and Stuedemann then had sex while Reiman slept. Reiman testified, however, that he did not fall asleep immediately after he and Stuedemann had sex and that he was certain that Stuedemann did not have sex with appellant.

Appellant fell asleep. Stuedemann left at 3:30 a.m. while appellant was sleeping. Reiman woke appellant and told him to leave as well. Appellant left at approximately 4 a.m. and eventually returned to the group home.

Because appellant had been reported as a runaway the night before, the house parent notified police of appellant's return to the group home, and a Woodbury police officer interviewed appellant. Appellant told the officer that he had been with Reiman the night before. The officer then left the group home and responded to a call that resulted in discovery of Stuedemann's body. Investigators discovered part of a set of headphones under Stuedemann's body. A piece of crumpled paper was found in Stuedemann's mouth with a fingerprint on it, later identified as appellant's, and a blood-stained screwdriver was found near her body.

Eventually, the house parent learned of blood-stained clothing that had been placed in a trash bag in the garage of the group home and that belonged to appellant, and she notified authorities. The lower half of a set of headphones was found in the group home's kitchen garbage. A forensic scientist determined that the headphones found in the garbage and the part of a set of headphones found under Stuedemann's body could have been a match. Authorities also found blood-stained underwear and a walkman with no headphones attached in appellant's bedroom.

The state offered DNA evidence at trial that was obtained from DNA testing of samples taken from the crime scene and the group home. The DNA testing was conducted by the BCA using the PCR-STR method. The DNA evidence showed that the DNA profile of blood samples taken from the screwdriver and appellant's personal property found at the group home matched Stuedemann's DNA profile and that semen samples taken from Stuedemann's body matched appellant's DNA profile. Before trial, appellant requested a *Frye-Mack* hearing to determine first, whether the PCR-STR method of DNA testing is generally accepted within the relevant scientific community and second, whether the state could establish the necessary foundation for admission of the test results in this case. The trial court granted a hearing only on the second issue. Following the limited *Frye-Mack* hearing, the court ruled the DNA test results admissible.

Appellant was found guilty by a Washington County jury of murder in the first degree while committing or attempting to commit criminal sexual conduct and premeditated murder in the first degree.... Appellant appeals the decision of the trial court denying a *Frye-Mack* hearing on the general acceptance of the PCR-STR method of testing DNA....

We must determine whether the trial court erred when it denied appellant's request for a pretrial *Frye-Mack* hearing to determine whether the PCR-STR method of testing DNA has gained general acceptance within the relevant scientific community. We begin our analysis with a brief overview of the *Frye-Mack* standard for determining admissibility of scientific evidence and its development in Minnesota.

In our decision in *State v. Kolander*, 52 N.W.2d 458, 465 (1952), we adopted the standard for the admissibility of evidence obtained from new scientific techniques that was set forth in *Frye v. United States*, 293 F. 1013, 1014 (D.C.Cir.1923), which requires "general acceptance in the particular field in which [the scientific principle or discovery] belongs." *Frye*, 293 F. at 1014. Subsequently, we stated in our decision in *State v. Mack*, 292 N.W.2d 764, 768 (Minn.1980), that "the results of mechanical or scientific testing are not admissible unless the testing has developed or improved to the point where experts in the field widely share the view that the results are scientifically reliable as accurate." We stated that the particular evidence must have a foundation that is scientifically reliable. As a result of *Frye* and *Mack*, a two-pronged standard has emerged in Minnesota that must be satisfied before scientific evidence may be admitted. First, a novel scientific technique that produces evidence to be admitted at trial must be shown to be generally accepted within the relevant scientific community, and second, the particular evidence derived from the technique and used in an individual case must have a foundation that is scientifically reliable. Put another way, the *Frye-Mack* standard asks first whether experts in the field widely share the view that the results of scientific testing are scientifically reliable, and second whether the laboratory conducting the tests in the individual case complied with appropriate standards and controls.

The trial court determines whether the *Frye-Mack* standard has been satisfied by means of a pretrial hearing. When the scientific technique that produces the scientific evidence is no longer novel or emerging, then the pretrial hearing should focus on the second prong of the *Frye-Mack* standard.

In this case the trial court denied appellant's request for a hearing on general acceptance of the PCR-STR method within the relevant scientific community. We must determine, then, whether evidence obtained from the PCR-STR method of testing DNA is novel, such that a pretrial hearing should have been conducted to determine whether ... [it] ... has gained general acceptance within the relevant scientific community.

We have considered the general acceptance within the scientific community of DNA testing and the admissibility of DNA evidence in earlier decisions. DNA typing is generally acceptable, and we do not question the theory of human genetics underlying DNA testing and the basic validity of DNA analysis.

Our previous analysis was of the RFLP method of testing DNA, however. Relying on *Schwartz* [*State v. Schwartz*, 447 N.W.2d 422 (Minn. 1989)], we stated in *Jobe* [*State v. Jobe*, 486 N.W.2d 407 (Minn. 1992),] that the required *Frye-Mack* hearing "should focus only on whether the laboratory which did the testing was in compliance with the appropriate standards and controls. It should not be a forum for challenging the basic DNA RFLP testing procedures themselves." *Jobe*, 486 N.W.2d at 420 (footnote omitted). We concluded in *Jobe* that the RFLP method should no longer be challenged in a pretrial *Frye-Mack* hearing because the general acceptance of the RFLP method had been established at the trial court level by means of a *Frye-Mack* hearing and affirmed by this court in *Schwartz*, 447 N.W.2d at 425.

The state points to the decisions of other appellate courts that have upheld admission of DNA evidence obtained from PCR-STR testing to argue that a *Frye-Mack* hearing on general acceptance ... is unnecessary. However, other jurisdictions have different standards for the admissibility of evidence obtained from scientific techniques, some adhering to the federal *Daubert* standard and others to state rules of evidence. In addition, even those appellate decisions that affirmed the admissibility of DNA evidence obtained from PCR methods of testing DNA generally did so only after reviewing the findings and conclusions of the trial court following an evidentiary hearing. The decisions of other appellate courts may be relevant evidence at an evidentiary hearing on the general acceptance of a scientific technique within the relevant scientific community. To rely exclusively on decisions of other appellate courts rather than on the testimony of expert witnesses to establish general acceptance, however, would be a departure from our precedent requiring a *Frye-Mack* hearing to determine general acceptance within the relevant scientific community.

General acceptance within the relevant scientific community of the PCR-STR method of testing DNA is not a matter this court has previously addressed. The PCR-

STR method is a new method of testing DNA that has emerged as an evidence-producing scientific technique. The state asserts that because the PCR-STR method has been used by the BCA since February 1999, it is no longer a novel scientific technique and a *Frye-Mack* hearing is therefore unnecessary to determine its general acceptance within the relevant scientific community. However, we have not decided general acceptance for Minnesota courts. The BCA's practice is not dispositive of the issue, but may instead be relevant evidence at the *Frye-Mack* hearing to determine whether the technique has in fact gained general acceptance within the relevant scientific community. Once this court has reviewed and confirmed the general acceptance of a scientific technique, then the evidence produced by the technique may be admitted without the need for a pretrial hearing on the first prong of the *Frye-Mack* standard, as with RFLP DNA.

Because the PCR-STR method is a new scientific technique that this court has never before considered, and because it is sufficiently different from the RFLP method, the evidence obtained from the technique is novel scientific evidence. It therefore requires not only a *Frye-Mack* hearing on the procedures and controls involved in the individual case but also a hearing on the general acceptance of the technique within the relevant scientific community before evidence obtained from the method is admissible. That the RFLP method of testing DNA has gained general acceptance does not permit evidence obtained from significantly different methods of DNA testing to be admitted without holding a hearing on the first prong of the *Frye-Mack* standard.

Even if it appears likely that in the course of a *Frye-Mack* hearing on the PCR-STR method of testing DNA the trial court will determine that the method has gained general acceptance within the relevant scientific community, the *likelihood* of such a determination should not be the basis for denying a *Frye-Mack* hearing.... We therefore conclude that the trial court improperly denied appellant his right to a pretrial *Frye-Mack* hearing on the general acceptance within the relevant scientific community of the PCR-STR method of testing DNA.

Appellant is entitled to a new trial only if the evidence was erroneously admitted and he suffered prejudice, however.... To determine whether the evidence was admissible, we remand the case to the trial court for a hearing on ... general acceptance within the relevant scientific community....

Notes and Questions

1. The court in *Roman Nose* makes clear that even if prior decisions of Minnesota courts have accepted RFLP analysis for DNA, STR testing would require a new *Frye*-type hearing to evaluate the issue of "general acceptance." Why is it necessary to have a new hearing on STR if RFLP has already been approved? Why not just take judicial notice of other state courts' acceptance of STR and move on?

2. STR testing begins with a count of the number of base pair repeats at each of thirteen standardized loci, and then calculates the overall probability of the sequence of base pair combinations using the product rule. KAYE & SENSABAUGH,

4 Modern Scientific Evidence § 30:54. As Forensic DNA Evidence: Science and the Law succinctly states:

> The random match probability for a DNA profile is calculated by multiplying the genotype (i.e., the observed allele(s)) frequencies (i.e., how often that allele or pair of alleles can be expected to occur at random in a human population) for each locus in an STR profile with the genotype frequency for every other locus in the profile. This process is an application of the "product rule."

Justice Ming W. Chin, et al., Forensic DNA Evidence: Science and the Law § 5.1 (2017 ed.). The product rule, however, depends on each contingency in question being independent of one other, like separate coin flips or consecutive rolls of dice. At one point, the application of the product rule in calculating random match probabilities may have been controversial, but courts have since acknowledged the general acceptance of these calculations. *See, e.g., People v. Soto*, 981 P.2d 958, 997 (Cal. 1999); *People v. Reeves*, 109 Cal. Rptr. 2d 728, 747–48 (Cal. Ct. App. 2001). *See also United States v. Gaines*, 979 F. Supp. 1429, 1440–41 (S.D. Fla. 1997).

3. As we consider the calculation of random match probabilities (RMP) using the product rule, let us consider *exactly* what the RMP calculation is telling us, and what it is not. When a researcher compares a known DNA sample to an unknown sample, if they "match," then the researcher must quantify the likelihood of the match using the product rule. The resulting final product is the random match probability, which the National Research Council explained as follows:

> Suppose that a DNA sample from a crime scene and one from a suspect are compared, and the two profiles match at every locus tested. Either the suspect left the DNA or someone else did. We want to evaluate the probability of finding this profile in the "someone else" case. That person is assumed to be a random member of the population of possible suspects. So we calculate the frequency of the profile in the most relevant population or populations. The frequency can be called the random-match probability, and it can be regarded as an estimate of the answer to the question: What is the probability that a person other than the suspect randomly selected from the population, will have this profile? The smaller that probability, the greater the likelihood that the two DNA samples came from the same person.[29]

RMP therefore is all about probative value. Even with a "match," does the evidence strongly support the inference the proponent makes? Or is it weaker? Only the RMP will establish the weight of the evidence, because "[w]ithout the probability assessment, the jury does not know what to make of the fact that the patterns match: the jury does not know whether the patterns are as common as pictures

29. National Research Council, National Academy of Sciences, The Evaluation of Forensic DNA Evidence 127 (1996).

with two eyes, or as unique as the Mona Lisa." *United States v. Yee*, 134 F.R.D. 161, 181 (N.D. Ohio 1991).

The following case discusses the scientific reliability of PCR testing, as *Roman Nose* requested, and also discusses the calculation and meaning of random match probabilities. Afterward, we see a court describing the misuse of DNA evidence with the "prosecutor's fallacy."

United States v. Gaines
979 F. Supp. 1429 (S.D. Fla. 1997)

GOLD, District Judge.

INTRODUCTION

The United States of America (hereinafter "the Government") filed a motion for a pre-trial determination of the admissibility of the results of DNA analysis performed by the FBI laboratory.... By order dated August 28, 1997, the Court required the Government to make the requisite showing under *Daubert v. Merrell Dow Pharmaceuticals, Inc.*, 509 U.S. 579 (1993) as a precondition to the admissibility of expert testimony regarding the Polymerase Chain Reaction ("PCR") DNA analysis performed in the case....

In accordance with *Daubert*, the Court heard testimony from the Government's experts, Melissa Smrz, with the FBI's DNA Analysis Unit, and Dr. Martin Tracey, a biologist with an expertise in DNA and population genetics, concerning (1) whether the PCR DNA based analysis, consisting of sample processing, match determination, and random match probability, is based upon reliable scientific knowledge, and (2) whether it will assist the trier of fact. The Defendants presented no expert testimony, but, argued instead by memoranda, that the evidence presented was insufficient to satisfy the *Daubert* standards.

Contrary to the Defendants' position, the Court previously has concluded that the reasoning and methodology underlying the PCR DNA based analysis performed in this case is scientifically valid and would assist the jury in determining a fact in issue (the identity of the robber), and, therefore, the Court held, prior to the commencement of trial, that it was admissible under Fed. R. Evid. 702. Accordingly, the Court permitted expert testimony as to each aspect of the PCR DNA based analysis conducted with respect to Defendant Liddell and the bandanna referred to as Q10.... This memorandum opinion sets forth the basis for the Court's ruling.

II. *FACTS*

The superseding indictment charges Defendants Bogard Liddell and Leetavious Gaines with the commission of six armed robberies between August 20, 1997, and August 30, 1997, and with conspiracy to commit these robberies. The DNA analysis in this case relates solely to the robbery charged in Count 10 of the superseding indictment. In that count, the Defendants are charged with robbing the McDonald's ... in Davie, Florida, on August 27, 1996. At the time of the robbery, the lobby was closed and the doors were locked. The perpetrators entered the McDonald's via the drive-thru window. One of the perpetrators was wearing a dark ski mask and the other was wearing an orange ski cap. After the robbery, a witness noticed a black bandanna outside the drive-thru window, which had not been there shortly before the robbery. This bandanna was seized by Davie police Detective Tony Phillips....

The bandanna ... [was] sent to the FBI laboratory for analysis.... The laboratory was also sent known blood samples taken from Defendants Bogard Liddell and Lee-tavious Gaines, and from Terrence Gaines, the brother of Leetavious who resided with him at the Gaines residence ... The DNA analysis was performed by Supervisory Special Agent Melissa Smrz, using the Polymerase Chain Reaction (PCR) technique ... Her analysis, dated May 20, 1997, was entered into evidence as Government's Exhibit 117. In brief, the results were as follows:

> The bandanna seized from the McDonalds contained sufficient DNA for analysis, and Bogard Liddell was identified as a potential source of this DNA. The probability of selecting an unrelated individual at random having the same DNA types as detected on the bandanna is approximately 1 in 6.1 million in the Black population, 1 in 67 million in the Caucasian population, 1 in 110 million in the Southeastern Hispanic population, and 1 in 170 million in the Southwestern Hispanic population....

III. ADMISSIBILITY OF DNA EVIDENCE

A. BASIC CONCEPTS OF DNA—AN OVERVIEW

The following is a basic description of DNA as set forth by Judge Barbadoro in his memorandum opinion in *United States v. Shea*, 957 F. Supp. 331, 333 (D. N.H.1997):

> DNA, an acronym for deoxyribonucleic acid, is the chemical blueprint for life. Most human cells other than reproductive cells contain identical copies of a person's DNA. Although 99.9% of human DNA does not vary from person to person, no two persons other than identical twins have the same DNA.

> Human DNA is organized into 23 pairs of chromosomes and each chromosome contains a DNA molecule. DNA molecules have a double stranded helical structure that can be envisioned as a spiral staircase. Running between the two sugar-phosphate strands forming the handrails of the staircase are millions of steps comprised of two loosely bound nitrogen bases. Each step is referred to as a base pair. There are four types of bases: adenine (A), thymine (T), guanine (G), and cytosine (C). A's ordinarily pair only with T's, and C's ordinarily pair only with G's. Thus, if the sequence of bases on one side of a DNA molecule is known, the corresponding sequence of bases on the other side can be deduced. The arrangement of base pairs in chromosomal DNA comprises the genetic code that differentiates humans from non-humans and makes every person unique.

> In total, the DNA molecules in the 23 pairs of human chromosomes contain approximately 3.3 billion base pairs. Most of the base pairs are arranged in the same sequence in all humans. However, every DNA molecule has regions known as polymorphic sites where variability is found in the human population. Each possible arrangement of base pairs that occurs at a poly-

morphic site is referred to as an allele. Alleles can result from differences in a single base pair, differences in multiple base pairs, or differences in the number of base pairs that comprise a site.

The combination of alleles from corresponding sites on a chromosome pair is sometimes referred to as the site's genotype. One allele for each single locus genotype is inherited from each parent. If both parents contribute the same type of allele, the child's genotype is considered to be homozygous. If each parent contributes a different type of allele, the child's genotype is considered to be heterozygous. To illustrate, if only two alleles for a locus are found in the population, A and a, two homozygous genotypes, AA and aa, and one heterozygous genotype, Aa, will be found in the population. Although an individual's genotype consists of either two copies of the same allele or one copy of each of two different alleles, many different alleles may be found in the population for a single locus.

B. *THE PCR METHOD OF DNA ANALYSIS.*

The PCR method of DNA analysis has been succinctly described in *United States v. Beasley,* 102 F.3d 1440, 1445 (8th Cir. 1996), where the Eighth Circuit quoted (and adopted) Judge Doty's findings which were rendered following a *Daubert* hearing. The quoted findings provide:

> The PCR method [of DNA analysis] is based upon the natural DNA replication process. By utilizing the PCR method, one can produce a substantial number of specific segments of human DNA which can then be typed. Because 99 percent of the DNA molecule is the same for every individual, the DNA segments amplified for purposes of PCR DNA typing are ones which exhibit genetic variation within the population. These variations provide the basis for DNA typing.

> The PCR method recognizes that the base pairs along the DNA molecule are joined by hydrogen bonds which can be broken by heating. When exposed to heating, the two complementary strands of DNA separate or "denature." Because the bases on a DNA strand are always complementary, a denatured DNA strand forms a template that allows the manufacture of a new strand that is identical to the former complementary strand. This denatured strand is then exposed to two synthetic primers, each complementing a sequence at one end of the target sequence and which bind with their complementary sequences on the separated strands.... The new strand is complementary to the sample strand, and thus identical to the other denatured strand of the original DNA sample.

> The replication process can be repeated by reheating the sample to again cause denaturation and with each new cycle, the DNA replicated grows exponentially. Eventually, the amplification produces a sufficient quantity of a relatively pure sample for an investigator to determine the gene type of the sample....

The second phase of the PCR method of DNA typing involves comparing the DNA profile from the unknown source with the DNA profile of a known source from a possible suspect. If the profiles are different the suspect is excluded. However, if the profiles match a question is raised as to the frequency with which such a profile occurs in the population. Based upon a population database developed by the BCA, the frequency with which an individual allele occurs in the comparison population is determined. These individual probabilities are then multiplied to produce a frequency of the DNA profile in the comparison population.

C. JUDICIAL RECOGNITION OF PCR DNA ANALYSIS.

The first two federal circuit courts to consider the question of the scientific reliability of PCR DNA based analysis have readily found that it satisfies the standards established by *Daubert*. In *United States v. Beasley*, 102 F.3d 1440 (8th Cir.1996), the Eighth Circuit held that "[t]he reliability of the PCR method of DNA analysis is sufficiently well established to permit the courts of this circuit to take judicial notice of it in all future cases."

In *Beasley*, the defendant claimed that the District Court erred by admitting DNA evidence of two hairs found in a ski mask used in a robbery. Before trial, the district court conducted a *Daubert* hearing concerning the admissibility of the DNA evidence using the PCR method of DNA typing and entered extensive finding as quoted above. Upon appeal, the Eighth circuit held that the district court had carefully considered the *Daubert* factors in its assessment of the reliability of the PCR method and rejected the appellant's (defendant) claim that PCR testing does not meet the *Daubert* standard of reliability. It added, however, that "[I]n every case, of course, the reliability of the proffered test results may be challenged by showing that a scientifically sound methodology has been undercut by sloppy handing of the samples, failure to properly train those performing the testing, failure to follow appropriate protocols, and the like."

The Eighth Circuit recognized that, while it appeared to be the first federal court of appeals to examine the PCR method of DNA typing, a number of state appellate courts have examined the PCR method. It found that the vast majority of them have sustained the admission of DNA evidence derived from the PCR method.

In *United States v. Hicks*, 103 F.3d 837 (9th Cir.1996), the Government's expert proposed to testify that, as a result of a PCR DNA testing procedure, none of the three perpetrators could be excluded as a contributor to the sample. Upon appeal, the Ninth Circuit concluded that, although PCR forensic testing is relatively new..., "... its novelty should not prevent the district court from exercising its sound discretion in admitting such evidence once a proper *Daubert* showing has been made." *United States v. Hicks, supra*, 103 F.3d at 846–47.

PCR DNA analysis has been accepted in two recent federal district court opinions. In *United States v. Shea, supra*, 957 F.Supp. 331, the district court judge was so convinced of the admissibility of PCR tests, that he concluded that courts could take judicial notice of their general reliability.... In *United States v. Lowe*, 954 F.Supp. 401

(D.Mass.1996), Judge Saris conducted an extensive *Daubert* hearing to consider the admissibility of DNA profiles obtained with PCR analysis.... In his memorandum opinion, Judge Saris, after considering each of the factors set forth in *Daubert*, denied the defendant's motion to exclude the PCR DNA evidence. In concluding that the Government had established the scientific validity, and thus the evidentiary reliability, of the tests and techniques employed in the PCR-based DNA analysis, Judge Saris relied on the testimony of the forensic examiner at the FBI's DNA Analysis Unit, and Dr. Martin L. Tracey, a biologist with an expertise in DNA and population genetics (who also testified in this case). This Court finds Judge Saris' analysis to be extremely persuasive....

D. *ENUMERATION AND APPLICATION OF* DAUBERT *FACTORS.*

Daubert sets forth the criteria for determining whether expert scientific evidence is admissible at trial. A district court confronted with a proffer of expert testimony must at the outset, pursuant to Fed.R.Evid. 104(a) and 702, determine whether the expert is proposing to testify about "(1) scientific knowledge that (2) will assist the trier of fact to understand or determine a fact in issue." *Daubert*, 509 U.S. at 592, 113 S.Ct. at 2796. "[T]he trial judge must ensure that any and all scientific testimony or evidence admitted is not only relevant, but reliable." 509 U.S. at 589, 113 S.Ct. at 2795. Among the non-exclusive factors that a court should consider in determining whether scientific testimony is reliable are: (1) whether the expert's opinion can be or has been tested; (2) whether the theory or technique on which the opinion is based has been subjected to peer review and publication; (3) the technique's known or potential error rate; (4) the existence and maintenance of standards controlling the technique's operations; and (5) "general acceptance." *Daubert*, 509 U.S. at 593–94, 113 S.Ct. at 2796–97. No single factor is necessarily dispositive in this analysis and other factors might also warrant consideration in the appropriate case. *Daubert*, 509 U.S. at 594, 113 S.Ct. at 2797.

E. *APPLICATION OF* DAUBERT *FACTORS TO THE EVIDENCE ...*

RANDOM MATCH PROBABILITY

There are two determinations that must be made with respect to the calculation of the random match probability. First, the population databases must be scientifically valid. Second, the method used to calculate the frequencies must be scientifically valid. Dr. Tracey, a well-established expert in the field of population genetics, provided extensive testimony concerning the scientific validity of the random match probability calculated in this case. The Court finds that his testimony fully supports the calculations provided by SSA Melissa Smrz with respect to the use of the FBI's population database and the probability of selecting an unrelated individual at random who had the same DNA types as detected on the black bandanna. This probability is 1 in 6.1 million in the African American population.

A. *The Method for Determining the Random Match Probability Has Been Tested*

With respect to the population databases used by the FBI, Dr. Tracey testified that he was familiar with those databases, and that their validity had been tested by comparing the frequencies that appeared in those databases with other databases. Although there were slight variations between the databases, the frequencies were consistent and established that the FBI's databases contained a sufficient number of samples to determine the frequency of alleles appearing in the four populations which comprise the database—Caucasian, African American, Southeast Hispanic and Southwest Hispanic. In addition, he testified that tests had established that the genetic markers which were used in this case were independent of each other, and that the product rule could be used to determine the probability of a random match. That is, based upon well-established scientific principles, the frequencies with which each of the identified alleles appeared in the relevant population could be multiplied together to obtain the frequency with which they would all appear in one individual in the relevant population. A factor known as "theta" is then applied to reduce this frequency where there are homozygous alleles. This is the method that SSA Smrz testified she used in this case. In addition, Dr. Tracey concurred with the recommendation in the 1996 NRC Report that the jury also be advised of the "confidence level," or margin of error of this frequency. That is, although in any given population of African Americans, the most likely frequency for the genetic profile found in this case is 1 in 6.1 million, in some populations, it could be a frequent as 1 in 600,000, or as rare as 1 in 61 million.

B. *The Method for Determining the Random Match Probability Has Been Subjected to Peer Review and Publication*

The expert testimony establishes that the tests conducted to determine the validity and reliability of the population databases used to calculate the random match probability, as well as the use of the product rule, have been published in peer-reviewed literature ... Other references are contained in the Reference Section of the FBI protocol. Neither expert was aware of any published articles which found this method to be scientifically invalid. The 1996 NRC Report specifically recommends that the product rule be used to calculate the DNA profile frequency....

C. *The Method for Determining Random Match Probability Has an Acceptable Rate of Error, and There are Standards Which Control this Determination*

To account for any possible variations between databases used in the frequency determinations, Dr. Tracey testified that he concurred with the NRC recommendation that a margin of error of ten percent be used. According to Dr. Tracey, this is a conservative estimate which would account for any differences in population databases. Dr. Tracey also testified that the standards which are used to control the use of the product rule and to determine the adequacy of the population database are well established, and demonstrate that the alleles of each of the genetic markers are inherited from each parent independently of each other, and that each of the genetic markers used to comprise the genetic profile in this case are inherited independently of each other.

D. *The Method for Determining Random Match Probability is Generally Accepted Within the Scientific Community*

The expert testimony establishes that the method for determining random match probability is generally accepted in the scientific community of population geneticists, although Dr. Tracey acknowledged that there was some disagreement over whether the margin of error correction was sufficient.

In concluding that the match probability analysis is in conformance with the *Daubert* standards, the Court finds persuasive that District Judge Barbadoro, in *United States v. Shea*, 957 F.Supp. 331 (D. N.H.1997), also addressed the concern over margin of error, accepted Dr. Tracey's testimony in this regard, and concluded that the probability of a random match, when adjusted in accordance with the 1996 NRC guidelines, satisfied the *Daubert* standard for admissibility. In so doing, the district court noted specifically that *Daubert* did not require scientific consensus.

IV. *CONCLUSION*

In sum, the Court is satisfied that the Government has established the scientific validity, and thus the evidentiary reliability, of the tests and techniques employed in the PCR-based DNA analysis conducted in this case, as required by *Daubert*.

People v. Pike

53 N.E.3d 147 (Ill. App. Ct. 2016)

PUCINSKI, Justice.

. . .

Prosecutor's Fallacy

A common mistake in attempting to understand the varying DNA statistical probability calculations is to conflate either a probability of inclusion/exclusion, or a random match probability, with the probability (or likelihood ratio) that a particular defendant is or is not the source of the DNA. This mistaken assumption is referred to as the "prosecutor's fallacy," which "is the assumption that the random match probability is the same as the probability that the defendant was not the source of the DNA sample." *McDaniel v. Brown,* 558 U.S. 120, 128 (2010) (quoting NAT'L RES. COUNCIL, THE EVALUATION OF FORENSIC DNA EVIDENCE 133 (1996)). Alternatively, it is called the "fallacy of the transposed conditional." Brief of 20 Scholars of Forensic Evidence as *Amici Curiae* in Support of Respondent, *McDaniel v. Brown,* 558 U.S. 120 (2010). "In other words, if a juror is told the probability a member of the general population would share the same DNA is 1 in 10,000 (random match probability), and he takes that to mean there is only a 1 in 10,000 chance that someone other than the defendant is the source of the DNA found at the crime scene (source probability), then he has succumbed to the prosecutor's fallacy." *McDaniel,* 558 U.S. at 128. "This faulty reasoning may result in an erroneous statement that, based on a random match probability of 1 in 10,000, there is a 0.01% chance the defendant is innocent or a 99.99% chance the defendant is guilty." *Id.* This is an important distinction to make, and yet it is a distinction that has not been clearly explained in our jurisprudence in Illinois. This same error can occur with the use of the probability of inclusion or probability of exclusion, which can be confused with source probability.

The prosecutor's fallacy is "the incorrect belief that the chance of a rare event happening is the same as the chance that the defendant is innocent." Helen Joyce, *Beyond Reasonable Doubt*, Plus, Aug. 31, 2002. "For instance, most United States senators are men, but very few men are senators. Consequently, there is a high probability that an individual who is a senator is a man, but the probability that an individual who is a man is a senator is practically zero." David H. Kaye & David A. Freeman, *Reference Guide on Statistics*, in Reference Manual on Scientific Evidence 83, 131 n. 167 (2d ed. 2000). "The obvious but absolutely wrong thing to do is to say: 'The rarity of this profile is 1 in 2 million. So there's only a 1 in 2 million chance that it came from someone other than the suspect.... We've got him!'" Philip Dawid & Rachel Thomas, *It's a Match!*, Plus, July 12, 2010. This is the prosecutor's fallacy — "misinterpreting the match probability (the probability that a random person's profile matches the crime sample) as the probability this particular person is innocent on the basis of the evidence." *Id.*

Compare the following variations on the same numbers. Assume that the correct statement is: The chance is 1 in 7000 that *some particular person* other than the suspect would leave a stain like the actual stain (random match probability). Now turn it around for the prosecutor's fallacy: The chance is 1 in 7000 that *someone, anyone*, other than the suspect left the stain. Then consider how often the same facts are carelessly paraphrased: The chance is 1 in 7000 for *someone other than the suspect* to produce the observed evidence.

It is a fallacy because it falsely equates that the probability that the suspect might be the donor (source probability) can be computed from the DNA evidence alone, which implies illogically that other evidence in the case makes no difference at all....

Notes and Questions

1. In *Gaines*, the court notes that the FBI lab agent reported that the match for the bandanna had different random match probabilities, when compared to different population subgroups (Black, Caucasian, Southeastern Hispanic, Southwestern Hispanic). Is all of this evidence relevant? Why or why not?

2. Creating a population database usually involves source data from a wide variety of sources including blood banks, genetics laboratories, hospitals, clinics, and other sources. National Research Council, National Academy of Sciences, The Evaluation of Forensic DNA Evidence 126 (1996). Then, when an unknown sample matches the known sample, the probative value of the match depends on the variation of the particular allele patterns within the appropriate database. Christopher D. Steele & David J. Balding, *Choice of Population Database for Forensic DNA Profile Analysis*, 54 Sci. & Just. 487 (2014). Steele and Balding note that in those comparisons, "[t]he most appropriate population is the one that best matches the ancestry of X, the true source of the DNA ... [and] when the ancestry of X is unknown, it is common to consider multiple population databases and choose the one that generates the lowest [probative value]." *Id.*

3. In certain situations, a defendant may claim that the comparison population used to establish the RMP in the case was improper. In *Dayton v. State*, the defendant argued the use of a population database of Eskimos for DNA comparison was meaningless, as Dayton was an Athabascan Indian not an Eskimo. 89 P.3d 806 (Alaska Ct. App. 2004). Why would the Defendant be making this claim? What might he expect would be different about an Athabascan database comparison compared to an Eskimo one?

4. A RMP is calculated, as we have learned, using the product rule and "multiplying the genotype (i.e., the observed allele(s)) frequencies (i.e., how often that allele or pair of alleles can be expected to occur at random in a human population) for each locus in an STR profile with the genotype frequency for every other locus in the profile." Justice Ming W. Chin et. al., Forensic DNA Evidence: Science and the Law § 5.1 (2017 ed.). Using this method, an RMP value answers the question: What is the probability that a person randomly selected from the appropriate population will have this profile?

Justice Pucinski makes clear in *Pike* that the RMP most certainly **does not** represent the likelihood the defendant is innocent. To understand why, consider a hypothetical case where the RMP is 1 in 10,000. If one misreads the RMP as the likelihood of innocence, the accused is almost certainly guilty. Instead, what the RMP of 1 in 10,000 tells us is that, considering the assortment of allele patterns in the sample, the probability that a person randomly selected from a similar population database will have this profile. In a city of 500,000 people, like Des Moines, Iowa, if the RMP is 1 in 10,000, then there are likely to be around 50 people with the matching allele pattern (assuming everyone belongs to the same population database). If so, the RMP here—instead of demonstrating overwhelming guilt—now is quite probative of lack of guilt. True, the accused could not be ruled out, but 50 other people could have been the source of the DNA sample in question. Unless other evidence is presented, the accused should be found not guilty. Mark Buchanan, *The Prosecutor's Fallacy*, N.Y. Times, May 16, 2007 (discussing the prosecutor's fallacy, and its potential to lead to injustice).

Court decisions discussing misuse of DNA evidence with the "prosecutor's fallacy" are unfortunately common. *See, e.g., McDaniel v. Brown*, 558 U.S. 120, 128–9 (2010); *Brown v. Farwell*, No.3:03-CV-00712-PMP-VPC, 2006 WL 6181129, at *5 (D. Nev. 2006); *State v. Abdullah*, 348 P.3d 1, 34–5 (Idaho 2015); *State v. Wright*, 253 P.3d 838, 845 (Mont. 2011); *State v. Ragland*, 739 S.E.2d 616, 624 (N.C. Ct. App. 2013). Whether these errors result in appellate relief, however, is a topic we will explore next, in Part C.

C. DNA Problems That Persist Today

The perception of DNA evidence as the quintessential methodology of individual identification, unerringly excluding or identifying suspects with scientific rigor, is obviously flawed at a fundamental level. Of course, DNA can definitively exclude the suspect from consideration, should the allele patterns of the known and unknown samples not match, but at best, when a positive "match" has been declared, there remains always the possibility that the sample came from another source which matches at the relevant allele locations. That explains the importance of RMP, and why a "match" can have widely varying probative force. We have also seen that the selection of a population database for comparison purposes can drastically affect the RMP calculation, and may itself become a subject of debate (as in cases like *Dayton*). Finally, we know that misuse of DNA statistics with the "prosecutor's fallacy" leads the jury to improper inferences.

These and similar issues dominated DNA case law in the 1990s and 2000s, but as the technology and its application advances, these issues likely will reduce in frequency. Instead, we must now consider what I call the "modern DNA problems." David Kaye has described these modern DNA considerations as follows: "most of the problems with DNA testing have not been errors of high theory or the introduction of methods that did not work. Rather, they have been production-line problems in the generation of the evidence for specific cases...." DAVID H. KAYE, THE DOUBLE HELIX AND THE LAW OF EVIDENCE 257 (2011). As we begin these materials, we will focus on three sources of continuing error, those that happen 1) prior to sample collection (contamination), 2) during sample analysis (lab error), or even 3) after litigation has ended (inadequate remedies). Even as the technology advances, these considerations will remain problematic long into the foreseeable future.

William C. Thompson,
Tarnish on the "Gold Standard":
Understanding Recent Problems in Forensic DNA Testing
CHAMPION, Jan./Feb. 2006, at 10

DNA evidence has long been called "the gold standard" of forensic science. Most people believe it is virtually infallible — that it either produces the right result or no result. But this belief is difficult to square with recent news stories about errors in DNA testing. An extraordinary number of problems related to forensic DNA evidence have recently come to light. Consider, for example, the following:

• The Houston Police Department (HPD) shut down the DNA and serology section of its crime laboratory in early 2003 after a television expose revealed serious deficiencies in the lab's procedures, deficiencies that were confirmed by subsequent investigations. Two men who were falsely incriminated by botched lab work have been released after subsequent DNA testing proved their innocence. In dozens of cases, DNA retests by independent laboratories have failed to confirm the conclusions of the HPD lab. The DNA lab remains closed while an outside investigation continues.

• In Virginia, post-conviction DNA testing in the high-profile case of Earl Washington, Jr. (who was falsely convicted of capital murder and came within hours of execution) contradicted DNA tests on the same samples performed earlier by the State Division of Forensic Sciences. An outside investigation concluded that the state lab had botched the analysis of the case, failing to follow proper procedures and misinterpreting its own test results. The outside investigators called for, and the governor ordered, a broader investigation of the lab to determine whether these problems are endemic. Problematic test procedures and misleading testimony have also come to light in two additional capital cases handled by the state lab.

- In 2004, an investigation by the *Seattle Post-Intelligencer* documented 23 DNA testing errors in serious criminal cases handled by the Washington State Patrol laboratory.

- In North Carolina, the *Winston-Salem Journal* recently published a series of articles documenting numerous DNA testing errors by the North Carolina State Bureau of Investigation.

- The Illinois State Police recently cancelled a contract with Bode Technology Group, one of the largest independent DNA labs in the country, expressing "outrage" over poor quality work.

- LabCorp, another large independent lab has recently been accused of botching DNA paternity tests.

While these scandals are bad enough, the problems with DNA evidence do not end there. A close look at the field shows that DNA testing errors have been popping up all over the country. Many of the mistakes arise from cross-contamination or mislabeling of DNA samples. Problems of this type have been documented in Minnesota, North Carolina, Pennsylvania, Nevada, and California. Tellingly, one of the private labs hired to retest DNA evidence in cases that were botched by the Houston Police Department Crime Lab has itself produced false matches due to sample mix-ups. A particularly ominous sign of underlying problems is that accidental transfers of DNA among samples from *different cases* being processed by the same laboratory have produced several false "cold hits."

While most of the problems are due to inadvertent mistakes, a number of cases involving dishonesty have also come to light. DNA analysts have recently been fired for scientific misconduct, and specifically for falsification of test results, by a number of forensic laboratories, including labs operated by the FBI, Orchid-Cellmark (another large private DNA laboratory), the Office of the Chief Medical Examiner in New York City, and the United States Army. In all of these cases, the analysts were caught faking the results of control samples designed to detect instances in which cross-contamination of DNA samples has occurred.

So what is going on with DNA testing? How can we explain this sudden rash of problems with "the gold standard" of forensic science? How can a test that has long been advertised as virtually infallible produce so many errors? And what is behind the recent spate of dishonesty among DNA analysts? The answers to these questions are, in my view, interconnected. Some serious underlying problems with DNA testing that have existed for a long time are beginning to come to light. What we are seeing is not a sudden deterioration in the quality of DNA testing. It is the inevitable emergence and recognition of problems that existed all along but heretofore were success-fully hidden. In this article, I will describe these underlying problems, comment on why they are occurring, and discuss what defense lawyers can do about them.

Bad Labs

One chronic problem that is now being recognized is the uneven quality of forensic DNA laboratories. Laboratories vary greatly in the care with which they validate their methods and the rigor with which they carry them out. Quality control and quality assurance procedures that are followed religiously in some labs are ignored or followed intermittently in others.

While there have always been bad labs, their shoddy work has been difficult to detect because the worst labs tend to be found in jurisdictions that have historically shielded crime labs from external scrutiny. For example, it is now recognized that the Houston Police Department (HPD) Crime Laboratory did grossly inadequate, incompetent and biased DNA and serology work for well over a decade before a team of television journalists exposed the problems in late 2002. Defense lawyers did not (and probably could not) expose the lab's problems because Harris County (Houston) judges routinely denied requests for discovery of underlying laboratory notes and for expert assistance in evaluating DNA evidence. Indeed, under a policy of the Harris County District Attorney's Office, that defense lawyers rarely challenged, the defendant could not even get a copy of laboratory reports in his case until the trial began.

Crime labs in Virginia and North Carolina have also received little scrutiny in the justice system due to severe limitation in those states on the availability of discovery, funding for independent experts, and funding for indigent defense in general.

But these problems could not remain hidden forever. Journalists have played a big role. In Houston, the problems were first exposed in a series of exposes by television reporters who were assisted by academic experts. Excellent investigative journalism also helped expose problems in Washington State, Virginia and North Carolina. Another important factor has been post-conviction DNA testing. A number of errors have come to light because post-conviction DNA tests contradicted tests performed by government crime labs. The work of Peter Neufeld, Barry Scheck, and their colleagues at the Cardozo Law School Innocence Project has been instrumental in exposing problems, particularly in Texas and Virginia.

Surprising Frequency of Cross-Contamination and Sample Mix-Ups

Another problem now emerging into the light is an unexpectedly high rate of laboratory errors involving mix-up and cross-contamination of DNA samples. Errors of this type appear to be chronic and occur even at the best DNA labs. This is a problem that forensic scientists have largely managed to keep under wraps (perhaps because it is always embarrassing). Practitioners have long claimed that the rate of laboratory error in DNA testing is so low as to be negligible, but growing evidence suggests otherwise.

An important source of evidence on the nature and frequency of these problems is "contamination logs" and "corrective action files" that are maintained by some

DNA laboratories. Under a guideline issued by the FBI's DNA Advisory Board in 1998, forensic DNA laboratories are required to "follow procedures for corrective action whenever proficiency testing discrepancies and/or casework errors are detected" and "shall maintain documentation for the corrective action." While many laboratories ignored this guideline, some laboratories (probably the better ones) have begun to keep records of instances in which, for example, samples are mixed up or DNA from one sample is accidentally transferred to another samples.

The surprise for defense lawyers who have managed to gain access to these files is how voluminous they are. Errors occur regularly. Files from Orchid-Cellmark's Germantown, Maryland facility, for example, show dozens of instances in which samples were contaminated with foreign DNA or DNA was somehow transferred from one sample to another during testing. I recently reviewed the corrective action file for an accredited California laboratory operated by the District Attorney's Office of Kern County (Bakersfield). Although this is a relatively small laboratory that processes a low volume of samples (probably fewer than 1,000 per year), during an 18-month period, it documented multiple instances in which (blank) control samples were positive for DNA, an instance in which a mother's reference sample was contaminated with DNA from her child, several instances in which samples were accidentally switched or mislabeled, an instance in which an analyst's DNA contaminated samples, an instance in which DNA extracted from two different samples was accidentally combined into the same tube, falsely creating a mixed sample, and an instance in which a suspect tested twice did not match himself (probably due to another sample-labeling error).

The errors documented in these files are disturbing, in part, because they probably represent just the tip of an ominous iceberg. The documented errors are, of course, those that the laboratory itself caught and corrected. In most instances, these errors produced unexpected results that flagged the problem, such as positive results in a control sample that was supposed to contain no DNA or a second DNA profile in a sample that was supposed to be from a single person. Upon noticing such problems, labs typically throw out the results of that test and start over. Accordingly, analysts usually argue that most of the incidents documented in these files are "not really errors" because they did not affect the final results of the analysis and, in fact, are evidence that "the system is working" to detect errors when they occur.

However, the same processes that cause detectable errors in some cases can cause undetectable errors in others. If DNA from a suspect is accidentally transferred into a "blank" control sample, it is obvious that something is wrong; if the suspect's DNA is accidentally transferred into an evidentiary sample, the error is not obvious because there is another explanation—i.e., that the suspect is the source of the evidentiary DNA. Errors that incriminate a suspect are unlikely to be detected as errors; they are likely to be treated as incriminating evidence. Consequently, the fat files full of errors that a lab was able to catch should not be taken as reassuring evidence that "the system is working." They are a warning signal that we need to worry about errors the lab did not catch.

Dishonest DNA Analysts

A third problem now emerging is dishonest DNA analysts who falsify test results. I suspect this third problem is closely related to the second problem: DNA analysts are faking test results to cover up errors arising from cross-contamination of DNA samples and sample mix-ups.

Given the unexpectedly high frequency of contamination in DNA testing we have just discussed, it is interesting, and not at all surprising, that the major form of fakery discovered to date involves control samples known as extraction blanks that are designed to detect contamination. These samples are supposed to contain no DNA. When they produce positive results, it indicates there was a problem—DNA somehow ended up in a sample where it did not belong. If that happened to a control sample, it could also have happened to other samples, so the analyst must throw out the whole test and start over.

The temptation to fake controls probably arises partly from production pressures and partly from the collision between the public image of DNA testing as infallible and the reality that it is easier than one might expect to botch a DNA test by cross-contaminating samples. Police and prosecutors have demanded DNA tests in an ever-expanding number of cases, putting pressure on labs to keep pace. Some labs have become high-tech sweatshops in which analysts are under pressure to maintain productivity. In this environment, the failure of a scientific control can be a big problem for a DNA analyst—it forces the analyst to redo the entire case, putting him or her behind schedule.

Furthermore, the presence of DNA in an extraction blank can be embarrassing for an analyst because contamination is often the result of sloppy laboratory technique. Having to redo the analysis can also lead to uncomfortable questions about why the analyst needed two or more tries to get the test right. DNA tests themselves are viewed as infallible, so any problem that occurs in testing tends to be attributed (fairly or not) to the analyst's incompetence. Consequently, a single mistake can end an analyst's career. After an accidental sample switch caused an embarrassing false incrimination in a North Carolina case, for example, the lab director reported that "the analyst working this case was removed from casework through retirement" and "will not be reemployed by this agency to conduct any type of forensic testing."

So what is a DNA analyst to do if problems (such as positive results in blank control samples) occur too often? For an analyst who thinks that the test results are right anyway, it must be very tempting just to hide the problem. This can be done in a number of ways. The DNA analysts in the Houston Police Crime lab came up with an easy solution—they simply failed to run extraction blanks (although they claimed in testimony that they had run all necessary controls).

According to the Inspector General of the Justice Department, FBI analyst Jacqueline Blake followed only a slightly more subtle approach. Although she prepared extraction blanks along with other samples and recorded the creation of these samples in her notes, she dumped the portion of these samples that might have contained contaminating DNA before sending the samples through the computer-operated genetic analyzer that typed the DNA. Interestingly, although Blake's misconduct could have been detected by close examination of the electronic files produced by the genetic analyzer, no one either inside or outside the Bureau checked this aspect of her work. Hence, "Blake's record of contamination-free testing for more than two years did not receive scrutiny." The analyst fired by the Office of the Chief Medical Examiner in New York used a similar strategy and was caught only after confiding her activities to another analyst, who then made an anonymous report to the laboratory managers.

Analyst Sarah Blair of Orchid-Cellmark used yet another approach. She manipulated the computer files produced by the genetic analyzer, replacing the computerized results for problematic control samples with the results of "clean controls" from other cases. This manipulation was uncovered when another Orchid-Cellmark analyst who reviewed Blair's work noticed that the same control file (which happened to contain an unusual anomaly) appeared in two different cases. According to Robin Cotton, a Technical Director for the lab, a subsequent review of computer files in Blair's cases found approximately 25 instances in which Blair had substituted controls. Dr. Simon Ford, an independent DNA consultant in San Francisco who has reviewed some of Blair's work for the Los Angeles County Public Defender's Office, has reported finding additional instances of data manipulation in Blair's cases based on close examination of printouts of the computer data. Dr. Ford also recently reported discovering a case in which an Arizona DNA analyst surreptitiously manipulated computer files in order to cover up an error involving mislabeling of samples.

What Defense Lawyers Need to Do

Criminal defense lawyers can play a key role in further exposing DNA testing problems and advocating for laboratory reform. The first step, when handling a case involving DNA evidence, is to fight relentlessly for full disclosure of the underlying laboratory records and for appointment of an independent expert to help review those records. As noted above, some of the worst laboratory work, such as flawed DNA testing by the Houston Police Department Crime Laboratory, has occurred in jurisdictions where laboratory work has rarely received outside scrutiny. Analysts who know that no one will ever check or challenge their conclusions tend to become sloppy, to cut corners, and to shade their findings in ways they find convenient. The criminal defense bar has an important role to play in maintaining the quality of forensic science....

Discovery of Electronic Data

A key aspect of discovery in DNA cases is the electronic data produced by the computer-controlled genetic analyzers that are currently used to "type" DNA samples. Analysis of the computer files can not only reveal undisclosed problems and support alternative interpretations of the findings, but also, as discussed above, these files can be crucial for detecting instances of scientific fraud, such as that committed by Jacqueline Blake and Sarah Blair....

The great majority of forensic DNA laboratories in the United States will, on receiving a proper request, provide complete copies of the electronic data in a case. The electronic files are typically burned onto a CD-Rom in a simple operation similar to copying digital music or photos. Although the files are in a proprietary format that is readable only by software created by vendors of the genetic analyzers, a number of independent experts have access to this software and can use it to reanalyze the results from the genetic analyzer, check the lab's interpretations, and look for other problems.

Taking Contamination Seriously

After obtaining complete laboratory records in the case, defense lawyers need to review them carefully with the assistance of an expert in order to identify all possible explanation for the laboratory findings that might be consistent with innocence. In light of the frequency of contamination and mislabeling problems, it is particularly important to consider whether accidental cross-contamination or mislabeling of samples could account for incriminating findings.

One sure pathway to a false incrimination is accidental contamination of an evidentiary sample with DNA from a suspect's reference sample. Given the known danger of cross-contamination among samples being processed together as a batch, most DNA laboratories take care to process the evidentiary samples at a different time or place than reference samples. However, some laboratories (the bad ones) insist on processing reference samples and evidentiary samples from a case all at the same time, a practice that seems irresponsible, even outrageous, given the danger that a laboratory accident could produce a false incrimination.

A false incrimination can also occur through cross-contamination among evidentiary samples. Even labs that are careful to test reference samples separately from evidentiary samples often process all of the evidentiary samples from a case together, creating the potential for false matches. I recently reviewed a case processed by the Los Angeles Police Department DNA laboratory in which samples from a bloody murder scene were being processed in the same batch as samples from items collected in a suspect's house. Due to an analyst's error in the case, DNA from the murder victim accidentally ended up in a control sample. This error was detected because the control sample was a "blank" which was supposed to contain no DNA. However, it was merely happenstance that the accidental transfer of DNA ended up in a blank control rather than another sample in the same batch. If the victim's DNA had instead ended up in one of the samples from the suspect's house, I believe that the error would not have been detected and would have led to a false laboratory report saying that the murder victim DNA had been found on an item collected in the suspect's house. Defense lawyers need to think carefully about the potential for such errors because experience shows that they can and do occur.

In several instances accidental cross-contamination of DNA samples in a laboratory have caused false "cold hits" (*i.e.*, false matches to an individual who was identified only because his or her DNA profile was in a government database). For example, the Washington State Patrol laboratory accidentally contaminated samples from a rape case with DNA from the reference sample of a juvenile felon. Luckily, the case in question was an old one. Because the juvenile offender had been a young child when the rape occurred he could not plausibly be connected to the case. According to the lab's Contamination/Extraneous DNA Log, "it was determined that the felon's sample was being used as a training sample by another analyst" when the rape case was being analyzed. In the Orange County, California, Sheriff-Coroner's crime lab an analyst accidentally cross-contaminated samples from two rape cases being processed at the same time, producing another false cold hit. False cold hits due to accidental cross-contamination of samples from different cases have also been reported in New Zealand and Australia.

In one particularly interesting Australian case, DNA on the clothing of a murdered toddler named Jaidyn Leskie was linked, via a "cold hit," to a young "mentally challenged" woman who lived hundreds of miles away and who, by all accounts, had never left her own village. Police could find no way to link the young woman to the Leskie murder and at first dismissed the "cold hit" as an "adventitious" (coincidental) match. However, a coroner's investigation established that DNA from the young woman had been processed through the same laboratory at about the same time as the toddler's clothing. The young woman had allegedly been the victim of a sexual assault involving a condom. Although laboratory personnel maintain that accidental transfer of samples between cases is impossible, it now appears almost certain that the young woman's DNA from the outside of the condom accidentally contaminated samples from the toddler's clothing. The alternative explanation—that there was a coincidental match between the young woman and another person who was involved with the toddler's murder—has become increasingly unlikely because additional DNA testing, and re-analysis of the lab's electronic data, has reduced the likelihood of such a coincidence to one in many trillions.

The facts of some recent cases in the United States have also raised suspicions about false cold hits due to contamination across cases. For example, in 2002, while investigating the 1969 murder of University of Michigan law student Jane Mixer, the Michigan State Police Crime Laboratory in Lansing found DNA of two men on her clothing. The profiles were searched through a database and matched two Michigan men, Gary Leiterman and John Ruelas. Police immediately suspected that Leiterman and Ruelas had been involved in the murder, but there was a problem—Ruelas was only four years old when Mixer was killed and had been living with his parents in another city. According to news accounts, police could find no link between young Ruelas and Mixer. That did not deter Washtenaw County Assistant Prosecutor Steven Hiller who charged Leiterman with the murder. Hiller "created a scenario placing a young Ruelas at the [murder] scene as a chronic nose-bleeder whose blood dropped on Mixer." There is, however, another possible explanation for this "cold hit." Examination of laboratory records revealed that known samples of DNA *from both Leiterman and Ruelas* were being processed in the Michigan State lab *on the same day* as the old samples from the Mixer murder. Both men were being tested in connection with other cases unrelated to the Mixer murder. Although the Michigan State laboratory maintains that cross-contamination of samples across cases was impossible, it seems a very strange and unlikely coincidence that two men who, according to the prosecutor, were present when Mixer was murdered in 1969 just happened to have their DNA tested (for other cases) on the very same day as samples from the Mixer case were tested. Leiterman was nevertheless convicted of Mixer's murder in 2005.

Lawyers who represent clients who are incriminated through "cold hits" would be well advised to investigate carefully whether a laboratory accident could explain the test results....

Potential Reforms

Defense lawyers should also play an active role in advocating for laboratory reform. Perhaps the sole positive aspect of the recent spate of DNA testing problems is that legislators, judges, and even prosecutors are gradually becoming aware of underlying problems in forensic science, making this an opportune time to press for reforms.

One such reform is the creation of independent commissions to supervise the operation of forensic laboratories. New York state's successful forensic science commission is a good model. It is encouraging that, in the wake of crime lab scandals in those states, Texas and Virginia have both recently adopted similar legislation. The Virginia legislation creates a scientific review panel with the authority to review laboratory operations, adopt qualification standards for the lab director and other staffers, and establish an audit process to be used when errors occur. The panel will also be available to review lab reports and test results at the request of the governor or lab officials.

This very positive development in Virginia would never have happened without the effective advocacy by members of the defense bar. Steven Benjamin and Betty Layne DesPortes of Richmond played a particularly important role in advocating for reform, as did Peter Neufeld and Barry Scheck of the Innocence Project....

Another reform worth pursuing is external blind proficiency testing of forensic DNA laboratories. Although most DNA laboratories participate in periodic proficiency tests, these are open tests in which the analysts know that they are being tested. These tests have also been criticized as too easy to detect problems that might arise in tough casework. A better approach is to occasionally ask the lab, without the analysts' knowledge, to analyze a simulated case that is constructed to test the lab's performance.

Conclusions

DNA evidence is difficult to challenge in the courtroom because most people think it is virtually infallible. It is not just jurors, fed on a media diet of *CSI*-style fantasies, who think so. Most members of the academic and legal community believe it as well. Even scholars who are critical of other areas of forensic identification science have argued that DNA is an exception—calling DNA testing "a model for scientifically sound identification science."

While there is no doubt that DNA testing rests on a stronger scientific foundation than many other forensic disciplines, recent events have proven that DNA evidence is hardly infallible. The solid scientific foundation for DNA testing is no guarantee that DNA tests will be carried out in a reliable manner that produces accurate results. Bad laboratory work is all too common and laboratory accidents and errors can occur even in good labs. Whether DNA evidence is trustworthy is a question that must be examined carefully in each case....

McDaniel v. Brown

558 U.S. 120 (2010)

PER CURIAM.

In *Jackson v. Virginia*, 443 U.S. 307 (1979), we held that a state prisoner is entitled to habeas corpus relief if a federal judge finds that "upon the record evidence adduced at the trial no rational trier of fact could have found proof of guilt beyond a reasonable doubt." A Nevada jury convicted respondent of rape; the evidence presented included DNA evidence matching respondent's DNA profile. Nevertheless, relying upon a report prepared by a DNA expert over 11 years after the trial, the Federal District Court applied the *Jackson* standard and granted the writ. A divided Court of Appeals affirmed. We granted certiorari to consider whether those courts misapplied *Jackson*. Because the trial record includes both the DNA evidence and other convincing evidence of guilt, we conclude that they clearly did.

I

Around 1 a.m. on January 29, 1994, 9-year-old Jane Doe was brutally raped in the bedroom of her trailer. Respondent Troy Brown was convicted of the crime. During and since his trial, respondent has steadfastly maintained his innocence.[1] He was, however, admittedly intoxicated when the crime occurred, and after he awoke on the following morning he told a friend "'he wished that he could remember what did go on or what went on.'"

Troy and his brother Travis resided near Jane Doe in the same trailer park. Their brother Trent and his wife Raquel lived in the park as well, in a trailer across the street from Jane Doe's. Both Troy and Trent were acquainted with Jane Doe's family; Troy had visited Jane Doe's trailer several times. Jane did not know Travis. The evening of the attack, Jane's mother, Pam, took Jane to Raquel and Trent's trailer to babysit while the three adults went out for about an hour. Raquel and Trent returned at about 7:30 p.m. and took Jane home at about 9:30 p.m. Pam stayed out and ended up drinking and playing pool with Troy at a nearby bar called the Peacock Lounge. Troy knew that Jane and her 4-year-old sister were home alone because he answered the phone at the bar when Jane called for her mother earlier that evening.

Troy consumed at least 10 shots of vodka followed by beer chasers, and was so drunk that he vomited on himself while he was walking home after leaving the Peacock at about 12:15 a.m. Jane called her mother to report the rape at approximately 1 a.m. Although it would have taken a sober man less than 15 minutes to walk home, Troy

---

1. He denied involvement when a police officer claimed (wrongly) that the police had found his fingerprints in Jane's bedroom, and he even denied involvement when the sentencing judge told him that acceptance of responsibility would garner him leniency.

did not arrive at his trailer until about 1:30 a.m. He was wearing dark jeans, a cowboy hat, a black satin jacket, and boots. Two witnesses saw a man dressed in dark jeans, a cowboy hat, and a black satin jacket stumbling in the road between the two trailers shortly after 1 a.m.

The bedroom where the rape occurred was dark, and Jane was unable to conclusively identify her assailant. When asked whom he reminded her of, she mentioned both Troy and his brother Trent. Several days after the rape, she identified a man she saw on television (Troy) as her assailant but then stated that the man who had sent flowers attacked her. It was Trent and Raquel who had sent her flowers, not Troy. She was unable to identify Troy as her assailant out of a photo lineup, and she could not identify her assailant at trial. The night of the rape, however, she said her attacker was wearing dark jeans, a black jacket with a zipper, boots, and a watch. She also vividly remembered that the man "stunk real, real bad" of "cologne, or some beer or puke or something."

Some evidence besides Jane's inconsistent identification did not inculpate Troy. Jane testified that she thought she had bitten her assailant, but Troy did not have any bite marks on his hands when examined by a police officer approximately four hours after the attack. Jane stated that her assailant's jacket had a zipper (Troy's did not) and that he wore a watch (Troy claimed he did not). Additionally, there was conflicting testimony as to when Troy left the Peacock and when Pam received Jane's call reporting the rape. The witnesses who saw a man stumbling between the two trailers reported a bright green logo on the back of the jacket, but Troy's jacket had a yellow and orange logo. Finally, because Jane thought she had left a night light on when she went to bed, the police suspected the assailant had turned off the light. The only usable fingerprint taken from the light did not match Troy's and the police did not find Troy's fingerprints in the trailer.

Other physical evidence, however, pointed to Troy. The police recovered semen from Jane's underwear and from the rape kit. The State's expert, Renee Romero, tested the former and determined that the DNA matched Troy's and that the probability another person from the general population would share the same DNA (the "random match probability") was only 1 in 3,000,000. Troy's counsel did not call his own DNA expert at trial, although he consulted with an expert in advance who found no problems with Romero's test procedures. At some time before sentencing, Troy's family had additional DNA testing done. That testing showed semen taken from the rape kit matched Troy's DNA, with a random match probability of 1 in 10,000.

The jury found Troy guilty of sexual assault and sentenced him to life with the possibility of parole after 10 years. On direct appeal, the Nevada Supreme Court considered Troy's claim that his conviction was not supported by sufficient evidence, analyzing "whether the jury, acting reasonably, could have been convinced of [Troy's] guilt beyond a reasonable doubt." The court rejected the claim.... Respondent also argued on appeal that the trial court erred in failing to conduct a pretrial hearing to determine whether the DNA evidence was reliable. The court found respondent had not raised this issue in the trial court and concluded there was no plain error in the trial court's failure to conduct a hearing.

In 2001, respondent sought state postconviction relief, claiming, *inter alia,* that his trial counsel was constitutionally ineffective for failing to object to the admission of the DNA evidence. He argued that there were a number of foundational problems with the DNA evidence, and that if trial counsel had objected, the evidence would have been excluded or at least its importance diminished. He noted that because trial counsel "totally failed to challenge the DNA evidence in the case," counsel "failed to preserve valid issues for appeal." The state postconviction court denied relief and the Nevada Supreme Court affirmed.

Respondent thereafter filed this federal habeas petition, claiming there was insufficient evidence to convict him on the sexual assault charges and that the Nevada Supreme Court's rejection of his claim was both contrary to, and an unreasonable application of, *Jackson.* He did not bring a typical *Jackson* claim, however. Rather than argue that the totality of the evidence admitted against him at trial was constitutionally insufficient, he argued that some of the evidence should be excluded from the *Jackson* analysis. In particular, he argued that Romero's testimony related to the DNA evidence was inaccurate and unreliable in two primary respects: Romero mischaracterized the random match probability and misstated the probability of a DNA match among his brothers. Absent that testimony, he contended, there was insufficient evidence to convict him.

In support of his claim regarding the accuracy of Romero's testimony, respondent submitted a report prepared by Laurence Mueller, a professor in ecology and evolutionary biology (Mueller Report). The District Court supplemented the record with the Mueller Report, even though it was not presented to any state court, because "the thesis of the report was argued during post-conviction." ... Relying upon the Mueller Report, the District Court set aside the "unreliable DNA testimony" and held that without the DNA evidence "a reasonable doubt would exist in the mind of any rational trier of fact." The court granted respondent habeas relief on his *Jackson* claim.

The Ninth Circuit affirmed. The court held the Nevada Supreme Court had unreasonably applied *Jackson.* The Court of Appeals first reasoned "the admission of Romero's unreliable and misleading testimony violated Troy's due process rights," so the District Court was correct to exclude it. It then "weighed the sufficiency of the remaining evidence," including the District Court's "catalogu[e] [of] the numerous inconsistencies that would raise a reasonable doubt as to Troy's guilt in the mind of any rational juror." In light of the "stark" conflicts in the evidence and the State's concession that there was insufficient evidence absent the DNA evidence, the court held it was objectively unreasonable for the Nevada Supreme Court to reject respondent's insufficiency-of-the-evidence claim....

We granted certiorari to consider two questions: the proper standard of review for a *Jackson* claim on federal habeas, and whether such a claim may rely upon evidence outside the trial record that goes to the reliability of trial evidence.

II

Respondent's claim has now crystallized into a claim about the import of two specific inaccuracies in the testimony related to the DNA evidence, as indicated by the

Mueller Report. The Mueller Report does not challenge Romero's qualifications as an expert or the validity of any of the tests that she performed. Mueller instead contends that Romero committed the so-called "prosecutor's fallacy" and that she underestimated the probability of a DNA match between respondent and one of his brothers.

The prosecutor's fallacy is the assumption that the random match probability is the same as the probability that the defendant was not the source of the DNA sample. In other words, if a juror is told the probability a member of the general population would share the same DNA is 1 in 10,000 (random match probability), and he takes that to mean there is only a 1 in 10,000 chance that someone other than the defendant is the source of the DNA found at the crime scene (source probability), then he has succumbed to the prosecutor's fallacy. It is further error to equate source probability with probability of guilt, unless there is no explanation other than guilt for a person to be the source of crime-scene DNA. This faulty reasoning may result in an erroneous statement that, based on a random match probability of 1 in 10,000, there is a .01% chance the defendant is innocent or a 99.99% chance the defendant is guilty.

The Mueller Report does not dispute Romero's opinion that only 1 in 3,000,000 people would have the same DNA profile as the rapist. Mueller correctly points out, however, that some of Romero's testimony—as well as the prosecutor's argument—suggested that the evidence also established that there was only a .000033% chance that respondent was innocent. The State concedes as much. Brief for Petitioners 54. For example, the prosecutor argued at closing the jury could be "99.999967 percent sure" in this case. And when the prosecutor asked Romero, in a classic example of erroneously equating source probability with random match probability, whether "it [would] be fair to say ... that the chances that the DNA found in the panties—the semen in the panties—and the blood sample, the likelihood that it is not Troy Brown would be .000033," Romero ultimately agreed that it was "not inaccurate" to state it that way.

Looking at Romero's testimony as a whole, though, she also indicated that she was merely accepting the mathematical equivalence between 1 in 3,000,000 and the percentage figure. At the end of the colloquy about percentages, she answered affirmatively the court's question whether the percentage was "the same math just expressed differently." She pointed out that the probability a brother would match was greater than the random match probability, which also indicated to the jury that the random match probability is not the same as the likelihood that someone other than Troy was the source of the DNA.

The Mueller Report identifies a second error in Romero's testimony: her estimate of the probability that one or more of Troy's brothers' DNA would match. Romero testified there was a 1 in 6,500 (or .02%) probability that one brother would share the same DNA with another. When asked whether "that change[s] at all with two brothers," she answered no. According to Mueller, Romero's analysis was misleading in two respects. First, she used an assumption regarding the parents under which siblings have the lowest chance of matching that is biologically possible, but even under this stingy assumption she reported the chance of two brothers matching (1 in 6,500) as much lower than it is (1 in 1,024 under her assumption). Second, using the assumptions Mueller finds more appropriate, the probability of a single sibling matching respondent is 1 in 263, the probability that among two brothers one or more would match is 1 in 132, and among four brothers it is 1 in 66.

In sum, the two inaccuracies upon which this case turns are testimony equating random match probability with source probability, and an underestimate of the likelihood that one of Troy's brothers would also match the DNA left at the scene.

III

Although we granted certiorari to review respondent's *Jackson* claim, the parties now agree that the Court of Appeals' resolution of his claim under *Jackson* was in error. Indeed, respondent argues the Court of Appeals did not decide his case under *Jackson* at all, but instead resolved the question whether admission of Romero's inaccurate testimony rendered his trial fundamentally unfair and then applied *Jackson* to determine whether that error was harmless.

Although both petitioners and respondent are now aligned on the same side of the questions presented for our review, the case is not moot because "the parties continue to seek different relief" from this Court. *Pacific Bell Telephone Co. v. linkLine Communications, Inc.*, 555 U.S. 438 (2009). Respondent primarily argues that we affirm on his proposed alternative ground or remand to the Ninth Circuit for analysis of his due process claim under the standard for harmless error of *Brecht v. Abrahamson*, 507 U.S. 619 (1993). The State, on the other hand, asks us to reverse....

Respondent no longer argues it was proper for the District Court to admit the Mueller Report for the purpose of evaluating his *Jackson* claim, and concedes the "purpose of a *Jackson* analysis is to determine whether the jury acted in a rational manner in returning a guilty verdict based on the evidence before it, not whether improper evidence violated due process." There has been no suggestion that the evidence adduced at trial was insufficient to convict unless some of it was excluded. Respondent's concession thus disposes of his *Jackson* claim. The concession is also clearly correct. An "appellate court's reversal for insufficiency of the evidence is in effect a determination that the government's case against the defendant was so lacking that the trial court should have entered a judgment of acquittal." *Lockhart v. Nelson*, 488 U.S. 33, 39 (1988). Because reversal for insufficiency of the evidence is equivalent to a judgment of acquittal, such a reversal bars a retrial. See *Burks v. United States*, 437 U.S. 1, 18 (1978). To "make the analogy complete" between a reversal for insufficiency of the evidence and the trial court's granting a judgment of acquittal, *Lockhart*, 488 U.S., at 42, "a reviewing court must consider all of the evidence admitted by the trial court," regardless whether that evidence was admitted erroneously.

Respondent therefore correctly concedes that a reviewing court must consider all of the evidence admitted at trial when considering a *Jackson* claim. Even if we set that concession aside, however, and assume that the Court of Appeals could have considered the Mueller Report in the context of a *Jackson* claim, the court made an egregious error in concluding the Nevada Supreme Court's rejection of respondent's insufficiency-of-the-evidence claim "involved an unreasonable application of . . . clearly established Federal law."

Even if the Court of Appeals could have considered it, the Mueller Report provided no warrant for entirely excluding the DNA evidence or Romero's testimony from that court's consideration. The Report did not contest that the DNA evidence matched Troy. That DNA evidence remains powerful inculpatory evidence even though the State concedes Romero overstated its probative value by failing to dispel the prosecutor's fallacy. And Mueller's claim that Romero used faulty assumptions and underestimated the probability of a DNA match between brothers indicates that two experts do not agree with one another, not that Romero's estimates were unreliable.

Mueller's opinion that "the chance that among four brothers one or more would match is 1 in 66," is substantially different from Romero's estimate of a 1 in 6,500 chance that one brother would match. But even if Romero's estimate is wrong, our confidence in the jury verdict is not undermined. First, the estimate that is more pertinent to this case is 1 in 132—the probability of a match among two brothers—because two of Troy's four brothers lived in Utah. Second, although Jane Doe mentioned Trent as her assailant, and Travis lived in a nearby trailer, the evidence indicates that both (unlike Troy) were sober and went to bed early on the night of the crime. Even under Mueller's odds, a rational jury could consider the DNA evidence to be powerful evidence of guilt.

Furthermore, the Court of Appeals' discussion of the non-DNA evidence departed from the deferential review that *Jackson* and § 2254(d)(1) demand. A federal habeas court can only set aside a state-court decision as "an unreasonable application of . . . clearly established Federal law," § 2254(d)(1), if the state court's application of that law is "objectively unreasonable," *Williams v. Taylor*, 529 U.S. 362, 409 (2000). And *Jackson* requires a reviewing court to review the evidence "in the light most favorable to the prosecution." Expressed more fully, this means a reviewing court "faced with a record of historical facts that supports conflicting inferences must presume—even if it does not affirmatively appear in the record—that the trier of fact resolved any such conflicts in favor of the prosecution, and must defer to that resolution." The Court of Appeals acknowledged that it must review the evidence in the light most favorable to the prosecution, but the court's recitation of inconsistencies in the testimony shows it failed to do that.

For example, the court highlights conflicting testimony regarding when Troy left the Peacock. It is true that if a juror were to accept the testimony of one bartender that Troy left the bar at 1:30 a.m., then Troy would have left the bar after the attack occurred. Yet the jury could have credited a different bartender's testimony that Troy left the Peacock at around 12:15 a.m. Resolving the conflict in favor of the prosecution, the jury must have found that Troy left the bar in time to be the assailant. It is undisputed that Troy washed his clothes immediately upon returning home. The court notes this is "plausibly consistent with him being the assailant" but also that he provided an alternative reason for washing his clothes. Viewed in the light most favorable to the prosecution, the evidence supports an inference that Troy washed the clothes immediately to clean blood from them.

To be sure, the court's *Jackson* analysis relied substantially upon a concession made by the State in state postconviction proceedings that "absent the DNA findings, there was insufficient evidence to convict [Troy] of the crime." But that concession posited a situation in which there was no DNA evidence at all, not a situation in which some pieces of testimony regarding the DNA evidence were called into question. In sum, the Court of Appeals' analysis failed to preserve "the factfinder's role as weigher of the evidence" by reviewing "*all of the evidence* ... in the light most favorable to the prosecution," *Jackson,* at 319, and it further erred in finding that the Nevada Supreme Court's resolution of the ... claim was objectively unreasonable.

IV

Resolution of the *Jackson* claim does not end our consideration of this case because respondent asks us to affirm on an alternative ground. He contends the two errors "in describing the statistical meaning" of the DNA evidence rendered his trial fundamentally unfair and denied him due process of law. Because the Ninth Circuit held that "the admission of Romero's unreliable and misleading testimony violated [respondent's] due process rights," and in respondent's view merely applied *Jackson* (erroneously) to determine whether that error was harmless, he asks us to affirm the judgment below on the basis of what he calls his "DNA due process" claim.

As respondent acknowledges, in order to prevail on this claim, he would have to show that the state court's adjudication of the claim was "contrary to, or involved an unreasonable application of, clearly established Federal law." 28 U.S.C. § 2254(d)(1). The clearly established law he points us to is *Manson v. Brathwaite,* 432 U.S. 98, 114 (1977), in which we held that when the police have used a suggestive eyewitness identification procedure, "reliability is the linchpin in determining" whether an eyewitness identification may be admissible, with reliability determined according to factors set out in *Neil v. Biggers,* 409 U.S. 188 (1972). Respondent argues that the admission of the inaccurate DNA testimony violated *Brathwaite* because the testimony was "identification testimony," was "unnecessarily suggestive," and was unreliable.

Respondent has forfeited this claim, which he makes for the very first time in his brief on the merits in this Court. Respondent did not present his new "DNA due process" claim in his federal habeas petition, but instead consistently argued that Romero's testimony should be excluded from the *Jackson* analysis simply because it was "unreliable" and that the due process violation occurred because the remaining evidence was insufficient to convict. In the Ninth Circuit, too, respondent presented only his *Jackson* claim, and it is, at the least, unclear whether respondent presented his newly minted due process claim in the state courts. Recognizing that his *Jackson* claim cannot prevail, respondent tries to rewrite his federal habeas petition. His attempt comes too late, however, and he cannot now start over....

We have stated before that "DNA testing can provide powerful new evidence unlike anything known before." *District Attorney's Office for Third Judicial Dist. v. Osborne,*

557 U.S. 52, (2009). Given the persuasiveness of such evidence in the eyes of the jury, it is important that it be presented in a fair and reliable manner. The State acknowledges that Romero committed the prosecutor's fallacy and the Mueller Report suggests that Romero's testimony may have been inaccurate regarding the likelihood of a match with one of respondent's brothers. Regardless, ample DNA and non-DNA evidence in the record adduced at trial supported the jury's guilty verdict under *Jackson,* and we reject respondent's last minute attempt to recast his claim under *Brathwaite.* The Court of Appeals did not consider, however, the ineffective-assistance claims on which the District Court also granted respondent habeas relief ... [and so] the case is remanded for further proceedings consistent with this opinion.

Notes and Questions

1. In modern DNA analysis, PCR/STR with the commonly-used 13 loci, often results in matches with RMPs numbering in the millions, billions, or even trillions. William C. Thompson, Laurence D. Mueller & Dan E. Krane, *Forensic DNA Statistics: Still Controversial in Some Cases*, Champion, Dec. 2012, at 12 (stating "random match probabilities of one in billions, trillions, or even quadrillions and quintillions are typical ..."). If so, the probative value of the DNA evidence is more likely to be weakened by attacking the collection, processing, or management of the samples, what Kaye calls "production-line problems." David H. Kaye, The Double Helix and the Law of Evidence 257 (2011).

   In the *Gold Standard* article, we see some examples of contamination errors resulting in mismatch. After detailing these concerns, Professor Thompson makes some suggestions on how to respond. Do you find these suggestions adequate to react to the problems identified? Which of the suggestions seems more likely to limit future error? On the other hand, are any of these suggestions unlikely to help?

2. Considering that RMP and lab error considerations both go to the issue of probative value of "match" evidence, it could be tempting to mix the issues. Yet even with that facial similarity, lab error and RMP must remain separate considerations. In *People v. Reeves*, the defendant claimed that RMP calculations must necessarily be modified to take into account lab error rates, since lab error is so much more likely to contribute to erroneous identification than random chance, especially when there are very low RMPs. 109 Cal. Rptr. 2d 728 (2001). The court concluded that mixing these considerations was against the weight of scientific opinion, citing the National Research Council's 1996 report and its rejection of combining the two considerations. *Id.* at 751 (*citing* National Research Council, National Academy of Sciences, The Evaluation of Forensic DNA Evidence 85–7 (1996)). In essence, lab error rates are uncertain, and RMP simply measures something different: the value of a match, considering the allele patterns in the samples. Finding that the two should not be mixed, *Reeves* concluded by noting that nothing precludes consideration of both considerations in any specific case.

3. The DNA analyst in *McDaniel* made two critical errors in presentation of the DNA evidence in that case: 1) she embraced the "prosecutor's fallacy" when she

affirmed the prosecutor's misuse of the RMP as the likelihood of innocence and 2) she misstated the probability of a DNA match with the brothers of the accused. Yet despite these clear errors, Defendant Brown is not granted any relief by the Nevada state courts or the federal courts in his habeas action. What is the obstacle to granting a remedy here, or how is it possible that these claims—which everyone agrees show factual inaccuracies—never merit relief?

Federal *habeas corpus* law is a complex area of criminal procedure, one meriting its own upper-division course to cover adequately. Yet even a surface-level familiarity with it from *McDaniel* reveals its failure to provide relief remedies to claimants with clear factual errors at trial. There are reasons for this stingy approach to relief, yet we must ask: are they valid in light of the enormous power of DNA evidence? Is DNA different enough to merit separate and more lenient standards for relief? Since 1989, the Innocence Project has used DNA evidence to exonerate over 350 convicted offenders, many from death row.[30] This is not just an academic distinction, rather it has real-world implications for many prisoners convicted of serious crimes.

Tying It Together

The Lucky 8 Motor Lodge had been the location of several crimes before but never a violent crime until now. Everything changed on the morning of August 31, 2010, when the housekeeping staff discovered a body in Room 237. After they called 9-1-1, the Polk City Police arrived within minutes and discovered a grisly scene of murder. The victim, a 32-year-old woman named Victoria Vasquez, had been bound and gagged, sexually assaulted, then strangled. Even the hardened Polk City Police CSI team found the scene particularly disturbing.

At the scene, CSI technicians collected DNA samples from the victim's body and from the bedspread on which the victim was found. Each sample was placed in a storage tube and separately marked with the identification of the CSI tech who collected the sample, the location of the sample, and the date of collection.

Back at the crime lab, forensic DNA specialist Martin Espinosa has been assigned the case. Espinosa has been a DNA technician at the Polk City crime lab since 1982, and the supervisor of the lab since 2010. A copy of his *Curriculum Vitae* is in Appendix B at the end of this book. Upon receiving the samples from the Lucky 8 Motor Lodge homicide, Espinosa decided to analyze the samples using PCR/STR analysis. However, without a known sample to compare the samples to, the tests would be of limited use (and would only provide a DNA profile of the murderer, but no more).

It took several years of police work and a lucky break to solve the Vasquez murder. In the summer and fall of 2010, the police catalogued any man who could have been the source of the DNA at the crime scene using employment records, hotel records,

---

30. INNOCENCE PROJECT, https://www.innocenceproject.org/dna-exonerations-in-the-united-states/ (last visited July 21, 2018) (detailing demographics and facts about the project's many exonerations).

surveillance tape, and eyewitness interviews. Yet after identifying a group of forty-four possible suspects, the case went cold. That changed on the evening of September 4, 2013.

That night Polk City Police received a 9-1-1 call from a panicked guest at the Elm Street Budget Hotel. The caller reported screaming, loud thuds against the wall, and other odd sounds in room Room 237 next door. Polk City police responded immediately, arriving within 60 seconds and just in time to observe a man walk out of Room 237 toward a grey Ford Focus. Officer Cortez immediately arrested the man, Donald Douglass, and other officers quickly found an unconscious woman in Room 237. She had been beaten and required a long stay in the hospital, but eventually did recuperate. Back at the station, Douglass stated that he had been in an argument in Room 237, heard sirens on Elm Street so left, but that he had never been in Polk City before. After those statements, he asked for a lawyer.

It turns out that Donald Douglass was one of the twenty men on the "suspects list" for the Vasquez homicide, because a car registered to him had been seen at the Lodge that night. Until now, the police had no further leads to implicate Douglass.

Because of the similarities of the Elm Street Budget Hotel and Lucky 8 Motor Lodge events, and that Douglass's car was at the scene of the homicide, the Polk City Police received a court order to take a DNA swab from Douglass. Martin Espinosa personally took the sample, and then returned to the crime lab to test the sample against the two samples from the Lucky 8 Motor Lodge. When he does, he declares that the samples match. The sample from the victim's body showed a match with a random match probability for Caucasian men of 1 in 100 billion, while the sample from the bedspread, due to degradation of the sample, matched at an RMP of 1 in 40,000. Based on the DNA evidence, Donald Douglass was charged, tried, and convicted of the murder of Victoria Vasquez.

Only after the murder trial does the Vasquez family discover that Douglass is heir to a large fortune. They retain your firm, Plaintiffs 'R' Us, as counsel in the case, and soon they file a wrongful death lawsuit in the U.S. District Court for the Southern District of Polk. Judge Chen has entered a scheduling order, accepting the stipulation of the parties that all experts in the case must be disclosed as "retained or specially employed" experts under Rule 26(a)(2)(B), and that the Plaintiffs must file all fact and expert disclosures within thirty days.

Paula Partner has called you into her office at Plaintiffs 'R' Us to discuss the *Vasquez v. Douglass* case. She has decided that since she is in trial next week, it will be your job to complete the disclosures. In fact, Paula says, the disclosures are complete except for the endorsement of Martin Espinosa. She reminds you that Espinosa is to receive payment of $125 an hour for his time preparing for, and testifying in, the case, on behalf of the Plaintiffs.

Assignment: Please draft the Rule 26 endorsement for Espinosa, including all appropriate details required by the Rules of Civil Procedure and Rules of Evidence.

Chapter 6

Fingerprint Comparison

DNA's unique combination of scientific testing and evidentiary force has led the National Academy of Sciences to single it out as the quintessential forensic tool when compared to other methods: "*With the exception of nuclear DNA analysis*, however, no forensic method has been rigorously shown to have the capacity to consistently, and with a high degree of certainty, demonstrate a connection between evidence and a specific individual or source."[31] So while it has the potential for error, as discussed in detail in Chapter 5, the reliability of DNA is firmly rooted in scientific research.

As we begin to evaluate other disciplines, we must consider how these other fields base their reliability on something else, often but not exclusively on the training and experience of the testifying expert. Our first foray into those fields will be with fingerprint analysis. Recent scholarship traces the development of the field to the turn of the last century, with the first use in a civil case in Argentina in 1892 and in the United States in 1904.[32] The first American case affirming admission of fingerprint evidence, *People v. Jennings*, occurred in 1911 in Illinois, and within a short span of time almost all jurisdictions had accepted it.[33] Faigman and his coauthors comment "[t]hat swiftness is somewhat surprising considering that fingerprint identification presented the courts with a claim that was still novel (infinite and absolute individualization) in a remarkably strong form (infallibility); and rapid considering the recent shortcomings and abandonment of anthropometry,[34] the first child of scientific attempts at individualization."[35] During this period, the official FBI handbook on fingerprint analysis shows unshakable confidence in the technique: "Of all the methods of identification, fingerprinting alone has proved to be both infallible and feasible."[36]

Why then did the courts so quickly and unequivocally accept fingerprint evidence, and is the FBI's confidence in the technique justified? To explore those issues, we will

---

31. NATIONAL RESEARCH COUNCIL, NATIONAL ACADEMY OF SCIENCES, STRENGTHENING FORENSIC SCIENCE IN THE UNITED STATES: A PATH FORWARD 7 (2009) (emphasis added).

32. Lyn Haber & Ralph Norman Haber, *Scientific Validation of Fingerprint Evidence Under* Daubert, 7 LAW, PROBABILITY & RISK 87, 87 (2008) (*citing* SIMON COLE, SUSPECT IDENTITIES: A HISTORY OF FINGERPRINTING AND CRIMINAL IDENTIFICATION (2001)).

33. DAVID L. FAIGMAN ET AL., MODERN SCIENTIFIC EVIDENCE: FORENSICS § 32.2, at 421 & 421 n. 4 (2016).

34. *Id.* at § 32.2, at 421 & 421 n. 3 (noting "Anthropometry ... developed in the early 1880s by Alphone Bertillon ... relied on the measurements of 11 different physical features of prisoners....").

35. *Id.* at § 32.2, at 420–21.

36. FED. BUREAU OF INVESTIGATION, U.S. DEP'T OF JUST., THE SCIENCE OF FINGERPRINTS: CLASSIFICATION AND USES iv (1985).

first look at some foundational materials on the methodology of fingerprint analysis in order to understand how examiners make individual identifications. We will read cases from the period of unquestioning acceptance of fingerprint comparison to see why courts invariably admitted expert testimony on the technique. Afterward, we need to consider the mandate of *Daubert*—to rigorously evaluate the underpinnings of the claimed expertise to decide if it is "good science"—and see how courts weigh the scientific foundation of fingerprint identification evidence. We will finish with a discussion of the current state of affairs, considering the National Academy of Sciences Report, *A Path Forward,* and current efforts to add foundational research to the field. As with the chapter on DNA, the focus here is not on being able to personally perform the comparison of samples, but instead to understand how the science is used—and sometimes misused—in litigation.

A. An Introduction to the Methodology and Controversies of Fingerprint Comparison Evidence

Robert Epstein, *Fingerprints Meet* Daubert: *The Myth of Fingerprint "Science" Is Revealed*

75 S. Cal. L. Rev. 605 (2002)

I. INTRODUCTION

For the past ninety years, law enforcement fingerprint examiners have been matching partial latent fingerprint fragments detected at crime scenes to inked fingerprints taken directly from suspects. In many, if not most of these cases, the fingerprint identifications have been seen as dispositive of the defendant's guilt. From the very outset, law enforcement has claimed that latent fingerprint identification is a science. Over the years, this claim has achieved almost universal acceptance.[3] Recently, however, some of the leading voices in the forensic science community have begun to question the scientific foundation of the fingerprint field and suggest that latent fingerprint identifications may not be nearly as reliable as people have long assumed. Indeed, some commentators have even gone so far as to suggest that fingerprint experts are vulnerable to challenge pursuant to the Supreme Court's seminal decision in *Daubert v. Merrell Dow Pharmaceuticals, Inc.* Defense attorneys have started to pick up on these suggestions. To date, there have been at least ten *Daubert* challenges filed in federal courts seeking to preclude fingerprint examiners from testifying....

---

3. A survey, for example, of 978 jurors revealed that 93% of them believed that fingerprint identification is a science....

II. THE BASICS OF LATENT FINGERPRINT
IDENTIFICATION EVIDENCE

Fingerprints are impressions of the ridged skin surface of the fingers and palm. Fingerprint identifications in criminal cases are typically made from small distorted fingerprint fragments detected at crime scenes. These fragments are commonly referred to as "latent fingerprints." The Department of Justice has recently suggested that the average size of a latent fingerprint fragment is only one-fifth the size of a full fingerprint. After a latent fragment is detected at a crime scene, it is then compared by a fingerprint examiner with inked or digitally scanned fingerprints taken directly from a suspect's fingers. An examiner makes an identification if he or she believes there is a sufficient number of common "ridge characteristics," both in terms of type and location, between the latent and inked print under comparison. The ridge characteristics are points along the ridge path where something dramatic occurs: For example, the ridge might come to an end or bifurcate into two ridges.

An average human fingerprint contains between seventy-five and 175 ridge characteristics. These ridge characteristics generally consist of a few different types, although there is no standard agreement among fingerprint examiners as to either the precise number or nomenclature of the different characteristics. The ridge characteristics most commonly referred to are: 1) islands, also referred to as dots, which are single independent ridge units; 2) short ridges, in which both ends of the ridge are readily observable; 3) ridge endings, where a ridge comes to an abrupt end; 4) bifurcations, in which a ridge forks into two; 5) enclosures, which are formed by two bifurcations that face each other; 6) spurs, where the ridge divides and one branch comes to an end; and 7) crossovers, in which a short ridge crosses from one ridge to the next. Illustrations of these various characteristics are provided in the following box.

RIDGE ENDING	
BIFURCATION	
SHORT RIDGE	
DOT OR ISLAND	
ENCLOSURE	
SPUR	
CROSSOVER	

While some occasional research has been conducted with respect to the relative frequencies with which these and other characteristics occur, no weighted measures of the characteristics have ever been adopted by fingerprint examiners on the basis of these studies. Research, moreover, has shown that different fingerprint examiners hold widely varying opinions regarding which characteristics appear most commonly.

All prints, both inked and latent, are subject to various types of distortions and artifacts. The most common is pressure distortion, which occurs when the print is being deposited. Other types of distortion can be caused by the shape of the surface on which the print has been deposited and by the media used to develop and lift the print. Significantly, distortion can cause a ridge characteristic to appear as something other than what it really is. For example, powder used to develop a latent print may cause a ridge ending to appear as a bifurcation. No study has been conducted to determine the frequency with which such distortions occur.

Latent fingerprint fragments found at crime scenes are often very distorted. Given the limited size of these latent prints, and given the amount of distortion that many latent prints suffer, fingerprint examiners often are in the position of making identifications on the basis of fifteen or fewer visible ridge characteristics.

... [T]here is considerable disagreement among fingerprint examiners as to how many common ridge characteristics should be found before an identification is made. Examiners historically have employed identification standards ranging from between eight and sixteen matching characteristics, or "points of similarity." Many examiners, however, including those at the FBI, currently believe that there should be no minimum standard whatsoever and that the determination of whether there is a sufficient basis for an identification should be left to the subjective judgment of the individual examiner.

It has been well documented that fingerprints from different people can share a limited number of ridge characteristics in common. Israeli fingerprint examiners, for example, have found fingerprints from two different people that contain seven matching ridge characteristics. As these examiners candidly acknowledge, "an expert with many years of experience behind him" could make a false identification when comparing two such prints.[30] No scientific study has been performed that reasonably indicates the probabilities of fingerprints from different people having varying numbers of matching ridge characteristics.

Lacking any such probability studies, latent print examiners do not offer opinions of identification in terms of probability. Indeed, latent print examiners are prohibited from doing so by the rules of their primary professional association, the International Association for Identification ("IAI"). Instead, latent print examiners make the claim of "absolute certainty" for their identifications.[33] In other words, examiners opine

---

30. Y. Mark & D. Attias, *What Is the Minimum Standard of Characteristics for Fingerprint Identification?*, 22 FINGERPRINT WHORLD 148, 150 (Oct. 1996).

33. David L. Grieve, *Possession of Truth*, 46 J. FORENSIC IDENTIFICATION 521, 527-28 (1996). Examiners have historically been taught that they are testifying not to their opinions, but to scientific fact that cannot be properly contradicted.... Examiners are still being taught the same lesson today....

that the latent print at issue was made by a particular finger to the exclusion of all other fingers in the world. But, fingerprint examiners themselves have recognized that such assertions of absolute certainty are inherently unscientific. For example, one leading law enforcement fingerprint examiner has noted:

> [I]mposing deductive conclusions of absolute certainty upon the results of an essentially inductive process is a futile attempt to force the square peg into the round hole.... [T]his categorical requirement of absolute certainty has no particular scientific principle but has evolved from a practice shaped more from allegiance to dogma than a foundation in science. Once begun, the assumption of absolute certainty as the only possible conclusion has been maintained by a system of societal indoctrination, not reason, and has achieved such a ritualistic sanctity that even mild suggestions that its premise should be re-examined are instantly regarded as acts of blasphemy. Whatever this may be, it is not science.[35]

The notion that a latent fingerprint fragment can be identified to the exclusion of all other fingers in the world stems from the fingerprint field's basic premise that no two people in the world have the same fingerprints. But, as discussed further below, this is a premise that, though fervently subscribed to by all fingerprint examiners, has never been scientifically established. Even assuming, moreover, that it is true that no two people in the world have the same fingerprint, this premise is logically flawed when it comes to the identification of latent fingerprint fragments. It simply does not follow from that premise that a fingerprint examiner can reliably make an identification from a small distorted fingerprint fragment that might reveal only a small number of ridge characteristics. As discussed above, fingerprints from different people can have a limited number of characteristics that appear to match. Furthermore, fingerprint examiners in making their comparisons must rely on the "naked eye ... along with their judgment to decide when two things are alike or different." Thus, even if all fingerprints are in some sense unique, the undisputable reality remains that fingerprint examiners sometimes make false identifications. Accordingly, the fundamental question in fingerprint analysis is one of reliability, not uniqueness....

Lyn Haber & Ralph Norman Haber, *Scientific Validation of Fingerprint Evidence under* Daubert
7 LAW, PROBABILITY & RISK 87 (2008)

2. The ACE-V method

Fingerprint examiners argue that there are unique and permanent combinations of features on the skin of fingers (and palms and feet, though we confine ourselves in this article to fingers). Further, they argue that images of these patterns (called

---

35. *Id.*

fingerprints) can be used to individuate people by the proper application of a comparison method. When a perpetrator of a crime touches a surface with a finger and leaves an image of the unique pattern from that finger (called a latent fingerprint), that latent fingerprint image can be found, lifted and compared to the images of the fingers of a suspect (called exemplar fingerprints, and usually recorded by a trained technician on a 10-print card). Following a method of fingerprint comparison such as the ACE-V, and depending on the examiner's training and experience in the comparison method, the examiner can offer an opinion about ground truth: whether the crime scene latent fingerprint was made by the suspect or by someone else.

The FBI claims in *Daubert* hearings that all examiners now use the ACE-V method to make these conclusions, and that there are no other methods in use by fingerprint examiners today. Ashbaugh makes a similar claim. Although alternative methods are mentioned in textbooks, practicing examiners uniformly refer to the fingerprint comparison method they employ as the ACE-V. Therefore, we restrict our discussion to evidence for the validity of the ACE-V method.

2.1 A Description of ACE-V

Because the ACE-V method may not be familiar to some readers outside the fingerprint profession, we provide a brief overview. However, neither the International Association for Identification (IAI) as the professional organization of fingerprint examiners, the FBI, nor any other professional fingerprint organization has provided an official description of the ACE-V method, so our description is based on the most detailed of the published sources.

Huber first described the structure of this method, which he applied to every forensic identification discipline, but without suggesting a name. The classic FBI Science of Fingerprints (1958, 1988) contains only a few pages on comparison procedures, but neither refers to that method as ACE-V nor distinguishes among its different steps. Ashbaugh provides much more detail and examples, in what has become the most influential textbook available....

What follows is a theoretical description, distilled primarily from the authors cited above, and from our own training in IAI-sponsored latent fingerprint courses. We know from examiner testimony offered in *Daubert* hearings and in trials involving testimony from fingerprint examiners that most practicing fingerprint examiners deviate from this description. (We consider below the implications of the facts that there is no agreed-upon description of the ACE-V method in the fingerprint profession, no professional body has approved any one description as the official ACE-V method and that individual examiners vary in their practice.)

2.1.1 Analysis stage.

The analysis stage begins when a fingerprint examiner looks at a latent fingerprint and decides whether it contains sufficient quantity and quality of detail so that it exceeds the standard for value. If the quantity and quality of detail do exceed the value standard, then the examiner continues the analysis. If the value decision is negative, the latent fingerprint is not used further. The majority of latent prints found at crime scenes are rejected as of no value.

If the fingerprint examiner continues analysis of the latent print (he has not yet seen the suspect's exemplar prints), he uses the physical evidence contained in the latent print and that produced by the crime scene investigation to determine which finger made the print, the nature of the surface on which it was deposited, the amount and direction of pressure used in the touch and the matrix (such as sweat) in which the ridge details of the finger were transferred onto the surface. This analysis is necessary to specify each of the sources of distortion in the latent print that causes the inevitable differences between the latent fingerprint and the patterns of features found on the skin (and on the exemplar image).

The examiner then chooses one feature-rich area of the latent print (preferably near a core or delta). Within this area, he selects the particular features along the various ridge paths in the latent print, in their spatial locations relative to one another, to use to start the comparison between the crime scene latent and the suspect's exemplar prints.

2.1.2 Comparison stage.

In the comparison stage, for the first time, the examiner looks at the suspect's 10 exemplar fingerprints. He starts with the most likely finger of the exemplar image, based on what he found during the analysis of the latent print. The examiner goes to the same area of the suspect fingerprint that he had selected in the latent print to determine whether the same patterning of features occurs. If it does not, the examiner concludes that that finger of the suspect cannot be the finger which made the latent print: an exclusion of that finger. He then goes to the next finger of the exemplar image, and repeats this process. If all 10 fingers can be excluded as the source of the crime scene latent print, the examiner excludes the suspect as the donor.

If the same pattern of features initially noted in the latent print is found in the corresponding area of one of the suspect's exemplar prints, the examiner goes back to the latent print, selects another area and locates the features there and their relative positions to each other. Then the exemplar is again examined in the new area to determine whether the corresponding features are also present. This latent-to-exemplar comparison (always in that order) continues until all the features in the latent print have been compared for agreement of features in corresponding locations in the suspect's exemplar. If substantial agreement is found, the examiner goes to the evaluation stage.

Throughout comparison, the examiner keeps track of every failure to find a correspondence between the latent and the suspect fingerprint. Any failure in agreement that cannot be accounted for by one of the distortions previously described and labelled in the analysis stage is a necessary and sufficient condition to exclude the suspect as the perpetrator with the application of the one unexplained discrepancy standard. The most common conclusion of the comparison stage is exclusion.

2.1.3 Evaluation stage.

In evaluation, the examiner applies a sufficiency standard to the amount of corresponding agreement between the latent and the exemplar that dictates his conclusion. If the amount of corresponding agreement exceeds the sufficiency standard, then the examiner concludes that the crime scene latent print can be individuated to the suspect. If the amount of agreement does not exceed the standard, then the conclusion is neither an individuation nor an exclusion—an inconclusive conclusion. Two kinds of sufficiency standards obtain. The first is numeric, in which the amount of agreement is stated as a number, and the threshold for sufficiency is determined by the profession or the crime laboratory. The second is experiential, based on the individual examiner's training and experience.

2.1.4 Verification stage.

Verification is employed in larger laboratories for cases in which an examiner has concluded individuation. A second examiner confirms the conclusion of the first. A verification standard describes the rules by which a verifier is selected, informed of the history of the latent print's comparisons and reports his findings, and how conflicting conclusions are resolved.

2.2 Scoring the accuracy of the four conclusions

In the overview of ACE-V presented above, the examiner has made four kinds of conclusions: value, exclusion, individuation or inconclusive. These are described in two reports by the Scientific Working Group on Friction Ridge Analysis, Study and Technology (SWGFAST). The classification of these four conclusions as either correct or incorrect requires knowledge of the ground truth. The accuracy of the method in reaching true conclusions or its converse, its error rate, is critical to admissibility under *Daubert*. We review here the meaning of correct or incorrect for each of the four conclusions. We then present the evidence for ACE-V accuracy with respect to these four conclusions.

2.2.1 Ground truth.

Ground truth is certain knowledge that the latent and an exemplar fingerprint came either from the same donor or from two different donors. Ground truth cannot be known in casework, and therefore, research using results from casework cannot be used to establish the validation of the method. In casework, the purpose of investigation, fingerprint comparison, indictment and trial is to find out as much as possible about ground truth. Neither the examiner's opinion nor the jury's verdict is ground truth, though both (or neither) may be consistent with it.

2.3 Classification of the four ACE-V conclusions

Table I shows the classification of each of the four conclusions as a function of a known ground truth.

Table 1: Classification of ACE-V Conclusions[Ed.]

Examiner's conclusion	Ground truth	
	Same donor	Different donor
No value	Missed individuation	Missed exclusion
Value + inconclusive	Missed individuation	Missed exclusion
Value + exclusion	Erroneous exclusion	Correct exclusion
Value + individuation	Correct individuation	Erroneous individuation

Consider the first two lines of Table 1. The no value and the inconclusive conclusions always miss the correct answer. Whether the prints came from one donor or from two, neither of these conclusions agree with ground truth. When an examiner reaches either of these conclusions, either an innocent suspect still remains at risk of indictment and conviction or a guilty perpetrator still remains at large.

Consider the last two lines of Table 1. The exclusion conclusion is correct when the two prints are from two different donors (and an innocent suspect is released from suspicion), and erroneous when the same donor made both prints (and a guilty perpetrator remains at large). The individuation conclusion is correct when one donor made both fingerprints (and indictment and conviction of the perpetrator are likely), and erroneous when two different donors made the two fingerprints (and an innocent suspect is at risk of indictment and conviction)....

Notes and Questions

1. Both Epstein and Haber & Haber make clear that the job of a fingerprint examiner is a straightforward assessment of the similarities and differences between a known and unknown print, to find areas of similarity and difference. Significant unexplained differences can result in an "exclusion" where the unknown print is found to not be from the known source. However, even if the technique is straightforward, when will a technician be able to claim there is a "match"? What standards exist to decide when the two prints are "close enough" to say the known source created the unknown print?

2. Fingerprint examination requires a visual inspection of the distinct characteristics of the unknown and known prints, using the naked eye. To get a sense of the type of characteristics they are looking for, a quick video segment (six minutes) provides additional perspective on their work:

    – https://www.youtube.com/watch?v=IrpTqKkgygA

    In this example, we can see how the ideal technique will work: because the two fingerprints are clear and have many points of similarity, a "match" can be declared. However, as Epstein and Haber & Haber make clear, latent fingerprints

---

[Ed.] Table 1 has been moved by the Author for clarity purposes.

in the field are not often done under ideal settings. They can be partial prints—the Justice Department study cited by Epstein says latent prints average size is 20% of a whole print—or there can be distortion, which affect the print quality but also can be used to explain incongruities.

3. As we begin to consider judicial evaluation of fingerprint comparisons, keep in mind the amount of subjective judgment of the examiner involved in each stage of the analysis.

B. Long-Standing Admission of Fingerprint Comparison in Court

People v. Jennings

96 N.E. 1077 (Ill. 1911)

CARTER, C.J.

Plaintiff in error, Thomas Jennings, was found guilty in the criminal court of Cook county of the murder of Clarence B. Hiller, the jury fixing the penalty at death.... This writ of error is sued out to review the record in that case.

The errors assigned are in reference to two questions: First, the introduction of evidence of other ... offenses ... by plaintiff ...; and second, the admission of evidence as to finger prints.

At the time of the murder, September 19, 1910, Clarence B. Hiller, with his wife and four children, lived in a two-story frame house facing north on West 104th street, just east of Waldon parkway, in Chicago. Immediately west of Waldon parkway, which runs north and south, and separated from the street by a wire fence, are the suburban tracks of the Chicago, Rock Island & Pacific Railway Company. East of the Hiller house was a vacant lot, and east of that was the residence of a family named Pickens. South of the Hiller house was a vacant space, beyond which were two houses facing west on Waldon parkway, the southern one being occupied by the McNabb family. The north or front door of the Hiller house leads into a hallway on the east side of the house and from the south end or rear of this hallway a stairway leads up to the second floor. The south bedroom nearest the head of the stairs was occupied by the daughter Florence, 10 years of age. Then came the bedroom of the daughter Clarice, 15 years of age, and at the north or front end of the second floor was a bedroom occupied by Mr. and Mrs. Hiller and the two younger children. At the head of the stairs, near the door leading to Florence's room, a gas light was kept burning at night. Shortly after 2 o'clock on Monday morning of September 19, 1910, Mrs. Hiller was awakened and noticed that this light was out. She called her husband's attention to the fact and he went in his night clothes to the head of the stairway, where he encountered an intruder, with whom he grappled, and in the struggle both fell to the foot of the stairway, where Hiller was shot twice, dying in a few moments. Just a little before the shooting the daughter Clarice had seen the form of a man at her doorway holding a lighted match by his body, but not so as to show his face. As it was the practice of her father to get up and see if the children were all right in the night she was not frightened. The form disappeared from her doorway, and she heard footsteps shuffling toward the room of her sister Florence, after which she heard a little sound made by Florence. She next heard her father going through the hallway. Then came the struggle and the shooting. Florence was awakened by somebody on her bed whom she supposed was her little brother, and she asked, 'Is that you, Gerald?' No reply being made, she asked, 'Who is this?' and a man's voice—not her father's—answered, 'It is me.' She testified that she tried to scream but was unable to do so; that the man pushed up her nightgown and felt of her bare limbs and body; that he also placed his prickly cheek upon her face and moved about in various ways upon the bed. The stranger then hurried out and met the father. The Pickens family were awakened by the screams of Mrs. Hiller and her children, and the father, John C. Pickens, partially dressed and ran to the Hiller house. He reached there at about the same time as his son, Oliver Pickens, and Officer Beardsley. The son had been visiting friends on the north side in Chicago and had left the train at the suburban station, about a block away, and was walking towards home when he heard the screams from the Hiller house and ran there, meeting a police officer, Floyd Beardsley, who had also heard the screams and was searching for the cause. They were let in by the daughter Clarice, and found the body of Mr. Hiller lying near the bottom of the stairway, his nightgown saturated with blood. The shooting occurred about 2:25 a.m. The witnesses who reached the house shortly after found three revolver cartridges undischarged and two leaden slugs. Neither of the shots fired had lodged in the body of the deceased, one entering the upper part of the left arm and passing out through the shoulder and neck, and the other entering the right breast and passing out through the lung and heart. Shortly thereafter Mrs. Pickens, going upstairs to get a cover for the body, found particles of sand and gravel on Florence's bed near the foot.

About three-quarters of a mile east of the Hiller house is Vincennes road, running southerly, with a slight inclination to the west, and which is occupied by a street car line. This street is intersected at 103d street by the tracks of the Panhandle railroad, which run southerly, with a slight inclination to the east. The street car line connects with the Chicago City Railway system at Seventy-Ninth street, and extends in a southerly direction from 103d street through Blue Island to Harvey, about 8 1/2 miles south of 103d street. On the west of Vincennes road, at 103d street, is a crossing gate. Early in the morning on which the murder occurred, four police officers, who shortly before had gone off duty in that neighborhood, were sitting on a bench just north of the gate, waiting for a north-bound street car. The gate was up, so that the officers were not easily seen by one approaching from the south. About 2:38 a. m., Jennings approached the place from the south. The officers spoke to him, and he continued walking for a few steps with his right hand in his trousers pocket, holding a loaded revolver. They searched him and took the weapon away. They did not know at this time of the murder. Jennings was perspiring, and the officers testified that fresh blood appeared at different places on his clothing. About three inches above his left wrist they found a slight wound, fresh and bleeding slightly. Jennings told the policemen that the blood came from a wound on his left little finger, received from falling off the street car at Seventy-Ninth street the evening before, when he was on his way to Harvey. Dr. Clement, who examined Jennings about half-past 3 that morning at the police station, found the wound on the little finger scabbed over and not of recent origin. He also found the wound on the left arm fresh and bleeding, clean cut, with recent blood coming from it, not coagulated. The doctor testified that it looked like a bullet wound and not like an injury received from falling off a street car. Dr. Springer also examined Jennings, and his testimony, so far as it covered the same ground, was practically to the same effect. It was testified that the holes in the sleeves of the shirts, which were introduced in evidence as exhibits, were continuous with this fresh cut in the arm. The officers took Jennings to the station on the street cars, and when examined there, sand was found in his shoes. Jennings, when arrested, first told the officers that he lived at 1244 State street, Chicago, and later 577 Twelfth street; that he left for Harvey about 7 or 8 o'clock the evening before to visit friends, and that when he started to return from Harvey, about 12 o'clock, not finding a street car, he had walked back to that point.

In August, 1910, Jennings had been released on parole from the penitentiary at Joliet, where he had been sentenced on a charge of burglary. He had been paroled before, but had been returned for a violation of the parole. Two weeks after his second parole, on August 16, 1910, he purchased a new .38 caliber revolver, giving his name as Will Jones, of Peoria. On September 9th following he had pawned this revolver for $2 under the name of Will Jackson, getting it back September 16th. On the 18th he pawned it to Elroy Jones, a saloonkeeper, getting it back about 7:00 p. m. on the night of September 18, 1910. It was this revolver that the officers found on Jennings' person when he was arrested. It was loaded with five cartridges, which were marked, 'A.P.C. 38 Smith & Wesson.' The testimony showed that these cartridges were identical in appearance, size and markings with the three undischarged cartridges found in the hallway of the Hiller house near the dead body. Jennings testified that he had not fired the revolver since he owned it and knew of no one else firing it. The officers testified that in their judgment it had been fired twice within an hour before his arrest, arriving at this conclusion from the smell of fresh smoke and the burned powder in two chambers of the cylinder. Later, chemical tests and the evidence of a gunsmith corroborated this testimony that the chambers contained burned particles of powder.

Over the objection of the plaintiff in error evidence was admitted to the effect that about 2:00 a.m. September 19, 1910, just before the shooting of Hiller, someone entered the McNabb house. Mrs. McNabb was awakened and saw a man standing in the door with a lighted match over his head. The man was tall, broad shouldered, and very dark. He came over to her and placed his hand on her shoulder twice, then put his hand under her clothes against her bare body. She kept shoving his hand away, and cried out, 'What is the matter?' The man did not reply, but went to the dresser and stood there a minute and then went down the stairs. Jessie McNabb, a daughter, who occupied the same bed with her mother, was awakened and saw the intruder. She testified he wore a light-colored shirt and figured suspenders; that he was large, with broad shoulders. From the shirt and suspenders which were introduced in evidence, and from the build of Jennings, she was of the opinion he was the man that was in their room. Mrs. McNabb also testified that she thought the man in the room was Jennings, from his size and build and from what she saw of him. Jennings was 6 feet tall and weighed about 175 pounds.

About 12:05 o'clock on the same morning, Clarence Halsted, living at 11,303 Church street, one block west of Vincennes road and about a mile and a quarter south of the Hiller house, was awakened by a man entering his bedroom window on the ground floor of his residence. The intruder, while he sat on the window sill with one leg in the room, lighted a match. When he saw Halsted, who had raised himself in bed on his elbow, he swung out of the window again. Halsted jumped up and grabbed at the man, his right hand catching in the curtain and his left hand in the pocket of the man's coat. As the man pulled away he tore the pocket of the coat off from the right side, thus breaking loose. Jennings' coat was found thus torn when he was arrested. Halsted identified Jennings as the man in question. Jennings told several witnesses that this tear was caused by his fall from the street car, and he and his half-brother testified at the trial that it had been torn by the door of a sand car falling against him on the Tuesday preceding the murder.

While Jennings told several witnesses, at the time of his arrest, that he left Chicago on the evening of September 18th to go to Harvey about 7 o'clock, he testified on the trial, and one or two other witnesses also testified, that he did not leave the downtown part of the city until after 10 o'clock on Sunday evening, September 18th. He stated once or twice after his arrest that he went to Harvey to visit acquaintances named Robinson, and gave the officers to understand that after visiting with them he missed the street car and walked back. The state proved by the Robinsons that he did not call on them on the night in question, and later Jennings testified in his own behalf that he knocked at the Robinsons' door and no one responded, so he went to a place called Phoenix, a short distance from Harvey, where he visited a saloon. No other witness corroborated him as to his presence in Harvey, Phoenix, or at any other point south of the Halsted residence on the night in question. He denied being at the Halsted house, the McNabb house or the Hiller house, or having anything to do with the shooting. When arrested he denied that he had ever been arrested before, giving his name as Will Jones.

Mrs. Hiller testified that their house had but recently been painted, the back porch, which was the last part done, being completed on the Saturday preceding the shooting. Entrance to the house had been gained by the murderer through a rear window of the kitchen, from which he had first removed the window screen. Near the window was a porch, on the railing of which a person entering the window could support himself. On the railing in the fresh paint was the imprint of four fingers of some one's left hand. This railing was removed in the early morning after the murder by officers from the identification bureau of the Chicago police force and enlarged photographs were made of the prints. Jennings, when returned to the penitentiary for the violation of his parole, in March, 1910, had a print of his fingers taken and another print was taken after this arrest. These impressions were likewise enlarged for the purpose of comparison with the enlarged photographs of the prints on the railing. Four witnesses, over the objection and exception of counsel, testified that in their opinion the prints on the railing and the prints taken from Jennings' fingers by the identification bureau were made by the same person. Their testimony will be referred to later.

The plaintiff in error insists that reversible error was committed in receiving the testimony of Halsted, Mrs. McNabb and Jessie McNabb.

The general rule is, that evidence of a distinct substantive offense cannot be admitted in support of another offense. But to this rule there are several well-known exceptions. If evidence is admissible on other general grounds, it is no objection to its admission that it discloses other offenses, even though they are the subject of indictment. 'Whatever testimony tends directly to show the defendant guilty of the crime charged is competent, although it also tends to show him guilty of another and distinct offense. A party cannot, by multiplying his crimes, diminish the volume of competent testimony against him.' *State v. Adams*, 20 Kan. 311. The test of admissibility is the connection of the facts proved with the offense charged. Evidence which has 'a natural tendency to establish the fact in controversy' should be admitted. One of the well-known exceptions to the settled rule as to the admission of evidence as to collateral crimes is when evidence of an extraneous crime tends to identify the accused as the perpetrator of the crime charged. When an alibi is disputed it is admissible to prove a collateral offense to prove that at the time the accused was in the vicinity.

In view of plaintiff in error's statements, after his arrest and before the trial, as to his whereabouts on that night, it was competent for the state to prove that shortly before the crime was committed he was near the scene of the crime, even though when seen by some of the witnesses he was engaged in the commission of other crimes. The evidence objected to tended strongly to contradict his statements as to his whereabouts at that time.

It is further insisted in this connection by plaintiff in error that the evidence of Halsted, Mrs. McNabb, and Miss McNabb was inadmissible because of the uncertain character of the identification. A great deal has been written and said in the past concerning the doubtful nature of testimony identifying persons. Men's faces, like their handwriting, may be so similar that the keenest observer may be baffled in seeking to discover differences. 'The witness,' says Wharton, 'is asked how he knows that the prisoner at the bar is the person who fired the fatal shot, and his answer is, 'I infer it from a similarity of eyes, of hair, of height, of manner, of expression, of dress.' Human identity, therefore, is an inference drawn from a series of facts, some of them veiled, it may be, by disguise and all of them more or less varied by circumstances.' WHARTON ON CRIM. EVIDENCE (8th Ed.) § 13.... It has been frequently held that a witness may testify to a person's identity from his voice or from observing his stature, complexion, or other marks. This testimony was competent. The weight to be given it was a question for the jury, in view of all the other circumstances and evidence in the case.

It is further contended that the evidence as to the comparison of photographs of the finger marks on the railing with the enlarged finger prints of plaintiff in error was improperly admitted. No question is raised as to the accuracy of the photographic exhibits, the method of identifying the photographs, the taking of the finger prints of the plaintiff in error or the correctness of the enlargements, as shown by the exhibits introduced in evidence. It is earnestly insisted, however, that this class of testimony is not admissible under the common-law rules of evidence, and as there is no statute in this state authorizing it the court should have refused to permit its introduction. No case in which this question has been raised has been cited in the briefs, and we find no statutes or decisions touching the point in this country. This class of evidence is admitted in Great Britain. In 1909 the Court of Criminal Appeals held that finger prints might be received in evidence, and refused to interfere with a conviction below though this evidence was the sole ground of identification. While the courts of this country do not appear to have had occasion to pass on the question, standard authorities on scientific subjects discuss the use of finger prints as a system of identification, concluding that experience has shown it to be reliable. 10 ENCY. BRITANNICA (11th Ed.) 376; 5 NELSON'S ENCY. 28. *See also*, GROSS' CRIM. INVESTIGATION (Adams' Transl.) 277; FULD'S POLICE ADMINIS-TRATION, 342; OSBORN'S QUESTIONED DOCUMENTS, 479. These authorities state that this system of identification is of very ancient origin, having been used in Egypt when the impression of the monarch's thumb was used as his sign manual, that it has been used in the courts of India for many years and more recently in the courts of several European countries; that in recent years its use has become very general by the police departments of the large cities of this country and Europe; that the great success of the system in England, where it has been used since 1891 in thousands of cases without error, caused the sending of an investigating commission from the United States, on whose favorable report a bureau was established by the United States government....

Four witnesses testified for the state as to the finger prints. William M. Evans stated that he began the study of the subject in 1904; that he had been connected with the bureau of identification of the Chicago police department in work of this character for about a year; that he had personally studied between 4,000 and 5,000 finger prints and had himself made about 2,000; that the bureau of identification had some 25,000 different impressions classified; that he had examined the exhibits in question, and on the forefinger he found 14 points of identity, and on the second finger 11 points; that in his judgment the finger prints on the railing were made by the same person as those taken from the plaintiff in error's fingers by the identification bureau.

Edward Foster testified that he was inspector of dominion police at Ottawa, Canada, connected with the bureau of identification; that he had a good deal to do with finger prints for six years or more; that he had special work along that line in Vancouver and elsewhere in Canada; that he had studied the subject at Scotland Yard; that he began the study in St. Louis in 1904 under a Scotland Yard man and had taken about 2,500 finger prints; that he had studied the exhibits in question and found 14 points of resemblance on the forefinger; that the two sets of prints were made by the fingers of the same person.

Mary E. Holland testified that she resided in Chicago; that she began investigation of finger print impressions in 1904, studied at Scotland Yard in 1908, passed an examination on the subject, and started the first bureau of identification in this country for the United States government at Washington; that they have over 100,000 prints at Scotland Yard; that she also had studied the two sets of prints and believed them to have been made by ... the same person.

Michael P. Evans testified that he had been in the bureau of identification of the Chicago police department for 27 years; that the bureau had been using the system of finger print impressions since January 1, 1905, and that they also used the Bertillon system; that he had studied the question since 1905 or 1906 and had made between 6,000 and 7,000 finger prints; that he had charge of the making of the photographs of the prints on the railing; that in his judgment the various impressions were made by the fingers of the same person.

All of these witnesses testified at more or less length as to the basis of the system and the various markings found on the human hand, stating that they were classified from the various forms of makings, including those known as 'arches,' 'loops,' 'whorls' and 'deltas.'

When photograph was first introduced it was seriously questioned whether pictures thus created could properly be introduced in evidence, but this method of proof, as well as by means of X-rays and the microscope, is now admitted without question. We are disposed to hold from the evidence of the four witnesses who testified, and from the writings we have referred to on this subject, that there is a scientific basis for the system of finger print identification, and that the courts are justified in admitting this class of evidence; that this method of identification is in such general and common use that the courts cannot refuse to take judicial cognizance of it. Such evidence may or may not be of independent strength, but it is admissible, the same as other proof, as tending to make out a case. If inferences as to the identity of persons based on the voice, the appearance, or age are admissible, why does not this record justify the admission of this finger print testimony under common-law rules of evidence? The general rule is that whatever tends to prove any material fact is relevant and competent....

It is further insisted, as we understand the briefs and oral argument, that expert testimony on this subject was not permissible. Expert testimony is admissible when the subject-matter of the inquiry is of such a character that only persons of skill and experience in it are capable of forming a correct judgment as to any facts connected therewith. It is an elementary rule that where the court or jury can make their own deductions they shall not be made by those testifying. Except evidence is not confined to classed and specified professions, but is applicable wherever peculiar skill and judgment applied to a particular subject are required to explain results or to trace them to their causes. Expert evidence is admissible when the witnesses offered as experts have peculiar knowledge or experience not common to the world, which renders their opinions, founded on such knowledge or experience, an aid to the court or jury in determining the questions at issue.

From the evidence in this record we are disposed to hold that the classification of finger print impressions and their method of identification is a science requiring study. While some of the reasons which guide an expert to his conclusions are such as may be weighed by any intelligent person with good eyesight from such exhibits as we have here in the record, after being pointed out to him by one versed in the study of finger prints, the evidence in question does not come within in the common experience of all men of common education in the ordinary walks of life, and therefore the court and jury were properly aided by witnesses of peculiar and special experience on this subject.

It is objected that some of these witnesses were not qualified by such special experience. The question of the qualification of an expert rests largely in the discretion of the trial court. There can be no arbitrary of fixed test but necessarily only a relative one, dependent somewhat on the subject and the particular witness.

These witnesses were qualified to testify as experts on this subject. In view of the knowledge and experience of men in identifying by footprints as compared with their knowledge and experience in identifying finger prints, it is manifest that opinions by experts might be entirely proper as to the latter class of testimony when they would not be with reference to footprints. The jury, if the facts were all stated, would be able to draw conclusions as to footprints as well as could expert witnesses....

It is further insisted that some of the witnesses testified positively that the finger prints represented by the photographs were made by a certain person whose finger print impressions had been photographed, enlarged, and introduced in evidence, when they should have only been permitted to testify that such was their opinion. 'In general, though a witness must depose to such facts, only, as are within his own knowledge, yet there is no rule that requires him to speak with such expression of certainty as to exclude all doubt in his mind.' 1 GREENLEAF ON EVIDENCE (Lewis' Ed.) § 440.... 'On questions of identity of persons and of handwriting it is every day's practice for witnesses to swear that they believe the person to be the same or the handwriting to be that of a particular individual, although they will not swear positively, and the degree of credit to be attached to the evidence is a question for the jury.' 1 STARKIE ON EVIDENCE (10th Am. Ed.) 172.... While it is usual for expert witnesses to testify that they believe or think, or in their best judgment, that such and such a thing is true, no rule of law prevents them from testifying positively on such subjects. It is for the jury to determine the weight to be given to their testimony....

Stevenson v. United States
380 F.2d 590 (D.C. Cir. 1967)

DANAHER, Circuit Judge.

Jointly indicted, Stevenson and Borum after a jury trial were found guilty of house-breaking and robbery....

On July 2, 1965, one Davis received work, and presently confirmed that his house had been forcibly entered. Its contents were in great disarray, and many items of value had been stolen. Money had been taken from a metal box, from underneath a glass top on a bedside table, and from a tea canister. Davis knew neither appellant and had never given them permission to enter his home.

A Metropolitan Police Department expert on July 2, 1965 had removed several fingerprints from the various named objects, each of which had been in the Davis home for some three to twelve years. Three prints were identical to known fingerprints of the appellant Borum, two having been lifted from the metal box and the third from the bedside table glass. A fourth fingerprint identical to a known fingerprint of the appellant Stevenson, had been lifted from the bottom of the tea canister.

Stevenson has argued that his conviction cannot be sustained since there was no showing that his fingerprint had been placed on the container on July 2, 1965 or that the container was located on the premises when the Stevenson print was superimposed. Thus, he contends, the evidence was insufficient to justify his conviction. The trial court instructed the jury that before a verdict of guilty could be returned, the jurors must be satisfied beyond a reasonable doubt that the housebreaking and robbery had occurred on July 2, 1965 as had been testified, and that Stevenson was one of those who had perpetrated the crimes.

An officer testified that when he arrived at the house about 10:30 in the morning of July 2, 1965, 'Everything was strewn all over the house, there were things out all over the bed and in the living room.' He proceeded to lift fingerprints from various objects. Stevenson was arrested the following evening, and some two to three hours later was fingerprinted by the police. The officer compared the known prints thus secured with that taken from the tea canister. The prints were identical, the expert testified, and both were prints made by Stevenson. He argues now that the evidence was insufficient to permit a jury to return a guilty verdict. We do not agree. Stevenson did not testify, and there was no suggestion from any source that Stevenson on any account could have had legitimate access to the canister upon which his fingerprints were found.

A like argument has been advanced by Stevenson's brother-in-law, the appellant Borum. Like Stevenson, Borum did not testify.

Under correct instructions the jury was bound to weigh the evidence and from such facts as it might find, to draw appropriate inferences respecting the guilt of the appellants. It is abundantly clear that the jury properly might conclude that Davis's house had been burglarized on July 2, 1965; that the thieves had left their fingerprints as found by the police; and that the identification of the two accused had been adequately established.

Fingerprint identification has long been recognized by the courts as entirely appropriate.[4] The accuracy of fingerprint identification is a matter of common knowledge[5] and no case has been cited, and we have found none, where identification so established[6] has been rejected.[7] Under the circumstances here shown, the jury was fully justified in concluding that these two appellants in the course of their crime had impressed their fingerprints upon the objects described in a location to which the appellants had been accorded no lawful access. We reject the contentions of the respective appellants that the evidence was insufficient to establish their complicity, as charged....

Notes and Questions

1. In *Jennings*, the court rests the admissibility decision on several different bases. Even though the court recognizes that no court in the United States had yet decided admissibility of fingerprint testimony, "standard authorities on scientific subjects" such as the *Encyclopedia Britannica* indicate its reliability for identification. The court also notes the qualifications of the experts in the case, each having some training and experience in the field. Do these sources provide an adequate basis for admission? In MODERN SCIENTIFIC EVIDENCE, the authors note what is missing:

   > Nowhere in the opinion, however, does the court articulate the basis of the expertise it is evaluating, or discuss any scientific evidence in support of the expertise, or illuminate the technique's theoretical premises, or explain why one would believe that fingerprint examiners can do what they claim the ability to do. Nor do the cited sources fill that gap.

   DAVID L. FAIGMAN ET AL., MODERN SCIENTIFIC EVIDENCE: FORENSICS § 3:2, at 177 (2008). Part of the problem is the individual weaknesses of opinions like *Jennings*, but there is another concern. Once a court accepts fingerprint evidence, then others will be more likely to follow their lead. In the years 1911–1940, all

---

4. Fingerprinting 'is known to be a very certain means devised by modern science to reach the desired end, and has become especially important in a time when increased population and vast aggregations of people in urban centers have rendered the notoriety of the individual in the community no longer a ready means of identification.' *United States v. Kelly*, 55 F.2d 67, 69 (2d Cir. 1932)....

5. For informational background, see *State v. Kuhl*, 42 Nev. 185, 175 P. 190 (1918).

6. Other methods, but none superior to fingerprinting have been employed over the years where the courts were concerned with problems of identification. *See, e.g., Shaffer v. United States*, 24 App.D.C. 417, 425, 426 (1904); *United States v. Kelly*, 55 F.2d at 69; *State v. Kuhl*, 175 P. at 190.

7. *See generally* BRIDGES, PRACTICAL FINGERPRINTING (1963) as to the 'invincibility' of the identification so shown....

but five states had explicitly accepted fingerprint evidence, heavily relying on out-of-state precedent in doing so. *Id.* at 176 n. 9.

2. Why did the court in *Stevenson* decide that fingerprint evidence was admissible, and what record did they have to support that conclusion? If asked, what might Judge Danaher say is the potential error rate for fingerprint identification?

The reality is that in the pre-*Daubert* era, admissibility of fingerprint evidence depended largely on the qualifications of the expert, and the court would pay little to no attention to the underlying procedures or methodologies of comparison. Typical court analysis of the issue from this era include the following unredacted excerpts:

– *People v. Richardson*, 65 Cal. Rptr. 487, 491 (1968):

> Defendant next maintains that the trial court erred in finding the prosecution's fingerprint identification expert to be qualified as an expert, and that the fingerprint expert's testimony was insufficient to identify the defendant's fingerprint on the cigarette lighter. However, the prosecution's witness certainly qualified as a fingerprint expert inasmuch as he had been on the staff of the F.B.I. from 1960–1965, and during his tenure with the federal agency, had consistently worked with the identification of latent prints. The trial court's determination as to an expert's qualification will not be disturbed on appeal unless there has been a clear abuse of discretion. (*People v. Busch*, 56 Cal. 2d 868, 878, 16 Cal. Rptr. 898, 366 P.2d 314; *People v. Murray*, 247 Cal. App. 2d 730, 735, 56 Cal. Rptr. 21.) Here, the witness had identified thousands of fingerprints and had the training and experience necessary to quality as an expert. Once the trial court determined that the witness was an expert, the witness was certainly entitled to give his opinion to the effect that the fingerprint found on the cigarette lighter was that of the defendant. The print found on the lighter and the defendant's print had numerous similar points. The weight to be given to the expert's opinion was a matter for the jury's determination.

– *State v. Murdock*, 689 P.2d 814, 818 (Kan. 1984):

> An expert witness who is shown to be qualified may testify as to the identity of fingerprints. 23 C.J.S. *Criminal Law* § 876; 22A C.J.S. *Criminal Law* § 616; 31 Am. Jur. 2d *Expert and Opinion Evidence* § 123; 2 *Jones on Evidence* § 435 (5th ed. 1958). The purpose of such testimony is, of course, to establish the identity or non-identity of a person accused and one whose fingerprints are found at the scene of a crime. The qualifications of expert witnesses and the admissibility of expert testimony are matters which lie within the sound discretion of the trial court. Its ruling thereon will not be disturbed on appeal unless the appellate court finds an abuse of discretion. *State v. Jones*, 233 Kan. 112, 660 P.2d 948 (1983); *State v. Churchill*, 231 Kan. 408, 413, 646 P.2d 1049 (1982). The opinion testi-

mony of an expert is to be considered as any other testimony and should receive only such weight as the factfinder determines proper. *In re Adoption of Irons*, 235 Kan. 540, Syl. ¶ 2, 684 P.2d 332 (1984); and see *A.T. & S.F. Rld. Co. v. Thul*, 32 Kan. 255, 261, 4 Pac. 352 (1884).

— *Wilson v. State*, 574 So. 2d 1324, 1334 (Miss. 1990):

> The admissibility of a fingerprint expert's testimony concerning his comparison of the background materials lifted with the latent print has not been addressed by this Court.

> The qualifications of an expert in applicable fields of scientific knowledge is left to the sound discretion of the trial judge. His determination on this issue will not be reversed unless it clearly appears that the witness was not qualified. *Smith v. State*, 530 So.2d 155, 162 (Miss.1988). Fingerprint examination is a field of knowledge which has gained a "general acceptance." Agent Jones was qualified to testify as a fingerprint expert. The practice of fingerprint examination necessarily involves the observation and comparison of background materials lifted with the latent prints. It is an integral part of fingerprint examination.

> This expert testimony was admissible.

Needless to say, none of these courts rejected the fingerprint expert testimony. In fact, in a more recent case, *People v. Luna*, an Illinois court noted: "Indeed, defendant has not cited a published opinion of any court suggesting that ACE-V methodology is not generally accepted within the relevant scientific community or holding that finger or palm print evidence is inadmissible." 989 N.E.2d 655, 672 (Ill. App. Ct. 2013). The Defendant did cite an unpublished Maryland trial court order, *Maryland v. Rose*, No. K06-0545 (Cir. Ct. Baltimore Co. Oct. 19, 2007); but to the *Luna* court, this confirmed rather than rebutted the general acceptance of fingerprint identification. *Id.* at 672 n. 2.

C. The Impact of *Daubert*— A Challenge to Fundamental Assumptions

Back in Chapter 2.D.ii, we covered the Supreme Court decision *Daubert v. Merrell Dow Pharmaceuticals, Inc.*, 509 U.S. 579 (1993), in which the Court instructed district court judges to screen expert evidence for reliability prior to admission at trial. We also discovered that reliability screening applies not only to labcoat-and-beaker scientists, but also to experience-based fields. *Kumho Tire Co. v. Carmichael*, 526 U.S. 137 (1999). That should include fingerprint examiners.

How have courts handled the mandate of *Daubert/Kumho* in the area of fingerprints? To get at that question, let's further examine the fingerprint article by Robert Epstein, in which he considers the reliability of fingerprint evidence under the *Daubert* factors. Afterward, we will see how courts handled the same issues, with one of the first *Daubert* challenges to fingerprint evidence in federal court, *United States v. Havvard*. When you read the case, ask whether Judge Hamilton's analysis is true to the mandate of *Daubert* to reliability screen for "good science."

Robert Epstein, *Fingerprints Meet* Daubert: *The Myth of Fingerprint "Science" Is Revealed*
75 S. Cal. L. Rev. 605 (2002)
IV. *DAUBERT* MEETS FINGERPRINTS

A. Has the Method or Technique Been Tested?

While fingerprint examiners have long claimed the mantle of science so as to bolster the credibility of their profession, the reality is that the fingerprint community has never conducted any scientific testing to validate the premises upon which the field is based. The most fundamental premise of the fingerprint field, like that of all other forensic identification disciplines, is that fingerprint examiners can make reliable identifications from the type of small distorted latent fingerprint fragments that are typically detected at crime scenes. Incredibly, there has been only one published study that even remotely addresses this issue. That study, an utter embarrassment to the fingerprint community, was done by two British researchers who were commissioned by Scotland Yard to review the sixteen point identification standard which, up until very recently, governed in both England and Wales.[96] As part of their review, the two researchers sent photographs of ten pairs of latent and inked fingerprints to fingerprint bureaus in England and Wales requesting that experts with ten or more years of experience undertake the ten comparisons independently of each other. Nine of the pairs that were supplied were taken from past casework of Scotland Yard. Six of these pairs were properly identifiable to one another, while the other three were considered borderline cases. The tenth pair provided by the researchers consisted of two prints that were made by different fingers. The participating examiners were asked to decide whether each of the pairs were identifiable and, if so, the number of corresponding points of similarity that could be seen. Replies were received from 130 participants. The variation in the responses was extraordinary. With respect to one of the pairs, for example, the number of points of comparison that the examiners reported ranged from ten to forty. As to another pair, the range was fourteen to fifty-six. There was also considerable disagreement as to whether identifications could properly be effectuated. On one of the pairs, 44% of the examiners found that an identification could be made, while 56% said that it could not. As the researchers appropriately concluded from these results, "[t]he variation [in the responses] confirms the subjective nature of points of comparison." "[E]xperts vary widely in their judgments of individual points." The British experiment thus suggests that fingerprint analysis is not nearly as reliable as most people have assumed. As the study reveals, fingerprint examiners can reach extremely different conclusions regarding the same … fingerprints, at least,

---

96. *See* Ian W. Evett & R. L. Williams, *A Review of the Sixteen Point Fingerprint Standard in England and Wales*, 46 J. Forensic Identification 49 (1996).

that is, when they are unaware of the results that prior law enforcement examiners have reached.

In addition to the lack of basic reliability studies, no testing has been conducted to determine the probability of two different people having a number of fingerprint ridge characteristics in common. This is in sharp contrast to the relatively new field of DNA analysis, where scientific testing has been done to calculate the probability of a coincidental match. Commentators have recently recognized that the lack of testing in the fingerprint field is a critical problem. David Stoney, for example, a leading forensic science scholar, and a trained fingerprint analyst, has written:

> [T]here is no justification [for fingerprint identifications] based on conventional science: no theoretical model, statistics or an empirical validation process.

> Efforts to assess the individuality of DNA blood typing make an excellent contrast. There has been intense debate over which statistical models are to be applied, and how one should quantify increasingly rare events. To many, the absence of adequate statistical modeling, or the controversy regarding calculations, brings the admissibility of the evidence into question. Woe to fingerprint practice were such criteria applied!

> Much of the discussion of fingerprint practices in this and preceding sections may lead the critical reader to the question "Is there any scientific basis for an absolute identification?" It is important to realize that an absolute identification is an opinion, rather than a conclusion based on scientific research. The functionally equivalent scientific conclusion (as seen in some DNA evidence) would be based on calculations showing that the probability of two different patterns being indistinguishably alike is so small that it asymptotes with zero.... The scientific conclusion, however, must be based on tested probability models. These simply do not exist for fingerprint pattern comparisons.

The DOJ, in a stunning admission, has recently conceded that Stoney is indeed correct—that basic validation studies in the fingerprint field have never been conducted and that they now must be performed. This admission is in the form of a formal "Solicitation" for "Forensic Friction Ridge (Fingerprint) Examination Validation Studies," which was issued by the DOJ's research arm, the National Institute of Justice ("NIJ"), in March of 2000.... The purpose of this Solicitation is nothing less than an attempt to provide fingerprint examiners with the necessary ammunition to survive *Daubert* challenges.

The Solicitation explicitly recognizes that testing in the fingerprint field "needs" to be conducted in two basic areas. First, it calls for "[b]asic research to determine the scientific validity of individuality in friction ridge examination based on measurement of features, quantification, and statistical analysis." As the DOJ admits in this regard, "the theoretical basis for [fingerprint] individuality has had limited study and needs additional work to demonstrate the statistical basis for identifications."

This is quite an admission. For the past ninety years, fingerprint examiners have been testifying in court that the basic premise of fingerprint identification evidence is the individuality of all fingerprints. Indeed, the notion of fingerprint individuality—that everyone has unique fingerprints—is deeply ingrained in our popular culture. Yet we now discover from the DOJ 's Solicitation that fingerprint individuality has never in fact been scientifically established and that basic research in this area needs to be conducted....

The second area of testing that the Solicitation calls for concerns the fundamental question of reliability. The DOJ recognizes that the fingerprint field "needs" to develop "standardized" procedures for comparing fingerprints and that these "[p]rocedures must [then] be tested statistically in order to demonstrate that following the stated procedures allows analysts to produce correct results with acceptable error rates." As the DOJ candidly concedes, such testing "has not yet been done."

The ramifications of this Solicitation are thus enormous. The DOJ has effectively admitted that latent fingerprint analysis fails the primary criterion of science and, by extension, the primary criterion for admissibility under *Daubert*: There has been no testing of the field 's basic underlying premises.

In addition to releasing the Solicitation, the DOJ has also recently conducted some experiments for litigation purposes.... In sum, at the present time, the fingerprint field fails the first and most critical of the *Daubert* factors. The premises underlying the field have never been scientifically validated.

B. Has an Error Rate Been Established?

The answer to this question is plainly no. Because of the lack of testing, there are no established error rates for latent fingerprint examiners, another fact that the DOJ has explicitly conceded in the recently issued Solicitation. There can be no dispute, moreover, that latent fingerprint examiners do make misidentifications. There are numerous documented cases in which latent fingerprint examiners have made erroneous identifications that have led to the imprisonment of innocent people. What remains unknown, however, is the rate at which misidentifications take place. As commentators have recognized, "[i]t is difficult to glean information about cases of error because they rarely produce a public record, and the relevant organizations and agencies tend not to discuss them publicly."[153]

Just how prevalent the problem of false identifications may actually be, however, can be seen, at least to some extent, in the poor performance of latent print examiners on proficiency exams. Such tests are typically taken by examiners for purposes of crime lab accreditation. While these exams do not constitute controlled scientific studies, they nevertheless do provide some indication of the proficiency, or lack thereof, of examiners throughout the United States. On these exams, latent fingerprint examiners typically are provided with several latent prints along with a number of "ten print" inked impressions for comparison. The 1995 exam is a useful starting

153. Simon A. Cole, *Witnessing Identification: Latent Fingerprinting Evidence and Expert Knowledge*, 28 Soc. Studies of Sci. 687, 701 (1998).

point, because it was the first test authorized by the fingerprint examiners own professional association, the IAI.[154]

The results of the 1995 exam were, in the words of a leading law enforcement examiner, both "alarming" and "chilling." Of the 156 examiners who participated, only sixty-eight (44%) were able to both correctly identify the five latent print impressions that should have been identified, and correctly note the two elimination latent prints that were not to be identified. Even more significantly, thirty-four of these examiners (22%) made erroneous identifications on one or more of the questioned prints for a total of forty-eight misidentifications. Erroneous identifications occurred on all seven latent prints that were provided, including thirteen errors made on the five latent prints that could be correctly identified to the supplied suspects. In addition, one of the two elimination latents was misidentified twenty-nine times.

These shockingly poor results, moreover, could not be blamed on the test. The 1995 proficiency exam was recognized by David Grieve, a leading law enforcement fingerprint examiner, as being "a more than satisfactory representation of real casework conditions."[160] A "proficiency test composed of seven latents and four suspects was considered neither overly demanding nor unrealistic." Accordingly, the fingerprint profession's dreadful performance on this test has been, and continues to be, a matter of significant concern. As Grieve, the head of Forensic Sciences for the Illinois State Police, has written:

> Reaction to the results of the CTS 1995 Latent Print Proficiency Test within the forensic science community has ranged from shock to disbelief. Errors of this magnitude within a discipline singularly admired and respected for its touted absolute certainty as an identification process have produced chilling and mind-numbing realities. Thirty-four participants, an incredible 22% of those involved, substituted presumed but false certainty for truth. By any measure, this represents a profile of practice that is unacceptable and thus demands positive action by the entire community.

… The proficiency testing thus suggests that when the DOJ validation studies are ultimately conducted, there may well be a substantial rate of error for latent fingerprint examiners. In this regard, it should be kept in mind that it is the prosecutor who bears the burden of establishing the reliability of the expert evidence that he or she is seeking to admit. Accordingly, when it comes to the *Daubert* factor of error rate, the prosecution cannot, at this point in time, satisfy its burden. As a district court has recognized in a case concerning handwriting analysis, "[c]ertainly an unknown error rate does not necessarily imply a large error rate[;] [h]owever if testing is possible, it must be conducted if forensic document examination is to carry the imprimatur of 'science.'"

154. David L. Grieve, *Possession of Truth*, 46 J. FORENSIC IDENTIFICATION 521, 523 (1996).
160. *Id.* at 524.

C. Are There Objective Standards to Govern the Technique 's Operation?

Latent fingerprint examiners in the United States currently operate in the absence of any uniform objective standards. The absence of standards is most glaring with respect to the ultimate question of all fingerprint comparisons: What constitutes a sufficient basis for making a positive identification? The position of the FBI, as well as the IAI, is that no minimum number of corresponding points of identification is necessary for an identification. Instead, the determination of whether there is a sufficient basis for an identification is left to the subjective judgment of the particular examiner. As one of the world's leading fingerprint practitioners, David Ashbaugh, has candidly acknowledged, a fingerprint examiner's opinion of identification is "very subjective."

While the official position of the FBI is that there is no basis for a minimum point requirement, many fingerprint examiners in the United States continue to employ either their own informal point standards or standards that have been set by the agencies for which they work. In addition, while there is no uniform identification standard in the United States, many other countries have set such standards. Australia, for example, has a minimum standard of twelve matching ridge characteristics; France and Italy each have sixteen. The obvious purpose of establishing such standards is to try to insure against erroneous identifications.

As commentators have recognized, the question of whether there should be a minimum point standard for latent print identifications has bitterly divided the fingerprint community. While latent print examiners have somehow managed to maintain a united front in the courtroom, they have been at odds in the technical literature. Ashbaugh, for example, has written that "[i]t is unacceptable to use the simplistic point philosophy in modern day forensic science." ... Here, for example, is Ashbaugh's explanation as to how a latent print examiner, in the absence of a minimum point standard, is supposed to know when a sufficient basis exists to make an identification:

> A frequently asked question is, "How much is enough?" The opinion of individualization or identification is subjective. It is an opinion formed by the friction ridge identification specialist based on the friction ridge formations found in agreement during comparison. The validity of the opinion is coupled with an ability to defend that position, and both are founded in one's personal knowledge, ability, and experience....
>
> How much is enough? Finding adequate friction ridge formations in sequence that one knows are specific details of the friction skin, and in the opinion of the friction ridge identification specialist that there is sufficient uniqueness within those details to eliminate all other possible donors in the world, is considered enough. At that point individualization has occurred and the print has been identified. The identification was established by the agreement of friction ridge formations in sequence having sufficient uniqueness to individualize.

The utter meaninglessness of this explanation speaks for itself. Ashbaugh's prior writings on this subject provide little in the way of additional insight. He has stated, for example, that while "[i]n some instances we may form an opinion on eight ridge characteristics[,] [i]n other instances we may require twelve or more to form the same opinion." Ashbaugh's explanation for this sliding scale is that some ridge characteristics are more unique than others. But, no weighted measures of the different characteristics have ever been adopted by the fingerprint community, and different examiners vary considerably in terms of their subjective beliefs as to the relative frequencies with which different characteristics appear. Accordingly, as Ashbaugh has ultimately recognized, a particular examiner's determination of whether eight or twelve matching characteristics is sufficient in a particular case is entirely "subjective."

The lack of uniform standards for latent print comparisons extends well beyond the question of what ultimate standard should apply for a positive identification. Objective standards are lacking throughout the entire comparison process. As discussed above, fingerprint examiners are not even in agreement as to what it is that they are looking for when comparing fingerprints. Examiners hold widely varying beliefs as to the number, nomenclature, and frequency of the standard ridge characteristics. Some examiners, moreover, such as ... Ashbaugh, do not limit their analysis to the traditional ridge characteristics, but instead rely heavily on what they refer to as third level detail, for example, sweat pores and ridge edges. Other examiners, however, strongly question the reliability of identifications that are made on the basis of such detail. For example, John Thornton, a leading forensic science commentator and trained fingerprint analyst, has recognized that "[i]dentifications based on level three detail have yet to be rigorously tested either in a scientific venue or in court." Thornton further states that he has not "ever seen a level 3 detail comparison of a latent fingerprint that didn't require some level of rationalization." ...

The lack of standards in the fingerprint field can even be seen with respect to the one rule apparently agreed upon by fingerprint examiners, the so called "one dissimilarity doctrine."[191] Pursuant to this rule, if two fingerprints contain a single genuine dissimilarity, then the prints cannot be attributed to the same finger or individual. This doctrine is well recognized in the fingerprint community. But, it is effectively ignored in practice. As Thornton has written, once a fingerprint examiner finds what he or she believes is a sufficient number of matching characteristics to make an identification, the examiner will then explain away any observed dissimilarity as being a product of distortion or artifact....

In response to recent *Daubert* challenges that have been lodged against fingerprint evidence, the DOJ has suggested that fingerprint examiners around the world all employ a standard methodology known as "ACE-V": analysis, comparison evaluation, and verification.... The problem ... [is that the DOJ and others never] ... provide much in the way of guidance beyond the ACE-V acronym. How exactly is the "Analysis" and "Comparison" to be conducted? How are examiners supposed to make their judgments as to whether various characteristics are in agreement or disagreement or

---

191. *See generally* John I. Thornton, *The One-Dissimilarity Doctrine in Fingerprint Identification*, 306 Int'l Crim. Police Rev. 89 (1977).

whether a characteristic is even genuine or is just the product of distortion? And, most fundamentally, how is an examiner to make his final "Evaluation" as to whether there is enough similarity to declare a match? The ACE-V "methodology" does not offer any assistance to an examiner who is grappling with these questions. Nor does it provide a court or a juror with any sort of standard by which the examiner's opinion can be evaluated.

Finally, the lack of standards in the fingerprint community extends to the training and experience requirements for latent print examiners. Put simply, no such requirements currently exist. As one leading fingerprint commentator has recognized, "people are being hired directly into latent print units without so much as having looked at a single fingerprint image." Once hired, the training that examiners receive is typically minimal....

Thus, as the above quoted practitioner has recognized, fingerprint examiners are not required to take any kind of objective test before they start giving their expert opinions in court. There is not even any type of licensing requirement in the field. The fingerprint professional association, the IAI, did start a certification program back in 1980. But approximately half the examiners that have taken the certification test have failed it. And since certification is not required, many, if not most, of the examiners who failed the test are still practicing.... The obvious result of not having any training or experience requirements is deficient examiners....

In sum, latent print examiners operate without the benefit of any objective standards to guide them in their comparisons. There also are no objective standards or minimum qualifications with respect to their hiring and training. Accordingly, another critical *Daubert* factor is unsatisfied.

D. Has the Method or Technique Been Subjected to Peer Review and Publication?

Very little has been written regarding the comparison and identification of fingerprints, a fact recognized by those within the fingerprint community itself. While a technical journal does exist..., *The Journal of Forensic Identification*, an examination of this journal reveals that the vast majority of its articles concern the lifting and developing of latent fingerprints, rather than the process of comparison and identification. There has been, moreover, very little in the way of analysis concerning the fundamental premises of the field.

The major texts in the field also provide little analysis of the comparison and identification of latent fingerprints. Take, for example, the FBI publication, The Science of Fingerprints. Only three pages of this 211-page text even concern the subject of latent fingerprint comparisons. The rest of the text is primarily concerned with classifying ten print patterns, recording ten print patterns, and the lifting of latent prints. As to the three pages that concern latent fingerprint comparisons, there is no discussion whatsoever about the fundamental premises that underlie latent print identifications or how such comparisons should be conducted.

Even when the premises of latent print identifications have been considered in the fingerprint literature, they have rarely been critically examined. A perfect example is the editorial *Nature Never Repeats Itself*, written by Alan McRoberts.[212] In this editorial, McRoberts cites with approval the following statement which was originally made by Harris Wilder and Bert Wentworth in their 1916 text, *Personal Identification*:

> Finally, there is never the slightest doubt of the impossibility of the duplication of a finger print, or even of the small part of one, on the part of any one who has carefully studied the subject at first hand, whether finger-print expert or anatomist; the only doubters are those who have never taken the trouble to look for themselves, and who argue from the basis of their own prejudices and preconceived opinions.

It is probably statements such as these that have led David Ashbaugh to bemoan the "failure of the identification community to challenge or hold meaningful debate."

… As a district court recently stated with respect to the field of handwriting analysis, the literature of latent fingerprint examiners "fails to meet the expectations of the *Daubert* Court — that a competitive, unbiased community of practitioners and academics would generate increasingly valid science."[216]

E. Is There a General Consensus?

It can hardly be disputed, of course, that a consensus exists in the general public, as well as the judiciary, that latent fingerprint identifications are perfectly reliable. But the pertinent inquiry, for purposes of *Daubert*, is whether a general consensus has been reached by a "relevant scientific community." And, as has been recognized in several post-*Daubert* cases, in defining a relevant scientific community, it is necessary to look beyond the practitioners of the technique.…

There has never been a scientific community, beyond fingerprint examiners, that has expressed a general acceptance of latent fingerprint identifications. To the contrary, mainstream scientists, by and large, have ignored the question of whether individuals can be reliably identified through small, distorted latent fingerprint impressions. And the leading forensic science commentators that have examined the issue recently have found the fingerprint field to be scientifically deficient. Michael Saks, an editor of one of the leading treatises in the field, *Modern Scientific Evidence: The Law and Science of Expert Testimony*, has written that "[a] vote to admit fingerprints is a rejection of conventional science as the criterion for admission." … Accordingly, fingerprint examiners cannot even properly satisfy the general acceptance prong of *Daubert*.

F. Are There Any Non-*Daubert* Factors That Establish the Reliability of Latent Fingerprint Identifications?

… In responding to recent *Daubert* challenges, the government has argued that fingerprint identifications "have been tested empirically over a period of 100 years." What the government apparently means by this is that fingerprint identifications have a long history of being used in court. But the obvious reply to this argument

212. Alan L. McRoberts, *Nature Never Repeats Itself*, PRINT, Sept.–Oct. 1996, at 1.
216. United States v. Starzecpyzel, 880 F. Supp. 1027, 1038 (S.D.N.Y. 1995).

is that there is simply no way of telling how many cases of error have gone undetected. There has been very little scrutiny of fingerprint evidence in the courtroom since it gained judicial acceptance in the early 1900s. From then on, virtually everyone, including most of the defense bar, simply assumed the reliability of the evidence....

The government, in responding to recent *Daubert* challenges, has also argued that all that needs to be done at this point in time is for defendants to hire their own fingerprint experts who can then check the identifications made by the prosecution. But to the extent that there are reliability problems inherent to fingerprint methodology itself, the retention of a defense expert might not do any good. Just as two polygraph examiners might reach the wrong conclusion about whether someone is telling the truth, because of deficiencies in the polygraph, so too might several fingerprint examiners make a false identification with respect to a particular fingerprint because of deficiencies in the standards and procedures of the fingerprint profession....

This argument by the government also betrays a fundamental misunderstanding of Federal Rule of Evidence 702. Under that Rule, the proponent of expert testimony must be able to demonstrate the reliability of the expert's methodology or technique as applied to the particular case. A litigant cannot satisfy this test simply by pointing out that his adversary has the ability to retain the same type of expert to give a conflicting opinion. If that were the case then virtually any expert could gain admittance, even astrologers and psychics.

In sum, the government will not be able to cite to any non-*Daubert* factors that support the reliability of latent fingerprint identification evidence.

United States v. Havvard

117 F.Supp.2d 848 (S.D. Ind. 2000)

HAMILTON, J.

Defendant Wade Havvard was charged with being a felon in possession of firearms and ammunition.... Before trial, Havvard filed a motion *in limine* seeking to bar the government from offering an expert opinion on whether a latent fingerprint recovered from one of the firearms in question matched Havvard's left index finger. Havvard contends that opinion evidence on latent fingerprint identification does not meet the standards of reliability for admissible expert testimony under *Daubert* and *Kumho Tire.*

Before trial, the court held an evidentiary hearing on the motion. The court denied defendant's motion and provided an oral explanation. The court's decision may strike some as comparable to a breathless announcement that the sky is blue and the sun rose in the east yesterday. Nevertheless, *Daubert* and *Kumho Tire* invite fresh and critical looks at old habits and beliefs. This entry provides the court's explanation in written form at the government's request because it may be useful to other courts.

I. *The Requirements of* Daubert *and* Kumho Tire *for Expert Testimony*

Daubert and *Kumho Tire* require district judges to act as "gatekeepers" of expert testimony, to ensure that proffered expert testimony is sufficiently (a) relevant and (b) reliable to justify its submission to the trier of fact. *See Kumho Tire*, 526 U.S. at 152; *Daubert*, 509 U.S. at 589. In this case there is no issue of relevance. An expert's opinion that Havvard's left index finger was the source of a latent print on a firearm found under a mattress is highly relevant to show that Havvard had possession of that firearm at a relevant time.

The issue here is reliability. The gatekeeping requirement is designed "to make certain that an expert, whether basing testimony upon professional studies or personal experience, employs in the courtroom the same level of intellectual rigor that characterizes the practice of an expert in the relevant field." *Kumho Tire*, 526 U.S. at 152. In *Daubert* the Court identified several factors that may be relevant in evaluating the reliability of an expert's method for developing a relevant professional opinion. These include whether the theory or technique can be … tested; whether it has been subjected to peer review and publication; whether there is a … known or potential rate of error; whether there are standards controlling the technique's operations; and whether the theory or technique enjoys general acceptance within a relevant scientific … community. See *Kumho Tire*, 526 U.S. at 149–52 (citing *Daubert*, 509 U.S. at 592–4).

In *Kumho Tire,* the Court explained that the *Daubert* gatekeeping function applies to all kinds of experts, without drawing distinctions between scientific experts and other types. The Court also explained in *Kumho Tire* that the *Daubert* factors on reliability were neither mandatory nor exclusive.…

In this case, Havvard contends in essence that an opinion about whether a given latent fingerprint is from a particular finger is a subjective opinion that is not sufficiently reliable to be admitted. Although the argument may seem improbable, Havvard pointed out that the examiner designated to testify at trial about the fingerprint refused to identify a given standard in terms of the number of "points" or features that must be identical between the latent print and the comparison print before an identification opinion can be given. In addition, when that examiner testified at Havvard's trial, he described his opinion as "subjective."

The refusal to provide a clear standard and the expert's description of his opinion as "subjective" at least raise a fair question about identification opinions under *Daubert* and *Kumho Tire.* Havvard argues further that there is no reliable statistical foundation for fingerprint comparisons and no reliable measure of error rates in latent print identification, especially in the absence of a specific standard about the number of points of identity needed to support an opinion as to identification. Havvard thus compares latent fingerprint identification to handwriting analysis or hair fiber comparisons, which also have been challenged [after] *Daubert.*

For decades courts have been allowing persons trained and experienced in latent fingerprint identification to testify about their opinions as to whether a given individual was the source of a latent print. The government suggested in response to Havvard's motion that fingerprint identification is so well-established that the court should not even hold a hearing on the issue, citing *United States v. Cooper,* 91 F.Supp.2d 79, 82–83 (D.D.C.2000) (rejecting non-specific request for pretrial hearing on government's expert testimony in well-established and generally accepted fields). The government proposed that the court essentially take judicial notice of the reliability of latent print identification and leave any further challenges to cross-examination. Cases prior to *Daubert* support this approach. See, *e.g., People v. Jennings,* 96 N.E. 1077, 1081–82 (1911) (early leading case recognizing validity of fingerprint identification testimony)....

Although a trial court has some degree of discretion in determining *how* to evaluate the reliability of expert testimony, it is clear that the court has no discretion as to *whether* to evaluate reliability. See *Kumho Tire,* 526 U.S. at 159 (Scalia, J., concurring) (district court's discretion is not discretion "to abandon the gatekeeping function" or to perform the function inadequately). This court therefore held an evidentiary hearing and has considered the issue in some detail.

II. *Identification from Latent Fingerprints*

Against that legal background, the court turns to the evidence in this case. The only evidence presented in the evidentiary hearing was the testimony of Stephen Meagher, a Latent Print Unit Chief in the Forensic Analysis Section of the FBI's Laboratory Division. Meagher has not examined the latent fingerprint in this case and did not testify at trial. He testified instead about the methods and scientific bases of latent print identification....

The evidence establishes that the patterns of friction ridges on fingertips, palms, toes, and the soles of the feet are unique and permanent to each individual. The prints are unique as to each finger and toe of each person. In addition, there is a biological, embryological basis for the claim of uniqueness. Friction ridge patterns are affected by genetics, but even twins with identical genes have different fingerprints.

That claim of uniqueness and permanence is a scientific claim in the sense that it can be falsified. Such falsifiability is the hallmark of a scientific claim. See *Daubert,* 509 U.S. at 593 ... In the roughly 100 years since fingerprints have been used for identification purposes, no one has managed to falsify the claim of uniqueness by showing that fingers of two persons had identical fingerprints. Nor has anyone shown that the distinctive characteristics of one person's fingerprints changed over time (apart from readily explainable changes such as ... scarring).

For purposes of identification, an examiner generally uses a full "rolled" set of fingerprints taken under controlled circumstances. The process is a familiar one. Ink or some other substance is put on the fingers. One can then obtain a clear, high quality impression of the entire surface by carefully rolling the fingers on a card or piece of paper.

Latent prints are left by substances such as sweat, oil, or blood on the friction ridges and deposited on a surface, such as glass, paper, or the metal surface of a gun.

The latent prints provide an image of the friction ridges. Persons skilled in recovery of latent fingerprints can use various techniques to obtain a clear image of the latent print that can then be used for purposes of comparison to known exemplars. Latent prints are usually prints of only a relatively small portion of the friction ridges on a particular finger. Latent prints can also vary widely in terms of the quality and clarity of the image.

Comparison of fingerprints for purposes of identification focuses on three different levels of details. Level one is the largest scale of information, such as the general type of the central area of the fingerprint, such as an arch, whorl, or loop. Other level one details may include such matters as the overall ridge count, focal areas of the print, such as "delta regions.... Showing that level one details are identical is not enough to make an identification....

Level two detail focuses on the characteristics of ridge paths, such as places where ridges bifurcate or end or create dots or islands. These features provide a great deal of detail. Each feature can be identified in terms of the type of feature (end, bifurcation, etc.), its direction, and its location with respect to other identifiable features in the print. Level two detail can be used to identify one ... finger from among the entire human population as the source of the ... print.

Level three detail can be described as "ridge detail," with such tiny features as pores on a ridge and the width and shape of the ridge itself and its edges.... Meagher's testimony shows that when the latent print is sufficiently clear, level three detail can contribute to the identification of the source of a latent print.

According to Meagher, a fingerprint examiner goes through a four-step process with the acronym "ACE-V," for analysis, comparison, evaluation, and verification. At the first, analysis stage, the examiner studies the latent print closely and identifies the key features at levels one, two, and (if possible) three that can be used for identification purposes. The examiner then looks at a known exemplar print and analyzes it for key features. At the second, comparison stage, the examiner simply compares the latent print and the known exemplar feature by feature to see if they match up or if there are any unexplained discrepancies.

... Havvard objects to the third step, evaluation, in which the examiner forms and later testifies to an opinion as to whether the latent print and the known exemplar are from the same finger, or are not from the same finger, or whether the examiner has insufficient information to make a determination either way.

Meagher testified that there is no single quantifiable standard for reaching an identification opinion because of differences in both the quantity of characteristics shown in the latent print and the quality of the image. For example, if a latent print shows a relatively small portion of a fingerprint but has a very clear image—one that allows clear identification of level three detail such as the shapes of ridges, locations of pores, and the like, a reliable identification may still be possible even with relatively few level two "points."

Meagher's explanation makes sense, and the court credits it....

The most important point at the evaluation stage, however, is that a single unexplained discrepancy between the latent print and a known exemplar is sufficient to prove conclusively that the exemplar was not the source of the latent print.

The final step in the process is verification. Meagher testified that the general rule is that all ... opinions must be verified by a second qualified expert. The second expert may repeat the entire process, but the comparison may not be blind. That is, the second expert may know from the outset that another examiner has already made the positive identification.

III. *Applying* Daubert *to Latent Fingerprint Identification*

The court has adapted the *Daubert* reliability factors to this case, and those factors strongly support the reliability of latent print identification despite the absence of a single quantifiable threshold.

First, the methods of latent print identification can be and have been tested. They have been tested for roughly 100 years. They have been tested in adversarial proceedings with the highest possible stakes—liberty and sometimes life. The defense has offered no evidence in this case undermining the reliability of the methods in general. The government points out correctly that if anyone were to come across a case in which two different fingers had identical fingerprints, that news would flash around the legal world at the speed of light. It has not happened in 100 years.

Further, the methods can be tested in any individual case. Any identification opinion must be based on objective information—the latent image and the known exemplar—that is equally available to any qualified examiner for comparison and possible disagreement. A single unexplained discrepancy between a latent print and a known exemplar is enough to falsify an opinion of identification.

Next, the methods of identification are subject to peer review. As just stated, any other qualified examiner can compare the objective information upon which the opinion is based and may render a different opinion if warranted. In fact, peer review is the standard operating procedure among latent print examiners.

Daubert refers to publication after peer review, which is important in evaluating scientific evidence because it shows that others qualified in a field have evaluated the method or theory outside the context of litigation and have found it worthy of publication. The factor does not fit well with fingerprint identification because it is a field that has developed primarily for forensic purposes. The purpose of the publication factor is easily satisfied here, however, because latent fingerprint identification has been subject to adversarial testing for roughly 100 years, again in cases with the highest stakes possible. That track record provides far greater assurance of reliability than, for example, publication of one peer-reviewed article describing a novel theory about the cause of a particular disease at issue in a civil lawsuit.

Another *Daubert* factor is whether there are standards for controlling the technique. There are such standards through professional training, peer review, criticism, and presentation of conflicting evidence.

Another *Daubert* factor is whether there is a high known or potential error rate. There is not. The defense has presented no evidence of error rates, or even of any errors. The government claims the error rate for the method is zero. The claim is breathtaking, but it is qualified by the reasonable concession that an individual examiner can of course make an error in a particular case. Most important, an individual examiner's opinion can be tested and challenged for error by having another qualified examiner compare exactly the same images the first one compared....

Even allowing for the possibility of individual error, the error rate with latent print identification is vanishingly small when it is subject to fair adversarial testing and challenge. It is certainly far lower than the error rate for other types of opinions that courts routinely allow, such as opinions about the diagnosis of a disease, the cause of an accident or disease, whether a fire was accidental or deliberate in origin, or whether a particular industrial facility was the likely source of a contaminant in groundwater. As these examples indicate, the fact that some professional judgment and experience is required also does not mean that expert testimony is inadmissible. It is instead the hallmark of expert testimony, so long as it can otherwise meet the standards of reliability set forth in *Daubert* and *Kumho Tire*.

In sum, despite the absence of a single quantifiable standard for measuring the sufficiency of any latent print for purposes of identification, the court is satisfied that latent print identification easily satisfies the standards of reliability in *Daubert* and *Kumho Tire*. In fact, after going through this analysis, the court believes that latent print identification is the very archetype of reliable expert testimony under those standards. At the request of the government, the court has prepared this written opinion so that other courts might avoid unnecessarily replicating the process of establishing these points as they try to ensure they comply with the Supreme Court's directive to ensure that *all* types of expert testimony are subject to screening for reliability.

For the foregoing reasons, defendant Havvard's motion to exclude the government's proffered opinion testimony on the source of the latent fingerprint on one of the firearms in this case was denied....

Notes and Questions

1. Did Judge Hamilton's assessment of fingerprint analysis hold true to the mandate of *Daubert* to screen expert testimony for reliability prior to admission? Or are we not convinced that fingerprint analysis is "good science" after reading *Havvard*? If convinced, what factors from *Daubert* support admission? If skeptical, why doesn't the reasoning of the court prove convincing?

2. Just as in 2000, when *Havvard* was decided, fundamental principles of fingerprint analysis have not yet been rigorously tested. Paul Giannelli has noted the weaknesses of fingerprint analysis as follows: "[t]he basic problem with fingerprint identification is the lack of empirical testing, something that has been recognized by both courts and commentators." Paul C. Giannelli, Daubert *Challenges to Fingerprints*, 42 Crim. L. Bull. 624, 641 (Sept.–Oct. 2006). The lack of testing continues to today, as a 2017 report on fingerprints by the American Association for

the Advancement of Science concluded, after reviewing all available research in the field, that

> ... latent print examiners may well be able to exclude the preponderance of the human population as possible sources of a latent print, but there is no scientific basis for estimating the number of people who could not be excluded and, consequently, *no scientific basis* for determining when the pool of possible sources is limited to a single person. Moreover, research on examiners' accuracy when comparing known-source prints has provided ample evidence that false identifications can and do occur. Consequently, we have concluded that latent print examiners should *avoid claiming that they can associate a latent print with a single source* and should particularly avoid claiming or implying that they can do so infallibly, with 100% accuracy.[37]

3. Concerns with lack of testing and rigorous standards for fingerprint analysis are not ivory tower musings divorced from the real world. They can have major consequences, as the curious case of Brandon Mayfield can attest. Following the March 11, 2004, Madrid train bombings, the FBI matched a latent fingerprint collected on a plastic bag near the scene of the crime to Mr. Mayfield, an attorney in Portland, Oregon and a U.S. Army veteran. *Mayfield v. United States*, 599 F.3d 964, 966 (9th Cir. 2010). Even after Spanish authorities disagreed with the FBI's "100% positive identification," the FBI arrested and held Mayfield in custody for two weeks while his family was told he was being charged with a capital crime. *Id.* at 967. Only after the Spanish authorities matched the latent fingerprint to an Algerian suspect did the U.S. release Mayfield. Mayfield would settle his civil claims with the U.S. government, but the FBI mismanagement of the case's fingerprint evidence led to high-profile scrutiny and a Justice Department OIG Report.[38] More recently, PBS's *Frontline* made the Mayfield case a major part of their program highlighting weaknesses in forensic science. *Frontline: The Real CSI* (PBS Television broadcast Apr. 17, 2012), http://www.pbs.org/wgbh/frontline/film/real-csi/. *See also* William C. Thompson & Simon A. Cole, *Lessons from the Brandon Mayfield Case*, CHAMPION, Apr. 2005, at 42; Simon A. Cole, *More Than Zero: Accounting for Error in Latent Fingerprint Identification*, 95 J. CRIM. L. & CRIMINOLOGY 985 (2005); Sarah Kershaw et al., *Spain and U.S. at Odds on Mistaken Terror Arrest*, N.Y. TIMES, June 5, 2004, at A1.

4. Amid criticism of cases like *Havvard* for their weak application of the *Daubert* standards and as high-profile errors like the Mayfield case made headlines, the National Academy of Sciences issued their 2009 report on forensic science. NATIONAL RESEARCH COUNCIL, NATIONAL ACADEMY OF SCIENCES, STRENGTHENING

---

37. William Thompson et al., *Latent Fingerprint Examination*, FORENSIC SCIENCE ASSESSMENT: A QUALITY AND GAP ANALYSIS, AM. ASS'N FOR THE ADVANCEMENT OF SCI. 60 (Sept. 15, 2017) (emphasis added).

38. U.S. DEP'T OF JUST., OFF. OF THE INSPECTOR GEN., A REVIEW OF THE FBI'S HANDLING OF THE BRANDON MAYFIELD CASE (2006), https://oig.justice.gov/special/s0601/exec.pdf.

Forensic Science in the United States: A Path Forward (2009). We will review portions of the 2009 report in detail in Chapter 7, but in regards to fingerprint analysis, the authors noted:

> Because of the amount of detail available in friction ridges, it seems plausible that a careful comparison of two impressions can accurately discern whether or not they had a common source. Although there is limited information about the accuracy and reliability of friction ridge analyses, claims that these analyses have zero error rates are not scientifically plausible.

Id. at 142. How have courts reacted to these criticisms of forensics in more recent cases? To answer that question, let's look at a case that came after the NAS report (and cites it):

United States v. Aman
748 F. Supp. 2d 531 (E.D. Va. 2010)

Ellis, District Judge.

At issue in this arson prosecution is whether the proffered testimony of the government's three expert witnesses is admissible under Fed. R. Evid. 702 and *Daubert v. Merrell Dow Pharmaceuticals, Inc.*, 509 U.S. 579 (1993). Defendant Aman has moved to exclude ... (ii) the testimony of Charles Kubilus with respect to his fingerprint and palmprint analysis.... For the reasons that follow, this motion must be denied.

I.

A brief factual recitation provides useful context for resolution of defendant's motion. On November 1, 2009, at approximately 3:30 a.m., the City of Fairfax Fire Department responded to a fire alarm signal from Bridges, a large commercial establishment that includes a restaurant, bar, pool tables, lounge, and dance club. Bridges is on the ground floor of a seven-story commercial office building. On arrival at the scene, the firefighters located the one remaining active fire and extinguished it. Thereafter, fire officials inspected the property and found two bottles of charcoal lighter fluid sitting on a hostess stand. Circa this time, defendant approached fire officials outside Bridges and explained that he had been inside Bridges when he discovered the fire. Fire-medics detected an odor of ignitable liquids on defendant, and one of the medics escorted defendant to the back of an ambulance for evaluation. Defendant explained that he had been alone in Bridges when the fire broke out, and that he left his keys and cell phone in a box that also contained lighter fluid.

Shortly thereafter, two assistant fire marshals arrived on the scene to investigate the cause of the fire. Upon meeting the defendant, both fire marshals smelled ignitable liquid on defendant's person. One fire marshal, Lt. David Whitacre, stayed with defendant while the other fire marshal, Captain Gary Orndoff, investigated the Bridges interior. Defendant told Whitacre that he had been handling ignitable fluids in Bridges, but intended to take the fluids home with him after leaving work. Defendant also stated that he had driven to work, but had left his keys inside his office in Bridges. Orndoff made numerous observations inside Bridges, including finding two bottles of charcoal lighter fluid on the bar and a cardboard box in defendant's office containing five plastic jugs, a bottle of lighter fluid, car keys, and a cell phone.

A short time later, three additional officials arrived from the Fairfax County Fire Marshal's Office to investigate the fire.... While inspecting the premises of Bridges, [they] observed irregular burn patterns on the wooden dance floor, as well as a charred piece of baseboard separate from the burn patterns on the floor. The office also contained heavy fire damage separate and distinct from both the baseboard charring and the burn pattern on the dance floor. Robbins oversaw the delayering of the office, which revealed two books of matches, a partially burned black shirt that reeked of an ignitable liquid, and the bottom half of a water bottle that had been partially melted. The half-bottle contained a liquid that smelled like gasoline.

Defendant was arrested later that same morning and charged with arson. A later search of defendant's vehicle, which was located in an open parking lot near Bridges, revealed a bottle of lighter fluid, a pair of scissors, and the top half of a water bottle that was consistent in shape and size with the bottom half of the bottle recovered from the office at Bridges.

II.

The standards governing the admissibility of expert testimony are well-recognized. Under Rule 702, an expert witness may present opinion testimony "if (1) the testimony is based upon sufficient facts or data, (2) the testimony is the product of reliable principles and methods, and (3) the witness has applied the principles and methods reliably to the facts of the case." Although the Supreme Court in *Daubert* recognized that testing, peer review, the existence of a known error rate or controlling standards, and the general acceptance of the relevant scientific community may establish that testimony is based on "reliable principles and methods," the Supreme Court expressly cautioned that "[m]any factors will bear on the inquiry, and we do not presume to set out a definitive checklist or test," emphasizing that "the inquiry envisioned by Rule 702 is ... a flexible one." *Daubert*, 509 U.S. at 593–94. Importantly, the *Daubert* inquiry focuses on the reliability of the expert's principles and methodology, rather than the conclusions generated. Finally, it should be noted that "vigorous cross-examination, presentation of contrary evidence, and careful instruction on the burden of proof are the traditional and appropriate means of attacking shaky but admissible evidence." And as always, the exercise of a district court's gate-keeping role should not transform a *Daubert* hearing into a trial on the merits. In this regard, courts have sensibly held that a district court has broad discretion in deciding how to resolve a *Daubert* challenge. In particular, a hearing is not necessary in all cases, as the submissions of the parties may provide a sufficient basis to determine if the proffered testimony is admissible.

III.

. . .

B. Testimony of Charles Kubilus

Charles Kubilus is a fingerprint specialist with the Bureau of Alcohol, Tobacco, Firearms, and Explosives ("ATF") Forensic Science Laboratory. He will testify that he examined the latent fingerprints and palmprints from Bridges and, with the exception of one palmprint, matched all the prints to defendant's known prints. Defendant contends both that the methods of fingerprint analysis are unreliable and that the methods were not reliably applied in this case.

Kubilus has significant experience in fingerprint analysis. For nine years, Kubilus worked at the Federal Bureau of Investigation ("FBI") as a fingerprint examiner. Following his time at the FBI, he served as a fingerprint specialist with the United States Secret Service for four years. In 2006, he left the Secret Service for his current post at the ATF. Kubilus has completed a two-month course in fingerprint examination and collection at the FBI, and he serves as an instructor in processing and comparing fingerprints. He has been certified as a fingerprint specialist by the FBI, Secret Service, ATF, and the International Association for Identification. He is plainly a well-qualified fingerprint analyst.

Defendant first attacks the reliability of the methodology Kubilus followed, namely the well-known Analysis-Comparison-Evaluation-Verification ("ACE-V") method for fingerprint identification. In his affidavit, Kubilus described each of the four steps in the ACE-V method: (i) analysis, (ii) comparison, (iii) evaluation, and (iv) verification.

The *analysis* phase relies on a "qualitative and quantitative" assessment of friction ridge detail at three levels of granularity: (i) ridge flow, which is the direction of the friction ridges; (ii) individual ridge examination, including bifurcations, ridge endings, and ridge dots; and (iii) poroscopy, which is the examination of pores. The first level of detail can be used to exclude, but not to identify, a print, while a combination of the second and third levels of detail may allow for either identification or exclusion. The latent print is analyzed first, followed by the known print. If either the latent or the known print is unsuitable for examination, the analysis ends.

The *comparison* phase involves side-by-side observation of friction ridge detail to determine if the details match in similarity, sequence, and spatial relationship. According to Kubilus, differences in the fingerprints do not necessarily end the analysis; rather, the examiner must determine whether the dissimilarity is explainable given pressure differences, surface texture, print medium (*e.g.*, ink, sweat, or blood), and other expected variations.

In his testimony, Kubilus stated that no set number of similarities—sometimes known as "points"—indicates a match, since it is both the quantity and quality of similarities that allow for identification. Likewise, the number of explained dissimilarities—that is, dissimilarities believed to be the result of expected variations—is not dispositive either for or against finding a match.

The third phase in the ACE-V method—*evaluation*—requires the examiner to form a conclusion about the prints. The examiner can conclude that the prints are a match (known as "individualization" or "identification"), that they are not a match (known as "exclusion"), or that the result is inconclusive. Both the comparison and evaluation phases involve the exercise of judgment by an examiner based on that examiner's training and experience.

Following the evaluation phase is the fourth and final phase: *verification*. In the verification phase, a second examiner is provided the same prints and asked to check the work of the first examiner. Notably, the second examiner is aware of the first examiner's conclusion. In Kubilus's experience, only once has a verifying examiner ever disagreed with the finding of the first examiner.

To determine whether Kubilus's testimony is admissible requires examining, first, the underlying method and, second, Kubilus's application of that method in this case. The ACE-V method is not without criticism. Although fingerprint examination has been conducted for a century, the process still involves a measure of art as well as science. The Fourth Circuit has noted that while not "scientific law," the principles underlying fingerprint examination "bear the imprimatur of a strong general acceptance, not only in the expert community, but in the courts as well." *United States v. Crisp*, 324 F.3d 261, 265–66 (4th Cir.2003). But of course, a history of judicial and expert community acceptance does not obviate the government's burden to demonstrate in this case reliability of the expert's testimony under *Daubert*. The [National Research Council of the National Academy of Sciences] Report devotes significant attention to friction ridge analysis, noting the "subjective" and "interpret[ive]" nature of such examination. Additionally, the examiner does not know, *a priori,* which areas of the print will be most relevant to the given analysis, and small twists or smudges in prints can significantly alter the points of comparison. This unpredictability can make it difficult to establish a clear framework with objective criteria for fingerprint examiners. And unlike DNA analysis, which has been subjected to population studies to demonstrate its precision, studies on friction ridge analysis to date have not yielded accurate population statistics. In other words, while some may assert that no two fingerprints are alike, the proposition is not easily susceptible to scientific validation.

Furthermore, while fingerprint experts sometimes use terms like "absolute" and "positive" to describe the confidence of their matches, the NRC has recognized that a zero-percent error rate is "not scientifically plausible." Kubilus has pointed out that some studies have demonstrated a high degree of accuracy in the work of fingerprint examiners, but the small sample sizes used in such studies diminish their persuasiveness. For example, a recent pilot study of the ACE-V process found no errors in any of the trials in which examiners found two prints to be a match.[11] But this study involved just six examiners in sixty ACE-V trials, and other studies have yet to test the accuracy of fingerprint examiners on a larger scale.

Additionally, the steps in the ACE-V method raise concerns about scientific validity, not only because of the subjective nature of the analysis, but also the lack of "blind" verification. This is so because the second examiner in the verification phase generally knows the conclusion reached by the first examiner, which calls into question whether the verification may be biased. Yet, it is worth noting that

---

11. *See* Glenn Langenberg, *A Performance Study of the ACE-V Process: A Pilot Study to Measure the Accuracy, Precision, Reproducibility, Repeatability, and Biasability of Conclusions Resulting from the ACE-V Process*, 59 J. of Forensic Identification 219 (2008).

the Langenberg pilot study examined this phenomenon and found that even after attempting to bias the examiners by stating that a prior examiner found a match where none existed, no examiner found the same pair of prints to be a match. That is, no examiner incorrectly verified a false-positive. Nevertheless, as stated previously, a study on the accuracy of friction ridge analysis has yet to be replicated on a large scale.

The absence of a known error rate, the lack of population studies, and the involvement of examiner judgment all raise important questions about the rigorousness of friction ridge analysis. To be sure, further testing and study would likely enhance the precision and reviewability of fingerprint examiners' work, the issues defendant raises concerning the ACE-V method are appropriate topics for cross-examination, not grounds for exclusion. Defendant's most significant criticism of the ACE-V method is that the process requires the exercise of judgment.... [T]he fact that ACE-V involves judgment does not render the method unreliable for *Daubert* purposes. *See United States v. Mitchell,* 365 F.3d 215, 241 (3d Cir.2004) (finding that the subjective nature of fingerprint analysis weighs against, but does not bar, its admissibility under *Daubert*). Judgment is, and must be, ubiquitous in science. Indeed, experts across various fields routinely must rely on the exercise of judgment in their work, and this fact alone does not prevent them from offering reliable, admissible opinions in court.

Furthermore, it can hardly be questioned that the ACE-V method has achieved widespread acceptance in the fingerprint examination community. The Scientific Working Group on Friction Ridge Analysis, Study and Technology ("SWGFAST"), which is composed of fingerprint specialists from numerous local, state, and federal law enforcement agencies, has established standards for fingerprint analysis for more than fifteen years. SWGFAST has supported ACE-V and published standards governing its application. According to Kubilus, SWGFAST has consistently concluded that there is no scientific basis for a predetermined number of points of ridge similarity to warrant an identification. In sum, the ACE-V method, although perhaps not worthy of the pedestal on which it has been historically placed, is sufficiently reliable to overcome *Daubert*'s bar to admissibility.

As to Kubilus's application of the ACE-V method, his testimony and reports make clear that he applied the ACE-V method reliably to the prints in this case. Kubilus examined two latent fingerprints and six latent palmprints recovered from Bridges. He found that both fingerprints and five of the six palmprints matched defendant's known prints, and each of these conclusions was verified by a second examiner. Kubilus identified between eleven and seventeen points of similarities in each print. As to the sixth palmprint, Kubilus stated that the print lacked sufficient clarity and completeness to allow for identification, and as such, the evaluation of that print was deemed inconclusive.

Because the ACE-V method is based on sufficiently reliably principles and methods, and because those principles and methods were reliably applied in this case by an expert with sufficient knowledge, skill, training, and experience, Kubilus's testimony passes muster under Fed. R. Evid 702 and *Daubert*....

Notes and Questions

1. In reading *Aman*, how is the analysis of the court here different than in *Jennings*, the 1911 case from Illinois? How is it similar? What about a comparison to *Havvard*? What does this analysis tell you about the impact of criticisms of fingerprint comparison methodology?

2. Lest one believe that lenient application of reliability standards is limited solely to judges applying the *Daubert* standard, it appears *Frye* jurisdictions also admit latent fingerprint analysis due to its long-standing acceptance. *See People v. Luna*, 989 N.E.2d 655, 679 (Ill. App. Ct. 2013) (affirming decision of the trial court to take judicial notice of the "general acceptance" of fingerprint comparison); *Markham v. State*, 984 A.2d 262 (Md. Ct. Spec. App. 2009) (same). In *State v. Dixon*, 822 N.W.2d 664 (Minn. Ct. App. 2013), the trial court held a *Frye* hearing on admissibility but found the technique to meet the "general acceptance" standard since the "relevant scientific community" included experts who were "actually involved in latent-print analysis and those who actually research the reliability of latent-print analysis." *Id.* at 674. It should surprise no one to learn that, within the community of latent print examiners, the acceptance of the technique was never in doubt.

3. Courts' unwillingness to rigorously vet fingerprint evidence has led one prominent scholar to lament:

   > Despite the ruckus created by *Llera Plaza* and the Mayfield fiasco, examiner testimony remained unchanged. Testimony such as "zero error rates," "matches to the exclusion of all other fingerprints," and "100 percent certainty"—which had been used for decades—continued, while the fingerprint community remain oblivious that such statements were scientifically implausible.

   Paul C. Giannelli, *Forensic Science:* Daubert*'s Failure*, 68 Case W. Res. L. Rev. 869, 927 (2018). Giannelli concludes that "*Daubert* had little effect." *Id.*

4. Whether the situation will change depends on many factors, including the willingness of the judiciary and law enforcement to challenge conventional wisdom. It also depends, however, on the completion of baseline research into the methodologies and assumptions about fingerprint analysis. The Epstein article, *Fingerprints Meet Daubert*, highlights the current weaknesses in the scientific basis for ACE-V analysis. But that does not mean the technique is irrevocably and fundamentally flawed. Even the NAS Report stated that it "seems plausible that a careful comparison of two impressions can accurately discern whether or not they had a common source."[39]

   Therefore, fundamental baseline research—into the patterns of fingerprints, accuracy and standards for matching, and other basic assumptions—is urgently

---

39. National Research Council, National Academy of Sciences, Strengthening Forensic Science in the United States: A Path Forward 142 (2009).

needed. PRESIDENT'S COUNCIL OF ADVISORS ON SCI. AND TECH., FORENSIC SCI-
ENCE IN CRIMINAL COURTS: ENSURING SCIENTIFIC VALIDITY OF FEATURE-COM-
PARISON METHODS 87–95 (2016) (recognizing the need for, and reviewing the
results from, early proficiency testing studies on fingerprint analysis).

Tying It Together

Imagine that after the District Court ruling in *Aman*, the case goes to trial and
the jury convicts the Defendant of all charges. He then appeals to the Fourth Circuit,
asking for the conviction to be overturned due to the admission of the fingerprint
comparison evidence.

Assignment: You have been assigned his case as a federal public defender, and there
is a pending deadline for filing the petitioner's brief. Draft a brief on behalf of your
client, explaining why his conviction must be overturned by the Court of Appeals.

Alternative Assignment: You are clerking for one of the three Judges assigned the
Aman appeal. Draft a preliminary decision on the case, either denying or granting
petitioner's appeal.

Chapter 7

Other Forensic Identification Methodologies

We began our assessment of forensic identification techniques with DNA evidence, a discipline that has been thoroughly tested and, when done properly, can offer a statistically-based high degree of certainty of a positive identification. Our next step was to consider fingerprint evidence, a discipline where fundamental baseline research into the patterns of fingerprints, accuracy and standards for matching, and other basic assumptions is urgently needed.[40] Yet even without that testing, the National Academy of Sciences Report *A Path Forward* from 2009 stated that it "seems plausible that a careful comparison of two impressions can accurately discern whether or not they had a common source."[41] So the discipline has strong theoretical underpinnings, even if baseline research remains to be done.

As we continue our assessment of forensic identification techniques, we now move into more controversial areas, including hair analysis, handwriting comparison, and toolmark identification. It may seem that each of these disciplines is separate and distinct; it is not obvious at first glance what comparison of hair, handwriting, and a knife wound all have in common. Yet, at their core, each discipline rests on a similar, unstable foundation, namely that the basis for admissibility has been, and likely will continue to be, the training and expertise of the expert.

Why have courts admitted testimony from these experts? And has the warning of the Supreme Court in *General Electric Co. v. Joiner*[42] (to not admit expert testimony solely based on the *ipse dixit* of the expert) had any effect on admissibility? To consider those issues, we need to break our assessment into separate sections for each discipline and consider the methodology of each technique and why courts have admitted it. We will then, for each, consider the effect of the mandate of *Daubert*—to rigorously evaluate the underpinnings of the claimed expertise to decide if it is "good science"— by looking at current criticism of each technique as well as whether those criticisms have had an effect in the courtroom. As with the chapters on DNA and fingerprints, the focus here is not on being able to personally perform the comparison in question, but instead on how the science is used and misused in litigation.

---

40. President's Council of Advisors on Sci. and Tech., Forensic Science in Criminal Courts: Ensuring Scientific Validity of Feature-Comparison Methods 87–95 (2016).

41. National Research Council, National Academy of Sciences, Strengthening Forensic Science in the United States: A Path Forward 142 (2009).

42. Gen. Elec. Co. v. Joiner, 522 U.S. 136, 146 (1997).

A. Microscopic Hair Comparison

Paul C. Giannelli, Edward J. Imwinkelreid & Joseph Peterson, *Reference Guide on Forensic Identification Expertise*

REFERENCE MANUAL ON SCIENTIFIC EVIDENCE
112–16 (3d ed. 2011)[Ed.]

. . .

X. Microscopic Hair Evidence

The first reported use of forensic hair analysis occurred more than 150 years ago in 1861 in Germany. The first published American opinion was an 1882 Wisconsin decision, *Knoll v. State*.[355] Based on a microscopic comparison, the expert testified that the hair samples shared a common source. Hair and the closely related fiber analysis played a prominent role in two of the most famous twentieth-century American prosecutions: Ted Bundy in Florida and Wayne Williams, the alleged Atlanta child killer. Although hair comparison evidence has been judicially accepted for decades, it is another forensic identification discipline that is being reappraised....

A. The Technique

Generally, after assessing whether a sample is a hair and not a fiber, an analyst may be able to determine: (1) whether the hair is of human or animal origin, (2) the part of the body that the hair came from, (3) whether the hair has been dyed, (4) whether the hair was pulled or fell out as a result of natural causes or disease, and (5) whether the hair was cut or crushed.

The most common subject for hair testimony involves an attempt to individuate the hair sample, at least to some degree. If the unknown is head hair, the expert might gather approximately 50 hair strands from five different areas of the scalp (the top, front, back, and both sides) from the known source. Before the microscopic analysis, the expert examines the hair macroscopically to identify obvious features visible to the naked eye such as the color of the hair and its form, that is, whether it is straight, wavy, or curved. The expert next mounts the unknown hair and the known samples on microscope slides for a more detailed examination of characteristics such as scale patterns, size, color, pigment distribution, maximum diameter, shaft length, and scale count. Some of these comparative judgments are subjective in nature: "Human hair characteristics (e.g., scale patterns, pigmentation, size) vary within a single individual.... Although the examination procedure involves objective methods of analysis, the subjective weights associated with the characteristics rest with the examiner."[361]

[Ed.] Reprinted with permission from the National Academy of Sciences, Courtesy of the National Academies Press, Washington, D.C.

355. 12 N.W. 369 (Wis. 1882).

361. Larry S. Miller, *Procedural Bias in Forensic Science Examinations of Human Hair*, 11 LAW & HUM. BEHAV. 157, 157–58 (1987).

Often the examiner determines only whether the hair samples from the crime scene and the accused are "microscopically indistinguishable." Although this finding is consistent with the hypothesis that the samples had the same source, its probative value would, of course, vary if only a hundred people had microscopically indistinguishable hair as opposed to several million. As discussed below, experts have often gone beyond this "consistent with" testimony.

B. The Empirical Record

The 2009 NRC report contained an assessment of hair analysis. The report began the assessment by observing that there are neither "scientifically accepted [population] frequency" statistics for various hair characteristics nor "uniform standards on the number of features on which hairs must agree before an examiner may declare a 'match.'" The report concluded,

> [T]estimony linking microscopic hair analysis with particular defendants is highly unreliable. In cases where there seems to be a morphological match (based on microscopic examination), it must be confirmed using mtDNA analysis; microscopic studies are of limited probative value. The committee found no scientific support for the use of hair comparisons for individualization in the absence of nuclear DNA. Microscopy and mtDNA analysis can be used in tandem and add to one another's value for classifying a common source, but no studies have been performed specifically to quantify the reliability of their joint use.[363]

There is a general consensus that hair examination can yield reliable information about class characteristics of hair strands. Indeed, experts can identify major as well as secondary characteristics. Major characteristics include such features as color, shaft form, and hair diameter. Secondary characteristics are such features as pigment size and shaft diameter. These characteristics can help narrow the class of possible sources for the unknown hair sample.

There have been several major efforts to provide an empirical basis for individuation opinions in hair analysis. In the 1940s, Gamble and Kirk investigated whether hair samples from different persons could be distinguished on the basis of scale counts.[367] However, they used a small database of only thirty-nine hair samples, and a subsequent attempt to replicate the original experiment yielded contradictory results.

In the 1960s, neutron activation analysis was used in an effort to individuate hair samples. The research focused on determining the occurrence of various trace element

---

363. National Research Council, National Academy of Sciences, Strengthening Forensic Science in the United States: A Path Forward 160 (2009).

367. Lucy L. Gamble & Paul L. Kirk, *Human Hair Studies II. Scale Counts*, 31 J. Crim. L. & Criminology 627, 629 (1941); Paul L. Kirk & Lucy L. Gamble, *Further Investigation of the Scale Count of Human Hair*, 33 J. Crim. L. & Criminology 276, 280 (1942).

concentrations in human hair.[369] Again, subsequent research tended to show that there are significant hair-to-hair variations in trace element concentration among the hairs of a single person.

In the 1970s, two Canadian researchers, Gaudette and Keeping, attempted to develop a "ballpark" estimate of the probability of a false match in hair analysis. They published articles describing three studies: (1) a 1974 study involving scalp hair, (2) a 1976 study using pubic hair, and (3) a 1978 followup.[373] In the two primary studies (1974 and 1976), hair samples were analyzed to determine whether hairs from different persons were microscopically indistinguishable. The analysts used 23 different characteristics such as color, pigment distribution, maximum diameter, shaft length, and scale count. Based on those data, they estimated the probability of a false match in scalp hair to be 1 in 4500 and the probability of a false match in pubic hair to be 1 in 800.

In the view of one commentator, Gaudette and Keeping's probability estimates "are easily challenged."[375] One limitation was the relatively small database in the study. Moreover, the studies involved samples from different individuals and sought the probability that the samples from different persons would nonetheless appear microscopically indistinguishable. In a criminal trial, the question is quite different: Assuming the samples appear microscopically indistinguishable, what is the probability that they came from the same person?

Early in the twenty-first century, the Verma research team revisited the individualization issue and attempted to develop an objective, automated method for identifying matches.[378] The authors claimed that their "system accurately judged whether two populations of hairs came from the same person or from different persons 83% of the time." However, a close inspection of the authors' tabular data indicates that (1) relying on this method, researchers characterized "9 of 73 different pairs as 'same' for a false positive rate of 9/73 = 12%"; and (2) the researchers characterized "4 sets of hairs from the same person as 'different' for a false negative rate of 4/9 = 44%."[379]

---

369. Rita Cornelis, *Is It Possible to Identify Individuals by Neutron Activation Analysis of Hair?*, 12 MED. SCI. & L. 188 (1972); Lima et al., *Activation Analysis Applied to Forensic Investigation: Some Observations on the Problem of Human Hair Individualization*, 1 RADIO CHEM. METHODS OF ANALYSIS 119 (Int'l Atomic Energy Agency 1965); A.K. Perkins, *Individualization of Human Head Hair*, PROCEEDINGS OF THE FIRST INT'L CONF. ON FORENSIC ACTIVATION ANALYSIS 221 (V. Guin ed., 1967).

373. B.D. Gaudette, *Some Further Thoughts on Probabilities in Human Hair Comparisons*, 23 J. FORENSIC SCI. 758 (1978); B.D. Gaudette, *Probabilities and Human Pubic Hair Comparisons*, 21 J. FORENSIC SCI. 514, 514 (1976); B.D. Gaudette & E.S. Keeping, *An Attempt at Determining Probabilities in Human Scalp Hair Comparison*, 19 J. FORENSIC SCI. 599 (1974). [Author note—the footnotes for these three articles have been consolidated into this single footnote, for clarity purposes.]

375. DAVID KAYE, SCIENCE IN EVIDENCE 28 (1997)....

378. M.S. Verma et al., *Hair-MAP: A Prototype Automated System for Forensic Hair Comparison and Analysis*, 129 FORENSIC SCI. INT'L 168 (2002).

379. NATIONAL RESEARCH COUNCIL, NATIONAL ACADEMY OF SCIENCES, STRENGTHENING FORENSIC SCIENCE IN THE UNITED STATES: A PATH FORWARD 159 (2009).

Commonwealth v. McCauley

588 A.2d 941 (Pa. Super. Ct. 1991)

TAMILIA, Judge.

At approximately 11:00 p.m. on Saturday, June 25, 1977, the 21-year old victim was hitch-hiking to her home in Boalsburg after finishing her shift at a waitressing job in State College, Centre County, Pennsylvania. The evidence suggests she was forced by appellant and Jessie Taylor, who were riding as passengers, into a van owned and operated by Robert Brown. At one point, the victim attempted to jump from the moving van but was forcibly constrained by appellant and Taylor. Disregarding the victim's pleas not to be harmed, they drove to a secluded area at a ski resort where appellant, who had been using cocaine, and Taylor, in an act of animal brutality, forcibly raped, beat and choked the victim. Afterwards, appellant and Taylor hog-tied the victim's arms and legs with her panty hose, gagged her mouth with a bandana and, because, as appellant stated, "[d]ead people don't talk," threw her off the Route 322 Thompsontown overpass, where she fell 44 feet to her death. By-passers found the victim's partially nude, bound and gagged body the following day.

The eleven-year murder investigation took several turns. Shortly after the murder, Brown's van was identified as the possible vehicle used in the abduction. When state police questioned Brown, he gave a false alibi and committed suicide a few days after being confronted with the suspicions against him.

In 1979, the state police suspected appellant's possible involvement in the crime. Thereafter, they questioned appellant and although placing himself at the murder scene, he exculpated himself. The break in the case came sometime in 1985 when Prisk, who, in 1983, had been appellant's cell-mate while appellant was serving time on an unrelated charge, informed the state police that appellant admitted to raping and taking part in the murder of Frink. State police also followed leads which resulted in the questioning of Catherine Crossley, appellant's girlfriend. Crossley, apprehensive of divulging admissions made to her by her boyfriend, gave little information which could corroborate Prisk's story. In 1987, Crossley was called to testify before the grand jury investigating the Frink murder and, under oath, she fully reiterated admissions appellant made to her concerning his role in the rape and murder. Additionally, state police obtained evidence developed by Janice Roadcap, a forensic criminalist with 32 years experience in microscopic hair examination. Roadcap, in her testimony, concluded that a hair found on the victim's calf closely resembled appellant's chest hair.

Due to time constraints and lack of resources, the Juniata County District Attorney made a request to the Office of the Attorney General to take over the investigation and prosecution of the case. On September 30, 1988, based on the evidence and testimony set forth above, the grand jury issued a presentment recommending that murder charges be brought against McCauley. A criminal complaint was filed and appellant was tried and convicted by a jury in 1989, twelve years after the murder was committed.

Appellant raises nine issues for our review....

... Appellant next asserts it was error to admit the testimony of Janice Roadcap, the Commonwealth forensic criminalist, allegedly because she was not qualified as an expert.

The Pennsylvania Supreme Court in *Commonwealth v. Topa*, 369 A.2d 1277, 1281 (Pa. 1977) established the standards by which scientifically adduced evidence may be qualified for presentation at trial in this Commonwealth when it adopted the notions so vividly expressed in *Frye v. United States*, 293 F. 1013 (D.C. 1923):

> Just when a scientific principle or discovery crosses that line between the experimental and demonstrable stages is difficult to define. Somewhere in this twilight zone the evidential force of the principle must be recognized, and while courts will go a long way in admitting expert testimony deduced from a well-recognized scientific principle or discovery, *the thing from which the deduction is made must be sufficiently established to have gained general acceptance in the particular field in which it belongs.*

Commonwealth v. Topa, 369 A.2d at 1281 (quoting *Frye*, 293 F. at 1014) (emphasis in original).

Our Supreme Court proceeded in *Commonwealth v. Topa* to pronounce the rationale for its adoption of the *Frye* standard:

> The requirement of general acceptance in the scientific community assures that those most qualified to assess the general validity of a scientific method will have the determinative voice. Additionally, the *Frye* test protects prosecution and defense alike by assuring that a minimal reserve of experts exists who can critically examine the validity of a scientific determination in a particular case. Since scientific proof may in some instances assume a posture of mystic infallibility in the eyes of a jury of laymen, the ability to produce rebuttal experts, equally conversant with the mechanics and methods of a particular technique, may prove to be essential.

Commonwealth v. Topa, 369 A.2d at 1282 (quoting *United States v. Addision*, 498 F.2d 741, 744 (D.C. Cir. 1974)). Roadcap has 32 years [of] experience in microscopic hair examination. She has concentrated in this area for over 20 years completing more than 2,000 comparisons. She testified for both the defense and prosecution in over 40 cases and was accepted therein as an expert in microscopic hair examination. In testifying in the instant case, she referred to the practice as a science, and made reference to her reliance on treatises and the FBI manual concerning microscopic hair examination.

Although we are unpersuaded by the authority cited by both the Commonwealth and appellant, we hold microscopic hair comparison evidence satisfies the *Frye* standard. Various federal and state courts have held the same. *United States v. Cyphers*, 553 F.2d 1064 (7th Cir. 1977), *cert. denied*, 434 U.S. 843 (1978) (armed robbery prosecution, expert opinion that human hairs found on items used in robbery could have come from defendants was admissible for whatever value jury might give it); *United States v. Haskins*, 536 F.2d 775 (8th Cir. 1976), *cert. denied*, 429 U.S. 898 (1977) (bank robbery, expert testimony identifying hair sample found in a silk stocking near bank as matching known sample of defendant's hair admissible; credibility of expert and weight given was for jury to determine and testimony was not invasion of jury's province); *People v. Columbo*, 455 N.E.2d 733 (Ill. App. 1983), *cert. denied*, 467 U.S. 1208 (1984) (expert testimony that defendant's hair was similar in color and characteristics to hair found on murder victim's T-shirt had probative value, and although not conclusive, was properly considered by the jury, and neither exclusionary character of hair comparisons nor lack of absolute scientific certainty rendered hair expert's testimony inadmissible); *Paxton v. State*, 282 S.E.2d 912 (Ga. App. 1981), *writ denied*, 283 S.E.2d 235 (Ga. 1982) (expert testimony pubic hairs found at scene of rape matching defendant's admissible); *State v. Pratt*, 295 S.E.2d 462 (N.C. 1982); *State v. Kersting*, 638 P.2d 1145 (Or. 1982); *State v. Melson*, 638 S.W.2d 342 (Tenn. 1982), *cert. denied*, 459 U.S. 1137 (1983); *State v. Clayton*, 646 P.2d 723 (Utah 1982).

Accordingly, Roadcap's testimony was legally relevant insofar as it was more probative than prejudicial. It did not mislead, prejudice or confuse the jury but gave a demonstrable accepted form of tying appellant to the crime.... Judgment of sentence affirmed.

Notes and Questions

1. *McCauley* is an example of the typical depth of analysis contained within pre-*Daubert* cases challenging microscopic hair analysis, in which a court notes the objection but then quickly dismisses it based on the expert's qualifications, prior cases accepting the evidence, or lack of prejudice to the defendant. *See, e.g., People v. Pride*, 833 P.2d 643 (Cal. 1992); *People v. Vettese*, 489 N.W.2d 514 (Mich. Ct. App. 1992); *State v. Harrison*, 357 N.W.2d 201 (Neb. 1984); *State v. Lerch*, 677 P.2d 678 (Or. 1984); *State v. White*, 621 S.W.2d 287 (Mo. 1981); *People v. Allweiss*, 396 N.E.2d 735 (N.Y. 1979). It comes as no surprise, then, to learn that an overwhelming majority of cases addressing the issue of microscopic hair analysis have resulted in affirming admission of the evidence on appeal. Paul C. Giannelli, *Microscopic Hair Comparisons: A Cautionary Tale*, 46 Crim. Law Bull. 7 (2010); Edward J. Imwinkelried, *Forensic Hair Analysis: The Case Against the Underemployment of Scientific Evidence*, 39 Wash. & Lee L. Rev. 41, 62 (1982).

2. The combination of judicial acceptance of hair comparison evidence and the jury's perception of hair comparison (in addition to other similar types of evidence) as strong evidence[43] led to the significant potential for its misuse. A more recent study evaluating causes of wrongful conviction found a number of cases — 42 out of 200 cases — involved improper hair comparison evidence. Brandon L. Garrett, *Judging Innocence*, 108 Colum. L. Rev. 55, 83 (2008); *see also* Giannelli, *Microscopic Hair Comparisons*, at Part I.G. As we move on to examine the effect of *Daubert* on the admissibility of hair comparison evidence, keep in mind the overwhelming pre-existing authority in favor of admission.

---

43. Paul C. Giannelli et al., Scientific Evidence § 24.01, 799 (5th ed. 2012) (noting trace evidence seen as highly persuasive to juries); *see also* Jonathan Koehler, *Intuitive Error Rate Estimates for the Forensic Sciences*, 57 Jurimetrics J. 153, 162 (2017) (finding mock jurors estimate error rate for hair comparison as 1 in 1 million).

Williamson v. Reynolds

904 F. Supp. 1529 (E.D. Okla. 1995)

Seay, Chief Judge.

Petitioner was convicted of First Degree Murder and condemned to death in 1988 by the District Court of Pontotoc County, Oklahoma. On direct appeal, the Oklahoma Court of Criminal Appeals affirmed Petitioner's conviction and death sentence. Petitioner now seeks ... [habeas corpus relief,] ... asserting that his conviction and death sentence were obtained in violation of the U.S. Constitution. Petitioner has not previously sought habeas corpus relief in federal court.

The facts, according to the trial record, are presented here as follows. On December 8, 1982, twenty-one-year-old Debbie Carter was found dead in her garage apartment in Ada, Oklahoma. She was discovered by her father, who had come to check on her at her mother's request, fearing that something might be wrong. Walking up the stairs to the second floor apartment, Mr. Carter observed glass on the landing and saw the screen door and front door standing wide open. Continuing through the apartment to the bedroom, he found Debbie's body lying face down on the floor with a washcloth stuck in her mouth. The police were called, and the investigation into the murder began.

Detective Dennis Smith of the Ada Police Department was among the first to arrive at the scene. He testified at trial that the apartment showed signs of a struggle. Broken glass was found both inside and outside the front door. In the living room, the sofa cushions and a nightgown were on the floor. On the wall, written in what was later determined to be fingernail polish, were the words, "Jim Smith next will die." On top of the kitchen table was written, "don't look fore [sic] us or ealse [sic]." Approaching the bedroom, he found the bed blocking entry into the room. The room was in complete disarray with clothing, sheets, blankets and stuffed animals on the floor. Debbie Carter's body, nude except for a pair of white socks, was on the floor between the bed and the wall. Written on her back in catsup were the words "Duke Graham." The word "die" was written on her chest in fingernail polish. A blood-soaked washcloth was stuffed into her mouth and down into her throat. Underneath the body was an electric cord and a belt. The bathroom, connected to the bedroom, showed no signs of a disturbance.

Four years and five months later, on May 8, 1987, Petitioner and Dennis Fritz were charged with the murder of Debbie Carter. Separate trials were held, and approximately two weeks before Petitioner's trial began, Dennis Fritz was found guilty and sentenced to life imprisonment.

Petitioner asserts seventeen grounds for relief....

III. *HAIR EVIDENCE*

Petitioner alleges ... that the unreliability and inherent subjectivity of microscopic hair comparison should prohibit its admissibility....

The prosecution's only physical evidence, apart from the semen evidence, were hairs allegedly found to be "microscopically consistent" with Petitioner and his co-defendant Dennis Fritz. Dennis Smith, retired detective captain of the Ada Police Department, testified that he and OSBI Agent Gary Rogers collected several hundred hairs at the crime scene. Individual hairs were placed in paper bindles which are pieces of paper that have been folded over several times. The victim's stuffed animals which had hairs attached to them were placed in bags. Head hair, pubic hair and saliva samples were taken from the victim's family and friends shortly after the murder. Samples were also collected from Glen Gore, who likely was the last person seen with the victim, and Mike Carpenter, whose fingerprint was found in her car. Smith and Rogers transported these samples to the Oklahoma State Crime Bureau.

In March 1983 the police department asked Petitioner and Dennis Fritz to submit hair and saliva samples, and they complied. These samples were also taken to the OSBI for analysis....

Mary Long, OSBI criminalist, testified that she collected pubic combings from the victim and hairs from articles found in the victim's apartment. She also collected known pubic hair and known scalp hair from the victim. Long sent this evidence to Susan Land, another OSBI criminalist. In all, Long submitted 45 hair sample containers to Land.

Susan Land testified that although she had hair samples from many individuals, the only samples she mounted on microscope slides were those from the victim, Petitioner and Fritz. She stated that she may have commenced a microscopic examination of some of the hair samples, but stopped because she did not feel she could be objective in her analysis due to the "stress and strain" from working on numerous homicide cases. Consequently, she turned the mounted and unmounted hair samples over to Melvin Hett on September 19, 1983.

Hett, the third OSBI criminalist to examine the evidence, testified that he had been engaged in the science of hair identification approximately 13 years and that about 90% of his time was devoted to hair and fiber comparisons and analysis. He brought charts prepared at his request to demonstrate the major racial characteristics of hair: Caucasian, Negroid and Mongoloid. He stated that in Oklahoma, however, there are many mixtures of the three racial types. He explained that a cross section of a human hair shows the three areas of human hairs: the cuticle or outer layer of scales, the cortex which gives hair its color, and the medulla which is usually just an air sack running down the center of the hair. Hett further testified that there are approximately 25 characteristics used in hair comparisons. He used his exhibits to demonstrate other characteristics and variations used in hair analysis and discussed factors such as bleaching, dying, sun bleaching and brushing which can change the characteristics of an individual hair. He explained that the root of an individual hair can have different characteristics from its far tip, and the hairs on an individual's head do not all look exactly the same. Therefore, when a known hair sample is to be used for comparison, the OSBI usually requests at least 30 hairs to account for variations of an individual's hair.

Hett testified he uses a stereo microscope which magnifies approximately 30 times for low power hair comparisons and a comparison microscope which allows the viewer to look at and compare 2 different hair samples simultaneously at a magnification of 50 to 400 times. He stated he spent several hundred hours in his examination of the hair samples in this investigation.

Hett said he received hair samples from Susan Land on September 19, 1983, some of which were mounted on slides and some of which were in bindles. He also received additional samples directly from the Ada Police Department....

With regard to Petitioner's hair, Hett testified he found 2 pubic hairs from the bedding that were "consistent microscopically and *could have* the same source as Ron Williamson's known pubic hair." He also found 2 scalp hairs on the washcloth which were "consistent microscopically and *could have* the same source" as Petitioner's known scalp hair.

The prosecutor questioned Hett about what "could have the same source" meant. Hett explained, "When a hair *matches*, if you will, it is consistent microscopically to a known source." After an objection by defense counsel, Hett went on to say he meant that

> [T]he hairs either did originate from that [known] source, or there could be or might be another individual in the world somewhere that might have the same microscopic characteristics. In other words, hairs are not an absolute identification, but they either came from this individual or there is — could be another individual somewhere in the world that would have the same characteristics to their hair.

Hett testified he received scalp and pubic hairs from a number of individuals, including Glen Gore. These persons were eliminated as possible sources of the questioned hairs after Hett's "direct comparisons" indicated the known samples were not "microscopically consistent" with the questioned hairs.... Under cross-examination, Hett testified that he could not determine with certainty that a particular hair came from a certain person, but he could only state whether a questioned hair "might" have come from a certain individual. He admitted that hair comparisons are not absolute identifications like fingerprints.

A. Admissibility of Hair Evidence

Petitioner argues that the State's hair evidence presented by its expert was inadmissible due to its unreliability and inherently subjective nature. The State asserts that the reliability of hair evidence is a jury question, rather than an admissibility issue.

Of the hundreds of hairs submitted to OSBI for analysis, 2 scalp hairs and 2 pubic hairs were found to be "consistent microscopically" with Petitioner's known scalp and pubic hairs. However, the State's expert did not explain which of the "approximately" 25 characteristics were consistent, any standards for determining whether the samples were consistent, how many persons could be expected to share this same combination of characteristics, or how he arrived at his conclusions.[11] Hett did acknowledge that "consistent microscopically" is not the same as a positive identification.

---

11. There is an apparent lack of consensus among hair examiners about the number of characteristics, and it has been suggested that there is a need for more accurate definitions of hair features in microscopic hair examination....

Forensic examination of human hair was conducted as early as 1861. Hair comparison in a criminal prosecution was first considered over one hundred years ago by the Wisconsin Supreme Court. *Knoll v. State*, 12 N.W. 369 (Wis. 1882). The hair expert in *Knoll* visually compared hair samples and concluded that they came from a common source. On appeal the court held that "such evidence is of a most dangerous character," and reversed the conviction.

At the time of the *Knoll* decision, hair analysis was a new area of forensics. Since then, it has become a familiar and common component of criminal prosecutions with contemporary hair analysis relying heavily upon conventional microscopes. Modern hair experts generally state their results in testimony that samples are "similar" and "could have" come from the "same source." Critics of hair evidence have criticized the admission of hair evidence on the grounds that it is too subjective and it has a high error rate.

In 1993, the United States Supreme Court held that "the trial judge must ensure that any and all scientific testimony or evidence admitted is not only relevant, but reliable." *Daubert v. Merrell Dow Pharms., Inc.*, 509 U.S. 579 (1993). Reliability refers to trustworthiness of the evidence. "In a case involving scientific evidence, evidentiary reliability will be based upon scientific validity." *Daubert*, 509 U.S. at 590 n. 9. This standard applies both to "'novel' scientific techniques" and "well-established propositions."

Acknowledging that it would not be reasonable to require scientific testimony to be "'known' to a certainty," the Supreme Court held that

> [I]n order to qualify as "scientific knowledge," an inference or assertion must be derived by the scientific method. Proposed testimony must be supported by appropriate validation—i.e., "good grounds," based on what is known. In short, the requirement that an expert's testimony pertain to "scientific knowledge" establishes a standard of evidentiary reliability.

In deciding whether proffered expert testimony is admissible, the trial judge must initially determine "whether the reasoning or methodology underlying the testimony is scientifically valid" and "whether that reasoning or methodology properly can be applied to the facts in issue." *Daubert*, 509 U.S. at 593. The Supreme Court recognized that many factors must be evaluated, and there is no set formula to follow, but the Court did give some "general observations" which it deemed appropriate.

> Ordinarily, a key question to be answered in determining whether a theory or technique is scientific knowledge that will assist the trier of fact will be whether it can be (*and has been*) tested. "Scientific methodology today is based on generating hypotheses and testing them to see if they can be falsified; indeed, this methodology is what distinguishes science from other fields of human inquiry." "[T]he statements constituting a scientific explanation must be capable of empirical test." "[T]he criterion of the scientific status of a theory is its falsifiability, or refutability, or testability."

An important consideration is "whether the theory or technique has been subjected to peer review and publication," a means of increasing the likelihood of detecting methodological flaws. In addition, when a particular scientific method is employed, "the court should ordinarily consider the known or potential rate of error." The "general acceptance" within the relevant scientific community may also be considered. Finally, if the probative value of relevant evidence is "substantially outweighed by the danger of unfair prejudice, confusion of the issues, or misleading the jury," the expert testimony can be excluded.

This court agrees with the Oklahoma Court of Criminal Appeals' finding that the decision whether expert testimony is admissible requires an "independent, thorough review." However, in analyzing Petitioner's case under the guidelines of *Daubert*, this court has found an apparent scarcity of scientific studies regarding the reliability of hair comparison testing. The few available studies reviewed by this court tend to point to the method's _un_reliability. Although probability standards for fingerprint and serology evidence have been established and recognized by the courts, no such standards exist for human hair identification. Since the evaluation of hair evidence remains subjective, the weight the examiner gives to the presence or absence of a particular characteristic depends upon the examiner's subjective opinion. Consequently, any conclusion regarding whether a particular hair sample came from a certain individual depends upon the value judgment and expertise of the examiner.

In response to studies indicating a high percentage of error in forensic analysis, The Law Enforcement Assistance Administration sponsored its own Laboratory Proficiency Testing Program. Between 235 and 240 crime laboratories throughout the United States participated in the program which compared police laboratories' reports with analytical laboratories' findings on different types of evidence, including hair. Overall, the police laboratories' performance was weakest in the area of hair analysis. The error rates on hair analysis were as high as 67% on individual samples, and the majority of the police laboratories were incorrect on 4 out of 5 hair samples analyzed. Such an accuracy level was below chance.[16]

Two studies by B.D. Gaudette of the Royal Canadian Mounted Police attempted to establish the probability of error when a questioned hair sample is found to be microscopically similar to known hair samples. Gaudette placed the probability that a single head hair which is microscopically similar to samples from a known source actually came from another source at about 1 in 4,500.[17] The estimated probability for this type of error in pubic hair analysis was 1 in 800. Courts have disagreed on whether these probability estimates are admissible, and other researchers have severely criticized the studies, concluding that they are invalid. Assertions have even been made that the Canadian probability estimates are virtually meaningless and grossly in error due to experimental bias resulting in an inaccurately low probability estimate. Gaudette has conceded that hair comparison is "still somewhat subjective,"

---

16. Edward J. Imwinkelried, *Forensic Hair Analysis: The Case Against the Underemployment of Scientific Evidence*, 39 WASH. & LEE L. REV. 41, 44 (1982).

17. B.D. Gaudette & E.S. Keeping, *An Attempt at Determining Probabilities in Human Scalp Hair Comparison*, 19 J. FORENSIC SCI. 599 (1974).

and that "hair is not generally a basis for positive personal identification." He contends his critics misunderstood his research, but he did revise his probability figures to 1 in 57 for scalp hair and 1 in 17 for pubic hair for the relevant population of individuals.[22]

In one revealing study students enrolled in advanced college crime laboratory courses were trained to examine hair samples. All the students received training that met the level required for qualification to testify as human hair experts. This study found a 30.4% error rate in conventional hair comparisons when a questioned hair from a fictitious crime scene was compared with known hair samples from a fictitious suspect.... The researcher in this study concluded that the conventional method is subject to unintentional bias among hair examiners. As with eyewitness identification, it appears that the accuracy rate for hair identification increases when multiple suspects are presented. Also, as with eyewitness identifications, erroneous conclusions can increase when the examiner is told which hair sample is from the suspect in the crime. A preconceived conclusion that questioned hairs and known hairs are from the same individual may affect the examiner's evaluation. This court notes that hair expert Melvin Hett testified in the preliminary hearing that this conventional method of comparison was precisely the procedure used in Petitioner's case.

Other forms of expert examination and testimony have been criticized because jurors may be awed by an "aura of special reliability and trustworthiness" which may cause undue prejudice, confuse the issues or mislead the jury. In the case of hair expert testimony, the jurors do not have the opportunity for direct evaluation. Instead, they hear an abbreviated summary of the characteristics of hair and testimony of the expert's overall conclusions....

The clear implication from the expert's testimony in Petitioner's trial was that 4 of the hairs found at the victim's apartment belonged to Petitioner. As witness to the incorrect conclusion that could result from this testimony, the prosecutor said in his closing argument, "[T]here's a match." Even the Court of Criminal Appeals misinterpreted and overstated the hair evidence by writing, "Hair evidence *placed [Petitioner] at the decedent's apartment.*"

This court finds that the prosecutor's mischaracterization of the hair evidence misled the jury, the trial court and the appellate court to believe "microscopically consistent" equates with reliability and to conclude there was a "match" between questioned hairs and Petitioner's hairs. Actually, the most to be drawn from Hett's testimony was that the questioned hair samples could have come from Petitioner. This also means, of course, that the hair samples might not have been his. While it may be possible to exclude an individual as the source of a hair sample, it is not possible to prove questioned hairs are from a particular person.

This court has been unsuccessful in its attempts to locate *any* indication that expert hair comparison testimony meets *any* of the requirements of *Daubert*. Not even the

---

22. B.D. Gaudette, *A Supplementary Discussion of Probabilities and Human Hair Comparisons*, 27 J. FORENSIC SCI. 279, 283 (1982).

"general acceptance" standard is met, since any general acceptance seems to be among hair experts who are generally technicians testifying for the prosecution, not scientists who can objectively evaluate such evidence.

This court has previously addressed the issue of hair expert testimony in the context of a criminal proceeding where the death penalty was sought. Such testimony by a special agent with the Federal Bureau of Investigation in Washington, D.C. was held inadmissible. Based in part on the hair expert's own testimony that there is no research to indicate with any certainty the probabilities that two hair samples are from the same individual, this court held that hair expert testimony was too speculative to be admissible. Admission of such testimony would have been "extremely unfair" and could "prejudice the defendants without any real probative value." This court is not persuaded to change those conclusions.

This court, therefore, finds that the introduction into evidence of expert hair testimony at Petitioner's trial was irrelevant, imprecise and speculative, and its probative value was outweighed by its prejudicial effect. The state of the art of hair analysis has not reached a level of certainty to permit such testimony. Although the hair expert may have followed procedures accepted in the community of hair experts, the human hair comparison results in this case were, nonetheless, scientifically unreliable. This court recognizes the long history of admissibility of such evidence, but as the *Daubert* Court stated, "[H]ypotheses ... that are incorrect will eventually be shown to be so." *Daubert*, 509 U.S. at 597. Based on the reasons above, this court holds that hair comparison evidence based on forensic procedures employed in Petitioner's case is inadmissible.

Notes and Questions

1. In addressing the admissibility of hair comparison evidence in *Williamson*, how faithful was Judge Seay to the holding of *Daubert*? Was this type of strict analysis of the methodology and its basis what *Daubert* expected judges to do, or not?

2. The *Williamson* court is not the sole example of a court rejecting the basis for hair comparison evidence. In 1996, the Indiana Court of Appeals in *McGrew v. State* also found an inadequate basis in the record for a finding of reliability. 673 N.W.2d 787 (Ind. Ct. App. 1996). However, on appeal, the Indiana Supreme Court vacated the holding of inadequate reliability. *McGrew v. State*, 682 N.E.2d 1289, 1292 (Ind. 1997). The final result in *McGrew* (conviction affirmed) is indicative of the approach taken by the vast majority of courts, even post-*Daubert*: to admit, and to do so without detailed assessment of the underlying scientific merit of hair comparison evidence. For a detailed review of the extensive case law admitting hair comparison evidence on appeal, see PAUL C. GIANNELLI ET AL., SCIENTIFIC EVIDENCE § 24.03, at 827–32 (5th ed. 2012).

3. Lest one think that the admission of this evidence is based solely on a laissez-faire interpretation of *Daubert* in forensic cases, it appears that *Frye* jurisdictions are also commonly admitting hair comparison evidence. In many cases, the courts refuse to apply the *Frye* standard, finding it only applies to new or novel scientific

techniques and, since hair comparison has always been admitted, it should not be reviewed again. *McDonald v. State*, 952 So. 2d 484, 498 (Fla. 2006). In other cases, the court simply notes that there has been long-standing admission of the evidence without a detailed review of the general acceptance standard. *Common-wealth v. Chmiel*, 30 A.3d 1111, 1140–42 (Pa. 2011); *People v. Huggins*, 131 P.3d 995, 1014 (Cal. 2006).

4. In response to judicial inability or unwillingness to reject hair comparison evidence, the FBI and Department of Justice decided to review a large number of cases on their own:

> Starting in 2012, the Department of Justice and FBI undertook an unprecedented review of testimony in more than 3,000 criminal cases involving microscopic hair analysis. Their initial results, released in 2015, showed that FBI examiners had provided scientifically invalid testimony in more than 95 percent of cases where that testimony was used to inculpate a defendant at trial.[44]

Considering this shockingly high error rate, the President's Commission rejected the FBI's finding that the technique is valid, instead finding that the methodology lacks foundational validity. Paul C. Giannelli, *Forensic Science:* Daubert's *Failure*, 68 Case W. Res. L. Rev. 869, 888 (2018).

B. Handwriting Comparison

Paul C. Giannelli, Edward J. Imwinkelreid & Joseph Peterson, *Reference Guide on Forensic Identification Expertise*
Reference Manual on Scientific Evidence
112–16 (3d ed. 2011)[Ed.]

...

VII. Handwriting Evidence

The Lindbergh kidnapping trial showcased testimony by questioned document examiners. Later, in the litigation over Howard Hughes' alleged will, both sides relied on handwriting comparison experts. Thanks in part to such cases, questioned document examination expertise has enjoyed widespread use and judicial acceptance.

---

44. President's Council of Advisors on Sci. and Tech., Forensic Science in Criminal Courts: Ensuring Scientific Validity of Feature-Comparison Methods 87–95 (2016), *available at* https://obamawhitehouse.archives.gov/sites/default/files/microsites/ostp/PCAST/pcast_forensic_science_report_final.pdf.

[Ed.] Reprinted with permission from the National Academy of Sciences, Courtesy of the National Academies Press, Washington, D.C.

A. The Technique

Questioned document examiners are called on to perform a variety of tasks such as determining the sequence of strokes on a page and whether a particular ink formulation existed on the purported date of a writing. However, the most common task performed is signature authentication — that is, deciding whether to attribute the handwriting on a document to a particular person. Here, the examiner compares known samples of the person's writing to the questioned document. In performing this comparison, examiners consider (1) class and (2) individual characteristics. Of class characteristics, two types are weighed: system and group. People exhibiting system characteristics would include, for example, those who learned the Palmer method of cursive writing, taught in many schools. Such people should manifest some of the characteristics of that writing style. An example of people exhibiting group characteristics would include persons of certain nationalities who tend to have some writing mannerisms in common. The writing of arthritic or blind persons also tends to exhibit some common general characteristics.

Individual characteristics take several forms: (1) the manner in which the author begins or ends the word, (2) the height of the letters, (3) the slant of the letters, (4) the shading of the letters, and (5) the distance between the words. An identification rarely rests on a single characteristic. More commonly, a combination of characteristics is the basis for an identification. As in fingerprint analysis, there is no universally accepted number of points of similarity required for an individuation opinion. As with fingerprints, the examiner's ultimate judgment is subjective.

There is one major difference, though, between the approaches taken by fingerprint analysts and questioned document examiners. As previously stated, the typical fingerprint analyst will give one of only three opinions: (1) the prints are unsuitable for analysis, (2) the suspect is definitely excluded, or (3) the latent print is definitely that of the suspect. In contrast, questioned document examiners recognize a wider range of permissible opinions: (1) definite identification, (2) strong probability of identification, (3) probable identification, (4) indication of identification, (5) no conclusion, (6) indication of nonauthorship, (7) probability of nonauthorship, (8) strong probability of nonauthorship, and (9) elimination. In short, in many cases, a questioned document examiner explicitly acknowledges the uncertainty of his or her opinion. Whether such a nine-level scale is justified is another matter.

B. The Empirical Record

The 2009 NRC report included a section discussing questioned document examination. The report acknowledged that some tasks performed by examiners are similar in nature "to other forensic chemistry work."[184] For example, some ink and paper analyses use the same hardware and rely on criteria as objective as many tests in forensic chemistry. In contrast, other analyses depend heavily on the examiner's subjective judgment and do not have as "firm [a] scientific foundation" as the analysis of inks

---

184. NATIONAL RESEARCH COUNCIL, NATIONAL ACADEMY OF SCIENCES, STRENGTHENING FORENSIC SCIENCE IN THE UNITED STATES: A PATH FORWARD 164 (2009).

and paper. In particular, the report focused on the typical task of deciding common authorship. With respect to that task, the report stated:

> The scientific basis for handwriting comparisons needs to be strengthened. Recent studies have increased our understanding of the individuality and consistency of handwriting ... and suggest that there may be a scientific basis for handwriting comparison, at least in the absence of intentional obfuscation or forgery. Although there has been only limited research to quantify the reliability and replicability of the practices used by trained document examiners, the committee agrees that there may be some value in handwriting analysis.[186]

Until recently, the empirical record for signature authentication was sparse. Even today there are no population frequency studies establishing, for example, the incidence of persons who conclude their "w" with a certain lift. As a 1989 article commented,

> our literature search for empirical evaluation of handwriting identification turned up one primitive and flawed validity study from nearly 50 years ago, one 1973 paper that raises the issue of consistency among examiners but presents only uncontrolled impressionistic and anecdotal information not qualifying as data in any rigorous sense, and a summary of one study in a 1978 government report. Beyond this, nothing.[187]

This 1989 article then surveyed five proficiency tests administered by CTS in 1975, 1984, 1985, 1986, and 1987. The article set out the results from each of the tests and then aggregated the data by computing the means for the various categories of answers: "A rather generous reading of the data would be that in 45% of the reports forensic document examiners reached the correct finding, in 36% they erred partially or completely, and in 19% they were unable to draw a conclusion."[189]

The above studies were conducted prior to *Daubert*, which was decided in 1993. After the first post-*Daubert* admissibility challenge to handwriting evidence in 1995, a number of research projects investigated two questions: (1) are experienced document examiners better at signature authentication than laypersons and (2) do experienced document examiners reach correct signature authentication decisions at a rate substantially above chance?

1. Comparison of experts and laypersons

Two Australian studies support the claim that experienced examiners are more competent at signature authentication tasks than laypersons. The first study was reported in 1999.[191] In this study, document examiners chose the "inconclusive" option

---

186. *Id.* at 166−67.

187. D. Michael Risinger et al., *Exorcism of Ignorance as a Proxy for Rational Knowledge: The Lessons of Handwriting Identification "Expertise,"* 137 U. Pa. L. Rev. 731, 747 (1989).

189. *Id.*

191. Bryan Found et al., *The Development of a Program for Characterizing Forensic Handwriting Examiners' Expertise: Signature Examination Pilot Study,* 12 J. Forensic Doc. Examination 69, 72–76 (1999).

far more frequently than did the laypersons. However, in the cases in which a conclusion was reached, the overall error rate for lay subjects was 28%, compared with 2% for experts. More specifically, the lay error rate for false authentication was 7% while it was 0% for the experts. The second Australian study was released in 2002.[192] Excluding "inconclusive" findings, the error rate for forensic document examiners was 5.8%; for laypersons, it was 23.5%.

In the United States, Dr. Moshe Kam, a computer scientist at Drexel University, has been the leading researcher in signature authentication. Dr. Kam and his colleagues have published five articles reporting experiments comparing the signature authentication expertise of document examiners and laypersons. Although the last study involved printing, the initial four were related to cursive writing. In the first, excluding inconclusive findings, document examiners were correct 92.41% of the time and committed false elimination errors in 7.59% of their decisions.[194] Lay subjects were correct 72.84% of the time and made false elimination errors in 27.16% of their decisions. In the second through fourth studies, the researchers provided the laypersons with incentives, usually monetary, for correct decisions. In the fourth study, forgeries were called genuine only 0.5% of the time by experts but 6.5% of the time by laypersons.[195] Laypersons were 13 times more likely to err in concluding that a ... document was genuine.

Some critics of Dr. Kam's research have asserted that the tasks performed in the tests do not approximate the signature authentication challenges faced by examiners in real life. In addition, critics have claimed that even the monetary incentives for the laypersons do not come close to equaling the powerful incentives that experts have to be careful in these tests. Yet by now the empirical research record includes a substantial number of studies. With the exception of a 1975 German study, the studies uniformly conclude that professional examiners are much more adept at signature authentication than laypersons.

2. Proficiency studies comparing experts' performance to chance

Numerous proficiency studies have been conducted in the United States and Australia. Some of the American tests reported significant error rates. For example, on a 2001 test, excluding inconclusive findings, the false authentication rate was 22%, while the false elimination rate was 0%. Moreover, as previously stated, on the five CTS proficiency tests mentioned in the 1989 article, 36% of the participating examiners erred partially or completely.[202] Further, critics have claimed that some of the

192. Jodi Sita et al., *Forensic Handwriting Examiners' Expertise for Signature Comparison*, 47 J. FORENSIC SCI. 1117 (2002).

194. Moshe Kam et al., *Proficiency of Professional Document Examiners in Writer Identification*, 39 J. FORENSIC SCI. 5 (1994).

195. Moshe Kam et al., *Signature Authentication by Forensic Document Examiners*, 46 J. FORENSIC SCI. 884 (2001).

202. Risinger, *supra* note [187], at 747–48.

proficiency tests were far easier than the tasks encountered in actual practice, and that consequently, the studies tend to overstate examiners' proficiency.

The CTS proficiency test results for the 1978–2005 period addressed the comparison of known and questioned signatures and other writings to determine authorship. In other exercises participants were asked to examine a variety of mechanical impressions on paper and the use of photocopying and inks.

— Between 1978 and 1999, fewer than 5% of the mechanical impression comparisons were in error, but 10% of the replies were inconclusive where the examiner should have excluded the impressions as having a common source. With regard to handwriting comparisons, the examiners did very well on the straightforward comparisons, with almost 100% of the comparisons correct. However, in more challenging tests, such as those involving multiple authors, as high as 25% of the replies were inconclusive and nearly 10% of the author associations were incorrect.

— In the 2000–2005 time period, the participants generally performed very well (some approaching 99% correct responses) in determining the genuineness of documents where text in a document had been manipulated or where documents had been altered with various pens and inks. The handwriting exercises were not as successful; in those exercises, comparisons of questioned and known writings were correct about 92% of the time, inconclusive 7% of the time, and incorrect 1% of the time. Nearly all incorrect responses occurred where participants reported handwriting to be of common origin when it was not.

During these tests, some examiners characterized the tests as too easy, while others described them as realistic and very challenging.

Thus, the results of the most recent proficiency studies are encouraging. Moreover, the data in the five proficiency tests discussed in the 1989 article can be subject to differing interpretation. The critics of questioned document examination sometimes suggest that the results of the 1985 test in particular prove that signature authentication has "a high error rate." However,

[t]hese results can be characterized in different ways. [Another] way of viewing the result would be to disaggregate the specific decisions made by the experts.... [S]uppose that a teacher gives a multiple-choice test containing fifty questions. There are different ways that the results could be reported. One could calculate the percentage of students who got any of the fifty questions wrong, and report that as the error rate. A more customary approach would be to treat each question as a separate task, and report the error rate as the mean percentage of questions answered incorrectly.[207]

---

207. Roger Park, *Signature Identification in the Light of Science and Experience*, 59 HASTINGS L.J. 1101, 1114 (2008).

If the specific decisions made by the examiners were disaggregated, each examiner had to make 66 decisions regarding whether certain pairs of signatures were written by the same person. Under this approach, the false authentication error rate was 3.8%, and the false elimination error rate was 4.5%. In that light, even the 1985 study supports the contention that examiners perform signature authentication tasks at a validity rate considerably exceeding chance....

United States v. Buck

No. 84 Cr. 220-CSH, 1987 WL 19300
(S.D.N.Y. Oct. 28, 1987)

HAIGHT, District Judge.

Defendants Marilyn Buck and Mutulu Shakur have brought joint motions *in limine* challenging several categories of evidence the Government seeks to introduce at trial. First, defendants contend that the Government should not be permitted to offer expert testimony from a 'questioned documents examiner' because handwriting comparison lacks the demonstrable scientific basis necessary before expert testimony on the subject is properly admissible....

Admission of expert testimony is a matter left to the discretion of the trial judge under Fed. R. Evid. 702.... When expert testimony pertaining to a subject not yet judicially recognized as one susceptible of expert analysis is offered, the proponent of that evidence must show that scientific knowledge of the subject "has reached a level of reliability sufficient to warrant its use in the courtroom." *United States v. Williams*, 583 F.2d 1194, 1198 (2d Cir. 1978). Defendants argue that handwriting comparison has not reached that level, despite the conceded fact that "modern case law permits a handwriting 'expert' to testify in opinion form concerning the identification of handwriting on a questioned document."

The case law admitting expert testimony on handwriting identification is "fatally flawed," defendants contend, because none of the cases apply the *Williams* analysis to determine reliability of the methodologies employed by questioned documents examiners.[2] ... Instead of the [standard] *Frye* test, *Williams* directs the trial court to weigh "the probativeness, materiality, and reliability of the evidence, on the one side, and any tendency to mislead, prejudice, or confuse the jury on the other," *Id.* at 1198, to determine admissibility.

Williams determined that spectrography, the science of voice comparisons, was sufficiently reliable for expert testimony although the defendant contended that most scientists opposed the use of spectrographic evidence in the courtroom. In doing so, the court reiterated its view that reliability of the proffered testimony "cannot rest solely on a process of 'counting (scientific) noses'... [although] a technique unable to garner *any* support, or only minuscule support, would be found unreliable by a

2. Defendants actually contend that the proper framework for analysis is "the rigorous *Frye-Williams* analysis," referring to *Frye v. United States*, 293 F. 1013 (1923) as well as to *Williams*....

court." One observation made by the court in the course of its analysis of reliability is particularly relevant here:

> Like handwriting exemplars and gun barrel striations, spectrograms are variable, but contain sufficient points of similarity or dissimilarity to enable a trained expert to reach a conclusion.

Williams, 583 F.2d at 1199. Of course, the court's mention of handwriting exemplars is merely *dicta*, but I think its choice of examples demonstrates widespread judicial acceptance of expert testimony on handwriting comparisons.

The court also noted that the proponent of expert testimony need not show that scientific knowledge on the subject is infallible. All that need be shown is that the discipline is reasonably reliable, based on criteria such as the potential rate of error, the existence of uniform standards, the degree of care attendant on the scientific technique employed, and the presence of "failsafe characteristics" such as the likelihood that poor exemplars would lead an expert to the conclusion that two samples are dissimilar rather than similar. 583 F.2d at 1198–99.

The Government argues that I need not consider the *Williams* test for admissibility of expert handwriting comparison testimony because that test is only necessary when the proffered opinion evidence is of "a novel form of expertise which has not yet received judicial sanction[.]" I agree that this position states the better view, but neither the Government's brief nor my own research reveal controlling authority on the point. I need not adopt this view of the rule ... because when I consider the reliability of handwriting comparison as a proper subject for expert testimony under the *Williams* test, I conclude that such evidence is sufficiently reliable....

The sheer number of cases admitting such evidence is itself probative of the reliability of handwriting expert testimony. *See, e.g., United States v. Green*, 523 F.2d 229 (2d Cir. 1975); *United States v. Liquori*, 373 F.2d 204 (2d Cir. 1967); *Robles v. United States*, 279 F.2d 401, 404 (9th Cir. 1960) ("It is well settled that ... an expert may testify and state his opinion as to whether different documents or signatures were written by the same person ..."); *People v. Hunter*, 34 N.Y.2d 432 (1972).

In addition, the Federal Rules of Evidence presuppose the admissibility of expert handwriting testimony. F.R.E. 901(3); *see also* Notes of Advisory Committee on Proposed Rules, F.R.E. 901(2) ("Testimony based on familiarity [with handwriting exemplars] acquired for purposes of the litigation is reserved to the expert under [F.R.E. 901(3)]").

Defendants argue that specific factors of reliability considered in *Williams* are not present with respect to handwriting comparisons, and thus that handwriting comparisons should be considered less reliable. Specifically, they point to the lack of any statistical formulation on the potential rate of error, and the lack of any uniform standards. The lack of these factors, and the ability to explain away any dissimilarities as "variation[s] within the person's handwriting[,] ... illustrate the imprecision and subjectivity of handwriting comparison techniques."

Notwithstanding the imprecision of handwriting analysis which defendants have identified, it is indisputable that a large professional community of document examiners exists. For example, the Government has submitted on this motion an affidavit from Gus R. Lesnevich, a "forensic document examiner," whose curriculum vitae shows that a body called the American Board of Forensic Document Examiners issues Certificates of Qualification in the field. I am satisfied that professional scientific knowledge in the subject area is sufficiently reliable to be of assistance to the jury.

As with any expert testimony, there is a danger that the jury may be awed by an "'aura of mystic infallibility' surrounding 'scientific techniques,' 'experts,' and the 'fancy devices' employed." *Williams*, 583 F.2d at 1199. Like spectrographic analysis, however, the "critical step in [the comparison handwriting exemplars] ... is the simple step of visual pattern-matching, a step easily comprehended and evaluated by a jury. Moreover, ... it is not expected that the jury will participate only as passive listeners.... The danger of improper influence is therefore much less with expert handwriting comparison testimony than ... with other forms of expert testimony."

Having found expert handwriting comparison testimony sufficiently reliable for admission, I still must consider whether such testimony will assist the trier of fact in this case. F.R.E. 702; *Williams*, 583 F.2d at 1200, n. 11. Defendants argue that jurors can perform visual comparisons of handwriting samples as easily as experts can, and that therefore expert testimony on the subject will not assist the jury. Defendants cite two cases for the proposition that a substantial danger of unfair prejudice exists when expert testimony is admitted about "matters within the ordinary understanding of the jurors given the 'aura of reliability' that surrounds expert testimony." Brief at 4, (citing *United States v. Amaral*, 488 F.2d 1148 (9th Cir. 1973) (holding that the trial court did not err by refusing to admit expert testimony for the defense on the effects of stress on perception)); *United States v. Fosher*, 590 F.2d 381 (1st Cir. 1979) (holding trial court did not err by refusing to admit expert testimony for the defense on the unreliability of eyewitnesses perception and memory).

As noted *supra*, the ability of jurors to perform the crucial visual comparisons relied upon by handwriting experts cuts against the danger of undue prejudice from the mystique attached to "experts." *Weinstein on Evidence* is in accord with this view. At pp. 702–9, 10 ("Must a court exclude expert testimony if the subject is within the comprehension of the average juror? Such a test is incompatible with the standard of helpfulness expressed in Rule 702. First, it assumes wrongly that there is a bright line separating issues within the comprehension of jurors from those that are not. Secondly, even when jurors are well equipped to make judgments on the basis of their common knowledge and experience, experts may have specialized knowledge to bring to bear on the same issue which would be helpful"). To the extent the cited cases disagree with this view of Rule 702, I disagree with them.

In my experience, expert testimony on handwriting comparison aids the jurors by focusing their attention on the minute similarities and dissimilarities between exemplars that lay jurors might otherwise miss. It is largely in the location of these similarities and dissimilarities that the professional document examiner has an advantage over a lay juror. In that advantage lies the expert's ability to assist the lay juror. I will, therefore, admit expert testimony on handwriting comparison.

Notes and Questions

1. Just as with hair comparison testimony, courts evaluating handwriting analysis often fall back upon assessment of the expert's qualifications, prior acceptance of the evidence, or lack of prejudice to the defendant in order to admit. Judge Haight's analysis in *Buck* is a more detailed examination of the reliability issue, also notable for its hesitation to allow expert testimony overwhelming the jury. *Compare with United States v. Brown*, 615 F.2d 1020 (4th Cir. 1980); *United States v. Wilson*, 441 F.2d 655 (2d Cir. 1971); *Wood v. United States*, 357 F.2d 425 (10th Cir. 1966); *United States v. Ruth*, 42 M.J. 730 (A. Ct. Crim. App. 1995).

2. An overwhelming majority of cases addressing the admissibility of handwriting analysis resulted in the court affirming the trial court's decision to admit the testimony. *See* Paul C. Giannelli et al., Scientific Evidence § 21.07, at 452–56 (5th ed. 2012); David L. Faigman et al., Modern Scientific Evidence: Forensics § 4:3, at 257 (2008) ("In the half century after [the Lindbergh baby case in 1936], no reported opinion rejected handwriting expertise nor was much skepticism displayed toward it. Rather, it became universally accepted as scientific and dependable.").

3. Even before the *Daubert* opinion in 1993, scholars and researchers had raised significant questions about the admissibility of handwriting comparison evidence. In their 1989 article, *Exorcism of Ignorance as a Proxy for Rational Knowledge: The Lessons of Handwriting Identification "Expertise,"* professors Risinger, Denbeaux, and Saks noted the near-complete lack of valid, reliable research into the methodologies and proficiency of experts in this field.[45] Since then, some testing has shown improvement in expert proficiency. Giannelli et al., *supra*. During the same time period, judges have been directed by the Supreme Court in *Daubert* to more thoroughly screen for reliability of expert evidence. As we consider the effect of *Daubert*, remember the scientific basis as discussed above in the *Reference Guide on Forensic Identification Expertise*.

United States v. Lewis

220 F. Supp. 2d 548 (S.D. W. Va. 2002)

Goodwin, District Judge.

Edward Lee Lewis was indicted on four counts of mailing threatening communications, one count of mailing a threat to the President, and one count of being a felon in possession of a firearm. Prior to trial, Lewis filed a motion in limine to exclude the testimony of the Government's expert witness, forensic document analyst John W. Cawley, III, under Fed. R. Evid. 702. The court granted the motion, finding that Mr. Cawley's testimony was not sufficiently reliable to meet the standards for expert testimony under Rule 702, as explicated by the Supreme Court in *Daubert v. Merrell Dow Pharmaceuticals, Inc.*, 509 U.S. 579 (1993) and *Kumho Tire Co. v. Carmichael*, 526 U.S. 137 (1999).... The court writes to further explain its rulings.

---

45. D. Michael Risinger et al., *Exorcism of Ignorance as a Proxy for Rational Knowledge: The Lessons of Handwriting Identification "Expertise,"* 137 U. Pa. L. Rev. 731, 747 (1989).

I. Background

At issue in this case are five letters mailed within Kanawha County, West Virginia, between January 2 and January 11, 2002, each of which contained an unidentified white powder, a cigarette butt, and a note. Of the notes, four are identical photocopies of a handwritten note reading "I were you [sic], I'd change my attitude." The fifth letter, received by a private citizen, Robert Burford, in Kelley's Creek, contained a different note reading, "It is on." Letters were addressed and sent to the following: Robert Burford; Kanawha County Circuit Judge Charles King; Chief United States District Judge Charles H. Haden II; Bob Wise, Governor of West Virginia; and President George Bush.

Many people who incidentally were exposed to the mailings testified that they felt intense fear and apprehension upon the observation of the powdery substance.... All of these persons believed that they possibly were exposed to the lethal anthrax virus.

The return address for each envelope bore the name "Gloria Fields" and an address in Cross Lanes, West Virginia. The United States Postal Inspector, W. Burl Fluharty, questioned Gloria Fields on January 7, 2002, and again on January 11, 2002. During these interviews Ms. Fields said that she did not send the letters. The return addresses on the letters did not accurately reflect Ms. Fields's address. When presented with copies of the notes, Ms. Fields acknowledged that they were photocopies of her hand-writing. Ms. Fields also told the inspectors that the text of the notes was taken from a letter she had written ... to her ex-boyfriend, Edward Lee Lewis.

On January 11, 2002, United States Magistrate Judge R. Clarke VanDervort signed an arrest warrant and criminal complaint charging Lewis with mailing threatening communications.... That evening, federal agents arrested Lewis at the home of his aunt and uncle. Based on observations made during the arrest, agents obtained a warrant to search Lewis's truck. While executing that search warrant, federal agents recovered several photocopied notes identical to those found in the mailings; the original note from which the copies apparently had been made; an envelope bearing the handwritten addresses of two recipients of the threatening notes, Chief Judge Haden and Governor Wise; two out-dated typewriters with ribbon; a twelve-gauge shotgun; and thirty-one twelve-gauge shotgun shells.

In an interview following his arrest, Lewis told Inspector Fluharty and F.B.I. Special Agent Allen Little that everything in the truck, with the exception of "some trash," belonged to him. Lewis, however, denied sending the threatening letters. As support for his denial, Lewis further explained that the officers would see he was not guilty when the letters kept coming after he was in jail.

On February 7, 2002, the defendant, Edward Lee Lewis, was indicted on four counts of mailing threatening communications, one count of mailing a threat to the President, and one count of being a felon in possession of a firearm.

Lewis's jury trial took place on August 13 through August 15, 2002. On August 6, 2002, Lewis's attorney filed a motion in limine under *Daubert* to exclude the anticipated handwriting analysis testimony of John W. Cawley, III. The court held a *Daubert* hearing on August 13, 2002. At the conclusion of the hearing, the court granted the defendant's motion, finding that the Government did not meet its burden under Rule 702 to demonstrate that Cawley's testimony as an expert was reliable....

II. Discussion

A. Admissibility of Handwriting Expert

The primary question posed by the defendant's motion to prohibit the testimony of forensic document analyst John W. Cawley, III was whether his handwriting identification evidence was sufficiently reliable to be admissible pursuant to Rule 702 and *Daubert*. The Government argued that the court was not required to apply *Daubert* to handwriting identification analysis and that, in any event, Mr. Cawley's testimony was reliable.

The court first notes that Rule 702 provides:

> If scientific, technical, or other specialized knowledge will assist the trier of fact to understand the evidence or to determine a fact in issue, a witness qualified as an expert by knowledge, skill, experience, training, or education, may testify thereto in the form of an opinion or otherwise, if (1) the testimony is based upon sufficient facts or data, (2) the testimony is the product of reliable principles and methods, and (3) the witness has applied the principles and methods reliably to the facts of the case.

As the Supreme Court explained in *Daubert* and *Kumho Tire*, under Rule 702, the district judge must ensure that the expert's testimony is both relevant and reliable before it may be admitted, regardless of whether the testimony is scientific or based on technical or other specialized knowledge. *See Kumho*, 526 U.S. at 147; *Daubert*, 509 U.S. at 589. When the expert's testimony's "factual basis, data, principles, methods, or their application are called sufficiently into question, ... the trial judge *must* determine whether the testimony has 'a reliable basis in the knowledge and experience of the relevant discipline.'" *Kumho*, 526 U.S. at 149.

In performing this gate-keeping responsibility, the Supreme Court has articulated four factors the court may consider:

> (1) Whether a theory or technique can be or has been tested;
>
> (2) Whether it has been subjected to peer review and publication;
>
> (3) Whether, in respect to a particular technique, there is a high known or potential rate of error and whether there are standards controlling the technique's operation; and
>
> (4) Whether the theory or technique enjoys general acceptance within a relevant scientific community

Id. at 149–50 (citing *Daubert*, 509 U.S. at 592–94) (internal quotations marks and alterations omitted). These various factors are not an exhaustive list of all possible ways to assess reliability, nor must all of the factors be applied in every case. Depending on the facts of the case and the type of testimony being challenged, it may very well be unreasonable to apply all of these factors. Accordingly, the trial judge is given discretion in determining how and in what manner to make reliability determinations pursuant to *Daubert*.

Where, however, the *Daubert* factors are reasonable measures of the testimony's reliability, the Supreme Court has instructed that the trial judge *should* consider them. While district courts have considerable leeway in determining how to assess reliability, they do not have the discretion to simply abandon their gate-keeping function by foregoing a reliability analysis. *Id.* at 158–59 (Scalia, J., concurring). Significantly, "[i]n a particular case the failure to apply one or another of [the *Daubert* factors] may be unreasonable, and hence an abuse of discretion." *Id.* (Scalia, J., concurring).

This court is not persuaded by the Government's argument that the court need not apply the *Daubert* factors. For support, the Government cites several cases where circuit panels have affirmed a district court's admission of a handwriting expert. *See, e.g., United States v. Jolivet*, 224 F.3d 902, 905–06 (8th Cir. 2000) (affirming under plain error review the district judge's decision to admit handwriting expert's testimony without applying *Daubert* factors); *United States v. Paul*, 175 F.3d 906, 910–11 (11th Cir. 1999) (concluding summarily that *Daubert* factors do not necessarily apply to admission of handwriting expert, but failing to address any alternative measures of reliability); *United States v. Velasquez*, 64 F.3d 844, 849–50 (3d Cir. 1995) (cautioning against strict application of the reliability requirement and finding that the ultimate touchstone is helpfulness to the trier of fact).

While these cases all emphasize the district judge's discretion in choosing how to assess the expert's reliability and the "flexibility" afforded the court under *Daubert* and *Kumho*, they do not provide any rationale for declining to apply the *Daubert* factors. These courts simply downplay their rejection of the *Daubert* factors by minimizing the importance of reliability. The rationale given in these cases is that reliability in the handwriting identification context is a less significant concern due to the fact that the jury is able to see for itself whether the writings are similar. *See, e.g., Paul*, 175 F.3d at 911; *United States v. Jones*, 107 F.3d 1147, 1160–61 (6th Cir. 1997) (citing *United State v. Buck*, No. 84 Cr. 220-CSH, 1987 WL 19300, at *3 (S.D.N.Y. Oct. 28, 1987)).

The Supreme Court's mandate in *Daubert*, however, runs contrary to this rationale. There, the Court explained that Rule 702's requirement that evidence "assist the trier of fact in reaching its conclusion" goes primarily to relevance; an assessment of reliability is an *additional* component of the judge's gatekeeper function. *Daubert*, 509 U.S. at 591–92. Simply put, expert testimony that does not relate to any issue in the case is not relevant, and thus, not helpful. Reliability, on the other hand, is an assessment of whether the expert's reasoning or methodology is valid and warrants the relaxation of the common law first-hand knowledge requirement for witnesses.

Here, the court finds that all of the *Daubert* factors reasonably apply to handwriting analysis and thus are helpful to the court in assessing the reliability of Mr. Cawley's testimony. As a branch of forensic science, handwriting analysis has many characteristics that are resonant with the traditional concept of "science." Handwriting analysis proposes a theory that each person's handwriting is unique, and involves a method by which a trained expert can identify each writing's author. The sufficiency of that theory and method can be tested through the basic factors set forth in *Daubert*.

For instance, because the results in handwriting analysis are based on identification, there must be a corresponding probability of error. *See* D. Michael Risinger & Michael J. Saks, *Science and Nonscience in the Courts:* Daubert *Meets Handwriting Identification Expertise*, 82 Iowa L. Rev. 21, 36 (1996). In other words, it is possible to calculate the number of times a handwriting expert correctly identifies the author of a handwriting sample. This number can then be used by courts as an indicative error rate. Other qualities of handwriting analysis, such as the theory that penmanship characteristics are separable from each other, and that there is a base rate of penmanship characteristics in a population of potential authors, are also capable of measurement.

Yet despite the relative ease with which such measurements could be made, the Government did not offer any evidence of reliable testing and error rates, or of any of the other *Daubert* factors through Mr. Cawley's testimony. The Government had the burden of establishing by a preponderance of the evidence that Mr. Cawley's expert testimony was sufficiently reliable to be admissible under Rule 702. The court found that the Government did not meet its burden.

On direct, Mr. Cawley testified that he

1) currently works as a forensic document analyst at the U.S. Postal Inspection Service Crime Laboratory in Dulles, Virginia, and has been employed there since 1977.

2) is certified as a questioned document analyst, a certification he received after completing two years of formal training with the U.S. Postal Service Crime Laboratory and one year of training under "recognized experts."

3) has testified approximately seventy times in courts as a questioned documents expert and has taught basic inspector training classes for the Postal Inspection Service.

With respect to the theories and principles behind handwriting analysis, Mr. Cawley testified to the following:

1) The central tenet behind handwriting identification is that no two individuals write identically. He supported this testimony by stating that "this basic principle of handwriting identification has been proven time and time again through research in my field, as well as recently through a study that was conducted out of the University of Buffalo by a Dr. Srihari."

2) Document analysts have performed research studies in the field and have published papers in the relevant journals, though Mr. Cawley could not recall specific names of articles or authors.

3) These research studies are subject to a peer review process, namely symposia and annual meetings of the American Society of Questioned Document Examiners. Mr. Cawley also discussed a system in his own office by which each document examiner's work is re-examined by another examiner.

4) The laboratory where Mr. Cawley works submits each examiner to a proficiency test each year, which it administers, and since 1989, Mr. Cawley's passage rate has been 100%.

5) The error rate of questioned document analysts has been determined by one study by Dr. Moshe Kam, and that study states the error rate of professional document examiners is 6% and the error rate of lay persons is 38%; these rates only applied to cursive writing.

6) Generally, the field of handwriting analysis is an old and venerated profession, however, Mr. Cawley would not categorize his skills as those gained by scientific knowledge, but rather as a skill gained through specialized knowledge, training, or experience.

On cross-examination and upon questioning by the court, the following testimony was elicited:

1) Mr. Cawley does not possess a college or masters degree in forensic science, but is currently working toward completing his degree requirements for a B.S. in personnel labor relations.

2) When asked about the error rate of print writing as opposed to cursive writing, he asserted that he could not speak on the error rate. When asked about the existence of other studies than the ones he mentioned on direct examination, Mr. Cawley testified generally as to the existence of "[r]esearch papers throughout the community ... published articles in various journals." When asked to elaborate, he stated the existence of studies addressing the frequency of certain handwriting characteristics, European handprinting analysis, and class characteristics of Latin American, African, and Asian handprinting. A few of the authors' names were provided, but the titles of the articles were not supplied. When asked by the court about the error rate of these studies and whether any of the studies had been replicated, Mr. Cawley admitted that he did not know. He also stated that other than the Kam studies mentioned in his testimony, he was unaware of any studies that address the potential error rate of forensic document examiners. When asked about the error rate of the Srihari study that he mentioned, Mr. Cawley again admitted that he did not know.

In sum, Mr. Cawley could not testify about the substance of the studies he cited. He did not know the relevant methodologies or the error rates involved in these studies. His bald assertion that the "basic principle of handwriting identification has been proven time and time again through research in [his] field," without more specific substance, is inadequate to demonstrate testability and error rate.

There were aspects of Mr. Cawley's testimony that undermined his credibility. Mr. Cawley testified that he achieved a 100% passage rate on the proficiency tests that he took and that all of his peers *always* passed their proficiency tests. Mr. Cawley said that his peers *always* agreed with each others' results and *always* got it right. Peer review in such a "Lake Woebegone" environment is not meaningful.

Mr. Cawley also failed to offer any substantive explanation of the standards used in the field of handwriting analysis. Although he stated that stroke similarities are required to make a positive match, he was unclear as to how many similarities are required for positive identification. Mr. Cawley had no explanation for why twenty-five samples of writing were necessary for a comparison of handwriting. He simply said that twenty-five samples was the number generally used. Finally, while there may be general acceptance of the theories and techniques employed in handwriting analysis among the "forensic evidence community," this acceptance does not demonstrate reliability. If courts allow the admission of long-relied upon but ultimately unproven analysis, they may unwittingly perpetuate and legitimate junk science.

After a careful review of the *Daubert* factors, the court found that it would have been improper to admit expert testimony based on principles and methodologies that have yet to be proven through proper testing. By excluding Mr. Cawley's testimony, the court did not hold that handwriting identification testimony is not reliable. Rather, the court narrowly held that handwriting analysis is susceptible to testing for reliability. The Government failed to offer evidence to prove that such testing had been done and the court granted the motion in limine ...

Notes and Questions

1. In addressing the admissibility of handwriting comparison evidence in *Lewis*, how faithful was Judge Goodwin to the holding of *Daubert*? Was this type of strict analysis of the methodology and its basis what *Daubert* expected judges to do, or not?

2. While *Lewis* represents one approach to the assessment of handwriting analysis post-*Daubert*, most courts have not been so rigorous in their review of the testimony and have continued admitting testimony over objection. The decision of the Fourth Circuit in *United States v. Crisp*[46] is indicative of the issue. Facing objections to both fingerprint and handwriting evidence, the court decided:

   > Our analysis of *Daubert* in the context of fingerprint identification applies with equal force here: like fingerprint analysis, handwriting comparison testimony has a ***long history of admissibility*** in the courts of this country. *See, e.g., Robinson v. Mandell*, 20 F. Cas. 1027 (D. Mass. 1868). The fact that handwriting comparison analysis has achieved ***widespread and lasting acceptance in the expert community*** gives us the assurance of reliability that *Daubert* requires.

   Crisp, 324 F.3d at 271 (emphasis added). In addressing the admissibility of handwriting evidence in *Crisp*, how faithful was Judge King to the holding of *Daubert*? Consider that many courts have agreed with the finding of the Fourth Circuit in *Crisp*. *See, e.g., United States v. Prime*, 431 F.3d 1147, 1154 (9th Cir. 2005) (noting that the district court's admission of the evidence was consistent with "all six circuits that have addressed the admissibility of handwriting expert testimony" and have found it to be reliable).

---

46. 324 F.3d 261 (4th Cir. 2003).

3. Just as with hair comparison evidence, there is no reason to think the broad admissibility standard of handwriting evidence is based solely on a laissez-faire interpretation of *Daubert* in forensic cases. *Frye* jurisdictions often admit handwriting evidence. In many cases, the courts refuse to even apply the *Frye* "general acceptance" standard because it only applies to "new or novel" scientific techniques under state interpretations of *Frye*. See Spann v. State, 857 So. 2d 845, 853 (Fla. 2003) ("Florida still considers the admissibility of new and novel scientific evidence under the test set forth in *Frye*. Because expert forensic handwriting identification is not new or novel, *Frye* has no application."). Other *Frye* courts have held contested hearings on the admissibility of handwriting comparison, but even then, the evidence is found to be generally accepted and therefore admissible. See, e.g., Pettus v. United States, 37 A.3d 213, 217–25 (D.C. 2012); State v. Hull, 788 N.W.2d 91, 103–04 (Minn. 2010).

4. The 2009 National Academy of Sciences Report, *A Path Forward*, noted that, after reviewing the evidence in favor of the reliability of handwriting analysis, "there has been only limited research to quantify the reliability and replicability of the practices used by trained document examiners."[47] However, a recent study by Jonathan Koehler measured the preconceived beliefs of mock jurors regarding certain forensic techniques, and while handwriting was not considered the most error-free (DNA was), it was thought to have an error rate of 0.00001 or 1 in 100,000. Jonathan Koehler, *Intuitive Error Rate Estimates for the Forensic Sciences*, 57 JURIMETRICS J. 153, 162 (2017). Considering the apparent disconnect between the scientific validity of handwriting comparison evidence and the jury's perception of validity, there is clearly a significant risk of its misuse.

C. Toolmark Identification

Paul C. Giannelli, Edward J. Imwinkelreid & Joseph Peterson, *Reference Guide on Forensic Identification Expertise*

REFERENCE MANUAL ON SCIENTIFIC EVIDENCE
96–100 (3d ed. 2011)[Ed.]

. . .

9. Toolmarks

Toolmark identifications rest on essentially the same theory as firearms identifications.[254] Tools have both (1) class characteristics and (2) individual characteristics;

---

47. NATIONAL RESEARCH COUNCIL, NATIONAL ACADEMY OF SCIENCES, STRENGTHENING FORENSIC SCIENCE IN THE UNITED STATES: A PATH FORWARD 167 (2009).

[Ed.] Reprinted with permission from the National Academy of Sciences, Courtesy of the National Academies Press, Washington, D.C.

254. Alfred A. Biasotti, *The Principles of Evidence Evaluation as Applied to Firearms and Tool Mark Identification*, 9 J. FORENSIC SCI. 428, 432 (1964)....

the latter are accidental imperfections produced by the machining process and subsequent use. When the tool is used, these characteristics are sometimes imparted onto the surface of another object struck by the tool. Toolmarks may be impressions (compression marks), striations (friction or scrape marks), or a combination of both. Fracture matches constitute another type of examination.

The marks may be left on a variety of different materials, such as wood or metal. In some cases, only class characteristics can be matched. For example, it may be possible to identify a mark (impression) left on a piece of wood as having been produced by a hammer, punch, or screwdriver. A comparison of the mark and the evidence tool may establish the size of the tool (another class characteristic). Unusual features of the tool, such as a chip, may permit a positive identification. Striations caused by scraping with a tool can also produce distinguishing marks in much the same way that striations are imprinted on a bullet when a firearm is discharged. This type of examination has the same limitations as firearms identification: "[T]he characteristics of a tool will change with use."[256]

Firearms identification could be considered a subspecialty of toolmark identification; the firearm (tool) imprints its individual characteristics on the bullet. However, the markings on a bullet or cartridge case are imprinted in roughly the same way every time a firearm is fired. In contrast, toolmark analysis can be more complicated because a tool can be employed in a variety of different ways, each producing a different mark: "[I]n toolmark work the angle at which the tool was used must be duplicated in the test standard, pressures must be dealt with, and the degree of hardness of metals and other materials must be taken into account."[257]

The comparison microscope is also used in this examination. As with firearms identification testimony, toolmark identification testimony is based on the subjective judgment of the examiner, who determines whether sufficient marks of similarity are present to permit an identification. There are no objective criteria governing the determination of whether there is a match.[259]

B. The Empirical Record

In its 2009 report, NRC summarized the state of the research as follows:

> Because not enough is known about the variabilities among individual tools and guns, we are not able to specify how many points of similarity are necessary for a given level of confidence in the result. Sufficient studies have not been done to understand the reliability and repeatability of the methods. The committee agrees that class characteristics are helpful in narrowing the pool of tools that may have left a distinctive mark. Individual patterns from manufacture or from wear might, in some cases, be distinctive enough to

---

256. Emmett M. Flynn, *Toolmark Identification*, 2 J. FORENSIC SCI. 95, 102 (1957).
257. *Id.* at 105.
259. As one commentator has noted: "[I]t is not possible at present to categorically state the number and percentage of the [striation] lines which must correspond." David Q. Burd & Roger S. Greene, *Tool Mark Examination Techniques*, 2 J. FORENSIC SCI. 297, 310 (1957).

suggest one particular source, but additional studies should be performed to make the process of individualization more precise and repeatable.[260]

The 1978 Crime Laboratory Proficiency Testing Program reported mixed results on firearms identification tests. In one test, 5.3% of the participating laboratories misidentified firearms evidence, and in another test 13.6% erred. These tests involved bullet and cartridge case comparisons. The Project Advisory Committee considered these errors "particularly grave in nature" and concluded that they probably resulted from carelessness, inexperience, or inadequate supervision. A third test required the examination of two bullets and two cartridge cases to identify the "most probable weapon" from which each was fired. The error rate was 28.2%.

In later tests,

> [e]xaminers generally did very well in making the comparisons. For all fifteen tests combined, examiners made a total of 2106 [bullet and cartridge case] comparisons and provided responses which agreed with the manufacturer responses 88% of the time, disagreed in only 1.4% of responses, and reported inconclusive results in 10% of cases.[262]

Proficiency testing on toolmark examinations has also been reported.[263]

For the period 1978–1999, firearms examiners performed well on their CTS proficiency tests, with only 2% to 3% of their comparisons incorrect, but with 10% to 13% of their responses inconclusive. The scenarios that accompanied the test materials asked examiners to compare test-fired bullets and/or cartridge cases with evidence projectiles found at a crime scene. Between 2000 and 2005, participants, again, performed very well, averaging less than 1% incorrect responses, but with inconclusive results about 10% of the time. Most of the inconclusive results in these tests occurred where bullets and/or cartridge cases were actually fired from different weapons. Examiners frequently stated they were unable to reach the proper conclusion because they did not have the actual weapon with which they could perform their own test fires of ammunition.

In CTS toolmark proficiency comparisons, laboratories were asked to compare marks made with such tools as screwdrivers, bolt cutters, hammers, and handstamps. In some cases, tools were supplied to participants, but in most cases they were given only test marks. Over the entire 1978–2005 period, fewer than 5% of responses were in error, but individual test results varied substantially. In some cases, 30% to 40% of replies were inconclusive, because laboratories were unsure if the blade of the tool in question might have been altered between the time(s) different

---

260. National Research Council, National Academy of Sciences, Strengthening Forensic Science in the United States: A Path Forward 154 (2009).

262. Joseph L. Peterson & Penelope N. Markham, *Crime Laboratory Proficiency Testing Results, 1978–1991, Part II: Resolving Questions of Common Origin*, 40 J. Forensic Sci. 1009, 1018 (1995).

263. *Id.* at 1025 ("Overall, laboratories performed not as well on the toolmark tests as they did on the firearms tests.").

markings had been made. During the final 6-year period reviewed (2000–2005), laboratories averaged a 1% incorrect comparison rate for toolmarks. Inconclusive responses remained high (30% and greater) and, together with firearms testing, constitute the evidence category where evidence comparisons have the highest rates of inconclusive responses.

Questions have arisen concerning the significance of these tests. First, such testing is not required of all firearms examiners, only those working in laboratories voluntarily seeking accreditation by the ASCLD. In short, "the sample is self-selecting and may not be representative of the complete universe of firearms examiners."[265] Second, the examinations are not blind—that is, examiners know when they are being tested. Thus, the examiner may be more meticulous and careful than in ordinary case work. Third, the results of an evaluation can vary, depending on whether an "inconclusive" answer is counted. Fourth, the rigor of the examinations has been questioned. According to one witness, in a 2005 test involving cartridge case comparisons, none of the 255 test-takers nationwide answered incorrectly. The court observed: "One could read these results to mean that the technique is foolproof, but the results might instead indicate that the test was somewhat elementary."[266]

In 2008, NAS published a report on computer imaging of bullets.[267] Although firearms identification was not the primary focus of the investigation, a section of the report commented on this subject. After surveying the literature on the uniqueness, reproducibility, and permanence of individual characteristics, the committee noted that "[m]ost of these studies are limited in scale and have been conducted by firearms examiners (and examiners in training) in state and local law enforcement laboratories as adjuncts to their regular casework." The report concluded: "The validity of the fundamental assumptions of uniqueness and reproducibility of firearms-related toolmarks has not yet been fully demonstrated."[270] This statement, however, was qualified:

> There is one baseline level of credibility ... that must be demonstrated lest any discussion of ballistic imaging be rendered moot—namely, that there is at least some "signal" that may be detected. In other words, the creation of toolmarks must not be so random and volatile that there is no reason to believe that any similar and matchable marks exist on two exhibits fired from the same gun. The existing research, and the field's general acceptance in legal proceedings for several decades, is more than adequate testimony to that baseline level. Beyond that level, we neither endorse nor oppose the fundamental assumptions. Our review in this chapter is not—and is not

---

265. United States v. Monteiro, 407 F. Supp. 2d 351, 367 (D. Mass. 2006).

266. *Id.*

267. NATIONAL RESEARCH COUNCIL, NATIONAL ACADEMY OF SCIENCES, BALLISTIC IMAGING (2008), *available at* http://www.nap.edu/catalog.php?record_id=12162.

270. *Id.* at 81.

meant to be—a full weighing of evidence for or against the assumptions, but it is ample enough to suggest that they are not fully settled, mechanically or empirically.

Another point follows directly: Additional general research on the uniqueness and reproducibility of firearms-related toolmarks would have to be done if the basic premises of firearms identification are to be put on a more solid scientific footing.[271]

The 2008 report cautioned:

Conclusions drawn in firearms identification should not be made to imply the presence of a firm statistical basis when none has been demonstrated. Specifically, ... examiners tend to cast their assessments in bold absolutes, commonly asserting that a match can be made "to the exclusion of all other firearms in the world." Such comments cloak an inherently subjective assessment of a match with an extreme probability statement that has no firm grounding and unrealistically implies an error rate of zero.[272]

The issue of the adequacy of the empirical basis of firearms identification expertise remains in dispute,[273] and research is ongoing. A recent study reported testing concerning 10 consecutively rifled Ruger pistol barrels. In 463 tests during the study, no false positives were reported; 8 inconclusive results were reported. "But the capsule summaries [in this study] suggest a heavy reliance on the subjective findings of examiners rather than on the rigorous quantification and analysis of sources of variability."[275]

Commonwealth v. Graves

456 A.2d 561 (Pa. Super. Ct. 1983)

VAN DER VOORT, J.

A jury found appellant guilty of third degree murder for the death of Lynette Weston, age 10, and of first degree murder for the death of Lloyd Weston, age 10, and recommended a death sentence on the first degree murder conviction. Trial Judge Joseph Ridge refused post-trial motions for a new trial and in arrest of judgment, but did grant a motion to vacate the death sentence....

---

271. *Id.* at 81–82.

272. *Id.* at 82.

273. ... AFTE disputed the Academy's conclusions. *See The Response of the Association of Firearm and Tool Mark Examiners to the National Academy of Sciences 2008 Report Assessing the Feasibility, Accuracy, and Capability of a National Ballistic Database August 20, 2008*, 40 AFTE J. 234 (2008) (concluding that underlying assumptions of uniqueness and reproducibility have been demonstrated, and the implication that there is no statistical basis is unwarranted)....

275. NATIONAL RESEARCH COUNCIL, NATIONAL ACADEMY OF SCIENCES, STRENGTHENING FORENSIC SCIENCE IN THE UNITED STATES: A PATH FORWARD 155 (2009).

Appellant was the stepbrother and boarder of Yvonne Weston, the mother of the two children. At about 11:00 P.M. on February 16, 1979, Mrs. Weston left her home, entrusting the care of the two children to the appellant. The children were asleep. From about 11:30 P.M. to about 4:45 A.M. the next morning, Mrs. Weston's brother Daniel Anderson was in the home drinking beer and listening to records. When he departed, the living room was in reasonably good order; appellant was present; and the children apparently sleeping in their beds. At about 7:00 A.M. on February 17, 1979, when Mrs. Weston returned home she found the living and dining rooms in complete disarray; the bodies of the two children were lying on the living room floor, and the appellant was missing.

Shortly thereafter appellant telephoned Mrs. Weston several times from some undisclosed phone, asking if the children were all right. He claimed he had been visited in the home by three men looking for another of Mrs. Weston's brothers who forced him to leave the home. On a fourth phone call, appellant was advised that the children were dead; he revealed his whereabouts. A police car picked him up at that location and took him to Police Station No. 5. He was locked up for about twenty minutes and then taken to Police Station No. 1, where he was interrogated through most of the day, finally being placed formally under arrest at 5:30 P.M.

Prior to the formal arrest, he surrendered hair and saliva samples and fingernail clippings, and agreed to the making of wax impressions of his fingernails. The police also took photographs of several fresh scratches on his back. These bits of "physical evidence" were used as part of the circumstantial evidence by which the prosecution attempted to identify the appellant as the perpetrator of the murders....

Over the objection of appellant and after an extended examination of their qualifications on voir dire outside the presence of the jury, Judge Ridge permitted the prosecution to put in the testimony of four expert witnesses, as follows:

> Dr. Michael N. Sobel, a dentist specializing in orthodontics, and forensic odontology employed from time to time as a consultant and expert on dental problems, bite marks and related topics;
>
> Dr. Robert Levine, a criminalist employed by the Allegheny County Crime Laboratory, with considerable experience in making comparisons of tool-marks and firearm-related marks;
>
> Dr. Lowell J. Levine, from New York, a dentist specializing in forensic odontology; and
>
> Dr. Homer Richardson Campbell, Jr., a dentist and Board certified specialist in forensic odontology for the State of New Mexico, with experience in bite-mark cases.

Scratch marks were found on the back of Lloyd Weston's body near the base of the neck. Dr. Sobel made an impression or cast of one of those scratch marks, using a compound of the same general type as dentists use in making impressions of teeth. He then compared that impression with an impression made from the nail on appellant's fourth (left) finger, using among other things, a comparison microscope.

On the basis of these comparisons he testified that: "it was highly likely that the nail of the fourth finger, left hand, of Bennie Graves had made the mark in the neck of Lloyd Weston, Jr."

Dr. Robert Levine, characterizing a fingernail mark in the skin as "a tool mark," based upon an examination of the impression made by Dr. Sobel, and of a wax impression of appellant's left little finger, again using the comparison microscope concluded that: "the fingernail impression as seen on the wax mold had the same class characteristics as the fingernail." He testified further that "there is probably a fair degree of probability that this nail or any nail of this shape made this kind of mark...." Over appellant's objection, he was later permitted to say that "this would be one (case) of high probability," although the nail could not be characterized as "unique."

Dr. Lowell J. Levine testified based upon his examination of finger nail clippings, photographs, slides and Dr. Sobel's impression, testified to a "fractured edge" on the impression of appellant's finger nail, and to his opinion that "it is highly probable" that appellant's finger nails made the mark on the neck of Lloyd Weston, Jr.; and that it was "very unlikely" that "some person other than Bennie Graves ... made these marks."

Dr. H.R. Campbell, Jr. utilizing photographs and slides of the decedent's body and finger nail clippings of appellant, testified to his opinion "that the left-little finger and the left-ring finger (of appellant) were consistent with the injury patterns shown in the photographs" of the deceased; that there was "a high degree of certainty in this case"; and finally that there was "[a]n extremely high degree of probability to the point of practical impossibility of finding two other nails on two fingers adjacent to each other that would make these marks."

Appellant contends at the appellate level, as he did below, that the opinion testimony of these four doctors should not have been received.

The Commonwealth contends, as the court determined below, that the witnesses were "experts" in the broader field of "tool-marks"; that a finger nail and the impression it leaves, are analogous to "tool-marks"; and that the general procedures utilized in this case to make comparisons and draw conclusions, are the same as used in tool-mark identification. The Commonwealth contends the expert witnesses have special qualifications, as to which the jurors needed and were entitled to assistance in the form of expert testimony.

Appellant concedes that the initial question of whether a witness is qualified to testify as an expert lies within the sound discretion of the trial court and will not be overturned absent an abuse of that discretion. He argues however that in this case: 1) none of the witnesses had the requisite special training, knowledge, and experience on the subject of finger nail identification, *Commonwealth v. Crawford*, 364 A.2d 660 (Pa. 1976); 2) there is no scientific recognition of a method of identification through finger nails, *Frye v. United States*, 293 F. 1013 (D.C. 1923); and 3) there are no established minimum standards in this field. At first glance, it would appear that the identification of teeth marks comes more often within dentists' usual field of knowledge than does the identification of finger nail scratchings. Nonetheless, the methods and techniques used and evaluated in this present case — the photographs; the casts of the wounds; the preparation of wax impressions of appellant's finger nails; the superimposing of images of the molds of the wound and the finger nail by use of comparison microscope — all were consistent with standards of general scientific acceptance in the field of tool-marks, of which, according to the witnesses, testimony as to finger nail wounds is a part. These were comparisons the witnesses were accustomed to make.

The current case is quite different from *Crawford*, where the witness testified as an expert regarding the dating of fingerprints only to later admit that such a procedure was not possible. Such testimony was held to be inadmissible. Here, while the comparison between scratch and nail may have been beyond the ability of the average juror, the witnesses had a "reasonable pretention to specialized knowledge" in making such comparisons. These witnesses were qualified to testify as they did and it was for the jury, who had the enhanced comparisons before it, to determine what weight to give to such testimony.

We also agree with the lower court that this area is one which is scientifically recognized. Wound marks here referred to as tool marks, whether made by a firearm, knife, blunt instrument or finger nails, are a proper area in which experts may assist juries. Our attention has been invited to *Commonwealth v. Topa*, 369 A.2d 1277 (Pa. 1977), where our Supreme Court granted a new trial after a conviction for murder. In that case, the trial court admitted opinion testimony of an expert concerning spectography, or voice print analyses. In the *Topa* case, Chief Justice Jones quoted *Frye*, reading in part, that:

> while courts will go a long way in admitting expert testimony deduced from a well-recognized scientific principle or discovery, the thing from which the deduction is made must be sufficiently established to have gained general acceptance in the particular field in which it belongs. *Frye v. United States*, 293 F. 1013, 1014 (1923).

More recently the Pennsylvania Supreme Court has found refreshing recollection by hypnosis has not gained sufficient acceptance in the scientific or legal community. *Commonwealth v. Nazarovitch*, 436 A.2d 170 (Pa. 1981).

Appellant has overlooked a subtle, but very important distinction. In *Topa,* the heart of the controversy was whether a person's voice recorded by a mechanical device was so distinguishable that it would allow one to identify its owner. Here the question *is not*, given a certain finger nail, whether its owner could be identified, *but instead* given a certain scratch and a known finger nail(s), can it be determined to a certain degree of probability that the nail caused the scratch. To demonstrate this distinction, we will review two cases from other jurisdictions upon which appellant relies.

People v. Marx, 126 Cal. Rptr. 350 (1975), involved a situation similar to the present, except the wound consisted of teeth marks and not scratches. The authorities had a victim with a bite-mark and a suspect whose teeth matched the bite mark.

Both the bite mark and the suspect's dentition reflected the same irregularity. The court noted that whether the specific technique of comparison was generally accepted or recognized was not determinative of the admissibility. The witnesses relied upon approved, established, scientific techniques (similar to those used here) to solve a particular problem, which though novel, was well within the capability of the techniques employed.

In contrast is *People v. Wesley*, 303 N.W.2d 194 (Mich. App. 1981), there the court found that finger nail identification was not scientifically recognized and was therefore inadmissible. The investigating authorities found a finger nail during the course of their investigation. Samples taken from a suspect were compared with the nail found in the investigation, much in the same manner as finger prints or hair samples are compared. The court found an absence of recognition and acceptance of finger nail identification in the forensic community. The court was dissatisfied that given a finger nail the experts could determine who it belonged to.

The distinction we draw here is as follows: in the *Marx* situation we are not dealing with an attempt to identify an individual based on some of his personal characteristics as the case was in *Wesley*, instead we have a wound, which the Commonwealth refers to as a "tool mark" and we have a suspected weapon (here a finger nail) and we wish to know the probability that the suspected weapon inflicted the injury. To relate this to Pennsylvania law, we need only to look at a few cases.

In *Topa*, supra, the accuracy of a voice print identification was questioned. There the Commonwealth claimed that given a voice print it could be determined that a certain individual made the recording. The Supreme Court was unwilling to accept this premise. While, in other situations, testimony as to size and shape of a wound in the body and the likeness of the thing causing the wound is frequently admitted to demonstrate that a suspect used a certain method in perpetrating a crime. *Commonwealth v. Hoyle*, 418 A.2d 376 (Pa. Super. Ct. 1979) (screwdriver); *Commonwealth v. Oates*, 409 A.2d 112 (Pa. Super. Ct. 1979) (knife). We find no reason to distinguish between a distinctive knife and an irregular finger nail. Therefore, we find it unnecessary to resolve whether finger nail identification is generally recognized.

Appellant further complains that the prosecution was permitted to rehabilitate Dr. Robert Levine's testimony from "a fair degree of probability" to "high probability." The extent to which a party may cross examine its own witness lies generally within the discretion of the trial judge. We find no abuse of discretion, and no demonstration of improper harm to appellant as the three other expert witnesses for the prosecution testified substantially as did ... Dr. Robert Levine.

Notes and Questions

1. In *Graves*, the defendant challenged the expert testimony linking his fingernail to the scratch marks found on the victim. On what basis did the court find the expert testimony was properly admitted? Does it matter that three out of four of the experts in question were dentists rather than police toolmark experts? Does it matter that the "toolmark" in question was from a fingernail rather than, say,

a screwdriver? Does it matter that the expert changes his opinion from "fair degree of probability" to "high probability"? Why or why not?

2. As with the other forensic fields we have covered, pre-*Daubert* courts failed to skeptically assess toolmark evidence. In fact, in MODERN SCIENTIFIC EVIDENCE, the authors note the absence of any court opinions excluding toolmark evidence between 1929 and 1989. DAVID L. FAIGMAN ET AL., MODERN SCIENTIFIC EVIDENCE: FORENSICS §5:2, at 399 (2008). Typical court assessment of toolmark evidence during this era is illustrated by the following unredacted excerpts:

○ *United States v. Bowers*, 534 F.2d 186, 193 (9th Cir. 1976):

A government witness was allowed to testify that he had made a microscopic comparison of one of the bullets found in the ranger's body with a bullet found in appellant's attache case and that in his expert opinion the marks on these bullets indicated they had been loaded into the same gun (not the murder weapon). Appellant objected to the admission of this opinion on the ground that there was no showing that "tool mark identification" was generally accepted as sufficiently reliable to justify admission of expert opinion based upon its use. Appellant fails to distinguish between the procedure and its application to the particular case. The record was sufficient to permit the trial court to conclude that "tool mark identification" rests upon a scientific basis and is a reliable and generally accepted procedure. Whether its use in the particular case resulted in a reliable opinion was a different question, to be explored in cross-examination of the expert witness. The jury was properly instructed to give the expert testimony such weight as the jury thought it deserved.

○ *State v. Churchill*, 646 P.2d 1049 (Kan. 1982):

Defendant next contends that the trial court erred in admitting, over objection, the opinion testimony of Michael Kelty, the firearm and toolmark examiner. It is well established that the qualifications of expert witnesses and the admissibility of expert testimony are matters which lie within the sound discretion of the trial court; its rulings upon such testimony will not be disturbed on appeal, unless the appellate court finds an abuse of discretion. K.S.A. 60-456; *State v. Bright*, 229 Kan. 185, 190, 623 P.2d 917 (1981); *State v. Reed*, 226 Kan. 519, Syl. P 1, 601 P.2d 1125 (1979); *Curtis v. Freden*, 224 Kan. 646, 585 P.2d 993 (1978); *Spraker v. Lankin*, 218 Kan. 609, 613, 545 P.2d 352 (1976).

Mr. Kelty had been employed for many years as a toolmark and firearms examiner; he had made hundreds of toolmark comparisons and had testified frequently as an expert during that period of time. He testified that he had not previously performed tests to determine whether marks upon the human body were made by a given tool, but he testified that toolmark examinations in human tissue were conducted by the same procedures and governed by the same principles applicable generally in toolmark examinations, and that the procedure used was acceptable in his profession. It would appear from the record that he has the requisite skill and training to perform the tests, and that the methods used were reliable. The defendant presented expert testimony to the jury in order to call into question Kelty's methods and conclusions. The witness's experience or lack of experience in previously performing similar examinations goes to the weight of the testimony, not to its admissibility. *See State v. Peoples*, 227 Kan. 127, 133, 605 P.2d 135 (1980). We hold that the trial court did not abuse its discretion in admitting the testimony.

- *Fletcher v. Lane*, 446 F. Supp. 729 (S.D. Ill. 1978):

     Petitioner's second contention is that expert testimony, that a screwdriver found in petitioner's trailer made the prymarks on the trailer door at the murder scene, was "impossible." A screwdriver was found by police underneath petitioner's clothing in a chest of drawers, in a search of petitioner's trailer. A toolmark identification expert testified that in his opinion the screwdriver positively made the prymarks on the door of the trailer in which the murder was committed. In addition to his claim that the expert testimony is "impossible," petitioner requests that the screwdriver be reexamined and additional expert opinions given.

     Petitioner's second contention is essentially an attack on the credibility of the expert testimony. The credibility of a witness is a matter for jury determination, and, as such, is not reviewable in a habeas corpus action. *United States ex rel. Bracey v. Petrelli*, 356 F. Supp. 699 (N.D. Ill. 1973). Federal habeas corpus is not merely an additional appeal available to state prisoners, and attacks on evidence and on the credibility of witnesses can only be challenged on appeal. *Concepcion Diaz v. Morales Bergeat*, 409 F. Supp. 749 (D.P.R. 1975). Therefore, petitioner's challenge to the credibility of this testimony does not state a sufficient ground for issuance of a writ of habeas corpus. *United States ex rel. Bracey v. Petrelli*, 356 F. Supp. 699 (N.D. Ill. 1973).

3. As we shift to consider the effect of *Daubert* on toolmark evidence, remember this reluctance of courts to reject long-standing forensic evidence.

Ramirez v. State

810 So. 2d 836 (Fla. 2001)

Shaw, J.

We have on appeal the judgment and sentence of the trial court imposing the death penalty on Joseph J. Ramirez following his third trial for the first-degree murder of a night courier. We reverse the convictions and vacate the sentences for the same reason as before—i.e., the trial court erroneously admitted evidence based on the knife mark identification....

I. FACTS

This is an appeal following the third trial of Ramirez for a 1983 murder. The prior reversals were based on the trial court's admission ("For the first time in the history of the Florida courts," as the first trial court put it) of testimony by Miami crime technician Robert Hart wherein he stated that, based on his knife-mark identification procedure, Ramirez's knife was *the* murder weapon to the exclusion of all others. The facts underlying the first trial are set forth in *Ramirez v. State*, 542 So. 2d 352 (Fla. 1989) (*Ramirez I*):

> The relevant facts are as follows. Early Christmas morning in 1983, the body of a twenty-seven-year-old woman was discovered in the Miami Federal Express building where she worked as a night courier. She had died of multiple stab wounds to her body and blunt trauma to her head. Additional injuries included cuts on her hands and back and one stab wound into her chest cartilage. At the scene, police found blood spatters and pools throughout the dispatch area and break room indicative of a struggle. A bloody paper napkin and bloodstained fragments of a missing sixty-seven-pound telex machine were also discovered. The hot water faucet in the women's restroom was turned on full force. One truck had been tampered with and one of the loading bay doors was unlocked. The desk of an employee who sold jewelry had been opened, and a mail bag containing approximately $430 was missing. A hair was discovered on the victim's hand. Experts compared hair samples taken from Ramirez with that hair and determined that the hair found on the victim's hand did not belong to Ramirez.

> The police discovered a bloody fingerprint on a doorjamb near the victim's body. From a photograph of the patent partial left thumbprint, a technician found ten points of similarity. Despite the fact that only approximately ten percent of the fingerprint area was discernible, the technician positively identified the fingerprint as belonging to Ramirez, an employee of an independent janitorial company which serviced the Federal Express offices. Based upon the fingerprint identification, Ramirez was arrested and charged with first-degree murder.

> Police investigation established that Ramirez had cleaned the Federal Express office on the afternoon of December 24. A week earlier, on December 17, the victim was unable to locate her keys to the building and had duplicates made. The lost keys were never found.... Ramirez inquired about the amount of revenues coming in and was told by the supervisor that they had a good business. Several people including Ramirez were also working in the area that day when the money was counted and placed in the mail bag.

> [Ramirez's] girlfriend testified that at approximately 6:00 p.m. on Christmas Eve Ramirez returned to their residence. She stated that Ramirez left at around 9:00 p.m. in her Renault automobile to visit the home of some friends and that he was wearing a navy blue sweater with a fox emblem on the front. He

remained at his friends' home until approximately 11:00 p.m. The appellant's girlfriend testified that Ramirez had returned home at some time during the night, but that she had not noted the time. However, when she arose at 5:30 a.m., Ramirez was at home. From the time Ramirez left his friends' home until sometime in the early hours of Christmas Day, his whereabouts were unknown.

When asked to produce the clothing he wore on Christmas Eve night, Ramirez told police the sweater he had worn was at Alvarez Cleaners, but the police were unable to locate a dry-cleaning establishment of that name. An inquiry of other dry cleaners in the area did not turn up the sweater. On December 28, Ramirez volunteered to the police a sweater he claimed to have worn Christmas Eve. The sweater was devoid of any emblem. Ramirez claimed the fox emblem had fallen off in the wash. When the police arrested Ramirez on December 28, they found a department store sales receipt in his wallet which indicated he had purchased the sweater that day. A store employee remembered selling Ramirez the sweater because she noticed his expensive watch. According to his girlfriend, Ramirez had purchased the watch on December 26. His old watch, found in the bedroom of his residence, appeared to have traces of blood on the band.

In the search of the Renault, police found a knife which Ramirez's girlfriend kept in the car for protection. The girlfriend testified that after Christmas she had found the knife in her kitchen sink and washed it. Her daughter returned the knife to the Renault when Ramirez, while cleaning the car, requested it to cut some string. Traces of some type of blood were detected on the knife, but in insufficient amount to determine their origin. No blood stains were detected on either Ramirez's sneakers or the pants he purportedly wore on the night of the murder. A police technician, who was qualified as a tool mark expert, testified that the knife found in the trunk of the Renault was the specific knife which produced the victim's chest wound.

Hart's specific knife mark identification evidence played a crucial role in the trial:

The trial court allowed the expert to state, "The result of my examination made from the microscopic similarity, which I observed from both the cut cartilage and the standard mark, was the stab wound in the victim was caused by this particular knife *to the exclusion of all others*." The technician explained that he had compared a piece of cut cartilage from the body of the victim to knife impressions, using the knife in question, but had made no comparisons with other knives.

Ramirez was convicted and sentenced to death.

This Court reversed the conviction, ruling that while the knife itself was admissible, Hart's testimony that this particular knife was conclusively the murder weapon was "self-serving" and inadmissible: "In reviewing the record, we find that no scientific predicate was established from independent evidence to show that a specific knife can be identified from the marks made on cartilage. The only evidence received was the expert's self-serving statement supporting this procedure...." *Ramirez I*, 542 So. 2d at 354–55.

Prior to the second trial, the court conducted a hearing wherein Hart testified concerning the reliability of his identification theory and submitted an article he had written on the subject; Ramirez was not allowed to present opposing evidence at the hearing. The court ruled the State's evidence admissible, and Ramirez again was convicted and sentenced to death. This Court again reversed: ... "Without the testimony of experts presented by both parties, the trial judge is denied a full presentation of relevant evidence. This is especially important in a criminal trial where the defendant is guaranteed certain constitutional rights...." *Ramirez v. State*, 651 So. 2d 1164, 1168 (Fla. 1995) (*Ramirez II*).

Prior to the third trial, the court conducted a hearing wherein the State presented the testimony of six experts to support Hart's identification methodology. The defense presented one expert in rebuttal. The trial court again admitted the evidence, and Ramirez was convicted and sentenced to death.... Ramirez raises nine issues on appeal, but we find a single claim dispositive.

Ramirez asserts that the trial court erred in allowing the State's experts to testify that the knife found in Ramirez's car was the murder weapon to the exclusion of every other knife in the world. He contends that Hart's identification method is novel and untested and the State has failed to present sufficient proof of its reliability.

II. RELIABILITY

An expert witness is normally permitted to testify relative to generally accepted scientific theory in the witness's area of expertise.... When a court is faced with expert testimony based on a new or untried scientific theory, however, ..."scientific" reliability must be established as a predicate to "legal" reliability.

A. *"Legal" Reliability — The Balancing Test*

Under the Florida Evidence Code, expert testimony is admissible if it will assist the trier-of-fact in his or her task:

> **90.702 Testimony by experts** — If scientific, technical, or other specialized knowledge will assist the trier of fact in understanding the evidence or in determining a fact in issue, a witness qualified as an expert by knowledge, skill, experience, training, or education may testify about it in the form of an opinion; however, the opinion is admissible only if it can be applied to evidence at trial.

All evidence, including expert testimony, is subject to the requirements of [Florida statutory law] which address relevancy and reliability....

B. *"Scientific" Reliability — The Frye Test*

Evidence based on a novel scientific theory is inherently unreliable and inadmissible in a legal proceeding in Florida unless the theory has been adequately tested and accepted by the relevant scientific community.... This Court, in adopting the *Frye* test for use in Florida, pointed out the underlying reason for the rule:

> The underlying theory for this rule is that a courtroom is not a laboratory, and as such it is not the place to conduct scientific experiments. If the scientific community considers a procedure or process unreliable for its own purposes, then the procedure must be considered less reliable for courtroom use.

Stokes v. State, 548 So. 2d 188, 193–94 (Fla. 1989). In keeping with the State's burden in a criminal trial (i.e., the State must prove each element of the charged offense beyond a reasonable doubt), this Court has continued to use the *Frye* test when evaluating novel scientific evidence proposed by the State even though the United States Supreme Court, in a civil case, has adopted a different rule.[8]

When applying the *Frye* test, a court is not required to accept a "nose count" of experts in the field. Rather, the court may peruse disparate sources—e.g., expert testimony, scientific and legal publications, and judicial opinions—and decide for itself whether the theory in issue has been "sufficiently tested and accepted by the relevant scientific community." In gauging acceptance, the court must look to properties that traditionally inhere in scientific acceptance for the type of methodology or procedure under review—i.e., "indicia" or "hallmarks" of acceptability. A bald assertion by the expert that his deduction is premised upon well-recognized scientific principles is inadequate to establish its admissibility if the witness's application of these principles is untested and lacks indicia of acceptability.

The trustworthiness of expert scientific testimony is especially important because oftentimes "[t]he jury will naturally assume that the scientific principles underlying the expert's conclusion are valid"....

III. KNIFE MARK EVIDENCE

Traditional "knife mark" evidence is a subgroup of the broad category of evidence commonly referred to as "tool mark" evidence. The theory underlying tool mark evidence, which is explained below, is generally accepted in the scientific community and has long been upheld by courts. Many of the analytical methods that were developed for use with tool marks in general have been applied to knife marks in particular and have similarly been accepted by courts. Hart's theory of knife mark identification, however, departs from traditional knife mark identification theory in significant ways, and the State has cited no appellate decision upholding his theory.

A. *Traditional Knife Mark Evidence*

The term "tool mark" refers to the mark left by a hard material when striking a softer material, and such a mark generally falls into one of two classes, i.e., (1) an impression marking, or (2) a striation marking....

---

8. The United States Supreme Court in *Daubert v. Merrell Dow Pharmaceuticals, Inc.*, 509 U.S. 579 (1993), eschewed a rule of "general acceptance" in favor of a rule of "scientific soundness" wherein the trial court must assess the scientific validity of the theory in issue based on various criteria including general acceptance....

An identification procedure commonly used by tool mark experts is as follows: (1) the expert attempts to duplicate the original crime-scene mark by using the suspected tool to create a comparable mark on a similar test medium; (2) the test mark (i.e., the "exemplar") is compared to the original mark via microscopic examination; (3) patterns of impressions or groups of striations are matched up under a three-dimensional stereoscopic comparison microscope; (4) two-dimensional photomicrographs (i.e., photos) of the comparison are taken for record purposes; and (5) if the marks are sufficiently similar, the expert may conclude that they were made by the same tool (i.e., the suspected tool). Marks left by various tools have been studied in this manner, including screwdrivers, chisels, wire-cutters, hammers, axes, and knives.

Unlike wood, metal, plastic, and other hard surfaces, human tissue is pliable and does not readily retain detailed marks. Thus, knife mark analysis in human tissue traditionally has been limited to a gross observation of the wound itself and a microscopic examination of the interior and exterior surfaces of the wound to detect alterations in the cellular structure of the tissue or the presence of fibers or other trace materials. From this analysis, an examiner may deduce, for instance, the general length, width, shape, or contour of the knife blade....

Specifically, courts have permitted experts to attest to the following: that a particular knife could have been the murder weapon; that a particular knife was consistent with the victim's wounds; that a victim's wounds were caused either by a particular knife or a knife similar thereto; and that a victim's wounds could not have been caused by a particular knife. On the other hand, courts have approached with caution an expert's testimony that a victim's wounds were caused by a particular knife.

B. *Hart's Knife Mark Evidence*

Hart's testing procedure is based on the premise that every knife blade is unique due to microscopic imperfections in the steel caused by the manufacturing process. These imperfections, he contends, leave lines—i.e., striations—when a knife is plunged into human cartilage, and because cartilage is a relatively firm material, as compared to human flesh, it retains the marks. The striations in the cartilage, i.e., the striation "signature," may be matched by a skilled technician to the imperfections in the blade of the knife that made the wound.

Hart employs the following technique: (1) he conducts a mock stabbing with the suspected knife in a test medium; (2) he separates the cut faces of both the incision in the exemplar and the incision in the victim's cartilage; (3) he makes a hard cast of the cut faces of both incisions; (4) he compares the casts under a firearms comparison microscope to match up the striations; (5) he makes a subjective determination concerning the degree of the match; and (6) if the marks are sufficiently similar—i.e., if the striation "signatures" are sufficiently similar—he concludes to a degree of scientific certainty that both incisions were made by the suspected knife to the exclusion of every other knife in the world.

According to Hart, a technician's ability to identify microscopic similarities in casts is developed by training and is passed on from one technician to another in the workplace. A "match" under his method is declared if there is "sufficient similarity" in the striated marks on the casts to eliminate the possibility of coincidence. This determination is entirely subjective and is based on the technician's training and experience; there is no minimum number of matching striations or percentage of agreement or other objective criteria that are used in this method. No photographs are made of the casts, Hart explained, because lay persons and those not trained in this procedure would be unable to understand the comparison process; similarly, no notes are made describing the basis for identification. Once a match is declared under his theory, no other knives are examined because an identification under this method purportedly eliminates all other knives in the world as possible sources of the wound. Under Hart's method of identification, a team of expert technicians trained by him would be virtually impossible to challenge notwithstanding the fact that his procedure is untested and yet to be accepted by the relevant scientific community. There is no objective criteria that must be met, there are no photographs, no comparisons of methodology to review, and the final deduction is in the eyes of the beholder, i.e., the identification is a match because the witness says it is a match.

IV. THE PRESENT CASE

At the pre-trial hearing below, the State presented the live testimony of Hart and four other tool mark experts, all of whom are or were at one time affiliated with law enforcement agencies, and one bite mark expert. The State's experts all testified in a manner that supported Hart's methodology. In counterpoint, the defense presented a single expert who testified that the validity of Hart's method has never been tested and that the underlying principle is suspect.

A. *The Frye Hearing*

After Hart explained the principle underlying his ... procedure for knife mark identification, he testified that Ramirez's knife was *the* murder weapon to the exclusion of all others.... The State's experts subsequently testified that the principles underlying Hart's testing procedure are generally accepted in the field.

One of the State's experts, Lonny Harden, testified that he too examined the evidence prepared by Hart in the present case and agreed with Hart that Ramirez's knife was the murder weapon to the exclusion of all other knives....

The defense expert, Dale Nute, on the other hand, testified that Hart's knife mark identification procedure has not been properly validated. Nute testified that because Hart's procedure applies to an unusual receiving material, i.e., cartilage, and involves a stabbing rather than cutting motion, it cannot be assumed that this method is as reliable as other tool mark comparisons. Nute further stated that it is not scientific to say "it was a match because I say so," as Hart does, rather than using objective criteria and articulating the bases for making an identification. At the conclusion of the ... hearing, the court ruled ... the evidence was admissible.

B. *Hart's Method Fails the Frye Test*

Although several of the State's experts testified that the underlying principle employed by Hart is generally accepted in the field, we conclude that this testimony standing alone is insufficient to establish admissibility under *Frye* in light of the fact that Hart's testing procedure possesses none of the hallmarks of acceptability that apply in the relevant scientific community to this type of evidence. This is particularly true in light of the extraordinarily precise claims of identification that Hart makes under his testing procedure—i.e., he claims that a "match" made pursuant to his method is made with absolute certainty. Such certainty, which exceeds even that of DNA testing, warrants careful scrutiny in a criminal—indeed, a capital—proceeding.

First, the record does not show that Hart's methodology—and particularly his claim of infallibility—has ever been formally tested or otherwise verified. At the *Frye* hearing below, the State submitted no substantive proof of scientific acceptance of such testing and its reliability. In fact, the only record evidence that even hints at general acceptance of Hart's testing procedure is a single published article describing an experiment wherein German forensic scientist Wolfgang Bonte examined the wounds left in cartilage by twelve different types of serrated-blade knives. Bonte, however, did not conduct a "blind" study; he was concerned only with documenting the relationship between the nature of the wound and the size and shape of the corresponding blade. Microscopic imperfections in knife blades—i.e., the key to Hart's test—was a non-issue in the Bonte study; the Bonte blades were *grossly* dissimilar to one another.

Second, the record does not show that Hart's test has ever been subjected to meaningful peer review or publication as a prerequisite to scientific acceptance. At the *Frye* hearing below, the court reviewed two groups of published articles addressing knife mark evidence—one group North American, the other European. The North American articles were written by law enforcement technicians and while several of those articles address principles related to Hart's theory none undertakes the kind of searching, critical review that is the *sine qua non* of scientific acceptance. The European articles, on the other hand, were written by medical doctors and professors and are far more discerning; they delineate general studies and contain extensive analyses. The articles in that group, however, address only *traditional* knife mark theory relative to striation signatures. None address Hart's testing methodology and the absolute certainty of identification deduced from such a test....

Fourth, the record does not show that the error rate for Hart's method has ever been quantified. On the contrary, the State's experts testified that the method is infallible, that it is impossible to make a false positive identification. Fifth, the record does not show that this method is governed by objective scientific standards. The State's experts repeatedly testified that the method is entirely subjective and that objective standards would be impractical. This testimony, however, is contrary to language in Hart's own published article wherein he refers to the existence of objective scientific standards used in assessing the degree of match in striation marks. And finally, the record contains no written authority—including Hart's own published article—that upholds his current methodology.

We conclude that the State has failed to show by a preponderance of the evidence that Hart's procedure is generally accepted by scientists active in the field to which the evidence belongs. In applying the *Frye* criteria, general scientific recognition requires the testimony of impartial experts or scientists. It is this independent and impartial proof of general scientific acceptability that provides the necessary *Frye* foundation.... We hold that while the knife that was recovered in Ramirez's constructive possession may be admitted as conventional evidence of guilt, testimony based on Hart's knife mark identification procedure, which we find to be new and novel, does not reach the threshold for admissibility under *Frye* and is therefore unreliable and inadmissible. Because this evidence played a key role in the trial below, the trial court's error in admitting the evidence was harmful beyond a reasonable doubt and requires reversal....

Notes and Questions

1. The *Ramirez* court makes clear that the analysis required to examine the proposed expert evidence under Florida state law is a *Frye*-based approach. However, one can also see that the court examines in detail many factors relevant to a *Daubert*-based analysis. Would the opinion in *Ramirez* have been different if the expert standard was different?

2. As with other forensic disciplines we have reviewed, most courts — even after *Daubert* — have not been so skeptical and willing to exclude expert testimony on toolmark identification. *See, e.g., United States v. Otero*, 849 F. Supp. 2d 425 (D.N.J. 2012); *United States v. Natson*, 469 F. Supp. 2d 1253 (M.D. Ga. 2007). In some cases, courts do limit the strength of the final opinion offered to the jury, as in *United States v. Ashburn*, where the court prohibited an expert from stating he was "100% sure the items matched." 88 F. Supp. 3d 239, 249 (E.D.N.Y. 2015). Yet even in a 2016 opinion in the District of Columbia, the court remarked:

    > We are aware of only one state supreme court decision and no federal appellate decisions limiting the opinion testimony of firearms and toolmark examiners. Indeed, as one federal district court judge has observed, "[a]lthough the scholarly literature is extraordinarily critical" of toolmark pattern-matching, it appears that courts have made little effort to limit or qualify the admission of such evidence.

    Williams v. United States, 130 A.3d 343, 348 (D.C. 2016) (quoting *United States v. Green*, 405 F. Supp. 2d 104, 122 (D. Mass. 2005)). However, one federal judge did analogize toolmark identification evidence not to "highly developed firearm identifications" but instead to the "similarly controversial polygraph test." *United States v. Smallwood*, No. 5:08-CR-38, 2010 WL 4168823 (W.D. Ky. Oct. 12, 2010). It should surprise no one to learn that the evidence was excluded, and while that decision was affirmed on appeal, the Sixth Circuit mostly focused on the expert's individual lack of qualifications rather than the weaknesses of the discipline. *United States v. Smallwood*, 456 Fed. Appx. 563, 566 (6th Cir. 2012).

3. After considering the current state of research in the field of toolmark identification, the National Academy of Sciences wrote, in their 2009 Report *A Path Forward*, that

Toolmark and firearms analysis suffers from the same limitations discussed above for impression evidence. Because not enough is known about the variabilities among individual tools and guns, we are not able to specify how many points of similarity are necessary for a given level of confidence in the result. Sufficient studies have not been done to understand the reliability and repeatability of the methods.

NATIONAL RESEARCH COUNCIL, NATIONAL ACADEMY OF SCIENCES, STRENGTH-ENING FORENSIC SCIENCE IN THE UNITED STATES: A PATH FORWARD 154–55 (2009); *see also* Paul C. Giannelli, *Forensic Science: Daubert's Failure*, 68 CASE W. RES. L. REV. 869, 909–15 (2018).

A bit of "good news" might however be in order. When we examined hair and handwriting comparison evidence, we learned that juries often overvalue the testimony. Jonathan Koehler, *Intuitive Error Rate Estimates for the Forensic Sciences*, 57 JURIMETRICS J. 153, 162 (2017) (finding juries believe error rates of one in one million for hair comparison, and one in 100,000 for handwriting). Considering that those disciplines also have significant weaknesses in their research background, this faith seems unwarranted. However, when we look at toolmark identification testimony, a recent study suggests that jurors are much more skeptical. In fact, almost all study participants valued toolmark identification as the least persuasive forensic methodology, less persuasive than lip print or handwriting analysis and only analogous to boot print comparisons. Craig M. Cooley, *Forensic Individualization Sciences and the Capital Jury: Are* Witherspoon *Jurors More Deferential to Suspect Science than Non-*Witherspoon *Jurors?*, 28 S. ILL. U. L.J. 273, 336–41 (2004). Perhaps, then, the utility of admitting toolmark evidence is so compromised that it will fade into obscurity. Until that day, however, skepticism of the procedures and methodologies should suggest this area as "low hanging fruit" for *Daubert* challenges.

Tying It Together

The Model Rules of Professional Conduct ("MRPC") or similar state rules or statutes regulate attorney behavior. Violations of these rules can result in sanctions or disbarment. Consider the following rules from the MRPC:

Rule 3.1 Meritorious Claims and Contentions

A lawyer shall not bring or defend a proceeding, or assert or controvert an issue therein, unless there is a basis in law and fact for doing so that is not frivolous, which includes a good faith argument for an extension, modification or reversal of existing law....

Rule 3.3 Candor Toward the Tribunal

(a) A lawyer shall not knowingly:

(1) make a false statement of fact or law to a tribunal or fail to correct a false statement of material fact or law previously made to the tribunal by the lawyer; ... [or]

(3) offer evidence that the lawyer knows to be false. If a lawyer, the lawyer's client, or a witness called by the lawyer, has offered material evidence and the lawyer comes to know of its falsity, the lawyer shall take reasonable remedial measures, including, if necessary, disclosure to the tribunal. A lawyer may refuse to offer evidence, other than the testimony of a defendant in a criminal matter, that the lawyer reasonably believes is false.

(b) A lawyer who represents a client in an adjudicative proceeding and who knows that a person intends to engage, is engaging or has engaged in criminal or fraudulent conduct related to the proceeding shall take reasonable remedial measures, including, if necessary, disclosure to the tribunal....

Rule 3.8 Special Responsibilities of a Prosecutor

The prosecutor in a criminal case shall:

(a) refrain from prosecuting a charge that the prosecutor knows is not supported by probable cause; ... [and]

(d) make timely disclosure to the defense of all evidence or information known to the prosecutor that tends to negate the guilt of the accused or mitigates the offense, and, in connection with sentencing, disclose to the defense and to the tribunal all unprivileged mitigating information known to the prosecutor, except when the prosecutor is relieved of this responsibility by a protective order of the tribunal; ...

Rule 8.4 Misconduct

It is professional misconduct for a lawyer to:

(a) violate or attempt to violate the Rules of Professional Conduct, knowingly assist or induce another to do so, or do so through the acts of another;

(b) commit a criminal act that reflects adversely on the lawyer's honesty, trustworthiness or fitness as a lawyer in other respects;

(c) engage in conduct involving dishonesty, fraud, deceit or misrepresentation;

(d) engage in conduct that is prejudicial to the administration of justice; ...

Assignment: You are an attorney within the ethics complaint office of the State Bar. You have received an ethics complaint, alleging that the prosecutor in a case (one of the three listed below) acted unethically in presenting the evidence listed.

Choose one of the three cases listed below and write a memo to your supervisor explaining whether there is probable cause to believe the prosecutor violated a rule of professional conduct. "Probable cause" means that the facts and circumstances of the situation would lead a person of reasonable caution to believe a violation has occurred.

- Case #1: *Williamson v. Reynolds*: testimony of crime lab technician Melvin Hett;
- Case #2: *United States v. Lewis*: testimony of document analyst John W. Cawley, III; or
- Case #3: *Ramirez v. State*: testimony of Miami crime technician Robert Hart.

D. Why It Matters — The Case of Cameron Todd Willingham

During our review of specific forensic disciplines in Chapters 5, 6, and 7, we have often seen discussion of the weaknesses of the underlying scientific bases for these methods (save, possibly, for DNA) in both the National Academy Report of 2009 and the President's Commission report of 2016. In calling for additional research, the National Academy Report described the problem in forensics as follows:

> The fact is that many forensic tests — such as those used to infer the source of toolmarks or bite marks — have never been exposed to stringent scientific scrutiny. Most of these techniques were developed in crime laboratories to aid in the investigation of evidence from a particular crime scene, and researching their limitations and foundations was never a top priority....
>
> Some non-DNA forensic tests do not meet the fundamental requirements of science, in terms of reproducibility, validity, and falsifiability....[48]

Similarly, in 2016, the President's Commission noted the weaknesses of the bases and called for basic foundational research to be performed by objective arbiters:

> It is important that scientific evaluations of the foundational validity be conducted, on an ongoing basis, to assess the foundational validity of current and newly developed forensic feature-comparison technologies. To ensure the scientific judgments are unbiased and independent, such evaluations should be conducted by an agency which has no stake in the outcome.[49]

These problems, however, are not confined to the lab. Since DNA evidence became widely-used, The Innocence Project has challenged many convictions and exonerated over 350 offenders.[50] Of those 350 exonerations, twenty offenders served time on death row.

For many years, defenders of the current system claimed there had never been an execution of an innocent person.[51] Justice Antonin Scalia boldly proclaimed, in his concurrence in *Kansas v. Marsh*, that:

> It should be noted at the outset that the dissent does not discuss a single case — not one — in which it is clear that a person was executed for a crime he did not commit. If such an event had occurred in recent years, we would

---

48. National Research Council, National Academy of Sciences, Strengthening Forensic Science in the United States: A Path Forward 42–43 (2009).

49. President's Council of Advisors on Sci. and Tech., Forensic Science in Criminal Courts: Ensuring Scientific Validity of Feature-Comparison Methods 14 (2016).

50. The number of exonerated cases changes all the time and is updated on the website of The Innocence Project, here: https://www.innocenceproject.org/dna-exonerations-in-the-united-states/.

51. *See* Andrew Cohen, *Yes, America, We Have Executed an Innocent Man*, Atlantic (May 14, 2012), *available at* https://www.theatlantic.com/national/archive/2012/05/yes-america-we-have-executed-an-innocent-man/257106/; Michael L. Radelet, *The Role of the Innocence Argument in Contemporary Death Penalty Debates*, 41 Tex. Tech L. Rev. 199 (2008).

not have to hunt for it; the innocent's name would be shouted from the rooftops by the abolition lobby.[52]

In fact, Justice Scalia would not have to wait long to learn the sad truth that he was wrong.

In April 2004, the State of Texas executed Cameron Todd Willingham for murder after the deaths of his three children in a house fire in 1991. As you read the article below, consider the evidence presented by the prosecution and what arguments you might have brought against the forensic evidence.

Paul C. Giannelli, *Junk Science and the Execution of an Innocent Man*

7 N.Y.U. J. L. & Liberty 221 (2013)

I. Introduction

Two-year-old Amber Willingham, along with her younger twin sisters, Karmon and Kameron, died in a fire on December 23, 1991 in Corsicana, Texas. Their father Cameron Todd Willingham escaped from the fire, was tried, and eventually executed for their deaths. The expert testimony offered against him to prove arson was "junk science." The case has since become infamous—the subject of an award-winning New Yorker article, numerous newspaper accounts, and several television shows. It also became enmeshed in the death penalty debate and the reelection of Texas Governor Rick Perry, who refused to grant a stay of execution after a noted expert submitted a report debunking the arson "science" offered at Willingham's trial. The Governor later attempted to derail an investigation by the Texas Forensic Science Commission into the arson evidence presented at Willingham's trial.

Whatever else the Willingham case may stand for, it is a trenchant illustration of the judicial acceptance of expert testimony devoid of empirical support and the legal system's inability to effectively police such testimony. The National Academy of Science's landmark 2009 report on forensic science, Strengthening Forensic Science in the United States: A Path Forward, made the breathtaking observation that, "[a]mong existing forensic methods, only nuclear DNA analysis has been rigorously shown to have the capacity to consistently, and with a high degree of certainty, demonstrate a connection between an evidentiary sample and a specific individual or source." The report went on to observe: "In a number of forensic science disciplines, forensic science professionals have yet to establish either the validity of their approach or the accuracy of their conclusions, and the courts have been utterly ineffective in addressing this problem." Moreover, recent studies document the role that forensic science played in convicting the innocent. The Willingham case also highlights the corrosive effect of death-penalty politics—the extraordinary lengths a state has undertaken to avoid investigating the possibility that it had executed an innocent man.

---

52. Kansas v. Marsh, 548 U.S. 163, 182 (2006) (Scalia, J., concurring).

II. The Trial

A. The Arson Evidence

Willingham's capital trial began in August 1992. Proclaiming his innocence from the beginning, Willingham refused to plead guilty in exchange for life imprisonment in lieu of the death penalty.

1. *Arson Investigations*

The arson evidence was critical. No arson, no crime. The prosecution proffered two experts: Manuel Vasquez, a deputy state fire marshal, and Douglas Fogg, an assistant fire chief in Corsicana. With years of experience, they came from the "old school" of investigators — those who used intuition and a number of rules of thumb to determine whether a fire was incendiary. In Vasquez's words: "The fire tells a story. I am just the interpreter.... And the fire does not lie. It tells me the truth."

Critics of this approach complained that it lacked a scientific foundation. Rather, it was based on folklore that had been passed down from generation to generation without any empirical testing. As early as 1977, a government report noted that common arson indicators had "received little or no scientific testing" and "[t]here appears to be no published material in the scientific literature to substantiate their validity." Through the 1980s, proponents of a science-based approach to arson investigations waged an uphill battle, finally winning a major victory in 1992 when the National Fire Protection Association (NFPA) published its Guide for Fire and Explosion Investigations (NFPA 921). Although NFPA 921 would subsequently become the bible in fire and arson investigations, it was published weeks after Willingham's trial.

2. *The Willingham Fire*

Deputy Fire Marshal Vasquez told the jury that he had found twenty indicators of arson during his post-fire investigation of Willingham's house. One indicator was a low burning fire. "All fire goes up," Vasquez testified. Thus, burn patterns on the lower walls and floor suggested that an accelerant was used.

This common-sense notion, however, has its limitations, especially when a fire occurs in a contained area, such as a house. Due to buoyancy, a thermal plume initially rises once a fire is ignited. As the fire continues, the plume reaches the ceiling, which causes it to spread outward towards the walls. When it reaches the walls, the combustion products press down from the ceiling creating an upper level, which continues to increase in depth and temperature. Eventually thermal radiation replaces convection as the principal method of heat transfer. When the temperature of the hot gas layer reaches approximately 1100–1200 degrees Fahrenheit, every exposed combustible surface in the room will burst into flames. This phenomenon, known as "flashover," can occur within minutes. After flashover, the entire room is engulfed in flames, including the lower walls and floor. Flashover, according to one authority, is the point at which the fire transitions from a "fire in a room" to a "room on fire." Consequently, a low burning fire is not necessarily indicative of an incendiary origin.

Moreover, some of Vasquez's other "indicators"—splotchy looking areas called "puddle configurations" and "pour patterns"—are present after flashover in an accidental fire. Similarly, additional indicators such as "alligatoring" marks on wood (char blisters) are explained by flashover. Flashover also accounts for another fact that Vasquez thought incriminatory. Willingham told investigators that he had attempted to save his daughters, but the heat was too great and he was forced to run from the house without shoes. Willingham's feet were not burnt, and in Vasquez's mind, burnt debris on the floor made that impossible. However, if Willingham left his home before flashover, his feet would not have been burnt. (Willingham exaggerated his attempts to save his children—a common occurrence when a parent survives a fatal fire.)

Still another clue was charring under an aluminum threshold of an interior door. Here, again, this may occur in a flashover. Still other arson indicators—melted bedsprings, multiple points of origin, and brown stains on a concrete floor—are also consistent with an accidental blaze. In addition, Vasquez relied on the presence of "crazed glass"—spider-web patterns on the windows as an indication of arson. It was long believed that crazed glass resulted from a fire that burned fast and hot—i.e., one fueled by a liquid accelerant. Yet, subsequent research demonstrated that crazing occurs only from rapid cooling when water from fire hoses is sprayed on heated windows.

In retrospect, the most damning piece of evidence involved one of the numerous debris samples submitted for laboratory analysis. It came from an area near the front door and was the only sample that tested positive for a chemical commonly used in charcoal lighter fluids. Nevertheless, this finding can be explained by the fact that a charcoal grill and lighter fluid were on the front porch at the time of the fire. Eyewitnesses reported no fire at the front door when they first saw Willingham on the porch. In fact, the negative results from the other samples support Willingham's case.

The cause of the fire remains unknown, and the scene cannot be reconstructed due in part to the disappearance of records....

IV. Texas Forensic Science Commission

After Willingham's execution, two seemingly unrelated statutes were enacted that ensured that the case would not die. In November 2004, Congress passed the Justice for All Act. Because of numerous crime laboratory scandals, this legislation included a requirement that each state receiving federal funds designate an entity to investigate forensic misconduct and incompetence.

One of the major scandals involved the Houston crime laboratory. According to a state senator, "the validity of almost any case that has relied upon evidence produced by the lab is questionable." As described by a later investigation, "the DNA Section was in shambles—plagued by a leaky roof, operating for years without a line supervisor, overseen by a technical leader who had no personal experience performing DNA analysis and who was lacking the qualifications required under the FBI standards, staffed by underpaid and undertrained analysts, and generating mistake-ridden and poorly documented casework." As a consequence, the state legislature created the

Texas Forensic Science Commission (TFSC) in 2005. Among other duties, the Commission was tasked with investigating claims of professional negligence or misconduct as required by the federal act.

A. Innocence Project Complaint

By this time, the Chicago Tribune ... began examining the Willingham case. The Tribune retained three independent experts to review the arson evidence, all of whom concluded that the evidence was seriously flawed. Next, the Innocence Project requested five experts to reexamine the case pro bono. These experts submitted a scathing forty-three page report, finding that "each and every one of the indicators relied upon have since been scientifically proven to be invalid." The report even raised questions about Fire Marshal Vasquez's general knowledge of the field. For example, Vasquez testified that of the 1200 to 1500 fires he had investigated, most were arson. Yet, the Texas Fire Marshal Office reported that between 1980 and 2005, only fifty percent of investigated fires were arson. Vasquez also testified that fifty percent of his fires involved injuries and deaths. In contrast, between 1995 and 2005, the annual percentage of fires that resulted in death was 0.23% and the percentage of those resulting in injuries was 1.22%.

In May 2006, the Innocence Project petitioned the Commission to review the arson testimony in the Willingham and Ernest Ray Willis cases. The expert evidence in both cases was comparable, but Willis was lucky. His death penalty conviction was overturned on procedural grounds, and the prosecutor subsequently refused to reindict him after Dr. Hurst wrote the same type of critical report in Willis's case that he had written in Willingham's. Willis, who had spent seventeen years on death row, was subsequently exonerated on grounds of actual innocence.

The TFSC was not authorized to determine guilt or innocence. Instead, the Innocence Project argued that the State Fire Marshal's Office should have reinvestigated the Willingham and other old arson cases, in which its experts had testified, after NFPA 921 was published in 1992—a full twelve years before Willingham's execution.

B. The Beyler Report

The Commission's work was hampered from the beginning. Initially, the legislature did not provide funding, and then the Governor and Lieutenant Governor delayed the appointment of Commission members. When funding was finally appropriated, the Commission spent a year formulating its procedures under the guidance of the Texas Attorney General's Office. In late 2008, more than two years after the Innocence Project complaint was received, the Commission retained an independent consultant, Dr. Craig Beyler, another nationally recognized expert, to review the arson evidence. Beyler's fifty-one page report dissected the expert testimony, concluding:

> The investigations of the Willis and Willingham fires did not comport with either the modern standard of care expressed by NFPA 921, or the standard of care expressed by fire investigation texts and papers in the period 1980–1992. The investigators had poor understandings of fire science and failed to acknowledge or apply the contemporaneous understanding of the limi-

tations of fire indicators. Their methodologies did not comport with the scientific method or the process of elimination. A finding of arson could not be sustained based upon the standard of care expressed by NFPA, or the standard of care expressed by fire investigation texts and papers in the period 1980–1992....

V. Conclusion

There is little dispute that the arson evidence in Willingham's case, based on myths that had permeated fire investigations for years, was invalid. Every independent expert, including the top experts in the country, has concluded that there was no evidence of arson. Without the arson evidence, there never would have been an arrest, much less a trial or execution. The other evidence introduced at trial (e.g., jail-informant testimony and demeanor evidence) was suspect. While Willingham was executed, Willis, who was convicted on comparable evidence, was exonerated after spending seventeen years on death row.

Although NFPA 921 was published in 1992 just weeks after Willingham's trial, many of its findings had been reported during the prior decade. After NFPA 921 was published, the State Fire Marshal's Office became aware of its but did not take corrective action in old cases during the dozen years Willingham waited on death row. Indeed, the Office still maintains it did everything right.

Moreover ... the Texas pardon board and Governor Perry had the opportunity to stay the execution to investigate further. They did not. Although the United States Supreme Court has called clemency the "failsafe" procedure in death penalty cases, the Texas procedure was known as "death by fax" because the pardon board is not required to meet or discuss a case; each member can vote by fax. "Between 1976 and 2004, when Willingham filed his petition, the State of Texas had approved only one application for clemency from a person on death row." In another case, a Texas appellate judge wrote: "Applicant's complaints about the inadequacies of our Texas executive clemency procedures are not unheard of. Not only are they not unheard of, but her complaints are pretty much accurate. I would say that clemency law in Texas is a legal fiction at best...."

Notes and Questions

1. *Junk Science and the Execution of an Innocent Man* is one of many reviews of the Willingham case. For popular media coverage of the case, see David Grann, *Trial by Fire*, NEW YORKER (Sept. 7, 2009); Bob Herbert, *Innocent but Dead*, N.Y. TIMES, Aug. 31, 2009, at A29. PBS Frontline reviewed the case in 2010 as well.[46]

2. The National Academy Report in 2009, assessing fire investigations in general, found that "[d]espite the paucity of research, some arson investigators continue to make determinations about whether or not a particular fire was set. However,

---

46. *Frontline: Death by Fire* (PBS television broadcast Oct. 19, 2010), *available at* http://www.pbs.org/wgbh/pages/frontline/death-by-fire/.

according to testimony presented to the committee, many of the rules of thumb that are typically assumed to indicate that an accelerant was used have been shown not to be true."[47] For a detailed review of the weaknesses of arson forensics, see Jennifer D. Oliva & Valena E. Beety, *Evidence on Fire*, 97 N.C. L. Rev. ___ (2019) (forthcoming).

3.   Sadly, the Willingham case is not the sole example of the possibility of a wrongful execution. In fact, it is not the only one in Texas. For a review of the Carlos DeLuna case, and the issue in general, see Andrew Cohen, *Yes, America, We Have Executed an Innocent Man*, Atlantic (May 14, 2012); *see also* Daniel H. Benson et al., *Executing the Innocent*, 3 Ala. C.R. & C.L. L. Rev. 1 (2013); Aliza B. Kaplan, *Oregon's Death Penalty: The Practical Reality*, 17 Lewis & Clark L. Rev. 1 (2013); Jessica Dwyer-Moss, *Flawed Forensics and the Death Penalty: Junk Science and Potentially Wrongful Executions*, 11 Seattle J. Soc. Just. 757 (2013).

4.   In 2015, the State Bar of Texas received a formal grievance from The Innocence Project against the prosecutor in the Cameron Willingham case.[48] After an investigation, the State Bar of Texas filed disciplinary charges against the prosecutor, John Jackson, for false statements, concealing evidence, and obstruction of justice.[49] The trial on these charges occurred in May 2017, and the jury acquitted Jackson of all charges. Maurice Possley, *Former Prosecutor Cleared of Misconduct in Texas Death Penalty Case*, Wash. Post, May 11, 2017.

---

47. National Research Council, National Academy of Sciences, Strengthening Forensic Science in the United States: A Path Forward 173 (2009).

48. *Grievance Against John Jackson*, Innocence Project (2014), *available at* https://assets.documentcloud.org/documents/1237292/willingham-final-draft-of-bar-complaint.pdf.

49. *John Jackson Disciplinary Petition*, Marshall Project (2015), *available at* https://www.themarshallproject.org/documents/1688574-jackson-disciplinary-petition-fm-3-5-15.

Chapter 8

Medical Standards of Care and Causation Testimony

The first half of Part II focused on expert fields that are mainly applicable to criminal trials. While DNA, fingerprints, and handwriting can become involved in civil cases, their predominant use remains in criminal forensics. Moving forward in Part II, we now shift to issues that are relevant primarily in civil litigation, with the caveat that these expert issues can likewise arise in the criminal law context on occasion. As we begin our analysis of these materials, remember the fundamental principle that the rules of evidence (with few exceptions) are rules of general applicability. Therefore, on their face, they apply to both civil and criminal issues with equal vigor. Yet as we engage with the different specialties, we must question whether that neutral proposition of equal vigor has been honored by the courts.

In that context, we will start our civil case expertise with the issue of medical negligence. Testimony on medical practice will clearly require significant expertise, and in that regard, it is similar to the science-based field of DNA forensics. We begin this chapter on medical negligence with an overview of the claims available and then quickly move to testimony on standards of care and causation in those cases. After medical claims in Chapter 8, Chapter 9 will discuss accident reconstruction, a discipline broadly analogous to fingerprint analysis, because while it is based on plausible grounds, there remains significant subjectivity in the field. We finish Part II with a discussion of economic valuation. This area is a component of nearly all civil cases and one in which attorneys often receive their first expert assignments.

In each of these fields, our assessment of the issue will include an introduction to the underlying scientific principles of the discipline, followed by materials related to controversies within the field. As with forensics, these disciplines may or may not be something a particular attorney uses on a regular basis in their practice. Instead, the text exposes students to areas that they could cover as junior attorneys while also providing a template of evaluation that is likely replicable in other fields. As always, we will write about expert evidence in some practical exercises as we simultaneously learn the substantive law of the field.

We begin the chapter with an overview of the components of a medical negligence claim before looking in detail at the main contested issues of standard of care and causation.

John D. North, *Medical Negligence*

BUSINESS & COMMERCIAL LITIGATION IN FEDERAL COURTS,
Ch. 86 (4th ed. 2017)[Ed.]

LIABILITY

Medical malpractice is negligence litigation. The basic structure of a medical malpractice case is the same as that of the most fundamental slip-and-fall or auto negligence case: a standard of care owed to the plaintiff; a breach of the standard; proximate causation; and an injury....

What sets medical malpractice apart from ordinary negligence cases is the setting. Medical malpractice cases all arise out of medical care or treatment rendered to a patient who is already injured or sick. Rather than a "reasonable man" standard of care, there is a professional standard of care. Rather than an injury that would not have occurred "but for" the defendant's conduct, the plaintiff's injury or sickness was aggravated, or was not reversed or cured, by the defendant's alleged failure to meet the standard of care.

Thus, although the basic structure of a medical malpractice case is the same as that of an ordinary negligence case, the facts are highly specialized, technical and scientific. Consequently, other than the plaintiff, almost all the players in medical malpractice litigation are specialized—the lawyers, the defendants, and third-party treating physicians or healthcare providers, as well as the expert witnesses.

One result of this specialization is that, in most cases, the liability issues are well defined by the time a case reaches trial. Generally, there is little dispute over whether the defendant owed the plaintiff a duty or over the standard of care. There are cases in which the plaintiff alleges he was abandoned by the defendant, in which the defense is that the physician-patient relationship had terminated. There are also cases where a new technique or protocol is at issue, and there is an evolving standard of care as experience accumulates. However, the liability issue most often turns out to be whether the defendant deviated from the standard of care. This issue pits the plaintiff's expert against the defendant and his expert. The subject matter of all the testimony of all of these witnesses is the same, and it will invariably be specialized....

EXPERT TESTIMONY NECESSARY

It is universally recognized that in order to establish the standard of care in a medical malpractice case, expert testimony is required, with the exception of "common knowledge" cases.... A jury of lay persons cannot have the technical knowledge of how medicine is practiced that is necessary to determine the applicable standard of care. By the same token, a jury cannot have the technical knowledge necessary to determine whether there has been a deviation from the applicable standard of care. Education is required. Thus, the first element of a medical malpractice case—a deviation from the applicable standard of care—will always require expert testimony, except

---

[Ed.] Used with the permission of Thomson Reuters.

in "common knowledge" cases. Since in "common knowledge" cases, the deviation from the applicable standard of care is self-evident, few "common knowledge" cases go to trial. As a practical matter then, medical malpractice trials will necessarily require expert testimony.

It is well established now in almost all jurisdictions that the standard of care that must be proved is a national standard. The standard is usually expressed in terms of the physician of "average" competence, or, in some states as "minimal" competence. However, in all cases, the standard requires competence. The argument that physicians in a rural locality affiliated with a small community hospital are not required to have the same minimal or base level of knowledge concerning medical conditions or are not required to observe the same precautions as physicians in more urban areas, is no longer available.

There is one qualification, however. Not all of the state-of-the-art facilities and procedures that are available in urban centers or tertiary referral hospitals are available in community hospitals. Therefore, a physician cannot be held to a standard that would require knowledge and experience in specialized techniques or procedures that are not possessed by physicians reasonably available for referral, or that would require the use of equipment that is not reasonably available. This qualification may come into play when the plaintiff has sustained an acute illness or injury in a remote location, sometimes on vacation, and the nearest facility offering the state-of-the-art care is too distant to render the care timely.

The other standard of care issue that has undergone recent evolution is whether the defendant should be held to the standard of a specialist or a general practitioner. The standard that applies to a specialist has been seen as a higher standard, and more favorable to the plaintiff. However, "general practice" is now for the most part performed by family practitioners and internists. Family practice and internal medicine are themselves recognized specialties. By and large, the "general practitioner" standard of care is seldom appropriate. Physicians are to be measured by the standards of their specialty.

While the plaintiff must offer expert testimony on the issue of liability, the defendant is not required to call an expert to refute the plaintiff's expert. In the first place, the plaintiff has the burden of proof, and is not entitled to any presumptions. Therefore, purely as a matter of technical legal requirements, except in exceptional circumstances..., the defendant has no burden of proof to sustain, and no burden of going forward with the evidence after the plaintiff's expert has testified.

On a more practical level, however, the defendant must meet the plaintiff's proofs. Most often, the defendant will retain an outside expert. However, the defendant may testify on his own behalf as well. The defendant will be competent to testify as to the standard of care, and how his care and treatment met the standard.... [T]he defendant, in the course of explaining his care and treatment of the plaintiff, why he decided on the course of treatment he did and how he carried it out will inevitably testify as to accepted practice and why the procedures and techniques he utilized were appropriate in the plaintiff's case. Such testimony is, in substance, testimony that the defendant observed the applicable standard of care ... [, and therefore] the defendant in a medical malpractice case gives what amounts to expert testimony.

The defendant then may call his own outside expert witness to refute plaintiff's expert, and to approve the defendant's care and treatment—and thus the defendant's testimony as well. The defendant thus has the natural advantage of being able to call two witnesses on the standard of care issues.

Defendants, however, do not always take advantage of the opportunity to call an expert witness. While calling an expert to corroborate and support the testimony of the physician expert in most cases gives the defendant a natural advantage, there are risks. Inevitably, in a case of any complexity, there will be points in the testimony of the physician and that of the expert witness that do not harmonize. Also inevitably, the expert witness will not have as firm a grasp on the facts of the case. A skilled plaintiff's attorney may use inconsistencies in the testimony of the physician and the expert, or the expert's lack of familiarity with the underlying facts, to undermine their credibility.

In order to avoid such risks, there are cases in which the defendant will make the tactical decision, at trial, not to call the expert witness, even though the expert has been properly identified ... and would easily meet the requirements of Fed. R. Evid ... 702 for expert testimony. This decision is usually made after the defendant has testified, and an evaluation can be made as to how well he has matched up against the plaintiff's expert....

The other strategy call that counsel must make regarding liability experts is the selection of the expert most appropriate for the case. In many states, "tort reform" statutes dictate the minimum credentials of expert witnesses in medical malpractice cases. As a general rule, in such states, the expert witness must practice in the same specialty or subspecialty as the defendant physician, and possess the same credentials. Thus, it takes a board-certified pediatric neuroradiologist to testify for or against another board-certified pediatric neuroradiologist.

Even in states where no such requirements have been imposed, meeting the minimum requirements of Fed. R. Evid. 702—"scientific, technical or other specialized knowledge [that] will help the trier of fact"—will not be enough to persuade the jury. In order to persuade a jury, the expert witness who criticizes or defends the defendant physician will have to have comparable training and experience, and be well versed in the specific procedure or treatment that is involved. A general orthopedic surgeon may meet the minimum standard under Fed. R. Evid. 702 to testify for or against an orthopedic surgeon who performs cervical fusions or reverse total shoulder replacements, but would not likely make a convincing witness....

On the other hand, the over-qualified expert may also lack credibility. In a case where the defendant is a local physician, practicing in a community hospital, an expert from a university hospital or tertiary referral hospital may be seen as out of touch with the realities of practice ... and his version of the standard of care discredited as well above and beyond what would be required of the "average practitioner" in the defendant's specialty.

CAUSATION

Medical malpractice cases raise causation issues that are unique. Other than in surgical cases where the surgeon has caused a direct injury to the plaintiff, physician error is not the sole cause of the plaintiff's ultimate outcome. In most cases, the ultimate outcome is the result of both the plaintiff's preexisting condition … and the physician's alleged negligence.

This combination of causes gives rise to a number of issues that have been addressed in a variety of ways. The physician's alleged negligence may be seen as aggravating the plaintiff's preexisting condition. Or, depending on the case, diminishing the plaintiff's chances for a cure or at least a better outcome.

The common example is a delay in diagnosis. Had the patient been diagnosed with cancer at Stage I of the disease, his chances of survival would have been 80%. As a result of the defendant's negligence, he was not diagnosed until Stage III, when the chances of survival are only 20%.

Such a plaintiff … cannot prove that, "but for" the defendant's negligence he would have been cured or would have survived. Despite a diagnosis at Stage III, 20% of the patients live anyway. Despite a diagnosis at Stage I, 20% of the patients die anyway. It is usually impossible to prove the plaintiff fell within the 60% of patients for whom timely diagnosis makes a difference. The plaintiff can do no better than to prove his chances were diminished.

The states have arrived at various solutions to this problem. Application of traditional causation doctrine can yield the anomalous outcome of a clearly negligent doctor escaping liability. When the severity of a preexisting condition is such that the plaintiff's statistical probability of survival is less than 51%, "but for" causation dictates that physician negligence could not have been the proximate cause of the patient's injury. It is "more likely than not" that the patient died from the preexisting condition. Conversely, where there is a 51% or greater chance of patient survival, the defendant is held responsible for any award as it is "more likely than not" that the plaintiff died as a result of physician negligence. Not surprisingly, the traditional causation approach to medical malpractice claims came to be known as the "all or nothing" rule. Notwithstanding the resulting unfairness to some plaintiffs (and physicians), until relatively recently, this "but for" analysis governed medical malpractice cases.

Gradually, courts and commentators came to question the suitability of traditional causation rules for medical malpractice claims. They reasoned that it is fundamentally inequitable and contrary to the purpose of tort law to ignore the fact that the plaintiff came to the doctor because of the very preexisting condition that reduced her chance of survival. In other words, the loss of a chance to survive is itself an injury deserving of compensation[, and therefore] … courts have crafted a relaxed causation standard.

While variations exist between and among jurisdictions adopting the relaxed approach, as a general matter they share the concept that a negligent physician should be held responsible for diminishing a plaintiff's chance of survival—irrespective of the plaintiff's overall chances of surviving a preexisting condition. Thus, if physician negligence is determined to have diminished the chance of recovery, the physician is held responsible for the increased risk of injury/lost chance of cure. Most jurisdictions have adopted some form of relaxed causation in medical malpractice cases.

However, a sizeable minority of states reject relaxed causation for medical malpractice suits. These jurisdictions continue to embrace the traditional "but for" approach. The rationale typically advanced for rejecting a relaxed causation approach is that it will allow recovery in dubious cases which will, in turn, result in higher insurance and medical costs.

The states have addressed these issues in a variety of ways. Therefore, in every medical malpractice case in federal court, it will be necessary to determine how the controlling state law addresses causation and the measure of damages.

A. Standard of Care Testimony

As North makes clear, duty to the patient is almost never contested. This leaves the appropriate standard of care for the physician as the first major component of a medical negligence case. To evaluate standard of care, we begin with the reasons for the "locality rule," its ultimate demise, and what it tells us about modern claims. Afterward, we address other modern case issues such as expert qualifications, and the basis and reliability of opinion testimony.

i. The Locality Rule and Its Demise

Wilson v. Sligar

516 N.E.2d 1099 (Ind. Ct. App. 1987)

RATLIFF, Chief Judge.

In June of 1977, Marilyn J. Wilson began to suffer from pain in her hip, which was previously operated on after an automobile accident in 1964. Wilson ... eventually was referred to William M. Sligar, M.D.... After [non-surgical] treatments failed, Dr. Sligar recommended and eventually performed total hip replacement surgery. After the operation Wilson suffered from a burning sensation in her left foot and developed a condition called "foot drop". Dr. Sligar treated Wilson for the "foot drop" condition and recommended additional surgery.

Wilson refused to have Dr. Sligar perform additional surgery, and instead sought medical opinions and treatment from William Naldo Capello, an orthopedic surgeon. Dr. Capello determined that Wilson had sciatic nerve palsy, and referred Wilson to Robert Worth, a neurosurgeon. Drs. Capello and Worth jointly operated on Wilson.

During surgery the doctors observed a kink in Wilson's sciatic nerve, which apparently had been caused by a retractor used during the surgery performed by Dr. Sligar. According to the testimony at trial, sciatic nerve palsy results from total hip replacement in up to five percent (5%) of the cases. (*i.e.* 50 per 1000), depending on the area in the country where the operation is performed. The surgery performed by Drs. Capello and Worth partially corrected Wilson's sciatic nerve palsy.

Wilson filed a complaint against Dr. Sligar in accordance with Indiana's Medical Malpractice Act ... On October 27, 28, and 29, 1986, a trial was held. During the trial, Wilson attempted to elicit testimony from Dr. Sligar and Dr. Capello on the standard of care for board certified orthopedic surgeons doing total hip replacement surgery. After objection and argument, the trial court prohibited the proffered testimony as being incompetent and without adequate foundation, because the questions sought testimony which did not connect the standard of care to the "same or similar community" as that in which Dr. Sligar performed the surgery. Wilson challenges the trial court's rulings.

ISSUE

Wilson raises one (1) issue on appeal: Whether the trial court erred by excluding testimony as to a standard of care which was not defined in terms of the "same or similar locality".

DISCUSSION AND DECISION

Wilson argues that the trial court erred by excluding expert testimony on the standard of care for board certified orthopedic surgeons. In challenging the trial court's evidentiary rulings, Wilson confronts a strong standard of review. The trial court is empowered with broad discretion in determining the competency of an expert witness and the admissibility of his testimony. On appeal, this court will not disturb the trial court's rulings absent an abuse of discretion.

The rulings Wilson challenges all involve the application of the "same or similar locality" rule to the standard of care for medical specialists. In Indiana, an expert witness may not testify as to the standard of care unless the record shows that the witness is familiar with the standard of care in the same or similar locality as the one in which the complained of services were performed. *Iterman v. Baker*, 15 N.E.2d 365, 371 (Ind. 1938). This rule stems from the standard of care that a specialist owes to a patient. The standard of care is defined as follows:

> The degree of skill and care required of the physician or surgeon who is employed because he is a specialist, is that degree of skill and knowledge which is ordinarily possessed by physicians and surgeons who devote special attention to the ailment, its diagnosis and treatment, agreeable with the state of scientific knowledge at the time of the operation or treatment, in similar localities generally.

Worster v. Caylor, 110 N.E.2d 337, 339 (Ind. 1952). Thus, the specialist's standard of care is measured with reference to the same or a similar locality as that in which the services were performed. *Joy v. Chau*, 377 N.E.2d 670, 675 n. 1 (Ind. Ct. App. 1978).

The "same or similar locality" rule developed in part as a compromise to the decreasing justification and logic behind the strict "locality" rule. The strict "locality" rule originated during a time when substantial discrepancies existed between rural and urban communities with regard to medical opportunities, equipment, facilities, and knowledge of new procedures and when the ability to travel between rural and urban communities was more restricted. The rule was intended to prevent the inequity that would result from holding rural doctors to the same standard of care as urban doctors. However, the discrepancies between rural and urban areas with regard to opportunities, equipment, facilities, and available knowledge have lessened over time. Furthermore, the advances in communication networks, travel means and modern educational opportunities have all but eliminated the justifications for a strict "locality" rule. In response to the decreased justifications, many courts have abrogated the "locality" rule. However, Indiana and other jurisdictions have adhered to a modified, less stringent version of the locality rule. Indiana currently measures a physician's conduct and defines the physician's standard of care in relation to the "same or similar localities".[2] The main purpose of the ... locality rule ... is aimed at insuring that, "the physician's professional conduct [will] be judged in light of the conditions and facilities with which he must work". *Purtill v. Hess*, 489 N.E.2d 867, 874 (Ill. 1986).

The "same or similar locality" rule's definition and application is flexible and not governed by precise criteria. *Hansborough v. Kosyak*, 490 N.E.2d 181, 186 (Ill. App. Ct. 1986).... However, in determining the scope and application for the "same or similar locality rule", the Illinois Appellate Court stated in *Hansbrough*, that,

> "The term 'locality' itself has no precise meaning, and varies with the facts of each particular case The applicable locality should be narrowed no further than necessary to promote the rationale of the rule. However, where it is determined that only one uniform standard of care for treatment exists, the national standard and the community standard may be synonymous. Further, as the supreme court recently recognized, a doctor will not necessarily be disqualified as an expert even if he is unfamiliar with the practices of a particular community as long as there are certain minimum standards of care uniform throughout the country for the particular practice."

Hansbrough, 490 N.E.2d at 186. This court agrees that the foregoing principles should be applied in determining the scope and application of the rule and in determining whether the trial court abused its discretion in ... ruling based on the "same or similar locality" rule.

In the present case, Wilson failed to establish that the trial court committed reversible error in making the evidentiary rulings based upon the application of the

---

2. We note that today even the less stringent "same or similar locality" rule is under attack with regard to nationally board certified specialists.... However, regardless of the merit of changing the standard for specialists to a national standard of care, as an intermediate appellate tribunal this court is not at liberty to depart from the standard of care embodied in our supreme court's precedent. Therefore, this court will apply the "same or similar locality" rule to the specialist in the present case.

locality rule to the proffered testimony. Wilson's challenges to the trial court's rulings involve questions to Dr. Sligar and Dr. Capello. These questions asked whether board certified orthopedic surgeons doing total hip replacements have the same standard of care regardless of where they are performed. These questions were objected to based upon lack of foundation and upon the ground that they did not sufficiently define or relate the standard of care to the locality in which Dr. Sligar operated or to other similar localities. The trial court sustained the objections on foundational and competency grounds, and excluded the proffered testimony.

The trial court improperly excluded the proffered testimony which sought to establish the scope and applicability of the "same or similar locality" rule in the present case. Although Dr. Sligar correctly argues that testimony delineating the standard of care cannot be admitted without an adequate foundation, only one of Wilson's questions directly asked for the specific standard of care. The other questions were directed toward establishing a foundation for the competency of the witness to testify as to the applicable standard of care. The witnesses' testimony involving the standard of care could not be presented until the evidence demonstrated either (1) that the witnesses were familiar with the standard of care in the same or similar locality as the one in which Dr. Sligar performed surgery or (2) that the witnesses were testifying with regard to certain minimum standards of care that are uniform throughout the country for the particular practice. However, to present evidence under the second foundation, the proponent must show that the available conditions and facilities were irrelevant to a determination of the standard of care. In the present case, Wilson was attempting to establish this foundational evidence and not the actual testimony on the standard of care. Therefore, the trial court's ruling was erroneous.

Although the trial court erred in excluding this foundational testimony, Wilson failed to establish that reversal is warranted. Any error in the trial court's evidentiary rulings and exclusions of testimony was rendered harmless when Wilson presented to the jury the same evidence on the standard of care in other evidence and testimony that was not excluded. First, the record reflects that Wilson's attorney was permitted to read the deposition of Dr. Norman V. Lewis to the jury. The record reflects the following:

> . . .
>
> **Q:** Would it be your opinion that the standard of care for board certified orthopedic surgeons doing total hip replacements is the same no matter where they do them? . . .
>
> **A:** Yes.

Second, the in court testimony of Dr. Capello related also that the standard of care for board certified orthopedic surgeons was the same regardless of the locality . . . [:]

> **Q:** Dr. Capello, are you familiar with the standard of care exercised by board certified orthopedic surgeons doing total hip replacements in December of 1979 generally?
>
> **A:** Yes sir.

Q: Is that standard of care, uh, any different or was it any different in New Albany or Clark County, Indiana than it was in Indianapolis or Louisville or indeed for any other city in the United States?

...

A: No I don't believe it [is different]

Q: Are you familiar with the standard of care exercised by board certified orthopedic surgeons doing total hip replacements in areas and communities similar to Jeffersonville, Indiana?

A: Yes.

Q: Doctor, based upon Dr. Sligar's description of his operation here in open court earlier this afternoon and based upon your familiarity with his operative note ... and based upon what you saw and found when you participated in the operation on Marilyn Wilson ... do you have an opinion as to whether Dr. Sligar ... comported and complied with the standard of care customarily exercised by board certified orthopedic surgeons doing that operation?

A: I have an opinion.

Q: What is your opinion?

A: My opinion is that I think there was excessive retraction on the nerve which would be out of keeping with the standards as I understand them.

Therefore, the jury obtained ... evidence on the standard of care, and any error was rendered harmless. Since Wilson failed to establish reversible error, the ... trial court is affirmed.

Vergara v. Doan
593 N.E.2d 185 (Ind. 1992)

SHEPARD, C.J.

Javier Vergara was born on May 31, 1979, at the Adams Memorial Hospital in Decatur, Indiana. His parents, Jose and Concepcion, claimed that negligence on the part of Dr. John Doan during Javier's delivery caused him severe and permanent injuries. A jury returned a verdict for Dr. Doan and the plaintiffs appealed.... We grant transfer to examine the standard of care appropriate for medical malpractice cases.

In most negligence cases, the defendant's conduct is tested against the hypothetical reasonable and prudent person acting under the same or similar circumstances. *Miller v. Griesel*, 308 N.E.2d 701 (Ind. 1974). In medical malpractice cases, however, Indiana has applied a more specific articulation of this standard. It has become known as the modified locality rule: "The standard of care ... is that degree of care, skill, and proficiency which is commonly exercised by ordinarily careful, skillful, and prudent [physicians], at the time of the operation and *in similar localities*." *Burke v. Capello*, 520 N.E.2d 439, 441 (Ind. 1988). Appellants have urged us to abandon this standard, arguing that the reasons for the modified locality rule are no longer applicable in today's society. We agree.

The modified locality rule is a less stringent version of the strict locality rule, which measured the defendant's conduct against that of other doctors in the same community. When the strict locality rule originated in the late 19th century, there was great disparity between the medical opportunities, equipment, facilities, and training in rural and urban communities. Travel and communication between rural and urban communities were difficult. The locality rule was intended to prevent the inequity that would result from holding rural doctors to the same standards as doctors in large cities. *Wilson v. Sligar*, 516 N.E.2d 1099, 1101 (Ind. Ct. App. 1987).

With advances in communication, travel, and medical education, the disparity between rural and urban health care diminished and justification for the locality rule waned. The strict locality rule also had two major drawbacks, especially as applied to smaller communities. First, there was a scarcity of local doctors to serve as expert witnesses against other local doctors. Second, there was the possibility that practices among a small group of doctors would establish a local standard of care below that which the law required. *Pederson v. Dumouchel*, 431 P.2d 973, 977 (Wash. 1967). In response to these changes and criticisms, many courts adopted a modified locality rule, expanding the area of comparison to similar localities. This is the standard applied in Indiana. *Wilson v. Sligar*, 516 N.E.2d 1099 (Ind. Ct. App. 1987) (recognizing the modified locality rule).

Use of a modified locality rule has not quelled the criticism. Many of the common criticisms seem valid. The modified locality rule still permits a lower standard of care to be exercised in smaller communities because other similar communities are likely to have the same care. *Shilkret v. Annapolis Emergency Hosp.*, 349 A.2d 245 (Md. 1975). We also spend time and money on the difficulty of defining what is a similar community. *Cf. id.* The rule also seems inconsistent with the reality of modern medical practice. The disparity between small town and urban medicine continues to lessen with advances in communication, transportation, and education. In addition, widespread insurance coverage has provided patients with more choice of doctors and hospitals by reducing the financial constraints on the consumer in selecting caregivers. These reasons and others have led our Court of Appeals to observe that the modified locality rule has fallen into disfavor. *See Wilson v. Sligar*, 516 N.E.2d at 1101 n. 2. Many states describe the care a physician owes without emphasizing the locality of practice. Today we join these states and adopt the following: a physician must exercise that degree of care, skill, and proficiency exercised by reasonably careful, skillful, and prudent practitioners in the same class to which he belongs, acting under the same or similar circumstances. Rather than focusing on different standards for different communities, this standard uses locality as but one of the factors to be considered in determining whether the doctor acted reasonably. Other relevant considerations would include advances in the profession, availability of facilities, and whether the doctor is a specialist or general practitioner. *See Shilkret*, 349 A.2d at 253.

We now turn to whether the instruction given at trial, legally correct at the time, requires a reversal in light of our decision today. Appellant urges us to remand for a new trial, claiming that the jury instructions overemphasized the same or similar locality.... The court gave the following instructions regarding the standard of care:

> I instruct you that the degree of skill and care required of a general practice physician who is employed prior to and during May, 1979 is that degree of skill and knowledge which ordinarily was possessed by general practice physicians who devote attention to obstetrics and its treatment in Decatur and similar localities of similar size in 1979.

> Therefore, in determining whether or not John Doan, M.D. exercised due care in treating and delivering the child of Concepcion Vergara during the period in question, you may consider his background, training and the care and skill required of general practice physicians rendering similar care under similar circumstances in areas similar in size to the area of Decatur, Indiana or similar localities in 1979.

[and]

> If you find from the testimony of the experts, by a preponderance of the evidence, that certain minimum standards of care, uniform throughout the country, existed for a particular practice then you may judge the doctor's conduct by that minimum standard of care for the particular practice.

Although our holding that the modified locality rule no longer applies makes [the top instruction] erroneous, the standard we have adopted today hardly prohibits consideration of the locality of practice. Locality of practice remains a proper subject for evidence and argument because it may be relevant to the circumstances in which the doctor acted.

Moreover, although [the top instruction] mentions Decatur or similar localities, [the next instruction] refers to a national standard of care. Plaintiff was permitted to present his expert witness, Dr. Harlan Giles, even though he was from Pittsburgh, Pennsylvania (not Decatur or a similar locality). Dr. Giles testified regarding his experience and knowledge of the standard of care in communities similar to Decatur and in hospitals similar in size to Adams County Memorial Hospital. He testified that in his opinion, considering all the factors incident to the pregnancy and birth of Javier Vergara, the standard of care required Dr. Doan to have delivered the baby by cesarean section. He stated that this opinion was based on the standard of care as it existed in 1979 in Decatur or similar communities.... Evidently the jury disagreed with Dr. Giles and found Dr. Doan's conduct reasonable under the circumstances.

We regard our new formulation of a doctor's duty as a relatively modest alteration of existing law. It is unlikely to have changed the way this case was tried. We are satisfied that an instruction without the locality language would not lead a new jury to a different conclusion.

Therefore, we hold that [the instruction error] was harmless and does not require reversal. In a different factual situation, however, an erroneous instruction with the locality language present might well constitute reversible error. The standard that we set out today, without the locality language, should be used from today forward.

GIVAN, J., concurring in result.

Although the majority opinion states that it is abandoning the modified locality rule, they claim the rule now to be that the physician must exercise the care and skill of practitioners in the same class to which he belongs and "acting in the same or similar circumstances." They go on to state that "[o]ther relevant considerations would include advances in the profession, availability of facilities, and whether the doctor is a specialist or general practitioner."

I do not perceive this "new standard" to differ materially from the modified locality rule. The ability of a physician to perform may well be vastly different in a small rural community hospital than ... in a large well-equipped metropolitan hospital.

I believe the majority has articulated a distinction without a difference. I would not confuse the issue by purporting to do away with the modified locality rule.

Notes and Questions

1. In *Wilson*, the court provides some of the reasons for the adoption of the "locality rule." Are there other reasons, beyond what the court mentions, that might support continued use of a locality rule (even if in modified form)? Also, why does the court in *Wilson* (at footnote 2) make a distinction between specialists and general practitioners? For a look at the origin and purpose of the locality rule, see Marc D. Ginsberg, *The Locality Rule Lives! Why? Using Modern Medicine to Eradicate an Unhealthy Law*, 61 DRAKE L. REV. 321, 325–31 (2013); Theodore Silver, *One Hundred Years of Harmful Error: The Historical Jurisprudence of Medical Malpractice*, 1992 WIS. L. REV. 1193, 1226–34.

2. The *Wilson* court continued to use the modified locality rule even after it acknowledged the rule was losing support in other jurisdictions. Within five years, the Indiana Supreme Court in *Vergara* revisited the issue, overturning the locality rule even in its modern form. What changes to society and the medical profession justified this abandonment?

3. To Justice Givan, the standard adopted by the Chief Justice in *Vergara* was not, in fact, modifying the previous standard. Considering the Chief Justice's discussion of the standard moving forward, was Justice Givan right? To help answer the question, also consider why the instruction error in *Vergara* was harmless.

4. Clearly the majority approach has been to move away from the locality rule, in both its strict or modified forms. For a detailed review of the origin, demise, and remaining use of the locality rule, see Ginsberg, 61 DRAKE L. REV. at 331–33. Ginsberg cites Idaho and Tennessee as states that adhere to the strict locality rule, while Arizona, New York, Virginia, and Washington maintain vestiges of the rule. *Id.* at 333–55 (citing *Suhadolnik v. Pressman*, 254 P.3d 11 (Idaho 2011); *Shipley v. Williams*, 350 S.W.3d 527, 536 (Tenn. 2011)). For attorneys practicing in these jurisdictions, detailed understanding of the state limits of the locality rule is fun-

damental. Attorneys in most states, however, will apply the general national standards—which we turn to next.

ii. Standard of Care in Modern Litigation

Hill v. Medlantic Health Care Group

933 A.2d 314 (D.C. 2007)

BLACKBURNE-RIGSBY, Associate Judge.

In this consolidated appeal, Vincent and Peggy Hill, appellants, challenge the trial court's grant of appellees' motion for judgment as a matter of law at the close of appellants' case. Appellants contend that, contrary to the trial court's ruling, they established a *prima facie* case on their claims of negligence, abandonment, and informed consent....

We first discuss the trial judge's proper grant of Judgment as a Matter of Law on appellants' remaining claims after the close of appellants' case. We conclude that appellants' expert, though initially qualified as an expert, failed to provide a basis for his knowledge of the applicable national standard of care, or a basis for his opinion that Mr. Hill's physicians breached the national standard of care in their treatment of his injuries. We require that an expert provide an independent basis for his knowledge of the applicable national standard of care and for his opinion regarding compliance with or breach of such standard. Absent such a basis and linkage, the expert would simply be providing a personal opinion as to the course of treatment he would have taken in treating the patient. This is insufficient for a medical malpractice case. An expert in a medical negligence case must establish that his opinion is grounded in a national standard of care and not merely his personal opinion. The expert must demonstrate that the doctor in question failed to do what a reasonable doctor nationally would have done in the same course of treatment. Appellants' expert failed to meet this standard.

I. Factual Background

On July 21, 1997, Mr. Hill fractured the tibia and fibula bones in his lower left leg in a motorcycle accident and was taken by ambulance, at his request, to the emergency room at Washington Hospital Center. Dr. Levitt recommended to Mr. Hill that an external fixation procedure be performed on his leg, however, Mr. Hill did not want an external fixation because he thought it looked painful based on what he saw in a movie. Mr. Hill informed Dr. Levitt that he preferred an internal fixation instead because he knew his bones took a long time to heal, and he was afraid of getting infected because of "those rods and stuff being outside going inside my leg." Dr. Levitt performed the internal fixation operation on Mr. Hill. Prior to the operation, Mr. Hill signed a consent form, but added a handwritten note on the form indicating that he wanted a board certified anesthesiologist to administer the anesthesia.

On October 20, 1998, during a follow-up visit with Dr. Levitt, Mr. Hill expressed concern that his "leg was starting to look like it was charcoal ... it looked dead, lifeless" in the area of the operation. Dr. Levitt told Mr. Hill that some darkness was to be expected. Mr. Hill scheduled a follow-up visit for December 1998, but was unable to make it because he was sick. Mr. Hill testified that by then his leg had "developed like a blister and ... had pus coming out of [it]." Mr. Hill did not think the blistering or dark color of the skin were related to the operation, so he decided to see a dermatologist, Dr. Lindgren. Dr. Lindgren took a skin culture and informed Mr. Hill that he had a staphylococcal infection. She treated the infection, but told him to return to Dr. Levitt if he had further concerns about his leg, which Mr. Hill did. A few days later, Dr. Levitt informed Mr. Hill that the hardware in his leg was infected and had to be removed immediately. Dr. Levitt performed a second surgery on Mr. Hill on February 11, 1998, which Mr. Hill thought was intended to remove every piece of metal in his leg.... On March 4, 1998, Mr. Hill called Dr. Levitt's office complaining of pain in his leg and that he heard a "crack" in his leg. He scheduled an appointment with Dr. Levitt for that day, and an x-ray revealed that he still had two screws on each side of his leg where it was broken.[5] On April 6, 1998, after several follow-up visits, Dr. Levitt informed Mr. Hill that another surgery was needed to remove over one-inch of the infected bone which would result in a 50% loss of the strength in that bone. During that visit, Mr. Hill ... "fired" Dr. Levitt.

Dr. Levitt referred Mr. Hill to Dr. DiPasquale, an orthopedic surgeon, and noted that she was known for her knowledge about osteomylitis (infections of the bone). Mr. Hill contends that Dr. Levitt never informed him, until that time, that he had osteomylitis. He contends that Dr. Levitt had only informed him that his "hardware" was infected. Mr. Hill met with Dr. DiPasquale, and she recommended a treatment plan which included performing an operation on April 16, 1998, to remove the infected bone and then inserting antibiotic beads into the leg.

Prior to the April 16, 1998 operation, Dr. DiPasquale informed Mr. Hill that Dr. Levitt would have to assist on any future operations, to which Mr. Hill strongly objected. Mr. Hill, however, consented to Dr. Levitt's presence in the operating room as long as Dr. Levitt did not touch him. When Mr. Hill received the consent form for his operation, both Dr. DiPasquale and Dr. Levitt's names were listed, at which point Mr. Hill "lost it" and "hit the ceiling." He felt as though Dr. Levitt had butchered his leg, and he did not want Dr. Levitt to touch him again. Later that day, Dr. DiPasquale informed Mr. Hill that she was canceling the surgery and provided him with the names of three doctors who could provide care for him.

Mr. Hill eventually went home, conducted his own internet research, and located Dr. Tetsworth, who was not one of the three doctors recommended by Dr. DiPasquale. After an initial appointment, Dr. Tetsworth then scheduled a surgery for May 7, 1999, at which point he partially removed the infected bone and inserted antibiotic beads into the infected leg. Over the course of the following year, Mr. Hill had several subsequent surgeries ... and on October 5, 1999, his bone was deemed healed. One leg is now permanently shorter than the other one, however, and he has a [muscle] deformity....

---

5. Appellees argued ... that the screws were left in the bone intentionally to provide support.

On July 17, 2000, Mr. Hill and Mrs. Hill filed the present action. On July 23, 2003, the trial court granted defendants, Dr. Levitt's and Dr. Danziger's,[9] Motion for Partial Summary Judgment as to punitive damages; and defendants' Dr. DiPasquale and WHC, Motion for Partial Summary Judgment as to punitive damages. On April 5, 2005, the trial court granted summary judgment [on some counts].... Mr. and Mrs. Hill appeal each of these orders.

On May 16, 2005, the matter went to trial by jury ... [on the remaining counts, including negligence]. Appellant testified and also presented the testimony of his wife, Peggy Hill, his expert, Dr. Bryant Bloss, Dr. Barrington Barnes (appellant's primary care physician) and Dr. Buck (Mr. Hill's radiologist). At the close of appellants' case, appellees made a Motion for Judgment as a Matter of Law, which the trial judge granted, on all of the remaining claims. This consolidated appeal followed. This ... appeal followed.

I. Analysis

A. The trial court correctly granted appellees' Motion for Judgment as a Matter of Law.

Our review of the trial court's grant of a Motion for Judgment as a Matter of Law is *de novo*, and we view the evidence in the light most favorable to the opposing party. "A verdict may be directed only if it is clear that the plaintiff has not established a *prima facie* case." *Strickland v. Pinder*, 899 A.2d 770, 773 (D.C. 2006).

1.   Appellants' expert failed to establish the basis for his national standard of care testimony.

Dr. Bloss failed to establish a basis for his knowledge of the national standard of care for the treatment of osteomyelitis. We do not agree, as appellants contend, that Dr. Bloss's general knowledge in the field of orthopedic surgery, which was sufficient for him to satisfy the first threshold requirement for qualifying as an expert, was sufficient to satisfy the second threshold requirement of demonstrating that his opinion testimony was grounded in and based on a national standard of care. Standing alone, Dr. Bloss' testimony regarding his educational and professional background, was insufficient to establish a basis for his knowledge of a national standard of care, and merely amounts to the expert's personal opinion.

Appellants' counsel attempted to elicit testimony from Dr. Bloss that to treat Mr. Hill's infection, all of the "hardware" should have been removed during the second operation with Dr. Levitt. Further, counsel attempted to elicit testimony establishing that when Dr. Levitt left two screws in Mr. Hill's leg, his conduct did not comport with the national standard of care. However, appellee's counsel objected, based on lack of foundation, and the objections were sustained by the trial court.... The trial court correctly concluded that the appellant ... never established the basis for Dr.

---

9. Dr. Danzinger was originally named in appellants' lawsuit; however, Dr. Danzinger was dismissed during the summary judgment stage and his dismissal is not being appealed.

Bloss' knowledge of a national standard of care, what the national standard of care was, or the basis for his opinion that Mr. Hill's doctors deviated from the national standard. Instead, Dr. Bloss repeatedly stated *his personal views* and *his* practices and procedures. He failed to link his views to a national standard of care.

… Dr. Bloss's testimony was fatally flawed in two respects: first, Dr. Bloss appeared to be giving his personal opinion based on his experience; and second, Dr. Bloss never referenced the basis for knowledge of a national standard of care, what the national standard was, or the basis of his opinion that Dr. Levitt's conduct fell below the standard of care.

As we have previously held, an expert in a medical malpractice case must establish the basis for his knowledge of the applicable national standard of care and link his opinion testimony to the applicable national standard. In a medical malpractice case, the plaintiff must establish the applicable standard of care, a deviation from that standard and a causal relationship between the deviation and the injury. Through expert testimony regarding the applicable national standard of care, the plaintiff must establish, "the course of action that a reasonably prudent doctor with the defendant's specialty would have taken under the same or similar circumstances." *Strickland*, 899 A.2d at 773. The personal opinion of the expert is insufficient, the expert must establish "that a particular course of treatment is followed *nationally* either through reference to a published standard, discussion of the described course of treatment with practitioners outside the District at seminars or conventions, or through presentation of relevant data." *Strickland*, 899 A.2d at 773–74; *Hawes v. Chua*, 769 A.2d 797, 806 (D.C. 2001).

In *Snyder*, this court reversed a trial court's grant of a directed verdict holding that the physician's expert testimony was sufficient to establish a national standard of care and deviation from that standard. [*Snyder v. George Wash. Univ.*, 890 A.2d 237, 239 (D.C. 2006).] In *Snyder*, the expert did not use the exact term "national standard of care" but testified that his knowledge of the standard of care was *based upon* attendance at national meetings and keeping up to date with literature with regard to the national standard.

Likewise, in *Hawes*, we concluded that the expert's testimony was minimally sufficient for admission into evidence. In *Hawes*, the court laid out seven principles that are important in assessing the sufficiency of national standard of care testimony, when an expert has already been qualified to give an expert opinion:

> First, the standard of care focuses on the course of action that a reasonably prudent doctor with the defendant's specialty would have taken under the same or similar circumstances. Second, the course of action or treatment must be followed nationally. Third, the fact that District physicians follow a national standard of care is insufficient in and of itself to establish a national standard of care. Fourth, in demonstrating that a particular course of action or treatment is followed nationally, reference to a published standard is not required, but can be important. Fifth, discussion of the course of action or treatment with doctors outside this jurisdiction, at seminars or conventions,

who agree with it; or reference to specific medical literature, may be sufficient. Sixth, an expert's personal opinion does not constitute a statement of the national standard of care; thus a statement only of what an expert would do under similar circumstances is inadequate. Seventh, national standard of care testimony may not be based upon mere speculation or conjecture.

Hawes, 769 A.2d at 806. When the expert in *Hawes* was asked the basis for his opinion with respect to the national standard of care, he testified that his testimony was *based on* reading literature in his specialty, attendance at national meetings and the standard of the American College of Obstetrics and Gynecology, which provided an accepted national standard of care to physicians in his field. Similarly, in *Washington v. Washington Hosp. Ctr.*, 579 A.2d 177, 182 (D.C. 1990), we concluded that there was sufficient evidence to establish a national standard of care. The expert in *Washington* did state his personal opinion, but also testified that the *basis of* his conclusion, that carbon dioxide monitors were required in operating rooms, was founded on several national publications.

This case is distinguishable from *Washington*, where we concluded that there was other evidence in the record, which in combination with the expert's testimony, established a standard of care.... In contrast to *Washington* and *Hawes*, Dr. Bloss was never asked by counsel what was the basis of his knowledge of the national standard of care and what was the basis of his opinion that appellant's doctors deviated from the national standard. Nor did Dr. Bloss provide an independent basis that his opinion, regarding the removal of the hardware, was based upon literature, speaking with other doctors around the country, attending medical conferences, or reviewing published national standards. Additionally, in contrast to *Washington*, there was no evidence admitted from which the national standard could have been inferred, although appellant's counsel did pose several questions to Dr. Bloss with respect to the national standard of care. For instance, here, appellants' counsel asked "when you testify here today are you here to testify to local standards or to national standards," and "are you aware of practices of other physicians with respect to removal of the hardware after a person has osteomyelitis and he has had open reduction and internal fixation." However, the objections to these questions were appropriately sustained because no proper foundation was established to demonstrate the *basis* of Dr. Bloss' knowledge of the national standard of care.

To the contrary, this case is more like our cases where we have concluded that the expert's testimony failed to establish the national standard of care. In *Strickland*, we concluded that the expert's testimony had failed to establish a national standard of care and, we affirmed the trial court's grant of a Motion for Judgment. In that case, appellant's expert was offered to establish that the appellees breached the national standard of care by failing to "perform additional tests when the decedent initially reported to the emergency room complaining of chest pains." We reasoned that mere reference to an expert's educational and professional background was insufficient to establish a national standard of care. We ... held that the expert's testimony amounted to nothing more than that expert's personal opinion.

Like the expert in *Strickland*, Dr. Bloss failed to establish the basis for his testimony and opinion regarding the national standard of care for the treatment of osteomyelitis. Although counsel for appellant asked "when you testify here today are you here to testify to local standards or to national standards," even if Dr. Bloss had responded in the affirmative, merely noting that the testimony was based upon a national standard was insufficient, unless he had first established the basis for his knowledge of the national standard. Further, Dr. Bloss was asked, "are you aware of practices of other physicians with respect to removal of the hardware." This question lacked a proper foundation because a basis was never established for his knowledge of the practices of other physicians on the removal of hardware. Mr. Hill's counsel also asked Dr. Bloss "is it standard practice in the field of orthopedic surgery to remove hardware after a person has had open reduction and internal fixation." The objection to this question was properly sustained because Dr. Bloss could not testify as to what the national standard was without the adequate foundation establishing the basis for his knowledge of a national standard....

It is counsel's duty to lay the necessary foundation to establish the national standard of care. It is not sufficient to rely on an expert's background or professional experience, nor is a simple statement that something does or does not comport with the national standard of care sufficient. The expert must explicitly indicate the *basis* for his or her knowledge of the national standard of care, state what the national standard of care is, and provide a basis for his or her opinion testimony that another doctor has deviated from that standard. That was not done here. As such, the trial court did not err in granting judgment to appellees on this issue....

Lundgren v. Eustermann

370 N.W.2d 877 (Minn. 1987)

Simonett, J.

In this case we conclude that plaintiffs' expert, a licensed consulting psychologist, is not qualified to give opinions in a medical malpractice action on the standard of care required of the defendant medical doctor. We reverse the contrary ruling of the court of appeals.

Plaintiff-respondents Judith Lundgren and her husband, Gary, sued defendant-appellant John Eustermann, M.D., claiming Dr. Eustermann was negligent in treating Judith's mental and emotional illness with the drug Thorazine. Plaintiffs included in their complaint a separate count for punitive damages. Dr. Eustermann is a family physician, with training in internal medicine, and has practiced in Mankato for approximately 30 years.

In March 1984, some 14 months after the suit had been started, defendant served a motion for partial summary judgment to dismiss plaintiffs' claim for punitive damages. The motion was made on the depositions that had been taken of Mr. and Mrs. Lundgren, a brief affidavit of Dr. Eustermann, and plaintiffs' answers to defendant's interrogatories directed to plaintiffs' expert medical testimony. Plaintiffs' answers to these interrogatories consisted of a detailed written response dated May 29, 1983, by William B. Rucker, Ph.D., a licensed consulting psychologist. After receiving the motion papers, plaintiffs obtained a supplemental letter report from Dr. Rucker in which the psychologist elaborated on why he thought the defendant doctor's treatment exhibited willful indifference to the patient's rights and safety....

The trial court ruled that Dr. Rucker was not qualified to give an opinion on the standard of medical care involved and granted defendant's motion for partial summary judgment dismissing the punitive damages claim. Although this is a nonappealable order, the court of appeals granted plaintiffs' petition for discretionary review. The court of appeals limited its review to "Whether evidence of the opinion of Dr. William Rucker, a licensed consulting psychologist, submitted to the trial court by petitioners, was sufficient to raise a genuine issue of material fact on the claim for punitive damages." Thereafter the court of appeals reversed the trial court, ruling that Dr. Rucker had the requisite competence to give expert opinion on the physician's standard of care, and reinstating the punitive damages claim for trial. *Lundgren v. Eustermann*, 356 N.W.2d 762 (Minn. Ct. App. 1984). We granted Dr. Eustermann's petition....

Judith Lundgren is a housewife, in her forties, with a history of mental and emotional problems. In 1973 she was hospitalized at Fairview Hospital by her attending psychiatrist (who is not sued, any claim against him being time barred), receiving electro-convulsant treatments and medication. While in the hospital and upon her discharge, she was treated with Thorazine. She apparently treated with this psychiatrist until October 1974. Beginning about April 1975 and continuing to January 1981, Judith came under the care of Dr. Eustermann at the Mankato Clinic, and during this period of time, Dr. Eustermann also prescribed Thorazine for the patient.

Dr. Rucker's view, stated in his answers to defendant's interrogatories, was, in part, that Thorazine, an antipsychotic drug, was less appropriate for Judith Lundgren than antidepressant drugs; that the continued prescription of Thorazine over a 6-year period was inappropriate; that the treating physician has an obligation to monitor the patient for adverse side effects from use of the drug; that there was no medical record that Dr. Eustermann had monitored for side effects; that the patient over the 6-year period had reported various symptoms which "could be" related to Thorazine treatment; that customary medical treatment would require a weighing of the relative benefits and risks of the continued use of a particular medication; and that, under the circumstances, the continued use of Thorazine was not acceptable medical practice.

We do not understand defendant to challenge Dr. Rucker's knowledge of Thorazine, its purposes, characteristics, and side effects. Defendant does, however, challenge Dr. Rucker's qualifications to give opinions on the standard of care to be exercised by a medical doctor in prescribing the drug for a patient. It is incumbent, in a medical malpractice action of this kind, for the plaintiff to offer expert testimony to establish the standard of care and the doctor's departure from that standard. *See, e.g., Cornfeldt v. Tongen*, 262 N.W.2d 684, 692 (Minn. 1977). The standard of care to be applied is that standard of skill and learning ordinarily possessed and exercised under similar circumstances by physicians in good standing in the same or similar localities. *Swanson v. Chatterton*, 160 N.W.2d 662, 666 (Minn. 1968).

To establish the foundation necessary to qualify a witness as an expert on whether a physician has exercised that degree of care required of a physician in administering Thorazine, the witness must have both the necessary schooling and training in the subject matter involved, plus practical or occupational experience with the subject. *Cornfeldt*, 262 N.W.2d at 692. Ordinarily, this foundation is best supplied if the expert witness is also a physician, especially a physician in the same area of practice, but this need not always be so. At least some courts have allowed a variety of cross-overs on medical expert testimony in malpractice actions if the proposed expert's knowledge and experience of the specialty or profession in question is apparent. In any event, theoretical expertise is not enough. There must also be some practical knowledge or experience. Thus, in *Swanson* we refused to let an internist testify to the standard of care required of an orthopedist in the treatment of an arm fracture, not because the witness was an internist, but because the witness lacked experience and expertise in treating fractures. What is required, we said, is "a practical knowledge of what is usually and customarily done by physicians under circumstances similar to those which confronted the defendant." *Swanson*, 160 N.W.2d at 668. In *Cornfeldt*, to give another example, we intimated that a nurse anesthetist might have been a competent expert witness on the standard of care for the defendant anesthesiologist "[i]f he [the nurse anesthetist] otherwise had sufficient scientific and practical experience." 262 N.W.2d at 697.

In this case the expert witness was not a physician but a psychologist. He has admirable qualifications as a psychologist, with extensive training and experience in the areas of psychology and pharmacology, including a doctorate in biopsychology. Dr. Rucker has also done consultant work for drug companies and has engaged in research and laboratory studies on the psychopharmacologic aspects of drug dependence. He has read books and journals, attended lectures, and trained graduate students, and he may well have the requisite scientific knowledge to testify about the nature of Thorazine, its dangers and uses. What the witness lacks, however, is practical experience or knowledge of what physicians do. He himself has never prescribed Thorazine for a patient. It is one thing to study Thorazine in the laboratory and to discuss it in the classroom, but it is quite another thing to prescribe the drug for a patient under the circumstances of a family medical practice. Dr. Rucker does not know how physicians themselves customarily use Thorazine in treatment of their patients. In his response to defendant's interrogatories, Dr. Rucker concedes, "I have not worked with physicians in the Mankato area who have dealt with the question of when and under what circumstances to prescribe Thorazine to their patients. I have received a small but continuing flow of information about prescription practices in Minnesota from students * * *, from other Licensed Consulting Psychologists in the state, and from people for whom such drugs have been prescribed."

Clearly, plaintiffs' expert does not have the practical knowledge and experience contemplated by the medical witness rule. We hold, as a matter of law, that Dr.

Rucker was not competent to give an opinion on the standard of medical care required of Dr. Eustermann nor to give an opinion on whether Dr. Eustermann had departed from that standard, much less to characterize the degree of that departure.

As mentioned earlier, plaintiffs submitted a supplemental letter from Dr. Rucker to the trial court at the time of the hearing on the motion for summary judgment. The trial judge refused to consider the letter in making his ruling because it was not made part of the record and because the letter was written by Dr. Rucker "not only as a medical expert but also as a legal advisor" and was an opinion on the very question at issue. Strictly speaking, Dr. Rucker's letter is not part of the record. It was unsworn, *see* Minn. R. Civ. P. 56.05, and was untimely presented, *see* Minn. R. Civ. P. 56.03. Nevertheless, it seems to us these technical defects should not in this instance preclude consideration of the letter, particularly since defendant's attorney made at best an extremely vague objection to its consideration. Nor do we understand the trial judge to have relied so much on the technicalities of making a record as on the fact that the contents of the letter were argumentative and incompetent evidence. Dr. Rucker begins his letter by stating he is responding to the request of plaintiffs' counsel to address the issue of whether the defendant had shown a willful indifference to the rights or safety of others in his treatment of Judith Lundgren, and his letter then proceeds, simply elaborating on the essential facts already in the record, to argue that, indeed, the defendant doctor had shown such willful indifference. It seems to us that Dr. Rucker's letter adds nothing to what was already in the record. As for the opinions expressed in the letter, we need only say that since Dr. Rucker was not qualified to give opinions on the defendant's conduct in the answers to interrogatories, neither was he qualified to elaborate on these opinions in his subsequent letter.

The case comes to us in a rather odd posture. Defendant chose to limit his summary judgment motion to only the punitive damages claim. Consequently, the trial court assumed *arguendo* that the facts presented a jury issue on negligence (presumably if supplemented by testimony of a qualified medical expert). The trial court then ruled that any negligence here "cannot be elevated to justify a punitive award on the basis of the conclusionary [sic] statements" of an unqualified expert. It is incumbent on the party opposing a summary judgment motion made on depositions or affidavits to counter with sufficient specific facts to raise a jury issue. We agree with the trial judge that there is no evidence of any willful indifference by the defendant's doctor to his patient's rights or safety.... Plaintiffs argue that defendant's failure to keep a medical record of any monitoring of the drug's side effects on his patient somehow constitutes willful indifference. Assuming this lack of documentation fails to meet the standard of care required of a physician, something more egregious is required in this case to afford a basis for the extraordinary sanction of punitive damages.

We hold, therefore, that the evidence presented is insufficient, as a matter of law, to present any genuine issue of material fact on the claim for punitive damages. We affirm the trial court's ruling granting defendant partial summary judgment on punitive damages....

Notes and Questions

1. The *Hill* case shows a court applying the post-locality rule — national standard of care — to the testimony of an expert witness, Dr. Bloss. If Dr. Bloss is an expert in orthopedic surgery, as the court acknowledged, then why was he unable to opine on the bone injury in that case? We see in the case different fact scenarios where courts have found the basis for national standard of care testimony sufficient (*Snyder, Hawes*) and insufficient (*Washington, Hill* itself). To decide whether the foundation is sufficient, the court notes seven "*Hawes* factors" to apply. When you apply the *Hawes* factors to all of the fact scenarios contained within *Hill* (*Snyder, Hawes, Washington,* and *Hill*), do they explain the different results? If not, what else might we want to consider?

2. In *Hill*, Dr. Bloss is testifying in his capacity as an orthopedic surgeon to the standard for proper care and management of a complex fracture resulting in osteomyelitis. Even if his testimony was insufficient for other reasons, his specialty clearly "matches" the plaintiff's injury. What if, instead of an orthopedic surgeon, the plaintiff offered a general surgeon, or an emergency room physician, or an infectious disease specialist? The *Lundgren* court makes clear that, despite any other knowledge, the expert must be able to speak intelligently about the practical knowledge and experience of a physician in the same specialty area ("... theoretical expertise is not enough. There must also be some practical knowledge or experience."). Thus, just as Dr. Bloss was clearly an expert orthopedic surgeon but disallowed from giving an opinion on the treatment in *Hill*, Dr. Rucker in *Lundgren* had experience in the pharmacological properties of Thorazine and yet was still unable to testify. What is the key ingredient of his testimony that is lacking?

   In many ways, the issue of physician specialties and "fit" is just a subset of the standard witness qualification issues under Rule 702, which we covered in Chapter 2. Remember that the witness here is being asked to opine not on all issues, but on the "standard of care" for a treating physician. Therefore, courts will necessarily require the expert to have a basis of knowledge to give that opinion. The *Lundgren* court engaged in a qualifications analysis here, just as other courts did in the cases contained within *Lundgren, Swanson,* and *Cornfeldt*. Note also that the court decided *Lundgren* in 1984 and therefore applied a modified locality rule requiring an expert familiar with practice in "the same or similar localities." Per our discussion in Chapter 8.A.i, this requirement would no longer be relevant (particularly for a specialist), except in a limited group of states. *See* Marc D. Ginsberg, *The Locality Rule Lives! Why? Using Modern Medicine to Eradicate an Unhealthy Law*, 61 DRAKE L. REV. 321, 331–33 (2013) (noting six states which retain some version of the locality rule).

3. While inadequate qualifications may result in expert preclusion, not all attacks on the expert will lead to that remedy. For example, it is common for attorneys to question experts about their professional time devoted to testifying as an expert. Some courts even permit examination into total income or percentage of income

earned as an expert. *See Wrobleski v. de Lara*, 727 A.2d 930 (Md. 1999); *Trower v. Jones*, 520 N.E.2d 297 (Ill. 1988). In *Wrobleski*, the court explains why and to what extent this inquiry is allowed:

> Exposure of potential bias based on self-interest is often attempted through cross-examination directed at how much the witness is being paid for his or her services in the case at bar, the frequency with which the witness testifies in similar kinds of cases, whether the witness customarily appears for a particular type of party (usually plaintiff or defendant), whether the witness is frequently employed by a particular party or attorney and, if so, how much income the witness derives from that employment, and, as in this case, the amount or the percentage of the witness's total income that is derived from lawyer referrals or testimony in lawsuits.

Wrobleski, 717 A.2d at 933–34.

Even if these questions are permitted at trial, courts do not always permit discovery of an expert's personal financial circumstances, calling it burdensome and tangential. *See Cooper v. Schoffstall*, 905 A.2d 482 (Pa. 2006); *Primm v. Isaac*, 127 S.W.3d 630 (Ky. 2004); *Wrobleski*, 727 A.2d at 938. However, other courts will permit discovery in this area. *See Falik v. Hornage*, 991 A.2d 1234 (Md. 2010); *Laseter v. Regan*, 481 S.W.3d 613 (Tenn. Ct. App. 2014).

Questioning an expert about fees from and time devoted to expert witness work is ubiquitous, but it is an open question whether the answers matter to factfinders. A recent survey of jurors, judges, lawyers, and experts found that there was no group where a majority of respondents agreed with the following statement: "an expert's compensation is an important factor in weighing the expert's bias." Andrew W. Jurs, *Expert Prevalence, Persuasion and Price: What Trial Participants Really Think About Experts*, 91 Ind. L.J. 353, 385 (2016). Only 36% of jurors, 44% of judges, and 16% of experts agreed with the statement. *Id.* Perhaps most interestingly, fewer than one in four (22%) of lawyers surveyed agreed with the statement. *Id.*

4. Independent of the issues of witness qualifications and basis of knowledge, which as we have seen can sometimes be intermingled, the final issue to consider (after the problem) is judicial gatekeeping of expert testimony on standard of care for reliability under *Daubert*. As we review these issues, consider how they are similar and different to reliability considerations in the forensic sciences, discussed *supra* in Chapters 5 to 7.

Tying It Together

During her first pregnancy, Eileen Cooper sought prenatal care from Dr. Eduardo Gomez, a licensed physician with board-certification in obstetrics and gynecology. The pregnancy was uneventful until the 28th week (of 40), when Cooper arrived at Capital City Hospital's emergency room at midnight with complaints of fever and pain. She saw Dr. Brenda Torres, a board-certified emergency room physician, who performed a pelvic examination showing no dilation. Torres then called Dr. Gomez. The two physicians agreed that Dr. Torres would stabilize the patient and then discharge her to meet with Dr. Gomez at 8:00 a.m. The next morning, Cooper showed up to her appointment and received a pelvic examination from Dr. Gomez. At this time, Dr. Gomez found blood pooling and dilation of the cervix. Gomez immediately ordered her transfer back to Capital City Hospital, where he performed an emergency cesarean section. Since the baby was premature, she weighed slightly under three pounds and died several days later. Cooper sued Drs. Gomez and Torres for negligence.

To prove her case, Plaintiff has hired Dr. Carlos Ramirez as an expert witness. Ramirez graduated from medical school in 1991 and had residencies in obstetrics and gynecology before becoming board-certified as an obstetrician in 1997. From 1997 to 2011, Ramirez engaged in private practice. In 2011, Ramirez was diagnosed with cancer, causing him to stop seeing patients and change his license status to "inactive." For several years after that change, Ramirez's sole source of income was from consulting work for medical negligence cases where all 150 of his cases were on behalf of plaintiffs. In the past two years, Ramirez has also earned a secondary source of income by teaming up with a nationally-recognized plaintiff's attorney to give a series of lectures on birth injury cases at plaintiff's bar association conferences.

Having reviewed the Cooper case, Dr. Ramirez found that Drs. Torres and Gomez both breached the standard of care when they allowed Cooper to leave the E.R. without additional testing. He believes that blood tests would have indicated the potential for placental abruption and resulted in delivery of the baby shortly after midnight instead of late in the morning. Cooper's attorney endorses Dr. Ramirez based on these opinions.

Shortly after the expert disclosures, the defense filed a motion to exclude the plaintiff's expert testimony under Rule 702. After a hearing where Ramirez testified, the court rules:

> Dr. Ramirez has not been a practicing obstetrician, or physician in any specialty, during the past seven years. Instead, Dr. Ramirez informed the Court that he has been doing a variety of consulting work, including consulting as an expert witness in approximately 150 cases. Dr. Ramirez testified that during the past year, he has worked exclusively on cases in which he writes reports or gives testimony on behalf of plaintiffs. Dr. Ramirez has not acted as an expert on behalf of a defendant in a single case during the past year. The Court finds that this track record indicates a bias in favor of plaintiffs. Furthermore, by withdrawing from practice and the corresponding supervision of the licensing board, Dr. Ramirez has set the stage for a line of work in which he need not provide impartial diagnoses of patients. This lack of control casts serious doubt over the degree to which Dr. Ramirez's testimony would be consistent with that of a responsible physician who is subject to oversight by a medical licensing board. Dr.

Ramirez's testimony is unlikely to be fair and impartial and therefore is excluded at trial.

After the court excludes the expert testimony, the case is dismissed on summary judgment. Plaintiff Cooper appeals the order excluding Dr. Ramirez as a witness.

Assignment: As counsel for Plaintiff Cooper or for Defendant Dr. Gomez, draft a brief explaining why the District Court's order should be affirmed or overturned.

– Also, are there any other legal issues presented by the facts that merit discussion?

Sullivan v. United States Department of the Navy
365 F.3d 827 (9th Cir. 2004)

Noonan, Circuit Judge.

Mary Sullivan appeals the grant of summary judgment to the United States in this action under the Federal Tort Claims Act. The central question is whether the district court properly excluded the proffered testimony of the plaintiff's medical expert....

FACTS

... On April 2, 1999, Mary Sullivan underwent surgery at the Naval Medical Center. A mastectomy was performed by Thomas Nelson, M.D., on her left breast to remove cancer. Then Amy Wandel, M.D., F.A.C.S., performed by endoscope the reconstruction of Sullivan's left breast by relocating a flap consisting of the latissimus dorsi muscle together with overlying tissue and a small panel of skin, moved through the axilla to her chest. Dr. Wandel then performed a mastopexy or reduction of the right breast. According to Dr. Wandel's report of the two operations ... they began at 10:30 and ended at 23:50:

> The skin was incised superiorly and using electrocautery the skin was elevated off the deep fat of the back and the latissimus. The endoscope was brought up in the field to dissect up into the axilla to dissect the overlying skin off the latissimus and deep fat. The dissection was carried from the axilla down to the scapula and to the midline of the back. Once this was completed the inferior incision was made and using electrocautery the skin was elevated off the fat inferiorly, harvesting a maximum of fat with the flap....

> ... [A]n axillary incision was made and the endoscope was brought through the axillary incision and the dissection was carried inferiorly along the anterior border of the latissimus to complete the dissection. The tunnel for passing the latissimus into the chest wall was then completed using electrocautery. The muscle and skin were then passed into the chest wall and the remainder of the axillary dissection was performed using careful blunt dissection.

In lay terms, the report indicates (1) a cut into the skin where the deep back fat was; (2) a cut into this fat by the endoscope up to the ... armpit; (3) a continuation of the cut from the armpit to the scapula or shoulder bone and to the middle of the back; (4) a cut to harvest fat and flap; (5) a cut in the armpit to bring through the endoscope; (6) another cut along the border of the latissimus; and (7) a further cut in the armpit. After these events, so the report continues, "Two drains were placed, one Blake drain in the axilla and one Jackson-Pratt along the medial wall." According to the report, there were "no complications." …

Sullivan suffered severe scarring and experienced muscle weakness in her lower back. She had … surgery to correct the disfigurement of her back [and] plastic surgery on her breasts.

PROCEEDINGS

On March 9, 2001, Sullivan brought this suit. On May 15, 2002, Sullivan's deposition was taken. She testified that the morning after the operation, she felt a hole in her back. She asked Dr. Wandel what it was, and was told that it was a seroma or, as Dr. Wandel put it, "an area of skin and tissue that sometimes goes dead during surgery." A week later, according to Sullivan, she returned to the hospital, and Dr. Wandel took off the bandage on this area of her back and said to an intern, "I don't know what happened here. She must have laid on something." On April 14, 1999, … surgery was performed by Dr. Wandel to debride the hole.

Sullivan submitted a written report and deposition testimony of Anne M. Wallace, M.D., associate professor of clinical surgery at the University of California at San Diego, director of its Breast Care Unit, and the author of fourteen articles in the area.… Dr. Wallace had performed plastic surgery on Sullivan after the operations performed by Dr. Wandel. Dr. Wallace reported:

> There were complications with the equipment in the operating room and the surgery took approximately 13 hours. Post-operatively, the patient went on to develop fat nercrosis in the left latissimus flap and a full thickness necrosis of the donor site at the left back region and was told that she had had an infection. She went on to debridement and secondary closure of the back wound which left a large scar and indentation down to the underlying back musculature. The scar tissue then resulted in some chronic back pain.…

> Under normal circumstances this form of reconstruction takes 3 to 4 hours to perform. In this particular case, the reconstruction took approximately 13 hours after the mastectomy. That is near triple the time that a normal latissimus dorsi myocutaneous reconstruction should take. It is my opinion that complications which are possible to occur become much more probable to occur because of the length of surgical time. The time for which the wound was open, exposed and manipulated, to a reasonable degree of medical certainty, aggravated an already known complication of a latissimus dorsi flap.… The most likely and probable cause of her wound complication following the reconstruction was the prolonged time of surgery and resultant stress it put on the tissue.…

At the heart of Dr. Wallace's report was this opinion:

> It is difficult to always know when a patient is going to have a donor site complication. There are specific risk factors such as smoking, diabetes, etc.,

of which this patient had none. But stress on a wound because of an excessively long surgical time could result in such a complication. Even though this complication can happen when everything is done by the standard of care, the length of surgery led to a situation in which a possible ... complication became a probable ... complication.

The report included the following foundation:

2) **The Basis and Reasons for the Expert's Opinion** — The reason for my opinion is based on 7 years of surgical oncology and oncologic reconstruction experience, as well as a Fellowship at the MD Anderson Cancer Center where this was a common operation.

3) **The Data and Information [On] Which the Opinion is Based** — This information is based on experience with many patients who have had the latissimus dorsi flap reconstruction and second opinions on multiple patients from the community and elsewhere that have also had this procedure. I also have some experience with endoscopic latissimus dorsi harvesting from fellowship training.

In her subsequent deposition by defendant's counsel, Dr. Wallace stated:

The infection was up in the axilla. And when you turn the patient back to supine, that whole incision is still open, the flap has been turned into it, and then you spend the next hour shaping it, putting drains in it and closing the incision.

Dr. Wallace further testified as to the necrosis of the flap suffered by Sullivan. She could not [at this time] say with certainty that the infection caused this necrosis....

Sullivan subsequently submitted the affidavit of Dr. Wallace, dated August 22, 2002, stating that the laboratory report showed that "a wound culture was taken from the incision on Mrs. Sullivan's back" and that the report was "positive for an infection." Dr. Wallace then cited four standard medical texts that stated that the length of an operation was "an influencing factor for infection." She gave as her opinion that "the excessive length of the surgery increased the risk of infection by at least six times," and that it was below the standard of care for the reconstructive surgery to last 10-1/2 hours.

Dr. Wandel, deposed by plaintiff's counsel, testified:

Q: Was the outcome less than what you expected?

Dr. Wandel: Yes

Q: In what way?

Dr. Wandel: She had a back wound which required wound care.

Q: When you went into the surgery, did you expect that she would have a back wound following the surgery?

Dr. Wandel: I expected her to have a healing incision from where I took her flap from. She ended up having a breakdown of that area, which required wound care.

In her deposition, Dr. Wandel went on to deny that the wound was infected and to maintain that the debridement was of dead skin. However, the report from the hospital's lab on the culture taken at the time of the debridement [tested positive for Staphylococcus aureus].

Photographs of Sullivan's back taken on April 7, 1999, and on subsequent occasions up to September 9, 1999, show a hole in her lower back.

[On] July 19, 2002, the United States moved for summary judgment. Having maturely considered the matter, on October 2, 2002, the district court granted the motion. The district court made these findings of fact (the numbering is added):

1. Sullivan's three operations lasted "a total of approximately 13 hours."

2. The time "included an unforeseen 45 minute delay."

3. "After the operations, Plaintiff's back incurred bruising on a three-centimeter by three-centimeter area located just above the region from which the skin had been taken for Plaintiff's breast reconstruction. The area did not heal readily but scabbed over, leading to skin loss and scarring."

4. "Plaintiff also suffered a surgical drain site infection."

5. "Here, the infection occurred not in the [surgical] wound but rather in the area near the surgical drain.... It is clear from the record that Plaintiff's infection was located at the surgical drain site ... there is no issue as to the infection site's location."

With this firm conviction that the infection occurred near the drain site, the district court considered whether Dr. Wallace's testimony should be admitted. The district court stated: "Dr. Wallace has not set forth the steps used to reach the conclusion that literature addressing the effect of operative length on the incidence of surgical *wound* infections is analogous to the effect of operative length on the incidence of surgical *drain* infections, much less how that literature applies to bruising at the skin harvest site. Thus, the scientific literature provided by Plaintiff in the instant case does not support Dr. Wallace's opinions." (emphasis in original).

Accordingly, carrying out the gate-keeping function assigned the district court by *Daubert v. Merrell Dow Pharms., Inc.*, 509 U.S. 579 (1993), the district court ruled Dr. Wallace's expert testimony inadmissible. Sullivan was deprived of any evidence that medical malpractice had caused her injury. The district court granted the United States' motion for summary judgment. Sullivan appeals.

ANALYSIS

Disputed Facts.

In this action under the FTCA, the law of the state where the injury occurred is controlling. California law therefore applies. Sullivan must show that it is more probable than not that negligence caused her injuries. *Dumas v. Cooney*, 1 Cal. Rptr. 2d 584, 589 (1991). This court reviews a trial court's decision to exclude expert testimony for abuse of discretion. *Kumho Tire Co., Ltd. v. Carmichael*, 526 U.S. 137, 152 (1999).

It is hornbook law, carefully recited by the district court in its opinion, that "the court must view all inferences drawn from the underlying facts in the light most favorable to the nonmoving party. The court must not weigh the evidence ... or make credibility determinations in evaluating a motion for summary judgment." Having articulated these familiar rules, the district court failed to follow them. Each of the district court judge's findings that we have numbered above violates these canons.

1. According to Dr. Wandel's report, the total time of the two operations performed by her was 13-1/2 hours; the total time for all three surgeries was 14-1/2 hours.

2. The delay caused by the misplacing and then malfunctioning endoscope was between 1-1/4 and 1-1/2 hours.

3. "Bruising," the term used by the government and adopted by the district court — means injury to blood capillaries. As Webster's *Third New International Dictionary* defines it, a bruise is "an injury transmitted through unbroken skin to underlying tissue causing rupture of small blood vessels and escape of blood into the tissue with resulting discoloration." Sullivan's testimony was that there was a hole in her back. A hole is the opposite of a bruise: the skin is broken. Dr. Wandel herself described the area as a wound. An inference could be drawn that the skin had died from the infection. It is a disputed material fact whether there was bruising or a hole. The size of the injury at the site of the harvest is also disputed....

4. and 5. The infection arguably occurred not at a drain site but in a surgical wound as part of the operation. The district court believed Dr. Wandel's statement that a surgical wound made during the main operation was not infected and interpreted the lab report to refer to the drain site. Doing so, the district court made a judgment of credibility....

The district court also misinterpreted Dr. Wallace's deposition that "the infection was up in the axilla." The district court assumed that this statement places the infection at the drain site at the armpit. A reading of Dr. Wallace's testimony shows that she referred to Dr. Wandel "putting drains in" after the infection in the axilla. Her further testimony, quoted above, shows she believed that the infection was "coming through right along the axilla." At least inferentially, Dr. Wallace's testimony related to a wound inflicted during the surgery when the endoscope was "brought up in the field to dissect up into the axilla" as described by Dr. Wandel's report. Dr. Wallace clearly differentiated the drains from the wounds necessary to move the latissimus. They did not occur "after the operations."

Dr. Wandel testified to necrosis of the skin in the back wound. An inference could be drawn that the skin death was caused by infection. The inference may be supported by another inference to be drawn from Dr. Wandel's reference to "debridement of the wound." According to *Webster's*, debridement is "surgical removal of lacerated, devitalized or contaminated tissue." If the tissue was either contaminated or devitalized, infection could be inferred to be the cause.

On the basis of its misinterpretations of Dr. Wallace and its resolution of the disputes over material facts, the district court did not see the relevance of the medical literature relating the length of the operation to the risk of infection of the surgical wound.... Basing itself on the resolution of a disputed material issue of fact and making its own errors of fact, the district court excluded Dr. Wallace's testimony and committed reversible error.

The admissibility of the expert's testimony. Even if the district court had not abused its discretion by misapprehending the evidence, it applied an inappropriately rigid Daubert standard to medical expert testimony. The district court directed the exclusion of Dr. Wallace's testimony by virtue of *Daubert*. While *Daubert* remains relevant, the more apposite case is *Kumho Tire Co., Ltd. Kumho* resolved a doubt as to whether *Daubert* applied to experience-based testimony. Interpreting *Daubert* and Fed. R. Evid. 702, *Kumho* held the district court's gatekeeping should govern the admission not only of scientific but "technical" and "other specialized knowledge." Dr. Wallace's proffered testimony is, therefore, subject to the *Daubert-Kumho* criteria. The testimony must be both reliable and relevant.

Dr. Wallace's opinion that an abnormally long back operation substantially increased the risk of complications including wound infection and skin necrosis appears to be relevant to this case. Its reliability appears to be supported by the four textbooks to which Dr. Wallace referred. Each textbook identifies the length of operation as a major factor in causing infection during surgery. *Sabiston on Surgery* (15th ed. 1997) says an exogenous infection of a surgical wound "is uncommon and usually indicates a break in aseptic technique or an excessively lengthy procedure." *Schwartz on Principles of Surgery* (1999 ed.) lists under "Influencing Factors in Wound Infection" the "duration of operation." ... *Fry on Surgical Infections* (1995) states: "Several authors pointed out that the development of a seroma after mastectomy is strongly associated with the development of wound infection." Fry cites four authorities for "the length of the procedure" leading to "the development of complications." *Hoeprick on Infectious Diseases* (1994) states as to infection following surgery: "Technical factors, such as the skill and experience of the surgeon, affect the risk of SWI [surgical wound infection]. Increased tissue trauma and prolonged duration of surgery are contributing factors."

The principle that the duration of the surgery bears on the likelihood of infection appears to be generally accepted. It is a particular application of broader principles going back to Pasteur and Lister on the role of bacteria and the likelihood of bacteria infecting open wounds. The application of both the broader and narrower principles to the case at hand is properly the domain of a surgeon experienced in the field. The textbooks cannot say what increase in the risk of infection is probable in the case; that estimate may be made by the expert putting the principles to work. Therefore, the district court abused its discretion and invaded the province of the expert by requiring the texts to state the precise type of harm....

Notes and Questions

1. As with any reliability analysis, the issue in *Sullivan* involves a determination of whether the underlying methodology has a reliable basis within the discipline.

The court makes clear this consideration is one more akin to the technical expert analysis of *Kumho* than *Daubert* itself. As with most *Kumho* analyses, the court is left to examine the complete testimony and record as well as other relevant information to make its determination. Independent of the factual dispute, what materials in *Sullivan* provide the firm basis for the reliability of Dr. Wallace's testimony?

2. It may help to consider the language of *General Electric Co. v. Joiner*, 522 U.S. 136, 146 (1997), where the court cautions:

    [N]othing in either *Daubert* or the Federal Rules of Evidence requires a district court to admit opinion evidence that is connected to existing data only by the *ipse dixit* of the expert. A court may conclude that there is simply too great an analytical gap between the data and the opinion proffered.

In some standard of care situations, we may have little independent evidence supporting the expert's opinion that the defendant did or did not follow the standard of care beyond the expert's own experience. Cases like *Kumho* and *Joiner* require more. *See Adams v. Laboratory Corp. of Am.*, 760 F.3d 1322 (11th Cir. 2014) (noting but overturning the district court's exclusion of an expert based on following reasoning: "The deficiency with Dr. Rosenthal's methodology is that it is an *ipse dixit* assessment that is devoid of any methodology that would allow another expert to challenge it in any objective sense …").

Tying It Together

Paula Phillips had experienced years of discomfort and occasional hospital visits before Dr. Davis ultimately decided she needed her gallbladder removed. After Phillips agreed to the surgery, Davis performed the procedure laparoscopically using small instruments inserted into the abdominal cavity through small incisions. This surgery usually involves the clipping and removal of the gallbladder and cystic duct. However, while Davis removed both, he also removed the common bile duct (see diagram below).[57] The removal of the common bile duct resulted in complications and corrective surgery for Phillips, who later sued Dr. Davis for malpractice.

To prove her case, Phillips endorsed Dr. Karen Priebus, a board-certified Professor of Surgery at Northern Plains University Medical School. Dr. Priebus has been performing gallbladder surgeries since 1990 and has performed approximately 50 such procedures every year since. At her deposition, Dr. Priebus testified that "in any surgery, everything should be identified before anything is cut." When asked whether any medical literature or texts supported her opinion, Dr. Priebus replied, "Medical literature doesn't discuss standard of care."

The defense endorses Dr. Carl Weiss, a board-certified surgeon at the Mayo Clinic in Rochester, Minnesota. Dr. Weiss testifies that "There are instances where you can

---

57. Image from https://www.alamy.com/stock-photo-correct-vs-incorrect-cholecystectomy-gallbladder-removal-procedure-7711933.html.

NORMAL (PRE-OPERATIVE) ANATOMY

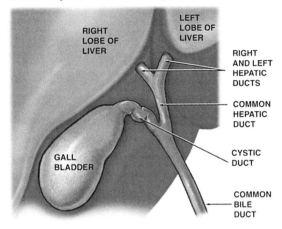

CORRECT POST-OPERATIVE CONDITION

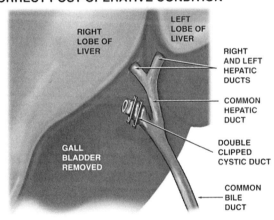

POST-OPERATIVE CONDITION

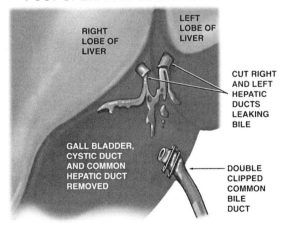

have an injury to the common [bile] duct and it could be malpractice and there are instances where it wouldn't be malpractice." When asked if any medical literature supported this theory, Dr. Weiss mentioned an editorial written by Dr. Jeff Foster in *The American Surgical Journal.* According to Dr. Weiss, the editorial stands for the proposition that "bile duct injuries can occur and are an inherent risk of the procedure without being below the standard of care. I have seen really excellent and highly experienced surgeons somehow damage the common duct inadvertently."

Prior to trial, the defense files a motion *in limine* to exclude the testimony of Dr. Priebus.

Assignment: Please prepare a brief explaining your argument in the context of the cases we have reviewed.

– As counsel for Defendant Davis, why are you objecting to Priebus's testimony?

– As counsel for Plaintiff Phillips, why is Priebus's testimony admissible?

B. Causation Testimony

i. Causation and Medical Error

Hankla v. Jackson

699 S.E.2d 610 (Ga. Ct. App. 2010)

DOYLE, Judge.

Zamarion Everett sustained a permanent brachial plexus injury[1] during his birth in 2003. His mother, Anita Jackson, filed the instant medical malpractice action, individually and as next friend of Zamarion, against Certified Nurse Midwife Vickie Hankla, who attended the birth, and Hankla's employer, Southern OB-GYN Associates, P.C. Jackson argued that Hankla breached the standard of care during delivery when she applied lateral traction[2] with enough force to cause Zamarion's injury during her attempts to deliver him during an obstetrical complication known as shoulder dystocia, which occurs when an infant's shoulders become lodged in the mother's pelvis after delivery of the head.

Hankla filed motions to exclude the testimonies of Jackson's expert witnesses, R.H. Allen, Ph.D., and Edith D. Gurewitsch, M.D. The trial court denied the motions to exclude, finding that the two witnesses were "qualified as experts in regards to matters involved in this civil matter." Upon the trial court's grant of a certificate of immediate review, the defendants applied for interlocutory appeal of the trial court's denial of their motions to exclude; this Court granted the application. We affirm in part and reverse in part for the reasons that follow.

---

1. The brachial plexus is a bundle of nerves at the base of the neck that control arm and hand movement.

2. Lateral traction is the force applied to the infant's head and neck when a provider moves the head to one side or another with the ear moving toward the shoulder.

1. Hankla argues that the trial court abused its discretion by denying her motion to exclude the testimonies of Allen and Gurewitsch without first determining that their expert opinions were reliable and relevant pursuant to OCGA § 24-9-67.1(b) and *Daubert v. Merrell Dow Pharmaceuticals, Inc.* "We review a trial court's ruling on a motion in limine for abuse of discretion. A motion in limine is properly granted when there is no circumstance under which the evidence under scrutiny is likely to be admissible at trial."

(a) Hankla first argues that the face of the trial court's order establishes that it applied the incorrect standard by determining only that Allen and Gurewitsch were "qualified" without also determining whether their testimonies were reliable and relevant. The trial court ... cited *Daubert* in its order and determined that the testimonies were admissible under *Daubert*'s guidelines as well as the guidelines of OCGA § 24-9-67.1. Thus, this argument is without merit.

(b) Next, relying heavily on this Court's opinion in *Hawkins v. OB-GYN Assoc.*,[5] Hankla contends that the trial court erred because Allen's and Gurewitsch's testimonies (1) failed to rule in a suspected cause of the injury, (2) failed to rule out other potential causes of the injury, (3) were based on an assumption that Hankla applied excessive traction that was not supported by the record based on her deposition testimony, (4) were based on the mere existence of the injury, which is prohibited in medical malpractice actions, and (5) have not been subject to testing or peer review. We disagree that the trial court erred and affirm the order denying the motion in limine to exclude the two experts' evidence.

Applying the *Daubert* standard, expert testimony is admissible if it is both relevant and reliable. And the Georgia statute provides that expert testimony is admissible if: (1) the testimony is based upon sufficient facts or data which are or will be admitted into evidence at the hearing or trial; (2) the testimony is the product of reliable principles and methods; and (3) the witness has applied the principles and methods reliably to the facts of the case. [*Shiver v. Ga. & Fla. Railnet*, 652 S.E.2d 819 (2007).]

(i) Gurewitsch is an assistant professor of obstetrics and gynecology and biomedical engineering at Johns Hopkins University, and she is board-certified in obstetrics and gynecology and maternal fetal medicine. Gurewitsch has performed numerous deliveries over her career as an obstetrician and has supervised midwives for the last eleven years, and she encounters shoulder dystocia in approximately three or four deliveries per year—approximately thirty to forty over her career. Gurewitsch deposed that approximately ten of those infants experienced a brachial plexus injury, one of whom sustained a permanent injury. She has been published extensively in peer-reviewed publications and has conducted clinical research on actual and simulated deliveries.

Gurewitsch deposed that based on her review of the medical records, including "[t]he neurological exam, EMG, and MRI" as well as Hankla's notes from delivery, "the nature and extent of injury, [her] research, training[,] and experience," Hankla

---

5. 660 S.E.2d 835 (2008).

"unnecessarily" applied excessive traction to Zamarion in an attempt to deliver his shoulders, causing the permanent brachial plexus injury to his right side.

Specifically, she explained that

> there is an injury to the posterior shoulder that is of a very severe nature and it involved the entire plexus, and an unusual sensory component to that injury which implies a locus of injury near the spinal cord. That locus of injury and the fact that all roots, all levels were involved, requires more than [forty] pounds of traction, which is at least four times what is normally used and at least twice as much as—would be the standard of care in a shoulder dystocia.

She also ruled out an inter-uterine injury, explaining that Zamarion showed no evidence of withering or lack of bulk in the affected arm, which would be apparent if the injury had resulted during gestation from the fetus's movements or as a result of a uterine mass or other maternal characteristic. Gurewitsch addressed the issue of brachial plexus injuries caused by normal maternal expulsive forces during labor and opined that a permanent injury such as Zamarion's could not result from such forces and that no such case had been reported in medical literature. Gurewitsch cited numerous studies that she had performed and published on the topic as well as studies published by other authors in support of her opinions.

Contrary to Hankla's assertion, she does not conclude that simply because there was a brachial plexus injury Hankla's negligence caused it, rather that based on "[t]he nature and extent of the injury" in conjunction with a "shoulder dystocia delivery," during which Hankla repeated the same obstetric maneuver followed by application of supra-pubic pressure in order to free Zamarion's shoulders, evinced that Hankla applied "excessive traction" at some point during the four minutes she spent trying to free the shoulders. Gurewitsch opined that in some cases applying lateral traction with sufficient force to cause a permanent brachial plexus injury in order to free an infant from the birth canal does not mean that the birth attendant has violated the standard of care; however, based on the circumstances of this case, Gurewitsch believed that Hankla had breached the standard.

(ii) Allen has a Ph.D. in civil engineering from Carnegie Mellon University and has been involved in the study of birth mechanics since 1986. He has held a number of teaching and research positions at various universities, and in 2000, he moved to Johns Hopkins University, where he has been teaching and researching in the field of bio-engineering, with specific research work in shoulder dystocia. Allen has created birthing models for study of the effects of labor and delivery, and he has authored or co-authored numerous journal articles appearing in various peer-reviewed publications; the majority of the articles address issues related to shoulder dystocia or brachial plexus injuries. His opinions are premised on his own peer-reviewed research as well as his assessment of other literature in the field.

During Allen's deposition, he offered his opinion on the mechanism of brachial plexus injuries generally, normal forces applied on an infant during delivery by the mother's body and by physicians, normal physician behavior in applying lateral force to an infant's head and neck during a shoulder dystocia delivery (i.e., documented behavior indicating that repeated attempts at delivering an infant led to increased force applied by a physician with each attempt), and the biophysical mechanics of the obstetric maneuver employed by Hankla and its use to free an infant during a shoulder dystocia delivery. Allen also deposed that based on Zamarion's medical records, Hankla's and Jackson's depositions, and other information regarding the birth, Hankla applied lateral traction to Zamarion at a force great enough to damage the brachial plexus nerve.

(iii) Based on this testimony, we cannot say that the trial court abused its discretion by denying Hankla's motion. Allen and Gurewitsch specifically ruled in Hankla's applied traction as the cause of Zamarion's injury, and they specifically ruled out all other potential causes of the injury. Allen and Gurewitsch based their opinions of causation on a number of factors related to the particular circumstances of Zamarion's delivery as well as their prior knowledge of permanent brachial plexus injuries and birth attendant behavior; their opinions were not merely based on the fact that the injury occurred. Hankla's contention that Allen's and Gurewitsch's research has not been submitted to peer review or has not been tested is wholly without support in the record.

With regard to *Hawkins*, we determine that the opinion does not require reversal in this case. In *Hawkins*, the expert testified only that the physician's application of traction was "more probably than not" the cause of the injury in that case. Here, Allen and Gurewitsch have presented extensive opinions regarding causation, in contrast to the opinion espoused by the expert in *Hawkins*. Moreover, because Allen's and Gurewitsch's testimonies regarding the causation of the injury are premised on more than the mere occurrence of the injury, we are not required to reverse the trial court's order on the basis that the opinions may conflict with Hankla's testimony that she applied only gentle force during the delivery.

Accordingly, we affirm the trial court's order with regard to Gurewitsch's testimony. With regard to Allen's testimony, although we find that he is qualified to render an opinion as to general causation with regard to brachial plexus injuries, and that his opinions are reliable and relevant, we reverse in part the trial court's denial of Hankla's motion to exclude his testimony, as stated in Division 2 below.

2. Hankla argues that the trial court abused its discretion by denying her motion to exclude Allen's testimony because he is a biomechanical engineer, rather than a doctor....

(a) First, Hankla contends that the trial court erred by denying her motion to exclude Allen's testimony on the basis that he inappropriately commented on the standard of care.

OCGA § 24-9-67.1(c) states in pertinent part that

the opinions of an expert, who is otherwise qualified as to the acceptable standard of conduct of the professional whose conduct is at issue, shall be admissible only if, at the time the act or omission is alleged to have occurred, such expert: ... (2) In the case of a medical malpractice action,

had actual professional knowledge and experience in the area of practice
or specialty in which the opinion is to be given as the result of having been
regularly engaged in: [The active practice of such area of specialty or the
teaching of his or her profession] and (C) ... (i) *Is a member of the same
profession.*...

Hankla explains that Allen characterized the lateral forces Hankla allegedly applied
during delivery as "excessive"; however, the citation to the record that Hankla provides
in support of her contention evinces no such statement. Moreover, Jackson explained
at the motion hearing that Allen would not be called to testify regarding the standard
of care, and Allen deposed that he has never delivered a baby and does not consider
himself competent as an expert to comment on the standard of care for physicians.
Nevertheless, to the extent that Allen would characterize the traction used as excessive,
we reverse. The trial court erred by failing to restrict Allen from commenting, even
indirectly, on whether Hankla's actions were a breach of the standard of care.[12]

(b) Hankla also argues that the trial court erred by finding that Allen was qualified ... as an expert on causation based on OCGA § 24-9-67.1(c) because he is not
a medical doctor.

The plain language of OCGA § 24-9-67.1(c) applies to experts testifying about the
"standard of conduct" in professional malpractice actions. Moreover, OCGA § 24-
9-67.1(b) explains: "If scientific, technical, or other specialized knowledge will assist
the trier of fact in any cause of action to understand the evidence or to determine a
fact in issue, a witness qualified as an expert by knowledge, skill, experience, training,
or education may testify thereto in the form of an opinion or otherwise...." Thus,
we do not read OCGA § 24-9-67.1(c) to prohibit in every instance expert testimony
regarding causation by those outside the profession of the defendant alleged to have
breached the standard of care.

With regard to the case at hand, looking to federal law, we find instructive *Bowers
v. Norfolk Southern Corp.*[15] In that case, the Middle District of Georgia explained the
current state of federal law regarding the admissibility of a biomedical engineer's
opinion pertaining to medical causation. *Bowers* explains that

> [b]iomechanical engineers apply the principles in mechanics to the facts of
> a specific accident and provide information about the forces generated in
> that accident. They may also explain how the body moves in response to
> those forces, and determine what types of injuries would result from the
> forces generated. Thus, biomechanical engineering is closely related to, and
> may sometimes overlap with, the field of medicine. However, the two dis-
> ciplines remain distinct. For instance, unlike medical doctors, biomechanical

12. *See Smith v. Harris*, 670 S.E.2d 136 (Ga. App. 2008) (holding that the trial court abused its
discretion by allowing a pharmacist to testify regarding a physician's standard of care).
15. 537 F. Supp. 2d 1343 (M.D. Ga. 2007).

engineers normally do not diagnose and treat human physical ailments, conditions, diseases, pain, and infirmities.

In the context of litigation, therefore, biomechanical engineers typically are found to be qualified to render an opinion as to the forces generated in a particular accident and the general types of injuries those forces may generate. However, biomechanical engineers ordinarily are not permitted to give opinions about the precise cause of a specific injury. This is because biomechanical engineers lack the medical training necessary to identify the different tolerance levels and pre-existing medical conditions of individuals, both of which could have an effect on what injuries resulted from an accident.[17]

In *Bowers*, the court granted the motion to exclude the engineer's testimony with regard to specific medical causation in that case, finding that although the engineer "may have trained in physiology and taught ... courses at a medical school, the record [did] not reflect that he [had] any experience either in examining patients, or in treating and diagnosing medical conditions."

We determine that a similar circumstance exists here. Allen is certainly qualified to render opinions regarding the myriad causes of brachial plexus injuries in general, the normal forces exerted by a mother and birth attendants during labor and delivery, and the current medical literature regarding causation of this type of injury. Turning to the complaint, Jackson has alleged that Hankla violated the standard of care by applying lateral traction, which in turn caused Zamarion's injury. Jackson did not allege that Hankla failed to correctly diagnose the shoulder dystocia. Thus, the trial court correctly determined that the testimony Allen was qualified to provide was relevant to the issues presented in the complaint and should not have been excluded. Nevertheless, Allen does not have any experience diagnosing or treating brachial plexus injuries. Therefore, the trial court erred by failing to preclude Allen from providing expert testimony regarding any questions of medical treatment or diagnosis.

Notes and Questions

1. The trial court in *Hankla* rejected the Defendants' motion to exclude the testimony of Drs. Gurewitsch and Allan, finding that the witnesses were "qualified as experts in regards to matters involved in this civil matter." On appeal, the court evaluated each expert separately under both *Daubert* and a state statute on medical negligence claims. Why did Hankla believe each witness could not testify against her? If Allan is a biomedical engineer and not a doctor, why could he testify against Hankla? What limits were there to that testimony?

2. In evaluating causation testimony for reliability, courts need to be especially careful to avoid the *ipse dixit* problem from *Kumho Tire Co. v. Carmichael* and

---

17. *Id.* at 1377.

General Electric Co. v. Joiner.[58] *Joiner* made clear that in evaluating expert testimony for reliability, "nothing in either *Daubert* or the Federal Rules of Evidence requires a district court to admit opinion evidence that is connected to existing data only by the *ipse dixit* of the expert." 522 U.S. at 146. The *ipse dixit* problem is particularly acute in the area of causation, since it necessarily involves testimony about injuries suffered by one or more claimants instead of a dispassionate examination of theoretical possibilities.

Tying It Together

In *McDowell v. Brown*, 392 F.3d 1283 (11th Cir. 2004), the plaintiff claimed that after he experienced significant back pain while incarcerated, a delay by jail officials in transporting him to the hospital for treatment caused his paralysis. To support that claim, plaintiff endorsed as experts the two neurosurgeons from the local hospital who treated his condition. Each doctor testified that the delay in treatment caused damage to plaintiff's spinal cord, based on the "'universal' axiom that expedited treatment is preferable to delayed treatment." *Id.* at 1299. They also testified that plaintiff would not have paralysis had surgery occurred even four hours earlier. When asked what supports their theory, each cited a study discussed in *Spinal Cord Compression*, a textbook on the subject, stating that 48-hour delays cause injury. *Id.* at 1300.

The defendants filed a motion *in limine* asking for the testimony of the neurosurgeons to be excluded. You are a clerk for Judge Forrester. The judge has read the briefs and is leaning toward excluding the testimony of the neurosurgeons. He asks you to draft a brief explaining why the testimony should be excluded, considering *Daubert* and related precedent.

Assignment: Draft a two-page bench brief explaining why the judge can exclude the evidence and why that opinion is unlikely to be overturned on appeal.

ii. Cause and Manner of Death — The Forensic Issue

Kolb v. State

523 S.W.3d 211 (Tex. App. 2017)

BOYCE, J.

Appellant Laura Lea Kolb pushed her boyfriend's four-year-old daughter off a bed while appellant was intoxicated and upset with the girl's father. The fall injured the girl's spinal cord, paralyzing her lungs and ultimately causing her death by asphyxiation. A jury convicted appellant of recklessly causing serious bodily injury to a child.

At issue in this appeal is ... (2) the trial court erred by admitting the medical examiner's expert testimony into evidence.... We affirm the trial court's judgment.

---

58. Kumho Tire Co. v. Carmichael, 526 U.S. 137 (1999); Gen. Elec. Co. v. Joiner, 522 U.S. 136, 146 (1997).

BACKGROUND

Appellant and her boyfriend, Kevin Moore, returned to their apartment from a bar just before midnight on March 22, 2013. Moore's four-year-old and 15-year-old daughters were asleep in the apartment.

Upon arriving home, Moore and appellant joined other residents from neighboring apartments who were playing dominos and drinking in the apartment courtyard. Appellant admitted to having at least six drinks over the course of the evening. At some point appellant went upstairs to the apartment, called for Moore to join her, and became upset when he did not join her and would not give her a cigarette. Appellant went into the bedroom where Moore's four-year-old daughter Taylor was sleeping and pushed the child head-first off the queen-sized bed onto the floor, which was strewn with toys. Appellant then picked Taylor up, "threw" her back on the bed, and left the room.

Appellant returned to the room 10 to 15 minutes later and realized that Taylor was not breathing. She went outside and told Moore. Moore went inside, was unable to elicit a response from Taylor, and called 911.

Moore carried Taylor downstairs, where he was met by police officers arriving from the police station next door. The officers performed CPR on Taylor until paramedics arrived. Taylor could not be revived and was pronounced dead at the hospital.

[The medical examiner testified that Taylor's cause of death was blunt force head trauma. The medical examiner explained that Taylor "had a hemorrhage in a small ligament of the spinal column," which "was a marker for the force applied to that part of the body that led to her death." The medical examiner testified that Taylor suffered blunt trauma to her head, either as a result of something hitting her in the head or her head hitting something else, and postulated that the trauma caused her head to rock forward "in a hyperflexion incident." Likening the injury to those seen in car accidents, the medical examiner testified that Taylor's head flexed forward "very quickly, very violently," causing the odontoid process—a portion of one of the vertebrae—to hit her spinal cord. This event disrupted electrical transmission through the spinal cord and "stopped her breathing immediately." Taylor then died from asphyxiation.

The medical examiner explained that a hyperflexion injury like the one he observed in Taylor results from moving the chin toward the chest very rapidly. He explained that "[t]he child has to be either impacted with something" that would push "the head forward ... extremely fast, extremely forcefully," or "the body is brought up to meet ... the chin." He clarified that to cause hyperflexion to the degree he observed, "you either hit the kid in the head; or you throw the kid against a wall and the hit [sic] on the head—and it flexes the head downwards, the chin down to the chest; or you throw the kid onto the floor and they land on the back of their head and their body kind of continues over them causing the chest to come down and meet the chin." When asked whether a child falling and landing on the back of her head with her body weight coming down over the head could cause the type of hyperflexion observed in Taylor, the medical examiner answered, "Absolutely." The medical examiner testified that such an injury could be caused as a result of the child being thrown from an average height bed, but that such an injury would not happen from a child merely falling backwards off a bed.

The medical examiner discounted any possibility that Taylor could have suffered the hyperflexion injury as a result of resuscitative efforts by the police or medical personnel. He also discounted any possibility that the injury could have been sustained when Moore carried Taylor down to the apartment courtyard to meet the police, noting that carrying a child in such a manner would ... bend the neck in the exact opposite direction from that needed to cause Taylor's injury.

... The jury heard substantial testimony from the medical examiner regarding his theory of the cause of Taylor's death. The medical examiner discussed a hemorrhage he observed in a ligament in Taylor's spinal column, which he relied upon to support his finding that the odontoid process hyperflexed and impacted the spinal column. The medical examiner discussed hemorrhages he observed on Taylor's head, suggesting her head impacted something or was impacted by something. The medical examiner also discussed petechia— pinpoint hemorrhages from broken blood vessels—that he observed on Taylor's face, neck, and larynx. The medical examiner testified that he believed the petechia corroborated his theory of death because they could be caused if the diaphragm were paralyzed and blood was unable to leave the head and return to the rest of the body. The medical examiner explained that he observed hemorrhages in Taylor's sternocleidomastoid and paraspinous muscles, which was consistent with a violent hyperflexion of her head down to her chest. The medical examiner concluded that Taylor "was traumatized by her head slamming into something or her head being slammed by something, causing a hyperflexion injury causing the odontoid process— the ligaments to loosen up, the odontoid bone to slam into the ... spinal cord, either stunning or injuring it, stopping her respirations immediately; and then she died from suffocation after that." The jury heard appellant's own interview in which she told the officer that Taylor moaned when she hit the floor, from which the jury reasonably could conclude that Taylor experienced pain from the fall caused by appellant's actions.][Ed.]

Appellant was charged with murder, but a jury convicted her of the lesser-included offense of reckless injury to a child.... Appellant timely appealed.

ANALYSIS

II. Medical Examiner's Testimony

In her third issue, appellant contends the trial court erred by admitting unreliable expert opinion testimony by the medical examiner. Appellant contends that the medical examiner's opinion testimony was unreliable because he failed to look for certain evidence that might contradict his own theory of Taylor's cause of death.

A. Standard of Review

A trial judge's ruling on the admissibility of expert testimony is reviewed under an abuse of discretion standard and will not be disturbed if the decision is within

---

[Ed.] The bracketed materials have been moved within the case by the Author for clarity purposes.

the zone of reasonable disagreement. *Wolfe v. State*, 509 S.W.3d 325, 335 (Tex. Crim. App. 2017). For expert testimony to be admissible, "the proponent of the expert scientific evidence must demonstrate by clear and convincing evidence that the testimony is 'sufficiently reliable and relevant to help the jury in reaching accurate results.'" *Id.* Because appellant challenges only the reliability of the medical examiner's testimony, we need not discuss whether the testimony was relevant....

To establish the reliability of scientific evidence, the proponent must prove that (1) the underlying scientific theory is valid; (2) the technique applying the theory is valid; and (3) the technique was properly applied on the occasion in question. *Id.* at 336....

B. Application

Appellant contends that the State failed to meet the reliability test's third prong by establishing that the medical examiner properly applied the pertinent scientific theory to the facts of the case. Specifically, appellant contends that the medical examiner neglected to "examine brain slides for evidence (*e.g.*, meningitis) which might have spoiled his theory of wrongdoing by Appellant," and that the medical examiner reached his conclusion on Taylor's cause of death without having reviewed Taylor's previous pediatric records, thereby "completely discount[ing] the possibility of viral infection."

The defense's main argument at trial was that something other than appellant pushing Taylor off the bed may have caused Taylor's death. The defense argued that Taylor had experienced a number of medical problems during her life, and that she may have died as a result of meningitis or some other serious medical illness. In support of this argument, the defense presented its own expert witness, Dr. Radelat, who disagreed with some of the medical examiner's conclusions and opined that the medical examiner's autopsy was inadequate because it did not involve a microscopic inspection of the child's brain.

The medical examiner testified that he did not review Taylor's previous pediatric medical records because it was unnecessary in this case. He testified that, even if Taylor's records revealed that she had suffered multiple viral and bacterial infections during her lifetime, his opinion on her cause of death would not change because she had "a physical mechanical cause of death" that had "nothing to do with viral or infectious processes." The medical examiner testified that, if Taylor had any other illness sufficient to cause her to die suddenly, he would have seen signs of such an illness. The medical examiner testified that he could rule out infection in this case even without performing a microscopic examination of the brain because he would have observed infection when he performed his gross examination of the brain. He testified that he did not find any evidence during the autopsy to suggest that the child had any such illness, and that from the autopsy it appeared that the child had been healthy.

Based on the foregoing evidence, the trial court could have concluded that the medical examiner's testimony was reliable despite his failure to inspect the brain microscopically or review the child's medical records. The defense was free to challenge the medical examiner's expert opinion through cross-examination and by presentation of its own expert testimony, both of which it did. *See Wolfe*, 509 S.W.3d at 336 (although the trial court serves as the gatekeeper of scientific evidence, that "does not supplant cross-examination as 'the traditional and appropriate means of attacking shaky but admissible evidence'")....

Pirolozzi v. Stanbro

No. 5:07-CV-798, 2009 WL 1441070
(N.D. Ohio 2009)

GWIN, District Judge.

[Plaintiff sued Defendant police officers and city under 42 U.S.C. § 1983, after the suffocation death of the decedent following handcuffing in a supine position]. On March 23, 2009, Defendants ... moved this Court to limit the expert testimony of Plaintiff Troy Pirolozzi's expert witnesses: Dr. Werner Spitz and Dr. Robert Stark.... After considering the parties' arguments, the Court concludes that the testimony of experts Spitz [and] Stark ... is admissible.

DAUBERT MOTIONS

Legal Standard

... Under Rule 702, testimony based on specialized knowledge is admissible if it "will assist the trier of fact to understand the evidence or to determine a fact in issue." Fed. R. Evid. 702.... As commentators have noted, Rule 702 evinces a liberal approach regarding admissibility of expert testimony. *See, e.g.,* WEINSTEIN'S FEDERAL EVIDENCE § 702.02, at 702–6....

Rule 703 governs the facts or data upon which an expert may base his expert testimony. So long as the facts and data are "of a type reasonably relied upon by experts in the particular field in forming opinions or inferences upon the subject," the basis for an expert's testimony need not be admissible as evidence at trial. In other words, expert witnesses may base their testimony on inadmissible materials, and if those materials are reliable in the expert's field, their inadmissibility does not stop the admissibility of the expert's testimony....

In *Daubert v. Merrell Dow Pharmaceuticals, Inc.,* 509 U.S. 579 (1993), the Supreme Court held that trial courts are to perform a "gatekeeper" function regarding the admissibility of scientific experts, and created a series of factors for courts to apply in determining reliability.... In *Kumho Tire Co. v. Carmichael,* 526 U.S. 137 (1999), the Supreme Court extended the gatekeeper function of district courts to cover non-scientific expert testimony....

For the instant *Daubert* motions, the Court restricts itself to determining whether the experts' purported testimony is admissible. To conduct this inquiry, the Court examines the prerequisites listed in Rule 702 and also asks whether the basis underlying the testimony meets ... Rule 703

Drs. Spitz and Stark

The Defendants move the Court to limit the testimony of the Plaintiff's medical experts, Dr. Werner Spitz and Dr. Robert Stark, on the issue of the cause of Shawn Pirolozzi's death, both because their testimony is not based on reliable scientific methods or principles and because, in the case of Dr. Stark, "he does not have the necessary qualifications to opine on asphyxia [the alleged cause of death]."

Generally, the Defendants argue that there is no scientific experiment supporting the theory of compressional asphyxiation in cases like this one, where a subject is held down by police officers. To support this conclusion, the Defendants rely on the scientific studies of their own expert, Dr. Tom Neuman, who has found that weight placed on the back of subjects does not affect the ventilatory response to exercise, or the amount of oxygen in the blood. Without refuting the existence of positional or compressional asphyxiation, the Defendants argue that "[t]his case is a question of degree." Allegedly, there is an analytical gap between this case and the kinds of circumstances under which asphyxiation can occur, and Defendants argue that the Plaintiff's medical experts have employed no reliable scientific methodology to bridge that gap.

Specifically, Dr. Spitz intends to testify that the decedent died from compressional asphyxia, because due to his emotional condition — his "fear of impending doom" — the decedent required more air than he otherwise would. The Defendants challenge this theory first on the basis of qualification, arguing that because Dr. Spitz is not a pulmonologist, he cannot testify regarding how much oxygen a person needs to live. Nor, according to the Defendants, is Dr. Spitz, as a pathologist, qualified to opine on the mental state of the decedent, whether he was experiencing "fear of impending doom." Further, on the issue of reliability, the Defendants argue that Dr. Spitz "has no scientific basis to conclude that one's state of mind creates the need for more oxygen." ...

As to Dr. Stark, the Defendants challenge his qualifications because he is a cardiologist and not board certified in pathology, pulmonary medicine, or emergency medicine. Further, the Defendants allege that Dr. Spark has neither conducted his own research on asphyxia, nor is he familiar with the vast array of research in the field. Therefore, he cannot present reliable expert testimony on the issue.

Defending his medical experts, Plaintiff Pirolozzi notes the impossibility of replicating the circumstances of a case like this for the purposes of scientific testing. In the absence of such simulations, however, the Plaintiff contends his experts can rely on principles of medicine and their own experience in similar situations to form reliable opinions. In support of the validity of the relationship between positional asphyxiation and the prone restraint, Plaintiff Pirolozzi offers several articles involving case studies. Further, the Plaintiff challenges the Defendants' reliance on the work of Dr. Neuman and his involvement in similar cases, because the Neuman studies were allegedly conducted in anticipation of litigation. As the Plaintiff points out, courts have allowed evidence of restraint asphyxia as a cause of death since Neuman's work began. [citing, e.g., *Johnson v. City of Cincinnati*, 39 F. Supp. 2d 1013, 1017 (S.D. Ohio 1999).] The Plaintiff concludes that Dr. Spitz and Dr. Stark are qualified physicians who relied upon their experience and training, supported by the medical literature, to form their opinions, and as such, their testimony should be admitted.

The Court first addresses the question of the doctors' qualifications to testify. Rule 702 considers "knowledge, skill, experience, training, or education" of experts, and Dr. Spitz and Dr. Stark have a sufficient combination of these factors to be able to testify in this case. Dr. Stark is board certified in both cardiology and internal medicine, and has vast experience from his actual treatment of patients.... Dr. Stark is therefore qualified to testify as to certain matters, although he may not be qualified regarding every issue.... Dr. Spitz, as a board-certified pathologist, is qualified to testify as to the cause of death.... The Court agrees that the doctors may not be able to testify as to the mental process of the decedent, but generally they are qualified to testify.

With respect to the reliability of both Dr. Stark and Dr. Spitz's expert testimony, to the extent that they rely on a theory of asphyxia as the cause of death, the Court also finds both experts' testimony admissible. The simple fact that the experts do not have lab results supporting their theory is insufficient to render their testimony unreliable. If, as both doctors testify, the mental or emotional state of the subject is a factor in death by asphyxia, it would be nearly impossible to simulate the extreme circumstances of police restraint in scientific experiments. And in looking to the scientific literature, the Court finds sufficient support for the idea that excitement, fear, psychosis, and drug use all may affect the body's need for oxygen, and thereby the possibility of asphyxia. Although these articles involved case studies rather than lab experiments, they were nonetheless published in the *American Journal of Forensic Medicine and Pathology*, a peer-reviewed publication. The materials thus meet one, if not another, of *Daubert*'s reliability factors. In its flexible discretion, the Court finds this evidence sufficient to admit the experts' testimony on the theory of asphyxiation as the cause of death.

Further, ... the Court notes that the Plaintiff raises questions as to the admissibility of the Defendants' experts' testimony on the same issue, arguing that Dr. Neuman conducted his scientific studies for the purposes of litigation and the results are therefore suspect. If the jury agrees and finds Dr. Neuman to be unbelievable because he is a hired gun and finds his experiments to be fraudulent because his subjects knew the circumstances of the experiment and so were no actually afraid, the jury could then choose to believe the Plaintiff's experts instead. If the jury agrees with the Defendants that the analytical gap cannot be adequately bridged to support the asphyxiation theory, they can choose to believe the Defendants' experts. Ultimately, the questions regarding the experts are questions of weight that should be given their testimony, which is the province of the jury to decide, rather than the reliability of the testimony....

Notes and Questions

1. In both cases above, the court decides that the expert testimony on cause of death is reliable enough to be admitted and any weaknesses of the testimony should be considered by the jury in making their final determination. Look closely at each case and identify the specific basis for the finding of reliability for each expert and ask: is this enough to make a finding of reliability under Rule 702/*Daubert*, or should the experts have been excluded? How does the standard of review — abuse of discretion — play into the review on appeal in *Kolb*?

2. The causation issue of "shaken baby syndrome" has recently received high profile media attention and judicial analysis. This condition "is defined by a constellation of symptoms known as the triad: brain swelling, bleeding on the surface of the brain and bleeding behind the eyes. For years, those three symptoms by themselves

were uniformly accepted as evidence that a crime had been committed, even in the absence of bruises, broken bones or other signs of abuse." Clyde Haberman, *Shaken Baby Syndrome: A Diagnosis That Divides the Medical World*, N.Y. Times, Sept. 13, 2015. *See* Jessica Pishko, *How Can Doctors Be Sure a Baby's Been Shaken?*, Atlantic, Nov. 14, 2014; Victor Zapana, *Shaken*, New Yorker, Nov. 26, 2012; *see also* Genie Lyons, *Shaken Baby Syndrome: A Questionable Scientific Syndrome and a Dangerous Legal Concept*, 2003 Utah L. Rev. 1109 (summarizing medical findings in the area); Sandeep Narang, *A* Daubert *Analysis of Abusive Head Trauma/Shaken Baby Syndrome*, 11 Hous. J. Health L. & Pol'y 505 (2011) (offering a similar summarization). Whether the syndrome exists and the extent to which it should be admissible in court are questions that have been hotly debated in the legal community as well. For an overview of this controversial topic, see 156 Am. Jur. Proof of Facts 3d *Proof of Admissibility of Expert Opinion Testimony in Criminal Prosecution Based on Shaken Baby Syndrome* §§ 4–7 (2016).

iii. Epidemiology and Mass Exposure Causation

Daubert v. Merrell Dow Pharmaceuticals ("*Daubert II*")
43 F.3d 1311 (9th Cir. 1995)

Kozinski, Circuit Judge.

On remand from the United States Supreme Court, we undertake "the task of ensuring that an expert's testimony both rests on a reliable foundation and is relevant to the task at hand." *Daubert v. Merrell Dow Pharms., Inc.*, 509 U.S. 579 (1993).

I

A. Background

Two minors brought suit against Merrell Dow Pharmaceuticals, claiming they suffered limb reduction birth defects because their mothers had taken Bendectin, a drug prescribed for morning sickness to about 17.5 million pregnant women in the United States between 1957 and 1982. This appeal deals with an evidentiary question: whether certain expert scientific testimony is admissible to prove that Bendectin caused the plaintiffs' birth defects.

For the most part, we don't know how birth defects come about. We do know they occur in 2–3% of births, whether or not the expectant mother has taken Bendectin. Limb defects are even rarer, occurring in fewer than one birth out of every 1000. But scientists simply do not know how teratogens (chemicals known to cause limb reduction defects) do their damage: They cannot reconstruct the biological chain of events that leads from an expectant mother's ingestion of a teratogenic substance to the stunted development of a baby's limbs. Nor do they know what it is about teratogens that causes them to have this effect. No doubt, someday we will have this knowledge, and then we will be able to tell precisely whether and how Bendectin (or any other suspected teratogen) interferes with limb development; in the current state of scientific knowledge, however, we are ignorant.

Not knowing the mechanism whereby a particular agent causes a particular effect is not always fatal to a plaintiff's claim. Causation can be proved even when we don't know precisely *how* the damage occurred, if there is sufficiently compelling proof that the agent must have caused the damage *somehow*. One method of proving causation in these circumstances is to use statistical evidence. If 50 people who eat at a restaurant one evening come down with food poisoning during the night, we can infer that the restaurant's food probably contained something unwholesome, even if none of the dishes is available for analysis. This inference is based on the fact that … it is highly unlikely that 50 people who have nothing in common except that they ate at the same restaurant would get food poisoning from independent sources.

It is by such means that plaintiffs here seek to establish that Bendectin is responsible for their injuries. They rely on the testimony of three groups of scientific experts. One group proposes to testify that there is a statistical link between the ingestion of Bendectin during pregnancy and limb reduction defects. These experts have not themselves conducted epidemiological studies on the effects of Bendectin; rather, they have reanalyzed studies published by other scientists, none of whom reported a statistical association between Bendectin and birth defects. Other experts proffered by plaintiffs propose to testify that Bendectin causes limb reduction defects in humans because it causes such defects in laboratory animals. A third group of experts sees a link between Bendectin and birth defects because Bendectin has a chemical structure that is similar to other drugs suspected of causing birth defects.

The opinions proffered by plaintiffs' experts do not, to understate the point, reflect the consensus within the scientific community. The FDA—an agency not known for its promiscuity in approving drugs—continues to approve Bendectin for use by pregnant women because "available data do not demonstrate an association between birth defects and Bendectin." Every published study here and abroad—and there have been many—concludes that Bendectin is not a teratogen. In fact, apart from the small but determined group of scientists testifying on behalf of the Bendectin plaintiffs in this and many other cases, there doesn't appear to be a single scientist who has concluded that Bendectin causes limb reduction defects.

It is largely because the opinions proffered by plaintiffs' experts run counter to the substantial consensus in the scientific community that we affirmed the district court's grant of summary judgment the last time the case appeared before us. The standard for admissibility of expert testimony in this circuit at the time was the so-called *Frye* test: Scientific evidence was admissible if it was based on a scientific technique generally accepted as reliable within the scientific community. *Frye v. United States*, 293 F. 1013, 1014 (D.C. Cir. 1923). We found that the district court properly applied this standard, and affirmed. The Supreme Court reversed, holding that *Frye* was superseded by [Rule 702], and remanded for us to consider the admissibility of plaintiffs' expert testimony under this new standard.

B. Procedural Issues

First, however, we address plaintiffs' argument that we should simply remand the case so the district court can make the initial determination of admissibility under the new standard announced by the Supreme Court. There is certainly something to be said for this position, as the district court is charged with making the initial determination whether to admit evidence. In the peculiar circumstances of this case, however, we have determined that the interests of justice and judicial economy will best be served by deciding those issues that are properly before us and, in the process, offering guidance on the application of the *Daubert* standard in this circuit ...

[The court begins with a discussion of the legal standard of review under *Daubert*. These materials appear in Ch. 1 of this volume. The court then begins to apply those standards to this case ...]

We have examined carefully the affidavits proffered by plaintiffs' experts, as well as the testimony from prior trials that plaintiffs have introduced in support of that testimony, and find that none of the experts based his testimony on preexisting or independent research. While plaintiffs' scientists are all experts in their respective fields, none claims to have studied the effect of Bendectin on limb reduction defects before being hired to testify in this or related cases.

If the proffered expert testimony is not based on independent research, the party proffering it must come forward with other objective, verifiable evidence that the testimony is based on "scientifically valid principles." One means of showing this is by proof that the research and analysis supporting the proffered conclusions have been subjected to normal scientific scrutiny through peer review and publication. HUBER, GALILEO's REVENGE at 209 (suggesting that "[t]he ultimate test of [a scientific expert's] integrity is her readiness to publish and be damned").

Peer review and publication do not, of course, guarantee that the conclusions reached are correct; much published scientific research is greeted with intense skepticism and is not borne out by further research. But the test under *Daubert* is not the correctness of the expert's conclusions but the soundness of his methodology. That the research is accepted for publication in a reputable scientific journal after being subjected to the usual rigors of peer review is a significant indication that it is taken seriously by other scientists, i.e., that it meets at least the minimal criteria of good science. *Daubert*, 509 U.S. at 593 ("[S]crutiny of the scientific community is a component of 'good science.'"). If nothing else, peer review and publication "increase the likelihood that substantive flaws in methodology will be detected." *Id.* ....

Establishing that an expert's proffered testimony grows out of pre-litigation research or that the expert's research has been subjected to peer review are the two principal ways the proponent of expert testimony can show that the evidence satisfies the first prong of Rule 702.[10] Where such evidence is unavailable, the proponent of expert scientific testimony may attempt to satisfy its burden through the testimony of its own experts. For such a showing to be sufficient, the experts must explain precisely how they went about reaching their conclusions and point to some objective source — a learned treatise, the policy statement of a professional association, a published article in a reputable scientific journal or the like — to show that they have followed the scientific method, as it is practiced by (at least) a recognized minority of scientists in their field. *See United States v.*

---

10. This showing would not, of course, be conclusive. ...

Rincon, 28 F.3d 921, 924 (9th Cir. 1994) (research must be described "in sufficient detail that the district court [can] determine if the research was scientifically valid").

Plaintiffs have made no such showing. As noted above, plaintiffs rely entirely on the experts' unadorned assertions that the methodology they employed comports with standard scientific procedures. In support of these assertions, plaintiffs offer only the trial and deposition testimony of these experts in other cases. While these materials indicate that plaintiffs' experts have relied on animal studies, chemical structure analyses and epidemiological data, they neither explain the methodology the experts followed to reach their conclusions nor point to any external source to validate that methodology. We've been presented with only the experts' qualifications, their conclusions and their assurances of reliability. Under *Daubert*, that's not enough.

This is especially true of Dr. Palmer—the only expert willing to testify "that Bendectin did cause the limb defects in each of the children." In support of this conclusion, Dr. Palmer asserts only that Bendectin is a teratogen and that he has examined the plaintiffs' medical records, which apparently reveal the timing of their mothers' ingestion of the drug. Dr. Palmer offers no tested or testable theory to explain how, from this limited information, he was able to eliminate all other potential causes of birth defects, nor does he explain how he alone can state as a fact that Bendectin caused plaintiffs' injuries.... "Personal opinion, not science, is testifying here." For this reason, Dr. Palmer's testimony is inadmissible as a matter of law under Rule 702.

The failure to make any objective showing as to admissibility under the first prong of Rule 702 would also fatally undermine the testimony of plaintiffs' other experts, but for the peculiar posture of this case. Plaintiffs submitted their experts' affidavits while *Frye* was the law of the circuit and, although they've not requested an opportunity to augment their experts' affidavits in light of *Daubert*, the interests of justice would be disserved by precluding plaintiffs from doing so. Given the opportunity to augment their original showing of admissibility, plaintiffs might be able to show that the methodology adopted by some of their experts is based on sound scientific principles ...

Were this the only question before us, we would be inclined to remand to give plaintiffs an opportunity to submit additional proof that the scientific testimony they proffer was "derived by the scientific method." *Daubert*, however, establishes two prongs to the Rule 702 admissibility inquiry. We therefore consider whether the testimony satisfies the second prong of Rule 702: Would plaintiffs' proffered scientific evidence "assist the trier of fact ..."?

C. No Visible Means of Support

In elucidating the second requirement of Rule 702, *Daubert* stressed the importance of the "fit" between the testimony and an issue in the case: "Rule 702's 'helpfulness' standard requires a valid scientific connection to the pertinent inquiry as a precondition to admissibility." Here, the pertinent inquiry is causation. In assessing whether the proffered expert testimony "will assist the trier of fact" in resolving this issue, we must look to the governing substantive standard, which in this case is supplied by California tort law.

Plaintiffs do not attempt to show causation directly; instead, they rely on experts who present circumstantial proof of causation. Plaintiffs' experts testify that Bendectin is a teratogen because it causes birth defects when it is tested on animals, because it is similar in chemical structure to other suspected teratogens, and because statistical studies show that Bendectin use increases the risk of birth defects. Modern tort law permits such proof, but plaintiffs must nevertheless carry their traditional burden; they must prove that their injuries were the result of the accused cause and not some independent factor. In the case of birth defects, carrying this burden is made more difficult because we know that some defects — including limb reduction defects — occur even when expectant mothers do not take Bendectin, and that most birth defects occur for no known reason.

California tort law requires plaintiffs to show not merely that Bendectin increased the likelihood of injury, but that it more likely than not caused *their* injuries. *See Jones v. Ortho Pharmaceutical Corp.*, 209 Cal. Rptr. 456, 464 (1985). In terms of statistical proof, this means that plaintiffs must establish not just that their mothers' ingestion of Bendectin increased somewhat the likelihood of birth defects, but that it more than doubled it — only then can it be said that Bendectin is more likely than not the source of their injury....

None of plaintiffs' epidemiological experts claims that ingestion of Bendectin during pregnancy more than doubles the risk of birth defects. To evaluate the relationship between Bendectin and limb reduction defects, an epidemiologist would take a sample of the population and compare the frequency of birth defects in children whose mothers took Bendectin with the frequency of defects in children whose mothers did not. The ratio derived from this comparison would be an estimate of the "relative risk" associated with Bendectin. *See generally*, JOSEPH L. FLEISS, STATISTICAL METHODS FOR RATES AND PROPORTIONS (2d ed. 1981). For an epidemiological study to show causation under a preponderance standard, "the relative risk of limb reduction defects arising from the epidemiological data ... will, at a minimum, have to exceed '2.'" [*DeLuca v. Merrell Dow Pharms.*, 911 F.2d 941, 958 (3d Cir. 1990)]. That is, the study must show that children whose mothers took Bendectin are more than twice as likely to develop limb reduction birth defects as children whose mothers did not.[16] While plaintiffs' epidemiologists make vague assertions that there is a statistically significant relationship between Bendectin and birth defects, none states that the relative risk is greater than two. These studies thus would not be helpful, and indeed would only serve to confuse the jury, if offered to prove rather than refute causation. A relative risk of less than two may suggest teratogenicity, but it actually tends to *dis*prove legal causation, as it shows that Bendectin does not double the likelihood of birth defects.

With the exception of Dr. Palmer, whose testimony is inadmissible under the first prong of the Rule 702 analysis,[18] the remaining experts proffered by plaintiffs were

---

16. A statistical study showing a relative risk of less than two could be combined with other evidence to show it is more likely than not that the accused cause is responsible for a particular plaintiff's injury.... Here, however, plaintiffs' experts did not seek to differentiate these plaintiffs from the subjects of the statistical studies. The studies must therefore stand or fall on their own.

18. Dr. Palmer's testimony would easily meet Rule 702's fit requirement, were it not rendered inadmissible by the total lack of scientific basis for his conclusions....

equally unprepared to testify that Bendectin caused plaintiffs' injuries; they were willing to testify only that Bendectin is "capable of causing" birth defects. Plaintiffs argue "these scientists use the words 'capable of causing' meaning that it does cause. This is an ambiguity of language.... If something is capable of causing damage in humans, it does." But what plaintiffs must prove is not that Bendectin causes some birth defects, but that it caused *their* birth defects. To show this, plaintiffs' experts would have had to testify either that Bendectin actually caused plaintiffs' injuries (which they could not say) or that Bendectin more than doubled the likelihood of limb reduction birth defects (which they did not say).

As the district court properly found below, "the strongest inference to be drawn for plaintiffs based on the epidemiological evidence is that Bendectin could *possibly* have caused plaintiffs' injuries." The same is true of the other testimony derived from animal studies and chemical structure analyses.... Plaintiffs do not quantify this possibility, or otherwise indicate how their conclusions about causation should be weighted, even though the substantive legal standard has always required proof of causation by a preponderance of the evidence. Unlike these experts' explanation of their methodology, this is not a shortcoming that could be corrected on remand; plaintiffs' experts could augment their affidavits with independent proof that their methods were sound, but to augment the substantive testimony as to causation would require the experts to change their conclusions altogether. Any such tailoring of the experts' conclusions would, at this stage of the proceedings, fatally undermine any attempt to show that these findings were "derived by the scientific method." Plaintiffs' experts must, therefore, stand by the conclusions they originally proffered, rendering their testimony inadmissible under ... Rule 702.

Conclusion

The district court's grant of summary judgment is affirmed.

Notes and Questions

1. Why does Judge Kozinski believe that to avoid summary judgment, the plaintiffs must show a doubling of the relative risk? Would there be any way to defeat summary judgment without making such a showing?

2. Epidemiologists have criticized Judge Kozinski's bright line doubling of risk approach, stating that determinations of disease causation cannot be distilled to that simple formula. Jan Beyea & Daniel Berger, *Scientific Misconceptions Among* Daubert *Gatekeepers: The Need for Reform of Expert Review Procedures*, 64 Law & Contemp. Probs. 353 (2001); Sander Greenland, *Relation of Probability of Causation to Relative Risk and Doubling Dose: A Methodologic Error That Has Become a Social Problem*, 89 Am. J. of Pub. Health 1166, 1168 (1999). In the *Reference Guide on Epidemiology*, Michael Green makes clear that doubling of risk *could be* the appropriate analysis in limited circumstances, though it requires multiple assumptions. Michael D. Green et al., *Reference Guide on Epidemiology, in* Reference Manual on Scientific Evidence 549, 612–18 (3d ed. 2011). For an overview of epidemiology on causation, see Green et al., at 608–18.

Chapter 9

Accident Reconstruction

We began our assessment of expertise in the context of civil litigation with medical negligence experts, in which specialists opine on standard of care and causation issues based on contemporary medical knowledge. Of course, we found that concerns of forensic science, such as *ipse dixit* reasoning and poor methodological bases, could undercut the scientific foundation of medical testimony as well. Our next step will be to consider the management of expert evidence in the drastically different context of accident reconstruction. This field entails engineers or specialists reconstructing automobile accidents to determine speed before impact or the location of impact. The large volume of auto-collision lawsuits ensures that experts from this field comprise a disproportionate number of overall expert endorsements. For this reason, knowledge of accident reconstruction is critical to proficiency in expert evidence.

Automobile accident reconstruction, like medical testimony, does have a scientific basis in materials science, engineering, and mathematics. Just as with previous chapters, a practicing attorney may never encounter an expert on accident reconstruction in a civil lawsuit (or a criminal prosecution). However, these materials also provide a template of evaluation that is replicable in other fields. We will also continue our focus on practical application of these materials as we simultaneously learn the substantive law of the field.

We begin this chapter with a discussion of the methodology of accident reconstruction, as we did with forensic specialty areas. We will then progress to materials examining controversies within the field, specifically regarding how expert testimony can be challenged under relevant rules of evidence. Remember that our focus is not on being able to personally perform the analysis, but instead on how it is used and misused in court.

Paul C. Giannelli, Edward J. Imwinkelried, Andrea Roth & Jane C. Moriarty, *Accident Reconstruction*

2 Scientific Evidence 1119–21, 1123–45 (5th ed. 2012)[Ed.]

§ 27.02 The Scientific Premises of Accident Reconstruction.

Accident reconstruction rests on principles and theories developed by the basic science of physics and the applied science of engineering. In part, the discipline rests

---

[Ed.] Reprinted from LexisNexis Matthew Bender with permission. Copyright 2018 Matthew Bender & Company, Inc., a LexisNexis company. All rights reserved.

491

on the laws of mechanics and motion formulated by Sir Isaac Newton. Those laws tell us the following:

- A body at rest tends to remain at rest. This is the law of inertia "[A]ny body will remain still unless moved by some force."

- A body in motion tends to remain in motion in a straight line at a uniform velocity. The body will move at a constant speed in a straight line "unless the body is acted upon by an unbalanced force."

- If an unbalanced force acts on a moving body, the body accelerates in the direction of the force. The acceleration is directly proportional to the unbalanced force and inversely proportional to the mass of the body. By way of example, a small push will move the object slowly or for a short distance. In contrast, a large push will move the object faster or for a greater distance.

- For every action, there is an equal and opposite reaction. Thus, if a person throws a ball against a wall, the ball will bounce back or react with the same amount of force it initially carried.

In addition to these laws, accident reconstruction experts rely on "hundreds of other equations." Some of these equations have been deduced from the Newtonian laws of motion while others have been derived inductively by empirical research.

Accident reconstructionists use these laws and equations to determine how the accident happened. Sections 27.04 through 27.09 of this chapter review some of the specific determinations which accident reconstruction experts can make. Of course, before solving an equation, the expert must know what values to insert or "plug in" for the various variables in the equation. Subsection 27.10[d] discusses the expert's minor premise, that is, the specific values plugged into the variables.

§ 27.04 Determining the Role of the Accident Participant: Driver, Passenger, or Pedestrian.

Armed with sufficient physical facts about the accident scene, the accident reconstruction expert can draw many inferences about various aspects of the accident. For example, the expert may be able to determine both whether a person was involved in a traffic accident and, if so, the person's role in the accident. Suppose, for instance, that the police find both the defendant and a decedent at an accident scene. An hour before the accident, the two were drinking together; and they left the bar together. The defendant owns the car involved in the accident, but he or she claims that the decedent was driving. It is undisputed that the defendant was present at the time of the accident, but the crucial question is whether the defendant was behind the wheel. There are several factors which an expert can weigh to determine the defendant's role in the accident.

On the one hand, the expert cannot rely solely on the final resting place of the bodies of the participants. The force of the accident may have thrown the participants around the interior of the vehicle or even entirely out of the vehicle.

On the other hand, the following factors are helpful clues to identifying the role of each participant in the accident:

Typical Injury Patterns

A pedestrian is likely to sustain lower leg bruises or even open fractures due to impact with the vehicle's bumper. The location of these injuries should roughly correspond with the height of the bumper. The bumper injuries tend to be lower if the driver applied the brakes before impact, since the front of the automobile dips. The absence of bumper injuries suggests that the pedestrian was side-swiped. Injuries to the abdominal area, hip, and buttocks are likewise common. Even when the visible injuries appear superficial, there may be serious subcutaneous hematomas, deep pockets of blood, or torn tissue. If the body is thrown from the hood onto the street, the body may have severe head or neck injuries. When the body is thrown violently onto the pavement, the body can exhibit road bums; and the clothing may suffer friction tearing.

A passenger's head frequently impacts the windshield during an accident and causes the windshield to form a spiderweb fracture pattern. Windshield injuries are often deep. In contrast, the shattering of tempered side windows tends to cause angled, dicing cuts. If the passenger is not wearing a seat belt, his or her entire body may fly forward; and the dashboard tends to force the kneecap between the femoral condyles.

The driver will frequently sustain closed chest injuries caused by the steering wheel. Impact with the steering wheel can result in multiple rib fractures, pulmonary tears and contusions, and cardiovascular injuries. If the driver's face comes into contact with a padded steering wheel or dashboard, the face may exhibit abrasions, lacerations, and fractures.

, Or suppose that an occupant of the vehicle is injured when a seat belt fails and the occupant is ejected from the vehicle. In that event, the occupant's injury pattern might include injuries to his or her outboard upper extremity (OUE) or head.

Matching Injuries to Trace Evidence within the Vehicle

The expert can attempt to correlate the injuries sustained by the accident participant and the trace evidence at the accident scene. For example, in a given case, it might be clear that something presumably impacting with the passenger's head caused a dent in the dashboard. If the defendant is the only accident participant who sustained that type of head injury, the injury is some evidence that the defendant was the passenger rather than the driver.

Textile-plastic Fusing (TPF)

This phenomenon is usually referred to as textile-plastic or fiber-plastic fusing. During a collision, a vehicle occupant's hair or fibres from his or her clothing may come into contact with parts of the vehicle's interior such as upholstery, roof, head liner, pillar covers, and dashboard. These parts of the interior are thermo plastic material. If part of a person's body strikes this material, the material can momentarily soften; and hairs or fibres from the body might become imbedded in the thermal surface. The imbedded hair and fibre is a contact trace, evidencing contact with the person's body. The imbedded hair or fibre can later be matched with the person's hair or clothing.

Airbag Particles

Like hair, particles from deployed airbags can be helpful. Hot gas inflates the airbags. The gas is so hot that it can singe the occupants' clothing. Research indicates that the singe patterns from the driver and passenger side airbags are different.

Other Clues

There might be fingerprints on the steering wheel. Similarly, there may be pedal imprints on the bottom of the driver's shoes. When the driver realizes that a collision is imminent, the driver may press down on the brakes; and that the pressure created by the impact can leave a pedal imprint on the sole of that person's shoe. In addition, biomechanical engineering principles can be used to help determine a person's physical posture during an accident.

It should be evident at this point that the determination of the accident participant's role can require the expertise of several disciplines: fingerprint examiners, trace evidence analysts, and forensic pathologists. In short, the resolution of the factual issues posed by an accident may necessitate a multidisciplinary team.

§ 27.06 Determining the Vehicle's Velocity.

In addition to identifying the direction of the vehicle, the expert often needs to determine the speed or velocity with which the vehicle was moving in that direction. Technically, there is a distinction between speed and velocity. As one commentator has stated, "[S]peed is 'rapidity in moving' [without regard to direction], where velocity is the 'time rate of change of position of a body in a specified direction.'" For the balance of this chapter, we shall use the expression, "velocity." In some cases, the expert is interested in the velocity of a vehicle after impact. There are recognized formulae for computing that velocity. Figure 27-1 sets out two of the formulae.

However, in most cases — especially prosecutions — the expert is more concerned about determining the velocity of the vehicle before impact. It is ideal if a police officer happened to be nearby and used radar, discussed in Chapter 28, to clock the vehicle. However, even absent a radar reading, there are several methods that an accident reconstruction expert may use to make a finding as to the vehicle's speed. In many cases, the expert will draw conclusions about the pre-impact velocity from one of the following types of data[:] skidmarks, yaw marks, and the damage to the vehicles.

[a] Skidmarks and ABS Deceleration Scuffs.

Assume that before collision, the driver attempts to apply his or her brakes. The wheels consequently lock rather than continue rotating. A locked wheel may produce skidmarks. The abrasive action between the sliding tire and the road surface can generate temperatures between 200 and 1,000 degrees [Fahrenheit]. Rubber particles are torn off the tire and deposited on the road surface. In order to estimate speed from these skidmarks, the expert must determine both the length of the skidmarks and the drag factor for the road surface.

Figure 27-1

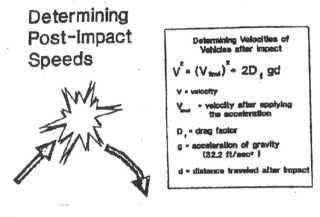

Ascertaining the skidmark length and drag factor

Determining Post-Impact Speeds

Determining Velocities of Vehicles after impact

$$V^2 = (V_{final})^2 + 2D_f gd$$

v = velocity

V_{final} = velocity after applying the acceleration

D_f = drag factor

g = acceleration of gravity (32.2 ft/sec²)

d = distance traveled after impact

Determining the Speed of a Vehicle after separation from a collision

$$SS = 5.45 \sqrt{fD}$$

SS = speed of vehicle after separating from collision

f = drag factor of road surface

D = length of skidmarks

Ascertaining the Skidmark Length and Drag Factor
—Skidmark Length

It is vital that the length of the skidmarks be measured accurately. The skidmarks should not be merely paced off. Experience indicates that although the person measuring the skidmarks may think he or she is consistently taking a 36-inch pace, the pace is often only 32 inches. The person making the measurement may have to get down on hands and knees to see parts of the skidmark and use a rolling wheel or tape to make accurate measurements.

The expert ought to measure the skidmarks left by all four wheels. At first blush, it may appear that there are only two skidmarks. However, if the car proceeded along a straight vector, the rear wheel skidmarks may overlap the front wheel skidmarks. In that case,

> the measurement started when the rear tires began to leave marks, and the measurement ends where the front tires stopped. If this is a case of one set of skidmarks overlapping another, the driver has been "cheated" by the length

Figure 27-2

Methods to Compute 4 Wheel Skid Length

Averaging		Brake Power	
Right Front	27.5	Right Front 27.5 x 30% = 8.25	
Right Rear	22	Right Rear 22 x 20% = 4.4	
Left Front	26	Left Front 26 x 30% = 7.8	
Left Rear	24	Left Front 24 x .20% = 4.8	
	99.5		25.25
99.5 / 4 = 24.875 feet			
4 Wheel Skid Distance of 24.875 feet		4 Wheel Skid Distance of 25.25 feet	

of the wheel base of the vehicle, because the measured skidding distance is that much longer than the actual skidding distance was.[45]

As Figure 27-2 indicates, after measuring the four skidmarks, the expert can use one of two methods to determine overall skid length. In one technique, the expert simply averages the four skidmarks to compute the mean. In the other technique, the expert adjusts for braking power.

The vehicle may pitch forward during braking. The second technique compensates for that factor.

— Drag Factor

Just as there is a technical distinction between speed and velocity, there is a difference between drag factor or friction number and friction coefficient. When the surface is inclined or wet and one or more of the wheels do not brake, the factor and the coefficient can differ. However, if the road surface in question is dry and level and the brakes on all four wheels locked, the coefficient and the factor are identical. They both represent "the resistance of sliding of two surfaces in contact: the force parallel to a surface required to keep an object sliding on that surface divided by the force of the object against the surface." In other words, it is "the horizontal force required to cause an object to move in the direction of the force, divided by the weight of the object being moved." The formula is:

$$f = F/W$$

If the force required were 19 pounds and the weight dragged were pounds, the drag factor would be 0.76.

There are several methods of determining drag factor. One is the use of a drag sled or box. Or the expert can employ an accelometer or electronic instrument attached to

45. Joseph E. Badger, *Reconstruction of Traffic Accidents*, 19 AM. JUR. PROOF OF FACTS 3D 115, 137 (1990).

Figure 27-3

Average Sliding and Peak Friction Coefficients for Passenger Car Tire

Surface Condition	Sliding Friction	Peak Friction
Concrete/Asphalt, polished to new, dry:	0.65 - 0.90	0.80 - 1.00
wet:	0.45 - 0.70	0.60 - 0.75
Gravel, loose to packed:	0.40 - 0.70	- - - - - -
Gravel, some grass:	0.35 - 0.40	0.40 - 0.50
Meadow, wet:	0.15 - 0.20	0.20 - 0.25
Meadow, dry, firm, short grass:	0.35	0.45
Off-road shoulder, firm, dry:	0.35	0.40
Soil, loose, moist, tires sink down appr. 2 in.:	0.60	0.70
Asphalt, wet leaves:	0.60	0.60
Road, snow covered:	0.30	0.30
Ice:	0.15	0.15

the vehicle involved in the accident or a substitute test vehicle. Alternatively, the expert may perform test skids with either the same vehicle or a similar exemplar vehicle.

In many cases, the person investigating the accident unfortunately does not bother to measure drag factor of the road. Instead, the person relies on published charts of average drag factors for certain types of surfaces. Figure 27-3 is illustrative. The difficulty is that some of these charts were generated in the late 1950s and early 1960s when rubber tire compounds were different and many road surfaces were aggregate. Further, motor vehicle braking systems were not as refined then. Moreover, little is known about the manner in which some of these charts were prepared. Nevertheless, in many cases—occasionally because the road in question has been resurfaced since the accident—the expert relies on generalizations from such a chart rather than a measurement carefully performed at the accident scene. The expert should consider a range of drag factors, since the true drag factor might fall outside the published chart values.

Our reviewer, Mr. Daily, points out that special problems arise when the vehicle in question was driving on a hilly road with changing slope. The analysis is relatively simple when there is a constant road slope, but in the real world the slope often varies. To compute the correct speed, the changing slope must be accounted for. The road should be divided into sections with a constant slope, and a separate drag factor ought to be determined for each such section.

Mr. Daily adds that peculiar problems also arise when, after collision, a vehicle rotates into a spin. In some cases, only one or two of the wheels have effective braking; and in many cases, at that point in the collision there is no driver-applied braking. The drag on the free-rolling tires will be a function of the angle that the tires make with respect to the vehicle motion. Ideally, in these situations the expert should consider the condition of each wheel. In particular, the expert ought to calculate drag factors for small distance increments in which the condition of the four wheels is constant.

Figure 27-4

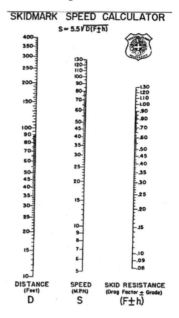

SKIDMARK SPEED CALCULATOR

$$S = 5.5\sqrt{D(F \pm h)}$$

DISTANCE
(Feet)
D

SPEED
(M.P.H.)
S

SKID RESISTANCE
(Drag Factor ± Grade)
(F±h)

Estimating Velocity

After determining the skidmark length and drag factor, the expert can estimate the velocity of the vehicle leaving the skidmarks in one of two ways.

—Formulae for Computing Velocity from Skidmarks

One way is to use a recognized equation and solve the equation for velocity. There are numerous equations which the expert may solve for velocity once he or she knows the values for skidmark length and drag factor. For example, one equation is:

$$S = \sqrt{30fd}$$

In this formula, S is the velocity, f is the drag factor, and d is the skidmark length. Another formula is:

$$v = \sqrt{2gfd}$$

In this equation, v is velocity in feet per second before the skid, g is the acceleration of gravity (32.2 feet per second squared), f is the drag factor, and d is the length of the skidmark.

—Nomograph Charts

Just as the expert can use a chart to estimate drag factor, the expert could resort to a chart to estimate velocity after determining the values for skidmark length and drag factor. These charts are referred to as speed calculators or nomographs. Figure 27-4 is a nomograph chart.

A "straight line [is] drawn to connect assumed values on [the] two scales" on the edges of the chart. The skidmark length column is on one edge, and the drag factor column is on the other. The expert connects the pertinent values in the two columns with a straight line. The line intersects the speed column in the middle of the nomograph, and the point of intersection is the velocity estimate.

There are several caveats about this method of determining velocity. The drag factor in particular is "susceptible to variation." There can be substantial imprecision in the estimate when the expert relies on a drag factor chart rather than meticulously measuring the factor at the accident scene.

The estimate is likely to be the minimum speed for the vehicle. Studies by Professors Reed and Keskin at the University of Texas suggest that "at least 20% of the vehicle's kinetic energy is lost before skidding commences." In the earliest braking stage, a vehicle sometimes leaves only the faint shadow of a skidmark. Twenty percent of the vehicle's energy can be "dissipated during this shadow period."

Due to these uncertainties, many accident reconstructionist experts concede that velocity determinations based on skidmarks are merely "ballpark" figures. Rather than citing a single estimate, some reconstruction experts prefer to report a range of probable velocities.

BCS Deceleration Scuffs

Our reviewer, Mr. Daily, points out that many of the techniques described above can be used to analyze BCS deceleration scuffs.

[b] Yaw Marks.

When the vehicle brakes, the resulting road mark is a skidmark or scuffmark. Assume, however, that before the accident, the driver was endeavoring to negotiate a curve. The driver begins to realize that he or she is losing control of the vehicle but tries to steer through the curve. Centripetal force (friction) tends to keep the vehicle on the road and in the curving movement while centrifugal force pushes the car on a tangent away from the curve. This maneuver results in a different type of road mark. The mark is called variously a yaw mark, scrub, scuff, or sideslip. The tire is still rotating but sliding. More precisely, the tire is rotating in one direction but sliding in another. The resulting mark is an arc portion of a circle—the circle the vehicle would have completed if it continued the arc. In a skidmark, the striations are usually parallel to the mark. In contrast, in a yaw mark, the striations can be oblique to the mark.

Of course, when the investigator finds a yaw mark at the accident scene, the investigator should record all the relevant dimensions of the mark. However, in truth, for the velocity estimate, the length of the mark is less important; but it should still be measured and recorded. It is much more important to determine the radius of the curve. Figure 27-5 depicts that determination. The expert initially establishes a chord on the curve by drawing a straight line from one point on the curve to another. The expert then draws another straight line from the midpoint of the chord perpendicularly to the yaw arc. That line represents the middle ordinate. Knowing the width of the vehicle's track, the expert can now solve the equation on Figure 27-5 to determine the radius of the yaw arc.

Figure 27-5

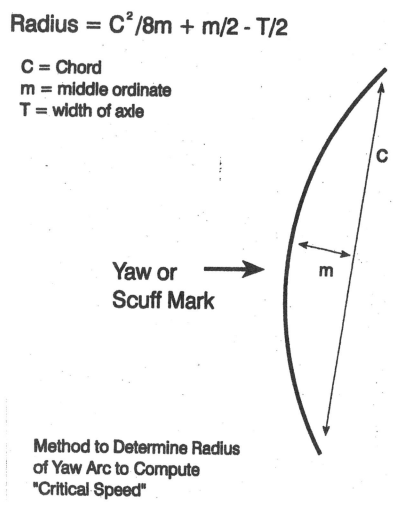

Radius = C²/8m + m/2 - T/2

C = Chord
m = middle ordinate
T = width of axle

Yaw or
Scuff Mark

m

c

Method to Determine Radius
of Yaw Arc to Compute
"Critical Speed"

Figure 27-6 sets out the formula which the expert can then utilize to estimate the critical speed of the vehicle. That speed is the maximum velocity which the vehicle can maintain before it begins to yaw or slide at the curve.

Our reviewer, Mr. Daily, adds several caveats about yaw analysis. In order for a vehicle to turn, an external, unbalanced force must be applied laterally to it. This applied force will change the direction of the velocity vector, which results in a lateral (centripetal) acceleration, because any change in velocity (either in magnitude or direction) causes an acceleration. Centrifugal force is sometimes called a pseudo force. It does not exist in an inertial reference frame. Consider the example of a pickup truck with a ball which is sitting in the bed of the pickup and is in equilibrium with the pickup. Initially, the pickup and the ball have the same velocity vector. However, turn the pickup. The driver applies steering, which then applies an unbalanced lateral force to the pickup, thereby

Figure 27-6

Formulae for Speed with Yawmarks or Scuff marks

Determining Radius of Yawmark

$$R = C^2/8m + m/2 - T/2$$

R = radius of curve

C = chord

m = middle ordinate

T = axle width (track)

Determining Critical Speed (Maximum Speed at which a vehicle can make a turn)

$$V = \sqrt{gfR}$$

V = Critical Speed

g = acceleration of gravity (32.2 ft/sec²)

f = drag factor of road

R = Radius of curve

changing its direction. However, that force is not applied to the ball in the back of the pickup. By virtue of Newton's First Law, the ball continues in a straight line, and that is what an outside observer (inertial reference frame) would see. Yet, to an observer in the bed of the pickup, the ball would appear to move to the side of the bed. The non-inertial observer might conclude that there was a force acting on the ball to move it to the side of the pickup bed. In reality, there is no unbalanced force acting on the ball.

Notwithstanding these caveats, if an automobile is actually in the yaw motion, this mode of analysis can be quite accurate. In the view of some authorities, "[a] speed correctly determined from a yaw mark is generally more accurate than one from a skidmark." The difficulty is that experts often employ this analysis when it is inappropriate. In Mr. Daily's view, the investigator should utilize this method of analysis only if the vehicle has gotten into the yaw by the application of steering. Thus, the analysis should not be used in post-impact trajectories. The expert *ought to* be confident that the vehicle was in a steady state maneuver before using yaw analysis.

[c] Damage to the Vehicles.

[The previous two subsections] ... both deal with inferences about velocity from highway marks. This subsection also deals with a velocity inference; but, in this case, the inference is drawn from the damage to the objects involved in the accident.

The key to drawing the inference is the law of the conservation of energy:

> [W]hen two or more vehicles or a single vehicle and another object collide, the conservation of energy principle states that the total linear energy of the system before the collision equals the total linear energy after the collision.

Hence, the energy of the system before the collision must be equal to "the energy of the bodies after the process, plus (or minus) the work or energy put into the system (or taken out)." The pertinent formula reads:

$$E \text{ before} = E \text{ after} \pm \text{Work in (out)}$$

To determine the pre-collision energy, the expert uses this formula:

$$KE = \tfrac{1}{2} MV^2$$

In this formula, KE is kinetic energy, M is the mass of the vehicle, and V is velocity in feet per second. Mass is determined by dividing weight by gravity. As previously noted, the acceleration due to gravity is 32.3 feet per second per second.

Collecting the Necessary Data

In effect, the expert works backward to solve the first equation for the pre-collision velocity. To do so, the expert needs to gather several items of information:

- The weight of the vehicle before collision. The expert ought to include the weight of any occupants or objects in the vehicle before collision. The expert can have the vehicle weighed after the accident. If parts of the vehicle broke off during the collision, those parts should be collected and weighed as well although this may not make a significant difference. Alternatively, the expert can use the weight stated in the manufacturer's specifications.

- The energy dissipated in the braking action prior to collision. When the vehicle leaves skidmarks, the expert can employ the length of the skidmarks to compute the energy dissipated in the braking process.

- The energy dissipated in post-collision movement. This action is referred to as separation movement.

- The energy spent in damaging one or both vehicles during the collision. Even if they are struck during the collision, some rubber parts of the vehicle may be capable of absorbing the impact and then making an elastic rebound to their original shape. Most parts, however, will suffer plastic deformation. The extent of the "crush" or plastic deformation is indicative of the amount of energy expended in damaging the vehicles.

Figure 27-7

Establishing a Crush Profile

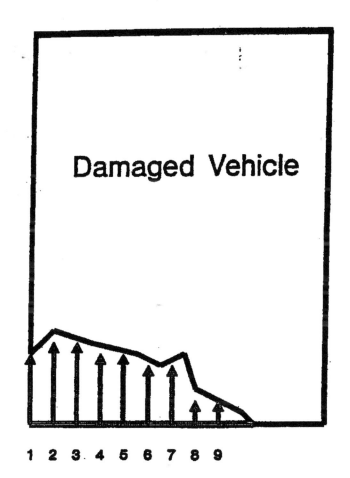

The person inspecting the damaged vehicle must carefully measure the crush in inches. As Figure 27-7 indicates, the inspector prepares a crush profile of the damage. The inspector draws a straight line along the undamaged plane of the vehicle. At regular intervals, the inspector measures the distance perpendicularly from the plane to the indented damage. The Society of Automotive Engineers has developed a system for classifying and assigning numerical values to damage of vehicles. The system is described in a document known as SAE J224 entitled Collision Deformation Classification. It is used as an input to some computer softwares.

Inferring Velocity from the Data

Having collected this information, the expert can then estimate speed in one of two ways. The expert may manually calculate the speed by using equations for deriving pre-collision speed from vehicle damage. Some of these equations are based on the empirical research of Rodolf Limpert; but our reviewer cautions that in some instances, Limpert's research data are rather old. Or the expert can use computer software programs specially designed for this purpose....

It is important to remember that if the accident involved two vehicles, their combined kinetic energy is the cause of the damage. The damage therefore reflects the speed of both vehicles. In most cases, the expert is ultimately interested in determining the speed of the individual vehicles. That computation is a simple matter if the witnesses to the accident establish that one of the vehicles was stationary at the time of the collision. Skidmarks will often permit the expert to determine the minimum velocity of one of the vehicles, and in some cases this allows an inference to be made about the speed of the other vehicle.

Our reviewer, Mr. Daily, adds several observations about vehicle damage analysis. In many instances, this analysis is based on the CRASH III model developed by McHenry. The model has two separate parts. The first part is the damage energy model, which uses the damage profile of the vehicle, along with empirically derived stiffness coefficients, to determine how much energy was required to crush the vehicle to its noted damage profile. The second component is the impact model. That model employs the crush energy together with vehicle mass and collision configuration to determine the velocity change in the crash. The expert must take care to ensure that the collision forces meet Newton's Third Law. The expert does so by calculating the collision forces for each vehicle. The velocity change is then added to the post-impact velocity by using the appropriate vector addition. Impact speeds in collinear collisions may be determined directly from the energy model by solving the energy model simultaneously with the Conservation of Linear Momentum (COLM) model.

A. Expert Qualifications in the Field

Wilson v. Woods

163 F.3d 935 (5th Cir. 1999)

JONES, Circuit Judge.

This case arose out of an automobile collision in which Joseph D. Woods, an 18-wheel truck driver employed by MCC Transportation Company, struck appellant's automobile as it proceeded forward after stopping at a highway intersection near Yazoo City, Mississippi. Wilson sued the appellees ... and appellees removed the case to the Southern District of Mississippi.

Appellant's suit alleged that Woods was negligent *per se* because he was exceeding the 55 mile per hour speed limit when the accident occurred. To support her theory, the appellant moved to qualify A.K. Rosenhan as an accident reconstruction expert. Rosenhan was prepared to testify that, based upon information contained in the accident report, his calculations determined that Woods's truck was traveling 63 miles per hour at the time of the accident. The appellees objected that Rosenhan was not sufficiently qualified as an accident reconstruction expert. The district court sustained the objection and refused to admit the testimony.

Without Rosenhan's testimony, Wilson was unable to prove that Woods exceeded the speed limit and accordingly, the jury returned a verdict for the defendants. Wilson appeals on the sole issue of the exclusion of Rosenhan's testimony.

STANDARD OF REVIEW

This court reviews a trial court's decision to exclude expert testimony under an abuse of discretion standard. *See Gen. Elec. Co. v. Joiner*, 522 U.S. 136 (1997). Accordingly, we have recognized that district courts are given "wide latitude in determining the admissibility of expert testimony, and the discretion of the trial judge ... will not be disturbed on appeal unless manifestly erroneous." *Watkins v. Telsmith, Inc.* 121 F.3d 984, 988 (5th Cir. 1997). In deciding whether the district court abused its discretion in refusing to qualify appellant's expert witness, we are guided by the Supreme Court's decision in *Daubert v. Merrell Dow Pharms., Inc.*, 509 U.S. 579 (1993), and Federal Rule of Evidence 702.

DISCUSSION

In *Daubert*, the Supreme Court instructed district courts to function as gatekeepers and permit only reliable and relevant expert testimony to be presented to the jury. *See Daubert*, 509 U.S. at 590–93. District courts must be assured that the proffered witness is qualified to testify by virtue of his "knowledge, skill, experience, training, or education." Fed. R. Evid. 702. A district court should refuse to allow an expert witness to testify if it finds that the witness is not qualified to testify in a particular field or on a given subject....

To support her theory that Woods exceeded the posted speed limit when the accident occurred, the appellant called Rosenhan as an expert in accident reconstruction. Rosenhan earned bachelor of science and master of science degrees in mechanical engineering, but he never completed his doctorate degree. After concluding his educational endeavors, Rosenhan taught courses in mechanical engineering and industrial engineering at various colleges and vocational schools. During the past 25 years, his consulting work has concentrated on fire reconstruction and investigation; however, he testified that he recently shifted his professional emphasis to automobile accident reconstruction.

Wilson moved to qualify Rosenhan as an expert in accident reconstruction. Before the court ruled on the motion, however, the appellees conducted voir dire of Rosenhan, which revealed that 1) although Rosenhan taught college level courses, he never held professorial rank; 2) he never taught an accident reconstruction course or any other course that involved automobile accident reconstruction; 3) he had no degree or certification in accident reconstruction (but he was enrolled in a correspondence course from the Northwestern Traffic Institute); 4) he had not completed the requirements for certification by the Association of Accident Reconstructionists; and, 5) although he had testified in various cases, one court had refused to qualify him as an expert in vehicle accident reconstruction based on his lack of qualifications. Appellees argued Rosenhan was not sufficiently qualified to testify as an expert in this case due to his lack of "training," "experience," and "qualifications." *See* Fed. R. Evid. 702.

The court also questioned Rosenhan and ascertained that he 1) had never conducted any studies or experiments in the field of accident reconstruction; 2) did not take any measurements or collect any data from the accident scene in this case; 3) did not examine the tires or other mechanical parts involved in the accident; 4) based his calculations on publicly accessible data published by the National Highway Transportation Safety Administration; and, 5) was unable to show that his training or experience as a mechanical engineer gave him expertise in the field of accident reconstruction that was distinguishable from training received by other mechanical engineers. Based on all these facts, the court refused to qualify Rosenhan as an expert witness and sustained the appellees' objection, stating:

> The court is concerned, as it has been directed to be concerned, by *Daubert* and its progeny, about the proliferation of so-called expert witnesses. This court personally is not convinced that there is any such thing as an accident reconstructionist as an expert field; under the rules and guidelines set forth by the Supreme Court in *Daubert*.

> None of the people who seem to be testifying have published in the field, have done experimentation in the field; and other than getting a correspondence course from this Northwestern Traffic Institute, which pads the resume, none seem to have anything other than, in most instances, a general scientific background.

> [T]he court is familiar with Mr. Rosenhan, who has testified in this court on other occasions as an expert in the cause and origin of fires. He knows that field, and I have had no hesitation in recognizing him as an expert in those fields. He's very good at what he does. As a professional witness, he's effective on the stand. For that reason, he has branched out into the field of accident reconstruction. And obviously, attorneys think that he's effective at what he does. That, however, does not make him an expert in that field, even assuming that the field is such.

> Here, we don't have simple physics questions. If we did, according to Mr. Rosenhan's testimony, then anyone who has any background in physics and mathematics, which any engineering graduate of any university in the country would have, would be capable of looking at whatever tables the government publishes and thereby become an expert. I don't think that's what an expert is supposed to be or is supposed to do in order to qualify as an expert.

Wilson contends that the district court was predisposed not to allow Rosenhan to testify as an expert in accident reconstruction because, in addition to the aforementioned comments, the judge stated that "I have never, at this stage, allowed, over objection, anyone to testify as an accident reconstructionist.... I don't know that there is such a thing other than some professional hired guns who go around and claim to be accident reconstructionists." Although this statement appears to illustrate a bias against accident reconstructionists, the court did not base its decision on the belief that accident reconstruction may be a bogus scientific field. In fact, the court gave the appellant the benefit of the doubt by expressly finding that "even assuming that the field" of accident reconstruction exists, Rosenhan was not qualified as such an expert.

The district court's finding that Rosenhan lacked the requisite qualifications is supported in the record. Appellees' voir dire and the court's own questioning revealed significant deficiencies in Rosenhan's experience and professional training, leading ineluctably to the impression that his "expertise" in accident reconstruction was no greater than that of any other individual with a general scientific background. In addition, the court noted that Rosenhan had never taught accident reconstruction courses, never experimented or conducted studies in the field, and never published anything on the subject. To the extent that accident reconstruction represents a specialized field of study, as Wilson contends, the district court did not clearly err in finding that Rosenhan had done little to acquire or practice the requisite expertise. Because Rosenhan's claimed professional status was legitimately in doubt, the court appropriately exercised its gatekeeping responsibility and did not abuse its discretion in refusing to qualify the witness. The judgment of the district court is accordingly affirmed.

Stevens Transport, Inc. v. Global Transport, LLC
No. 6:15-CV-552-MHS-JDL, 2016 WL 9244669
(E.D. Tex. May 24, 2016)

Love, U.S. Magistrate Judge

This lawsuit arises from a motor vehicle accident that occurred on January 9, 2015 on Interstate 20 in Gregg County, Texas, when Plaintiffs' tractor-trailer struck Defendants' tractor-trailer. Defendants' tractor-trailer was operated by Patricio Espinosa-Herzberg, who had pulled the tractor-trailer to the side of I-20. As noted by Plaintiffs in their motion, "[t]he position of Defendants' trailer is a hotly contested issue in this case." Plaintiffs contend that Defendants' trailer extended into the right lane of I-20 while Defendants contend that the trailer was pulled over completely onto the shoulder of I-20. Robert Harris, an employee driver for Plaintiff Stevens Transport, Inc., collided with the rear driver's side of Defendants' trailer. Harris suffered injuries and the tractor, the trailer, and the cargo burned as a result of the accident. Plaintiffs seek damages for the value of the tractor, the trailer, and the cargo, as well as for expenses incurred for the care of Harris' injuries. *Id.*

By their Motion, Plaintiffs seek to partially exclude the testimony of Corporal Darren Thomas, the Department of Public Safety lead investigator at the scene of the accident ...

LEGAL STANDARD

In accordance with Federal Rule of Evidence 104(a), when faced with expert testimony, the trial court acts as a "gatekeeper" and must perform "a preliminary assessment of whether the reasoning or methodology underlying the testimony is scientifically valid and of whether that reasoning or methodology properly can be applied to the facts in issue." *Daubert v. Merrell Dow Pharms., Inc.*, 509 U.S. 579, 592–95 (1993).

To admit expert testimony, a court "must determine at the outset, pursuant to Rule 104(a), whether the expert is proposing to testify to: (1) scientific knowledge that (2) will assist the trier of fact to understand or determine a fact in issue." *Daubert*, 509 U.S. 579, 113 S. Ct. 2786. Trial judges have traditionally been afforded wide discretion to admit or exclude expert evidence. *See Peters v. Five Star Marine*, 898 F.2d 448, 450 (5th Cir. 1990)....

Rule 702 of the Federal Rules of Evidence governs the admissibility of expert testimony and reports. "Whether the situation is a proper one for the use of expert testimony is to be determined on the basis of assisting the trier." *Peters*, 898 F.2d at 449. Assisting the trier of fact means "the trial judge ought to insist that a proffered expert bring to the jury more than the lawyers can offer in argument." *Salas v. Carpenter*, 980 F.2d 299, 305 (5th Cir. 1992) The district court's responsibility "is to make certain that an expert, whether basing testimony upon professional studies or personal experience, employs in the courtroom the same level of intellectual rigor that characterizes the practice of an expert in the relevant field." *Kumho Tire Co. v. Carmichael*, 526 U.S. 137, 152 (1999).

When evaluating expert testimony, the overarching concern is generally focused on whether it is relevant and reliable. *See Daubert*, 509 U.S. 579...."[T]he test of reliability is 'flexible,' and the *Daubert* factors neither necessarily nor exclusively apply to all experts or in every case. Rather, the law grants a district court the same broad latitude when it decides how to determine reliability as it enjoys in respect to its ultimate reliability determination." *Kumho Tire Co.*, 526 U.S. at 151, 119 S. Ct. 1167.

As a general rule, questions relating to the bases and sources of an expert's opinion affect the weight to be assigned that opinion rather than its admissibility. *See* Fed. R. Evid. 702 Advisory Committee's Notes, 2000 Amendments (citing *Rock v. Arkansas*, 483 U.S. 44, 61 (1987)). While the district court must act as a gatekeeper to exclude all unreliable expert testimony, "the rejection of expert testimony is the exception rather than the rule." *Id.* (citing *Daubert*, 509 U.S. 579; *Kumho Tire Co.*, 526 U.S. 137). Importantly, in a jury trial setting, the Court's role under *Daubert* is not to weigh the expert testimony to the point of supplanting the jury's fact-finding role; rather, the Court's role is limited to that of a gatekeeper, ensuring that the evidence in dispute is at least sufficiently reliable and relevant to the issue before the jury that it is appropriate for the jury's consideration....

ANALYSIS

Corporal Darren Thomas

Plaintiffs contend that Corporal Thomas is not qualified to provide some of the opinions contained in his deposition testimony, that he failed to follow proper methodology in investigating the accident, and that he has no factual basis for concluding that Plaintiffs' driver, Harris, was asleep or inattentive at the time of the accident. Plaintiffs challenge Corporal Thomas' qualifications to testify as to the location of the point of impact because he is not an accident reconstructionist. Plaintiffs also take issue with the fact that Corporal Thomas failed to document the skid mark which formed the basis for his conclusion that Defendants' tractor-trailer was on the shoulder of the highway and that he could not definitively state what formed the basis for his conclusion that Plaintiffs' driver, Harris, was asleep or inattentive.

Plaintiffs argue that Corporal Thomas is not qualified to opine as to the point of impact because he lacks certification in accident reconstruction and that is not a member of the DPS accident reconstruction team. Experts in accident reconstruction typically have a degree in engineering, as well as certification in accident reconstruction, and experience conducting studies and experiments, taking measurements, and collecting data from accident scenes, including examining tires and mechanical parts. *Moreno v. W.R. Davis Produce, Inc.*, 2007 WL 1731139, at *2 (W.D. Tex. 2007) (citing *Wilson v. Woods*, 163 F.3d 935, 937 (5th Cir. 1999)). Corporal Thomas admits that he has not received training in accident reconstruction and does not consider himself an accident reconstructionist.

Defendants counter that Corporal Thomas is designated as an expert in accident investigation, not as an accident reconstructionist, and is being offered to provide his opinion as the law enforcement officer who conducted the official investigation. The record shows that Corporal Thomas is trained in accident investigation with more than 15 years of experience investigating accidents.... As it relates to the distinction between accident investigation and accident reconstruction, Corporal Thomas testified that "[a]ccident investigation is responding to the scene, looking at the evidence, taking statements from witnesses, making a preliminary determination about what may have been a contributing factor to the crash, [and] writing [and] submitting the initial crash report" while "[a]ccident reconstruction involves a team coming out and using equipment ... to actually recreate the accident as best they can based on the evidence that, a lot of time, [was gathered] the day that the crash occurred."

The distinction between accident investigation and accident reconstruction was also discussed in *Cartwright v. Am. Honda Motor Co.*, 2011 WL 3648565, at *4 (E.D. Tex. 2011). In *Cartwright*, the DPS officer indicated on the accident report his conclusion regarding the cause of the accident. However, the DPS officer also conducted an experiment wherein he attempted to re-create the path of plaintiff's car with his patrol car to test plaintiff's assertion that she lost control of her vehicle after hitting a pothole. The court found that the officer was not qualified to re-create an accident and make findings from that re-creation but that, based on his experience and training to investigate accidents, he was qualified to offer opinions flowing from his accident investigation, including an opinion as to the cause of the accident.

Although Plaintiffs cite *Moreno v. W.R. Davis Produce, Inc.*, 2007 WL 1731139, at *2 (W.D. Tex. 2007)[1] and *Graves ex rel. W.A.G. v. Toyota Motor Corp.*, 2011 WL 4590772

---

1. In *Moreno*, the district court determined that a DPS officer was not qualified to provide opinion evidence in the field of accident reconstruction because he had received no such training, made no calculations related to the accident, and took no photographs related to his specific opinion that gouge marks were made by plaintiff's car.

(S.D. Miss. 2011)[2] as support for their position that Corporal Thomas' opinions are inadmissible due to lack of documentation and lack of reconstruction expertise, the Court finds no Fifth Circuit precedent and no consensus among the district courts regarding the admission of expert testimony by investigating officers at the scene of an accident. However, the Court finds persuasive the reasoning presented in *Cartwright*, as well as in [several similar cases, *Vigil* and *Main*], all of which concluded that experienced accident investigators at the scene of an accident are qualified to testify regarding their investigation and the conclusions flowing therefrom.

As noted above, the court in *Cartwright* concluded that a DPS officer was qualified to offer opinions flowing from his accident investigation, including an opinion as to the cause of the accident. In *Vigil*, the court held that a sheriff's deputy could call upon his experience to provide expert testimony regarding the accident scene, the cause of the accident, and other factors that came to light during his investigation of the accident scene. In *Main*, the court found that the officer designated as an expert in accident investigation was sufficiently qualified to testify regarding his investigation, observations ... at the scene, and contributing factors to the collision.

Having considered the arguments of the parties and reviewed the testimony of Corporal Thomas, and based on the reasoning presented in *Cartwright*, *Vigil*, and *Main*, the Court finds that Corporal Thomas possesses the requisite training and practical experience to testify regarding his investigation, observations he made at the scene, contributing factors to the collision, and his opinion regarding the position of Defendants' [truck] at the point of impact....

Koenig v. Beekmans

No. 5-15-CV-00822-RCL-RBF, 2017 WL 6033404
(W.D. Tex. Dec. 5, 2017)

FARRER, U.S. Magistrate Judge

This personal injury lawsuit arises from an October 2, 2013 head-on car accident involving Koenig and Beekmans. Koenig asserts claims for negligence and negligence per se, and seeks damages from Beekmans in excess of $1 million.... The parties ... dispute who, Koenig or Beekmans, caused the accident....

Defendant Beekmans designated accident reconstructionist Billy S. Cox to offer an expert opinion regarding the accident's causes and the sequence of events that led up to it. Cox conclude[d] that the accident occurred because Koenig was driving his vehicle eastbound in the westbound lane lawfully occupied by Beekmans' vehicle. According to Cox, Beekmans was traveling at or below the posted speed limit (45 mph) when he noticed Koenig's vehicle approaching his lane of travel. Cox concludes that once Beekmans noticed Koenig's vehicle approaching his lane, Beekmans reacted by steering his vehicle to his left and applying his brakes, which reduced Beekmans' speed to 2 to 5

---

2. In *Graves*, the court found that the officers were qualified to testify as to what they observed at the scene but were not allowed to testify as experts to any conclusions they reached as a result of observing that evidence.

mph. According to Cox, Koenig was traveling between 40 to 50 mph and also changed lanes to the impact point but did not apply his brakes before the collision. Cox concludes that Beekmans' decisions to steer to his left to the point of impact and apply his brakes to try to avoid the collision were appropriate. He also concludes that had Koenig properly applied his brakes, the parties could have avoided the accident altogether.

Koenig's motion attacks Cox's qualifications to testify as an expert....

II. Legal Standards

Koenig's challenges to the admissibility of Cox's expert testimony are governed by Federal Rule of Evidence 702, along with *Daubert v. Merrell Dow Pharms., Inc.*, 509 U.S. 579 (1993), and its progeny. Rule 702 provides that a witness "'qualified as an expert ... may testify ... in the form of an opinion ... if (1) the testimony is based upon sufficient facts or data, (2) the testimony is the product of reliable principles and methods, and (3) the witness has applied the principles and methods reliably to the facts of the case.'"

Daubert charges trial courts to act as evidentiary "gate-keepers" to ensure that proffered expert testimony is, among other things, sufficiently reliable. Courts enjoy wide discretion in deciding precisely how to make such a reliability determination in a given case. *Kumho Tire Co. v. Carmichael*, 526 U.S. 137, 142 (1999). The reliability inquiry focuses "on [experts'] principles and methodology, not on the conclusions that [experts] generate." *Daubert*, 509 U.S. at 594. The proponent of expert testimony is not required to show that the testimony is correct, but rather show—by a preponderance of the evidence—that the testimony is sufficiently reliable. *Moore v. Ashland Chem. Inc.*, 151 F.3d 269, 276 (5th Cir. 1998). Whether an expert is "basing testimony upon professional studies or personal experience," a court must ensure the expert "employs in the courtroom the same level of intellectual rigor that characterizes the practice of an expert in the relevant field." *Kumho Tire Co.*, 526 U.S. at 152.

At the same time, "the trial court's role as gatekeeper is not intended to serve as a replacement for the adversary system." *United States v. 14.38 Acres of Land*, 80 F.3d 1074, 1078 (5th Cir. 1996). "Vigorous cross-examination, presentation of contrary evidence, and careful instruction on burden of proof are the traditional and appropriate means of attacking shaky but admissible evidence." *Daubert*, 509 U.S. at 596. In general, "questions relating to the bases and sources of an expert's opinion affect the weight to be assigned that opinion rather than its admissibility and should be left for the jury's consideration." *14.38 Acres of Land*, 80 F.3d at 1077; *see also Viterbo v. Dow Chemical Co.*, 826 F.2d 420, 422 (5th Cir. 1987).

III. Analysis

Cox is qualified to provide an accident reconstruction analysis in this case, and his testimony regarding the vehicles' momentum prior to impact, as well as the parties' perception times and the reasonableness of each party's accident-avoidance maneuvers are sufficiently ... helpful to survive the motion to exclude....

Qualifications. Cox's qualifications satisfy Rule 702 and *Daubert*, which require that a "proffered witness is qualified to testify [as an expert] by virtue of his 'knowledge, skill, experience, training, or education.'" *Wilson v. Woods*, 163 F.3d 935, 937 (5th

Cir. 1999) (quoting Fed. R. Evid. 702). "Rule 702 does not mandate that the expert be highly qualified in order to testify about a given issue, and the issue of qualification has been described as presenting a 'low threshold' for the proponent to clear." *DiSalvatore v. Foretravel, Inc.*, No. 9:14-CV-00150, 2016 WL 7742824, at *10 (E.D. Tex. Jul. 20, 2016). As long as an "expert meets liberal minimum qualifications, then the level of the expert's expertise goes to credibility and weight, not admissibility." *Kannankeril v. Terminix Int'l*, 128 F.3d 802, 809 (3d Cir. 1997).

Cox's experience, training, and education with accident reconstruction qualify him to provide an expert opinion in this case. Cox's resume and deposition testimony reflect over 25 years of experience as a full-time forensic accident reconstructionist, and involvement in thousands of accident reconstruction cases. Cox is also accredited by the Accreditation Commission for Traffic Accident Reconstruction, the only accreditation available for accident reconstructionists, and has taken the necessary continuing education courses to keep his accreditation current for the past 20 years. In short, Cox's qualifications meet the "low threshold" set by *Daubert*. *DiSalvatore*, 2016 WL 7742824, at *10.

Koenig's arguments attacking Cox's lack of an undergraduate or advanced degree in either engineering or physics are unavailing. Neither a college degree nor an advanced degree is a requirement for an expert witness. Indeed, "the text of Rule 702 expressly contemplates that an expert may be qualified on the basis of experience" alone, or "experience in conjunction with other knowledge, skill training, or education." *Pipitone v. Biomatrix, Inc.*, 288 F.3d 239, 247 (5th Cir. 2002) (citing Fed. R. Evid. 702 advisory committee's note to 2000 amendment). And, in any event, Cox is approximately 40 hours shy of a degree in biomedical engineering, which consisted of courses in physics, calculus, design, statistics, and engineering, including specifically biomechanical or crash testing.

Notes and Questions

1. What qualifications do each of the experts in *Wilson*, *Stevens*, and *Koenig* bring in the field of accident reconstruction? Based solely on those qualifications, do you think they should have been permitted to testify to the accident reconstruction in their respective cases?

2. The expert witness in *Koenig* lacks both an undergraduate and advanced degree, yet is able to testify. Contrastingly, the expert witness in *Wilson* has a Bachelor of Science and Master of Science degree in mechanical engineering (and taught at the college level), yet is excluded from testifying. Did the courts err, or was their analysis correct in each case?

3. While the expert in *Wilson* was excluded and the expert in *Koenig* was admitted, the court in *Stevens* does not undertake an "all-or-nothing" approach to the admissibility of expert testimony. Instead, the court appears to draw a distinction between experts in accident reconstruction and experts in accident investigation. Based on this distinction, do you see any difference in what each expert will be allowed to testify about at trial?

4. Note that many of these cases, including the cases cited for precedent, are unpublished opinions (with *Wilson* being a notable exception cited in the other
   opinions). Why do you think that might be?

B. Gatekeeping Reliability and the
Ipse Dixit Problem

Mitchell v. Barnes

96 So. 3d 771 (Miss. Ct. App. 2012)

Griffis, Presiding Judge.

David Barnes filed a lawsuit against Leigh Mitchell for his personal injuries arising
from an automobile accident. The jury returned a verdict for Barnes in the amount
of $150,000. On appeal, Mitchell argues that the circuit court erred by: … admitting
James Hannah's expert testimony in the field of accident reconstruction; and … admitting Officer Michelle Foster's expert opinion testimony regarding fault and causation.…

FACTS

On July 11, 2004, Barnes was driving his motorcycle northbound on Old Canton
Road. Barnes and Mitchell were involved in a collision in front the Jitney Premier
[supermarket]. Prior to the accident, Mitchell's car was located in the entrance to
the Jitney Premier facing west. At this location, Old Canton Road has two northbound
lanes, a center turn lane, and two southbound lanes.

Officer Foster, a patrol officer with the Jackson Police Department, was dispatched
to the accident scene. She testified that when she arrived, Barnes's motorcycle was
on the opposite side of the road in the southbound lane of Old Canton Road, and
Mitchell's car was near the entrance area of the Jitney Premier. Officer Foster testified
that Mitchell was easing out into Old Canton Road when she clipped Barnes's motorcycle. She also testified that, at the time of the accident, Barnes was not driving
improperly and that Barnes's estimated speed at the time of the accident was thirty
miles per hour. Officer Foster did not indicate Mitchell's speed and did not issue
Mitchell a traffic citation for the accident.

Barnes testified he stopped at the red light before the Jitney Premier exit and gas
pumps. He testified that he drove through the light when it turned green and then
signaled to change lanes. As he was looking to see if the other lane was clear, Mitchell
pulled out into the road. Barnes testified that he did not have enough time to stop
and avoid hitting Mitchell. Barnes testified he was driving between twenty-five and
thirty miles per hour. He also testified that he was driving in between the two northbound lanes when the accident occurred.

James Hannah testified as an expert in accident reconstruction on behalf of Barnes.
In forming his expert opinion, Hannah surveyed the accident area and interviewed

Officer Foster on September 17, 2005, approximately fourteen months after the accident. Hannah also reviewed photographs of Mitchell's vehicle, but did not review any photographs of Barnes's motorcycle. Hannah testified that he had interviewed Barnes about what he remembered of the accident. Hannah estimated the final resting location of the motorcycle and, from that estimation, determined the speed of Barnes's motorcycle from an estimated friction coefficient calculation. Hannah concluded that Barnes was traveling thirty-miles per hour at the time of the accident.

Mitchell testified that, as she pulled up to the exit of the gas station, she heard Barnes speeding down the street. As Barnes's motorcycle came close to her car, he lost control of his motorcycle and struck her car while it was stopped. Mitchell testified that, at the time of the accident, Barnes was riding his motorcycle on the back wheel doing a "wheelie." Mitchell testified she had pulled up to the road to see around the bushes, but her vehicle was not in the road at the time of the accident. Mitchell stated that Barnes hit the edge of her bumper and then rolled off his motorcycle as it flipped.

Several eyewitnesses testified during the trial. Greg Parsons testified Barnes was speeding and driving the motorcycle on one wheel. Parsons testified that the accident occurred when Barnes applied his brakes and lost control of the motorcycle. Lorna Owens also testified that the motorcycle was speeding while on one wheel. Owens testified that when the motorcycle came down from being on one wheel, Barnes lost control of the motorcycle. Owens testified that Officer Foster did not ask her about the accident, and she did not give her statement to the police at the time of the accident. Mike Williams also testified that he saw Barnes on one wheel driving at a high rate of speed at the time of the accident. Williams testified that the accident occurred when Barnes used his brakes, causing him to lose control of the motorcycle and hit Mitchell ...

ANALYSIS

...

Whether the circuit court erred by admitting expert testimony of James Hannah.

Mitchell argues that it was error to allow James Hannah to testify as an expert witness in accident reconstruction claiming that Hannah's testimony was not based on sufficient facts or data. Mississippi Rules of Evidence 702 states:

> If scientific, technical, or other specialized knowledge will assist the trier of fact to understand the evidence or to determine a fact in issue, a witness qualified as an expert by knowledge, skill, experience, training, or education may testify thereto in the form of an opinion or otherwise if (1) the testimony is based upon sufficient facts or data, (2) the testimony is the product of reliable principles and methods, and (3) the witness has applied the principles and methods reliably to the facts of the case.

"Our well-settled standard of review for the admission or suppression of evidence is abuse of discretion." *Miss. Transp. Comm'n v. McLemore*, 863 So. 2d 31, 34 (Miss. 2004). The Mississippi Supreme Court has said that "the decision of the trial judge will stand 'unless we conclude that the discretion was arbitrary and clearly erroneous, amounting to an abuse of discretion.'" *Id.*

Under Rule 702, trial "courts are charged with being gatekeepers in evaluating the admissibility of expert testimony." *Watts v. Radiator Specialty Co.*, 990 So. 2d 143, 146 (Miss. 2008). Rule 702 "recognizes the gatekeeping responsibility of the trial court to determine whether the expert testimony is relevant and reliable." *Kilhullen v. Kan. City S. Ry.*, 8 So. 3d 168, 172 (Miss. 2009).

On August 18, 2006, Mitchell filed a motion in limine to exclude Hannah's expert testimony on the basis that his data was unreliable. On the date of trial, Mitchell requested the circuit court hear her motion to exclude Hannah as an expert witness. The circuit court ruled that the issue of Hannah's expert testimony should be addressed during trial under cross-examination. Thus, the circuit court did not conduct a *Daubert* evidentiary hearing on whether Hannah's testimony was admissible under Rule. 702.

In *McLemore*, 863 So. 2d at 35–42, the supreme court conducted an in-depth analysis of the admissibility of expert testimony adopting the modified *Daubert* standard. The *McLemore* court stated that "[t]he trial court is vested with a 'gatekeeping responsibility.'" *Id.* at 36 (citing *Daubert v. Merrell Dow Pharms., Inc.*, 509 U.S. 579, 589 (1993)). "The trial court must make a 'preliminary assessment of whether the reasoning or methodology underlying the testimony is scientifically valid and ... whether that reasoning and methodology can be applied to the facts in issue.'" *Id.* at 36.

Here, the circuit court did not make a preliminary assessment of Hannah's methodology or whether his reasoning and methodology could be applied to the facts in this case. *See McLemore*, 863 So. 2d at 36. Instead, the circuit court ruled that Hannah's expert testimony would be subject to cross-examination by Mitchell's counsel and that his expert opinions were matters for the jury to assess.[2] However, this approach fails to implement the circuit court's gatekeeping function required by *McLemore*.

When Hannah was called in Barnes's case-in-chief, the circuit court did allow Mitchell's counsel to conduct a proffer of Hannah's testimony outside the presence of the jury. Hannah's proffer reflected his expected testimony ... [including] his opinions about the accident.

During the proffer, Hannah admitted that there was no physical evidence to review to determine the final resting point of the two vehicles after the accident. He also testified that he did not know where the point of impact was or where Barnes's motorcycle came to rest. In determining the point of impact, Hannah relied upon Officer Foster's recollection, fourteen months after the accident, of the accident scene. At the time of the accident, Officer Foster did not note any physical evidence of the impact, nor did she record any measurements from the scene in the accident report.

---

2. Despite the court's ruling that counsel for Mitchell would be permitted to cross-examine Hannah regarding his expert opinions, the circuit court subsequently limited the cross-examination and instructed Mitchell's counsel on several occasions to move to other lines of questioning, particularly in regard to Hannah's testimony on his coefficient of friction calculations. Thus, Mitchell was deprived of a full cross-examination of Hannah's opinions. *See Denham v. Holmes ex rel. Holmes*, 60 So. 3d 773, 785 (Miss. 2011) (holding "[v]igorous cross-examination, presentation of contrary evidence, and careful instruction on the burden of proof are the traditional and appropriate means of attacking shaky but admissible evidence.")

Moreover, there were no skid marks, oil spots, gouges, or scratches in the road for Hannah to analyze. Hannah testified that he based his placement of the vehicles on Officer Foster's recollection and the eyewitnesses'. Hannah testified that he never viewed the motorcycle but was given information pertaining to where the damage was on the motorcycle. Hannah did not indicate where he obtained the information about the motorcycle. Because Officer Foster did not mark any landmarks in her drawing of the accident scent in the accident report, Hannah based his reconstruction of the accident on her visit to the accident site with him more than a year later.

Hannah also offered an expert opinion regarding the speed Barnes was traveling at the time of the accident. Hannah conceded that in order to determine Barnes's speed, he needed to know how far the motorcycle traveled from the point of impact with Mitchell's car to its final resting position. However, Hannah did not know the final resting position, as his calculations were based upon Officer Foster's recollection. Another essential calculation for Hannah to perform to determine Barnes's rate of speed is called the "coefficient-of-friction". This calculation takes into consideration how vehicles interact with different types of surfaces, e.g., asphalt, grass or rocks. In this instance, Hannah used a coefficient of friction calculation to determine how far Barnes's motorcycle slid on the asphalt after impacting Mitchell's car. Hannah testified he had little physical evidence to determine the coefficient of friction.

As to this calculation, Hannah testified in his deposition as follows:

> **Q.** All right. So, again, where did you come up with the number of using half of the coefficient of friction[?]
>
> **A.** Again, I was trying to give the benefit of the doubt. I don't like to go with the extreme. I always play devil's advocate, because I do accidents for everybody, criminal, civil, both sides, and I always like to come up with numbers that gives everybody the benefit of the doubt.
>
> **Q.** Is there any scientific basis for using half, or did you just pick a number?
>
> **A.** Well, I picked a number because this has ... proven to be true over the years, that this actually applies, that it has to be less than this. What I am giving is the absolute number.

The record before this Court reflects that Hannah: (1) did not know the distance the motorcycle traveled after hitting Mitchell's car; (2) did not know the exact location where the motorcycle came to rest; (3) was given an estimate of between fifty and one hundred feet by Officer Foster of the distance between impact and the motorcycle's resting place; (4) did not have any physical evidence from the scene of the accident to review; (5) "picked" a coefficient-of-friction number to determine the speed of Barnes's motorcycle at the time of the accident; (6) did not have photographs of the accident scene; (7) did not inspect Barnes's motorcycle; (8) relied on the recollections of Officer Foster and other eyewitnesses more than one year after the accident in formulating his expert opinions; and (9) did not record the interviews with Barnes or the other eyewitnesses.

We find the circuit court failed to conduct a *Daubert* evidentiary hearing on the admissibility Hannah's testimony as required by *McLemore*. We further find that Hannah's expert testimony does not meet the standards for admissibility under Rule 702 and *McLemore*. Applying a mathematical formula, such as a coefficient of friction, where the underlying facts relied on by the expert are the product of speculation and conjecture and cannot be substantiated with any degree of reliability, does not pass scrutiny under the modified *Daubert* standard applied in *McLemore*.

Therefore, it was error for the circuit court to accept Hannah as an expert and allow him to offer expert testimony regarding the accident.

. . .

Whether the circuit court erred by allowing Officer Foster to testify regarding fault and how the accident occurred.

Mitchell argues two assignments of error regarding the testimony of Officer Foster. First, Mitchell argues Officer Foster testified outside of her capacity as a lay witness and offered opinions that qualified as expert testimony. Second, Mitchell argues the circuit court erred by admitting portions of the police records that repeated the opinions of Officer Foster. The standard of review for the trial court's admission or suppression of evidence is abuse of discretion. *Haggerty v. Foster*, 838 So. 2d 948, 958 (Miss. 2002).

Officer Foster was not designated as an expert witness at trial. Mitchell argues that Barnes's counsel attempted to elicit expert testimony from Officer Foster based on her training and experience as a police officer. Specifically, Officer Foster indicated that the cause of the accident was due to Mitchell's "fail[ure] to yield the right-of-way." Officer Foster further concluded that Barnes's speed at the time of the accident was thirty miles per hour and that Barnes was not driving improperly.

Barnes argues that Officer Foster reached these conclusions from information that she obtained from Mitchell at the accident scene. Mitchell disputes that she ever spoke with Officer Foster.[3] This disputed fact is not material, however, to Officer Foster's opinion testimony as to the cause of the accident or Barnes's speed. It is undisputed that Officer Foster was not present at the time the accident occurred. Thus in order for her to render expert opinion testimony, she must be qualified under Rule 702. *See also Roberts v. Grafe Auto Co.*, 701 So. 2d 1093, 1099 (Miss. 1997) (holding trial court committed reversible error in allowing the police officer to give expert testimony without first being tendered and accepted as an expert in accident reconstruction). Since Officer Foster was never identified or tendered as an expert witness in accident reconstruction, her opinions are inadmissible under Rule. 702. While Officer Foster's opinions are not admissible under Rule 702, certain opinion testimony is admissible under Mississippi Rule of Evidence 701 as follows:

> If the witness is not testifying as an expert, the witness's testimony in the
> form of opinions or inferences is limited to those opinions or inferences

---

3. The accident report does not reflect that Officer Foster spoke with Mitchell at the accident scene.

which are (a) rationally based on the perception of the witness, (b) helpful to the clear understanding of his testimony or the determination of a fact in issue, and (c), not based on scientific, technical or other specialized knowledge within the scope of Rule 702.

The supreme court has held "Rule 701 opinions are by definition lay opinions and thus require no specialized knowledge, however obtained." *Miss. State Highway Comm'n v. Gilich*, 609 So. 2d 367, 377 (Miss. 1992). The supreme court has further stated: "There is a bright line rule. That is, where, in order to express the opinion, the witness must possess some experience or expertise beyond that of the average, randomly selected adult, it is a [Rule] 702 opinion and not a Rule 701 opinion." *Sample v. State*, 643 So. 2d 524, 530 (Miss. 1994).

Here, Officer Foster was required to possess specialized knowledge to testify about the cause of the accident and the rate of speed of Barnes's motorcycle at the time of the accident since she was not present at the time of the accident. On the accident report admitted into evidence, Officer Foster drew a diagram depicting the accident, the lanes where the vehicles were located ... and the point of impact of the collision. Officer Foster testified that she wrote the description of the accident in her report. Officer Foster further testified as to the cause of the accident that Mitchell had failed to yield to the right of way, and moreover, that Barnes was not driving improperly, and was traveling thirty miles per hour at the time of the accident.

We find this testimony by Officer Foster is Rule 702 opinion testimony, rather than Rule 701 lay witness testimony. Officer Foster clearly testified based on her knowledge and experience as a police officer investigating accidents and not based on personal observations. "[I]t is clear that a police officer's testimony as to the cause of the accident, based on training, experience in investigation, etc., would be considered accident reconstruction testimony, allowable as expert testimony under Rule 702, if the officer is properly qualified." *Couch v. City of D'Iberville*, 656 So. 2d 146, 153 (Miss. 1995). On remand, Officer Foster may testify as to her opinions if properly qualified and tendered as an expert witness.

Finally, Mitchell argues that the circuit court erred in allowing the portion of Officer Foster's accident report containing her opinions. We agree. To allow the portion of the accident report containing Rule 702 expert opinions would simply circumvent the proper exclusion of her opinion testimony. Therefore, the portion of the accident report containing Rule 702 opinion testimony is inadmissible unless Officer Foster is qualified as an expert witness....

Logan v. Cooper Tire & Rubber Co.
No. 10-3-KSF, 2011 WL 3267894
(E.D. Ky. July 30, 2011)

FORESTER, Senior District Judge.

Currently before the Court is the motion in limine of the defendant, Cooper Tire & Rubber Company to exclude the testimony of the plaintiff's proposed expert, Micky

Gilbert, pursuant to *Daubert v. Merrell Dow Pharamaceuticals, Inc.*, 509 U.S. 579 (1993) and *Kumho Tire Co. Ltd. v. Carmichael*, 526 U.S. 137, (1999), and Federal Rule of Evidence 702....

I. FACTUAL AND PROCEDURAL BACKGROUND

This products liability action arises out of a one-vehicle automobile accident which occurred on Interstate 64 in Montgomery County, Kentucky on February 12, 2009. At the time of the accident, James O. Gumm, Jr. was driving a 1994 Chevrolet C2500 pickup truck in the westbound lane when the left rear tire of his truck failed. Gumm lost control of the vehicle, crashed, and was rendered a brain-injured quadriplegic as a result of the accident. This products liability action was subsequently filed by Kim Logan, Gumm's legal guardian, on January 4, 2010 against Cooper Tire, the manufacturer of the failed tire.

The plaintiff intends to call Micky Gilbert as an accident reconstruction expert. While Cooper Tire does not dispute Gilbert's qualifications to reconstruct the accident at issue, it does seek to exclude Gilbert's opinions related to the following: (1) the controllability of the vehicle; (2) the reasonableness of Gumm's actions; and (3) the cause of the accident. According to Cooper Tire, Gilbert's opinions are based on testing of dissimilar, allegedly defective vehicles in turns that are different from the turns made by Gumm in the accident at issue, or on his "observations" when working as a driving instructor giving him a "sense" he has developed about driving behavior. Cooper Tire argues that any opinions based on this testing or his "sense" should be excluded because they are not reliable....

II. RULE 702 AND ... *DAUBERT* AND *KUMHO TIRE*

As amended in 2000, Rule 702 of the Federal Rules of Evidence states the requirements for admissibility of expert testimony:

> If scientific, technical, or other specialized knowledge will assist the trier of fact to understand the evidence or to determine a fact in issue, a witness qualified as an expert by knowledge, skill, experience, training, or education, may testify thereto in the form of an opinion or otherwise, if (1) the testimony is based upon sufficient facts or data, (2) the testimony is the product of reliable principles and methods, and (3) the witness has applied the principles and methods reliably to the facts of the case.

Fed. R. Evid. 702. Generally, this rule "should be broadly interpreted on the basis of whether the use of expert testimony will assist the trier of fact." *Morales v. American Honda Motor Co., Inc.*, 151 F.3d 505, 516 (6th Cir. 1998).

"[U]nder the Rules the trial judge must ensure that any and all scientific testimony or evidence admitted is not only relevant, but reliable." *Daubert v. Merrell Dow Pharms., Inc.*, 509 U.S. 579 (1993). As the Supreme Court stated in *Daubert*:

> Faced with a proffer of expert scientific testimony, then, the trial judge must determine at the outset, pursuant to Rule 104(a), whether the expert is proposing to testify to (1) scientific knowledge that (2) will assist the trier of

fact to understand or determine a fact in issue. This entails a preliminary assessment of whether the reasoning or methodology underlying the testimony is scientifically valid and of whether that reasoning or methodology properly can be applied to the facts at issue.

Id. at 592–93. The proponent of expert testimony must prove by a preponderance of the evidence that the testimony is reliable, not that it is scientifically correct. *Id.* at 593; Fed. R. Evid. 104(a).

In determining whether to admit or exclude proffered expert testimony, the court must act as a "gatekeeper" to ensure that the expert is duly qualified to render an expert opinion, that his testimony will assist the trier of fact, and that the proffered testimony is reliable. *Id.* However, the court's gatekeeper role under *Daubert* "is not intended to supplant the adversary system or the role of the jury." *Allison v. McGhan*, 184 F.3d 1300, 1311 (11th Cir. 1999). Rather, "[v]igorous cross-examination, presentation of contrary evidence, and careful instruction on the burden of proof are the traditional and appropriate means of attacking [debatable] but admissible evidence." *Daubert*, 509 U.S. at 596.

In *Kumho Tire Co. v. Carmichael*, 526 U.S. 137 (1999), the Supreme Court clarified that this "gatekeeper" function applies to all expert testimony, not just scientific testimony. *Id.* at 147 (explaining that Rule 702 makes "no relevant distinction between 'scientific' knowledge and 'technical' or 'other specialized' knowledge …"). The Supreme Court proceeded to provide the district courts with a checklist for assessing the reliability of expert testimony. This list of "specific factors" "neither necessarily nor exclusively applies to all experts or in every case." *Id.* at 141. Listed considerations include whether an expert's theory can be tested, "whether the theory or technique has been subjected to peer review and publication," "the known or potential rate of error," and "general acceptance." *Daubert*, 509 U.S. 593–94. Yet, the "list of factors was meant to be helpful, not definitive" and will vary from case to case. *Kumho Tire*, 526 U.S. at 151. Thus, the trial court must use its discretion in determining whether reasonable criteria of reliability were used by a proffered expert…. Nevertheless, "[t]he Rules' basic standard of relevance … is a liberal one," *Daubert*, 509 U.S. at 587, and the trial court's gatekeeping role does not permit it to reject admissible expert testimony.

In 2000, Rule 702 was amended in response to *Daubert* and cases applying it, such as *Kumho Tire*. It affirms the trial court's role as gatekeeper and provides general standards for the trial court to use to assess the reliability and helpfulness of proffered expert testimony. In fact, the advisory comments to the 2000 amendments to Rule 702 noted that "[a] review of the case law after *Daubert* shows that the rejection of expert testimony is the exception rather than the rule." Advisory Committee Comments to the 2000 Amendments to Rule 702.

III. ANALYSIS

The plaintiff's expert, Micky Gilbert, is a licensed mechanical engineer. There is no dispute that Gilbert is a qualified accident reconstructionist. He has published many peer-reviewed papers focused on traction issues, roll-over events, and yaw stability of vehicles during limit handling maneuvers. He has also taught classes and given presentations on accident reconstruction to attorneys, insurance adjusters, engineers and police officers He has testified numerous times in cases involving tread separation accidents on pickup trucks. As a result, he is qualified to render an opinion in this case.

The Court now turns to whether Gilbert's opinions will assist the trier of fact and whether they are reliable. Gilbert's opinions in this case are based on his inspection of the accident scene and his review of the police report and photographs. Additionally, Gilbert has also relied in part on tread separation testing he has previously conducted on the following vehicles: a 1998 Ford Explorer, a 2001 Mercury Mountaineer, a 1992 Chevy Cavalier, and a 2002 Volvo S80. The objective of this testing was "to measure how the vehicle handles with four good tires; and then second, with—with one failed tire at one corner of the vehicle, and to measure with instruments the difference in handling properties for the vehicle at a limit-type situation." Cooper Tire contends that the Court should exclude Gilbert's opinions based on these tests because the tests involved different vehicles and tires and were not "substantially similar" to the Gumm vehicle or the accident at issue.

However, as the plaintiff points out, Gilbert is not applying these tests as a "simulation" or "recreation" of the accident at issue here. Rather, the results of the test are used by Gilbert to demonstrate "general scientific principles." As a result, there is no requirement that the tests be substantially similar. *Muth v. Ford Motor Co.*, 461 F.3d 557, 566 (5th Cir. 2006) (holding "[w]hen the demonstrative evidence is offered only as an illustration of general scientific principles, not as a reenactment of disputed events, it need not pass the substantial similarity test.").

The fact that the testing did not include a pickup truck or tires the size involved in this accident also does not justify excluding Gilbert's opinions. Gilbert has explained that the difference between a pickup truck and the vehicles tested was irrelevant for the tread separation testing. Moreover, Cooper Tire's own tire expert, Geoff Germane, has agreed that the size of the tires had no effect on the driver's steering input. Any difference between the testing variables and the accident at issue here can be fleshed out during cross examination, but does not justify excluding any of Gilbert's opinions based on these test results.

Nor does the fact that Gilbert has based his opinions on his experience as a driving instructor justify excluding his testimony. As an expert with practical experience, Gilbert is entitled to rely on his experience in his field of driving instruction. In fact, the Advisory Committee Note to Rule 702 provides that if an expert relies on practical experience in the field, "then the witness must explain how that experience leads to the conclusion reached." In his deposition, Gilbert has clearly explained how his years of experience as a driving instructor have given him insight into the typical steering reactions of drivers in emergency situations. Moreover, his opinions are supported by the analysis of relevant evidence, investigation of the accident scene, consultation of peer-reviewed literature on tread separation, and his own testing on multiple vehicle types.

In conclusion, a review of Gilbert's deposition and his expert report reveals he has reviewed the relevant physical evidence, conducted testing on general engineering principles, and reviewed relevant third-party literature and studies. This review, coupled with his practical field experience, fully satisfies the requirements of *Daubert* and Rule 702. Accordingly, Cooper Tire's motion in limine to exclude the testimony of Micky Gilbert is hereby denied.

Notes and Questions

1. In reviewing Officer Foster's testimony, the court makes some general statements about the dividing line between Rule 701 lay opinion and Rule 702 expert opinion testimony. What standards does the court suggest constitute the difference? Are these standards an accurate representation of the dividing line between testimony under 701 and 702?

2. If *Daubert* tells us that "[v]igorous cross-examination, presentation of contrary evidence, and careful instruction on the burden of proof are the traditional and appropriate means of attacking [debatable] but admissible evidence," why not let James Hannah testify in *Mitchell* and then allow the opposing attorney to challenge his methodology?

3. In the *Mitchell* case, the court excludes the expert testimony of James Hannah as unreliable. However, the court in *Logan* finds the expert testimony of Micky Gilbert reliable and denies the motion to exclude. Look very carefully at the methodology of each expert and then compare the methods used to each other. Should both experts be excluded, both admitted, or were the courts right?

Tying It Together

After a serious auto accident occurring in an intersection, plaintiff sued defendant for damages. Following initial discovery, the defense endorsed an accident reconstruction expert and plaintiff decided to depose that expert. We will watch a portion of that deposition, in which plaintiff's counsel asks the defense's expert some questions.

Assignment: As plaintiff's counsel, draft a motion *in limine* to exclude the testimony of the defense expert.

C. Ultimate Issue Constraints on Testimony

Johnoff v. Watson

No. L-03-1245, 2004 WL 2924600
(Ohio Ct. App. Dec. 17, 2004)

PIETRYKOWSKI, Judge.

This case is before the court on appeal from the Lucas County Court of Common Pleas, which entered judgment on a jury verdict in favor of appellee Andrew Watson in this personal injury case. Because we find that the trial court did not err in admitting the expert testimony in question, we affirm the decision of the trial court.

This case involves an accident between a car driven by appellee and a bicycle ridden by appellant Joanne Johnoff. The accident occurred on July 31, 1998, on Fallen Timbers Lane in Lucas County, Ohio. The details of the accident are sketchy because appellant has no memory of it. Aside from appellee and his passenger, there were no eyewitnesses. Even the time of the accident is disputed, but it likely occurred sometime between 9:00 and 9:30 p.m., when it was at least dusk and possibly dark. Three experts testified; two believed that the car and the bike were traveling generally in the same direction at the time of the collision, and the other expert believed that they were traveling in opposite directions. However, the experts agreed that there was an angular collision between the bike and the car, with the bike traveling at some angle into the car's path. The exact angle is disputed. Also disputed is the extent to which appellant and her bike were discernable to appellee and whether he had sufficient time to react to appellant's presence in his path. All agreed that appellee was traveling below the speed limit. Drugs or alcohol were not factors in the accident.

Dennis Gunther, PhD., a mechanical engineer, testified on behalf of appellant. He is an expert in vehicle dynamics, or the "who, the what, the where, the when and the how of an accident on the highway," as he put it. He concluded that the bike and the car were traveling in the same general direction, that the bike was a discernable object to appellee, and that appellee had enough reaction time to avoid the accident.

David Uhrich, PhD., a physicist, testified on behalf of appellee. He is an accident reconstructionist who testified that the car and bike were traveling in opposite directions, that the bike came into the car's path, and that appellee did not have enough reaction time to slow his vehicle to any degree.

Finally, Trooper Gregory Rayot of the Ohio State Patrol testified, both as the officer responding to the scene of the accident and as an accident reconstructionist. Trooper Rayot testified that the car and the bike were traveling in generally the same direction just before the collision but that the car and bike collided at an angle. He considered the possibility that, due to the angle of the impact, the bike could have been making a U-turn when the bike and the car collided. A portion of Trooper Rayot's testimony given on cross-examination is the subject of this appeal. The following exchange took place on cross-examination between defense counsel and Trooper Rayot:

Q: Do you believe Andrew Watson did anything to cause this accident or contribute to this accident?

[**Appellant's counsel**]: Objection, that's what the jury is here for.

[**Appellee's counsel**]: Your Honor, that very question he was allowed to ask his expert this morning. I objected and you overruled it.

THE COURT: I'll allow[] it.

Q: Did Andrew Watson do anything to contribute to cause this accident?

A: No sir."

Following all of the testimony, the jury deliberated and found in favor of appellee. Appellant now appeals, setting forth the following assignment of error:

> The court committed reversible error when it permitted an expert witness to testify to the ultimate issue to be determined by the jury, where such testimony was not essential to the jury's understanding of the issue and the jury was capable of coming to a correct conclusion without it.

A trial court has discretion to admit or exclude evidence during the course of trial, and such a decision will not be reversed absent an abuse of that discretion. *Peters v. Ohio State Lottery Comm.*, 587 N.E.2d 290 (Ohio 1992), *cert. denied*, 506 U.S. 871 (1992). The Supreme Court of Ohio has stated that "[t]he term 'abuse of discretion' connotes more than an error of law or judgment; it implies that the court's attitude is unreasonable, arbitrary or unconscionable." *Blakemore v. Blakemore*, 450 N.E.2d 1140 (Ohio 1983).

Evid. R. 704 provides: "Testimony in the form of an opinion or inference otherwise admissible is not objectionable solely because it embraces an ultimate issue to be decided by the trier of fact."

Three issues are extant in this case: (1) Whether Rayot testified as to the "ultimate issue;" (2) whether the testimony was "otherwise admissible" under Evid. R. 704; and (3) whether admission of the evidence, even if improper, was harmless error.

In the context of jury instructions, the Supreme Court of Ohio has indicated that "ultimate issues" are synonymous with "determinative issues." The court stated,

> [D]eterminative issues are ultimate issues which when decided will definitely settle the entire controversy between or among the parties, so as to leave nothing for the court to do but to enter judgment for the party or parties in whose favor such determinative issues have been resolved by the jury. *Miller v. McAllister*, 160 N.E.2d 231 (Ohio 1959).

Here, it is not clear that the question to Rayot ("Do you believe Andrew Watson did anything to cause this accident or contribute to this accident?") is the ultimate issue. Rayot was testifying in a limited capacity: He is an accident reconstructionist whose opinions were limited to the direction the car and bike were traveling and the point of impact. The manner in which the accident physically happened is just one aspect of this case. Also important to this case is whether appellee should have been able to see appellant before he hit her and whether he should have been able to react to her presence in his path. Rayot neither expressed opinion on these subjects nor claimed to be an expert in this area. Therefore, the case was not resolved simply by having Rayot testify that, from an accident reconstruction standpoint, appellee did nothing to cause the accident. The jury still needed to resolve the other issues: discernability [sic] and reaction time. Therefore, Rayot's conclusion that appellee did nothing from an accident reconstruction point of view to cause the accident did not embrace the ultimate issue. *Compare McQueen v. Goldey*, 484 N.E.2d 712 (Ohio Ct. App. 1984) (trial court did not err in not permitting expert to testify as to ... the "cause of the accident and the percentage of fault of each party.")

Even if the testimony did embrace the ultimate issue, it need not have been excluded if it was "otherwise admissible." Evid. R. 704. Appellant contends that it is not otherwise admissible because it was not helpful to the jury. The Ohio Supreme Court has addressed this issue, holding:

> While testimony on an ultimate issue to be decided by the trier of fact is not *per se* inadmissible in Ohio, it is within the sound discretion of the trial court to refuse to admit the testimony of an expert witness on an ultimate issue where such testimony is not essential to the jury's understanding of the issue and the jury is capable of coming to a correct conclusion without it. *Bostic v. Connor*, 524 N.E.2d 881 (Ohio 1988).

Here the testimony was helpful to the jury. Accident reconstruction is a highly technical area and, after the expert has testified as to the various measurements he or she took and after coming to conclusions about the point of impact, it is helpful to a jury to know "what is all means." In this case, after hearing Rayot's testimony about which direction the bike and car were traveling and possible scenarios about how the bike came to be in the path of the car, it was helpful to the jury to know the import of this testimony. *See Blanton v. Int'l Minerals & Chem. Corp.*, 707 N.E.2d 960 (Ohio Ct. App. 1997) (trial court did not err in admitting expert testimony on an ultimate issue where the testimony helped the jury understand the import of the technical expert testimony). Additionally, since the trial court instructed the jury to give all expert testimony whatever weight the jury thought it deserved, we cannot see how allowing the testimony caused any undue prejudice.... We therefore find that the trial court did not abuse its discretion in admitting Rayot's testimony about whether appellee did anything to cause the accident.

Appellant cites a Butler County Court of Appeals holding that ultimate-issue testimony was impermissibly allowed in a car accident case involving a car and a pedestrian. *See McQueen*, 484 N.E.2d at 712. *McQueen* is distinguishable. The court in *McQueen* testified that the ultimate issues were "who caused the accident and the percentage of fault of each party." *Id.* The court held that the jury was just as qualified as the expert witness (an accident reconstructionist) to determine "whether [defendant] was paying proper attention or going too fast under the circumstances, or whether [plaintiff] was paying proper attention or misjudged the speed and location of the automobile." *Id.* (Defendant's speed was never seriously disputed.) In this case, the testimony was much more technical than whether a party was attentive enough or whether a party's speed was excessive. Trooper Rayot's testimony involved numerous measurements, calculations of angles, examination of dents, scuff marks, and scratches, all to re-create exactly how the accident occurred. Since the expert testimony was much more technical than in *McQueen*, we find that the testimony in question undoubtedly aided the jury.

Even if the testimony was improperly allowed, we find that it was harmless error. Civ.R. 61 provides, in pertinent part:

> No error in either the admission or the exclusion of evidence and no error or defect in any ruling or order or in anything done or omitted by the court

or by any of the parties is ground for granting a new trial or for setting aside a verdict ... or otherwise disturbing a judgment or order, unless refusal to take such action appears to the court inconsistent with substantial justice.

The Ohio Supreme Court has interpreted this rule to mean that an error "does not justify reversal of an otherwise valid adjudication where the error does not affect substantial rights of the complaining party, or the court's action is not inconsistent with substantial justice." *O'Brien v. Angley*, 407 N.E.2d 490 (Ohio 1980). Substantial justice has been done a party despite errors in the proceedings when a reviewing court weighs the errors and concludes that, had the errors not occurred, "the jury or other trier of the facts would probably have made the same conclusion." *O'Brien*, 407 N.E.2d at 490....

In this case, it is undisputed that appellee neither side-swiped nor rear-ended appellant's bicycle, and appellant's bicycle was at some angle into appellee's path of travel at the time of impact. Appellee and his passenger testified that the accident happened in a matter of seconds; appellee testified that the bicycle was perhaps 10 to 15 feet away from him when he first saw it, and he was traveling approximately 30 miles per hour at the time. Appellee's expert, Dr. Uhrich testified that there was insufficient time for appellee to have slowed to any degree before the impact. Appellant's expert, Dr. Gunther, was the only witness to testify that appellee could have avoided this accident. There is no dispute that appellee was traveling well below the speed limit and that drugs or alcohol were not involved. It is also undisputed that, though appellant had a rear reflector on her bike and was wearing an orange shirt, she had no reflectors in the spokes and no headlight. Finally, though there was testimony that appellant customarily rode her bike on the right-hand side of the road near the berm, there was no eyewitness testimony that she did so on the night of the accident. Given the state of the evidence, we conclude that the jury probably would have come to the same conclusion even without Trooper Rayot's testimony that appellee did nothing to contribute to or cause the accident. *See O'Brien*, 407 N.E.2d at 490. Therefore, even if the evidence in question was improperly admitted, it was harmless error. Accordingly, appellants' assignment of error is found not well-taken....

State v. Trahan

637 So. 2d 694 (La. Ct. App. 1994)

WATKINS, Judge.

Shane Trahan was indicted with three counts of vehicular homicide. He pled not guilty and, after trial by jury, was convicted as charged. On each count, the court sentenced him to serve a term of ten years imprisonment at hard labor and to pay a fine of $2,000 and court costs. The court imposed the sentences concurrently and credited defendant with time served. Defendant has appealed....

FACTS

The following facts were revealed at trial. At about 2:30 a.m. on June 16, 1991, Page Comeaux was driving a Buick LeSabre south on Highway 308 in Lafourche Parish. Accompanying her were Jessica Lee (in the middle of the front seat) and Kendalyn Cheramie (on the passenger side of the front seat). As the young women were talking, they saw headlights coming toward them and noticed that an oncoming northbound vehicle had gone off the road onto the shoulder. According to Ms. Cheramie, the vehicle went off the road on its right side, returned to the highway and crossed the centerline, went off the other side of the road, and then returned to the highway and struck the car driven by Ms. Comeaux. Although Ms. Comeaux took evasive actions, she was unable to avoid the accident. As a result of the accident, Ms. Comeaux died instantly and Ms. Lee died about an hour later. Ms. Cheramie survived the accident but suffered serious injuries.

Trooper Gregg Falgout with the Louisiana State Police arrived at the accident scene minutes later. Upon arrival, he saw the Buick LeSabre on fire on the southbound shoulder facing south. The Buick had sustained damage on the driver's side of the front of the vehicle. Another vehicle, a Mazda truck, was facing north on the northbound shoulder with the front of the truck up against a telephone pole. The damage to the truck was on the passenger's side of the front of the truck. Ms. Cheramie and Ms. Lee had already been pulled from the Buick; Trooper Falgout assisted others in trying to remove Ms. Comeaux from the burning car. Trooper Falgout determined that defendant and Petey Mejia had been the occupants of the truck. Defendant was lying about eleven feet from the Buick; Mr. Mejia, with his arm severed, was 111 feet northwest of the Buick. Mr. Mejia's arm was located on the ground about three feet from defendant near the rear quarter panel of the side of the Buick. According to the autopsy report, Mr. Mejia died about six hours after the accident as a result of his injuries.

Sgt. Ralph Mitchell, a fatality/homicide traffic accident investigator with the Louisiana State Police, was accepted by the court as an expert in the field of accident reconstruction. He arrived at the scene shortly after Trooper Falgout and assisted in the investigation. After viewing physical debris and marks on the roadway, Sgt. Mitchell and Trooper Falgout determined that the truck had been traveling northbound when it went completely off the highway in a curve and traveled about 140 or 180 feet on the shoulder. The truck then returned to the roadway, crossed over the centerline, and hit the Buick in the southbound lane approximately 43 feet from the point where the truck reentered the roadway. Sgt. Mitchell explained that the change in the surfaces (from shoulder to highway) and the tendency of people to oversteer to correct a problem resulted in the truck's being steered at a sharp angle across the roadway after it returned to the road, where it then struck the Buick at an angle. Sgt. Mitchell opined that after the impact, the truck started spinning counterclockwise and spun around twice before coming to rest. As a result of the accident, the occupants of the truck were thrown from the vehicle. The Buick rotated counterclockwise before it stopped moving.

The state introduced additional evidence to prove that defendant was operating the truck at the time of the accident and to prove that defendant was under the influence of alcoholic beverages and had a blood alcohol concentration of 0.10 percent or more....

EXPERT TESTIMONY BY SERGEANT MITCHELL

In assignment of error number eight, defendant argues the court erred when it allowed Sgt. Ralph Mitchell, Jr., to testify outside his expertise. In his brief, defendant specifically argues Sgt. Mitchell did not possess the qualifications necessary to be accepted as an expert in the field of accident reconstruction. Defendant also asserts that a portion of Sgt. Mitchell's testimony, wherein he testified that defendant was the driver of the truck and that alcohol was a contributing factor in the accident, violated [Louisiana's Code of Evidence Article] 704, which prohibits an expert in a criminal case from offering an opinion as to the guilt or innocence of the accused. Defendant further contends that the prejudicial effect of Sgt. Mitchell's testimony outweighed the probative value of the evidence and, thus, admission of this testimony violated [Louisiana's Code of Evidence Article] 403.

Initially, we note that, because defendant did not object on the ground that Sgt. Mitchell's qualifications were insufficient, he is barred from raising this issue on appeal. When Sgt. Mitchell was tendered as an expert, defendant objected and argued generally that Sgt. Mitchell's testimony would relate to an ultimate issue to be determined by the jury. However, defendant did not contest Sgt. Mitchell's qualifications. It is well-settled that defense counsel must state the basis for an objection when it is made, pointing out the specific error to the trial court. The grounds for objection must be sufficiently brought to the court's attention to allow it the opportunity to make the proper ruling and prevent or cure any error. Because defendant failed to object to this issue at trial, he cannot urge the issue on appeal. *See State v. LeBlanc*, 618 So. 2d 949, 958–59 (La. Ct. App. 1993). Moreover, Sgt. Mitchell's background as a certified accident reconstruction investigator with several years [of] experience in this field, his education, extensive formal training in accident investigation, position as an instructor in this field, and previous acceptance by other courts as an expert justified the court's acceptance of him as an expert in the field of accident reconstruction. *See State v. Honeyman*, 565 So. 2d 961, 966–67 (La. Ct. App. 1990). This portion of the assignment of error is without merit.

Defendant similarly has waived any objection he might have to Sgt. Mitchell's testimony that he believed alcohol was a contributing factor to the accident. Twice the state asked Sgt. Mitchell if he thought alcohol was a contributing factor in the accident and Sgt. Mitchell responded that alcohol was a contributing factor. However, on neither of these occasions did defendant object; his general objection ... was insufficient to preserve this particular issue. Thus, defendant may not now raise this issue on appeal.

Defendant has preserved the issue he raises concerning Sgt. Mitchell's testimony that defendant was the driver of the truck. On direct examination, Sgt. Mitchell extensively described the various factors he considered as he investigated this accident — damage to the vehicles, markings left at the scene, debris resulting from the accident, and injuries sustained by the occupants of the vehicles. After being asked if he was able to reach any conclusions insofar as the positioning of the occupants of the truck, Sgt. Mitchell twice testified that he concluded that Petey Mejia was the passenger in the truck based on the injuries Mr. Mejia sustained and the type of injuries he would expect the passenger of the truck to have had. When the state asked Sgt. Mitchell if he had drawn any conclusions concerning defendant based on the type of injuries defendant received, defense counsel objected and argued the witness was being asked to give an opinion on the ultimate issue of fact. The court overruled the objection, and Sgt. Mitchell responded, "It is my opinion without a doubt in my mind that Shane Trahan was driving based on the injuries he sustained...." Later, when asked if he had "any doubt" that defendant was the driver, that Petey Mejia was the passenger, or that alcohol was a contributing factor, Sgt. Mitchell responded to each question, "None whatsoever."

Article 704 of the Louisiana Code of Evidence regulates opinion testimony given by experts on an ultimate issue:

> Testimony in the form of an opinion or inference otherwise admissible is not to be excluded solely because it embraces an ultimate issue to be decided by the trier of fact. However, in a criminal case, an expert witness shall not express an opinion as to the guilt or innocence of the accused.

Thus, an expert's opinion in a criminal case is not inadmissible merely because it embraces an ultimate issue to be decided by the jury, except that the expert cannot express an opinion as to the guilt or innocence of the accused. *State v. Parker*, 596 So. 2d 315, 320 (La. Ct. App. 1992).

The comments to article 704 indicate the article "clarifies" prior Louisiana law and is in "harmony" with *State v. Wheeler*, 416 So. 2d 78 (La. 1982), which decision, according to the comments, "should continue to control." In *Wheeler*, the trial court accepted a police officer as an expert in the field of narcotics transactions. The state then presented the expert with a hypothetical set of facts resembling the facts of the case (possession with intent to distribute marijuana) and asked the officer what the likelihood was that the person involved in that hypothetical was involved in the distribution of marijuana. The officer responded that, in his opinion, the person was involved in the distribution of the substance. Finding this testimony "tantamount to an opinion that the defendant was guilty of the crime charged," the Louisiana Supreme Court found error in the court's admission of the evidence and reversed the conviction. 416 So. 2d at 81. In doing so, the court said that variables are present in the principles which guide a trial court in deciding whether or not to admit expert witness testimony and that all of the variables weighed heavily against the admission of expert testimony on such matters as how the case should be decided or as to whether or not a defendant is guilty:

> The evidence is not truly expert testimony because it relates to matters well within the jury's understanding and is wholly without value to the trier of fact in reaching a decision; the inference or opinion is abstract and indirect; and it relates to an ultimate issue rather than a collateral matter. When an objection is raised to the introduction of an expert's opinion or inference, care should be taken by the trial judge to assess the statement in light of each of the foregoing variables.

416 So. 2d at 81. The final sentence of article 704 codifies the position taken by the court in *Wheeler*, that expert testimony concerning whether or not a defendant is guilty is inadmissible.

Consistent with *Wheeler*, the Louisiana Supreme Court has said "it is reversible error for an expert to testify as to an ultimate issue of the defendant's guilt, even when couched in terms of a hypothetical situation." *State v. Code*, 627 So. 2d 1373, 1384 (La. 1993). In *Code*, the court found that article 704 was expressly violated when a fingerprint expert in a first degree murder case testified that he positively believed that palm prints left by the defendant on the victim's bathtub were left when the defendant drowned the victim. The court further found that article 704 was implicitly violated when an expert in fingerprint and crime scene analysis testified that palm prints lifted from the bathtub, which had been matched to the defendant's, were left by the perpetrator of the crime. *Code*, 627 So. 2d at 1384. The Louisiana Supreme Court has repeatedly reversed convictions in drug cases wherein a police officer, qualified as an expert in the field of narcotics transactions, was allowed to give an opinion based upon hypothetical facts resembling the particular case that the defendant intended to distribute the drugs, as opposed to merely possessing them. *See State v. White*, 450 So. 2d 648 (La. 1984); *Wheeler*, 416 So. 2d at 81–82.... Although finding such expert testimony inadmissible, the court has [allowed] ... certain expert testimony which amounts to a recitation of the characteristics of drug dealers....

Applying these principles to the instant case, it is apparent the court erred when it overruled defendant's objection. While it was proper for Sgt. Mitchell to testify concerning the types of injuries typically sustained by occupants of a vehicle damaged in a fashion similar to the truck, it was error to allow Sgt. Mitchell to offer his opinion that defendant was the driver of the truck. On appeal, the state argues the court properly overruled the objection because Sgt. Mitchell did not testify as to all of the elements necessary to find defendant guilty and did not comment on defendant's guilt or innocence. However, this position ignores the approach taken by the Louisiana Supreme Court in the drug cases cited above. In these cases, the court found expert testimony relating to the person's intent to distribute to be an expression of the defendant's guilt even though other elements also were required (i.e., the defendant's identity as the perpetrator and proof the substance was a controlled dangerous substance). Considering that defendant's main defense in the instant case was that he was not the driver, Sgt. Mitchell's testimony was tantamount to an opinion that defendant was guilty. *See Wheeler*, 416 So. 2d at 81.

Finding error under article 704, however, does not end our analysis. In *Code*, the Louisiana Supreme Court held that error resulting from the improper admission of an expert's opinion concerning the ultimate issue of a defendant's guilt is subject to a harmless error analysis. 627 So. 2d at 1384. The court then said that the proper analysis for determining harmless error in such a situation is "not whether, in a trial that occurred without the error, a guilty verdict would surely have been rendered, but whether the guilty verdict actually rendered in *this* trial was surely unattributable to the error." 627 So. 2d at 1384 (quoting *Sullivan v. Louisiana*, 508 U.S. 275, 279 (1993))....

After discussing ... harmless error standards, the Louisiana Supreme Court then found that, under either analysis, the error in admitting the expert testimony (that the defendant had left his palm prints on the bathtub when he drowned the victim) was harmless. In doing so, the court considered the following factors: five expert witnesses testified that the palm prints recovered from the bathtub matched the defendant's prints and were left on the recently cleaned bathtub near the time of the murder; the expert testimony made clear the prints were inconsistent with those that would be left as someone got in or out of the bathtub; expert testimony established the prints were in such a position that they could only have been left by someone who held the victim over the bathtub, and the position of the victim's body supported this conclusion; extensive evidence showed the defendant had never rented the victim's house and had never worked there as a plumber. The court instructed the jury that it alone, and not the experts, was to determine the ultimate issues and that it could accept or reject the testimony of the experts.

Under ... the harmless error standards discussed in *Code*, the record of the instant case shows the error at issue here, as in *Code*, was "unmistakably harmless." 627 So. 2d at 1385. Sgt. Mitchell explained that, at the time of an accident, occupants of a vehicle continue moving in the same direction. Because the truck rotated counterclockwise after impact, the occupants of the truck, by continuing to move forward, moved to the right side of the truck. Sgt. Mitchell explained the types of injuries he would expect the occupants to have suffered, based upon the physical damage to the truck. The damage to the truck is evident in the enlarged photographs introduced by the state, which show that the main damage occurred at the front of the truck on the passenger side. The doctor who performed the autopsy on Petey Mejia testified that, as a result of his examination, he determined that the impact Mr. Mejia received on his right side was of sufficient force to cause serious internal bleeding, broken ribs, and a dislocated collarbone. In the final instructions to the jury, the court told the jurors that they "are the sole judges of the law and the facts on the question of guilt or innocence" and that they should give an expert's opinion such weight as they thought it deserves and could disregard the opinion "entirely."

Considering the admissible evidence concerning the damage to the truck and the manner in which the accident occurred, no rational juror could find those facts without also finding the ultimate fact of defendant's guilt. As in *Code*, "[i]t is beyond doubt the guilty verdict in this case was unattributable to the erroneous testimony." 627 So. 2d at 1385....

Notes and Questions

1. In *Johnoff*, the court considers the prior precedent of *McQueen v. Goldey*, 484 N.E.2d 712 (Ohio Ct. App. 1984). In *McQueen*, the expert would have testified as to the "cause of the accident and the percentage of fault of each party," but the trial court excluded the testimony under Rule 704. Yet in the *Johnoff* case, when Trooper Gregory Rayot was asked, "Did Andrew Watson do anything to contribute to cause this accident?" and he responded, "No sir," the court permitted the testimony. How did the court distinguish *McQueen*? Was Judge Pietrykowski's argument persuasive?

2. In *Johnoff*, the court permitted Trooper Rayot to testify that Watson did not contribute to the accident, while in *Trahan*, the court excluded Sgt. Mitchell's testimony—that Trahan was the driver and alcohol contributed to the accident—for violating Rule 704. When we consider the two cases together, the testimony seems quite similar. Did the courts get these cases right? More precisely, is there a factual distinction between them justifying the different results or did one of the courts err?

3. Even if the expert testimony of Sgt. Mitchell in *Trahan* was erroneously admitted, the court found the error harmless and sustains the conviction. What argument could the defense have made that the testimony cannot be harmless? Considering our assessment of Federal Rule of Evidence 704, is that argument persuasive? If so, why did the court disagree? If not, then consider the *Code* case contained within *Trahan*. In that case, the fingerprint expert testified that the Defendant left the hand print on the tub when he committed the crime. What argument can the defense make that this expert testimony cannot be harmless? Considering our assessment of Federal Rule of Evidence 704, is that argument persuasive? If so, then why did the *Code* opinion find otherwise? If the defense is not persuasive, then has Louisiana redefined the harmless error standard of *Sullivan*, 508 U.S. at 279 (holding whether "the guilty verdict actually rendered in this trial was surely unattributable to the error")?

Tying It Together

Sam Davidson was running late that morning, so he was taking a few chances he normally would not take to get to work. As he took the Highway 30 exit off of Interstate 9, the ramp curved to merge with the traffic already traveling on the highway. Failing to check his rear- and side-view mirrors in his haste, Sam entered the right lane of traffic on Highway 30 and was immediately struck by a truck driven by Paula Prince. The impact caused both cars to careen off the highway and down the shoulder embankment, coming to a rest near a containment pond. While Sam was uninjured, Paula had not been wearing her seatbelt and broke several bones due to the initial impact and subsequent motion.

Immediately after the accident, Wendy Wilson of the Polk State Police arrived as a specialist in accident reconstruction. She took measurements of the intersection and of the damage to the cars, photographed the cars, skid marks on the road, and car damage, and spoke to the drivers and a few other witnesses who stopped to assist the injured. Based on all this information, Wilson concluded that Davidson failed to yield the right of way at the on-ramp from I-9 to Highway 30, causing Prince to strike his car and leading to a spinout. In the State of Polk, "Failure to Yield" is a traffic offense, defined by statute as follows:

> The driver of a vehicle approaching a yield sign shall slow to a speed reasonable for the existing conditions and, if required for safety, shall stop at the first opportunity at either the clearly marked stop line or before entering the crosswalk or before entering the intersection or at the point nearest the intersecting

roadway where the driver has a view of approaching traffic on the intersecting roadway. After slowing or stopping, the driver shall yield the right-of-way to any vehicle on the intersecting roadway which has entered the intersection or which is approaching so closely as to constitute an immediate hazard during the time the driver is moving across or within the intersection.

Since Failure to Yield is only an infraction, the State Police never bother to charge Davidson with the offense.

Prince decides to retain Getta, Lotta, & Dough to represent her, and she files a personal injury suit against Davidson based on the collision. To support her theory of the case, Prince calls Wilson at trial as her accident reconstruction expert. Wilson then testifies to her extensive credentials in the field and her opinion that Davidson caused the accident by failing to yield to Prince's truck when merging from the ramp. The defense objects to this testimony, but the trial court overrules the objection. The jury finds in favor of Prince.

On appeal, Davidson claims that the trial court erred in overruling his objection to Wilson's testimony and seeks a new trial.

Assignment: You have been assigned to the *Prince v. Davidson* case as a new associate at Getta, Lotta, & Dough. Draft Prince's response motion to Davidson's appeal brief.

Chapter 10

Economic Damages Valuation

In the vast majority of civil lawsuits—whether based on contract, patent, or tort—the ultimate remedy hinges on the question of monetary damages. As we shift away from the causes of action and supporting evidence for a finding of liability, we need to consider the types of expert evidence presented on economic and non-economic losses in civil cases. Our primary focus will be on tort losses, considering our exposure to these types of actions in previous chapters. However, note that many of these considerations can be transferred to other fields as well. Because the issues in damages valuation appear in nearly every civil case, newer attorneys or associates in civil litigation firms often receive their first expert assignments in this subject area. This is often problematic due to the mathematical illiteracy common among lawyers (students taking this class excepted, of course). In light of these considerations, it is imperative to examine the fundamentals of damages valuation and break down the constituent parts.

We will begin with an overview of the categories of damages available and how they differ for different causes of action. After this brief detour, we will quickly turn to damages calculations in the types of cases we discussed in Chapters 8 and 9, namely tort actions resulting in injury or death. Many different factors enter the equation on economic damages in a tort action. Thus, we will break this analysis down to individual components and see what each means and how it is calculated. We will then look at non-economic damages claims, evaluating what can and cannot be considered and how these damages have been statutorily limited in many states. Finally, we will shift over to a discussion of business valuation and the various methods of determining what a publicly or privately held company is worth. As with the chapters on specific areas of expertise, the focus here is not on being able to personally perform a complete damages valuation. Instead, the objective is to identify the components of various damages calculations and how experts can alter or manipulate the calculations by adopting different underlying assumptions.

Mark A. Allen, Robert E. Hall, and Victoria A. Lazear, *Reference Guide on Estimation of Economic Damages*
REFERENCE MANUAL ON SCIENTIFIC EVIDENCE 429–37 (3d ed. 2011)[Ed.]

I. Introduction

This reference guide identifies areas of dispute that arise when economic losses are at issue in a legal proceeding. Our focus is on explaining the issues in these disputes

---

[Ed.] Reprinted with permission from the National Academy of Sciences, Courtesy of the National Academies Press, Washington, D.C.

rather than taking positions on their proper resolutions. We discuss the application of economic analysis within established legal frameworks for damages. We cover topics in economics that arise in measuring damages and provide citations to cases to illustrate the principles and techniques discussed in the text.

We begin by discussing the qualifications required of experts who quantify damages. We then set forth the standard general approach to damages quantification, with particular focus on defining the harmful event and the alternative, often called the but-for scenario. In principle, the difference between the plaintiff's economic value in the but-for scenario and in actuality measures the loss caused by the harmful act of the defendant. We then consider damages estimation for two cases: (1) a discrete loss of market value and (2) the loss of a flow of income over time, where damages are the discounted value of the lost cash flow. Other topics include the role of inflation, issues relating to income taxes and stock options, adjustments for the time value of money, legal limitations on damages, damages for a new business, disaggregation of damages when there are multiple challenged acts, the role of random events occurring between the harmful act and trial, data for damages measurement, standards for disclosing data to opposing parties, special masters and neutral experts, liquidated damages, damages in class actions, and lost earnings.

Our discussion follows the structure of the standard damages study, as shown in Figure 1. Damages quantification operates on the premise that the defendant is liable for damages from the defendant's harmful act. The plaintiff is entitled to recover monetary damages for losses occurring before and possibly after the time of the trial. The top line of Figure 1 measures the losses before trial; the bottom line measures the losses after trial.[2]

Figure 1: Standard Format for a Damages Study[Ed.]

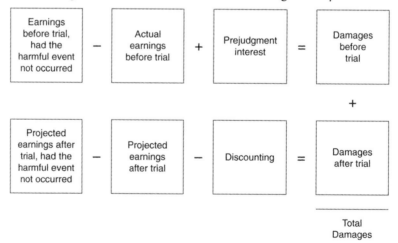

----

2. Our scope here is limited to losses of actual dollar income. However, economists sometimes have a role in the measurement of nondollar damages, including pain and suffering and the hedonic value of life. *See generally* W. KIP VISCUSI, REFORMING PRODUCTS LIABILITY (1991).

[Ed.] Figure 1 has been moved within the text by the Author for clarity purposes.

The goal of damages measurement is to find the plaintiff's loss of economic value from the defendant's harmful act. The loss of value may have a one-time character, such as the diminished market value of a business or property, or it may take the form of a reduced stream of profit or earnings. The losses are net of any costs avoided because of the harmful act.

The essential elements of a study of losses are the quantification of the reduction in economic value, the calculation of interest on past losses, and the application of financial discounting to future losses. The losses are the difference between the value the plaintiff would have received if the harmful event had not occurred and the value the plaintiff has or will receive, given the harmful event. The plaintiff may be entitled to interest for losses occurring before trial. Losses occurring after trial are usually discounted to the time of trial. The plaintiff may be due interest on the judgment from the time of trial to the time the defendant actually pays. The majority of damages studies fit this format; thus, we have used such a format as the basic model for this reference guide.

We use numerous brief examples to explain the disputes that can arise. These examples are not full case descriptions; they are deliberately stylized. They attempt to capture the types of disagreements about damages that arise in practical experience, although they are purely hypothetical. In many examples, the dispute involves factual as well as legal issues. We do not try to resolve the disputes in these examples and hope that the examples will help clarify the legal and factual disputes that need to be resolved before or at trial. We introduce many areas of potential dispute with a question, because asking the parties these questions can identify and clarify the majority of disputes over economic damages....

III. The Standard General Approach to Quantification of Damages

In this section, we review the elements of the standard loss measurement in the format of Figure 1. For each element, there are several areas of potential dispute. The sequence of issues discussed here should identify most of the areas of disagreement between the damages analyses of opposing parties.

A. *Isolating the Effect of the Harmful Act*

The first step in a damages study is the translation of the legal theory of the harmful event into an analysis of the economic impact of that event. In most cases, the analysis considers the difference between the plaintiff's economic position if the harmful event had not occurred and the plaintiff's actual economic position.

In almost all cases, the damages expert proceeds on the hypothesis that the defendant committed the harmful act and that the act was unlawful. Accordingly, throughout this discussion, we assume that the plaintiff is entitled to compensation for losses sustained from a harmful act of the defendant. The characterization of the harmful event begins with a clear statement of what occurred. The characterization also will include a description of the defendant's proper actions in place of its unlawful actions and a statement about the economic situation absent the wrongdoing, with the defendant's proper actions replacing the unlawful ones (the but-for scenario).

Damages measurement then determines the plaintiff's hypothetical value in the but-for scenario. Economic damages are the difference between that value and the actual value that the plaintiff achieved.

Because the but-for scenario differs from what actually happened only with respect to the harmful act, damages measured in this way isolate the loss of value caused by the harmful act and exclude any change in the plaintiff's value arising from other sources. Thus, a proper construction of the but-for scenario and measurement of the hypothetical but-for plaintiff's value by definition includes in damages only the loss caused by the harmful act. The damages expert using the but-for approach does not usually testify separately about the causal relation between damages and the harmful act, although variations may occur where there are issues about the directness of the causal link.

B. *The Damages Quantum Prescribed by Law*

In most cases, the law prescribes a damages measure that falls into one of the following five categories:

- **Expectation:** Plaintiff restored to the same financial position as if the defendant had performed as promised.

- **Reliance:** Plaintiff restored to the same position as if the relationship with the defendant or the defendant's misrepresentation (and resulting harm) had not existed in the first place.

- **Restitution:** Plaintiff compensated by the amount of the defendant's gain from the unlawful conduct, also called compensation for unjust enrichment, disgorgement of ill-gotten gains, or compensation for unbargained-for benefits.

- **Statutory:** Plaintiff's compensation is a set amount per occurrence of wrongdoing. This occurs in cases involving violations of state labor codes and in copyright infringement.

- **Punitive:** Compensation rewards the plaintiff for detecting and prosecuting wrongdoing to deter similar future wrongdoing.

Expectation damages often apply to breach of contract claims, where the wrongdoing is the failure to perform as promised, and the but-for scenario hypothesizes the absence of that wrongdoing, that is, proper performance by the defendant. Expectation damages are an amount sufficient to give the plaintiff the same economic value the plaintiff would have received if the defendant had fulfilled the promise or bargain

Reliance damages generally apply to torts and to some contract breaches. Such damages restore the plaintiff to the same financial position it would have enjoyed absent the defendant's conduct as well as, in the case of torts, compensation for nonpecuniary losses such as pain and suffering. Reliance most often includes out-of-pocket costs, but may also include compensation for lost opportunities, when appropriate. In such cases, reliance damages may approach expectation damages. For a tort, reliance damages place the plaintiff in a position economically equivalent to the position absent the harmful act.[10] For a breach of contract, measuring damages as the amount of compensation needed to place the plaintiff in the same position as if the contract had not been made in the first place will result in refunding the part of the plaintiff's reliance investment that cannot be recovered in other ways. Thus, reliance damages may be appropriate when the plaintiff made an investment relying on the defendant's performance ...

Restitution damages[13] are often the same, from the perspective of quantification, as reliance damages. If the only loss to the plaintiff from the defendant's harmful act arises from an expenditure that the plaintiff made that cannot otherwise be recovered, the plaintiff receives compensation equal to the amount of that expenditure.

Interesting and often difficult issues arise in cases that involve elements of both contract and tort. Consider a contract for a product that turns out to be defective. Generally, under what has become known as the economic loss rule, if the defective product only causes economic or commercial loss, the dispute is a private matter between the parties, and the contract will likely control their dispute. But if the product causes personal injury or property damage (other than to the product itself), then tort law and tort damages will likely control.

Fraud actions can present particularly difficult problems. For example, if the claim is that the defendant fraudulently induced the plaintiff to enter into an agreement that caused purely commercial losses, the economic loss rule may apply to limit the plaintiff's recovery to only commercial losses for breach of contract, and thus not allow recovery of additional damages recoverable under fraud, such as punitive damages....

Plaintiffs cannot normally seek punitive damages in a claim for breach of contract, but may seek them in addition to compensatory damages in connection with a tort claim. Although punitive damages are rarely the subject of expert testimony, economists have advanced the concept that punitive damages compensate a plaintiff who brings a case for a wrongdoing that is hard to detect or hard to prosecute....

In some situations, the plaintiff may have a choice of remedies under different legal theories. For example, in determining damages for fraud in connection with a contract, damages may be awarded under tort law for deceit or under contract law for breach....

---

10. *See, e.g.*, E. River S.S. Corp. v. Transamerica Delaval Inc., 476 U.S. 858, 873 n.9 (1986) ("tort damages generally compensate the plaintiff for loss and return him to the position he occupied before the injury")....

13. The objective of restitution damages is to put the *promisor* or breaching party back in the position in which it would have been had the promise not been made. Note the traditional legal distinction between restitution and reliance damages: Reliance damages seek to put the *promisee* or nonbreaching party back in the position in which it would have been if the promise had not been made....

Frank D. Tinari, *An Introduction to the Field of Forensic Economics*

FORENSIC ECONOMICS: ASSESSING PERSONAL DAMAGES IN
CIVIL LITIGATION 4–7 (2016)

... Let us first consider personal litigation.

The process by which the expert arrives at an opinion of loss is not particularly complicated. But it does require careful consideration of various facts and assumptions that touch upon every aspect of the expert's work. For example, had an alleged incident not occurred, the analyst would need to determine what would have been the likely annual earnings in subsequent years. If the plaintiff's earnings history over the past five years were provided, would it be appropriate for the analyst to average the five values to establish a reasonable base earnings as the foundation for projecting future years' earnings? Or would it be better to use the preceding two or three years? If there had been a dip in the earnings rate in the second and third years, but the dip had occurred during a recession, how would the analyst treat these values for purposes of making projections? Alternatively, the earnings history may have exhibited annual increases, year after year, for the past five years. In that case, taking an average of past, lower-earnings years would likely yield an unwarranted lower figure.

Another possible complication would involve projecting earnings for a person with no track record of past earnings, such as a student, who has been injured. In such cases, the analyst must project expected earnings or the earnings capacity of the individual. This generally entails consideration of the individual's potential educational attainment, the person's grade-point average, the educational attainment of the person's parents, and other related factors....

Given this brief sketch of the issues involved in determining a reasonable figure for projecting future earnings, it must be reiterated that the forensic economics methodology, though not complicated, requires consideration of numerous elements of each particular case. Choices must be made by the analyst at nearly every turn. Assumptions are unavoidable. And, over time, as knowledge expands, the expert's assumptions may change to reflect current research and statistical sources....

However, all of this rests on a basic, underlying approach used in every analysis. The FE is being asked to create a picture of what would have occurred absent the injury or incident. This is often referred to as the "but for" scenario. In other words, the analyst must examine the available information, consider relevant microeconomic and macroeconomic forces that might have a bearing on the case, make assumptions regarding numerical values needed for projecting future values, undertake research related to the assumptions, and carefully make the calculations necessary to arrive at an opinion of economic loss. The economic loss opinion represents what *most likely would have occurred* but for the incident. It is an alternative universe, but one grounded as best as possible on known facts and known economic and statistical trends....

... [A] related question involves determining the number of years over which such losses would likely occur. When would the individual have retired? During the entire time period until retirement, would the individual have been in the labor force every month and every year? ... Further, even when a person participates in the labor force, would there likely have occurred periods of layoffs or unemployment that would have adversely impacted annual earnings?

These important questions, and others like them, have led to the development of an extensive literature in forensic economics. Several academic journals regularly publish research related to the questions encountered by FEs. Two well-regarded publications, among others, are the *Journal of Forensic Economics* and the *Journal of Legal Economics*, published, respectively, by [the National Association of Forensic Economists] and the American Academy of Economic and Financial Experts. In their pages over the past three decades may be found articles about numerous topics including studies of statistical years to retirement and worklife expectancy. Many of the statistical-based articles rely on US government data and, as such, have been accepted by state and federal courts in civil litigation.

Because the research in forensic economics covers a wide variety of topics touching on all aspects of the calculation of economic losses, there is no single "theory" that underpins forensic economics. Rather, FEs use theories and methods based on numerous microeconomic and macroeconomic foundations. Publishers of the *Journal of Economic Literature* classify the sub-field of forensic economics within the broad Law and Economics category. Other sub-fields such as antitrust, environmental, health, sports, and many other economics specialties are assigned separate classification categories. And like these others, forensic economics dips into labor economics, statistics, and welfare analysis, to name a few. In some unusual situations, economists may venture into environmental economics, foreign exchange rate theory, and even international cost-of-living differences.

And, as in other sub-fields in economics, there are several unresolved or disputed findings. What is the best source or basis for determining a discount rate? Or, for a person who has lost a job due to discrimination, for how many subsequent years will the losses likely persist? What are the accepted methods for measuring the value of non-cash compensation such as the value of a medical insurance policy? For an injured person who takes twice as long to do household chores, should the additional hours be valued at the person's occupational wage rate, or at the cost of hiring someone to do the chores? The list could go on.

In addition to published articles, FEs also make use of data directly available from US government agencies such as the rich data sets on life expectancy, earnings by age, and unemployment statistics. Thus, for example, if the analyst determines that a particular element of damages would extend over the remaining life expectancy of the individual, then the analyst would rely on relevant life expectancy data for that calculation.

Once an earnings base is established, the analyst needs to determine what rate of growth would apply to annual earnings. Would it be a fixed growth rate over the entire remaining period of loss? Would the rate change over time due to specific assumed reasons? Again, research may have to be undertaken to support the analyst's earnings growth rate assumptions. Is there a union contract governing the person's wages? Are local, state, or national economic trends most applicable to the person's likely earnings trajectory?

Then there is consideration of non-cash forms of compensation such as employer-funded retirement plans and medical insurance policies. Employment contracts may have to be reviewed, and knowledge of the employee's contribution, if any, toward these benefits would have to be obtained. What if the medical insurance plan covered the injured party's family members, and would change once the children emancipated—how would the analyst value the changing nature of the medical insurance coverage?

In some state and federal jurisdictions, the loss of earnings must be reduced by likely amounts of federal and state income taxes. Consequently, the FE must determine the tax rates that would likely have been imposed on the person's future earnings. There is some debate within the profession about the scope of taxes to consider. One position is that Social Security taxes ("contributions") should also be incorporated while an opposing position says that they should not be viewed strictly as "income taxes."...

When analyzing losses in a wrongful death case, there is the added element of the extent to which the decedent devoted part of his or her income for personal use and that, consequently, would not have been available to surviving family members. The analyst would need to determine the magnitude of such personal expenses and subtract them from projected earnings. The literature contains many articles regarding not only the measurement of personal consumption or personal maintenance but also whether or not the subtraction should be made from total household income, or solely from the decedent's own earnings....

A. Personal Valuation

In the above excerpt, Tinari makes clear that any calculation of economic damages will include multiple separate inputs, each independently calculated using certain assumptions based on available data sources. As we consider economic damages calculations, we will now discuss several (but not all) of these inputs, focusing on the major issues likely to arise in a tort or wrongful death case. Practicing attorneys will attest that there is no one way to perform these calculations and that seasoned economists will often change their approach to meet the circumstances of each individual case. Understanding what components enter an economist's calculation will allow a savvy attorney to recognize when these changes have been made. Hopefully, attorneys in this situation will be able to provide insight into whether the changes are appropriate and which are unwarranted.

Finally, we will finish with noneconomic damages calculations. This will entail an examination of the component factors that create noneconomic claims and how they differ from economic loss valuations. As always, an attorney must pay close attention to the underlying assumptions of the expert's calculation to understand how the calculation can lead to divergent results.

i. The Lost Wage Component of Economic Damages

Johnson v. Walden University, Inc.

No. 3:08CV00045, 2012 WL 2087414
(D. Conn. June 8, 2012)

Squatrito, District Judge.

The Plaintiff, Greg V. Johnson brings this diversity action against the Defendant Walden University, Inc., raising claims of fraudulent misrepresentation, negligent misrepresentation … breach of implied contract, promissory estoppel, and breach of implied covenant of good faith and fair dealing. Now pending before the court is Walden's motion to exclude the expert testimony of Brett Steinberg, Ph.D.….

BACKGROUND

Johnson's claims all relate to his allegations that representations made by … Walden led Johnson to believe that he could become a practicing psychologist … by obtaining from Walden a doctorate degree in psychology with a specialization in health psychology. After Johnson had received his doctorate … from Walden, he was informed by an agent of the State of Connecticut that he would not be permitted to sit for Connecticut's psychology licensing examination because Walden lacked the necessary accreditation. Without a license to practice psychology issued by the State of Connecticut, Johnson cannot practice psychology in Connecticut.

Johnson has disclosed Brett Steinberg, Ph.D. as an expert witness.… Dr. Steinberg's report also offers his opinions on Johnson's lost income based upon his inability to practice as a psychologist in general and, more specifically, as a psychologist in private practice. Walden moves to exclude these opinions for the reasons that Dr. Steinberg is not qualified to provide an expert opinion on Johnson's earning potential as a practicing psychologist and that there is no proper factual basis for the opinion on lost income as a psychologist in private practice.

STANDARD

… "District courts have a 'gatekeeping' role under Federal Rule of Evidence 702 and are charged with the task of ensuring that an expert's testimony both rests on a reliable foundation and is relevant to the task at hand." … In order to satisfy the requirements of Rule 702, "the proffered testimony must 'fit' the factual dispute at issue—in other words, it must be 'sufficiently tied to the facts of the case that it will aid the jury in resolving a factual dispute.'" *In re Rezulin Prods. Liab. Litig.*, 441 F. Supp. 2d 567, 576 (S.D.N.Y. 2006) (quoting *Daubert v. Merrell Dow Pharms., Inc.*, 509 U.S. 579, 591 (1993)).…

Lost Income

Expert testimony must be presented by "a witness qualified as an expert by knowledge, skill, experience, training, or education.…" Fed. R. Evid. 702. Walden contends that Dr. Steinberg is not qualified to offer expert testimony on Johnson's earning potential. Walden further contends that Dr. Steinberg's opinion as to Johnson's lost income based on his inability to practice as a psychologist in private practice lacks a proper factual basis. Johnson argues that Dr. Steinberg's "extensive and long-standing experience as a clinical psychologist" and "extensive and long-standing contacts within the psychological community" qualify him "to apply reliable data concerning the compensation earned by practicing psychologists to the facts of the case."

"A witness's qualifications can only be determined by comparing the areas in which the witness has superior knowledge, skill, experience, or education with the subject matter of the witness's testimony." *In re Fosamax Prods. Liab. Litig.*, 645 F. Supp. 2d 164, 172 (S.D.N.Y. 2009). The "subject matter of the witness's testimony" at issue is Johnson's earning potential as a practicing psychologist. Dr. Steinberg clearly has "superior skill, experience, or education" with respect to certain areas of the practice of psychology. Dr. Steinberg testified at his deposition that "the core strongest expertise that I have ... would be as a forensic neuropsychologist, the diagnosis and treatment of emotional disorders and potential brain dysfunction in clinical patients ... and applying that knowledge in both clinical settings and forensic contexts." He also testified, however, that he has no expertise in income tax issues, employee benefits, mathematics, economics, accounting, or present value calculations. Dr. Steinberg's opinions relating to lost income are based entirely on his review of the results of a survey of members' salaries conducted by the American Psychological Association ("APA") in 2007. Apart from "very informal ... conversations with colleagues," Dr. Steinberg himself has never done any independent research or analysis into the salaries of psychologists.

The Court recognizes that "[q]ualification as an expert is viewed liberally and may be based on a broad range of knowledge, skills, and training." *In re Fosamax Prods. Liab. Litig.*, 645 F. Supp. 2d at 172. However, "[t]he Rules [of Evidence] recognize that there is some limit to every expert's expertise and that he cannot be allowed to go beyond it. For example, no medical doctor is automatically an expert in every medical issue merely because he or she has graduated from medical school or has achieved certification in a medical specialty." *O'Conner v. Commonwealth Edison Co.*, 807 F. Supp. 1376, 1390 (C.D. Ill. 1992). The Court's acceptance of Dr. Steinberg as an expert qualified to testify on the issue of Johnson's lost income would be tantamount to a determination that any and every practicing psychologist who has read an APA salary survey is, solely on that basis, qualified to present expert testimony as to the lost income of someone who has been prevented from practicing psychology. The Court does not find such a sweeping determination to be consistent with its function of "ensur[ing] that the expert will actually be testifying on issues or subject matter[s] within his or her area of expertise." *Arista Records LLC v. Lime Group LLC*, No. 06 CV 5936(KMW), 2011 WL 1641978 (S.D.N.Y. Apr. 29, 2011).

Even if the Court found Dr. Steinberg qualified as an expert on the issue of lost income, the question would remain as to "whether the proffered testimony has a sufficiently 'reliable foundation' to permit it to be considered." *Campbell v. Metro. Prop. & Cas. Ins. Co.*, 239 F.3d 179, 184 (2d Cir. 2001) (quoting *Daubert*, 509 U.S. at 597). While the inquiry into the reliability of expert testimony is a flexible one, "the district court should undertake a rigorous examination of the facts on which the expert relies, the method by which the expert draws an opinion from those facts, and how the expert applies the facts and methods to the case at hand." *Amorgianos v. Amtrak*, 303 F.3d 256, 267 (2d Cir. 2002).

As mentioned above, Dr. Steinberg's opinion as to lost income is based entirely on his review of a 2007 APA salary survey. At his deposition, Dr. Steinberg testified that he didn't know who had authored the survey, had no way of verifying that the report is accurately reflecting the information collected by the APA, and didn't respond to the survey himself. In his brief opposing Walden's motion to exclude, Johnson argues that the APA survey data is "methodical and highly reliable...." In support of that argument, Johnson represents that Dr. Steinberg testified at his deposition that "[b]ecause the American Psychological Association is the organization for practicing psychologists ... the vast majority of [practicing psychologists] are members of the APA." In fact, Dr. Steinberg testified at his deposition that "I don't have any specific numerical percentage [of psychologists in the United States who are members of the APA].... Because the American Psychological Association is the organization for practicing psychologists, *I would assume* that the vast majority of people are members of the APA. It appears from the Introduction section of the 2007 APA salary survey that approximately 52,000 individuals "were eligible for inclusion in the study," and approximately 13,000 individuals "responded to the survey either through the web or the paper version." Johnson has not established that "the proffered testimony has a sufficiently reliable foundation to permit it to be considered." *Campbell*, 239 F.3d at 184. On the basis of the evidence before it, the Court finds "that there is simply too great an analytical gap between the data and the opinion proffered." *Gen. Elec. Co. v. Joiner*, 522 U.S. 136, 146 (1997).

"The party seeking to rely on expert testimony bears the burden of establishing, by a preponderance of the evidence, that all requirements have been met." *Arista Records*, 2011 WL 1641978 (citing *Daubert*, 509 U.S. at 593 n.10). The Court concludes that in addition to not establishing that Dr. Steinberg is qualified to testify on the issue of lost income, Johnson has also not met his burden of establishing the reliability of the testimony proffered on that issue.

Vincent v. American Honda Motor Co.

No. CV 108-067, 2010 WL 11537725
(S.D. Ga. Feb. 4, 2010)

BOWEN, District Judge.

I. FACTUAL BACKGROUND

This is a products liability case involving the 1999 Honda Accord Coupe. Plaintiff was the passenger in a car of that make and model when he was involved in an accident that left him a quadriplegic. He alleges that the Honda Accord Coupe was defective because it was designed with neither an electronic stability control, nor vehicle stability assist system, and that this omission caused the accident and his resulting injuries.

Plaintiff testified that at the time of the accident, he was self-employed as a trim carpenter, trimming houses. Plaintiff dropped out of school in the ninth grade, and according to Dr. Coston, had no plans for further education. After dropping out of school, Plaintiff worked in various roles, including at lumber yards and bowling alleys, and eventually ended up working as a self-employed carpenter.

Dr. Coston, a retired economics professor from Georgia State University, was retained by Plaintiff to provide a lost earnings analysis.[1] When Dr. Coston contracts to be an expert in a case, he asks the hiring attorney or the attorney's client to fill out an information sheet that he created. The information sheet lists, among other things, the individual's birth date, educational background, and income history. Regarding income, it asks for five years of "income history" as well as W-2s and tax records

In this case, Plaintiff's counsel completed the information sheet and filled in the income history, but did not provide any pertinent documentation of Plaintiff's prior earning history. Dr. Coston testified that the only information he knew about Plaintiff's income history was "the information supplied to [him] on that form."

Based on this information, Dr. Coston assumed that Plaintiff would earn twenty (20) dollars per hour, forty (40) hours per week, fifty (50) weeks per year for the remainder of his working life. For base income, Dr. Coston assumed that Plaintiff's gross earnings would be $45,000 per year for the remainder of his working life. Dr. Coston then adjusted this amount for inflation and discounted the total to present value. Additionally, based upon the information provided by Plaintiff's counsel, Dr. Coston assumed that Plaintiff would earn an additional two hundred (200) dollars per day for weekend "side jobs," for a total supplemental income of $4,800 per year, which he also adjusted for inflation and discounted to present value. In total, Dr. Coston projected that Plaintiff will earn just short of $50,000 per year, as adjusted, for the remainder of his work life. Based on this projection, Dr. Coston estimates Plaintiff's lost earnings at $1,927,035.13.

Defendant argues that ... Dr. Coston's opinions regarding Plaintiff's lost earnings should be excluded as speculative and without foundation.

II. ANALYSIS

In *Daubert v. Merrell Dow Pharmaceuticals, Inc.*, 509 U.S. 579 (1993), the Supreme Court charged trial judges with the responsibility of acting as gatekeepers to exclude unreliable expert testimony. This obligation extends to all expert testimony, not just testimony based on science. *Kumho Tire Co. v. Carmichael*, 526 U.S. 137 (1999). Federal Rule of Evidence 702 reaffirms this responsibility and provides general standards that the Court must use to assess the reliability and helpfulness of proffered expert testimony.

---

1. Dr. Coston earned a Ph.D. degree in economics from the University of Arkansas in 1973. He was the head or acting head of Georgia Southern University's Department of Economics from 1972–1988. He taught economics at Georgia Southern until his retirement in 2001....

Rule 702 requires that an expert's testimony "assist the trier of fact to understand the evidence or to determine a fact in issue …" [and] "[t]his condition goes primarily to relevance." *Daubert*, 509 U.S. at 591. Expert testimony does not assist if it is based on factual assumptions that are not supported by the evidence. *United States v. City of Miami*, 115 F.3d 870, 873 (11th Cir. 1997).… The proponent of the expert testimony has the burden of establishing that the pertinent admissibility requirements of Rule 702 are met by a preponderance of the evidence.…

A review of the case law after *Daubert* shows that the rejection of expert testimony is the exception rather than the rule. Furthermore, a court has broad discretion in deciding whether an expert's relevant testimony is reliable. "The judge's role is to keep unreliable and irrelevant information from the jury because of its inability to assist in factual determinations, its potential to create confusion, and its lack of probative value." *Allison v. McGhan Med. Corp.*, 184 F.3d 1300, 1311–12 (11th Cir. 1999). However, this role "is not intended to supplant the adversary system or the role of the jury." *Id.* at 1311. "Vigorous cross-examination, presentation of contrary evidence, and careful instruction on the burden of proof are the traditional and appropriate means of attacking [debatable] but admissible evidence." *Id.*

…

Dr. Coston's opinion … that Plaintiff would earn $50,000 per year

With respect to Dr. Coston's opinion and testimony regarding Plaintiff's lost earnings, Defendant argues that Dr. Coston's opinion is based upon insufficient facts and should therefore be excluded. Specifically, Defendant challenges the factual basis of Dr. Coston's assumption that Plaintiff was earning close to $50,000 per year prior to the accident.

In support of this argument, Defendant points out that Dr. Coston relied entirely upon Plaintiff's counsel's representation that Plaintiff was making this sum prior to the accident. Dr. Coston did not conduct any independent research to determine the market rate of someone with similar skills in the same geographic location, and also did not base his assumption upon any of Plaintiff's prior employment records, pay stubs, or tax returns.

After Defendant challenged the factual basis of Dr. Coston's assumption, Plaintiff filed two supporting Affidavits. Plaintiff argues that the Affidavits "now provide more than sufficient facts or data to support Dr. Coston's opinions." The problem is that Dr. Coston did not rely upon the Affidavits as the basis of his opinion regarding Plaintiff's lost earnings. Federal Rule of Evidence 702 specifically requires that an expert's opinion "be based upon sufficient facts or data." While the Affidavits tend to support Dr. Coston's opinion, Plaintiff's attempt to engineer an "after-the-fact" factual basis for Dr. Coston's opinion is unpersuasive.

Nevertheless, I conclude that Dr. Coston's opinion is not without a factual basis. Plaintiff's counsel's representation of Plaintiff's past earnings, although not the best evidence, provided Dr. Coston with a factual foundation to calculate Plaintiff's future earnings. Nothing in the law suggests that an expert's opinion and pre-trial testimony regarding lost wages and future earning capacity must be initially founded upon tax returns, pay stubs, or employee records. Albeit minimal, Dr. Coston had a factual basis for his assumptions, and the purported deficiencies in Dr. Coston's opinion impact the weight and sufficiency of his opinion and testimony rather than its admissibility. *See United States v. 1.161 Acres of Land in Birmingham*, 837 F.2d 1036, 1040 (11th Cir. 1988) (holding that "the factual basis of an expert opinion goes to the credibility of the testimony, not admissibility, and it is up to the opposing party to examine the factual basis for the opinion in cross-examination"). At trial, Defendant will have ample opportunity to expose any weaknesses in Dr. Coston's opinion and testimony. Accordingly, Defendant's motion to exclude Dr. Coston's testimony based upon the assumption that Plaintiff would have earned $50,000 per year is denied....

Notes and Questions

1. Even when looking at the same basic rules for admissibility, the court in *Johnson* refuses to allow the proposed expert testimony on lost income, while the court in *Vincent* permits it. Of course, one difference between the cases involves the qualifications of the two experts in question. That alone could explain the results here. But what other differences are there that distinguish these cases?

2. Experts will always prefer to have the greatest amount of information available to them in making their calculations of future income, although *Vincent* shows that some professions tend to generate less documentation than others. In cases with sparse information, a court must decide if the calculation meets a minimal standard to admit, as Judge Bowen did. On the other hand, another common way that an expert economist might extrapolate from unknown to known data is to use reasonable assumptions. For example, in *Brown v. West Corp.*, the expert decided to use the annual average of the last three salary years to decide future incomes, despite the likelihood that more data from further years might have been available.[59] Why might an economist choose those years instead of a year-to-year analysis of the prior, say, ten years of income data? Often times, an assumption's reasonability is in the eye of the beholder. The court in *Brown* ultimately decided the expert could testify, saying:

   > The Court is satisfied that [the] expert testimony meets the minimum standards of sufficient facts and reliable methods set forth in *Daubert*. In addition, West has failed to show any prejudice or confusion that might flow from allowing the expert to testify regarding his opinion before the jury. The Court finds that [the] expert opinion could assist the jury in calculating damages, tipping the scales of Rule 403 in favor of admission.

3. Similarly, the issue of assumptions about the *length of time* a litigant planned to or would have worked can also be a point at issue. The "work life expectancy" difference can, especially in cases of many years' extrapolation, lead to divergent results. For example, in *Dunn v. United States*,[60] expert economists on each side

---

59. No. 8:11CV284, 2014 WL 1689662, at *1 (D. Neb. Apr. 29, 2014).
60. No. 04 Civ. 3035(MDF), 2007 WL 1087204, at *1 (S.D.N.Y. Apr. 11, 2007).

needed to calculate the lost wages after a 43-year-old man was severely injured in a workplace accident. One expert's assumption (work until 60) led to a valuation of the loss at $320,668.00, while another expert's assumption (work until 62.9) led to a valuation of $474,760.00.[61]

To resolve or at least ground these disputes in empirical research, many experts will look to third-party source materials. In the Tinari excerpt at the start of this chapter, he cites the *Journal of Forensic Economics* and *Journal of Legal Economics* as bases for forensic economists to make reasonable calculations:

> In their pages over the past three decades may be found articles about numerous topics including studies of statistical years to retirement and worklife expectancy. Many of the statistical-based articles rely on US government data and, as such, have been accepted by state and federal courts in civil litigation.

As with many areas of economic valuation, experts can make different choices on assumptions or inputs in their calculations that drastically alter the final results. Considering the cases above, however, unless these choices are wildly unsupportable or patently unreasonable, they are unlikely to result in exclusion of the testimony.

4. Finally, in addition to the base calculations of lost wages, experts will also adjust the final damages calculation to take into account the difference between the current value and past or future value of money. To put it another way, the damages must be adjusted to increase the dollars that have been withheld in the past (since they could have been invested) and to decrease the dollars paid for future losses (since giving less now will result in the correct amount over time with reasonable investments). To further examine prejudgment interest and discount rate issues, let us look at how courts handle them.

Mark A. Allen, Robert E. Hall, and Victoria A. Lazear, *Reference Guide on Estimation of Economic Damages*

REFERENCE MANUAL ON SCIENTIFIC EVIDENCE
452–53 & 457–58 (3d ed. 2011)[Ed.]

G. Is There a Dispute About Prejudgment Interest?

The law may specify how to calculate interest for losses prior to a verdict on liability, generally termed "prejudgment interest." The law may exclude prejudgment interest, specify prejudgment interest to be a statutory rate, or exclude compounded interest. Table 3 illustrates these alternatives. With simple uncompounded interest, losses from 5 years before trial earn five times the specified interest, and so compensation for a $100 loss from 5 years ago is $135 at 7% interest. With compound interest, the plaintiff earns interest on past interest. Compensation at 7% interest compounded is about

---

61. *Id.* at *10.

[Ed.] Reprinted with permission from the National Academy of Sciences, Courtesy of the National Academies Press, Washington, D.C.

$140 for a loss of $100 five years before trial. The difference between simple and compound interest becomes much larger if the time from loss to trial is greater or if the interest rate is higher. Because interest receipts in practice do earn further interest, economic analysis generally supports the use of compound interest.

Table 3. Calculation of Prejudgment Interest (in Dollars)[Ed.]

Years Before Trial	Loss Without Interest	Loss with Compound Interest at 7%
10	100	197
9	100	184
8	100	172
7	100	161
6	100	150
5	100	140
4	100	131
3	100	123
2	100	114
1	100	107
0	100	100
Total	1100	1579

Where the law does not prescribe the form of interest for past losses, the experts will normally apply a reasonable interest rate to bring those losses forward. The parties may disagree on whether the interest rate should be measured before or after tax. The before-tax interest rate is the normally quoted rate. To calculate the corresponding after-tax rate, one subtracts the amount of income tax the recipient would have to pay on the interest. Thus, the after-tax rate depends on the tax situation of the plaintiff. The format for calculation of the after-tax interest rate is shown in the following example:

1. Interest rate before tax: 9%

2. Tax rate: 30%

3. Tax on interest (line 1 times line 2): 2.7%

4. After-tax interest rate (line 1 less line 3): 6.3%

Even where damages are calculated on a pretax basis, economic considerations suggest that the prejudgment interest rate should be on an after-tax basis: Had a tax-

---

[Ed.] The Table has been simplified for clarity purposes by the Author.

paying plaintiff actually received the lost earnings in the past and invested the earnings at the assumed rate, income tax would have been due on the interest. The plaintiff's accumulated value would be the amount calculated by compounding past losses at the after-tax interest rate.

Where there is economic disparity between the parties, there may be a disagreement about whose interest rate should be used — the borrowing rate of the defendant or the lending rate of the plaintiff, or some other rate. There may also be disagreements about adjustment for risk....

2. *Are the Parties Using a Discount Rate Properly Matched to the Projection?*[Ed.]

For future losses, a damages study calculates the amount of compensation needed at the time of trial to replace expected future lost income. The result is discounted future losses; it is also sometimes referred to as the present value of future losses. Discounting is conceptually separate from the adjustment for inflation considered in the preceding section. Discounting is typically carried out in the format shown in Table 1.

Table 1. Calculation of Discounted Loss at 5% Interest

Years in Future	Loss	Discount Factor	Discounted Loss[A]
0	$100	1.000	$100
1	125	0.952	119
2	130	0.907	118
Total			$337

[A] Discounted Loss = Loss × Discount Factor.

"Loss" is the estimated future loss, in either escalated or constant-dollar form. "Discount factor" is a factor that calculates the number of dollars needed at the time of trial to compensate for a lost dollar in the future year. The discount factor is the ratio of the value at a future date of a cash flow received today to its value today. It is calculated from the discount rate, which is the interest rate that values a cash flow at a future date. If the current 1-year interest rate is 5%, then the discount rate is 1.05 — the value of $1 will be $1.05 a year from now. The discount factor will therefore be $1/$1.05. The 2-year discount rate is the square of 1.05, and the discount factor will be 1/(1.05 × 1.05) Thus, the discount factor is computed by compounding the discount rate forward from the base year to the future year and then taking the reciprocal.

For example, in Table 1, the interest rate is 5%. As discussed, the discount factor for the next year is calculated as the reciprocal of 1.05, and the discount factor for 2

[Ed.] The Section on Discount Rate has been moved within the text for clarity purposes by the Author.

years in the future is calculated as the reciprocal of 1.05 squared. Future discounts would be obtained by multiplying by 1.05 a suitably larger number of times and then taking the reciprocal. The discounted loss is the loss multiplied by the discount factor for that year. The number of dollars at time of trial that compensates for the loss is the sum of the discounted losses, $337 in this example.

To discount a future loss projected in escalated terms, one should use an ordinary interest rate. For example, in Table 1, if the losses of $125 and $130 are in dollars of those years, and not in constant dollars of the initial year, then the use of a 5% discount rate is appropriate if 5% represents an accurate measure of the current interest rate, also known as the time value of money. The ordinary interest rate is often called the nominal interest rate to distinguish it from the real interest rate.

To discount a future loss projected in constant dollars, one should use a real interest rate as the discount rate. A real interest rate is an ordinary interest rate less an assumed rate of future inflation. In Table 1, the use of a 5% discount rate for discounting constant-dollar losses would be appropriate if the ordinary interest rate was 8% and the rate of inflation was 3%. Then the real interest rate would be 8% minus 3%, or 5%. The deduction of the inflation rate from the discount rate is the counterpart of the omission of escalation for inflation from the projection of future losses....

Wiradihardja v. Bermuda Star Line, Inc.

No. 89 Civ. 3927 (DLD), 1993 WL 385817
(S.D.N.Y. Sept. 26, 1993)

DiCarlo, District Judge.

Plaintiff Martin Wiradihardja brings this action for personal injuries sustained while an employee aboard a vessel owned by Defendant Bermuda Star Line, Inc.... The court granted partial summary judgment in favor of Plaintiff on the claim of unseaworthiness. The issues of damages and retaliatory discharge were subsequently tried before a jury. A special verdict was rendered in the amount of $691,513.00. The award included $138,817.00 for lost past earnings, $482,696.00 for lost future earnings, $5,000.00 for past pain and suffering, $15,000.00 for future pain and suffering, and $50,000.00 for mental anguish resulting from the retaliatory discharge. The portion of the award attributable to lost future earnings remains to be adjusted for discounting to the present value.... The parties ... dispute issues regarding pre-judgment interest on the amounts of the award attributable to (1) past earnings and vacation pay; and (2) past pain and suffering and loss of enjoyment of life. In addition, the parties request that the court discount the portion of the award attributable to future earnings, to reflect its present value, at a rate previously stipulated to by the parties....

BACKGROUND

Plaintiff was employed as a food manager aboard the Queen of Bermuda, a luxury liner owned by Defendant. On June 30, 1988, when Plaintiff was working in his office, he was confronted by Mr. Wilson, a vegetable cook aboard the ship and one of the employees under Plaintiff's supervision. Mr. Wilson entered Plaintiff's office and hurled two bottles ten feet across the office. One of the bottles struck Plaintiff in his raised arm, and the force of the blow fractured his left ulna bone. Three days after the incident, Plaintiff underwent surgery. To set the fracture, a metal plate was inserted, with four screws attached to the bone.

Plaintiff returned to Defendant's vessel and continued in his position as food manager until February, 1989, when Plaintiff's replacement was brought on board. On February 25, Plaintiff was signed off of the ship in New Orleans. On February 28, at Defendant's request, Plaintiff visited a doctor chosen by Defendant. Following an examination and X-rays, the doctor recommended that Plaintiff undergo a second surgical procedure, excision of the distal ulna. On March 1, 1989, Defendant urged Plaintiff to undergo the recommended surgery. Plaintiff informed Defendant that he would need time to think it over and consult with his attorney. The following day, Defendant informed Plaintiff that if he did not agree to submit to surgery he would have to sign a paper relieving Defendant from a duty to pay for further medical care. Again, Plaintiff informed Defendant that he would have to consult with his attorney. The next day, March 3, 1989, Plaintiff was notified during a telephone conversation with Defendant's port captain, Captain Cross, that he was fired. This action ensued....

II. PREJUDGMENT INTEREST

A. Award of Prejudgment Interest

Plaintiff seeks prejudgment interest on the award for past lost earnings and on the award for past pain and suffering. Defendant does not dispute that plaintiff is entitled to the latter. The issue is whether Plaintiff is entitled to interest on that part of the award attributable to past lost earnings.

Prejudgment interest is added to the judgment on the theory that the defendant incurs liability to the plaintiff "the instant that the injury occurs." *McCrann v. U.S. Lines, Inc.*, 803 F.2d 771, 773 (2d Cir. 1986). Prejudgment interest is properly granted in admiralty cases in the absence of extraordinary or exceptional circumstances which mitigate against them. *Magee v. U.S. Lines, Inc.*, 976 F.2d 821, 823 (2d Cir. 1992). Instances of exceptional circumstances include situations where the plaintiff had "(1) unreasonably delayed in prosecuting its claim, (2) made a bad faith estimate of its damages that precluded settlement, or (3) not sustained any actual damages." *In re Banker's Tr. Co.*, 658 F.2d 103, 108 (3d Cir. 1981), *cert. denied*, 456 U.S. 961 (1982). In admiralty cases, the purpose of prejudgment interest is to make the plaintiff whole, not to punish the defendant. Therefore, it should only be denied in the event that such extraordinary circumstances exist. *Id.*

Defendant argues that prejudgment interest should not be awarded because the damage award for past earnings is not supported by any evidence that Plaintiff's injury resulted in this loss. However, any argument as to sufficiency of the evidence supporting the awarded damages is misplaced, and has ... been addressed in Defendant's motions for JNOV and a new trial. Defendant fails to bring to the court's attention any extraordinary circumstances which warrant the denial of prejudgment interest. Nor does the court find any such circumstances to be present. Accordingly, prejudgment interest is awarded to plaintiff on past lost earnings and on past pain and suffering.

B. Application of Prejudgment Interest

It is within the court's broad discretion to determine what rate of interest to apply to prejudgment interest. *Indep. Bulk Transp., Inc. v. Vessel "Morania Abaco"*, 676 F.2d 23, 25 (2d Cir. 1982). Upon due consideration, the court fixes the prejudgment interest rate at nine percent per annum.

When interest shall begin to accrue is also a decision that falls within the court's broad discretion. *Id.* In principle, "interest on damages is a form of compensation intended to make the injured party whole." *Mitsui & Co. v. Am. Exp. Lines, Inc.*, 636 F.2d 807, 824 (2d Cir. 1981). In keeping with this principle, interest generally accrues as of the date of injury.

Seeking application of the general rule, Plaintiff requests interest for past lost earnings as of the date of his original injury aboard Defendant's vessel. However, Plaintiff's employment with Defendant continued from the date of the incident until February 25, 1989. Therefore, there cannot be any award of interest on past earnings for the period between June 30, 1988 (date of original injury) and February 25, 1989 (when actual wage loss began) because Plaintiff suffered no wage loss during that period. Accordingly, interest shall begin to accrue on past lost earnings after February 25, 1989. Upon applying nine percent per annum prejudgment interest to the award of $138,817.00 for past earnings, the award is increased by $25,497.00. The adjusted award for past earnings is $164,314.00.

In contrast, Defendant's obligation to make plaintiff whole for his past pain and suffering did arise on the date of the incident. Therefore, interest on past pain and suffering shall commence on June 30, 1988, the date of the incident. Upon applying nine percent per annum prejudgment interest to the award of $5,000.00 for past pain and suffering, the award is increased by $2,362.50. The total adjusted award for past pain and suffering is $7,362.50.

III. DISCOUNTING TO PRESENT VALUE

Per stipulation by the parties, the award for future earnings is hereby discounted by two percent to its present value. The net discount applied to the future earnings award of $482,696.00 is $57,290.83. Following this adjustment, the total award for future earnings is $425,405.17....

Notes and Questions

1. The *Wiradihardja* case was an admiralty law claim, so it was decided by federal law. In admiralty cases, the court has enormous discretion to decide the prejudgment interest rate and discount rate to apply (although in this case, the discount rate was decided by stipulation). In other federal cases, however, 28 U.S.C. § 1961

establishes the prejudgment interest rate based on the weekly average Treasury yield rate from the Federal Reserve. 28 U.S.C. § 1961(a). Since Treasury notes are generally considered the safest investment possible, this is consistent with the Supreme Court's admonition that "The discount rate should be based on the rate of interest that would be earned on 'the best and safest investments.'" *Jones & Laughlin Steel Corp. v. Pfeifer*, 462 U.S. 523, 537 (1983) (citation omitted). The *Erie* doctrine also provides that in diversity jurisdiction cases, prejudgment interest will be set by applicable state law rules. *In re Exxon Valdez*, 484 F.3d 1098, 1101 (9th Cir. 2007) (collecting cases from a variety of circuit courts of appeal in support of state law rule when sitting in diversity).

The discount rate is similarly decided by state law when diversity jurisdiction cases appear in federal court. *See, e.g., BGB Pet Supply, Inc. v. Nutro Prods., Inc.*, No. 96-1337, 1997 WL 476519, at *11 (6th Cir. Aug. 19, 1997). For other cases, the issue may be resolved by presentation of evidence and a factual determination of the reasonable rate. *See, e.g., Teachers Ins. & Annuity Ass'n of Am. v. Criimi Mae Servs. Ltd.*, 763 F. Supp. 2d 665, 669 (S.D.N.Y. 2011). In the absence of any evidence, however, courts will use a discount rate of two percent. *Ammar v. United States*, 342 F.3d 133, 148 (2d Cir. 2003); *McCrann v. U.S. Lines*, 803 F.2d 771, 775 (2d Cir. 1986)

2. As for the issue of income tax offset for damages, the Tinari excerpt at the start of this chapter notes that "In some state and federal jurisdictions, the loss of earnings must be reduced by likely amounts of federal and state income taxes." Tinari, *supra*. Claims under the Federal Tort Claims Act generally involve an offset for income tax liability. *See, e.g., Shaw v. United States*, 741 F.2d 1202, 1206 (9th Cir. 1984); *Flannery v. United States*, 718 F.2d 108, 111 (4th Cir. 1983). However, as with discount rate and prejudgment interest, the issue is one of state law in diversity actions. Lauren Guest & David Schap, *Rationales Concerning the Treatment of Federal Income Taxes in Personal Injury and Wrongful Death Litigation in the State Courts*, 21 J. LEGAL. ECON. 85, 86 (2014). For a detailed look at the issue of taxation in civil litigation, see *id.*; Mark W. Cochran, *Should Personal Injury Damage Awards Be Taxed?*, 38 CASE W. RES. L. REV. 43 (1988); John E. Theuman, Annotation, *Propriety of Taking Income Tax into Consideration in Fixing Damages in Personal Injury or Death Action*, 16 A.L.R. 4th 589 (1982).

ii. Non-Wage Components of Economic Damages

Hedgepeth v. Diamond Offshore Drilling, Inc.

No. 01-12-01156-CV, 2013 WL 6097798
(Tex. Ct. App. Nov. 19, 2013)

HUDDLE, J.

Cindi Hedgepeth appeals a jury award in a wrongful death case.... A jury awarded Cindi $280,082 for the loss of her late husband's support and household services.

Cindi contends the award is inadequate and the evidence is factually insufficient to support the award. We affirm.

Background

John Timothy Hedgepeth (Tim) worked as an electrician for Diamond Offshore Drilling, Inc. In December 2008, Diamond sent Tim to the Ocean Lexington, an oil rig stationed off the coast of Libya. Diamond arranged Tim's travel itinerary, which included a layover in Malta. In Malta, Tim died from pneumococcal meningitis, a bacterial infection that affected his brain. Tim was 52 years old when he died.

Tim's widow, Cindi, sued Diamond under the Jones Act. Cindi alleged Diamond had a legal duty to provide Tim a safe place to work, Diamond breached its duty, and Diamond's breach caused Tim's death. Diamond generally denied the allegations and claimed Tim's negligence caused his death.

At trial, Cindi testified about her life with Tim. She testified that when Tim was working offshore, he worked 30 days on and 30 days off. She also testified that she and Tim were married 33 years, that Tim spent a lot of time with family when he was not working, that Tim raised show horses with their oldest daughter, and that the family frequently went to horse shows.

Cindi testified that Tim worked for Diamond on two separate occasions. Tim started working for Diamond in 1993, then left Diamond in 1996 to work for Georgia Pacific Paper Mill. Tim earned $50,000 less per year working for Georgia Pacific, but the paper mill was close to home and Tim wanted more time with his family. Cindi testified that Tim returned to Diamond in 2006 because Georgia Pacific changed management and Tim disliked the new owners.

Cindi introduced expert testimony valuing the loss of Tim's support and household services. Economist Thomas Mayor testified that he calculated three numbers: past lost support, future lost support, and lost household services. Mayor testified that in order to reach a lost support calculation, he first estimated Tim's annual net earning capacity.... Mayor then added 13 percent to those figures to account for lost fringe benefits, such as medical insurance benefits and retirement plans. The 13 percent was not based on Tim's actual fringe benefits, but rather, government statistics showing that the average value of fringe benefits is 13 percent of wages. On cross-examination, Mayor testified that information from Diamond indicated that its benefits were slightly better than average. Mayor deducted amounts attributable to payroll taxes, federal income tax, and state income tax, based on Tim's previous tax returns, to arrive at a net annual income figure of $79,249 for onshore work, and $136,252 for offshore work.

Mayor testified that he then subtracted from the net annual income figures an allowance for personal consumption, because part of what Tim earned would have been spent on items for his own personal consumption and would not have benefitted the family.... Mayor testified that combining the past and future lost support yielded a total lost support of $753,343, assuming onshore work, or $1,356,892, assuming offshore work.

Mayor also testified about the value of the household services provided by Tim. According to Mayor, household services can include, among other things, taking care of the yard, doing work inside, repairing the house, painting a house, taking care of vehicles, paying bills, contracting for people to take care of the house, going to the store to pick up things for the family, and taking care of small children. Mayor testified that, based on government statistics, the national average value of household services performed by a married man without small children who is employed full-time is $9,632 a year. Accounting for wage rates in Mississippi, where Tim lived, that figure was $7,705 per year. According to Mayor, if the man is retired, the figure adjusts to $12,979 a year. Mayor testified that he did not try to determine whether Tim was an above average, average, or below average provider of household services, and that he did not know how, on balance, Tim's working offshore would affect the level of household services he provided. Assuming a life expectancy of 79.4 years, Mayor testified that the total value of lost household services was $280,082.

Mayor testified that the sum of past and future lost support, assuming offshore work, plus household services, was $1,636,974.

Diamond's expert, economist Stuart Wood, offered alternative calculations. Like Mayor, Wood calculated two sets of lost support figures, one assuming that Tim continued to work offshore, and one assuming that he worked onshore. Wood based his net annual income figures on the same past income figures as Mayor.... Wood concluded that total lost support, assuming onshore work, was $467,807.24. Assuming offshore work, Wood calculated total lost support to be $739,387.53.

Regarding household services, Wood testified that "this is a thing that depends upon the specifics of the individual." Wood agreed with Mayor that there were "difficulties [with] trying to annualize for a man who works 50 percent of time offshore and at home." Like Mayor, Wood did not base his figure on specific information about the services provided by Tim, but rather, based his figure on an average derived from statistical studies. Wood reached his household services figure by using a general assumption regarding the time and value for Tim's household services, based upon a national average of 14 hours devoted to household services per week at 52 weeks a year, multiplied by the minimum wage. Using this calculation, Wood arrived at a figure for lost household services of $57,961.30.

In short, Wood testified that total lost support based on the assumption of onshore work, plus fringe benefits, and his estimate of household services, was $682,719.70. The same sum, assuming lost support based on offshore work, was $954,269.99.

The jury found both Diamond and Tim negligent, assessing 25% against Diamond and 75% against Tim.[1] The jury awarded $0 for Tim's pre-death pain, suffering, and mental anguish, and $280,082 for the loss of Tim's support and household services. Cindi moved for a new trial, contending the award for support and household services

1. In a cause of action under the Jones Act, a seaman's contributory negligence does not bar recovery, but diminishes damages on the basis of comparative negligence in proportion to the amount of negligence attributable to contributory fault....

was inadequate and the evidence was factually insufficient to support the award. The trial court denied Cindi's motion. This appeal followed.

Discussion

On appeal, Cindi contends that the jury's award of $280,082 for lost support and household services is supported by factually insufficient evidence.

A. Standard of Review

The Jones Act provides for a wrongful death action for maritime workers who die from injuries sustained in the course of employment. *See* 46 U.S.C.S. § 30104. When a state court hears an admiralty case, that court occupies essentially the same position occupied by a federal court sitting in diversity: the state court must apply substantive federal maritime law but follow state procedure. *Mar. Overseas Corp. v. Ellis*, 971 S.W.2d 402, 406 (Tex. 1998). We review a jury's award of pecuniary damages under the Jones Act under the traditional standard of review for factual sufficiency under Texas law, considering and weighing all of the evidence, not just that evidence which supports the verdict. We can set aside the verdict only if it is so contrary to the overwhelming weight of the evidence that the verdict is clearly wrong and unjust. *Ellis*, 971 S.W.2d at 407; *Cain v. Bain*, 709 S.W.2d 175, 176 (Tex. 1986).... Unless the record demonstrates otherwise, we presume the jury followed the trial court's instructions. We may not pass upon the witnesses' credibility or substitute our judgment for that of the jury, even if the evidence would clearly support a different result.

B. Applicable Law

Recovery of damages under the Jones Act is limited to pecuniary losses. *De Centero v. Gulf Fleet Crews, Inc.*, 798 F.2d 138, 141 (5th Cir. 1986). In a wrongful death case under the Jones Act, recoverable items include, among others, loss of support from past and future earnings, loss of household services, and recovery for pre-death pain and suffering. *Id.*

The jury generally has broad discretion to award damages within the range of evidence presented at trial. A jury is entitled to disbelieve or discount any part of an expert's testimony even though the basis of the jury's specific calculation cannot be determined from the record. A jury is entitled to make credibility determinations and weigh competing expert testimony and the variables and assumptions upon which that testimony is based. A jury "may disregard even uncontradicted and unimpeached testimony from disinterested witnesses," so long as the decision to disregard is reasonable. *City of Keller v. Wilson*, 168 S.W.3d 802, 820 (Tex. 2005). Pecuniary loss in a wrongful-death case is not subject to precise mathematical calculation, and the jury is given significant discretion in determining this element of damages. *Christus Health v. Dorriety*, 345 S.W.3d 104, 113 (Tex. App. 2011, pet. denied) (citing *Thomas v. Uzoka*, 290 S.W.3d 437, 454 (Tex. App. 2009, pet. denied). "[A] jury determining pecuniary loss may look beyond evidence of calculable financial contributions, and is not necessarily limited by an economist's testimony about some of the considerations included in pecuniary loss." *Id.*

C. Analysis

Here, the jury was asked to "[s]tate the amount of damages you award to Plaintiff Cindi Hedgepeth" for "[t]he loss of John Timothy Hedgepeth's Household Service and Support." The trial court's charge instructed the jury, if it found that Cindi was entitled to an award for the "loss of future support and services," to "reduce any loss of support ... by the amount you determine [Tim] would have consumed himself." The jury was also instructed to "consider loss after income taxes" and to "discount [any award] to present value by considering what return would be realized on a relatively risk free investment." Additionally, the trial court instructed the jury not to reduce the award by the percentage of contributory negligence it assigned to Tim, if any, because making that reduction was the court's responsibility. The jury awarded $280,082.

Cindi acknowledges that the jury is entitled to disregard or discount expert testimony, but asserts that, because Diamond sponsored Wood's testimony regarding lost support and household services, his testimony provides the absolute floor for the award of lost support and household services. In response, Diamond contends that the jury was not bound to accept either expert's testimony, and the jury's award is supported because the jury could have concluded that Tim was not going to continue working offshore and that Tim had a higher personal consumption percentage than assumed by either expert, because of his hobby of showing horses.

We agree with Diamond that Wood's testimony did not create an absolute floor for the jury's award. Because pecuniary loss is not subject to precise mathematical calculation, the jury had significant discretion in determining this element of damages. See Dorriety, 345 S.W.3d at 113. The jury was entitled to disbelieve or discount any part of either expert's testimony, to weigh both experts' testimony and the variables and assumptions upon which each expert's testimony was based, and to reject or discount each expert's testimony based on this review.

Both Mayor and Wood testified that their calculations of lost support were based upon various assumptions. The experts' assumptions differed, and in many cases were based upon generalized data or studies, not data unique to Tim. The jury was entitled to disbelieve or discount the assumptions made by either expert.

For example, the jury could have concluded that, based on the fact that Tim had previously decided to work onshore in order to be closer to his family, he would do so again, and therefore rejected the experts' offshore figures. The jury also could have concluded that a change to an onshore job may have resulted in less valuable pay and benefits than those Tim received from either Diamond or his previous onshore job at Georgia Pacific. The jury was not required to accept either expert's assumption about how long Tim would continue to work. Cindi testified that Tim was very involved with his family, and had previously taken a $50,000 pay cut to take a job onshore in order to spend more time with them. The jury also could have concluded that Tim would retire before the date that either expert assumed, ... to spend more time with his family.

Further, the jury could have determined that neither expert accurately calculated Tim's personal consumption allowance, because neither expert based his allowance on Tim's actual consumption rate. *See Weeks Mar., Inc. v. Salinas*, 225 S.W.3d 311, 320–21 (Tex. App. 2007, pet. dismissed). The experts' personal consumption allowance numbers differed greatly—Mayor applied a 12 percent allowance to offshore work and a 16 percent allowance to onshore work, while Wood applied a 33 percent allowance to both figures. But the jury could have disregarded these figures because, although Cindi contends that showing horses was not a personal expense since her adult daughter showed them with Tim, the evidence adduced at trial could permit the jury to determine that Tim's personal consumption allowance was higher because he showed horses and even Cindi described this as a "luxury."

In addition, the jury could have discounted both experts' figures regarding the value of lost household services because neither considered actual services rendered by Tim. Both experts used national averages even though they agreed that there were "difficulties" associated with calculating the value of household services contributed by a person who was offshore for 30 days at a time. Cindi's expert, Mayor, admitted that he didn't know "how much difference that makes," and stated that "[i]t's a hard— I think it's a hard issue to determine." Accordingly, the jury could have determined that neither expert's household services figure was accurate and that a lower figure was warranted.

We do not speculate on how the jury actually arrived at its award, but conclude based upon all of the foregoing that there is sufficient evidence in the record from which a rational jury could have determined an award lower than either expert estimated. Having considered all of the evidence, in light of the jury's significant discretion in determining pecuniary damages, we conclude that the jury's award of $280,082 for loss of support and household services is not so contrary to the overwhelming weight of the evidence that it is clearly wrong and unjust. *See Dorriety*, 345 S.W.3d at 113 (jury has significant discretion in determining pecuniary damages and is not necessarily limited by expert testimony); *Salinas*, 225 S.W.3d at 320 (jury is entitled to disbelieve or discount any part of an expert's testimony even though the basis of the jury's specific calculation cannot be determined from the record).

We overrule Cindi's sole issue.

Lind v. Slowinski

450 N.W.2d 353 (Minn. Ct. App. 1990)

FORSBERG, Judge.

Respondent Kelly A. Lind was injured when an auto she was a passenger in left the road. She sued the driver, appellant Michael Slowinski, and the owner of the car, appellant Paul Slowinski. Slowinskis in turn filed a third-party complaint against appellant Larry Bunnell, another passenger in the car at the time of the accident. The jury found Lind 5% negligent, Slowinski 55% negligent, and Bunnell 40% negligent. Damages of $323,074 were awarded and included $63,000 for future medical expenses.

Bunnell and Slowinskis appeal from judgment and denial of post-trial motions. We affirm in part and reverse in part.

FACTS

On October 24, 1984, Michael Slowinski and Bunnell had just completed the first phase of their architectural drawing curriculum at a state vo-tech school. After the two drank a 12-pack of beer, Bunnell purchased another and put it in Slowinski's car. He then called Lind, his girlfriend at the time, to arrange for her to accompany him and Slowinski on a drive to Hastings, Minnesota. Bunnell and Lind have since been married.

Bunnell testified he was intoxicated when he picked up Lind between 6:30 and 7:00 p.m. Lind smelled alcohol on Bunnell and Slowinski. Before entering the car, she noticed empty beer cans as well as the full 12-pack.

The back seat of Slowinski's 1978 Buick Skylark was down when Lind attempted to get in the car. She requested the back seat be put up, but both Slowinski and Bunnell urged her to ride in the front seat on Bunnell's lap. The testimony is unclear as to exactly what convinced her to do so, but she did get in the car partially on Bunnell's lap and partially on the front seat.

During the ride to Hastings, all three consumed beer. Both Bunnell and Lind noticed Slowinski's driving became erratic. There is testimony both passengers urged Slowinski to be more careful and perhaps to cease driving. He did not heed this advice.

Upon arriving in Hastings, Slowinski's ability to drive had seriously deteriorated. He swerved out of control at one point, smashing into the front fender of a parked car. Slowinski drove away from the scene and turned down a dirt road at a speed of between 35 and 40 miles per hour. He was unable to negotiate a turn and as a result his vehicle left the road, rolled over, and landed on its hood.

While Slowinski and Bunnell suffered only minor injuries, Lind sustained a severe cervical spine injury. She has undergone surgery and, while generally able to walk and function on a day-to-day basis, has a 25 percent permanent partial disability. She suffers from brown-sequard syndrome, manifested by muscular deficit on one side of her body with a corresponding loss of feeling on the other side.

In June 1986, Lind sued Michael Slowinski, the driver, and Paul Slowinski, the owner of the vehicle.... Slowinskis served a third-party complaint upon Bunnell, which alleged Bunnell was negligent in directing Lind to sit on his lap and preventing her from being in the rear seat where seat belts were available. Bunnell moved for summary judgment, claiming he owed Lind no legal duty. Bunnell's motion was denied and the case proceeded to trial.

Dr. Harry Fielden was Slowinskis' medical expert. Dr. Fielden testified in deposition, and over objection, the seating position of Lind in Bunnell's lap caused or increased the severity of her injuries. The court excluded this testimony based on lack of foundation....

At the close of Lind's case, Bunnell moved for a directed verdict. He argued since the record was devoid of any evidence showing how the seating position contributed to the injury, there was no evidence reasonably tending to support the allegations in Lind's complaint. The trial court denied this motion. The issue of Bunnell's negligence went to the jury.

Slowinskis moved, at the close of evidence, that the court find as a matter of law Lind had not met her burden in proving the certainty of amount of future medical expenses. The court denied the motion and allowed this question to go to the jury.

After the jury instructions were given, Lind moved to amend her third-party complaint "by way of alleging that Larry Bunnell was negligent in his affirmative conduct from the time of entering the car up to the rollover accident, which negligence was a concurring cause to the accident and the resulting injuries to the plaintiff." The motion was granted over objection.

The jury apportioned liability 55% to Slowinski; 5% to Lind; 40% to Bunnell. The total jury verdict was for $323,074.52. After no-fault and comparative liability setoffs, Lind's award was $264,528.12. Included in this award was $63,000 for future medical expenses....

Slowinskis and Bunnell have appealed from the judgment and from the order denying their post-trial motions. The two appeals have been consolidated by this court.

ISSUES

1. Did the trial court err in allowing the issue of Bunnell's negligence and liability to go to the jury?
2. Was there sufficient evidence to support the jury award of $63,000 for future medical expenses? ...

ANALYSIS

Bunnell claims the trial court erred in allowing his negligence to go to the jury since he owed no legal duty to Lind. The existence of a legal duty is a question of law to be determined by the court. On review, conclusions of law by the trial court are not binding on this court....

We believe *Olson v. Ische*, 343 N.W.2d 284 (Minn. 1984) is the controlling authority in this case. In *Olson*, driver-owner Ische was intoxicated while driving home a passenger, Fritz. Both Ische and Fritz had been drinking at a party earlier. Each man took a plastic cup of beer with him on the ride. Ische drove at an excessive speed, noticeably weaving, until he collided head-on with an auto operated by plaintiff Olson. Olson sued both Ische and Fritz. Several theories were advanced to support Fritz's liability.

The *Olson* court dismissed any cause of action against Fritz based upon the Restatement (Second) of Torts § 298 (1965), which imposes a duty of reasonable care on a passenger not to subject other persons to unreasonable risks of harm. In so doing, the court reasoned:

> A passenger has, of course, a legal duty to use care for his own safety, and his contributory negligence will bar or diminish his own claim. He may also

have a moral duty owed to others not to encourage the driver to drive when he should not be driving. But to impose a legal duty on the passenger, which makes him liable to others on the highway for what the driver himself chooses to do, seems to us, as a general proposition, inappropriate.... For Fritz to join Ische in the car ride as he did here may be encouragement of a sort, but not the kind that creates legal liability.

The *Olson* court further held, as a general rule, there must be either active interference with the driver or some special relationship to the injured party to create liability.

A passenger who interferes with his driver's operation of the motor vehicle, for instance by grabbing the steering wheel, may be liable to others, and a passenger who is the owner of the car may be liable, at common law, for negligent entrustment to an incompetent driver. This case, however, is different. *We hold that a passenger has no duty to members of the public to control the operation of a motor vehicle by its intoxicated owner*, where, as under the circumstances here, there is no special relationship between the driver-owner and the passenger....

No evidence was introduced here to show Bunnell in any way physically interfered with Slowinski's operation of the vehicle. Nor can such interference be inferred from Bunnell's furnishing alcohol to the operator of the vehicle ... In addition, there was no special relationship between Lind and Bunnell sufficient to impose a duty. Such relationships might include "parent-child, master-servant, land possessor, and custodian of a person with dangerous propensities." *Olson*, 343 N.W.2d at 288. Under certain circumstances, such a duty may also exist between husband and wife. Although Lind and Bunnell are now married, this was not the case at the time of the accident. The dependency relationship of the type required to impose a passenger duty to third parties was therefore absent in this case....

As none of the exceptions to the general rule against passenger liability outlined in *Olson* apply, we conclude Bunnell owed no duty to Lind as a matter of law. The trial court therefore erred in submitting his liability to the jury. Since we reach this result, it is unnecessary to determine Bunnell's additional assignments of error.

Slowinskis contend the jury's award of $63,000 in future medical expenses is not warranted by the evidence at trial. They argue the testimony is speculative and will not allow the award of any future medical expenses. Alternatively, they suggest under the most liberal reading possible of the evidence, an appropriate jury award would be $17,374.13.

There are two requirements in the award of future medical expenses. The first is whether future damages in the form of future medical treatments will be required. *Pietrzak v. Eggen*, 295 N.W.2d 504, 507 (Minn. 1980). The second requirement is that not only the necessity, but the amount of the damages be established by expert testimony. In particular, "the plaintiff must prove the reasonable certainty of such expenses by a fair preponderance of the evidence...." *Kwapien v. Starr*, 400 N.W.2d 179, 184 (Minn. Ct. App. 1987).

Kwapien affirmed the trial court's refusal to grant remittitur on an award of future medical expenses. To reach the award it did, the jury in *Kwapien* made certain inferences based upon expert testimony. The jury had information on the cost of physical therapy, that future physical therapy would be necessary, and the life expectancy of the plaintiff. This made it "possible for the jury to take respondent's life expectancy and factor it against the cost of her past physical therapy treatments to arrive at an approximate figure for future medical expenses."

Slowinskis note Dr. Fielden gave no estimate of future medical expenses. However, Dr. Fielden did state, "I think she will probably seek medical attention once in a while maybe over the years on the average of once every four or five years." Slowinskis also cite the testimony of Dr. John Bower, who stated: "With reasonable medical certainty I think she will need ongoing medical care on a sporadic basis." Slowinskis argue although there is some evidence ... it is not established to a reasonable probability what kind of care she will need.

The jury was provided with actuarial tables estimating Lind's life expectancy at 54 years. Dr. Fielden's testimony was that Lind takes, with varying frequency, Antiprox, Naprisin, Puronol, and Flexerol, and Advil. The jury also received as an exhibit Lind's past medical bills and records.

We agree this testimony does not support the $63,000 award. However, uncontradicted evidence does support allowing $70 per year for one examination by a physician, plus $450 for physical therapy, six sessions at $75 per hour; $40 for muscle relaxant which would reflect $20 each week for her two weeks of physical therapy. This would equal a total of $560, times her life expectancy of 54 years, which would total future medical expenses at $30,400. Applying a discount factor of 2.3 for adjustment to present value, her total allowable medical expenses are $17,374.13. The award of future medical expenses must therefore be reduced from $63,000 to $17,374.13....

Notes and Questions

1. Economic damage calculations involve more than just the lost wages and income calculations from cases like *Vincent*. Instead, additional expenses can include out-of-pocket expenses, medical expenses, loss of household services, or any other direct loss caused by the injury in question. To be clear, these other economic expenses will also be subject to adjustment for past and future value of money using discount rates and prejudgment interest, because they also serve to "compensate the plaintiff for loss and return him to the position he occupied before the injury." *East River S.S. Corp. v. Transamerica Delaval Inc.*, 476 U.S. 858, 873 n.9 (1986).

2. However, just as with wage loss calculations, the *Lind* court makes clear that non-wage economic damages claimed by the injured party should be presented by expert testimony and established by a preponderance of the evidence. Do you believe the testimony in *Lind* was sufficient to meet this burden? Why did the court find only some of the expenses valid? Should all or none of them have been credited?

3. Note also that to establish these claims of non-wage economic damages, there may need to be testimony from separate experts: the medical component established by a medical expert, and then the value of those expenses tallied and depreciated to present dollars by an expert economist. This becomes more critical as economic loss calculations become more complicated than those seen in *Lind*. *See, e.g., Carrier v. Novel Ins. Co.*, 817 So. 2d 126, 134–35 (La. Ct. App. 2002) (affirming $750,000 on future medical expenses based on testimony of three treating physicians and one economist).

iii. Components of Noneconomic Damages

Mississippi Baptist Health Systems v. Kelly

88 So. 3d 769 (Miss. Ct. App. 2011)

Ishee, J.

Mississippi Baptist Health Systems, Inc.... appeals the Hinds County Circuit Court jury award of $4,691,000 in favor of Jonathan Kelly and the estate of his wife, Ellen Kelly, for her wrongful death. The subject tort was committed in 2000, and the subsequent lawsuit was filed in 2001. Both occurred before the passage of Mississippi Code Annotated section 11-1-60 (Supp. 2011), which capped non-economic damages in medical-malpractice lawsuits at $500,000 and actual economic damages at $1,000,000.

Baptist argues the following on appeal: (1) the verdict is inconsistent because the jury found the doctors who cared for Ellen were not at fault, yet the jury held the nurses and their employer, Baptist, were responsible for Ellen's death; (2) portions of Ellen's medical records were improperly excluded; (3) there was insufficient evidence of Ellen's pain and suffering to support the award; (4) the verdict was contrary to the overwhelming weight of the evidence; and (5) the trial court's award of 8% interest on the judgment was improper. Finding no errors, we affirm.

FACTS AND PROCEDURAL HISTORY

Ellen was a twenty-nine-year-old attorney and mother of two sons, Adam O'Malley and Jacob Kelly, ages ten and two at the time of her death. She was married to Jonathan, and the family lived outside of Monticello, Mississippi. She was employed by the Mississippi Department of Human Services in the child-support-collection division. On July 10, 2000, Ellen was admitted to Baptist to undergo a hysterectomy and a partial vulvectomy, both of which were recommended by her gynecologist, Dr. Fred Ingram. Dr. Ingram had been Ellen's obstetrician-gynecologist since 1997....

On July 10, 2000, Dr. Ingram performed Ellen's surgery with the assistance of his partner, Dr. Doug Odom. It is undisputed Ellen regained consciousness after the surgery. However, Jonathan's expert physician, Dr. Eric Gershwin, testified Ellen experienced an allergic reaction to the latex she was exposed to during the surgery. She complained of itching, had blisters on her lips, redness of the face, and nausea following the surgery. She was given Benadryl for the itching and Phenergan for the nausea and vomiting....

Jonathan remained with Ellen throughout the afternoon and night following her surgery and spoke to her approximately every forty-five minutes. In the early morning, Jonathan heard Ellen making "gasping [and] gurgling sounds." When she was unable to respond to Jonathan, he contacted her nurse. The nurse then called Dr. John Brooks, an emergency physician. Dr. Brooks immediately intubated Ellen. She had also developed ventricular tachycardia, a condition where the heart is unable to maintain its rhythm, and she lost her pulse. Due to the intubation, Ellen was unable to breathe on her own. Thereafter, she was placed on a ventilator and transferred to the intensive care unit (ICU) at Baptist. Ellen had no neurological function following cardiac arrest and never regained consciousness. The family elected to take her off the ventilator four days later, and she died on July 14, 2000.

Jonathan brought a wrongful-death action in the Hinds County Circuit Court. He claimed Ellen died of anaphylactic shock due to the doctors' and Baptist's negligent failure to discover Ellen was allergic to latex and to thereafter take proper precautions. He asserted Ellen died as a result of the latex allergy, which caused her cardiac arrest.

At trial, Jonathan introduced Baptist's latex allergy policies and procedures. Those policies and procedures require that upon admission, "all patients should be assessed for [a] latex allergy." The policy also provided that patients should be questioned about certain items which would indicate a patient was at a high risk of having a latex allergy. The "ABC Food Allergies (Avocado, Banana, Chestnuts)" are an example of one such risk. On the Pre-Procedure/Surgery Check List, prepared on July 3, 2000, by Nurse Debra Priester (Priester), Ellen's allergies were listed as "sulfa, Lorcet, dairy products, seafood[,] and adhesive tape." The listing "old chart sent with patient" was also marked with an "X."

On a nursing admission history and assessment form, prepared a week before surgery, Ellen's allergies were listed as "sulfa, Lorcet, all dairy products and seafood, adhesive on Band-Aids." This form also included a subsection titled "Latex Allergy Alert" and listed various questions probing for a latex allergy. At the top of the form is the notation, "Notify MD if Yes." A nursing expert testified this notation meant the physician should be notified if the patient answered affirmatively to any of the questions. The first question on the form asked whether "[patient] knows allerg[y] to latex." Neither box was checked, but a dash was written beside "[n]o." ...

Priester, the nurse who completed the form, testified the Latex Allergy Policy/Procedure for Baptist required a nursing assessment for each patient to minimize the risk of patients having an allergic or anaphylactic reaction to latex during a surgical procedure. The assessment intended to discover the patient's known allergens to latex.... If a risk of a latex allergy was detected, the procedures required the nurse to indicate that risk on the assessment form. According to the protocol in Baptist's Latex Allergy Policy/Procedure, if a known allergy or sensitivity to latex is identified in the patient's admission history, an allergy sticker should be placed on the front of the patient's chart, signage should be placed on the patient's door, central supply and purchasing should be notified regarding any special supplies or products needed for the patient, and food and nutrition services should be notified to ensure servers would not wear latex gloves when serving the patient food.

Priester then testified regarding the form dated July 3, 2000. On the Latex Allergy Alert portion of the assessment regarding the question, "[patient] knows allerg[y] to latex," Priester stated neither box was checked because Ellen did not tell her she had a latex allergy. However, she had just testified she did not have any independent knowledge of Ellen's assessment completed some nine years before. When asked about the fact Ellen circled "chestnuts" as an allergy, Priester testified that in her opinion, "one item in and by itself would not have made her necessarily allergic." ... Priester said she did not follow the protocol because "[Ellen] did not have a latex allergy, so I did not notify a physician." When asked if she notified Ellen's doctors about a potential latex allergy, she replied: "No. [Ellen] did not give me any information about being allergic to latex." On cross-examination, Priester testified she based her opinion that Ellen was not latex sensitive on her experience in the "nursing process." She stated it was her interpretation of the latex-allergy procedure that she should only notify a doctor if the patient acknowledged she had a known allergy to latex.

To further his claim that an undetected latex allergy caused Ellen's death, Jonathan introduced a nursing admission history and assessment form from Ellen's admission to Baptist on October 15, 1997, during the early part of her second pregnancy. The form shows Ellen answered affirmatively to the question, "[patient] knows allerg[y] to latex," and she also noted a chestnut allergy. Rebecca Dawn Davis, the nursing clinical director for Baptist, testified regarding Baptist's latex-allergy procedures.... Davis testified the notation meant Ellen's record from 1997, which showed she was allergic to latex, would have been part of the record for her surgery. Davis also stated Priester did not follow Baptist's policies and procedures when she did not fill in an answer as to whether Ellen knew she was allergic to latex. Lang, Ellen's pre-operation nurse, stated Ellen told her she was allergic to "sulfur, Lorcet, dairy products, seafood[,] and adhesive tape." She testified she did not consult the form Priester filled out one week before the surgery to check for possible allergies.

A nursing expert, Dr. Beare, opined Baptist's nurses breached their duty of care to Ellen. Dr. Beare based this conclusion on the fact the nurses received positive responses from Ellen on latex-allergy questions but did not report it to the doctors. Significantly, Dr. Gershwin, Jonathan's main medical expert, testified that repeated exposure to latex worsens the reaction in an individual. He opined she developed the allergy during her previous surgeries in which latex products were used. According to Dr. Gershwin, Ellen suffered all the classic signs and symptoms of a latex allergy. The symptoms included itching, redness, blisters, and nausea. He concluded Ellen's cardiac arrest was a result of her allergy to latex....

Ellen's gynecologist, Dr. Ingram, and his partner, Dr. Odom, stated Ellen did not have an allergy to latex. Dr. Ingram testified he had been Ellen's gynecologist since 1997. He said he treated her throughout her second pregnancy and Caesarean-section, all the while using various latex products, without any adverse reaction from Ellen....

Dr. Ingram and Dr. Odom both testified they used their own files from their clinic instead of the hospital files for the surgery. They stated this was their standard practice. Dr. Ingram testified he had taken a complete history from Ellen, and there was no indication she was allergic to latex. He said he did not consult the hospital's forms concerning Ellen's allergies. Dr. Odom testified to the same.

Dr. Carroll McLeod, the anesthesiologist who treated Ellen at Baptist during her surgery, took a separate history from Ellen in which she indicated an allergy to adhesive tape. According to expert testimony, this indicates a possible latex allergy. However, Dr. Brooks, the emergency physician, testified, in his opinion, Ellen did not die of an adverse reaction to latex. He testified the itching was very common in post-operative patients who received morphine....

Baptist called Dr. Richard DeShazo, an allergist at the University of Mississippi Medical Center in Jackson, as an expert witness. He had reviewed Ellen's medical records, including the documents from her surgery. Dr. DeShazo concluded that Ellen did not have an allergy to latex and that she did not have an anaphylactic reaction to latex.

After hearing all of the testimony, the jury returned a verdict finding Baptist liable for Ellen's death through the negligence of its nurses. The jury exonerated the doctors. It further held Baptist's nurses were negligent by failing to notify the doctors of Ellen's latex allergies and for failing to follow the hospital's latex-allergy procedures. The jury awarded $516,000 to the wrongful-death beneficiaries and $4,175,000 to Ellen's estate....

DISCUSSION

...

III. ASSESSMENT OF DAMAGES

In its next claim, Baptist makes several arguments against the jury's assessment of damages, ultimately asserting a new trial should be held on damages. Baptist argues the following three main issues: (1) the jury incorrectly assessed the value of household services; [and] (2) the jury incorrectly assessed Ellen's medical expenses, funeral expenses, and compensation for Ellen's physical and emotional pain and suffering....

Mississippi's wrongful-death statute allows recovery of damages in the amount the jury determines to be just, taking into consideration all damages of every kind to the decedent and all damages of every kind to any and all interested parties in the suit. Miss. Code Ann. § 11-7-13. This statutory language provides for (1) medical and funeral costs; (2) the present net cash value of the life expectancy of the deceased if older than the beneficiaries; (3) the loss of the companionship and society of the decedent; (4) the pain and suffering of the decedent between the time of injury and death; and (5) punitive damages, when appropriate.[4]

"It is primarily the province of the jury ... to determine the amount of damages to be awarded[,] and the award will normally not be 'set aside unless so unreasonable

---

4. The parties agreed at the close of evidence that punitive damages would not be sought.

in amount as to strike mankind at first blush as being beyond all measure, unreasonable in amount[,] and outrageous.'" *Estate of Jones v. Phillips ex rel. Phillips*, 992 So. 2d 1131, 1150 (Miss. 2008). However, this Court may order a new trial if we find the damages are "excessive or inadequate for the reason that the jury or trier of the facts was influenced by bias, prejudice, or passion, or that the damages awarded were contrary to the overwhelming weight of credible evidence." Miss. Code Ann. § 11-1-55.

Finally, all three of Baptist's challenges to the damages awarded involve jury instructions; thus, we state the familiar standard of review that the instructions must be read as a whole. Once the jury has returned a verdict, we will not direct judgment be entered to the contrary unless we find, given the evidence as a whole and taken in the light most favorable to the verdict, no reasonable hypothetical juror could have found as the jury found.…

MEDICAL EXPENSES, FUNERAL EXPENSES, AND COMPENSATION FOR PHYSICAL AND EMOTIONAL PAIN AND SUFFERING

Baptist argues Jonathan provided no substantial evidence of Ellen's conscious pain and suffering. Baptist does not dispute the jury award for Ellen's funeral and medical expenses totaling $29,604.52. As previously discussed, expert testimony established the family lost $992,109 for the value of Ellen's household services. Dr. Glenda Glover, dean of the business college at Jackson State University, who is also a certified public accountant and attorney, testified regarding the amount of Ellen's lost wages. Using wages from the year of Ellen's death and considering her work-life expectancy, Dr. Glover testified Ellen's future lost wages totaled $1,415,881. Baptist did not offer any expert testimony to dispute this figure.

The actual damages awarded include: $29,604.52 for funeral and medical expenses; $992,109 for the loss of Ellen's household services; and $1,415,880 for Ellen's lost wages. Therefore, the actual damages awarded totaled $2,437,934.52. The total amount of the damages awarded by the jury totaled $4,691,000. Thus, the jury awarded $2,253,065.48 for pain and suffering.

As previously stated, Mississippi's wrongful-death statute allows for recovery of damages by the survivors for the pain and suffering of the decedent from the time of injury until their subsequent demise. Baptist cites *M & M Pipe & Pressure Vessel Fabricators, Inc. v. Roberts*, 531 So. 2d 615, 621 (Miss. 1988), as support for the proposition the plaintiff has the burden of proving survival and consciousness after the wrongful injury and the burden is not sustained "unless there is 'substantial proof' of consciousness after the [injury]." Baptist claims Jonathan submitted no evidence to show Ellen ever regained consciousness. Case law states pain and suffering damages are measured from "the time of injury and death[.]" *McGowan v. Estate of Wright*, 524 So. 2d 308, 311 (Miss. 1988). Baptist incorrectly states the "time of injury" was "the time between her cardiorespiratory arrest/resuscitation on July 11, 2000, and her death four days later." Clearly the "injury" was the surgery during which she was exposed to latex. It is uncontradicted that Ellen regained consciousness after the surgery. The jury found during this period that she suffered an allergic reaction, which included itching, redness of the face, blisters on the lips, and nausea. As her reaction progressed, she struggled to breathe due to the anaphylactic reaction. The reaction caused Ellen's bronchoconstriction, heart arrhythmia, respiratory arrest, and a severe drop in blood pressure. There is no doubt she suffered physical agony and mental anguish as she struggled to breathe. In fact, she had to be intubated in order to breathe. She also experienced heart arrhythmia, which is typically characterized by severe chest pain. As her reaction continued, the flow of blood to her brain decreased, which led to extreme swelling of her brain and ultimately a brain stroke and infarction. She remained in the ICU for four days until her family decided to end her suffering and disconnect the ventilator.

"Awards fixed by jury determination are not merely advisory and will not under the general rule be set aside unless so unreasonable in amount as to strike mankind at first blush as being beyond all measure, unreasonable in amount[,] and outrageous." *Jack Gray Transp., Inc. v. Taylor*, 725 So. 2d 898, 899 (Miss. 1998). Our courts have repeatedly recognized the amount of damages awarded is primarily a question for the jury. *S. Cent. Bell Tel. Co. v. Parker*, 491 So. 2d 212, 217 (Miss. 1986).

Furthermore, Jonathan points out the amount for pain and suffering is less than the actual damages. The Mississippi Supreme Court has upheld damages with far greater disparities than the award in this case. *Estate of Jones v. Phillips*, 992 So. 2d 1131, 1150 (Miss. 2008) (upholding a $5,000,000 verdict and finding although economic damages only totaled $440,511.46, the amount of the verdict was not so excessive as to shock the conscience); *Gatewood v. Sampson*, 812 So. 2d 212, 223 (Miss. 2002) (upholding jury verdict of $308,000 in compensatory damages although proof of lost wages and medical expenses only totaled $8,002.50); *Dorrough v. Wilkes*, 817 So. 2d 567, 575 (Miss. 2002) (upholding jury verdict of $1,500,000 although medical fees and loss of services only totaled $339,000).

It is clear Ellen was conscious after her surgery and experienced significant pain and suffering. The jury heard the testimony and rendered damages for pain and suffering in the amount of $2,253,065.48. We do not find the amount outrageous or unreasonable; therefore, we find this issue is without merit....

Blake v. Neurological Specialists, P.C.
No. (X02) CV940155265S, 2003 WL 21235295
(Conn. Super. Ct. May 9, 2003)

SHELDON, J.

On December 12, 2001, the jury in this case returned verdicts for the plaintiff, Elaine Blake, against the defendants, Lawrence M. Beck, M.D. and his medical group, Neurological Specialists, P.C., on both of her pending claims against them. On the plaintiff's claim for wrongful death, ... the jury awarded her $1,004,492.00 — $4,492.00 in economic damages for funeral expenses and $1 million in non-economic damages — based on findings that the defendants committed medical malpractice in their case and treatment of Mr. Blake, and thereby proximately caused his death.

On the plaintiff's claim of loss of consortium ... the jury awarded her $2 million, all in non-economic damages, based on findings that by negligently causing Mr. Blake's death, the defendants wrongfully deprived her of his companionship, services and support throughout what would otherwise have been the remainder of their married life.

The defendants have now moved this Court to order a remittitur as to the jury's $2 million verdict for loss of consortium. In support of that motion, the defendants insist that a verdict of that magnitude—twice as large as the jury's verdict on the plaintiff's underlying claim of wrongful death and ten times larger than the amount suggested by the plaintiff's own lawyer in his closing argument—is so excessive as to shock the sense of justice, and thus to require that it be set aside as a matter of law.

I. Rules for Deciding Motions for Remittitur

In ruling on a motion for remittitur, a trial judge must bear in mind that "[t]he amount of a damage award is a matter peculiarly within the province of the trier of fact, in this case the jury." *Gaudio v. Griffin Health Servs. Corp.*, 249 Conn. 523, 551 (1999). Accordingly, a jury's assessment of damages should only be set aside "when the verdict is plainly excessive and exorbitant." *Wochek v. Foley*, 193 Conn. 582, 586 (1984). Proper compensation for many forms of loss or injury cannot be computed mathematically, and thus the law furnishes no precise rule for its assessment. Accordingly, when a verdict is challenged for excessiveness, the test applied "is whether the award falls within the necessarily uncertain limits of just damages or whether the size of the award so shocks the sense of justice as to compel the conclusion that the jury was influenced by partiality, prejudice, mistake or corruption." *Gaudio*, 249 Conn. at 551.

Under this test, it is certainly not necessary to present independent evidence of juror mistake or misconduct to set aside a verdict. The focus, instead, is on the size of the verdict in relation to the evidence claimed to support it. In determining if the evidence is sufficient to support the jury's award, the court must view the evidence in the light most favorable to sustaining that award....

II. The Law Governing Loss of Consortium

The Connecticut Supreme Court first recognized the modern common-law claim for loss of ... consortium in *Hopson v. St. Mary's Hospital*, 408 A.2d 260 (1979). [There], the Court defined consortium:

> "as encompassing the services of the [injured spouse], the financial support of the [injured spouse], and the variety of intangible relations which exist between spouses living together in marriage. Prosser, Torts (4th ed. 1971) § 124, pp. 881–82. These intangible elements are generally described in terms of affection, society, companionship and sexual relations.... These intangibles have also been defined as the constellation of companionship, dependence, reliance, affection, sharing and aid which are legally recognizable, protected rights arising out of the civil contract of marriage...."

Jacoby v. Brinkerhoff, 735 A.2d 347 (2001) (quoting *Hopson v. St. Mary's Hosp.*, 408 A.2d 260 (1979)).

At common law, a spouse's right to recover damages for loss of consortium was strictly limited to the period of the marriage itself.... With the enactment of General Statutes § 52-555a, however, the bar to recovering damages for postmortem loss of consortium was abrogated.... Under the statute, the surviving spouse of an injured person who dies as a result of tortiously inflicted injuries can now recover damages from the tortfeasor for any loss of consortium she has suffered or will probably suffer as a direct and proximate result of her spouse's wrongful death. Logically, the only temporal limitation upon the surviving spouse's right to recover damages for post-mortem loss of consortium is the period of time in which the plaintiff and her deceased spouse would probably have continued to live together as a married couple, enjoying each other's companionship, society and support, were it not for the defendant's tortious conduct....

III. Defendants' Challenges to Plaintiff's Loss-of-Consortium Verdict

In support of their claim that a remittitur should be ordered as to the jury's $2 million verdict for loss of consortium, the defendants do not argue that there was no factual basis in the record for any finding of loss of consortium. To the contrary, they impliedly concede that the record contains substantial evidence of loss of consortium, for they devoted nearly half of their original nine-page brief on this Motion to describing and discussing that evidence. Instead, their challenge is directed to the amount of the jury's verdict, both in absolute terms and in relation to the size of its verdict on the plaintiff's underlying claim for wrongful death.

The challenged verdict, claim the defendants, is the largest loss-of-consortium verdict in Connecticut legal history, yet the loss of consortium for which it was awarded was that of a man who, had he survived the stroke that first put him in the defendants' care, would have suffered from serious disabilities for which the defendants were in no way responsible. During the remainder of his life, for which he concededly had but a fifteen-year statistical life expectancy because he suffered from sickle cell disease, it was highly unlikely, claim the defendants, that he could or would have remained the same fine source of companionship, society and service for his wife as he had been and she had become accustomed to before his stroke. This, then, they argue, is not the right case in which to set the State record for loss-of-consortium verdicts....

Another major part of the defendant's challenge to the amount of the jury's loss-of-consortium verdict is that that verdict was nearly twice the size of their verdict for wrongful death. Here, they argue, it is simply inconceivable that the plaintiff's loss of her husband's consortium during what would otherwise have been the final years of their married life had any greater value to her than that of own loss, over that same period, both of her consortium and of all the other pleasures of life itself. Even without a specific explanation as to how the jury might have reached their verdicts, the defendants argue that in context, having awarded the plaintiff $1 million in noneconomic damages on her representative claim of wrongful death, they could not reasonably have awarded her $2 million in non-economic damages on her individual claim for loss of consortium arising from that wrongful death. Such a result, they insist, "so shocks the sense of justice as to compel the conclusion that the jury was influenced by partiality, prejudice, mistake or corruption." *Gaudio*, 249 Conn. at 551....

IV. Plaintiff's Responses to Defendants' Challenges and Court's Disposition Thereof

A. *Claim That Verdict Was Excessive Because It Failed to Reflect the True Value of the Plaintiff's Loss of Consortium in Light of Her Husband's Stroke*

The defendants' first challenge to the size of the plaintiff's loss-of-consortium verdict is that the verdict is excessive in light of the likely deterioration of the Blakes' marital relationship, and the resulting diminution in value of Mr. Blake's consortium to the plaintiff, as a result of his stroke. Because Mr. Blake did not become the defendants' patient until after he had suffered the stroke, they argue that any damages awarded for loss of consortium in the post-stroke period should have been reflective of his diminished capacity to be a source of services, society and companionship for the plaintiff as a result of the stroke.

The plaintiff's response to this argument is that the defendants have improperly based it on a misapplication of the controlling standard for deciding motions for remittitur. She claims, in particular, that the defendants rely upon a misleading summary of the evidence that fails to view the evidence in the light most favorable to sustaining the challenged verdict.... The most favorable construction of the evidence in support of the jury's verdict, she argues, was provided by her expert, Stephen Goldman, M.D., who testified that, with proper post-stroke care and treatment, Mr. Blake would have "... returned to be able to walk, to ambulate, to speak conversantly, to understand, to interact with his family appropriately and to be independently functional in the house." The Court agrees with the plaintiff that if Dr. Goldman's optimistic prognosis for Mr. Blake was correct, as the jury was entitled to believe, there was ample evidence in the record to support a finding that Mr. and Mrs. Blake would probably have continued to enjoy the same kind of loving, trusting, mutually supportive relationship after the stroke as they had enjoyed before it. The Court concludes on this basis that the defendants' first argument in support of their Motion for Remittitur must be rejected.

B. *Claim That Verdict Is Excessive Because It Is the Largest Loss-of-Consortium Verdict in Connecticut Legal History*

As for the defendants' second argument—that the Court should order a remittitur as to the challenged verdict because it is the largest loss-of-consortium verdict in Connecticut legal history—the plaintiff responds in three ways. First, she correctly reminds the Court of Connecticut case law which holds that there is no mathematical formula or ironclad rule for assessing damages in wrongful death cases.... This important note of caution has been sounded with equal clarity in loss-of-consortium cases, where our Appellate Court has flatly stated that, "Since loss of consortium is incapable of precise measurement, considerable latitude is allowed a jury in estimating damages." *Musorofiti v. Vlcek*, 783 A.2d 36 (2001) (quoting *Shegog v. Zabrecky*, 654 A.2d 771 (Conn. Ct. App. 1995)).

Secondly, the plaintiff challenges the defendants' claim that her verdict is so large as to fall outside the range of verdicts actually returned for loss of consortium, in Connecticut or elsewhere. On this score, she first draws the Court's attention to the jury's verdict in *Guthrie v. Town of Groton*, where a plaintiff's total damages for loss of consortium were assessed at $1.7 million.... The plaintiff also draws the Court's attention to the $800,000 in-state loss-of-consortium verdict returned in *Talbot v. Nissanka* and to several out-of-state loss-of-consortium verdicts in amounts approaching or exceeding $1 million. *See, e.g., Wheat v. United States*, 630 F.2d 699, 722 (W.D. Tex. 1986) (death award of $1.8 million and loss-of-consortium award of $900,000); *Meek v. Dep't of Transp.*, 610 N.W.2d 250 (2000) (awards of $1.5 million for wrongful death and $1.5 million to decedent's wife for resulting loss of consortium after a 2-year marriage).

Third and finally, the plaintiff argues that her showing of loss of consortium was especially strong and convincing, as indeed it was. The evidence showed, and permitted the jury to find, that the plaintiff and her husband had an especially warm, supportive and loving relationship dating back many years, to when they first met in their native Jamaica. They moved to this country to obtain a better life for themselves and their family, and worked constantly together, with great love, affection and mutual respect, to build a life together here. Mrs. Blake testified that her husband was a loving, kind family man, for whom his family was the most important thing in the world. She testified that he worked hard to support the family as a porter at a New York hotel, but at all times played a singularly important role in helping her to raise and counsel their children. The Blakes eventually saved enough money to buy their own home in Bridgeport, which they purchased with great joy. Mr. Blake made great efforts at home improvement, which, though not always successful, betokened his love for the family and commitment to their home. Eventually, they hoped to retire to Florida.

While at home, the Blakes had a playful, affectionate relationship with one another, which they openly enjoyed in the presence of their children. In short, Mr. Blake was the consummate family man, living out the American dream with the plaintiff, his wife, while working together with her to raise a family of which any couple would be proud. When Mr. Blake died at the age of 45, it had a devastating emotional impact upon the plaintiff, who, according to her daughter Natalie, had never imagined being alone without her father. With his death, Mrs. Blake lost her constant helpmate and loving companion, and was forced to fill the roles of both mother and father in the lives of their children. She also lost the dream she shared with Mr. Blake of retiring to and living out their lives together in Florida.

In light of this evidence, which was presented with grace and feeling by the plaintiff, her daughter and Mr. Blake's niece, Marjorie Powell, who had lived with the family for several months, the plaintiff made a compelling case for a substantial award of damages for loss of consortium. On the basis of that evidence, the jury might well have concluded that the defendants, by their negligence, wrongfully deprived her of 15 years or more of love, support, caring and affection from, while sharing all the joys of a truly happy marriage with, an especially attentive, hardworking, proud and joyous man. Against that background, this Court cannot say that Mrs. Blake's damages award for loss of consortium should not be among the largest ever awarded by a Connecticut jury. It is not so far outside the range of loss-of-consortium verdicts in this or other states as to warrant setting it aside on that basis alone....

D. *Claim That Verdict Shocks the Sense of Justice in Light of Jury's Verdict for Wrongful Death*

To the defendants' fourth argument in support of their Motion for Remittitur—that the jury's verdict for loss of consortium was so large as to shock the sense of justice in light of its markedly smaller verdict on the plaintiff's underlying claim for wrongful death—the plaintiff responds in two ways. First, she argues that there is no absolute rule in our case law prohibiting the awarding of greater damages to a surviving spouse for loss of consortium than to the representative of the deceased spouse's estate for wrongful death. Though a loss-of-consortium claim is derivative, in the sense that it is based upon and cannot be maintained without a parallel claim by the deceased spouse's representative for wrongful death, the claim is otherwise independent and subject to separate valuation because the losses for which damages may be awarded thereunder are district and different....

Here, however ... the Court concludes that there is no rational basis for sustaining the jury's $2 million verdict for loss of consortium while awarding just over $1 million to the plaintiff, in her representative capacity, for her husband's wrongful death. This is so, the Court believes, because the entire theory of the plaintiff's claim for loss of consortium was based upon the great joy, positivity and productivity with which the decedent, Crafton Blake, had lived and shared his life with the plaintiff and would likely have continued to do so, notwithstanding his stroke, had his life not been cut short by the defendants' negligence. There is simply no basis in this record, read in the light most favorable to sustaining a large verdict for the plaintiff on her individual claim for loss of consortium, for assigning any greater value to her loss of his companionship, services and society during what should have been the final years of their marvelously happy, successful marriage than to his own loss of life and all its pleasures, as he would have enjoyed them in the context of that marriage. In sum, though this Court was impressed throughout the trial by the attentiveness and apparent seriousness of purpose of the jurors who served in this case, the Court must conclude that on this record, in light of their smaller, $1 million award of noneconomic damages for the wrongful death of Mr. Blake, their $2 million award of noneconomic damages for Mrs. Blake's resulting loss of consortium "so shocks the sense of justice as to compel the conclusion that the jury was influenced by ... mistake[.]" *Gaudio*, 249 Conn. at 551. Accordingly, the Court concludes that the defendants' Motion For Remittitur must be granted.

Against this background, the Court concludes that the largest verdict which the jury in this case could reasonably have returned on the plaintiff's individual claim of loss of consortium was one equal in amount to the noneconomic damages component of its verdict on her representative claim of wrongful death....

Notes and Questions

1. Why does the court find it inappropriate for the jury verdict on the loss of consortium claim in *Blake* to exceed the noneconomic damages component of the wrongful death claim? Note that a jury determination on a loss of consortium claim is entitled to great deference: "Since loss of consortium is incapable of precise measurement, considerable latitude is allowed a jury in estimating damages." *Shegog v. Zabrecky*, 654 A.2d 771, 779 (Conn. App. Ct. 1995). Considering that standard of review, was the court right to restrict the value of the claim using this analysis?

2. Why is the jury verdict for pain and suffering in *Kelly* upheld if the loss of consortium claim in *Blake* is deemed excessive? Is there a way to read these cases together for a consistent principle or are they hopelessly inconsistent?

3. In *Kelly*, the jury returned an award of $4.7 million, of which $2.4 million was economic damages and $2.3 was for pain and suffering. The court notes that the damage claim predated Mississippi Code § 11-1-60, which enacted a cap of economic damages at $1 million and a cap on non-economic damages at $500,000. If the incident in *Kelly* occurred now, the recovery would be limited by that statute to $1.5 million.

   Why would a legislature adopt this type of cap? Proponents of tort reform claim that by reducing liability exposure to personal injury lawsuits, they can reduce insurance rates and make a state's environment friendlier to business or medical practice.[62] Since the 1970s, many states have adopted tort reform measures limiting overall recoveries, noneconomic damages, or recovery in medical malpractice lawsuits.[63]

   Whether tort reform succeeds in creating the results intended remains an open question. Research has shown such reforms can result in reductions in tort filings and tort awards,[64] yet studies are mixed on whether this results in insurance rate reductions.[65] On the other hand, even without proven reductions in insurance rates, these caps can disproportionately affect female claimants.[66] Lucinda M.

---

62. *See* Scott DeVito & Andrew Jurs, *An Overreaction to a Nonexistent Problem: Empirical Analysis of Tort Reform from the 1980s to 2000s*, 3 STAN. J. COMPLEX LITIG. 62, 68–72 (2015).

63. *Id.* at 69 n.22 (citing Ronen Avraham, *Database of State Tort Law Reforms*, http://papers.ssrn.com/sol3/papers.cfm?abstract_id=902711).

64. Myungho Paik, Bernard Black & David Hyman, *The Receding Tide of Medical Malpractice Litigation Part 1: National Trends*, 10 J. EMPIRICAL LEGAL STUD. 612, 625 tbl.2. (2013) (finding a higher drop in filings during study years in states with tort reform (42%) than in states without it (24%)); David M. Studdert, Y. Tony Yang & Michelle Mello, *Are Damages Caps Regressive? A Study of Malpractice Jury Verdicts in California*, 23 HEALTH AFFS. 54, 58 (2004) (finding a 34% reduction in damage awards after cap enacted in California).

65. *Compare* Meredith Kilgore et al., *Tort Law and Medical Malpractice Insurance Premiums*, 43 INQUIRY 255, 265 (2006) (finding a 17.3% reduction), *with* Mark Paul Guis, *Using Panel Data to Estimate the Determinants of Medical Malpractice Insurance Premiums*, 5 APPLIED ECON. LETTERS 37, 37 (1998) (finding no effect).

66. *See, e.g.*, Lucinda M. Finley, *The Hidden Victims of Tort Reform: Women, Children, and the Elderly*, 53 EMORY L.J. 1263, 1285 (2004).

Finley writes that the effect of damages caps is nothing short of a "form of discrimination against women [that] contribute[s] to unequal access to justice...."[67] State Supreme Courts sometimes find that tort reform is unconstitutional, mainly for violating the claimant's right to a jury trial or equal protection. *Best v. Taylor Mach. Works*, 689 N.E.2d 1057 (Ill. 1997); *Ray v. Anesthesia Assocs. of Mobile, P.C.*, 674 So. 2d 525, 526 (Ala. 1995).

Considering this background, evaluate whether the Mississippi damages cap discussed in *Kelly* violates those rights.

Tying It Together

Consider the following passage, discussing how forensic economists calculate income and wage loss in personal injury litigation:

> U.S. government data clearly show that both average earning and the important worklife expectancy variables — participation rates and employment rates — significantly differ by gender, race, and ethnicity.... For adults with a work history, the earnings history for the particular person is used, and average earnings for statistical classes of persons are generally irrelevant.... The same is not true for worklife expectancy, because the combination of participation and employment rates contained in any worklife expectancy measure has typically been based on statistical tables disaggregated by age, education level, gender, and race or ethnicity. For example, the participation rate for U.S. women (the probability that a female will either have a job or be in the workforce seeking a job) has steadily grown toward the rate of U.S. men since World War II, although their participation rate has leveled in recent years. It is still true, however, that the participation rate of women is just over 80 percent of the rate for men....
>
> Many forensic economists believe it is their scientific duty to use reliable data that is as close as possible to the characteristics of the particular person. Others believe that discrimination is at least one factor in workforce differences by race and gender, and some believe that the use of data disaggregated by race and gender is ... wrong.[68]

Consider how race or gender-specific data can affect a real case with the example of *United States v. Bedonie*, a homicide case where the amount of restitution was at issue.[69] In performing the lost wages calculation, the expert economist found a likely wage loss of approximately $433,000 based on a finding that the average Native Amer-

67. *Id.* at 1313.

68. Michael L. Brookshire, *Some Special Cases and Issues, in* THE PLAINTIFF AND DEFENSE ATTORNEY'S GUIDE TO UNDERSTANDING ECONOMIC DAMAGES 101, 105–6 (Michael Brookshire et al., eds., 2007).

69. 317 F. Supp. 2d 1285, 1288 (D. Utah 2004) (discussed in detail in Martha Chamallas, *Civil Rights in Ordinary Tort Cases: Race, Gender, and the Calculation of Economic Loss*, 38 LOY. L.A. L. REV. 1435, 1438 (2005)).

ican male will only earn 58% of what the average white male will earn over a lifetime.[70] The judge then asked for a race-neutral income loss figure, which the economist determined was approximately $744,000.[71]

Assignment: You have been assigned to the *Bedonie* case prior to the final arguments motion for restitution. Your boss calls and asks you to prepare a brief memo outlining the arguments for the restitution hearing. As either the Assistant U.S. Attorney or defense attorney for Bedonie, prepare a two-page memo for your boss on what the appropriate restitution figure should be.

B. Business Valuation

Barry M. Wertheimer, *The Shareholders' Appraisal Remedy and How Courts Determine Fair Value*

47 DUKE L.J. 613 (1998)

II. How Courts Determine Fair Value

A. Approaches to Valuation

The key to the effectiveness of the appraisal remedy in protecting minority shareholder interests lies in the way in which courts appraise minority shares. If courts do not appraise shares in a manner consistent with the appraisal remedy's purpose of protecting minority shareholders, such shareholders will ignore the appraisal remedy in favor of other means of challenging fundamental transactions, principally breach of fiduciary duty claims, which may be less efficient and more time consuming to resolve.

The statutory command in an appraisal proceeding is to find the "fair value" of the dissenting shares, or sometimes the "fair market value" or "fair cash value." Fair value is typically defined by statute as "the value of the shares immediately before the effectuation of the corporate action to which the dissenter objects, excluding any appreciation or depreciation in anticipation of the corporate action." Statutes generally provide no further guidance with respect to ascertaining fair value in an appraisal proceeding.

Before *Weinberger*, the traditional means of determining fair value was the Delaware block method of valuation. [[This method] utilizes a weighted average of three separate valuations, one based on asset value, one based on earnings value, and one based on market value.[66] This mechanical approach to appraisal was not very hos-

---

70. *Id.* at 1313.

71. *Id.* at 1314.

66. To calculate fair value under the Delaware block method, it is first necessary to value the corporation based on its asset value, its earnings value, and its market value. Next, each of these three valuations is accorded a percentage weight. The fair value of the corporation is deemed to be the weighted average of the three separate valuations. *See, e.g.,* Francis I. duPont & Co. v. Universal City Studios, Inc., 312 A.2d 344, 348–52 (Del. Ch. 1973)....

pitable to the claims of dissenting shareholders, and did not accord with current financial methods of valuation. As a result, the court in *Weinberger* cast aside the block method as the exclusive means of valuation, opening the process up to all methods of valuation "generally considered acceptable in the financial community."[69] [Ed.] After *Weinberger* opened up the valuation process to [any acceptable technique] ... the most prominent method of valuation in Delaware has been the discounted cash flow (DCF) method. This valuation technique operates on the premise that the value of a company is determined by the present value of its projected future cash flows. The DCF method has been described by the Delaware courts as "the preeminent valuation methodology" and "[i]n many situations ... [theoretically] the single best technique to estimate the value of an economic asset." As described by the Delaware Court of Chancery:

> The DCF model entails three basic components: an estimation of net cash flows that the firm will generate and when, over some period; a terminal or residual value equal to the future value, as of the end of the projection period, of the firm's cash flows beyond the projection period; and finally a cost of capital with which to discount to a present value both the projected net cash flows and the estimated terminal or residual value.[81]

The DCF method, although probably the most prominent and frequently used post-*Weinberger* method of appraisal, has not been the exclusive valuation method employed. The Delaware courts have continued to use a variety of valuation techniques, depending on the facts and circumstances of the particular case, including the Delaware block method, valuation based on a comparison to other companies (the "comparable company approach"), valuation based on net asset value, valuation based on earnings and book value, and valuation based on combinations of these techniques.

The valuation technique used by a court is highly dependent on the valuation evidence presented by the parties.... Thus, if both parties present evidence of fair value utilizing the DCF method, the court's resolution of the dispute will likely employ a DCF analysis....

There are problems endemic to an appraisal proceeding that cannot be eliminated by the choice of appraisal methodology. Each appraisal technique is but a way of estimating the "fair value" or "true value" or "intrinsic value" of a company, and undeniably, " '[v]aluation is an art rather than a science.' "[90] The valuation "answer" given by each of these techniques is very dependent on the assumptions underlying the calculations employed. For example, even though the DCF approach is highly regarded, it relies heavily on a guess as to the future cash flows of the enterprise. This

---

69. Weinberger v. UOP, Inc., 457 A.2d 701, 713 (Del. 1983).

[Ed.] The bracketed material has been moved within the text by the Author for clarity purposes.

81. Cede & Co. v. Technicolor, Inc., No. CIV.A.7129, 1990 WL 161084, at *23 (Oct. 19, 1990), *rev'd on other grounds*, 684 A.2d 289 (Del. 1996).

90. In re Appraisal of Shell Oil Co., No. CIV.A.8080, 1990 WL 201390, at *16 (Dec. 11, 1990) (quoting testimony of expert witness), *aff'd*, 607 A.2d 1213 (Del. 1992).

"guess" may be informed by looking at historical data, operating trends, and other relevant factors, but it is still nothing more than a prediction of future events. Once these future cash flows are predicted, they must be discounted to a present value. What discount rate should be employed? Again, there is much room for guesswork and subjectivity. The DCF technique also requires that a terminal value be established and then discounted to a present value; both are further exercises in guesswork and subjectivity.

As a practical matter, this means that both parties to the appraisal proceeding will present expert testimony of valuation. Because of the inherent subjectivity and estimation involved, the parties' experts can compute dramatically different valuations, even if they utilize the same methodology.... It is not unusual for the opinions of the experts to differ by a factor of ten. It is, therefore, not surprising that courts have evidenced frustration with this process....[98]

Berens v. Ludwig
953 F. Supp. 249 (N.D. Ill. 1997)

ALESIA, District Judge.

Before the court is defendant Comptroller of the Currency's motion to dismiss plaintiff Mark H. Berens' complaint pursuant to F.R.C.P. 12(b)(6), or in the alternative, motion for summary judgment pursuant to F.R.C.P. 56(b). For the reasons that follow, the court denies the motion to dismiss, but grants the motion for summary judgment.

I. *BACKGROUND*

Plaintiff Mark H. Berens owned 33 shares of stock in Marquette Bank Shakopee, N.A., making him a minority shareholder in the bank. Marquette Bancshares, Inc. ("MBI"), was the bank's majority shareholder. Some time prior to January 1, 1995, MBI decided to consolidate the bank with 10 other banks. Berens voted against the consolidation, to no avail. On January 1, 1995, MBI consolidated the banks.... MBI gave Berens $12,071 per share of stock that he owned, but Berens felt that this price was too low.

Accordingly, Berens sought an appraisal of his stock by the Comptroller of the Currency pursuant to 12 U.S.C. § 215(d), which allows any interested party in a bank consolidation to request that the Comptroller appraise a dissenting shareholder's stock. The Comptroller's appraisal is final and binding on all parties.

Both Berens and MBI submitted information in support of their positions with respect to the value of the stock. The Comptroller considered the parties' materials, and conducted his own analysis. In his appraisal, the Comptroller considered the stock's market value, adjusted book value, and investment value. He gave no weight

---

98. *See* Kleinwort Benson Ltd. v. Silgan Corp., No. CIV.A.11107, 1995 WL 376911, at *5 (Del. Ch. June 15, 1995) (noting the "adversarial hyperbole that inevitably influences an expert's opinion in valuation proceedings").

to the market value, finding that the bank's stock traded too infrequently and sporadically for a true and accurate market value to exist. He gave greater weight to the investment value than the adjusted book value, such that his final appraisal reflected a three-to-one weighting of investment value to adjusted book value....

Using this methodology, the Comptroller determined that Berens' stock was worth $13,034 per share as of January 1, 1995. However, Berens' believes his stock is worth about $16,700 per share. Consequently, Berens filed this lawsuit against the Comptroller ... alleging that the Comptroller's appraisal was conducted in an arbitrary and capricious manner, and asking the court to set aside the appraisal. The Comptroller has moved to dismiss Berens' cause of action ... or alternatively, has moved for summary judgment....

II. *DISCUSSION*

Berens has two primary quarrels with the Comptroller's appraisal of his stock. He contends that the Comptroller failed to adjust its calculations to account for about $5,000,000 in excess capital that the bank carried. He also contends that the Comptroller should have used a discounted cash flow analysis to estimate the bank's value. Berens asserts that these errors by the Comptroller resulted in an arbitrary and capricious appraisal that undervalued his stock.

The Comptroller moves to dismiss Berens' action for failure to state a claim. He argues that because the Comptroller was not required to use any particular methodology in appraising the stock's value, Berens cannot bring a claim based on the Comptroller's decision not to follow Berens' suggested approaches. In the alternative, the Comptroller argues that even if Berens could bring a cause of action based on the Comptroller's failure to use a specific appraisal methodology, the Comptroller's methodology was not arbitrary and capricious. Therefore, the Comptroller contends he is entitled to summary judgment on Berens' cause of action.

A. *Motion to Dismiss*

When deciding a motion to dismiss under F.R.C.P. 12(b)(6), the court must accept all factual allegations in the complaint as true and draw all reasonable inferences in favor of the plaintiff. If, when viewed in the light most favorable to the plaintiff, the complaint fails to state a claim upon which relief can be granted, the court must dismiss the case. However, the court may dismiss the complaint only if it appears beyond doubt that the plaintiff can prove no set of facts in support of his claims that would entitle him to relief.

The Comptroller contends that under *Beerly v. Department of the Treasury*, 768 F.2d 942 (7th Cir. 1985), *cert. denied*, 475 U.S. 1010 (1986), this court cannot tell the Comptroller what methodology he should have used in conducting his appraisal of Berens' stock. According to the Comptroller, the essence of Berens' complaint is that the Comptroller should have used valuation methods other than the one he chose to use. Thus, the Comptroller argues, Berens' complaint asks the court to dictate the Comptroller's choice of appraisal methodology, which neither Berens nor the court can do. Therefore, Berens' cause of action should be dismissed....

The Comptroller contends that *Beerly* precludes this court from deciding whether the Comptroller should have used a particular methodology instead of the one that he used. This court does not read *Beerly* as so absolute. The *Beerly* court stated that the fact that the Comptroller used a conventional appraisal went far in shielding his results from review, not that it precluded review. Moreover, the court then proceeded to evaluate the merits of the Comptroller's appraisal.... In short, the Seventh Circuit went beyond deciding whether the Comptroller had used a particular appraisal methodology, and determined whether the Comptroller's appraisal methodology was reasonable. The reasonableness of the Comptroller's appraisal methodology is not a question to be decided on a motion to dismiss, but is more appropriately a question for summary judgment. *See, e.g., Simonds v. Guaranty Bank & Tr. Co.*, 492 F. Supp. 1079, 1080 (D. Mass. 1979); *Yabsley v. Conover*, 644 F. Supp. 689, 691 (N.D. Ill. 1986)....

Accordingly, the court denies the Comptroller's motion to dismiss, and will address the merits ... in the context of the Comptroller's motion for summary judgment.

B. *Motion for Summary Judgment*

A motion for summary judgment must be granted if "the pleadings, depositions, answers to interrogatories, and admissions on file, together with the affidavits, if any, show that there is no genuine issue as to any material fact and that the moving party is entitled to a judgment as a matter of law." The burden is on the moving party to show that no genuine issues of material fact exist. Once the moving party presents a *prima facie* showing that it is entitled to judgment as a matter of law, the party opposing the motion may not rest upon the mere allegations or denials in its pleadings but must set forth specific facts showing that a genuine issue for trial exists. All reasonable factual inferences must be viewed in favor of the non-moving party.

In this motion for summary judgment, the overarching question is whether the Comptroller's appraisal was reasonable. *See Yabsley*, 644 F. Supp. at 693. The court considers "whether the appraisal was based on a consideration of the relevant factors and whether there has been a clear error of judgment." *Id.*

In considering whether the Comptroller's appraisal was reasonable, the court is resolving a legal question; it must determine on the basis of the administrative record whether the Comptroller's appraisal procedure was arbitrary or capricious. Consequently, this court will examine the reasoning behind the Comptroller's appraisal in some depth.

The Comptroller stated that his appraisal uses three measures of value: market value, investment value, and adjusted book value, all as of the date of the consolidation on January 1, 1995. The Comptroller stated that he selected valuation methods that provide a market value for the shares being valued. He stated that market value is the price at which a willing buyer and willing seller would exchange a share of stock in an "arm's length" transaction; and that market value reflects an investor's perception and valuation of a bank as a going concern. However, because the bank's stock was not listed on a major exchange and was infrequently traded, and therefore had no active market, the Comptroller found that he could not establish a reliable market value to appraise the stock.

The Comptroller stated that investment value is a method of valuation that attempts to assess the earnings capacity of the bank and then apply the market perception of the value of banking organizations with similar earnings potential. Determining investment value is a two-step process that requires the Comptroller to establish a peer group comprised of banking institutions with similar earnings potential for which market data is readily available, and to analyze the historical earnings data of the bank.

The Comptroller determines investment value by multiplying the bank's earnings per share by the average price per earnings ratio for the banks in the peer group; this yields a market-based price per share, or investment value, for the bank. The Comptroller determined that the investment value of a share of the bank's stock was $12,018.50.

Adjusted book value is derived by multiplying the book value of a bank's assets per share by a ratio of market price to book value for a peer group. Book value is determined by dividing total equity capital by number of shares of common stock outstanding. The application of the market price to book value ratio measures the premium or discount to book value that investors attribute to the condition and prospects of similarly situated banking organizations. Since the bank had capital of $12,464,000 and 1,000 shares outstanding, its book value per share was $12,464. Multiplying the book value by the peer group's average ratio of market price to book value of 1.29 yielded an adjusted book value of $16,078.56 per share.

The Comptroller then considered the materials submitted by Berens, primarily consisting of the appraisal of Berens' stock by a private appraiser. The Comptroller described in detail the methodology used by the private appraiser. In particular, the private appraiser took into account the fact that the bank had excess capital of $4,900,000 when compared to regulatory capital requirements and the amount of capital held by the institutions in the peer group. It then applied the discounted cash flow method of appraisal, also adding $4,900 per share of implied excess capital to the present value calculations. The Comptroller rejected the private appraiser's methods, stating that the Office of the Comptroller does not employ a discounted cash flow approach or excess capital methodology for determining the value of dissenting shareholder stock. However, the Comptroller noted that the peer groups used by the Comptroller and the private appraiser contained many of the same banking institutions.

The Comptroller then reviewed his determinations of investment value and adjusted book value. He stated that investment value provides a reasonable estimate of the value to investors of a share in the future earnings of the bank, and therefore is income-based and values the bank as a going concern. In contrast, the adjusted book value is asset-based, and is more reflective of the value of the bank in voluntary liquidation. The Comptroller stated that he gives more weight to the investment value method, since banks' earnings are readily available to the public and historically are the primary factor used by investors in deciding the value of a bank's stock. Thus, the Comptroller gave investment value to adjusted book value a three-to-one weighting. That is, he added 75 percent of the investment value of $12,018.50 to 25 percent of the adjusted book value of $16,078.56 to arrive at an appraised value of $13,033.52.

Berens feels this value is too low. He first contends that the Comptroller should have used the widely accepted discounted cash flow method of appraisal, as did his private appraiser and MBI's appraiser. Berens contends that the Comptroller explicitly refused to consider his and MBI's appraisers' findings....

Berens is factually incorrect in his assertion that the Comptroller explicitly refused to consider the other appraisers' findings. In fact, the Comptroller explained in detail the discounted cash flow approach used by the other appraisers. Nonetheless, he chose to use his version of the Delaware Block method, and stated that the Comptroller does not use the discounted cash flow approach to valuing stock.

The court sees nothing unreasonable about the Comptroller's methodology. As the court in *Beerly* stated, "the fact that the Comptroller was following a conventional approach goes far to shield his results from judicial invalidation." *Beerly*, 768 F.2d at 945. Moreover, the Comptroller applied the same methodology in this case as he did in *Beerly*, and of which the *Beerly* court expressly approved. *See also Yabsley*, 644 F. Supp. at 693–95 (holding that Delaware Block method of appraisal ... was a reasonable method of appraisal). Thus, "mere use of the Delaware Block Method does not render the appraisal arbitrary and capricious."

Moreover, the Comptroller explained in great detail the basis of his appraisal, the calculations he used to reach his valuations, and his reasons for using his methodology. For example, the Comptroller fully explained why he used investment value and adjusted book value as the two benchmarks of the stock's value, and why he weighted investment value three times greater than adjusted book value. The ... explanation seems eminently reasonable.

Berens also argues that the Comptroller failed to consider the fact that the bank had excess capital of about $5,000,000, which is a relevant factor that the Comptroller is required to consider. Berens contends that the bank paid grossly inadequate dividends for 16 years, forcing the minority shareholders to suffer years of underpaid dividends, which resulted in the accumulation of the excess capital. Berens contends that because of the Comptroller's refusal to recognize these facts, Berens will not receive his share of the value of the excess capital accumulation from the forced sale of his shares.

The court notes again that the Comptroller recognized that Berens' private appraiser took into account the excess capital in reaching his appraised value of the stock. However, the Comptroller stated that he did not employ the excess capital method of appraisal. Therefore, the Comptroller did not totally disregard the possible existence of excess capital....

More important, the Comptroller's calculations accounted for the excess capital, at least indirectly. The Comptroller's determination of adjusted book value was based on the bank's total equity capital of $12,464,000, about $5,000,000 of which is the purported excess capital. Thus, the adjusted book value figure is based on total capital, including the excess capital. Obviously, if the bank has excess capital compared to other banks, all other things being equal, its adjusted book value should be higher than that of the other banks. Consequently, the court finds that the Comptroller considered the excess capital by considering total capital, and therefore did not fail to consider a relevant factor....

The court finds that the Comptroller sufficiently considered the relevant factors, including the amount of capital of the bank, in appraising Berens' stock. As the Eleventh Circuit noted, the court "do[es] not assess whether the appraisal was correct or utilized the best methods[, but] ... determine[s] only whether it was reasonable." *Lewis v. Clark*, 911 F.2d 1558, 1563 (11th Cir. 1990). Based on the administrative record, the court finds that the Comptroller's appraisal of Berens' stock was reasonable.

Accordingly, the court grants the Comptroller's motion for summary judgment....

Notes and Questions

1. Judge Alesia's decision in *Ludwig* is a fairly straightforward assessment of the methodology of the valuation, the appropriate legal standard, and the reasonableness of the overall calculation in light of the objections raised by the opponent. Note particularly that the judge is merely deciding if the method used is reasonable, not whether the method was correct or the best possible approach. Only when the determination is arbitrary and capricious can the judge overturn the valuation. In that regard, the valuation is given standard administrative deference.

2. In describing the valuation, the appraiser notes that market value would be the first major factor to consider. However, the bank's stock was not listed on a major exchange and was infrequently traded, so it had no active market. In cases of publicly traded corporations, the market-based approach is often used, since it sets a value based on disinterested third-party trading. *See* Barry M. Wertheimer, *The Shareholders' Appraisal Remedy and How Courts Determine Fair Value*, 47 DUKE L.J. 613, 631–32 (1998). In fact, Wertheimer notes a significant number of states that exempt publicly traded shares from an appraisal remedy by statute. *Id.* at 632 n.101 (counting 24 statutory adoptions of the market exception). *See also* Jeff Goetz, Note, *A Dissent Dampened by Timing: How the Stock Market Exception Systematically Deprives Public Shareholders of Fair Market Value*, 15 FORDHAM J. CORP. & FIN. L. 771, 772–73 (2010) (noting 35 states with market exception statutes by 2010, since "dissenting shareholders could more efficiently receive the fair value of their publicly traded shares through sale on the market....").

Part III

Looking Forward

Chapter 11

Changing Our Approach: Can We Do Better?

We reviewed the basic underlying rules of expert evidence in Part I and examined specific areas of expertise in both civil and criminal litigation in Part II. Having seen both the strengths and (many) weaknesses of expert evidence, we must now consider a fundamental question first raised in Chapter 1: can we do better?

Susan Haack, in her article *Irreconcilable Differences*, raised the question of significant reform in our very first reading of the text. She first reviewed the different methodologies of scientific and legal inquiry, and identified how their "marriage" can lead to distortion effects. Having reviewed the management of scientific evidence in the judicial system since then, we can see exactly how those distortions occur, and what courts do about them. In her piece, Haack decided, since "divorce is out of the question," that instead "[b]oth partners have tried to adapt,"[72] and then she offered suggestions on how to avoid distortion effects. For example, she suggests that if scientific inquiry into an issue is ongoing, then legal processes that are inconsistent with that approach (for example, statutes of limitation) should be changed.[73] Similarly, she suggests that if adversarial experts inherently come from the margins of a discipline, judges should appoint independent experts which can be nominated by neutral inquiry.[74]

Now, in our final chapter, we turn to consider whether—in light of the problems of expert evidence being presented in court—significant reforms to our current system are appropriate. As we think about these proposals, assess the extent to which each proposal has an effect on the current approach to expert witnesses. First, we must consider whether the proposal relies largely upon the current rules, or whether it significantly or even radically alters them. Second, consider the current relationship of the court to the expert and how the proposals might alter that balance. Finally, on a more fundamental level, consider how radically each proposal alters the structure of systems of expert witnesses and shifts away from an adversarial approach. When we distill those three considerations into policy, we will see that the proposals of this chapter can be lumped into low-, medium-, and high-level change categories based on the extent of their disruption.

---

72. Susan Haack, *Irreconcilable Differences? The Troubled Marriage of Science and Law*, 72 Law & Contemp. Probs. 1, 21 (2009).
73. *Id.*
74. *Id.*

As we move through these materials from low- to high-level changes, remember these fundamental questions: how does each proposal seek to address a weakness in the current system of expert evidence and how effective would it be in fixing the problem? By answering those questions, we can decide if each proposal has merit and should be adopted.

A. Low-Level Change Proposals

Daubert v. Merrell Dow Pharmaceuticals, Inc.

509 U.S. 579 (1993)

BLACKMUN, J.

… Faced with a proffer of expert scientific testimony, then, the trial judge must determine at the outset … whether the expert is proposing to testify to (1) scientific knowledge that (2) will assist the trier of fact to understand or determine a fact in issue. This entails a preliminary assessment of whether the reasoning or methodology underlying the testimony is scientifically valid and of whether that reasoning or methodology properly can be applied to the facts in issue. We are confident that federal judges possess the capacity to undertake this review. Many factors will bear on the inquiry, and we do not presume to set out a definitive checklist or test. But some general observations are appropriate.

Ordinarily, a key question to be answered in determining whether a theory or technique is scientific knowledge that will assist the trier of fact will be whether it can be (and has been) tested. "Scientific methodology today is based on generating hypotheses and testing them to see if they can be falsified; indeed, this methodology is what distinguishes science from other fields of human inquiry.…"

Another pertinent consideration is whether the theory or technique has been subjected to peer review and publication. Publication (which is but one element of peer review) is not a *sine qua non* of admissibility; it does not necessarily correlate with reliability, see S. Jasanoff, The Fifth Branch: Science Advisors as Policymakers 61–76 (1990), and in some instances well-grounded but innovative theories will not have been published, see Horrobin, *The Philosophical Basis of Peer Review and the Suppression of Innovation*, 263 JAMA 1438 (1990). Some propositions, moreover, are too particular, too new, or of too limited interest to be published. But submission to the scrutiny of the scientific community is a component of "good science," in part because it increases the likelihood that substantive flaws in methodology will be detected.…

Additionally, in the case of a particular scientific technique, the court ordinarily should consider the known or potential rate of error.…

Finally, "general acceptance" can yet have a bearing on the inquiry. A "reliability assessment does not require, although it does permit, explicit identification of a relevant scientific community and an express determination of a particular degree of acceptance within that community.…" Widespread acceptance can be an important factor in ruling particular evidence admissible, and "a known technique which has been able to attract only minimal support within the community," may properly be viewed with skepticism.

The inquiry envisioned by Rule 702 is, we emphasize, a flexible one. Its overarching subject is the scientific validity and thus the evidentiary relevance and reliability— of the principles that underlie a proposed submission. The focus, of course, must be solely on principles and methodology, not on the conclusions that they generate.

Throughout, a judge assessing a proffer of expert scientific testimony under Rule 702 should also be mindful of other applicable rules. Rule 703 provides that expert opinions based on otherwise inadmissible hearsay are to be admitted only if the facts or data are "of a type reasonably relied upon by experts in the particular field in forming opinions or inferences upon the subject." Rule 706 allows the court at its discretion to procure the assistance of an expert of its own choosing. Finally, Rule 403 permits the exclusion of relevant evidence "if its probative value is substantially outweighed by the danger of unfair prejudice, confusion of the issues, or misleading the jury...." Judge Weinstein has explained: "Expert evidence can be both powerful and quite misleading because of the difficulty in evaluating it. Because of this risk, the judge in weighing possible prejudice against probative force under Rule 403 of the present rules exercises more control over experts than over lay witnesses." Weinstein, 138 F.R.D., at 632.

General Electric Co. v. Joiner
522 U.S. 136 (1997)

BREYER, J., concurring

The Court's opinion, which I join, emphasizes *Daubert*'s statement that a trial judge, acting as "gatekeeper," must " 'ensure that any and all scientific testimony or evidence admitted is not only relevant, but reliable.' " This requirement will sometimes ask judges to make subtle and sophisticated determinations about scientific methodology and its relation to the conclusions an expert witness seeks to offer—particularly when a case arises in an area where the science itself is tentative or uncertain, or where testimony about general risk levels in human beings or animals is offered to prove individual causation. Yet, as *amici* have pointed out, judges are not scientists and do not have the scientific training that can facilitate the making of such decisions.

Of course, neither the difficulty of the task nor any comparative lack of expertise can excuse the judge from exercising the "gatekeeper" duties that the Federal Rules of Evidence impose—determining, for example, whether particular expert testimony is reliable and "will assist the trier of fact," ... or whether the "probative value" of testimony is substantially outweighed by risks of prejudice, confusion or waste of time.... To the contrary, when law and science intersect, those duties often must be exercised with special care.

Today's toxic tort case provides an example. The plaintiff in today's case says that a chemical substance caused, or promoted, his lung cancer. His concern, and that of others, about the causes of cancer is understandable, for cancer kills over one in five Americans. Moreover, scientific evidence implicates some chemicals as potential causes of some cancers. Yet modern life, including good health as well as economic well-being, depends upon the use of artificial or manufactured substances, such as chemicals. And it may, therefore, prove particularly important to see that judges fulfill their *Daubert* gatekeeping function, so that they help assure that the powerful engine of tort liability, which can generate strong financial incentives to reduce, or to eliminate, production, points toward the right substances and does not destroy the wrong ones. It is, thus, essential in this science-related area that the courts administer the Federal Rules of Evidence in order to achieve the "end[s]" that the Rules themselves set forth, not only so that proceedings may be "justly determined," but also so "that the truth may be ascertained."

I therefore want specially to note that, as cases presenting significant science-related issues have increased in number, judges have increasingly found in the Rules of Evidence and Civil Procedure ways to help them overcome the inherent difficulty of making determinations about complicated scientific, or otherwise technical, evidence. Among these techniques are an increased use of Rule 16's pretrial conference authority to narrow the scientific issues in dispute, pretrial hearings where potential experts are subject to examination by the court, and the appointment of special masters and specially trained law clerks....

In the present case, the New England Journal of Medicine has filed an *amici* brief "in support of neither petitioners nor respondents" in which the Journal writes:

> [A] judge could better fulfill this gatekeeper function if he or she had help from scientists. Judges should be strongly encouraged to make greater use of their inherent authority ... to appoint experts.... Reputable experts could be recommended to courts by established scientific organizations, such as the National Academy of Sciences or the American Association for the Advancement of Science.

Cf. Fed. Rule Evid. 706 (court may "on its own motion or on the motion of any party" appoint an expert to serve on behalf of the court ...). Given this kind of offer of cooperative effort, from the scientific to the legal community, and given the various Rules—authorized methods for facilitating the courts' task, it seems to me that *Daubert*'s gatekeeping requirement will not prove inordinately difficult to implement, and that it will help secure the basic objectives of the Federal Rules of Evidence..., the ascertainment of truth and the just determination of proceedings.

Joe S. Cecil & Thomas E. Willging,
Accepting Daubert's *Invitation: Defining a Role for Court-Appointed Experts in Assessing Scientific Validity*
43 Emory L.J. 995 (1994)

I. INTRODUCTION

In *Daubert v. Merrell Dow Pharmaceuticals, Inc.* the Supreme Court urged federal judges faced with a challenge to scientific testimony to undertake "a preliminary assessment of whether the reasoning or methodology underlying the testimony is scientifically valid and of whether that reasoning or methodology properly can be applied to the facts in issue." In response to concerns raised by Chief Justice Rehnquist, Justice Blackmun, writing for the majority, expressed confidence in the ability of federal judges to undertake such a review, noting that, among other thing, judges "should also be mindful" of the authority to appoint experts under Rule 706 of the Federal Rules of Evidence.

In offering this aside the Court joined a long list of recent proponents of court-appointed experts. The Court's invitation to consider court-appointed experts is likely to receive greater attention as the demanding requirements for admissibility of such evidence established in *Daubert* are applied to the growing volume of scientific and technical evidence....

II. AUTHORITY TO APPOINT AN EXPERT

Two principal sources of authority permit a court to appoint an expert, each envisioning a somewhat different role for the expert. Appointment under authority of Rule 706 of the Federal Rules of Evidence most directly addresses the role of the appointed expert as a testifying witness; the structure, language, and procedures of Rule 706 specifically contemplate the use of appointed experts to present evidence to the trier of fact. Supplementing this authority is the broader inherent authority of the court to appoint experts who are necessary to permit the court to carry out its duties, including authority to appoint a technical advisor to consult with the court during the decision-making process. The narrower testimonial focus and procedural confines of Rule 706 do not envision such a role....

A. Rule 706 of the Federal Rules of Evidence

Rule 706 of the Federal Rules of Evidence specifies a set of procedures governing the process of appointment, the assignment of duties, the reporting of findings, testimony, and compensation of experts. Other questions such as how to identify the need for a Rule 706 expert, how to shape pretrial procedures to reduce conflicts between the parties' experts, how to compensate experts, and how to reduce interference with the adversarial process are not addressed by the rule but are discussed in ... this Article.

The trial court has broad discretion in deciding whether to appoint a Rule 706 expert. Although it has been suggested that "extreme variation" among the parties' experts is the primary circumstance suggesting that such an appointment may be beneficial, courts frequently appoint experts because of the complexity of the issues or the evidence. Furthermore, the trial court retains discretion to refuse to appoint an expert despite extreme variations in the parties' expert testimony. Such experts should be appointed when they are likely to clarify issues under consideration; it is not an abuse of discretion for a trial court to refuse to appoint an expert under Rule 706 when "additional experts would ... add more divergence and opinion differences."

Appellate courts on occasion have reminded judges of this authority. Where a trial court has been unaware of or unclear on its authority to appoint a neutral expert under Rule 706 or its inherent power to do so, a reviewing court may order the trial court to exercise its discretion and decide whether appointment of a neutral expert is justified in the circumstances of the case. Indeed, in a case in which the experts' testimony is especially disparate on an issue of valuation, a trial court should consider the value of "a court-appointed witness who would be unconcerned with either promoting or attacking a particular estimate of ... plaintiff's damages."[17] The standard for review of a trial court's appointment of an expert under Rule 706 is whether the appointment constituted an abuse of discretion. One factor to consider in such a review is whether the expert selected by the court had any bias toward one party or one side of an issue....

B. Inherent Authority to Appoint a Technical Advisor

The court's authority under Rule 706 to appoint an expert to offer testimony represents a specific application of its broader inherent authority to invite expert assistance in a broad range of duties necessary to decide a case. The most striking exercise of this broader authority involves appointing an expert as a technical advisor to confer in chambers with the judge regarding the evidence, as opposed to offering testimony in open court and being subject to cross-examination. Although few cases deal with the inherent power of a court to appoint a technical advisor, the power to appoint remains virtually undisputed,[26] tracing a clear line from the 1920 decision of the Supreme Court in *Ex parte Peterson*[27] to the recent decision of the United States Court of Appeals for the First Circuit in *Reilly v. United States*.[28] Generally, a district court has discretion to appoint a technical advisor, but it is expected that such appointments will be "hen's teeth rare," a "last" or "near-to-last resort."[29] General factors that might justify an appointment are "problems of unusual difficulty, sophistication, and complexity, involving something well beyond the regular questions of fact and law with which judges must routinely grapple."[30] The role of the technical advisor, as the name implies, is to give advice to the judge, not to give evidence and not to decide the case....

III. USE AND NONUSE OF COURT-APPOINTED EXPERTS

A. Use of Court-Appointed Experts

Many commentators have mentioned that the use of court-appointed experts appears to be rare, an impression based on the infrequent references to such experts in published cases. To obtain an accurate assessment of the extent to which court-ap-

---

17. E. Air Lines, Inc., v. McDonnell Douglas Corp., 532 F.2d 957, 1000 (5th Cir. 1976).

26. In the words of the Advisory Committee on the Rules of Evidence, "[t]he inherent power of a trial judge to appoint an expert of his own choosing is virtually unquestioned." Fed. R. Evid. 706 advisory committee's note. *See also* United States v. Green, 544 F.2d 138, 145 (3d Cir. 1976) ("[T]he inherent power of a trial judge to appoint an expert of his own choosing is clear.")....

27. 253 U.S. 300 (1920).

28. 863 F.2d 149, 154, n.4 (1st Cir. 1988).

29. *Id.* at 157.

30. *Id.*

pointed experts have been employed, in 1988 we sent a one-page questionnaire to all active federal district court judges.

... [E]ighty-six judges, or 20% of those responding to the survey, revealed that they had appointed an expert on one or more occasions. The figures indicate that, taken together, these judges made approximately 225 appointments, far more than suggested by the paucity of published opinions dealing with the exercise of this authority....

Notes and Questions

1. These proposals fit within the category of low-level changes because they rely largely (or entirely) on existing rules, maintain the current relationship between the court and the expert, and do not radically alter the current system. Try to isolate each proposal and ask the following: is it likely to improve upon the current system? What problems can you anticipate with each proposal?

2. Are these proposals really change at all? Considering that they are suggestions for expert witness management contained within Supreme Court decisions, it may at first glance seem that the answer is "no." However, let's consider the broader context.

   In a 2012 article, *Questions from the Bench and Independent Experts: A Study of the Practices of State Court Judges*,[75] this Author surveyed state court judges about expert witness methodologies. The results were consistent with Cecil & Willging's 1988 survey, indicating that a low percentage (22%) of judges have ever actually appointed an independent expert.[76] When asked why judges are reluctant to do so, the most common explanation was "concern about interference with the adversarial system."[77] A more recent study supports this finding, and also found judges even more unlikely to appoint special masters under Rule 53.[78]

   If judges are reluctant or unwilling to use these methods, it *would be* a significant change for them to be more open to considering them. So the current shift could be seen not as a change in the rule, but rather as a change in the willingness to take advantage of the rule.

3. If appointment of a technical advisor, independent of a Rule 706 expert, is an "inherent power" and not subject to the procedural requirements of 706 (like testimony and cross-examination), is it a legitimate power? Would you be comfortable with your judge in a complex case consulting with a technical advisor in chambers without any ability to know the nature of the consultation or the opinions of the advisor? And yet courts have consistently upheld this power in the limited case

---

75. 74 U. Pitt. L. Rev. 47 (2012).

76. *Id.* at 58.

77. *Id.* at 64.

78. Andrew W. Jurs, *Gatekeeper with a Gavel: A Survey on Judicial Management of Challenges to Expert Reliability and Their Relationship to Summary Judgment*, 83 Miss. L.J. 325, 347 (2014).

law which addresses the issue. *Reilly v. United States*, 863 F.2d 149, 154, n.4 (1st Cir. 1988); *United States v. Green*, 544 F.2d 138, 145 (3d Cir. 1976).

B. Medium-Level Change Proposals

Christopher Tarver Robertson,
Blind Expertise

85 N.Y.U. L. Rev. 174 (2010)

The United States spends many billions of dollars on its system of civil litigation, and expert witnesses appear in a huge portion of cases. Yet litigants select and retain expert witnesses in ways that create the appearance of biased hired guns on both sides of every case, thereby depriving factfinders of a clear view of the facts. As a result, factfinders too often arrive at the wrong conclusions, thus undermining the deterrence and compensation functions of litigation. Court-appointment of experts has been widely proposed as a solution, yet it raises legitimate concerns about accuracy and has failed to gain traction in the American adversarial system.

Drawing on the notion of blind research from the sciences and on the concept of the veil of ignorance from political theory, this Article offers a novel and feasible reform that will make it rational for self-interested litigants to present unbiased experts to factfinders. The idea is to use an intermediary to select qualified experts who will render litigation opinions without knowledge of which party is asking. The result will be greater accuracy of both expert opinions and litigation outcomes compared to both the status quo and litigation with court-appointed experts....

II. The Blind Expert

... [W]hen hired-gun experts appear on each side of a case, it is exceedingly difficult for the factfinder to discern where the truth lies. The problem remains even with mandated disclosure, professionalism, exclusion, and the possibility of court-appointment.

Consider the absurdity of this situation. If we believed that when we consulted our neurologists or our aircraft engineers in the real world there was only a 50/50 chance that they would provide accurate advice, we would not call them experts at all, nor would we pay them handsomely to cure our diseases and build our planes. Yet, that is the story of litigation: One out of every two experts is wrong, and it is quite difficult to tell which one.

The fact-deficit in litigation is a familiar problem for scholars, and there have been calls for all sorts of interventions, from abandoning the adversarial process altogether to taking the fact-finding task away from juries. However, if the basic problem is that factfinders do not get reliable truth signals because experts are biased by the litigants who select, affiliate with, and compensate them, then the solution is simply to eliminate those contingent factors.

This Part lays out a solution that exploits our adversarial norms rather than tries to avoid them (as in court-appointment). Even if self-interested litigants bring the

experts to court, those experts can retain objectivity if they render their opinions behind blinds of ignorance....

A. *The Concept of Blinding in Justice and Science*

The concept of blind decisionmaking has deep roots. Consider Lady Justice, the
icon engraved on courthouse facades and bar cards: She stands on rocky ground,
wearing a blindfold. The rocky ground suggests that justice is contingent—dependent
on the particulars of the world—and the blindfold seems to concede that bias is a
real temptation, even for Lady Justice herself. The blindfold is a practical intervention—a tactical ignorance—that protects the decisionmaker from those biasing
temptations....

Scientists routinely use blinds. As one methodologist concludes, "[A]ny process
using a human as a perceptor, rater, or interpreter should be 'as blind as possible
for as long as possible.'" Indeed, the randomized, controlled "double-blind" study
is the scientific "gold standard." In such studies, subjects are randomly assigned to
treatment and control groups to avoid selection bias. In a single-blind study, the
human subjects are not informed about whether they are in the control group (e.g.,
receiving a placebo) or the treatment group (e.g., receiving the drug being tested).
In a double-blind study, the researcher is additionally prevented from knowing
which subjects are in the control group versus the experimental group. This second
blind prevents the researcher from exercising biased judgments along the way, both
in her interactions with the human subjects and in her management of the study
itself.

Blinds are also quite common in academia. In most scholarly journals (outside of
legal academia), double-blind review—where the reviewers do not know the identity
of the authors, and vice versa—is used for article selection. In order to avoid possible
favoritism for particular students, law professors routinely use blinds in grading
papers. The U.S. Supreme Court has specifically pointed to this grading practice to
demonstrate that it is possible to evaluate the quality of speech even if it is anonymous,
which was part of the Court's justification of constitutional protection for anonymous
speech....

In short, the concept of blinding is already well-developed in a variety of contexts.
Blinds work as a form of tactical ignorance that prevents conflicting interests from
creating biases.

B. *Operationalizing the Blind in Litigation*

Although blind expertise may have application wherever experts render opinions
under potential biases, civil litigation presents a particularly accessible area for initial
study. Court cases are discrete occurrences with identifiable parties who have speci-
fiable interests, working in a rule-governed space. This Section explores how the
blind can be operationalized in litigation, focusing first on the roles of the blinding
intermediary and the expert, second on the role of the sponsoring litigant exercising
discretion in whether to retain and use the expert, and finally on the role of the court
in facilitating the process.

1. *The Roles of the Intermediary and the Expert*

The blind procedure would center on an intermediary agency that functions as a broker between sponsors of research (e.g., plaintiffs) and potential expert witnesses (e.g., doctors). The intermediary would be set up as a generalized infrastructure, not created on an ad hoc basis for particular cases. For now, assume that there would be a single intermediary for all cases, such as the American Association for the Advancement of Science (AAAS), that would be truly neutral with regard to the outcome of any case and would be accredited by the courts to ensure quality and to minimize the need for ex post monitoring.... Alternatively, other not-for-profit or for-profit agencies could provide blinding services for litigants. For the model to be viable, however, the intermediary will need to aggressively maintain independence from the litigants, so as to avoid biases and signal to factfinders that it has done so. An advisory or governance board, consisting of plaintiffs' lawyers, defense lawyers, scientists, and judges may help in this regard.

The blind process would be initiated by a litigant, who would contact the intermediary and request an expert opinion on at least one aspect of his or her case, such as specific causation or damages. Although this service could be partially or completely subsidized by the government (for the purpose of improving the legal system), let us proceed on the assumption that it would be fee-based and that the intermediary would require the litigant to pay the intermediary's fee and the expert's fee, both in advance, before learning of the expert's identity or opinion. The intermediary would then provide two blinds: (1) a blind for litigants in retaining experts without selection bias, and (2) a blind for experts to render opinions without affiliation and compensation biases. Consider these functions in more detail.

First, the intermediary would select, through an unbiased mechanism, an expert that is qualified to render an opinion on the case. By avoiding selection bias, the sampled opinion will more likely be representative of the body of expert opinions than is the case under the status quo, where the hand-picked experts likely come from the extreme poles of expert opinions.

Prior to the selection, the litigant would identify the field of expertise and specify certain objective parameters for the desired expert (e.g., must be a board-certified neurologist and cost no more than $500 per hour). The sponsor could also identify additional criteria to avoid experts who may be already biased, for example, by previous interaction with the litigants. Any such screening criteria will be subject to later impeachment by the adversary to ensure that they are not pretexts for biasing the selection, and the intermediary may also limit the types of screens allowed in order to preserve the integrity of the blinding process. Finally, potential experts should be required to precommit to testify for either side as the facts warrant. After screening on these criteria, the intermediary would then select one of the qualified experts....

There are two ways that the intermediary could impartially select an expert. One way would be through random selection from a roster of qualified experts.... Alternatively, the blind expert could be hand-picked by the intermediary, using both objective and subjective criteria. To prevent such discretion from leading to a pro-plaintiff or pro-defendant bias, the intermediary could be bifurcated, separating the staff who deal with the attorneys from those who select and deal with the experts. Accordingly, the person selecting the expert would be unaware of whether the plaintiff or defendant was requesting the opinion.

Second, the intermediary would blind the experts to minimize affiliation and compensation biases. The intermediary would develop and assign the expert's question, provide the expert with a dossier of the necessary materials to review, and pay the expert, all without the expert knowing the identity or interests of the sponsoring litigant.

A key challenge at this stage will be for the intermediary to develop an unbiased litigation question and a dossier of the necessary predicate facts for the expert to review — one that is complete yet redacted of any biasing information. This stage will be self-policing to some extent because the adversary will eventually see that same dossier and will be able to impeach and undermine the blind expert's opinion if it was based on a skewed or incomplete set of predicate facts — indeed, the blind expert may even change his opinion upon learning the other side of the story. In addition, the intermediary should encourage the expert to specify any other information that she needs to see ... before rendering her opinion.

After receiving the dossier and research question, the expert will record her opinion in a structured report, affirming that she has received all information necessary to render a final and complete opinion. The report will disclose all the factors she considered and relied upon and will specify a confidence level for her opinions. The intermediary will check that the expert's report is explicit, concrete, and complete; and if so, it will pay the expert for her time regardless of the substance of her opinion. The intermediary will then incorporate into the expert's report information about how many blind experts the sponsoring litigant consulted and how the blinds were implemented. Thereafter, the intermediary will convey the combined report to the sponsoring litigant.

2. The Role of the Litigant

When the sponsoring litigant receives the expert's report, he will assess its usefulness. The sponsor's assessment of the report will depend on the substance and tenor of the expert's opinions, along with the credentials of the expert and any other factors that may affect her persuasiveness at trial. On net, the litigant will determine whether or not this opinion is likely to be favorable for improving the value of his case, or whether it will instead be useless or harmful all things considered. Thus, the litigant transforms a complicated question into a binary one (usable or not usable)....

Under the attorney work product doctrine, if a litigant consults with an expert but does not designate her as a trial witness, then the expert's opinions are generally not discoverable by the adversary. The rationale for work product protection is to permit an attorney to "assemble information, sift what he considers to be the relevant from the irrelevant facts, prepare his legal theories and plan his strategy without undue and needless interference," allowing him "to promote justice and to protect [his] clients' interests."[172] There is no reason why this privilege would not apply to a consulting, non-testifying expert simply because she rendered her opinions from behind a blind.

Therefore, if a litigant commissions a blind expert to render an opinion and it turns out to be unfavorable, then the opinion will not be discoverable by the adversary. Accordingly, when a blind opinion turns out to be unfavorable, the sponsoring party has lost only the cost of the initial opinion (perhaps a few thousand dollars). The blind expert's opinion cannot hurt the sponsor. This is a critical point that will make the procedure attractive to rational litigants, and particularly attractive compared to court-appointed experts, for whom the disclosure decision is out of the litigants' control.

On the other hand, if the blind expert's opinion is favorable to the sponsoring litigant, then the litigant can retain the expert for testimony. If the litigant does so, she must disclose the expert and her report to the adversary, just as in normal litigation. As noted above, the report would include the intermediary's disclosures about how the blind procedure was implemented, which should then help persuade the factfinder that the blind expert is entitled to extra credibility. The adversary would test the robustness of the procedure, rendering the process largely self-policing.

To ensure that sponsoring litigants do not create an iterative selection bias by making multiple requests for blind opinions, litigants who do designate a blind expert for testimony would be required to disclose how many blind experts (in that same field) they consulted before selecting one. Indeed, as noted above, this information would be included in the intermediary's report with each expert opinion. Of course this sort of disclosure is not required under the status quo. For the blind procedure, the disclosure requirement would arise from either of two existing exceptions to the work product doctrine. First, an opposing litigant could assert an "at issue" implied waiver of work product protection. The litigant that brings a blind expert, and thereby claims a lack of selection bias, cannot at the same time avoid discovery into selection bias. Likewise, the potential for a litigant to claim falsely that there was no selection bias would be an "exceptional circumstance" allowing discovery under the Federal Rules....

Ex ante knowledge of this disclosure rule would generally deter litigants from iterative use of the blind procedure. For a litigant, there is little value in bringing a favorable blind opinion if he also must disclose the existence of one or more unfavorable blind opinions; he would be better off resorting to traditional unblind experts or settling the case. Indeed, if an initial opinion is unfavorable, each subsequent attempt to secure an opinion will promise diminishing returns, both in the likelihood of the next opinion being favorable and in the persuasiveness to the factfinder of any favorable opinion received.

It is also important to specify when and how the blind will be lifted. If the opinion is favorable to the sponsor, the litigant will retain the expert, designate him for tes-

---

172. Hickman v. Taylor, 329 U.S. 495, 511 (1947).

timony, and lift the blind prior to the expert's deposition by the adversary. The litigant will pay the expert for subsequent work—including depositions, trial preparation, and testimony—based on a prearranged fee schedule. One might worry that such affiliation and compensation will create the very biases that the blind sought to avoid, but the expert's initial opinions are already locked-in in her disclosed report, written before she ever learns of her sponsor....

3. *The Role of the Court*

The blind procedure is designed to work within existing institutions and procedures, requiring no major changes to substantive or procedural law. Still, there are a few measures that the courts should take to ensure that the blind procedure is workable.

First, the courts should make it a safe choice for litigants. I have shown that the current doctrine of work product protection should allow a litigant to consult a blind expert without risk of an adverse opinion hurting his case. Courts must adhere strictly to this interpretation of the doctrine and signal their intention to do so, perhaps by amending the federal or local rules of procedure. It will be important for litigants to know that not only will adverse blind opinions be nondiscoverable by the adversary, but also that the very fact that a blind expert was consulted will be protected from discovery. In this way, litigants can be reassured that the worst-case scenario under the new procedure is that a blind opinion will be unusable.

Second, the courts should make the blind procedure attractive for litigants by allowing those who use blind experts at trial to use hired-gun experts as well. A blind expert will have additional credibility due to his lack of biases, but a hired gun may have other advantages, such as credentials, teaching skills, and the ability to stand up to tough cross-examination. The court should not force a litigant to choose. By allowing both types of experts on the same side, the court improves the ex ante incentives for litigants to use the blind procedure. Although an adversary may object that the additional expert is cumulative and therefore wastes time, the Federal Rules explicitly provide that when a court-appointed expert offers testimony, this does not preclude litigants from also offering their own hand-selected experts. The same should be true for the blind procedure. In this way, factfinders can get the best of both worlds: persuasive advocates from both sides and an objective assessment of the truth.

Third, the courts should ensure that the blind procedure is robust and that litigants can present it effectively at trial. Adversaries will want to conduct discovery about the procedures used to select and communicate with a blind expert, and the court should allow these....

Fourth, courts should assist juries in understanding the differences between blind experts and traditional experts. Currently, courts explicitly instruct jurors to consider the biases of expert witnesses. When a blind expert appears in trial, courts should issue a jury instruction that conveys the concept of blind expertise and explains why these experts may merit special consideration as compared to the other experts who were hand-selected by litigants and subject to affiliation and compensation biases....

Andrew W. Jurs, *Balancing Legal Process with Scientific Expertise: Expert Witness Methodology in Five Nations and Suggestions for Reform of Post-*Daubert *U.S. Reliability Determinations*

95 Marq. L. Rev. 1329 (2012)

V. Assessment of Methodologies from Other Nations That May Benefit Expert Witness Handling in the United States

Having reviewed expert methodologies in several nations, one can see that balancing technological or scientific expertise and legal process can be addressed by a variety of means. It is precisely this variety of approaches that provides a fertile source for law reform efforts, as Haack suggested: "Maybe we could learn something from the experiences of other countries that are equally technologically advanced, but have different regulatory and legal arrangements."[475] Other commentators agree with her premise. The question then becomes: what would work here?

A. *Procedures That Cannot Be Considered for Use in the United States*

Initially, it is important to note that many procedures used in other nations cannot be considered for transplantation to the U.S., whether or not they would address weaknesses in *Daubert*. Examples will help demonstrate the point.

One methodology that cannot be considered in the U.S. system is the Canadian practice of extensive judicial comment on the evidence, including the expert opinions. As allowed by Canadian law, the comment on evidence allows judges to state a personal opinion on the strength of the evidence, ostensibly to assist the jury. While it is perhaps helpful to the jury to hear the judge's viewpoints, judges in the United States are specifically prohibited from offering opinions on evidence, pursuant to the Judicial Code of Conduct and other ethical standards.

A second expert witness management device in use elsewhere that is inappropriate for reform in the United States is the Japanese practice of allowing experts to directly question witnesses. In Japan, an appointed expert commissioner may assume a role beyond the limits of an expert in the United States, so that the expert may be directly involved with in-court presentation of evidence including witness examination. While intended to efficiently facilitate the presentation of evidence, this expansive role exceeds the more limited role of experts in U.S. litigation. Experts in the United States are witnesses providing evidence, rather than parties directly involved in case management.... Without specific authorization, the use of experts to question witnesses would be an abuse of the court's discretion.

One final procedure other countries use that could not be directly adopted in the United States is the near-universal use of bench trials for complex torts.... Even in those systems that permit jury trials in civil cases—as Canada and the U.K. do for certain claims—torts requiring extensive scientific or technical evidence are removed from jury consideration. Part of the basis for removal, or assignment to the court

---

475. Susan Haack, *Irreconcilable Differences? The Troubled Marriage of Science and Law,* 72 Law & Contemp. Probs. 1, 23 (2009).

initially, is confidence in the judge's ability to handle complex cases that may be beyond the jury's capacity. Yet in the United States, the right to a jury trial in Federal court exists as a constitutional right....

B. *Methodologies That Should Be Considered for Adoption in the United States*

While many methodologies of expert witness management cannot be transplanted into the U.S. legal system, there are several that lawmakers should consider. Each procedure discussed represents a specific change to the current expert witness balance of legal process and scientific expertise, to fix areas of weakness within the *Daubert* regime. With these options, expert witness reform can develop not from unilateral development of the current U.S. system, but through limited transplantation of tested procedures already used in other major legal systems. We need not reinvent the wheel.

1. *Canadian Summary of the Evidence, and Additional Disclosures*

The first example of an expert management device from another nation that could assist expert management in the United States comes from Canada. In Canada, at the end of a trial, the judge summarizes the evidence, objectively stating the evidence and issues in the case for the jury. In the United States, however, we rely on the advocates to summarize the evidence at the end of the case for the jury. Even so, the idea of packaging and presenting issues offers a solution to a persistent *Daubert* problem: the management of the challenges to experts at "*Daubert* hearings."

Consistent with the Canadian example then, we should consider adopting mandatory summary of expert evidence for the judge to use at a *Daubert* hearing, to assist the judge in deciding what are the fundamental issues contested by the parties and the specific details of evidence to support each party's contention. This Article therefore proposes a new requirement for parties to file a joint disclosure in cases with contested *Daubert* issues. The disclosure would be completed by both parties, not unlike a pre-trial order, and must include these materials:

- Qualifications and background of each expert involved in the issues contested by the motion (whether the contested expert or the expert in response);

- Delineation of the specific areas of testimony that are contested as improper under the standard of *Daubert*/Evidence Rule 702; and

- For each contested issue:

  ○ Areas of agreement between the experts regarding the contested issue;

  ○ Areas of disagreement and each party's position on those issues;

  ○ Detailed support for each expert's opinions on the contested issue, including all scientific and technical bases for those opinions; and

  ○ Areas of scientific uncertainty with explanation of the basis of the uncertainty and the current state of research in the area.[493]

---

493. These suggested disclosures are similar to the proposed changes to Rule 56 suggested by the Advisory Committee on the Civil Rules in May 2008. STANDING COMM. ON RULES OF PRACTICE AND PROCEDURE, REPORT OF THE CIVIL RULES ADVISORY COMMITTEE 27–32 (2008)....

Upon filing of the disclosures, the court may schedule a hearing to take testimony on the motions, or may decide the issue without further evidence from the parties.

The expert disclosures mandated by this proposal serve several purposes. Benefits of the procedure will be classified by the stage in which the proceeding case receives assistance: the *Daubert* hearing itself; independent expert review—if desired by the court—pursuant to Federal Rule of Evidence 706; jury trial; or similar challenges before other courts.

At the first stage—the *Daubert* hearing—the court faces several obstacles with the potential to affect the court's reliability determination on the expert evidence. Among these obstacles are the selection bias from a litigant's selection of outlier experts, adversarial bias from the rigid framework imposed by cross-examination, and judicial inexperience with scientific or statistical issues.... More specific disclosures ... address all of these shortcomings. An outlying expert may or may not be identified as such by the judge under the current rules, but when forced to explain in detail the basis for each contested opinion, it becomes more likely that the testimony can be assessed within the context of the entire scientific field. The same benefit accrues regarding the adversarial methods of cross-examination. With cross-examination, a party has the ability to cast doubt—merited or otherwise—on the expert's position, while empirical evidence demonstrates that experts sometimes respond by expressing their opinions more unconditionally. Yet, if the issues are clearly delineated by the parties in the new disclosures, the judge should be better able to determine which cross-examination questions serve to cast genuine doubt upon the merits of the expert opinion, and which do not. Finally, the disclosures assist in addressing the judiciary's general inexperience with complex science or mathematics.... With additional disclosures, the court has a clear record of the disputed issues and the basis for each, and it becomes easier for the judge to apply the reliability test under *Daubert*....

Even with disclosures, however, some reliability issues will test the skills of even the most scientifically-capable juror. The disclosures suggested here have an additional benefit for these cases; the disclosures permit a quicker, more efficient review by an independent expert appointed by the court under Federal Rule of Evidence 706. While judges see independent review as beneficial, many are reluctant to appoint a Rule 706 expert. Two reasons for this reluctance are judicial concerns about interfering with adversarial process and potential case delay. The benefit of additional disclosures eliminates these two reasons....

So far, the focus has been on benefits at the *Daubert* hearing stage or for independent expert review, but the disclosures suggested here would also assist at the trial stage. At the *Daubert* hearing, the court has to determine whether the expert opinion is reliable enough for admission under Rule 702. Should the opinion be unreliable, the court precludes the expert from testifying. In many cases, however, the result of the hearing will be that the contested expert's opinion is deemed "reliable enough," and admitted. For those cases, then, the contested expert—and a counterpart from the opposing party or parties—will testify at trial for the jury. Yet, we know jurors may have the same difficulties in assessing complex evidence as judges. To the extent the reliability issue remains an issue at trial, then the disclosures can also assist the jury. Therefore, the disclosures submitted by the parties to the judge for the *Daubert* stage also should be admissible at trial, on motion of the parties or the judge *sua sponte*, when "good cause" has been shown. The disclosures will assist the jury to decide the contested expert reliability just as the disclosures helped the judge at the earlier stage. Use by the jury, after all, is the original purpose of summary on the evidence used in Canada, and in this form offers the same benefit.

The disclosures suggested here would have one final systematic benefit: they specifically delineate the state of the science on an issue at the time of the decision. Case opinions discussing complex science often serves as persuasive authority for other judges reviewing the same issue. Of course, scientific knowledge in a given field constantly changes. To the extent that any other court addresses the same issue, and considers the older opinion as precedent, the court will know exactly what evidence was presented in the previous case and served as a basis for the opinion. Knowing the evidentiary basis for the prior opinion permits the later judge to establish what evidence in his or her hearing was not considered before....

2. Civil Law Expert Selection Methods

A second example of a procedure based on one used abroad that could assist expert management in the United States originates in procedures used in Japan and Germany. In those countries, the judge selects an expert to assist the judge to decide contested issues of evidence, and sometimes for case management in Japan. The selection and role of the expert in these civil law systems contrasts significantly with the party-led expert practices in the United States. Yet aspects of the civil law expert selection procedures would offer benefits to U.S. expert management.

Because the expert selected by a judge in Germany or Japan will serve as the single neutral expert in the case, those nations place great emphasis on the fairness of the expert selection procedures, so that trials maintain legitimacy. As a result, these civil law systems have developed procedures to ensure that the single expert selected is suitable to serve by having recognized skills in the scientific field, but also by agreeing to neutral and detached assessment of the facts. Japan and Germany ensure experts will be vetted prior to the specific litigation in question, so that they may serve when needed by a judge in future cases. In some instances, the relevant professional society selects those members who wish to and who are well-qualified to serve. By these methodologies, the person will be seen as fair....

Since the U.S. courts lack systematic procedures to identify or vet experts prior to specific litigation, almost all expert selection is adversarial and inherently subject to selection bias and other ills.... This Article therefore proposes a new system, established through the federal judiciary, to identify experts both well-qualified in their field and dedicated to the principle of fair assessment of evidence.

The selection process would be modeled on the systems of both Japan and Germany. As in Germany, for those experts who are licensed and regulated by an administrative governing body—doctors, architects, lawyers, dentists, etc.—the proposal amounts to allowing that governing body to determine appropriate qualifications, and identify those experts who meet high standards for skill and ethics. All decisions of that self-governing body would be subject to oversight by the administrative body responsible for establishing lists for other expert areas. For all other experts not self-regulated—epidemiologists, some engineers, college professors—the expertise and qualifications of individuals would be vetted through a central administrative body maintained within the office of the U.S. Courts, governed by regulations adopted to ensure selected experts demonstrate both skill in their field and dedication to ethical assessment of the evidence in assigned cases.

Once selected, the experts from the lists will be available to serve in two separate situations. First, the experts may be called to serve as independent experts by judges under Rule of Evidence 706.... Independent of the use of experts by the judiciary under Rule 706, any listed expert could be retained by a litigant as his or her expert in the litigation.

The identification of experts through a civil-law screening process provides several important benefits, each addressing a current weakness in the *Daubert* management of experts. First, the identification of skilled neutral experts enables judges to quickly find and retain experts who can assist them in reviewing contested scientific or technical evidence. Empirical evidence demonstrates judges themselves may lack necessary skills to evaluate complex science in the courtroom, with the potential to effect reliability assessments in cases involving complex science. The use of independent experts under Rule 706 provides judges with a skilled assistant to help the judge in evaluating the litigant's expert in reliability determinations under *Daubert*. It also exposes those attacks on litigants' experts that are pro forma adversarial tactics, and those that actually expose weaknesses in the science discussed by the expert. Yet the Rule has, since its inception, been used sparingly. A list of available and appropriate experts neutralizes two of the major reasons why judges do not currently use Rule 706 procedures: delay, and inability to identify a qualified expert.... As a result, the expert lists proposed here would reinvigorate the Rule 706 neutral expert review procedure, allowing judges to seek help more often in cases involving complex science.

Independent of the benefit to the judge, expert lists identified through a civil-law screening procedure have separate benefits to the litigants stemming from the ability to use experts from the list as their party-expert in the litigation. Since the lists would be available for anyone, the experts identified through these procedures would provide litigants with a pre-approved list of experts, who a jury would likely consider fair. Any party could decide that the benefit of choosing an expert from the list—blunting attacks based on payment of fees or on non-neutrality—exceed the benefits of choosing an expert using adversarial techniques but who may be subject to those attacks. Over time, experts retained by litigants would have to blunt partisan over-reaching, because experts who overreach or who are inappropriate outliers in the field will be exposed as the non-neutral adversarial experts they are. In doing so, the focus can again shift from persuasion to the scientific merit of the testimony.

Finally, one other benefit of the proposed procedure is the maintenance of the general balance of power within our adversarial system. Neutral experts and additional use of the Rule 706 expert procedure may assist the judge in the performance of his or her duties, and assist in encouraging outcomes that reflect accurate scientific methodologies. The neutral expert procedure so described does not, however, take the decisionmaking authority away from those who already have that power: the judge and the jury.... Therefore, the balance of legal process and scientific expertise is not subject to radical ... shifts inconsistent with our nation's legal norms....

Adoption of a civil-law expert management system modeled on the Japanese and German systems would provide benefits in overcoming current problems with *Daubert*-era expert management in the United States. The current proposal offers significant advantages over previous attempts to manage neutral experts. It also demonstrates that, at least in the area of expert witnesses, the U.S. can and should consider alternative methodologies developed in other nations, if those methodologies are shown to offer advantages over the current system....

Notes and Questions

1. The proposals from Robertson and Jurs fit neatly within the category of medium-level changes, since they are not reliant on existing rules (like low-level changes) but build upon them, and require some investment of time or effort in adopting a new approach to experts thereby altering the relationship of the court to the expert. However, these changes do not constitute radical new approaches (like the high-level changes we will review next). As you consider each proposal, ask yourself: what is the problem the proposal is addressing, and is it likely to solve that problem? What problems do you anticipate with each? To the extent to which the two articles address the same problem, which is a more realistic response?

2. In the United States, law students might never examine the legal systems of other countries in detail unless they choose to take classes in International or Comparative Law (when offered at their institution). Yet as Susan Haack notes,[79] we truly can learn something from countries with different legal and regulatory environments. To put it another way, there is no reason to think that the United States—in creating and developing its legal system—has found the ideal approach to every complex issue. The proper balance of legal process and scientific expertise is not a uniquely American problem, as seen in the approaches other nations have taken in *Balancing Legal Process with Scientific Expertise.*

   Clearly some methods are impossible to consider, as the article notes, but other methodologies could be considered in response to the same problems of science and the law. Of course, it would be interesting to further investigate legal reform efforts in other nations in addition to those discussed in *Balancing Legal Process* (Canada, the U.K., Germany, and Japan). It would also be interesting to examine

---

79. Susan Haack, *Irreconcilable Differences? The Troubled Marriage of Science and Law,* 72 LAW & CONTEMP. PROBS. 1, 23 (2009) (appearing in excerpt by Jurs, *supra,* in text accompanying note 475).

the management of other complex legal issues beyond expert witness management. But at the most basic level, we should always remember that just because something is currently one way, it does not mean it cannot and should not change.

As we consider the next proposal, keep that exploratory spirit in mind. . . .

C. A High-Level Change Proposal

Andrew W. Jurs, *Science Court: Past Proposals, Current Considerations, and a Suggested Structure*

15 VA. J. L. & TECH. 1 (2010)

. . .

IV. PROPOSED STRUCTURE FOR AN ARTICLE III COURT OF SCIENTIFIC JURISDICTION

Having reviewed the need for a specialized court in the field of complex science, the next step is to sensibly design a court that maximizes the benefits of that specialization. In this section, this Article will discuss the design of a federal Court of Scientific Jurisdiction, beginning with the objectives for the court, followed by its jurisdiction, structure, and procedure. The experience of the Kantrowitz science court proposal guides these efforts.[Ed.] Finally, the discussion will review the benefits to be achieved by implementation of this proposal.

A. *Principles for the Court*

While perhaps designed to address different disputes than the Kantrowitz science court, the exact same goals would be served by the specialization of scientific knowledge in an Article III science court. Each of the following three objectives is an important consideration for the Court of Scientific Jurisdiction.

First, the court must be designed to purify the scientific inquiry occurring within its cases by focusing on the quality of scientific research, data, or opinions submitted by litigants. The goal is to have a finalized statement of the quality of the science presented by experts, the current state of knowledge in the field, and the extent to which the expert opinions are supported or rebuffed by the overall state of knowledge. In doing so, the court will ensure "defensible, credible, technical bases" for each opinion, increasing the accuracy and precision of the results.

Second, the CSJ should capture scientific expertise within the judiciary selected for service, to serve the goals of accuracy, consistency, and precision. Accordingly, the expertise of the judges is the central feature of the CSJ proposal.

Finally, the court must be structured to minimize the role of outside influences on the quality of decision making regarding science. Kantrowitz worried about the

---

[Ed.] The Author notes that mention in this excerpt of the Kantrowicz Science Court are referring to a 1970s proposal for adjudication of public policy disputes by quasi-judicial means, discussed in great detail in the unredacted article.

effect of political influences on the quality of scientific decisions. While political choices are not the usual contaminant of judicial analysis, the undue influence within the court system that affects analysis of science in court is the adversarialism of the proceeding. Reduction in adversarialism will be a necessary cost to increase accuracy and efficiency of the CSJ outcomes.

The CSJ must be designed to serve these goals, to achieve the greatest chance of success in efficiency, accuracy, consistency, and other benefits of the proposal. Learning from the Kantrowitz proposal provides useful insight for the design of the CSJ processes.

B. *Design of the Court*

Creating the right design for the court involves the delicate balancing of maximizing the benefits of specialization with minimizing the negative consequences of the changes.

1. *Jurisdiction*

The jurisdiction of the CSJ is perhaps the most critical element to its success, and the most likely pitfall. Too much jurisdiction and the court will collapse under the docket weight and be unable to function effectively. Too little jurisdiction and the court will fail to achieve the "critical mass" of expertise and cases necessary to achieve success.

As a federal court, the CSJ must have diversity of parties to achieve jurisdiction. The subject matter jurisdiction must therefore be tailored to the reasons for specialization. One of the primary reasons for the CSJ is the increased judicial analysis of the quality of proffered science — the "gatekeeping" — under *Daubert* and *Joiner*. As a result, the jurisdiction of the CSJ must include those cases most likely to involve complex scientific, technological, or other expert issues. Finally, the weakness of several specialized courts in the federal system has been identified by many scholars as too little jurisdiction, not too much. The court must be limited to a subset of cases truly requiring expertise, however, lest it be overrun by collecting every diversity case involving experts.

Considering and integrating these different strands of thought is a delicate balancing process. In a previous article, this author offered a potential jurisdictional framework, involving minimal diversity plus scientific issues of significant complexity. Expanding on those thoughts, this Article suggests jurisdiction be shaped by consideration of the following factors:

- Whether the case has diversity of citizenship, modeled on 28 U.S.C. § 1332(d);

- Whether the determination of admissibility of evidence under Federal Rule of Evidence 702 and *Daubert* involves complex scientific or technical information and is directly related to a claim "at issue" in the complaint or answer;

- Whether the determination of contested *Daubert* issues would be "substantially assisted" by judicial expertise in the scientific or technical field at issue in the case;

- Whether the scientific or technical information is very likely to be heard by other courts in unrelated cases;

   ○ Whether the use of existing procedures is unlikely to inform the judge on the expert claims "at issue" in the case; and

   ○ Whether the case involves "new or novel" scientific or technical controversies.

By applying these considerations, the jurisdiction of the CSJ would meet constitutional requirements and balance competing values. It would grant exclusive trial jurisdiction to the subset of expert cases in which new or novel scientific evidence is presented, cases likely to reappear in other courts, cases where judicial expertise offers substantial assistance, and cases where existing structures may be inadequate.... This balancing would allow expert judges to handle those cases where expertise is most essential....

2. *Structure*

To handle this subset of complex, new, and technologically- or scientifically-advanced cases effectively, the CSJ's structure would need a diversity of expertise among its trial judges, a method of determining case assignment, and a plan for appellate-level review.

Expertise is the central benefit of the CSJ proposal. The CSJ would select judges with significant experience in diverse complex fields — the natural sciences, applied science, technology, and engineering, to name a few — and then assign them cases according to their fields of experience. This structure would provide each case with a "decisionmaker ... who is fully capable of evaluating the particular claims in dispute." Assignment of cases directly related to a judge's expertise is, of course, ideal and should be used when possible. The benefits of this assignment structure include the increased ability to recognize the scientific merit in proffered testimony, greater capacity to handle cases quickly due to the decrease in need for case-by-case research, and more immediate recognition of the limitations of science offered by the parties. Expertise could be measured by a judge's background education in the field or by the development of a skills-based assessment method.

One aspect of the assignment of cases received significant attention during the Kantrowitz science court debate, and that discussion should be considered when planning the CSJ. Kantrowitz recognized that usually, when assigning decision-makers to particular matters, "one must choose between those who have gone deeply into the subjects under discussion and, accordingly, will have preconceived ideas about what the outcome should be, and those who are perhaps unprejudiced but relatively uninformed...."[260] To balance the need for expertise against the problem of preconceived notions when adjudicating issues in a particular field, Kantrowitz suggested selecting judges from experts in "neighboring fields." While the definition of "neighboring fields" requires further elaboration and discussion, applying this suggestion should ensure impartiality along with expertise. The general proposition that "the [scientist] will provide a more educated perspective than the nonscientist judge" ... even when operating outside his or her specific field, is relatively less controversial....

---

260. Arthur Kantrowitz, *Proposal for an Institution for Scientific Judgment*, 156 Sci. 763, 763 (1967).

The permanence of the CSJ, and the resulting responsibility its judges would assume, would be one of the major side benefits of this structure. Having a permanent court would avoid one of the major weaknesses of the Kantrowitz proposal: the lack of accountability for ad hoc panels.... For the CSJ, however, the permanent structure of the court would provide for both internal legal accountability (by appellate review) and external scientific accountability (by providing the external scientific community an opportunity to review the opinions ...).

Finally, the assignment of cases to the CSJ and to specific judges based on expertise would not violate random case assignment rules or law. Case assignments are not required to be random, by statute or otherwise, and a non-random assignment may be appropriate in consideration of other interests.

3. *Procedure*

With the selection of cases qualifying to be heard at the CSJ being determined by a jurisdictional statute, and the case selection process largely established by the court's structure, the third and final leg of the CSJ stool is the procedure by which the specialist judges will make the necessary determinations on the complex cases assigned to them.

As a federal trial-level court, the standard Federal Rules of Civil Procedure and Federal Rules of Evidence should apply. This is not to say that judges will not use the rules in a distinct manner at the CSJ, but the same rules, granting the same due process rights, should apply.

In making any decision that may be dispositive, whether a ruling on a Motion for Summary Judgment or *Daubert* challenge to an expert, the CSJ judges should formalize their decisions into distinct and separate components. As was the case in the Kantrowitz proposal, all opinions should include a statement of uncontested facts, a statement of contested facts, conclusions on the facts to the extent they can be determined, and a section discussing the areas lacking scientific data on which to base a determination.... The benefits of this procedure include the following: increased clarity of the bases for any decision, the express recognition of what areas are less well established, the clarity of the precedential value that will be applied to the *legal* determinations of the court but not to the factual findings, and the establishment of a methodological precedent for assessment of similar factual issues by future courts— whether at the CSJ, federal, or state level.

On the procedural issue of trial format, the CSJ would retain the jury trial right inherent in the Seventh Amendment to the U.S. Constitution.... [T]he Supreme Court has ... clarified that "[Congress] lacks the power to strip parties contesting matters of private right of their constitutional right to a trial by jury."[275] Forcing a bench trial on claims against the will of the litigants is therefore impermissible under any circumstances short of constitutional amendment.... [T]he CSJ would maintain the constitutionally protected jury trial right, while ensuring the jury hears only the best, legally admissible and vetted scientific evidence.

---

275. Granfinanciera v. Nordberg, 492 U.S. 33, 51–52 (1989).

Even if a jury is to hear previously vetted science, there is no reason to prohibit jurors at the CSJ from taking advantage of new mechanisms to maximize their abilities to handle the material. Professor Franklin Strier, in his article *Making Jury Trials More Truthful*, offers suggestions for several methods to increase jury accuracy: asking questions, note taking, videotape/transcripts of critical testimony, or even interim deliberations.[277] Because more complex material is even less well suited to juror comprehension, the CSJ provides an ideal environment to utilize these tools for greater juror accuracy.

Finally, the CSJ appellate right will be different than other district courts. Appeals should go to a single forum in order to maximize the expertise of the appellate-level review of its cases. Since the CSJ would be located in a single location[279] to take advantage of having all fields of expertise under the same roof, it makes the most sense that the appeals of the CSJ opinions would go to a single appellate court. The success of the Court of Appeals for the Federal Circuit makes it a natural location for the CSJ appeals. It makes sense that the same court, which is used to handling complex science and technology cases, would result in similar benefits for the CSJ appeals docket.... Over time, the Federal Circuit could handle the CSJ docket with the same skill with which it handles patent law.

C. Benefits of the Proposal

The proposed CSJ would involve immediate benefits to the analysis of complex cases involving science, technology, and related fields. These benefits include the commonly cited accuracy, efficiency, and consistency, but other tangible improvements as well.

1. The Basics: Efficiency, Accuracy, and Consistency

Specialized courts can increase judicial efficiency in handling dockets. Since 1990, the caseload of the federal district courts has increased significantly. Judicial delay has been an issue for much of this period. The CSJ would alleviate systematic strain in two ways: by taking the most difficult and technically challenging cases away from the standard district courts where they take great effort and time to resolve, and by streamlining the judicial analysis of those cases in a framework that can better handle the case.... Once at the CSJ, the judges who handle cases within or near their area of expertise would be in a better position to handle the complexities of the caseload, and would gain additional efficiency through their ... analysis of similar cases....

Accuracy is the second basic benefit of the CSJ. When CSJ judges receive a docket, the judge will be able to evaluate the case in light of his or her substantial background knowledge in the field. With that background knowledge, the judge can more critically assess the proffered testimony before applying the appropriate standards of the law. These trained judges will be better able to separate the genuine claims or assertions

---

277. Franklin Strier, *Making Jury Trials More Truthful*, 30 U.C. Davis L. Rev. 95, 137–41 (1996).

279. Since the CSJ should be located in a single location, the choice of Washington, D.C., provides the greatest benefits to the institutional mission....

from those not supported by the current state of scientific knowledge. We need not guess whether that result would happen, however. In examples of current specialized courts, the decisions and processes have been deemed objectively "better" as compared to generalist court....[296]

Third, the increase in consistency of decision making from a specialized court handling all cases of a similar nature cannot be doubted. Expertise feeds consistency through the prism of scientific accuracy. It also would be the result of a uniform interpretation of the appropriate legal standards. This single interpretation theory avoids a splintering of approaches regarding the same legal standard, more likely with more cases in more districts. As one example, the Federal Circuit has resulted in consistency in patent law since its jurisdictional consolidation of patent cases in 1982....[302]

Efficiency, accuracy, and consistency form the troika of initial benefits from the development of a complex science docket at the CSJ....

D. *Criticisms*

Any proposal of court specialization is bound to encounter serious criticism, whether by those opposed to any specialized courts or those concerned about the specifics of any particular proposal. The Kantrowitz proposal of the 1970's was attacked repeatedly and directly by critics opposed to both its goals and its methods before it faded into obscurity. The CSJ would likely see similar criticism.

One benefit of the CSJ is that the proposal has been formed in light of the Kantrowitz proposal. As a result, many significant criticisms of the Kantrowitz science court simply do not apply to the CSJ. These include the criticisms of the procedures for selection of advocates and judges, the issues to address, and the methods of dispute resolution incorporating too many adversarial procedures. All of these issues disappear as a case is filed in federal court, since the procedures, judge, advocates, and claims will immediately be apparent.

One criticism that critics leveled against the Kantrowitz proposal was that the decisions of the court would become the sole authority in the area, crowding out dissent; similar accusations might arise regarding the CSJ.[317] The CSJ would be extremely unlikely to suffer from a predisposition to authoritarianism, however, because the decisions would be created in a judicial framework where precedential effect of case law has a long history and known limits. While science subject to adversarial inquest

---

296. *See, e.g.,* Rochelle C. Dreyfuss, *Forums of the Future: The Role of Specialized Courts in Resolving Business Disputes,* 61 BROOK. L. REV. 1, 18–19 (1995) (assessing the Delaware Court of Chancery, which has "captured benefits of specialization fully, without paying a high cost in terms of quality erosion")....

302. Rochelle Cooper Dreyfuss, *The Federal Circuit: A Case Study in Specialized Courts,* 64 N.Y.U. L. REV. 1, 13–14 (1989) (stating that precision is a benefit "when similar issues arise repeatedly before the same group of adjudicators").

317. Critics of the Kantrowitz proposal thought the proposal was authoritarian in the sense that no one could question the judgment of the court, and those standing in opposition would be marginalized....

may be determined to be stronger or weaker within the framework of the law, it seems unlikely this will have the Orwellian *1984* effects critics ascribed to the Kantrowitz proposal....

Finally, critics of specialized judges often suggest that a specialized court is inherently susceptible to capture by particular interests. Kondo dismisses this idea as unsupported by the state of empirical work in specialized courts.[325] Dreyfuss, in her analysis of the Federal Circuit, similarly determined that the court did not suffer from capture concerns, and was, "[w]ith regard to its patent jurisdiction ... a fairly balanced court."[326] The design of the CSJ is even less likely than the Federal Circuit to succumb to capture. Capture is more likely to occur when the potential of any individual judge to affect policy increases, i.e., the addition of one "biased" judge would affect the overall judicial output. At the CSJ, judges would be trial-level judges grouped according to background specialty, able to hear cases on their area of background and its neighboring subject areas. Since any subject matter is likely to have multiple available judges who are qualified in the applicable area of expertise, the marginal value of each judge seems less likely to attract capture than even the Federal Circuit....

Notes and Questions

1. Science Court is a high-level, even radical (depending on who you ask) change to the current management of expert witnesses. The proposal significantly reconceptualizes the role of judge, altering the current adversarial balance toward a more continental model and requiring a significant commitment to a new judicial body (the centralized CSJ court). As with the earlier proposals, we need to decide: what is the problem the proposal is addressing and is it likely to solve that problem? What problems can you anticipate with the Science Court proposal?

2. One's willingness to consider a proposal like the Court of Scientific Jurisdiction may depend largely on one's opinion on the state of expert witness management today. Throughout the book, we have seen courts struggling with complex scientific evidence. However, the story is not so one-sided. Occasionally, there are moments of significant optimism indicating that change is imminent. *Daubert* was likely one of those moments. The impressive work of the National Academy of Sciences (in authoring its 2009 Report *A Path Forward*)[80] and the President's Council of Advisors on Science and Technology (in its 2016 report *Forensic Science in Criminal Court*)[81] offered hope that, at least in the forensic sciences, imminent foundational research would result in validity for some disciplines and exclusion

---

325. Leroy L. Kondo, *Untangling the Tangled Web: Federal Court Reform Through Specialization for Internet Law and Other High Technology Cases*, 2002 UCLA J. L. & TECH. 1 (2002)....

326. Dreyfuss, *supra* note [302], at 29.

80. NATIONAL RESEARCH COUNCIL, NATIONAL ACADEMY OF SCIENCES, STRENGTHENING FORENSIC SCIENCE IN THE UNITED STATES: A PATH FORWARD (2009).

81. PRESIDENT'S COUNCIL OF ADVISORS ON SCIENCE AND TECHNOLOGY, FORENSIC SCIENCE IN CRIMINAL COURTS: ENSURING SCIENTIFIC VALIDITY OF FEATURE-COMPARISON METHODS (2016), *available at*: https://obamawhitehouse.archives.gov/sites/default/files/microsites/ostp/PCAST/pcast_forensic_science_report_final.pdf.

for others. On the other hand, the Attorney General recently disbanded the National Commission on Forensic Science—an advisory panel of scientists, judges, crime lab leaders, prosecutors, and defense lawyers interested in pursuing independent forensic research in response to the 2009 National Academy Report—and also ended systematic Justice Department review of prior forensic errors. Spencer Hsu, *Sessions Orders Justice Dept. to End Forensic Science Commission, Suspend Review Policy,* WASH. POST., Apr. 10, 2017. Whether one is optimistic or pessimistic about future handling of scientific evidence might indicate whether more radical reform is needed.

Certainly, we should all have some optimism that this issue is one that has been prominently debated and will continue to be debated well into the future.

Tying It Together

You have been appointed to the Commission on Judicial Reform for the State of Polk. The Commission has recently begun to consider reform efforts for expert evidence. The Commission Chair anticipates debate on the multiple proposals under consideration, but wants to give the members of the Commission a chance to consider each proposal in detail before such debate ensues.

Assignment: Take any one of the proposals for change discussed above and draft a memo to the Commission Chair explaining either: a) why it offers significant benefits and should be adopted, or b) why it is unrealistic or harmful and must be rejected. Please be prepared to discuss your analysis with the other Commission members at its next meeting.

Appendix A

Statement of Qualifications for Roger Karp

Name	Roger Karp	Date	2/26/2015
Laboratory	Oakland County Forensic Science Laboratory		
Job Title	Forensic Laboratory Specialist II		

Indicate all disciplines in which you do casework:

☐ Controlled substances   ☐ Toxicology
☐ Firearms/Toolmarks   ☐ Biology
☐ Trace evidence   ☐ Questioned documents
☒ Latent Prints   ☒ Crime Scene
☐ Digital Evidence

Indicate all sub-disciplines in which you do casework:

None

Education: List all higher academic institutions attended:

Institution	Dates attended	Major	Degree completed
Michigan State University	1991 to 1995	Forensic Science	Bachelor of Science
Oakland Community College	1999	Oakland Police Academy	

Other Training: List continuing education, workshops, in-service and other formal training received.

Evidence Technician School—1999, Macomb Community College

Tire, Footwear, and Toolmark Documentation—2000, Oakland Community College

Serology and Trace Evidence—2000, Macomb Community College

Forensic Crime Scene Techniques—2000, Oakland Community College

Advanced Forensic Fingerprint Identification and Testimony Course—2000, Oakland Community College

Basic Videography for Law Enforcement—2000, Troy PD

Accident Investigation 3 (Photography)—2001, Lansing MSP

Judicial Preparatory Course—2001, Oakland Community College

Practical Homicide Investigation—2001, Romulus, MI

Forensic Ridgeology—2002, Lansing MSP

Homicide Investigation Seminar—2003, Oakland County

Forensic Science and Grave Excavation—2003, Oakland Community College

DOA Death Investigation—2006, Oakland County

DNA and the Law—2007, Frankenmuth, MI

Cogent (AFIS) Training—2008, Oakland County

AFIS21 Latent Course: GWS-L and Archive USER Methods & Operations—2008, Michigan State Police

IAI Conference—2008, Louisville, KY

Lifting Latent Prints off Unusual and Textured Surfaces (IAI-Louisville)—2008, Louisville, KY

Understanding the Henry Classification Formula (IAI-Louisville)—2008, Louisville, KY

Swipes, Wipes and Other Transfer Impressions (IAI-Louisville)—2008, Louisville, KY

Advanced Palm Print Comparison Techniques—2008, Southfield, MI

IAI Conference—2009, Tampa Bay, FL

Universal Latent Workstation Software (IAI-Tampa Bay)—2009, Tampa Bay, FL

Mock Crime Scene (IAI-Tampa Bay)—2009 Tampa Bay, FL

The Use of SPR for the Recovery of Wet Latent Fingerprints (IAI-Tampa Bay)—2009, Tampa Bay

Courtrooms Demonstrations for Latent Footwear & Fingerprint Evidence (IAI-Tampa Bay)—2009

12th Annual Cogent User Group International Conference (CUGI)—2009, Pasadena, CA

Analysis of Distortion in Latent Prints—2010, Troy, MI

IAI Conference—2010 Spokane, WA

The Use of Metal Detectors for the Recovery of Metallic Evidence (IAI-Spokane)—2010, Spokane, WA

Enough is Enough! Latent Selection: A study of sufficiency (IAI-Spokane)—2010, Spokane, WA

Techniques of Electrostatic Lifting at Crime Scenes (IAI-Spokane)—2010, Spokane, WA

IAI Conference—2011 Milwaukee, WI

Creases and Third Level Detail Workshop (IAI-Wisconsin)—2011, Milwaukee, WI

Universal Latent Workstation (ULW) Software (IAI-Wisconsin)—2011, Milwaukee, WI

Powder, Powder Everywhere: Which one does one use? (IAI-Wisconsin)—2011, Milwaukee, WI

Crime Scene Analysis and Reconstruction (IAI-Wisconsin)—2011, Milwaukee, WI

Child Death Investigation—2011, Oakland County

What Makes a Credible Witness? (Educational Webinar Series)—2013 online

ULW Software Workshop (FBI)—2013, Mt. Pleasant, MI (Hosted by MSP)

Fingerprint Error Rate Workshop—2013, Mt. Pleasant, MI (Hosted by MSP)

Recent Studies in Latent Prints lecture—2013, Mt. Pleasant, MI (Hosted by MSP) DNA Biological Screening for Law Enforcement (NFSTC)—2013, Oakland County IAI Conference—2013, Providence, RI

Applying the SWGFAST ACE-V Methodology Standard—2013, Providence, RI

So I've Got This Evidence … and I am perplexed about what Technique to Use!—2013, Providence, RI

Thermal Paper, Regular Paper … What's the Big Deal?—2013, Providence, RI

Trace Evidence Discovery & Collection—2013, Providence, RI

ASCLD/LAB-1nternational Assessor Training Course—2013, Grand Rapids, Ml

9th Annual AFIS Users Conference-Michigan State Police—2014, Mt. Pleasant, MI

Comparison of Plantar Impressions—2014, Mt. Pleasant, MI (Hosted by MSP)

Reducing Errors in Exclusion Decisions—2014, Mt. Pleasant, MI (Hosted by MSP)

IAI Conference—2014, Minneapolis, MN

Indanedione/Zinc Chloride ... Better than DFO and Ninhydrin?—2014, Minneapolis, MN

Recovery and Documentation of Footwear Evidence—2014, Minneapolis, MN

Analyzing and Documenting the Shooting Scene—2014, Minneapolis, MN

I.T. Security Awareness Training—2014 (OCSO-Online training)

Measurement Traceability-ASCLD/LAB Assessor Training—2014 (ASCLD/LAB-Online training)

2014 ASCLD/LAB Technical Assessor Refresher Training—2014 (ASCLD/LAB-Online training)

Courtroom Experience: List the discipline(s) in which you have qualified to testify as an expert witness and indicate over what period of time and approximately how many times you have testified in each.

Expert Fingerprint Comparison, 50th District Court (Pontiac)—1 time in 2000

Expert Fingerprint Comparison, 50th District Court (Pontiac)—1 time in 2001

Expert Fingerprint Comparison, 6th Circuit Court (Pontiac)—2 times in 2001

Expert Fingerprint Comparison, 50th District Court (Pontiac)—1 time in 2002

Expert Fingerprint Comparison, 6th Circuit Court (Pontiac)—1 time in 2002

Expert Fingerprint Testimony, 6th Circuit Court (Pontiac)—1 time in 2003

Expert Fingerprint Comparison, 6th Circuit Court (Pontiac)—1 time in 2004

Expert Fingerprint Comparison, 6th Circuit Court (Pontiac)—1 time in 2006

Expert Crime Scene Testimony, 6th Circuit Court (Pontiac)—1 time in 2007

Expert Fingerprint Comparison, 48th District Court (Bloomfield)—1 time in 2009

Expert Fingerprint Comparison, 6th Circuit (Pontiac)—4 times in 2009

Expert Fingerprint Comparison, Federal Court (Detroit)—1 time in 2009

Expert Fingerprint Comparison, 46th District Court (Southfield)—1 time in 2009

Expert Fingerprint Comparison, 52-1 District (Novi)—2 times in 2009

Expert Fingerprint Comparison, 6th Circuit Court (Pontiac)—2 times in 2010

Expert Fingerprint Comparison, Expert in Forensic Science, 50th District Court (Pontiac)—1 time in 2010

Expert Fingerprint Comparison, 45-B District Court (Oak Park)—1 time in 2010

Expert Fingerprint Comparison, 45-B District Court (Oak Park)—1 time in 2011

Expert Fingerprint Comparison, 6th Circuit Court (Pontiac)—4 times in 2011

Expert Fingerprint Comparison, 50th District Court (Pontiac)—1 time in 2011

Expert Fingerprint Comparison, 47th District Court (Farmington)—1 time in 2011

Expert Fingerprint Comparison, 52-2 District Court (Clarkston)—1 time in 2011

Expert Fingerprint Comparison, 6th Circuit Court (Pontiac)—3 times in 2012

Expert Fingerprint Comparison, 50th District Court (Pontiac)—1 time in 2012

Expert Fingerprint Comparison, 6th Circuit Court (Pontiac)—2 times in 2013

Expert Fingerprint Comparison, 45-B District Court (Oak Park)—1 time in 2013

Expert Fingerprint Comparison, 6th Circuit Court (Pontiac)—4 times in 2014

Expert Fingerprint Comparison, 47th District Court (Farmington)—1 time in 2014

Expert Fingerprint Comparison, Federal Court (Detroit)—1 time in 2014

Expert Fingerprint Comparison, Federal Court (Ann Arbor)—1 time in 2014

Expert Fingerprint Comparison, 6th Circuit Court (Pontiac)—4 times in 2015

Expert Crime Scene/Fingerprint Analysis, 44th District Court (Royal Oak)—1 time in 2016

Expert Fingerprint Analysis, 6th Circuit Court (Pontiac)—1 time in 2016

Expert in Forensic Science & Latent Print Identification, 6th Circuit Court (Pontiac)—1 time in 2016

Expert in Crime Scene Investigation & Latent Print Identification, 6th Circuit (Pontiac)—2 times in 2016

Expert in Crime Scene Investigation & Latent Print Identification, 6th Circuit (Pontiac)—2 times in 2017

Expert in Fingerprint Comparison, 6th Circuit Court (Pontiac)—2 times in 2018

Fingerprint Analysis, Federal Court (Port Huron)—1 time in 2018

Expert in Fingerprint Comparison, 45th District Court—1 time in 2018

Expert in Fingerprint Analysis, 3rd Circuit Court (Detroit)—1 time in 2018

Professional Affiliations: List any professional organizations of which you are or have been a member. Indicate any offices or other positions held and the date(s) of these activities.

Member of International Association for Identification 2008–present

Employment History: List all scientific or technical positions held, particularly those related to forensic science. List current position first. Be sure to indicate employer and give a brief summary of principal duties and tenure in each position.

ORGANIZATION: Oakland County Sheriff's Office	From: 07/07 To: present
YOUR TITLE: Forensic Laboratory Specialist	
DUTIES: Physical and chemical development of latent fingerprints, examination and comparison of fingerprint evidence, and crime scene investigation.	

ORGANIZATION: Pontiac Police Department	From: 07/06 To: 07/07
YOUR TITLE: Crime Scene Investigator	
DUTIES: Processed crime scenes to photograph, document, collect, and process evidence. I also did a great deal of work with inked and latent finger and palm impressions. I made several thousand ink to ink identifications along with several hundreds of latent to ink identifications.	

ORGANIZATION: **Pontiac Police Department**	From: To:	07/03 07/06
YOUR TITLE: Detective		
DUTIES:		

ORGANIZATION: **Pontiac Police Department**	From: To:	07/99 07/03
YOUR TITLE: **Crime Scene Investigator**		
DUTIES: Processed crime scenes to photograph, document, collect, and process evidence. I also did a great deal of work with inked and latent finger and palm impressions. I made several thousand ink to ink identifications along with several hundreds of latent to ink identifications.		

Curriculum Vitae of Martin Espinosa

Name of Lab	Polk Bureau of Investigation Crime Laboratory	Date	05-15-18
Name	Martin Espinosa	Job Title	Supervisor

Discipline(s): Indicate all areas in which you do casework.

☐ Controlled substances   ☒ DNA
☐ Toxicology   ☐ Firearms/tool marks
☐ Trace evidence   ☐ Questioned documents
☒ Serology   ☐ Latent prints

Education: List all higher academic institutions attended.

Institution	Dates attended	Major(s)	Degree completed
Springfield University	08/76–05/80	Chemistry, Biology, 2nd Ed	Bachelor of Science
Polk State University	01/85–05/94	Biology	Master of Arts

Other training: List continuing education, workshops, in-service and other formal training received.

1/10/83	Introduction to Hairs and Fibers
1/23/83	Basic Forensic Serology
4/26/83	Blood Spatter Interpretation: Midwestern Assoc. of Forensic Scientists
7/11/83	Polarized Light Microscopy
1/23/84	Seminal Fluid Analysis
3/26/84	Basic Fingerprint School
6/18/84	Advanced Latent Fingerprint School
6/25/85	An International Symposium on Forensic Hair Comparisons
10/22/85	Biochemical Methods in Bloodstain Analysis
3/17/86	Forensic Human Immunoglobin Allotyping
5/31/88	DNA Technology in Forensic Science
6/18/89	International Symposium on the Forensic Aspects of DNA Analysis
7/9/89	DNA Typing Methods
10/8/91	Identification of Bones: MAFS Meeting

4/12/93	MAFS DNA Autoradiograph Interpretation Workshop
4/19/93	Advanced Aspects of Forensic DNA Analysis
4/14/94	Genetic and Statistical Considerations for Forensic Analyses: MAFS Workshop
5/25/95	DNA Typing with STRs
10/8/94	Fifth International Symposium on Human Identification
10/10/95	Technical Working Group on DNA Analysis Methods (TWGDAM), Chemiluminescent Workshop
10/12/95	Sixth International Symposium on Human Identification
7/10/95	Forensic Amplitype PM and HLA DQA1 PCR Amplification and Typing Workshop, and New Methods in Forensic PCR Amplification and Typing Workshop
10/8/96	Introduction to Wood Identification: MAFS Meeting
6/19/98	TWGDAM Midwest Meeting
9/14/97	Quality Assurance in the Laboratory
1/21/99	Internal Lab Audits by AALA
3/10/99	STR's by Capillary Electrophoresis
1/11/00	Advanced AmpFISTR & ABI Prism 310 Genetic Analyzer Class
10/17/00	STR Instrumentation and STR Interpretation Workshop
10/18/00	STR Report Writing Workshop MAFS meeting
6/12/01	DNA Auditor Training
9/25/01	Population Statistics and Forensic DNA Analysis: MAFS Meeting
7/15/02	Courtroom Testimony Techniques — 16 hrs
10/6/02	SWGDAM Meeting — 5 hrs
10/7/02	Paternity Mini Symposium — 4 hrs
10/8/02	Int. Symposium on Human Identification — 23 hrs
12/11/02	Quarterly Lab In-Service (Workman's Comp, FMLA, Sudden Illness, Legislative Process, Criminal Profiling) — 8 hrs
2/12/03	Quarterly Lab Training — 8 hrs
4/10/03	Capillary Electrophoresis and DNA Applications — 4 hrs
7/14/03	DNA Technology — Promega Corp. — 5 hrs
10/13/03	Ethics in the Forensic Sciences — 8 hrs
12/2/03	Laboratory Safety Training Seminar — 8 hrs
12/9/03	Crime Scene Training — State Medical Examiner's Office — 4 hrs
2/25/04	Serial Offenders & Crime Scene from an investigator & profiler point of view
3/16/04	MO-KS Forensic DNA Conference — 15 hrs
6/14/05	Annual In-House Safety Training — 4 hrs
8/8/05	GeneMapper ID Software — 2 hrs
8/25/05	GeneMapper ID Software — 8 hrs
10/3/05	Forensic Statistics Workshop — 4 hrs
10/3/05	Gene Mapper ID Workshop/Real Time PCR Workshop — 8 hrs
4/3/06	MidAmerican DNA Conference & ISO 17025 Accreditation for Laboratories
10/9/06	Midwestern Association of Forensic Scientists — 35 hrs

11/2/06	Annual In House Safety Training—4 hrs
1/30/07	HID 310 Systems Training Program—28 hrs
4/3/07	Mid America 2007 Forensic DNA Conference—17 hrs
9/24/07	MAFS Annual Meeting & Various DNA Topics—33 hrs
10/17/07	Annual In-House Safety Training—4 hrs
4/15/08	Mid America 2008 Forensic DNA Conference—18 hrs
7/16/08	2008 Ethics Training—2 hrs
9/29/08	MAFS Annual Meeting—40 hrs
1/7/09	AB 3130 Genetic Analyzer HID Install Training—8 hrs
3/10/09	Promega's Plexor HY DNA Quantification Training—8 hrs
3/27/09	2009 Diversity Training—3.5 hrs
4/7/09	Forensic DNA, and ISO 17025 auditing—8 hrs
4/8/09	PTC Conference—16 hrs
6/9/09	DNA Symposium—20 hrs
7/31/09	2009 Annual Safety Training—4 hrs
1/11/10	Forensic Science Management-Best Practices Series—40 hrs
4/07/10	Biomek 3000 Software Training—4 hrs
5/21/10	2010 Annual Safety Training—4 hrs
7/12/10	Forensic Y STR Training—30 hrs
10/02/10	2010 MAFS Annual Meeting Board Meeting and Two workshops—40 hrs
10/25/10	NIJ Grant Management Summit—16 hrs
11/15/10	16th CODIS Conference—32 hrs
12/6/10	CODIS v5.7.4 Software Training Course—36 hrs
02/23/11	American Academy of Forensic Sciences—20 hrs
5/11/11	2011 "Spring CODIS State User's Meeting—12 hrs
09/18/11	MAFS Fall Meeting and Workshop—16 hrs
11/14/11	17th Annual CODIS National Conference—32 hrs
04/10/12	Mid American 2012 Forensic DNA Conference—14 hrs
04/16/12	Basic GeneMapper ID-X training—8 hrs
06/5/12	CODIS Instructor Led Software Training—19.5 hrs
09/24/12	MAFS 41st Annual Fall Meeting—28 hrs
11/13/12	18th Annual CODIS National Conference—24 hrs
01/07/13	Paternity Statistics—20 hrs
11/19/13	19th Annual CODIS National Conference—24 hrs
05/06/14	2014 Spring CODIS State Administrator Meeting—12 hrs
10/08/14	2014 Fall MAFS Meeting—12 hrs
11/18/14	20th Annual CODIS National Conference and State Admin. Meeting—24 hrs
01/28/15	Sorenson "Qiagen EZ 1 Advanced XL and QIACube Teachback—8.0 hrs
05/12/15	2015 Spring CODIS State Administrator Meeting—12 hrs
11/17/15	21st Annual CODIS National Conference and State Administrators Mtg.

05/10/16	Spring CODIS State Administrator Meeting—12 hrs
09/29/16	27th International Symposium on Human Identification (Promega)
11/15/16	22nd Annual CODIS Nat'l Conference & State Administrator's Mtg.
01/3/17	Armed Expert Software Training (NicheVision)
05/09/17	2017 Spring CODIS State Administrator Meeting—14 hrs
05/15/17	STR Mix Software Training (ESR)—30.0 hrs
11/14/17	23rd Annual CODIS National Conference and State Administrator's Mtg.
5/08/18	2018 Spring CODIS State Administrator Meeting—14 hrs

Courtroom experience: List the discipline(s) in which you have qualified to testify as an expert witness and indicate over what period of time and approximately how many times you have testified in each.

Trace Evidence	Jan. 83	>75 times
Serology	Jan. 83	>200 times
DNA	Jan. 87	>100 times
Blood spatter	June 93	4 times

Professional Affiliations: List any professional organizations of which you are or have been a member. Indicate any offices or other positions held and the date(s) of these activities.

Midwestern Association of Forensic Scientists   84 to present, Regular member
  – Have served an annual rotation as: Workshop Coordinator, Local Arrangements Chair,
                                         Program Chair, and President

American Board of Criminalistics: Diplomate   January 1997–present

Employment History: List all scientific or technical positions held, particularly those related to forensic science. List current position first. Give a brief summary of principal duties and tenure in each position.

ORGANIZATION: Polk Bureau of Investigation, Crime Laboratory		From Month Year 08/10
YOUR TITLE: Criminalist Supervisor State CODIS Administrator	NAME OF SUPERVISOR: Janice Yin, Lab Administrator	To Month Year present
DUTIES: Oversee the personnel and responsibilities of the DNA casework and convicted offender units of the laboratory. Oversees the State CODIS Database.		

ORGANIZATION: Polk Bureau of Investigation, Crime Laboratory		From Month Year **09/82**
YOUR TITLE: **Criminalist, 28 yrs** **DNA Technical Leader (10 yrs)**	NAME OF SUPERVISOR: **Allan Anderson**	To Month Year **08/10**
DUTIES: Responsibilities include collection and preservation of physical evidence, performance of scientific analyses, report writing, courtroom testimony, crime scene processing, methods development and instruction for external agencies. Responsible for overall technical operations of DNA unit.		

Other Qualifications: List below any scientific publication and/or presentation you have authored or co-authored, research in which you are or have been involved, academic or other teaching positions you have held, and any other information which you consider relevant to your qualification as a forensic scientist. (Use additional sheets if necessary.)

– Reviewer for: Sexual Assault: Polk Forensic and Medical Protocol, March 1998

– Reviewer for: Movie Sexual Assault Exam Franklin County Victim Services, 1997

– Past-President of Midwestern Association of Forensic Scientists

Index

Pages with tables, figures, or illustrations are indicated by page numbers followed by *table, fig.,* or *illus.* respectively.

valuation methodology, assessment of, 580–85

work life expectancy, 548–49

employment discrimination

age and disability, expert relevance in, 26–29

age discrimination, use of statistical evidence, 255–60

empirical data use, in criterion-related study of HSSTB test, 241–50

fact witnesses, required disclosures by, 165–70

regression analysis, of employment and performance factors, 270–76

Epstein, Robert, 338–41, 358–66, 378

Espinosa, Martin (expert witness, DNA evidence), *Curriculum Vitae* of, 623–27

The Evaluation of Forensic DNA Evidence (NAS), 307, 315, 334

expert opinion testimony, substantive rules for

bases for (Rule 703), 75–77, 77–80

disclosure of facts or data underlying (Rule 705), 77

inadmissible evidence, 80–86

judicial comment on, in Canada, 602, 603

expert relevance (Rule 702), 22–39

common knowledge *vs.* standards of care, 30–33

employment discrimination, 26–29

excessive force, expert testimony on, 33–39

helpfulness, 24–25

Rule 702, 22–23

testimony, on excessive force, 33–39

of testimony by expert witnesses (Rule 702), 21–22

expert witness oral depositions, strategies for, 231–35, 235–36

opposing experts, 233–35

surprises, follow up and, 235

your experts, 231–32

your preparation for trial, 232–33

expert witnesses. *See also* qualifications screening (Rule 702), substantive rules for

expert qualifications, accident investigation *vs.,* 507–10

expert qualifications, *Daubert* standard, 504–7

police, as expert witnesses to drunk driving, 104–13

scientific disciplines using, 4

scientists as, 12

use of, generally, 3–4

F

Faigman, David L. (*Modern Scientific Evidence*), 355

Federal Evidence (Weinstein), 73, 74

Federal Rules of Civil Procedure

Rule 26(a)(1)(A), duty to disclose, by standard fact witnesses, 162, 165

Rule 26(a)(1)(C) & (D), time for initial disclosures, 163

Rule 26(a)(2)(A)-(C), duty to disclose, by retained expert witnesses, 163–64, 175

Rule 26(a)(2)(B), expert heightened disclosure requirement, 184–88, 189–90

Rule 26(a)(2)(C), duty to disclose, by non-retained expert witnesses, 164

Rule 26(a)(2)(D), time to disclose expert testimony, 164

Rule 30, depositions by oral examination, 226–27

Rule 37(a), motion for order compelling disclosure or discovery, 194–95

Rule 37(b), failure to comply with court order, sanctions, 195–96

Rule 37(c), failure to disclose or supplement, sanctions, 196–99, 200

Federal Rules of Criminal Procedure, Rule 16, disclosure by government, 201–3